From Doubt to Unbelief
Forms of Scepticism in the Iberian World

LEGENDA

LEGENDA is the Modern Humanities Research Association's book imprint for new research in the Humanities. Founded in 1995 by Malcolm Bowie and others within the University of Oxford, Legenda has always been a collaborative publishing enterprise, directly governed by scholars. The Modern Humanities Research Association (MHRA) joined this collaboration in 1998, became half-owner in 2004, in partnership with Maney Publishing and then Routledge, and has since 2016 been sole owner. Titles range from medieval texts to contemporary cinema and form a widely comparative view of the modern humanities, including works on Arabic, Catalan, English, French, German, Greek, Italian, Portuguese, Russian, Spanish, and Yiddish literature. Editorial boards and committees of more than 60 leading academic specialists work in collaboration with bodies such as the Society for French Studies, the British Comparative Literature Association and the Association of Hispanists of Great Britain & Ireland.

The MHRA encourages and promotes advanced study and research in the field of the modern humanities, especially modern European languages and literature, including English, and also cinema. It aims to break down the barriers between scholars working in different disciplines and to maintain the unity of humanistic scholarship. The Association fulfils this purpose through the publication of journals, bibliographies, monographs, critical editions, and the MHRA Style Guide, and by making grants in support of research. Membership is open to all who work in the Humanities, whether independent or in a University post, and the participation of younger colleagues entering the field is especially welcomed.

ALSO PUBLISHED BY THE ASSOCIATION

Critical Texts
Tudor and Stuart Translations • *New Translations* • *European Translations*
MHRA Library of Medieval Welsh Literature

MHRA Bibliographies
Publications of the Modern Humanities Research Association

The Annual Bibliography of English Language & Literature
Austrian Studies
Modern Language Review
Portuguese Studies
The Slavonic and East European Review
Working Papers in the Humanities
The Yearbook of English Studies

www.mhra.org.uk
www.legendabooks.com

STUDIES IN HISPANIC AND LUSOPHONE CULTURES

Studies in Hispanic and Lusophone Cultures are selected and edited by the Association of Hispanists of Great Britain & Ireland. The series seeks to publish the best new research in all areas of the literature, thought, history, culture, film, and languages of Spain, Spanish America, and the Portuguese-speaking world.

The Association of Hispanists of Great Britain & Ireland is a professional association which represents a very diverse discipline, in terms of both geographical coverage and objects of study. Its website showcases new work by members, and publicises jobs, conferences and grants in the field.

STUDIES IN HISPANIC AND LUSOPHONE CULTURES

From Doubt to Unbelief

Forms of Scepticism in the Iberian World

❖

EDITED BY
MERCEDES GARCÍA-ARENAL AND STEFANIA PASTORE

l

LEGENDA

Studies in Hispanic and Lusophone Cultures 42
Modern Humanities Research Association
2019

Published by Legenda
an imprint of the Modern Humanities Research Association
Salisbury House, Station Road, Cambridge CB1 2LA

ISBN 978-1-78188-867-4 (HB)
ISBN 978-1-78188-868-1 (PB)

First published 2019
Paperback edition 2021

Copy-Editor: Richard Correll

CONTENTS

❖

ACKNOWLEDGEMENTS

❖

Most of the essays collected here were presented as papers at the conference 'Doubt to Unbelief: Forms of Skepticism in the Iberian World', which took place at the Consejo Superior de Investigaciones Científicas (CSIC) in Madrid in November 2015. That conference brought together scholars from different disciplines — history (social and cultural), philosophy, art history and literature — and from different academic traditions, to approach in a new way how doubt, unbelief, and scepticism were manifested in late medieval and early modern Iberia. The conference was organised by the editors of this volume under the auspices of the European Research Council's Advanced Grant project, the European Union's Seventh Framework Programme (FP7/2007–2013) ERC Grant Agreement 323316 project CORPI, 'Conversion, Overlapping Religiosities, Polemics, Interaction: Early Modern Iberia and Beyond', whose PI is Mercedes García-Arenal. Other essays that are included here, namely those by José Luis Villacañas and Miriam Bodian, were presented afterwards at the monthly CORPI seminar and added to the volume. The editors are especially grateful to David Nirenberg and to Felipe Pereda, with whom many of the ideas that formed the genesis of this book were initially discussed, but also to the members of the CORPI group who shared with us their research and their ideas.

We want to acknowledge the contributions, through discussion and debates, of all those who participated in the conference as well as the discussion that has occurred during the editorial process in which contributors have read and built upon each others' essays. Ryan Szpiech and Yonatan Glazer-Eytan read a first version of the 'Introduction' and improved it with their suggestions. We also gratefully mention the invaluable work done by Nicholas Callaway, who translated the Italian texts into English, by our American editor and translator Deirdre Casey, and in Spain, by Teresa Madrid Álvarez-Piñer, who compiled the bibliography and index. Last but not least, we must acknowledge the evaluation and revisions carried out by Trevor Dadson and an anonymous reader, which have helped to improve this book.

NOTES ON THE CONTRIBUTORS

❖

Luca Addante is currently associate professor of Modern History at the University of Turin. His primary research interests are the figures and the dynamics of the political and religious dissent, from the most radical heretics to the libertines and from Campanella to the Jacobins and the Carbonari. He has also focused on analysing the origin of modern liberties, Republicanism, Patriotism, and on the fortunes of Machiavelli. He is the author of several books, including *Eretici e libertini nel Cinquecento italiano* (Laterza, 2010) and *Tommaso Campanella. Il filosofo immaginato, interpretato, falsato* (Laterza, 2010).

Matthew Ancell (PhD in Comparative Literature, the University of California, Irvine) is now Associate Professor of Humanities and Comparative Literature at Brigham Young University. His research interests include the Baroque in Spain and Italy, early modern scepticism, and deconstruction. He has published articles on Luis de Góngora, Calderón de la Barca, Diego Velázquez, and Jacques Derrida in publications such as *Oxford Art Journal*, *Hispanic Review*, *Renaissance Drama*, *The Comparatist*, and *Revista de Estudios Hispánicos*. For the past three years he has co-directed BYU's International Cinema Program. Currently, he is co-editing (with Aneta Georgievska-Shine) a collection, 'The Dialectics of Faith and Doubt in Seventeenth-Century Spain: Visual and Literary Reflections', and is writing a monograph on Calderón de la Barca and visual art.

Harm den Boer is Professor for Iberoromance Literature at the University of Basel. He has researched and published extensively on Early Modern Iberian Literature with a particular focus on the literature, culture and intellectual history of Iberian Jews and Conversos, teaching courses at universities and academic centres worldwide. He is author of *La Literature sefardí de Amsterdam* and of the bibliography *Spanish and Portuguese Printing in the Northern Netherlands, 1584–1825*; he also coordinates the collection *Sephardic Editions* (from 2004 onwards). He has published monographic studies and editions together with Kenneth Brown (Edition and Studies on David Valle de Saldaña, Abraham Gómez Silveira). In 2012, with Jorge Ledo, he discovered the influential but hitherto 'lost' Spanish Translation of Erasmus's *Moria*, now published. His current interests include Cryptojudaism in Literature, the existence and validity of a 'Converso Canon', Black Legend and Exile, Sacred Texts and Cultural Transference; and Iberian Jewish Preaching.

Miriam Bodian is Professor of History and Director of the Institute for Historical Studies at the University of Texas at Austin. She has written extensively on the Judeo-Conversos and Portuguese Jews, including two books, *Hebrews of the*

Portuguese Nation: Conversos and Community in Early Modern Amsterdam and *Dying in the Law of Moses: Crypto-Jewish Martyrdom in Iberian Lands*. She is currently writing a book on the career and thought of the Portuguese Jew Isaac de Castro Tartas, based on his lengthy Inquisition trial.

Mercedes García-Arenal is PI of ERC project CORPI ('Conversion, Overlapping Religiosities, Polemics, Interaction. Early Modern Iberia and Beyond') at CCHS-CSIC, Madrid. Her research focuses on the religious history of Iberia and the Muslim West, mainly on religious minorities: conversion, polemics, messianism, religious dissidence and dissimulation. Among her last main publications are (ed.), *After Conversion: Iberia and the Emergence of Modernity* (Brill, 2016); with Gerard Wiegers (eds), *A Mediterranean Diaspora: The Expulsion of the Moriscos from Spain* (Brill, 2014); and as author with F. Rodríguez Mediano, *The Orient in Spain: Converted Muslims, the Forged Lead Books of Granada and the Beginnings of Orientalism* (Brill, 2013); *Visiones imperiales y profecía. Roma, España, Nuevo Mundo* (Abada, 2018).

Eleazar Gutwirth is the Professor of Hispano-Jewish History and Culture at Tel Aviv University. Recent publications include 'Pablo de Santa María y Jerónimo de Santa Fe. Hacia una re-lectura de la Epístola de Lorqui'; 'Coplas de Yocef from St. Petersburg'; 'Musical Lives: Late Medieval Hispano-Jewish Communities'; 'Rabbi Mose Arragel and the Art of the Prologue in Fifteenth-Century Castile'; 'Techne and Culture: Printers and Readers in Fifteenth-Century Hispano-Jewish Communities'; 'La cultura material hispano-judía. Entre la norma y la práctica'; 'Jewish Writings on Art in Fifteenth-Century Castile'.

Maurice Kriegel is Directeur d'études in l'École des Hautes Études en Sciences Sociales (EHESS), Paris. His research focuses on medieval and early modern Jewish history. Among his last articles are 'Devant le marranisme. Malaise dans l'opinion juive', 'L'Esprit tue aussi. Juifs *textuels* et Juifs *réels* dans l'histoire', and 'Paul de Burgos et Profiat Duran déchiffrent 1391'. He is author of *Les Juifs dans l'Europe méditerranéenne à la fin du Moyen Âge* (Hachette, [1979] 2006) and editor of *Cahier de l'Herne Scholem* (Éditions de l'Herne, 2009).

Stefania Pastore is Associate Professor of Early Modern and Cultural History at the Scuola Normale Superiore di Pisa. She is also member of the CORPI project. Her leading interest has been the cultural and religious history of late medieval and early modern Spain. In addition to numerous articles, she is the author of *Il vangelo e la spada. L'Inquisizione di Castiglia e i suoi critici, 1460–1598* (Edizioni di storia e letteratura, 2003) and *Una herejía española. Conversos, alumbrados e Inquisición, 1449–1559* (Marcial Pons, 2010).

Felipe Pereda is Fernando Zóbel de Ayala Professor of Spanish Art, Department of History of Art and Architecture, Harvard University and a member of the CORPI project. He has previously taught at the Johns Hopkins University, the Universidad Autónoma de Madrid, and the Instituto de Investigaciones Estéticas (Universidad Autónoma de México). He has worked on the history of architecture and cartography, architectural theory, and the religious imagery of late medieval and early modern Spain. Recent publications include *Crime and Illusion: The Art of Truth in the Spanish Golden Age* (Harvey Miller, 2018); *Las imágenes de la discordia. Política y poética de la imagen sagrada en la España del 400* (Marcial Pons, 2017), and with Mercedes García-Arenal, 'On the Alumbrados: Confessionalism and Religious Dissidence in the Iberian World'.

Isabelle Poutrin is Professor of Early Modern History at the Université de Reims Champagne-Ardenne and member of the Institut universitaire de France. Her present research focuses on the theorization of individual consent in canon law, and practices of coercion in Catholic States. She is director of the research project Pocram (Political Power and Religious Conversion, Late Antiquity-Early Modern Period, ANR 13-CULT-0008). In addition to her book *Convertir les musulmans. Espagne, 1491–1609*, she has co-edited *Pouvoir politique et conversion religieuse. 1. Normes et mots*. Essays recently published include 'La Captation de l'enfant de converti. L'Évolution des normes canoniques à la lumière de l'antijudaïsme des XVIe–XVIIe siècles', and 'The Jewish Precedent in the Spanish Politics of conversion of Muslims and Moriscos'.

Jeremy Robbins is Forbes Professor of Hispanic Studies and Head of the School of Literatures, Languages and Cultures at the University of Edinburgh. His books include *Challenges of Uncertainty* and *Arts of Perception*, and the translation and edition of *Baltasar Gracián: The Pocket Oracle and Art of Prudence* (Penguin Classics, 2011). His work has focused on Spanish Baroque literature and the history of ideas, and he is currently working on the articulation of space in European Baroque art, architecture and theatre.

Fernando Rodríguez Mediano is Research Scientist at the Spanish National Research Council (CCHS-CSIC, Madrid) and a member of the CORPI project. His areas of expertise are, among others, the relationship between Spain and North Africa (sixteenth to twentieth centuries) and the origins of Spanish modern Orientalism (seventeenth century). Among his publications, with Mercedes García-Arenal, is *The Orient in Spain: Converted Muslims, The Forged Lead Books of Granada and the Rise of Orientalism* (Brill, 2013).

José Luis Villacañas Berlanga is Professor of Philosophy at the Universidad Complutense de Madrid. He has dedicated himself to the history of philosophy, especially to the Philosophy of Enlightenment and German Idealism, as well as its legacy in the twentieth century, from Max Weber's thought to Hans Blumenberg's proposal. He is the founder of *Res Publica*, Journal of History of Political Ideas. Since 2002 he has directed the project of the Saavedra Fajardo Digital Library of Spanish Political Thought. His latest books are *History of Political Power in Spain*; *Populism*; *Imperial Political Theology and Community of Christian Salvation*; *Freud reads the Quijote*; *The Hispanic intelligentsia I. The Failed Cosmos of the Goths*; and *Empire, Reformation and Modernity*.

INTRODUCTION

❖

Mercedes García-Arenal and Stefania Pastore

This book was born out of an absence, and reflects all of the many and often contradictory developments which we encountered as we attempted to address it.

The absence in question is a history of doubt in the Iberian world, a world that has traditionally been left out of a historiography on doubt and secularization. Iberia has been typically viewed as confined to a Catholic and Inquisitorial obscurantism that left no space for the great anti-dogmatic philosophical constructions which, from Montaigne on, marked the history of European Scepticism. Neither was it in general believed that there was space, on a different plane, for the existence of any doubt or protest within everyday Catholic life which might have shaken the concept of revealed truth, or the increasingly heavy baggage of dogma that religious belonging came to entail. It is an absence largely due to a problem of perspective, a point to which we shall return further on.

One of the objectives of this volume is to identify the distinctiveness of the Iberian contribution to that period and to connect Catholic Europe to the narrative of modernity traditionally centred squarely on Northern Europe, where doubt is not only the foundation of modernity but the main reason for toleration. By assuming an absolute lack of tolerance in Spain — a lack of doubt, of internal debate — this narrative has left entire areas of Iberian intellectual and cultural history largely unexplored. What we aim to address is the basic question of how, in an Iberian world that was apparently far removed from the battlegrounds of modernity and secularization, doubt and unbelief found fertile soil, stimulated by the tensions of Iberia's singular social and religious development. Adopting a multidisciplinary perspective, this volume shows how the crisis of identity produced by forced mass conversion touched off inner crises about the nature of Truth.

Even a brief glimpse at the list of essays in this volume will reveal a number of difficulties and multiple developments concerning the real object of this study — doubt — and its manifold, mercurial nature. What is doubt? How, and to what extent, did it spread? Is it part of a hermeneutical process to arrive at the truth, an intrinsic element for all cognitive processes? Or is it rather an element that erases the possibility of reaching any form of certainty? Does it negate the very idea of finding firm, unshakeable truths in the human conscience and in the beliefs, particularly religious beliefs, that regulate peoples' lives?

Our book is situated at the confluence of these questions and, in chronological terms, covers a period in which, with the revival of ancient Scepticism, religious and epistemological doubt came to overlap with one another. Some essays will specifically address these problems, and will show the points where they converge. In any case, we must distinguish between, on the one hand, a philosophical or epistemological stance connected to well-defined philosophical schools (academic Scepticism, Pyrrhonism, etc.), and, on the other, a looser, less defined approach that cannot be traced back to a specific philosophical system, and which affects the truths of faith and brings into question a system of dogmas and rituals that are imposed and defined in increasingly oppressive and pervasive ways.

★　★　★　★　★

Our volume opens with a well-known image that represents a key story in the history of Christianity and Western thought: the episode in which the Apostle Thomas doubted Jesus's resurrection, even though he was seeing him with his own eyes; he was not sure that it was indeed Christ risen, and he asked for proof. Jesus then put Thomas's fingers inside his wounds and Thomas's doubt was instantly replaced by total conviction. In a recent book titled *Doubting Thomas*, Glenn W. Most suggests that Thomas, or rather the story about him in the Gospel of John, seems to have been introduced by the Apostle John as a means of invoking, exaggerating, and eventually resolving doubt. According to Most, the story that John inserted into his Gospel had an undesired long-term effect, giving doubt an ambiguous status, revealing it to be inseparable from judgment, evidence and testimony, part of a dialectical process needed to arrive at the Truth. What we believe is infused by what we doubt.[1]

Indeed, the essays in this book address the equivocal nature of doubt both as a producer of unbelief and free thinking, but also as a critical tool for arriving at the Truth. Doubt is important, especially in the Christian tradition, as a trial of faith, as an essential tool for religious life which serves to bring about religious reflection. In fact, this book presents doubt and belief as two facets of the same phenomenon. Therefore, in exploring doubt we will at the same time be considering the changing nature of belief.

Our point of departure is the premise that in Spain religious doubt stemmed mainly from two key events that revolutionized conceptions of identity and religious belonging. These were the forced conversions of Jews and Muslims to Christianity from the end of the fourteenth to the beginning of the sixteenth century, and the birth in 1478 of the Spanish Inquisition, an institution created to deal with false converts to Catholicism. These forced conversions are, in our view, one main factor of religious doubt. The imposition of a single faith took place simultaneously with the emergence of other new conceptions about faith and belief. The measure of allegiance that Catholicism demanded from the believer increased: it was now necessary to be knowledgeable in order to believe; the comfortable faith in the ancestral traditions of one's family or group was no longer enough.[2]

Changes in the conception of belief were engendered, at least in part, by fourteenth- and fifteenth-century Catholicism's simultaneous emphasis on inner focus and exterior action, mysticism and materiality.[3] Once the forced conversions had broken with the traditional medieval system whereby each community had a firm, clean-cut religious identity, faith and religious belonging ceased to be taken for granted, and were no longer seen as a merely hereditary matter. Rather, these aspects were now something that the judges of the Inquisition could verify and assess based on a person's knowledge and practice. Jean Wirth has written a crucial article on the passage from a medieval world, in which the word 'fides' could indicate religious and political belonging, to an early modern world that, alongside confessional plurality, discovers the many possible degrees and variables that belief and religious belonging can take on. In this process, the divide between internal and external grows wider and wider, until there is enough room to accommodate the modern conscience. Confessional belonging thus gradually separates from its effective adhesion to a faith and, even from a lexical point of view, the terms for defining faith, religious belonging and belief multiply, with nuances that reflect the gradual but irreparable fragmentation of a single 'fides' that is the same for everyone.[4]

In the Iberian world, the process described by Wirth begins to take place at least a century earlier. The fabric of identity and religious belonging is violently and irremediably torn apart starting in 1391, the moment of violent pogroms against Jewish communities and the subsequent forced conversions of Jews. As a consequence, the Iberian Peninsula had to face, before any other place in Europe, the problem of multiple religious beliefs and the possible discrepancy between religious adherence and inner belief, between the external and the internal. At the same time, the birth of the Spanish Inquisition completely breaks with a traditional canonical system that regarded the inner realm of the conscience as an inviolable private space that was neither judicial nor subject to judgment, as in the famous dictum, 'Ecclesia de occultis non iudicat'.[5]

This is precisely the starting point for our reflection on doubt. We explore the spaces opened up to doubt by the discrepancy between religious belonging and adhesion, and the many complex ways such as dissimulation in which this breach is reflected in the history of Iberia. As may be seen in our table of contents, this is a story that arises in the context of religious pluralism and of passage from one faith to another, but it does not remain confined to this setting. Rather, it spreads out and significantly complicates the life of Catholic and mono-confessional Spain as well. Indeed, one of this book's most significant challenges is to retrace the convoluted paths through which religious doubt stretches into sixteenth-century and Tridentine Spain.

The new religious situation in Iberia demanded that all people (not only converts) be familiar with religious dogma in order to be considered good Catholics. This pressure increased when Philip II became, in 1564, the first sovereign to approve the decrees of the Council of Trent, weeks before their papal promulgation. The Inquisition then had the new tasks of disseminating the doctrines clarified at Trent and developing ways to implement them correctly, of reducing the spheres of ignorance and doubt. It was not the only institution dedicated to the control of inner belief: oral confession became an extraordinary means which often produced another kind of doubt,[6] the scrupulous doubts of people who were anxious about their correct observance of every precept and ritual.[7] There were also the doubts of those who wanted 'seguridad de conciencia' when confronted with practical decisions.[8] The Inquisition considered inner conversion and total and full adhesion to the whole corpus of Catholic belief to be imperative. For the Inquisition, doubt about the faith was equated with infidelity. On account of its nature, doubt tended to lurk in attitudes that the Holy Office deemed hypocritical or defined as heresy, and it therefore had to be unearthed and then crushed.

★   ★   ★   ★   ★

Let us trace the rough outlines of the contemporary context in Europe and the prevailing historiographical approaches to this subject. The period of the late sixteenth and early seventeenth centuries was a time of crisis and paradigm shift in myriad areas of cultural, intellectual and spiritual life throughout Europe, as a long century of religious strife ended in a stalemate between Catholics and Lutherans but also culminated in the consolidation of numerous sects among the followers of the *Sola scriptura*. The main issue was defining true Christianity. 'Scripture alone' was not a solution to this problem — far from it. Beginning in the 1520s this doctrine raised questions about the nature of knowledge and evoked the spectre of radical doctrinal scepticism and relativism.[9] Jonathan Israel has argued that in about 1570 Christianity grew weary of confessional strife and explored a new and different complex of secular politico-economic thought that historians call mercantilism. According to Israel, an upsurge of radical scepticism characterized philosophy in the age of Montaigne, and Christianity embarked on a centuries-long retreat, compelled to compete with a host of rival outlooks and attitudes and, in particular, a rising tide of doubt, deism and atheism.[10]

Clearly, Israel's vision fits perfectly in an analysis that regards intellectual history as the privileged field for reflection. Obviously, from the seventeenth century onward, the experience of doubt was the breeding ground for philosophical ideas that would become the pillars of a definition of truth as being both verifiable and independent of divine revelation. But this way of thought fails to consider the many ways in which other sectors of the population expressed their convictions or lack thereof.

In contrast to this narrative of de-Christianisation, historians have applied a different model, which has become known as the confessionalization thesis. Developed by Wolfgang Reinhard and Heinz Schilling during the 1980s as an explanation for historical developments in Germany, this thesis sees the institutional and theological standardization of religious difference as a tool of political government and social discipline that was characteristic of the early modern period. According to the confessionalization thesis, the early modern period witnessed not so much a retreat of *religion* but rather the expansion of *religions*, and that it is this development toward religious pluralism that had its characteristic effects even outside the areas that were immediately affected by religious differentiation. The political fragmentation of Christianity went hand in hand with the early modern crisis of faith. The criteria for establishing the nature of Truth underwent irreversible transformations, as did the notion of proof, in an important dialogue between faith and science. Doubt was an important tool for reflection and for judgment.

A number of studies in recent years have shown how the pathways leading to modernity quite often intersected with those of doubt, not only in the mainstream Western philosophical tradition but also in the fields of Biblical philology, ethnography, and antiquarianism. And yet the relationship of Spain and the Spanish Empire to this history of the early modern genesis of doubt and modernity has scarcely been explored. Whether we turn to Paul Hazard's now classic account of the crisis of European conscience and the birth of a new critical conscience unhampered by dogmas and confessionalisms, or to the great master-narratives of European tolerance — from Richard Popkin's crucial history of European scepticism, to Guy Stroumsa's recent effort to spotlight the origins of the comparative study of religion, to Benjamin Kaplan's monograph on the birth of toleration — France, Holland, Germany, and England always take centre stage.[11] In general, Iberia figures at best in these narratives as the place whence certain individuals hurriedly depart or flee, as in Yirmiyahu Yovel's *Marranos*, where these individuals' 'split identities' and hence their modernity are explained exclusively in terms of their Jewish origins, without taking into account the social context in which those split identities were formed.[12] The 'Radical Enlightenment' that Spinoza put in motion is considered to be the product of debates that took place inside a Republic of Letters from which southern Europe was excluded.[13]

And yet, as (Spanish) explorers expanded the limits of the known world and scholars engaged the classical past in new ways, established truths were increasingly questioned.[14] The encounter with the Americas, and in consequence the emergence of comparative ethnography and religion, seem to be the only Iberian aspects considered in this literature about modernity. Recent scholarship has noted that the sheer diversity of non-European societies created a complex set of rhetorical aims and ideological possibilities that have yet to be fully appreciated and that impinge on the questions addressed in this book.[15]

For quite some time the two editors of this volume have been working, both together and separately, on the spaces for tolerance and dissent in early modern Iberia, and on the long-term effects of the forced conversions. We have both explored the violent world of the Inquisition, the debates and protests that the creation and imposition of the Tribunal sparked within Iberian society, the aftermath of the forced conversions, and the complex world of Iberian minorities and their fluctuating identities.[16] In studying Spain's passage from multi-confessional to mono-confessional society, the authors have examined the many traces of multiculturalism and non-conformism, of heresies or acts of resistance, that the Inquisition and the new rules from Trent were incapable of fully quashing. In doing so, we have paid particular attention to the ways in which individual identity emerged out of minority identity, a phenomenon that was to take hold not only in the Iberian world, but throughout Europe as a whole.

These concerns have accompanied us for quite some time, slowly taking the shape of an international conference and then a coherent volume, and were tested and presented on a number of occasions before being tackled independently. Recently, they have come back to influence our own work once more as we now focus on the polemical milieu in Iberia since the Middle Ages,[17] thus addressing doubt as separate from the emergence of modernity.[18] Among these discussions and previous publications of members of our research group, the work of Felipe Pereda has been particularly relevant. In his recent book on sacred images from the Spanish Golden Age, Pereda explores art as an exercise dedicated to dispelling doubt in those who see it, as a testimony of Truth, but he also explores the sceptical reflection of artists confronted with the link between images and truth.[19]

Naturally, along the way we have been aided by the various exceptional contributions in the historiography that came before us, which staked out the ground that we have attempted to explore in greater detail. As to Iberia, we have to refer in the first place to John Edwards's article 'Religious Faith and Doubt in Late Medieval Spain' (included in his book *Religion and Society in Spain, c. 1492*),[20] that first rejected the long-standing notion that religious dissent among converts should automatically be attributed to an unshakable attachment to Judaism or Islam. Edwards also was the first to link inquisitorial material on Judaizers with the general incidence of heresy and scepticism across Europe. He was the first to consider doubt and scepticism as part of the religious landscape of Iberia. Before him, but using literary fictional sources, Albert Mas had shown how Spanish humanists had used 'the Turk' as a means to express religious relativism.[21] Another landmark for us has been Stuart B. Schwartz's book *All Can Be Saved*.[22] This book focuses on the proposition 'cada uno se salva en su ley' (each person can be saved in his own law). Schwartz interprets the proposition uttered at Inquisitorial trials as evidence for a 'popular tolerance' which has gone unnoticed until now because historians have focused on the process by which religious identities were inculcated during this period rather than looking into the cracks that opened up during that process. In his view, expressions of tolerance in Spain did not differ from those spreading across other parts of Europe at the time. In our opinion, the words, deeds, and attitudes of those accused of believing the propositions — including Old Christians, conversos, Moriscos, and Lutherans — do indeed partake of a degree of relativism, a loss of faith, or at the very least a sense of detachment from religion, if not scepticism. Above all, as we interpret the records of these Inquisition trials, what they indicate is a desire to distance oneself from the contentious rhetoric of Truth and salvation, a rhetoric that was not confined to Counter-Reformation Spain but was wielded by all sides in the religious battles of Reformation Europe.

The works of Edwards, Schwartz, and others (such as Miriam Bodian)[23] frame doubt within an intellectual tradition, but they also show personal doubt as a key element in an individual's faith journey. We have to consider those two aspects of doubt but also doubt as sin, which was a problem of authority and for authorities. From the point of view of religious authorities, doubt gave rise to a space that lacked a defined identity, within which the solid outlines of mainstream religious identities were no longer recognizable. This is why doubt had to be monitored and supressed, because it was by its nature linked to attitudes judged by the Inquisition to be either hypocritical or facilitating unbelief and heresy. Some of the attitudes and manifestations of this crisis were also related to a widespread feeling of deep pessimism. Recent historiography has established a link between that feeling of pessimism and a sceptical attitude. Increasing interest in epistemological scepticism in late sixteenth-century Spain reflected an awareness of the moral and political consequences of human ignorance and a worldview predicated on the ubiquity of deceit and the incongruity between appearance and reality. Jeremy Robbins has vividly described the main features of a mentality steeped in epistemological (and thus moral) pessimism, largely fostered by the sustained creative interaction between scepticism and stoicism that was so characteristic of seventeenth-century Spain. This interaction forged a distinctive view of the nature and extent of human knowledge and had a decisive influence on questions related to agency, morality, reason of state, trust, and honour.[24]

The historical body of work which presents doubt as a producer of 'modernity' is also linked to a long-standing tradition claiming that unbelief, in the sense of cynicism, atheism, irreligion, and so on, was impossible in the pre-modern period: that prior to the eighteenth-century Enlightenment, nobody was mentally capable of thinking outside the accepted framework of religion.[25] According to the influential proposals of Jacques Le Goff and Lucien Febvre (in his book on Rabelais and the problem of disbelief in the sixteenth century),[26] disbelief was unthinkable and inexpressible until the late modern period, and mere doubting could be (and was) considered heresy. We do not want to go into this debate at length here because Luca Addante's contribution in this volume will analyse and discuss it. We do not agree with Febvre but rather follow other, more recent historiography that derives from the work of historians such as Jean-Pierre Cavaillé, particularly his demonstration that irreligion was expressed as much by individuals belonging to the popular classes as by the learned elites, and in similar terms; and this was true in very different regions of Europe.[27] The debate over whether it was possible to be an atheist in the sixteenth and early seventeenth century has distracted scholars from wider questions about popular expressions of scepticism and religious and epistemological idiosyncrasy, and a fixation on atheism has tended to obscure the fact that an individual can experience varying degrees of scepticism without necessarily being an atheist in the modern sense.[28] The distance between unquestioning belief at one extreme and absolute disbelief at the other is considerable, and the positions between them, which this book explores, are numerous.[29]

Although these works are our point of departure, our proposal is probably more radical: we focus on Iberia (as some of them do) but consider the problem of doubt in isolation from modernity. Our subject is an Iberia marked by religious pluralism, interfaith polemics, religious and communal conflict but also by various forms of coexistence. We will closely examine what happens in Southern Europe, in both Iberia and Italy from the late Middle Ages to the Early Modern Period.

The book is divided into three parts. The first one, 'The Medieval Iberian Legacy and its Aftermath', begins with two essays based on an early sixteenth-century chronicle, Solomon Ibn Verga's *Shevet Yehudah* — in Spanish *La Vara de*

Judá. Both focus on a parable in the book, the parable of the three rings. Ibn Verga's version of this well-known parable tells of a king who asks a Jew which is the best religion, and the Jew answers with the story of a father who bequeathed to each of his three sons a ring, all of them similar to one another, the question being if one is better than the others or whether we can know which is best. Both Kriegel and Gutwirth coincide in showing that the parable supports the opinion of those who maintain that the truth claims of different religions are too shaky for irrefutable conclusions about the superiority of one of them.

The first essay, 'Not Scepticism but Certainty: A Different Plea for Toleration in Late Medieval Spain', by Maurice Kriegel, considers the debate in the *Shevet* about religion, its social and political role, and its value. Three strands of thought are for Kriegel clearly discernible. The first is the legacy of a philosophical view of the role of religion, as found among Muslim thinkers, in different forms, since al-Fārābī, that had been shared by many Jewish authors in Christian Spain during the thirteenth and fourteenth centuries and was still influential even up to 1492. Ibn Verga intended to translate into a witty and entertaining parable the sceptical viewpoints that were part of Maimonides's thought. The second strand is linked to the legacy of the interreligious 'dialogue' in the Middle Ages. The parable of the three rings is not the only case in point: Kriegel insists on the importance of the Tortosa Controversy in 1413–14, particularly the debate about belief and faith, and on Ibn Verga's vindication of ideas aired on that occasion, such as the notion that faith is unassailable by doubt, is undemonstrable and based on tradition. The last strand gives evidence of Ibn Verga's familiarity with sceptical notions that circulated in the wider Christian world of the early sixteenth century, particularly the notion of the limits of human knowledge, and the correlative discussion of faith. Ibn Verga brought these strands together; indeed, on this issue even more than on others, he stands out as a thinker who, on the one hand, is heir to the 'Medieval Enlightenment', and, on the other, is closely associated with currents in Renaissance sceptical thought which were later tapped by the modern, eighteenth-century Enlightenment.

Eleazar Gutwirth also deals with the parable of the three rings in his essay 'The Three Rings: *Shevet Yehuda*-Lessig/Graetz-Fritz Ishaq Baer'. Gutwirth discusses the reading of the parable by different authors as an icon of Enlightenment scepticism and tolerance, especially by the famous historian of Spanish Jewry Ishaq Baer. But Gutwirth mainly dedicates his essay to his own reading and contextualization of the parable of the three rings and to understanding it from what he calls the 'creative ambiguity' between ancient and modern, Jewish and Christian, which he deems characteristic of fifteenth-century Iberian Judaism. He shows that Ibn Verga's is not just another version of the parable. From the classical motifs underlying the parable, to the meaning of the names of the protagonists, to the contemporary social context in Spain which would resonate for Ibn Verga's readers, Gutwirth demonstrates the multifaceted body of references included in the text and the extent to which it is intertwined with contemporary Jewish life in Castile. Gutwirth uses Inquisition files and in particular the trial records of those who deny life after death ('no hay sino nascer e morir') and those who maintain that all men can obtain salvation through their own law and therefore that to observe the followers of other religions fulfilling their own law leads to respect for them.

Inquisition files are a rich source of evidence on disbelief, scepticism, and religious doubt. It is necessary to read anew the documents of the Holy Office since, as we have said, doubt and related phenomena have not been generally associated with Iberia and are seldom considered as features of the intellectual or religious attitudes that developed in the Iberian world. 'What Faith to Believe? Vacillation, Comparativism and Doubt', Mercedes García-Arenal's essay, is based on the Inquisition trial cases of individuals (not necessarily converts) who alternated or vacillated between Judaism, Christianity, and Islam, without necessarily becoming convinced of any of the three, and thus not settling on a definitive religious identity. She focuses on converts from Judaism, now indifferent Christians, who claim to be ready, if need be, to become Muslims and seem to be detached from any of the Laws; people who vacillate between the three religions, never becoming convinced, as in the parable of the three rings, of the superiority of any of them; and people who seek their own truth by means of converting from one religion to the other and then to a third one, trying out different religious paths. In this essay, García-Arenal argues that forced conversion and forced indoctrination engendered unbelief and irreligion, scepticism and even 'libertinism' in many individuals, and that this is made manifest in the yearning for 'freedom of conscience'. She also contends that the resulting vacillation and doubt were considered by Catholic moralists such as Jerónimo Gracián as conducive to atheism.

Isabelle Poutrin's essay serves as a threshold to the second part of the book, 'Europe and the Iberian Connection'. Poutrin's ' "Dubius in fide infidelis est": Between Faith and Heresy, Is There a Place for Doubt?' begins with the definitions of heresy given by Catholic canonists and theologians (mostly sixteenth-century Spaniards, with the occasional Italian). These definitions at times mention 'dubiousness', though not 'doubt', and describe heresy as a set of false affirmations and certainties. Poutrin explores whether these doctors opened up a space for uncertainty and hesitation, whether they made heretics of anyone who doubted. She bases her analysis on the classics (the great commentaries to the *Decretals* and the *Summa Theologica*), moral theology, and even works of exegesis, but most particularly on the Jesuit Juan Azor and his *Institutionum moralium*, published in Rome in 1600. According to the sources used by Poutrin, doubt, when firmly established in an individual's consciousness and not resisted by the forces of the will, is a sign of disobedience to the Church and an inner rejection of the gift of faith, and as such constitutes an open door to heresy and atheism.

Stefania Pastore's 'Pyrrhonism and Unbelief: Diego Hurtado de Mendoza and the Spanish Tradition', focuses on the legacy of medieval Spain within a European perspective and traces a possible Spanish contribution to the great Pyrrhonian and sceptical tradition in France. In Lyon in 1562, the well-known humanist and printer Henri Estienne produced the first published Latin translation of Sextus Empiricus's *Outlines of Pyrrhonism*. This anthology, which made the ancient, non-

Academic sceptical tradition accessible to a much broader audience, was to become a best-seller in modern Europe, finding its way into virtually every library from that time on. Montaigne had mottos from Sextus's text carved into the rafters of his study, and Pedro de Valencia, in 1590, remarked on the wide circulation of the text. As Richard Popkin has pointed out, Sextus's text would become a sort of anti-dogmatic manifesto and would revolutionize not only the history of philosophy but also the history of religious tolerance in Europe, paving the way for religious relativism. However, between 1545 and 1549, a Latin translation had already been prepared by the Spanish humanist Juan Páez de Castro at the request of the imperial ambassador Diego Hurtado de Mendoza, working from a codex in Mendoza's own collection.

The mutual influence of the Radical Reformation and the Renaissance in sixteenth-century Italy, which tended to promote unbelief, is the subject of Luca Addante's chapter, 'Unbelief, Deism and Libertinism in Sixteenth-Century Italy'. This essay offers an overview of current scholarship about unbelief and proposes Addante's own interpretation of libertinism and unbelief that convincingly challenges Fevbre's thesis. The cases of Juan de Valdés and his followers are a clear example of the ideological and religious connections between Spain and Italy, as well as the influence of tendencies within the Reformation on Catholicism.

'Shifting Certainties in the Baroque' is the title of Part III, which shares with Part II a concern with rhetoric and moral issues, and finds its internal cohesion in a discussion of new forms of belief, of ideas about what constitutes belief. As we have noted with the example of the Apostle Thomas, doubt had been a fundamental rhetorical tool of dialectics since Antiquity, but in the period dealt with in this part of the book, doubt came to partake of Scepticism's power to dissolve, its importance in determining how judgment is defined, and in the construction of the moral subject. Part III starts with Jeremy Robbins's essay, 'All Things to All People: Baltasar Gracián, Dissimulation, and the Question of Interpretation'. The work of Baltasar Gracián, and in particular his *Oráculo manual y arte de prudencia* (1647), has long divided critics over its moral and indeed religious stance because of the absence of overt religious references and statements. How does one interpret the significance of absence when dissimulation played such a major part in early modern political, moral, and courtly discourse? One way is to contextualize Gracián within contemporary moral treatises, and in particular to analyse his own approach to the concept of dissimulation, which was considered by many as the acceptable face of non-truth telling. The use of stratagems to say the opposite of what he appears to be saying is not exclusive to Gracián. Another way to interpret this absence is to explore the nature not simply of early modern doubt and unbelief but, more importantly, of early modern belief. Placing Gracián within the Jesuit culture that formed him, and reading his aphorisms in the context of his use of the notions of dissimulation and of virtue, Robbins reassesses the moral ethos of the *Oráculo* in order to examine the nature of his belief.

Fernando Rodríguez Mediano's 'The Concept of Doubt in the Trial of Miguel de Molinos (1687) and in the Controversy over Quietism' also deals with the moral implications of doubt. The word 'doubt' appears in the propositions by Molinos that were condemned by the Roman Inquisition in 1687. These propositions are problematic, because they do not reflect the exact nature of mystical 'Molinosismo'. Rodríguez Mediano tries to explain Molinos's trial in the context of the great moral debates in seventeenth-century Europe around the 'Forum of conscience' and the limits to freedom of conscience. In these debates, doubt emerges as an essential instrument for guiding souls and, therefore, as one of the ways of constructing moral and religious authority. However, in the seventeenth century, moral doubt is inseparable from sceptical doubt, and because of this there is an important epistemological dimension to theological issues. These issues come to a head in Molinos's trial, where doubt plays a key role: the Roman Inquisition understood that Molinos's doctrine, in particular his advocacy of surrendering oneself to God, constituted an attack on religious authority and mediation. Molinos's trial and the construction of the category of 'quietism' demonstrate the centrality of doubt in the battle to control conscience in modern Europe.

Felipe Pereda's 'The *Art* of Believing in Golden Age Spain' takes a look at another kind of rhetoric — the language of visual arts — through the lens of the same kind of Inquisition materials that were used in the essays in the first part of the book. One Inquisition trial in which two people discuss the nature of belief is used to interpret three paintings by Francisco de Zurbarán, Alonso Cano, and Sebastián López de Arteaga depicting the arrival and the dinner at Emmaus, two New Testament episodes that are thematically related to Thomas, the disciple who doubted the evidence of his own eyes and had to use his hand. According to Pereda, the paintings suggest that true faith is not dependent on the evidence offered by our senses, that faith does not reside in those things that we can perceive. That is perhaps among the biggest questions of the time: whether true knowledge of God can be gained from human experience. The differences between faith as an act of allegiance and assent and the cognitive act of believing had opened a divide that was destined to increase wherever any kind of debate took place, even if it was between two lay persons in a tavern, as the trial used by Pereda shows. He also brings to his discussion of faith and belief the writings of the Spanish painter Francisco Pacheco, who argued that the aim of painting was persuasion, moving men and women and leading them to piety. He was proposing therefore a rhetoric in which convincing depends as much on the state of mind that the orator creates in his audience (or the painter in his viewers) as on the signs or proofs that make up his argument. Painting and rhetoric have to move between argumentation and emotion.

The fourth part of the book is entitled 'Marranisms: Inside and Outside Iberia' and continues the discussion of doubt as a rhetoric of caution, distance and irony, proposing an elective affinity between this rhetoric and people of converso descent. It begins with Matthew Ancell's 'Decircumcizing the Heart: The Eucharist and Conversion in Calderón's *Autos Sacramentales*'. Ancell takes up Pereda's discussion about concepts of faith and belief. In *autos sacramentales* such as 'El orden de Melquisedec' (*c.* 1652) and 'El socorro general' (1644), Calderón de la Barca employs the Pauline notion of the circumcision of Christ as baptism. By examining the figure of 'decircumcision' in Derrida's analysis of Michel de Montaigne, who coins it as a term for forced conversion, Ancell investigates Eucharistic discourse in Calderón's sacramental plays as both an allegory of the situation of the converso and an examination of the nexus between faith, belief and doubt. Whereas transubstantiation relies on the authority of the priest for the efficacy of the sacrament, other seventeenth-century interpretations of the Eucharist depend on the faith of the communicant. Seen in this light, the theological discourse of the *autos* reveals the converso's predicament, that conversion is a question of fidelity to a covenant (political and religious), rather than of belief versus doubt. One of the *autos* used by Ancell includes a person who affirms 'When I am with Jews I am a Jew, when I am with Christians, I am a Christian,' expressing a kind of religious flexibility (or lack of it) similar to the one described in the first part of the book (especially in García-Arenal).

The rest of the chapters are dedicated to individual 'doubters'. José Luis Villacañas deals with the physician of Ferdinand the Catholic and later of Empress Isabella, Charles V's wife, in 'Marrano Emotions: Francisco López de Villalobos'. Though his suggestive notion of 'marrano emotions' — which belong not strictly to those who are of Jewish descent but to those who feel in a place outside time or space, without a proper sense of belonging — seems uncertain to us, his reading of Villalobos's translation of Plautus's *Amphitryon* is full of insights: the translation as well as the notes of the translator contain ironic hints about Villalobos's suspicions and doubts, his secret misgivings about the possibility of having a religious identity, and irony towards those who believe yet do not know. It also shows how in early modern Spain the rhetoric of the self had a political dimension.

In his 'Literary Discourse between the Eternal Validity of the Torah and Philosophical Doubt: The Polemical Writings of Abraham Gómez Silveira (1656–1740)', Harm den Boer insists on the use of irony, even of irreverent and irrepressible humour towards religious matters, humour that does not preclude curiosity regarding Judaism, Christianity, or Islam. Abraham Gómez Silveira was born into a Portuguese converso family in Arévalo (Spain) in 1656. He migrated to Amsterdam at an early age, where he joined the Portuguese Jewish community and received a religious education at the congregation's institutions, and later became one of the most prolific authors of Jewish–Christian polemical literature written in the Spanish or Portuguese language. The polemical manuscripts written by Gómez Silveira take up thousands of pages, full of references to both Jewish and Christian works, and even the Qur'an. These works also cover a variety of literary genres, ranging from a mere listing of titles and phrases, to treatises, dialogues, and several forms of poetry. In fact, Silveira's persistent use of literary devices seems to Den Boer to be a way of expressing doubt or relativism, in contrast to the all-too-simple argument for adherence and obedience to Judaism's eternal truth, contained in the Torah. More emphatic in his denial of rabbinic authority is Uriel da Costa, the famous Amsterdam Jew of Portuguese extraction who, humiliated and expelled from the Jewish community of his town, committed suicide in 1640. Miriam Bodian's 'Uriel da Costa's Career: An Interpretation' is an analysis of the life and work of Da Costa and in particular his work *Exemplar humanae vitae* (1623), in which he set out his radical beliefs about religion. He argued that Scripture and all positive religions were fraudulent and that the 'law of nature' was the only law of God. Da Costa's central concern, like that of many individuals who appear in this book, is the human longing for salvation and the difficulties it has caused for mankind. The problem for him was further complicated because he did not believe in the afterlife: neither in eternal reward or punishment. Da Costa, according to Bodian, was aware of a certain male ideal of his period, the solitary and uncompromising seeker of truth. He had a disdain for authority and was not willing to allow his pursuit of truth to be constrained by the need for prudence and dissimulation. He is part of the evidence that Reformation rhetoric about individual conscience and the abuses of the clergy was widespread among crypto-Jews. But he is also extraordinary, unique: in the normative Jewish world of the seventeenth century, as Bodian shows, it was unthinkable for a Jew to compose and publish a treatise laying out an argument based on Scripture that there was no world beyond this one.

Conclusion

This book demonstrates the existence of religious doubt in the Iberian Peninsula in the period before the modern age, in a polemical, pluri-religious context that necessarily produced comparisons between the three monotheistic religions. The heightened awareness of multiple religious traditions — traditions that taught mutually exclusive paths to salvation — raised doubts and discomfort even among the faithful about their creed's monopoly on salvation. Anxiety about salvation set some people on heterodox courses impelling them into unexplored territory, such as the reading of Scripture or of the sacred texts of other religions. It inspired many others to pursue inner religiosity and contributed to the creation of a new idea of the self and a forum of conscience. We are dealing here with ideas and attitudes prevalent in the Europe of the Protestant Reformation, where a new religious plurality had appeared. The most intriguing aspect of these intellectual and religious phenomena, in our view, has been to see how those ideas interacted both with the confusion and blurring of religious identities produced by mass conversion, and with the comparativism inherent to polemical writing and religious indoctrination that accompanied the expansion of the Iberian world and the resulting contact with new peoples.

To our mind, there is a question that has not yet been sufficiently explored and that is how the crisis of the Protestant Reformation interlocks or overlaps in Iberia with the crisis produced by mass conversion and the existence of large numbers of 'converts' struggling painfully with their religious identities. This book provides food for thought on this question and unveils new connections between the two religious crises and between the identification, sometimes even by the Inquisition, between converts and Protestants.

The premises from which we started work on this book are confirmed by many chapters, mainly in its first parts. But there are also crucial lines of questioning that arise mainly from how Spain and Spaniards reacted to the religious transformations of the sixteenth and seventeenth centuries, as Protestant and Catholic Reformations compelled Europeans to confront conflicting claims to theological truth. These transformations also affected the Jewish communities in exile. Throughout the book we witness a battle for the control of conscience, how individuals deal with it or try to evade it, and how the 'individual conscience' starts to make its appearance. There is a tension between the imposition of orthodoxy by a political and religious power obsessed with the threat dissenters posed to domestic and international peace, and the desire of dissenters and minorities for freedom of conscience. 'Toleration' and 'freedom of conscience' were the terms more commonly used in contemporary France to defend the rights of religious minorities. We witness most importantly the formulation and discussion of the moral implications of doubt. The new religious plurality brought the need for a moral criterion. In Spain, by the seventeenth century moral doubt becomes inseparable from sceptical doubt. Spanish theologians reacted to these challenges in ways that reflected Spain's pluralistic past, one of which was probabilism, a strain of casuistic reasoning that was advanced by the Dominican Bartolomé de Medina around the last quarter of the sixteenth century and remained extremely influential up to the 1640s, through the work of Juan Caramuel. Probabilism held that, in the face of difficult moral choices, it is enough to choose the option that is not a sin. This doctrine was adopted by most moral theologians: it opened up new possibilities in moral reasoning by seeking moral assurance while daring to take intellectual risks. Although probability did not provide certainty, it did at least eliminate the danger of acting while in a state of doubt. Probabilism sought certainty, at least moral certainty by accommodating doubt and uncertainty in moral choices and decisions. It was a doctrine that was condemned by many for leading to moral laxity but perhaps we can also consider it inside the processes that in Europe led to 'toleration'.

The last part of this book took an unexpected turn and posed provocative and engaging questions, among which is how this early modern Spanish moral theology, in connection with political thought, may nuance paradigms of secularization. We must admit that it opens up new questions and lines of research that are far removed from those we had at the outset. The idea we started with was a coherent and homogeneous scenery, reflected in the first and second parts. However, the research into the legacy of that multi-religious and multi-cultural Spain, and into the doubt that permeated it in the period following the Council of Trent, has led the way to a wide variety of new panoramas and unexpected itineraries. In the attempt to disinter an absence, that of doubt at the heart of the history of the Iberian world, we have cast light on diverse and complex presences which are, perhaps, only contradictory in appearance. However, we have done so using multiple sources and perspectives, in an attempt not to relegate its existence to a purely intellectual history, but rather analysing its repercussions both in the everyday lives of ordinary people and in polemics, in the rich and complex artistic and literary production of the Spanish baroque, and how it was reflected on in the fields of philosophy and theology. Inquisition trials, polemical writings, treatises on theology and casuistry, language, rhetoric and visual art; each of these fields has clearly proven that Spain must be included in any *histoire mondiale* of doubt, and that we may now need to change our definition of 'modernity' or maybe reconsider if it is at all a good analytical tool.

Notes to the Introduction

1. Glenn W. Most, *Doubting Thomas* (Cambridge, MA: Harvard University Press, 2005), p. 223.
2. *Belief in History: Approaches to European and American Religion*, ed. by Thomas A. Kselman (Notre Dame, IN: University of Notre Dame Press, 1991), especially John van Engen, 'Faith as a Concept in Medieval Christendom', pp. 19–67.
3. Caroline Walker Bynum, *Christian Materiality: An Essay on Religion in Late Medieval Europe* (New York: Zone Books, 2011), pp. 272–73.
4. Jean Wirth, 'La naissance du concept de croyance (XII–XVII siècles)', *Bibliothèque d'Humanisme et Renaissance*, 45.1 (1983), 7–58 [reprinted in Wirth, *Saint Anne est une sorcière et autres essais* (Geneva: Droz, 2003), pp. 113–76].
5. Adriano Prosperi, 'Confessione e dissimulazione', *Les Dossiers du Grihl* (2009); Jacques Chiffoleau, ' "Ecclesia de occultis non iudicat". L'Eglise, le secret et l'occulte du XIIe au XVe siècle', *Micrologus*, 14 (2006), 359–481; and for the Iberian World Stefania Pastore, *Il vangelo e la spada. L'Inquisizione di Castiglia e i suoi critici (1449–1598)* (Rome: Edizioni di storia e letteratura, 2003), pp. 214–53. For a general overview see Stephan Kuttner, 'Ecclesia de occultis non iudicat. Problemata ex doctrina poenali decretalistarum a Gratiano usque ad Gregorium P. IX', in *Acta congressus iuridici internationalis VII saeculo a decretalibus Gregorii IX et XIV a codice iustiniano promulgates*, 5 vols (Rome: Pont. Instituti Utriusque Iuris, 1934–37), vol. III (1936), pp. 225–46; and, more recently, Paolo Prodi, *Una storia della giustizia. Dal pluralismo dei fori al moderno dualismo tra coscienza e diritto* (Bologna: Il Mulino, 2000), pp. 92–97.
6. Adriano Prosperi, *Tribunali della coscienza: Inquisitori, confessori, missionari* (Turin: Einaudi, 1996).
7. Manuel Peña Díaz, 'Cultura escrita, escrúpulos y censuras cotidianas (siglos XVI–XVIII)', *Estudis. Revista de historia moderna*, 37 (2011), 73–90.
8. Igor Sosa Mayor, *El noble atribulado. Nobleza y teología moral en la Castilla moderna (1550–1650)* (Madrid: Marcial Pons, 2018), especially chapter 1.
9. Brad S. Gregory, *The Unintended Reformation: How a Religious Revolution Secularized Society* (Cambridge, MA: Belknap Press of Harvard University Press, 2012).
10. Jonathan I. Israel, *European Jewry in the Age of Mercantilism, 1550–1750* (London: Littman Library of Jewish Civilization, 1998), p. 30.
11. Paul Hazard, *La crise de la conscience européenne, 1680–1715* (Paris: Boivin, 1935); Richard H. Popkin, *The History of Scepticism: From Erasmus to Spinoza* (Berkeley: University of California Press, 1979); Guy G. Stroumsa, *A New Science: The Discovery of Religion in the Age of Reason* (Cambridge, MA, and London: Harvard University Press, 2010); Benjamin J. Kaplan, *Divided by Faith: Religious Conflict and the Practice of Toleration in Early Modern Europe* (Cambridge, MA: Belknap Press of Harvard University Press, 2007). As an exception see Ronald W. Truman, *Spanish Treatises on Government, Society and Religion in the time of Philip II* (Leiden: Brill, 1999), especially chapter 6.
12. Yirmiyahu Yovel, *The Other Within. The Marranos: Split Identity and the Emerging Modernity* (Princeton, NJ: Princeton University Press, 2009); Yosef Kaplan, *An Alternative Path to Modernity: The Sephardi Diaspora in Western Europe* (Leiden: Brill, [1996] 2000).
13. Jonathan I. Israel, *Radical Enlightenment: Philosophy and the Making of Modernity, 1650–1750* (Oxford: Oxford University Press, 2001).
14. Anthony Pagden, *The Fall of Natural Man: The American Indian and the Origins of Comparative Ethnology* (New York: Cambridge University Press, 1982).
15. See, for example, *Implicit Understandings: Observing, Reporting and Reflecting on the Encounters between Europeans and Other Peoples in the Early Modern Era*, ed. by Stuart B. Schwartz (Cambridge and New York: Cambridge University Press, 1995); Joan-Pau Rubiés, *Travellers and Cosmographers:*

Studies in the History of Early Modern Travel and Ethnology (Aldershot: Ashgate, 2007). Also, Elvira Vilches, *New World Gold: Cultural Anxiety and Monetary Disorder in Early Modern Spain* (Chicago, IL: University of Chicago Press, 2010).

16. Stefania Pastore, *Il vangelo e la spada*; Pastore, *Un'eresia spagnola. Spiritualità conversa, alumbradismo e Inquisizione (1449–1559)* (Florence: L. S. Olschki, 2004).

17. *Polemical Encounters: Christians, Jews and Muslims in Iberia and Beyond*, ed. by Mercedes García-Arenal and Gerard Wiegers (University Park: Pennsylvania State University Press, 2018).

18. *After Conversion: Iberia and the Emergence of Modernity*, ed. by Mercedes García-Arenal (Leiden: Brill, 2016). A whole section of this book is dedicated to 'Conversion and Perplexity'; see in particular the essays included there authored by Stefania Pastore, 'Doubt in Fifteenth-Century Iberia', M. García-Arenal, '"Mi padre moro yo moro": The Inheritance of Belief in Early Modern Iberia', and Felipe Pereda, 'True Painting and the Challenge of Hypocrisy'.

19. Felipe Pereda, *Crimen e ilusión. El arte de la verdad en el Siglo de Oro* (Madrid: Marcial Pons, 2017). From a different but related perspective, Stefania Tutino, in her *Shadows of Doubt*, has examined the hermeneutical and epistemological anxieties assailing post-Reformation Catholicism, and has shown the point to which they ushered in modernity. Stefania Tutino, *Shadows of Doubt: Language and Truth in Post-Reformation Catholic Culture* (Oxford: Oxford University Press, 2014).

20. John Edwards, 'Religious Faith and Doubt in Late Medieval Spain: Soria circa 1450–1500', in *Religion and Society in Spain, c. 1492* (Aldershot: Variorum, 1996); originally published in *Past and Present*, 120 (1988), 3–25.

21. Albert Mas, *Les Turcs dans la littérature espagnole du Siècle d'Or*, 2 vols (Flers: Follope, 1967), I, 167 ff.

22. Stuart B. Schwartz, *All Can Be Saved: Religious Tolerance and Salvation in the Iberian Atlantic World* (New Haven, CT, and London: Yale University Press, 2008).

23. Miriam Bodian, 'In the Cross-Currents of the Reformation: Crypto-Jewish Martyrs of the Inquisition, 1570–1670', *Past and Present*, 176 (2002), 66–104; Bodian, *Dying in the Law of Moses: Crypto-Jewish Martyrdom in the Iberian World* (Bloomington: Indiana University Press, 2007), pp. 24–25.

24. This is the general argument of Jeremy Robbins, *Arts of Perception: The Epistemological Mentality of the Spanish Baroque, 1580–1720* (Abingdon: Routledge, 2007), especially chapters 1–2.

25. See a general overview in the first two chapters of Thomas Kselman, *Conscience and Conversion: Religious Liberty in Post-Revolutionary France* (New Haven, CT, and London: Yale University Press, 2018).

26. Lucien Febvre, *Le Problème de l'incroyance au XVIe siècle. La Religion de Rabelais* (Paris: Albin Michel, 1942).

27. Jean-Pierre Cavaillé, 'La question de l'irréligion populaire, à la rencontré de l'histoire et de l'anthropologie', *Institut d'histoire de la Réformation. Bulletin Annuel*, 36 (2014–15), 55–69. See also Wirth, 'La naissance du concept de croyance'; Alain Mothu, 'De la foi du charbonnier à celle du héros (et retour)', *Les Dossiers du Grihl* (2007) <https://dossiersgrihl.revues.org/3393>.

28. Nicholas Griffiths, 'Popular Religious Scepticism and Idiosyncrasy in Post-Tridentine Cuenca', in *Faith and Fanaticism: Religious Fervour in Early Modern Spain*, ed. by Lesley Twomey (Aldershot: Ashgate, 1997), pp. 95–128 (p. 99).

29. Mercedes García-Arenal, 'L'Estompe des identités en situation de conversion: Isaac Pallache, un converti insincère?', in *Les Musulmans dans l'histoire de l'Europe*, ed. by Jocelyne Dakhlia and Wolfgang Kaiser, 2 vols (Paris: Albin Michel, 2013), II, 35–60.

PART I

❖

The Medieval Iberian Legacy
and its Aftermath

CHAPTER 1

❖

Not Scepticism, but Certainty:
A Different Plea for Toleration in
Late Medieval Spain

Maurice Kriegel

Leaders of minority religions who felt responsible for the fate of their communities, as well as followers of the dominant religions who felt uneasy about policies of outright physical persecution or of abasement and humiliation, undertook, in medieval times, to foster well-wishing attitudes towards those who, in the phrase of Thomas Aquinas, 'were outside'.[1] They often combined, in their pleas, two closely related arguments. First, they contended, the evidence at our disposal in order to gauge the truth claims of the different religions is too shaky to allow us to arrive at irrefutable conclusions, so that the devotees of the majority religion are certainly entitled to hold to their creeds, but should also allow the worshippers of other faiths to do likewise, until all questions become settled and truth definitely established, in the afterlife or in some future redemptive era. Secondly, what, in the meantime, we are in a position to know reliably, through observation, is the quality of the moral behaviour among the followers of the competing religions, and we should have high regard for those people, whatever be their creed, who lead a virtuous life.

Those who made their case on such groundings often put forward one variant or another of the tale of the three rings, because they found it consonant with these views. In late eighth-century Baghdad, the head of the Christian Nestorian Church, Catholicos Timothy, told Caliph al-Mahdi a parable about a pearl: it once happened that many people were gathered in a house at night and that a pearl fell to the ground; all strove to pick it up; because of the dark only one person succeeded in doing so; the others, however, also believed that they had got hold of it, although what they in effect had in hand was but a stone, a piece of glass or a bit of earth. 'We children of man are in this perishable world as in darkness'. It is only at dawn, 'in the world to come', when 'the fog of ignorance' will dissolve, that we will know who is the real possessor of the pearl. Caliph al-Mahdi, Timothy wrote in the (real or fictional) account of his discussion, immediately grasped the lesson of the story and voiced his approval: 'The possessors of the pearl are not known in this world, O Catholicos'.[2] Timothy immediately mitigated the scepticism of this assertion by adding that the possessors of the pearl are nevertheless 'partially known [...] by good works [...] and pious deeds, and by the wonders and miracles that God performs through those who possess the true faith'. He then expatiated, on traditional lines, on the miracles recorded in the Bible and the New Testament as proofs of the truth of Christianity. When the Caliph protested that it might be difficult to distinguish real miracles from counterfeit ones, the Catholicos agreed. This was why, he observed, he had said that both 'good works and miracles are the lustre of the pearl of the faith': he could not abandon the argument from miracles, but was prepared to admit, it seems, that the devouts of any given belief may be well-advised to adduce the good deeds they perform as the more convincing proof on behalf of their faith.[3]

Boccaccio makes the same points as Patriarch Timothy, but his emphases are somewhat different. He has the same lesson to teach as his (unknown to him) predecessor Patriarch Timothy on the impossibility to establish with certitude which of the three rings that the father has given to his sons (which of the three monotheistic religions) is the true one:

> And the rings being found so like one to the other that it was impossible to distinguish the true one, the suit to determine the true heir remained pendent, and so remains. And so, my lord, to your question, touching the three laws given to the three peoples by God the Father, I answer: each deems itself to have the true inheritance, the true law, the true commandments of God; but which of them is justified in so believing, is a question which, like of that of the rings, remains pendent.

But he has only a passing reference to the ethical conduct displayed by the followers of the different religions: the three sons — who embody the three religions — were 'goodly and virtuous all, and very obedient to their father [God the father]'. It may well be that what Boccaccio found attractive in the story that had been handed down to him was less any lessons to be drawn from it on the limitations of human knowledge or on 'toleration', than the literary possibilities offered by the folkloristic motive of how a merchant outwitted the prince who wanted to entrap him.

This motive in Boccaccio (or in the other Italian versions of the tale) led, in turn, the Spanish-Jewish author Solomon Ibn Verga to retell the story in his Hebrew book *The Staff of Juda*,[4] written during the first decades of the sixteenth century.[5] Ibn Verga ascribes a number of character traits to the Jews, and he time and again mentions cleverness as one of the most salient. At the same time, he could feel all the more prompted to include the tale in his work if the two themes of the limits of human knowledge and of openness to persons beyond sectarian affiliation were foremost in his mind. On the first topic, he had only to tap his own cultural tradition. Thus, in one of the discussions he crafted between a king and his adviser, this latter, asked about the motion of the spheres, answers facetiously:

> By my life, O king, don't ask me about the heavens, and even what is above the roof of my house I do not know. The Sages have said that what is said in physics is for the most part truth, what is said in mathematics is for the most

part untruthfulness, and what is said in metaphysics [or theology] is totally
untruthfulness, for it is not in the power of man.[6]

It has been suggested[7] that Ibn Verga intended to translate into the language of
a witty and entertaining dialogue, as suited his programme of offering a piece of
light-hearted literature in Hebrew, those sceptical viewpoints that were part and
parcel of Maimonides's thought.[8] And he dedicated a significant part of his work to
the second issue, to the point that he may be said to have offered one of the earliest
principled defences of toleration.

A different line of argument was put forth by one of the Jewish participants in
the Tortosa Controversy in 1414. Pope Benedict XIII had convened this Jewish–
Christian disputation in the city where he resided, where it had opened on 8
February 1413. A year later, at one of the sessions of the fourth round of discussions,[9]
after the same issues had been discussed for a whole year, one of the three Jewish
scholars who had agreed to participate in the disputation, Astruc Halevi,[10] tried to
bring the proceedings to an end. There was no point, he said, in discussing articles
of faith:

> I say that all disputation about an article of faith is prohibited, so that a man may
> not stray away from the articles of his religion. David says: 'The mouth of the
> righteous uttereth wisdom, and his tongue speaketh justice. The law of his God
> is in his heart. None of his steps slide' (Psalm 37, verses 30–31). It seems that
> only science should be made the subject of dispute and argument; but religion
> and belief ought to be consigned willingly to faith, not argument, so that one
> may not retreat from it; everyone should make his root and foundation in faith
> and accept its conclusions as valid, firm and undoubted.[11]

In order to put this contention into proper perspective, and to better understand
both its underpinnings and its import, it may be useful to consider a text dealing
with the notion of faith, and authored by none other than the spokesman for
Christianity in the Tortosa disputation, to whom Astruc Halevi directed his plea,
Jerónimo de Santa Fe, formerly known, when he was still a Jew (that is, until
1412), as Joshua Halorki. When the most prominent convert of the 1390s, Paul
of Burgos, previously Shlomo Halevi, had made known his conviction that the
Messianic Biblical prophecies had been fulfilled in Jesus, Halorki, then a physician
close to the lay leader of the Jewish communities in Aragon, wrote a letter to Paul
in which he expressed his bewilderment, raised a number of objections concerning
the Christological interpretation of the Biblical prophecies, and in the sequel put
forward two questions on which he begged his correspondent to offer him an
answer.[12] In the first one, he asked:

> Is a man who professes a religion obliged, or is it proper for him, from the
> viewpoint of his professing a religion, to probe and investigate the cornerstones
> of his religion and faith as to whether it is true or another one is true? Or is one
> not obliged or allowed to do so?[13]

Any answer, he said, seems to entail difficulties. In particular, to support the notion
that one has indeed to 'examine and weigh the beliefs[14] of his religion and faith
with those of another religion, from the existent ones, until one decides where the

truth is according to his opinion', is objectionable on two accounts: first, one will never be 'stable in his faith',[15] but live permanently in doubt and perplexity, since there will be no end to a process of examination which will involve not only the three monotheistic religions, but also others; secondly, everyone will have to take a personal decision on religious truth, instead of relying on the tradition of the prophet who was the founder of the religion to which one happens to belong: if one professes a religion as the result of such a deliberation, his attitude cannot be aptly described as one of 'faith', if the word is understood in its strict sense.[16]

Astruc Halevi, in his declaration in 1414, and his opponent in Tortosa, Joshua Halorki/Jerónimo de Santa Fe, in his queries more than twenty years earlier, appear to share a preoccupation with the robustness of faith as against the assaults of doubt and are prone to contrast faith on the one hand with argument and reason on the other. It is no less telling that two other Jewish scholars, Ferrer Saladin and Joseph Albo — who were also among the disputants at Tortosa — bothered to give a definition of faith, which concurred, in fact, with that supplied by Halorki. Their disquisitions on the issue show that they also agreed with Halorki on the opposition between a religious attitude based on a claim to the right, or even the duty, to assess the truth claims of one's religion, and, by extension, of the different competing religions, and an attitude of reliance 'on the tradition of the prophet'.

Ferrer Saladin defined, as we learn from one of his recently published sermons,[17] what is referred to by the Hebrew term *emunah* in the following terms:

> it is the assent of the mind, which will occur to someone, to a thing, so that the opposite of it is impossible. It will not come from the senses, or from knowledge, or from generally accepted opinions. It has thus been defined in its genus, as an assent of the mind, and set apart from the first principles (it 'occurs in the mind'), from the opinion ('the opposite of it is impossible'), from what is known by the senses, by the intellect and on the basis of generally accepted opinions (it will not come... etc.).[18]

There are, Ferrer Saladin adds, three kinds of *emunah*, and, accordingly, three ranks among the believers: the highest rank is that of the prophets, whose *emunah* has its source in the 'divine science', whereas the *emunah* of those who rely on a tradition which has its origin in prophecy cannot be said to be perfect to the same degree, but nevertheless is highly commendable, and superior to the knowledge supplied by the senses or rational investigation. *Emunah* based on miracles displays less merit than the first two kinds, but should be given too its due recognition. *Emunah*, a term long understood in the sense of 'belief', has here become 'faith': it is characterized by certainty (so that the distinction, found for example in Maimonides, between 'belief' and 'certain belief',[19] is silently dropped),[20] and the certainty of *emunah* is not reached through sense perception or rational proof, but through Revelation, directly (as in the case of the prophets) or indirectly (through reliance on a trustworthy tradition).

The definition of *emunah* put forward by Joseph Albo in his *Book of Principles* seems at first to be less trenchant than that of Ferrer Saladin, since he characterizes as *emunah* any 'conception in the mind' that is held as certain, so that the mind 'cannot in any way imagine its opposite', whether certitude is reached through the senses, demonstration or 'experience'.[21] But it is clear that what Albo wants primarily to emphasize is that the experience of Revelation and the tradition that bears it out meet the criteria of certainty. He thus quotes Deuteronomy 5. 19: 'Did ever a people hear the voice of God speaking out of the midst of the fire, as thou hast heard, and live?' and comments: 'Though reason rejects it, it is absolutely true, since experience testifies to it, and it has been handed down by tradition continuously from father to son. It cannot therefore be denied'.[22] He then concludes his discussion of belief by emphasizing that 'belief applies to things which we have not perceived with our senses at the time of their occurrence, nor proved with our reason, but have only on the authority of continuous tradition'.[23] As, for him, the main feature of belief — or, better, of faith — is certitude, Albo can connect his discussion of belief and Halorki's question addressed to Paul of Burgos — which he reproduces in his book, without mentioning its author — and echo Halorki's first objection against a duty of examination:

> no religionist will be firm in his faith, and will therefore deserve no reward for belief, if he is not firm therein and free from doubt. For we cannot call a thing belief except when the mind cannot conceive the thing being otherwise, as we explained before.[24]

Paul of Burgos seems to have brandished, shortly after his conversion, the flag of 'faith', or at least to have insisted on a definition of it. This much — but hardly more — we can infer from the cryptic allusions of the Jewish author Profiat Duran in an epistle he sent to his ex-friend Bonet Bonjorn, who had converted under the influence of Paul of Burgos:

> Human Reason, Duran writes mockingly, will seduce thee never more to dwell with her in dark chambers, thou recognizest her as an enemy, 'a cruel poison of vipers' (Deuteronomy 32. 33). For she always hates faith and injures it. He is a fool who says: 'Reason and Religion are two lights', for reason with its syllogisms and demonstrations has no part thereof [...]. Faith alone ascendeth on high. Those who deny this go to hell. That is the meaning of the verse 'The righteous shall live by faith' (Habakkuk 2. 4), if the definition of faith [emunah] in the Hebrew language is as you and your teacher [Paul of Burgos] think.[25]

This description of Bonjorn's (and, by implication, Paul of Burgos's) view, positing a direct antithesis between faith and reason, is probably closer to Duran's own polemical presentation of Christianity than an authentic representation of Bonjorn's or Paul of Burgos's positions. It is worth discussing a bit in detail the last phrases of the passage just quoted, since it has been seen as a telling illustration of a general thesis on the role of the philosophical-intellectualistic currents in the collapse of Spanish Jewry in the late fourteenth- and early fifteenth-century Spain, and on the appeal, for those among Jews who felt frustrated when they faced a 'Judaism-of-the-elites' unable to satisfy their religious yearnings, of a Christianity extolling faith. In this spirit, Ishaq Baer has understood the sentences as if Bonjorn and Paul of Burgos had referred to the Apostle Paul's definition of faith, and had themselves stressed the contrast, put forward by Profiat Duran, in the manner of a moderate Maimonideanism, between the Apostle Paul's doctrine of salvation by faith and the stance which makes salvation dependent on both intellectual perfection and the right kind of conduct.[26] The lines in question are thus understood to mean that Bonjorn and Paul of Burgos claimed to adhere to a markedly Pauline theology of faith, even if, in fact, these lines do not expressly mention the Apostle Paul.[27] In such a reading, Paul of Burgos's trajectory largely reduplicated the path previously trodden by Alfonso de Valladolid (known, as a Jew, as Abner de Burgos), which led from a philosophical outlook that blended an interest in matters of science and a relative indifference to the specifics of religious worship, to a denunciation of *esprits forts*, a thirst for 'faith', and finally conversion to a fideistic brand of Christianity. Indeed, Paul of Burgos made in passing, in his answer to Halorki's letter, a scornful remark on 'your teacher, Averroes'.[28] Nevertheless, it may well be that Duran's sentences in his letter to Bonjorn are to be interpreted more prudently, as stating that the two converts made some assertion, in unspecified circumstances, concerning the definition of 'faith' in Hebrew; or, more precisely, that Paul of Burgos made this statement, and Bonjorn, who had become his follower, accepted it: which is plausible, since Paul of Burgos was in the habit, as his later writings show, of displaying his knowledge of the original language of the Biblical books. Paul of Burgos had probably his own definition of faith, when he was still the rabbi Solomon Halevi, while Ferrer Saladin and Albo had theirs: the three of them took up the task of providing such a definition, in the context of the turn in Jewish thought, from the late fourteenth century onwards, from speculation cast in the Maimonidean-Averroistic mould to anti-philosophical philosophies (with varying degrees of the anti-philosophical bent).

True, Paul of Burgos thought, as we learn from his answer to Halorki, that 'some of the great thinkers have put speculative knowledge as the locus of faith, and they erred in this, as wise men have proven'.[29] But he may have entertained this view not only after his conversion but when he was a learned Jew. Joseph Albo was no less convinced that 'faith stands higher than speculative knowledge'.[30] Both Ferrer Saladin and Joseph Albo seem to have been deeply sceptical about the power of natural reason, or, at least, to have adopted — even if they did so, admittedly, without acknowledging it by a direct quotation of *The Kuzari* — the views of Judah Halevi: on the primacy of experience, especially of the 'irrefutable' prophetical experience, and on the superiority of the unquestioning 'faith, free from doubts' on the kind of faith that needs to find a support in 'examination' (although such a lesser brand of faith is commended, we read in *The Kuzari*, for the 'perturbed soul').[31] Profiat Duran — who himself borrowed from Judah Halevi some of the building blocks of his own theology — argued against views on the matter of faith that were those of Ferrer Saladin and Albo no less than those of Paul of Burgos.

It is against this background that Astruc Halevi makes his case for toleration. One should commend his religion and belief to faith. Jews have their own way to understand the role of the Messiah, and this way is for them an article of faith. What is the exact content of this article of faith dealing with the Messianic issue, Astruc Halevi does not say at this point. He had asserted in another part of his brief that the issue of when the Messiah will come is not such a critical issue for Jews that they have to espouse one of the possible views as an article of faith,[32] but he may have contradicted himself, as Jerónimo de Santa Fe accused him of having done. The heart of his argument, in any case, is that as an examination and discussion of the validity of faith, in the manner of the scrutiny to which matters of science are submitted, can be conducted only at the risk of shaking it, they are prohibited, or should be: faith is too precious. Or, in order to place the main tenets of faith above dispute, he may have resorted to the argument used by Ferrer Saladin in his last speech, when he had to address the question, which had come to the fore, of the articulation between articles of faith and scriptural statements: Jews and Christians equally accept the articles of their faith 'through pure faith and tradition',[33] and the premises of faith — like premises in scientific reasoning — do not require any proof.[34]

Astruc Halevi tells also his Christian opponent, in the conclusion of his memorandum, that Jews should not be assailed on account of their stiff-neckedness, but on the contrary be praised for their commitment to the faith they inherited from their forebears, their indifference to temporal goods and their fortitude in the face of misfortunes and troubles. It should be recognized that these commendable features of their behaviour proceed from the 'firmness and stability of a good loyalty'.[35] The faith of the Christians and the faith of the Jews, Astruc Halevi adds, are indeed different: they are so much so that they should not conflict, since they are not nurturing opposing views on the same matters, and the respective beliefs they teach answer aspirations and queries of a different order. Christians believe in a Saviour that redeems souls, Jews expect a Messiah that will restore their former political independence.[36] Christians and Jews, Astruc Halevi thus says — more implicitly than in so many words — should live peacefully side by side and respect each other for the moral strength that stems from their faith.

Making a case for mutual respect on these grounds certainly did not compel Astruc Halevi to admit that the two religions, or for that matter the three monotheistic religions, are equally true. Joseph Albo insisted that faith is based on revelation and tradition, but did not infer from this, as Halorki had done, that one is under no obligation to investigate the foundations of his faith and to check the truth claims made by the different religions. To the contrary, it is in his opinion the duty of every believer to carry out this test. Such is Albo's method in conducting it that the Jewish believer will not have to waste much time in order to distinguish the one 'genuine' religion from the 'spurious' ones.[37] Astruc Halevi could in like manner decline to admit the inference that Halorki had made when he had dealt with the other horn of the dilemma he had expounded to Paul of Burgos: from the position that the believer of a given religion has no duty, or even is not allowed, to examine its core beliefs and its foundations, it does not necessarily follow, Halevi could argue, that everyone professing a religion will be saved in the religion which happens to be his, and that there is no superiority of one religion on another (this conclusion is inescapable, Halorki had claimed, unless we are prepared to accept the notion of an unjust God, and to maintain that God has made an obligation on the believers of the different religions to stay in the religious communities in which they are born, even if only one religion that leads to eternal happiness and if the members of the other religions will be punished despite their piety in the faith to which they have been enjoined to stick).[38] There were Christians as well as Jews at the time who claimed that everyone is saved in his faith — if we are to believe the testimony of Vicente Ferrer, who denounced them in a sermon he preached in Toledo in 1411.[39] It is debatable whether the proposition entails as a necessary consequence that the exclusive truth claims of the different religions are illusory, and we may surmise that those who subscribed to it did not bother to address this question. Thanks to his view that an undoubting faith is at the root of some of the character traits of the Jews which Christians may regard with appreciation, it was possible for Astruc Halevi to decline to relinquish the claim of his religion that truth is its exclusive preserve and at the same time to contend that the valuation, among all men, beyond any sectarian divide, of virtues fostered by religion, provides a basis for mutual recognition.

Astruc Halevi's stance thus turns out to bear surprising resemblances to that of Lessing four centuries later — or that ascribed to him by many critics. In their view, Lessing's discourse of toleration, if compared with the usual argumentations marshalled during the battles for tolerance of the eighteenth century, was very much in a class of its own. While many of those who campaigned for toleration espoused a deism of one variety or another, and were indifferent or hostile to the official religions, Lessing inveighed against the bigoted mindsets fostered by bickering Churches, but also recognized a kind of positive impulse that is channelled through the religious institutions. At the same time, he embraced Leibniz's perspectivism and was thus led to hold that truth is by its very nature refracted in as many ways as there are human beings who strive after it. Truth came to matter less than search for truth; as he said in 1778: 'If God held fast in his right hand the whole of truth and in his left hand only the ever-active quest for truth, albeit with the proviso that I should constantly err, and said to me: "Choose", I would humbly fall upon his left hand and say: "Father, give! For pure truth is for you alone"'.[40] His perspectivism led him at the same time to admit that the general truths of natural religion have to be complemented by beliefs that are in accordance with the circumstances of time and place in which those beliefs are enunciated. He thus gave his own version of the theory of accommodation, which Maimonides had developed and which had become popular among European learned circles in the seventeenth century:[41]

> The indispensability of a positive religion, whereby natural religion is modified in each state according to that state's natural and fortuitous condition, I call its inner truth; and this inner truth is as great in the one as in the other.[42]

This quotation encapsulates three contentions: the positive religions offer only approximations of the truth, these approximations are of equal value, they fill a necessary and positive role. Lessing appears to be uniquely equipped to give every religion its due recognition, and he should be seen, or so Jan Assmann has claimed, as an early proponent of that cosmopolitanism, making room both for the universal and the particular, which Ulrich Beck has contrasted with a uniformizing universalism.[43]

If we accept this perspective, we may be in a position to appraise the exact import of two motifs that Lessing added in *Nathan the Wise* to the tale of the three rings as he found it in Boccaccio (and some other medieval sources).[44] Nathan tells Saladin in the speech Lessing puts in his mouth that the three sons brought their quarrel before a judge, who was upset by the selfishness displayed by the brothers and concluded that none of them possessed the genuine ring. 'The real ring must have been lost':[45] this is Lessing's first addition. Lessing's intent at that point, it seems, is to persuade us that the historical positive religions have departed from the 'inner' religion common to them all to such an extent as to be in their present state bereft of any worth.[46] But then comes a reversal of sorts. The judge intimates that it does not too much matter if there is no true ring, and that the three sons should behave as if they possessed it:

> Let each of you rival the others only in uncorrupted love, free from prejudice. Let each of you strive to show the power of his ring's stone. Come to the aid of this power in gentleness, with heartfelt tolerance, in charity, with sincerest submission to God.

These lines, it is often asserted, convey the core message of the play, but their meaning is far from transparent. Is it that rites and dogmas, the usual stuff of the quarrels between the organized religions, do not matter, and that morals, benevolence and good deeds are what counts? Or is it, rather, that benevolence and good deeds flow, or should flow, from religious faith, and that consequently the different religions should emulate good deeds among their believers, and those latter should cherish the performers of these good deeds?[47] If we prefer the second reading, Lessing both vindicates the legitimate role of the institutionalized religions and insists that the followers of the divergent religions can develop feelings of appreciation for each other. Astruc Halevi's rationale for mutual respect between Christians and Jews, that takes certitude, or strong beliefs, as its starting point, and Lessing's call to friendship beyond confessional boundaries, grounded in, or tallied with, a principled rejection of the search for truth, or at least principled doubts towards the possibility of attaining truth, are polar opposites, but nevertheless have this in common that they conceive of religious conviction as of a resource for empathy and human connection as well as of an incentive for conflict.

Some Christians may have been responsive to Astruc Halevi's argumentation. The Spanish-Jewish writer Shem Tov Ibn Shaprut held a controversy in 1379 with a Christian opponent. If we are to believe him, he had the upper hand and the Christian interlocutor eventually declared: 'I have no compelling answer to your points. However, my faith is truth according to the tradition that is ours, and if you will not believe faith will not be wanting thereby'.[48] This Christian certainly did not say that the Jews were worthy of respect on account of their faith, but he did say that his own faith was undemonstrable and based on tradition; he implied, or a charitable interpretation may contend he implied, that the two religions should in parallel rely on their respective traditions. It is ironical that this Christian interlocutor was none other than Cardinal Pedro de Luna, the future pope (or antipope) Benedict XIII, who would later preside over the Tortosa Disputation, during which the Jewish participants, Astruc Halevi among them, had to be constantly on their guard and beware lest they be attacked for negating tenets of their own faith and be branded heretics, with all the imaginable consequences. Cardinal Pedro de Luna's utterance was very much in keeping with the spirit of *convivencia*, Pope Benedict XIII envisioned a Spain which would renounce it.

Notes to Chapter 1

1. *On the Government of Jews*: 'Eos qui foris sunt' — for our discussion, Jews and Muslims in the societies which define themselves as Christian, Jews and Christians in those which construe themselves as Islamic.

2. See Alphonse Mignana and Rendel Harris, 'Woodbrooke Studies: Christian documents in Syriac, Arabic, and Garshūni, edited and translated with a critical apparatus. Fasciculus 3: The apology of Timothy the Patriarch before the Caliph Mahdi', *Journal of the John Rylands Library*, 12.1 (1928), 137–298. Shlomo Pines called attention to this source in his study: 'The Jewish Christians of the Early Centuries of Christianity According to a New Source', *The Israel Academy of Sciences and Humanities, Proceedings*, 2.13 (1966), 1–72 (p. 38 n.139), and had this comment: 'The example implies that as far as human knowledge is concerned, there is nothing to choose between the various religions'. For the historical context of the debate, see Dimitri Gutas, *Greek Thought, Arabic Culture: The Graeco-Arabic Translation Movement in Baghdad and Early Abbasid Society (2nd–4th/8th–10th centuries)* (London and New York: Routledge, 1998), pp. 61–69.

3. For good measure, Patriarch Timothy expressed the hope that Christians will share the pearl with the Muslims, and added: 'God has placed the pearl of his faith before all of us, like the shining rays of the sun, and everyone who wishes can enjoy the light of the sun'. Iris Shagrir has suggested that the parable was the origin of the tale of the three rings: a version of the Baghdad story is found in a collection of Mozarabic manuscripts from the thirteenth and fourteenth centuries, discovered by Giorgio Levi della Vida in a mosque in Kairouan and this may substantiate the hypothesis already made long ago that the tale of the rings originated in Spain: see I. Shagrir, 'The Parable of the Three Rings: A Revision of its History', *Journal of Medieval History*, 23.2 (1997), 163–77. As to the Kairouan manuscripts, see the recent observations of Cyrille Aillet, *Les Mozarabes. Christianisme, islamisation et arabisation en péninsule Ibérique (IXe–XIIe siècle)* (Madrid: Casa de Velázquez, 2010), pp. 209 and 227. That versions of the tale of the three rings circulated in thirteenth-century Spain is shown by the instance of Abraham Abulafia's allegorical story (see below, n. 46). Friedrich Niewöhner has brought together an enormous amount of material on the 'journey' of the tale of the three rings from the Middle Ages to Lessing, but his historical reconstruction is fanciful: F. Niewöhner, *Veritas sive varietas. Lessings Toleranzparabel und das Buch Von den drei Betrügern* (Heidelberg: Lambert Schneider, 1988).

4. The title of the book, *Shevet Yehudah*, may also be translated: 'The Tribe of Judah'; or also: 'The Chastisement of Judah'. The play on the multiple meanings (of the word *sheveth*) is of course intentional.

5. That Ibn Verga borrowed the story from one of the Italian versions, with their unique insistence on the adroitness of the Jewish merchant, has been recognized by Yitzhaq-Fritz Baer; see his introduction in the Hebrew edition of the book (Jerusalem: Bialik Institute, 1947), pp. 14–15.

6. Ibn Verga, *Shevet Yehudah*, p. 86.

7. In the note on the passage in the edition of 1947.

8. Note that Ibn Verga's formulation does not fit exactly that of Maimonides in chapter I, 31 of *The Guide for the Perplexed*, where we read: 'Confusion prevails in metaphysical subjects, less in problems relating to physics, and is entirely absent in mathematics'. Whether this is by chance or because Ibn Verga was informed about discussions between philosophical schools in Italy, his formulation is close to that of Ficino, who scoffed at the Aristotelians: they know a few things in physics, know less in mathematics, and even less in metaphysics; see Miguel Granada, 'Apologétique platonicienne et apologétique sceptique: Ficin, Savonarole, Jean-François Pic de la Mirandole', in *Le Scepticisme au XVIe et au XVIIe siècle. Le Retour des philosophies antiques à l'âge*

classique, vol. II, ed. by P. F. Moreau (Paris: Albin Michel, 2001), pp. 11–47 (p. 25 n.1). Chapter I, 31, and chapter II, 24 of *The Guide* are at the core of what has often been termed the 'scepticism', or 'critical epistemology', of Maimonides. See, for recent discussions, the 'Aleph Forum on the Knowability of the Heavens and of Their Mover (Guide, 2: 24)', *Aleph. Historical Studies in Science & Judaism*, 8 (2008), 151–339; and Pierre Bouretz, *Lumières du Moyen Âge. Maïmonide philosophe* (Paris: Gallimard, 2016), pp. 343–82.

9. During a first round, in February 1413, the question whether the Messiah has already come or was yet to come was discussed informally. From late February, and until mid-April 1413, the same theme was debated, but the participants had to read from written memoranda. From May to August, the broader issues of the conception of salvation and of the role of the Messiah were brought up. During a fourth round (and after a long interruption), the discussion was again supposed to bear only on the topic disputed at the beginning of the disputation, but in the debates as they actually took place the two questions of the 'date' of the coming of the Messiah and that of the meaning of the Messianic expectation became to some point intertwined.

10. In fact, these three scholars (Astruc Halevi, Zerahia Halevi and Mattityahu Hayitzhari) had played the prominent role as speakers on the Jewish side from the very first days of the disputation, as both the Latin protocol and the Hebrew accounts show. Zerahia Halevi was also called Ferrer Saladin. In order to make it easier to differentiate between Astruch Halevi and Zerahia Halevi, I will refer to the latter by the name of Ferrer Saladin.

11. See Antonio Pacios López, *La Disputa de Tortosa. II, Actas* (Madrid and Barcelona: CSIC, Instituto Arias Montano, 1957), p. 440: 'Item dico quod omnis disputatio in articulo legis est prohibita, ut non deviet homo ab articulis sue legis, inquit David, psalmo 36: "os justi meditabitur sapienciam et lingua ejus loquetur judicium, lex Dei in corde ipsius, et non supplantabantur gressus ejus". Videtur quod scientia solum debet disputari, et in racionibus poni; sed legem et credenciam debet homo cordialiter fidei commendare, non autem disputacioni, taliter ut non fugiat vel recedat quis ab ea; ymo oportet quod omnis homo faciat radicem et fundamentum in fide et ponat conclusiones illius validas, stabiles et non dubias'. The text had already been published by Fritz-Yitzhak Baer in his study of the disputation on the basis of the manuscript in the Vatican Library, as appendix II: see Baer, 'Die Disputation von Tortosa (1413–1414)', *Spanische Forschungen der Görresgesellschaft. 1. Reihe: Gesammelte Aufsätze zur Kulturgeschichte Spaniens*, 3 (1931), 307–36 (p. 333). But in his comment on the passage, p. 318, as well as his later reference to it in his treatment of the disputation in *A History of the Jews in Christian Spain*, 2 vols (New York: Jewish Publication Society of America, 1961), vol. II, chapter 11 (whose text follows closely the German article, with only minor changes), Baer makes only a passing allusion to the argument that 'all disputation about an article of faith is prohibited', and does not differentiate between this specific argument and the protest, included in the same part of the memorandum then read by Astruc Halevi, against the set of pressures brought to bear on the Jewish scholars. Hyam Maccoby should be given credit for having stressed the import of what he rightly calls Astruc's 'plea for toleration', even if some of the remarks he appended are less than convincing: see Hyam Maccoby, *Judaism on Trial: Jewish-Christian Disputations in the Middle Ages* (London: The Littman Library of Jewish Civilization, [1982] paperback 1993), pp. 85–88.

12. See the analysis of this correspondence in Baer, *A History of the Jews*, II, 143–50; and in Benjamin Gampel, 'A Letter to A Wayward Teacher: The Transformations of Sephardic Culture in Christian Iberia', in *Cultures of the Jews: A New History*, ed. by David Biale (New York: Schocken Books, 2002), pp. 389–447 (pp. 389–426).

13. My translation. The Hebrew manuscripts read: 'the cornerstone' (in Hebrew: *pinah*), in the singular. But the following sentences in Halorki's question as well as the wording used by Paul of Burgos when he mentions the issue in his answer ('how is it desirable for a man professing a religion to investigate the fundamental principles of his religion') make it clear that the text should here be emended, and the term 'cornerstone' read in the plural (and see also the wording used by Albo, see below).

14. I choose to translate here the Hebrew *deot* by 'beliefs'. On the difficulties linked with the use by the medieval authors of the terms *emunah* (pl. *emunot*), *deah* (pl. *deot*), and the different translations by the medieval Hebrew translators of the Arabic *i'tiqād*, see, among many studies,

Georges Vajda, 'Études sur Saadia', *Revue des Études Juives*, 109 (1948–49), 1–37; and Shalom Rosenberg, 'The Concept of *Emunah* in Post-Maimonidean Jewish Philosophy', in *Studies in Medieval Jewish History and Literature*, ed. by Isadore Twersky, 2 vols (Cambridge, MA: Harvard University Press, 1984), II, 273–307.

15. Hebrew: *qayam be-emunato*.

16. Hebrew: *ve-az lo yitsdak aleihem shem emounah kefi horaot ha-milah*.

17. The only copy of this sermon is found in the Firkovitch collection in the Russian National Library in St Petersburg. The text has now been published by Ari Ackerman (ed.), *The Sermons of R. Zerahya Halevi Saladin* (BerSheva: Ben Gurion University Press, 2012), pp. 104–20 (for the discussion of *emounah*, see pp. 114–17). For an English translation of another sermon penned by Ferrer Saladin (as has been shown in the meantime by A. Ackerman), see Marc Saperstein, *'Your Voice Like a Ram's Horn': Themes and Texts in Traditional Jewish Preaching* (Cincinnati, OH: Hebrew Union College Press, 1996), chapter 13: '"Make Vows and Pay Them": A Newly Discovered Confraternity Sermon from Spain' (introduction, pp. 179–89; translation, pp. 190–222; Hebrew text, pp. 223–50).

18. See Ackerman, *The Sermons*, p. 114, and Ackerman's excellent discussion of the passage, pp. 60–64 of the pages in Hebrew numbering.

19. See *The Guide of the Perplexed*, I, chapter 50. See, on Maimonides' understanding of 'belief', Charles Manekin, 'Belief, Certainty, and Divine Attributes in the *Guide for the Perplexed*', *Maimonidean Studies*, 1 (1990), 117–41; Sarah Stroumsa, *Maimonides in his World: Portrait of a Mediterranean Thinker* (Princeton, NJ: Princeton University Press, 2009), p. 70.

20. On the shift from 'belief' to 'faith' in fifteenth-century Spanish-Jewish thought, see Charles Manekin, 'Hebrew Philosophy in the Fourteenth and Fifteenth Centuries: An Overview', in *History of Jewish Philosophy*, ed. by Daniel H. Frank and Oliver Leaman (London: Routledge, [1997] 2003), pp. 350–78 (pp. 353–58, esp. p. 356).

21. Joseph Albo, *Sefer ha-Ikkarim/Book of Principles*, ed. by Isaac Husik, 2 vols (Philadelphia, PA: Jewish Publication Society of America, [1929] 1946), vol. I, chapter 19, pp. 165–66.

22. Albo, *Sefer ha-Ikkarim*, p. 166.

23. Albo, *Sefer ha-Ikkarim*, p. 169.

24. See Albo, *Sefer ha-Ikkarim*, chapter 24, pp. 187–88. That Albo reproduces in this chapter, with negligible changes in the precise wording, the question asked by Halorki has been first recognized by Nehemiah Brüll, 'Paulus Burgensis and Geronimo de Santa Fe', in *Jahrbücher für Jüdische Geschichte und Literatur*, 7 vols (Frankfurt am Main: W. Erras, 1879), IV, 50–55 (p. 52). Albo gives also a (rather longish) paraphrase of Halorki's first objection to examination, but drops the second one. See Isaac Husik, *A History of Mediaeval Jewish Philosophy* (New York: Meridian Books, [1916] 1958), pp. 417–18.

25. See this passage of Profiat Duran's letter, 'Be Not Like Unto Thy Fathers', in English translations (which I used but also modified) in: Baer, *A History*, II, 153, or in Frank E. Talmage, *Disputation and Dialogue: Readings in the Jewish-Christian Encounter* (New York: Ktav Publishing House, 1975), p. 120. For a recent study of the letter, see Maud Kozodoy, *The Secret Faith of Maestre Honoratus: Profyat Duran and Jewish Identity in Late Medieval Iberia* (Philadelphia: University of Pennsylvania Press, 2015), chapter 8.

26. Baer, *A History*, II, 152–53.

27. Verses in the Epistles of Paul and the Epistle to the Hebrews include mentions of the verse in Habacuc referred to by Duran, but do not thereby give a 'definition' of faith. Such a definition is found in the Epistle to the Hebrews 11. 1.

28. Baer, *A History*, II, 150.

29. My tentative translation of the phrase (existing translations are here unsatisfactory): see the Hebrew text in Leo Landau, *Das apologetische Schreiben des Josua Lorki an den Abtrünnigen Don Salomon ha-Lewi (Paulus de Santa Maria)* (Antwerp: Teitelbaum & Boxenbaum, 1906). Who are the 'wise men' he had in mind, Paul of Burgos unfortunately does not say. He adds that 'this is not the place' to discuss the issue.

30. Joseph Albo, *Sefer ha-Ikkarim* (see above, n. 21), chapter 21, p. 177. Paul of Burgos and Albo use the same Hebrew expression translatable as 'speculative knowledge', *yediah mehqarit*. As has

often been observed, Albo was an unsystematic thinker, who fell heir to very different, and even conflicting, strands of thought.

31. *The Kuzari*, I, 5 (see, on these rather difficult lines, the English translation by Isaak Heinemann, *Three Jewish Philosophers: Philo, Saadya Gaon, Jehuda Halevi* (New York: Meridian Books, 1960), p. 31; and compare the French translation by Charles Touati, *Le Kuzari. Apologie de la religion méprisée par Juda Hallevi* (Paris: Verdier, 1994), p. 7); I, 25; II, 26 (the French translation by Touati is here especially telling: 'Quiconque accepte [le culte sacrificiel] d'un cœur entier, sans ratiociner et sans faire étalage de sa propre sagesse est supérieur à celui qui fait l'intelligent et se livre à des investigations'); V, 1–2.

32. He is thus in agreement with Albo (as has been pointed out by Baer, see 'Die Disputation von Tortosa', [above, n. 11], p. 318 n. 18). Albo said in one of the first meetings of the disputation that 'granted that you can prove to me that the Messiah has already come, I think I should not be worse a Jew for all that'. As Isaac Husik has rightly observed (*Philosophical Essays: Ancient, Mediaeval & Modern*, ed. by Milton C. Nahm and Leo Strauss (Oxford: Blackwell, 1952), p. 259), the statement is not entirely clear. It is easy to understand the contention that Judaism does not stand or fall with the belief in the *future* coming of the Messiah: with or without the promise of an earthly reward, Jews are bound to observe the commandments of the Law. But how to admit that the Messiah has come in the past? It may be possible to make sense of such a view by referring to one of the points made by Astruc Halevi concerning the messianic belief: a Jew who would be of the opinion that the Messiah had come to the Jews who live near the country of Prester John (that is, in a place where Jews were supposedly independent), while the other Jews have not yet been redeemed because of their sins, would be mistaken but would not thereby utter a heretical view. This claim is of course consistent with Astruc Halevi's view that the role of the Messiah is essentially to do all that is necessary in order for the Jews to live again in conditions of political freedom. On this understanding, Messiahs may have emerged in the past who did not complete their mission since the Jews then did not deserve to be redeemed.

33. Pacios López, *La Disputa*, vol. 2 (see above n. 11), p. 520. This is in line, we may observe, with Ferrer Saladin's standpoint when he discussed faith in his Hebrew sermon.

34. Pacios López, *La Disputa*: 'Premisse traducte et acquisite per fidem non requirunt aliquam probacionem, tam parum sicut prime intellective'. It remains to be elucidated in which manner this contention relates to the debates of the time, among Jewish theologians, on how to establish the dogmas of Judaism.

35. Pacios López, *La Disputa*, pp. 480–81: 'constanciam and stabilitatem bone legalitatis'. Note the insistence on *stabilitas*. One has, Astruc Halevi had earlier said, to accept the conclusions of his faith as 'firm and undoubted' — thereby following, as we saw, the line of thought previously developed by Halorki; see above notes 11 and 15.

36. Pacios López, *La Disputa*, p. 503: 'magister Ieronimus dicit quod major repugnancia quae inter judeum et christianum est quod judeus dicit Messiam venturus esse, christianus jam venisse. Item dico quod non repugnant. Qualiter enim repugnant, cum termini sententiarum utriusque sint diversi?' and see the following passage.

37. See Albo, *Sefer ha-Ikkarim*, chapter 24, pp. 190–93. Albo refers to the criteria defined in *The Guide of the Perplexed*, II, 40, and concludes: 'When he [Maimonides] says that a test of the law is, if it takes pains to inculcate true ideas about God, etc., he is alluding to that religion which ascribes to god corporeality and trinity. And when he speaks of testing the moral qualities of the founder of the religion, he is alluding to that man who claimed that he was a prophet of the Arabs'. Paul of Burgos had asserted in the same manner that every person professing a religion, and especially a Jew, has to probe the cornerstones of his faith, and had made the observation that such an investigation does not weaken faith, but reinforces it. He had likewise referred to *Guide*, II, 40 — in which he found support, we have to assume, for the claim that Christianity is the one genuine divine Law. This insistence on using this chapter of the *Guide* on behalf of Christianity is rather disconcerting: lines near the end of the chapter deal with Islam, since they allude, even if only implicitly, to the standard argument of the lustful behaviour of Muḥammad in order to brand him as an impostor, but it is difficult to see which sentences in the chapter Paul of Burgos adduced as having some bearing on the question of the status of Christianity. See Landau, *Das Apologetischen*, p. 19.

38. See Landau, *Das Apologetischen*, p. 17.

39. See Pedro Cátedra, *Sermón, sociedad y literatura en la Edad Media. San Vicente Ferrer en Castilla (1411–1412)* (Valladolid: Junta de Castilla y León, 1994), pp. 245–46: 'sciatis quod multi christiani et judei sunt in isto errore, dicentes quod quilibet tenendo suam legem potest salvari, scilicet judei tenendo legem Moysy, et sarraceni de Mahometi, et christiani de Christo, quod non est verbum christianum, est magnus error'. It is of interest that Giovanni da Capestrano repeatedly attacked the Jews, in the sermons he preached in German towns towards the mid-fifteenth century, for saying that salvation is possible through every faith: see Haim H. Ben-Sasson, 'Jewish-Christian Disputation in the Setting of Humanism and Reformation in the German Empire', *Harvard Theological Review*, 59.4 (1966), 369–90 (pp. 377–78). As is well known, a large number of sources from the Spanish Inquisition document this view for the late fifteenth century.

40. Lessing, *A Rejoinder*, quoted by Hugh Nisbet, *Gotthold Ephraim Lessing: His Life, Works, and Thoughts* (Oxford: Oxford University Press, 2013), p. 552. Lessing wrote in the same vein in a letter: 'Let each man say what he deems truth, and let truth itself be commended unto God!'. Hannah Arendt concludes her essay (see below, n. 45) by quoting this sentence.

41. See Sarah Stroumsa, *Maimonides in his World*, chapter 4; Guy G. Stroumsa, *A New Science: The Discovery of Religion in the Age of Reason* (Cambridge, MA, and London: Harvard University Press, 2010), chapter 4.

42. Lessing, *On the Origin of Revealed Religion*, quoted by Nisbet, *Gotthold Ephraim Lessing*, p. 301.

43. See the introduction of Ronald Schechter to *Nathan the Wise* by Gotthold Ephraim Lessing, *with Related Documents, Translated, Edited, and with an Introduction by Ronald Schechter* (Boston, MA, and New York: Bedford-St. Martin's, 2004), pp. 1–23, and esp. 12–16; Nisbet, *Gotthold Ephraim Lessing*, chapter 20 and *passim*; Jan Assmann, *Religio Duplex: How the Enlightenment Reinvented Egyptian Religion* (Cambridge: Polity Press, 2014), chapter 5 and conclusion.

44. *Nathan the Wise*, act III, scene 7.

45. It has been Hannah Arendt's central thesis in a celebrated essay that Lessing 'was glad that [...] the genuine ring, if it had ever existed, had been lost; he was glad for the sake of the infinite number of opinions that arise when men discuss the affairs of the world'; see Arendt, 'On Humanity in Dark Times: Thoughts on Lessing', in *Men in Dark Times* (New York: Harcourt Brace, 1993), pp. 3–31. This view is closely connected with themes in her political thought that run through all her writings. See the convergent discussions of Margaret Canovan, 'Friendship, Truth, and Politics: Hannah Arendt and Toleration', in *Justifying Toleration: Conceptual and Historical Perspectives*, ed. by Susan Mendus (Cambridge: Cambridge University Press, 1988), pp. 177–98; and of Alan Mittleman, 'Tolerance, Liberty, and Truth: A Parable', *Harvard Theological Review*, 95.4 (2002), 353–72, particularly pp. 362–71.

46. The distance between the present state of religions and the one that will eventually prevail is highlighted by the thirteenth-century Kabbalist Abraham Abulafia, in his particular version of the tale of the three rings (or, here, of a pearl). The genuine pearl, Abulafia recounts, has been thrown into a pit by the father (God), who has become angry with his sons (the Jews). Abulafia's version seems at first glance less than tolerant, since the quarrel about the pearl does not involve three sons, but one son and two servants (Christianity and Islam), and since we are told that 'the argument continues as to who has the pearl and the truth, we or our oppressors. Until there comes He who decides who will raise the pearl from the pit and give it to whom He desires, us or them'. But the lesson of the tale is that the father will give back the pearl to the son when the latter will raise up to the spiritual interpretation of the revealed teachings of which he has been thus far unable, and that concurrently the son and the servants will reconcile and be united in this spiritual religion. I follow here Moshe Idel's interpretation; see Moshe Idel, 'The Pearl, the Son and the Servants in Abraham Abulafia's Parable', *Quaderni di Studi Indo-Mediterranei*, 6 (2013), 103–35; and see Harvey J. Hames, *Like Angels on Jacob's Ladder: Abraham Abulafia, the Franciscans and Joachimism* (Albany: State University of New York Press, 2007), chapter 3: 'The Politics of Universal Salvation' (Idel and Hames provide English translations of Abulafia's Hebrew text).

47. We are reminded of the 'good works' extolled by Patriarch Timothy in eighth-century Baghdad.

48. See Norman E. Frimer and Dov Schwartz, *The Life and Thought of Shem Tov Ibn Shaprut* (in Hebrew) (Jerusalem: Ben-Zvi Institute, 1992), p. 16; José Vicente Niclós Albarracín, 'La Disputa religiosa de D. Pedro de Luna con el judío D. Shem Tov Ibn Shaprut en Pamplona (1379): el contexto en la vida y la predicación de Vicente Ferrer', *Revue des Études Juives*, 160.3/4 (2001), 409–33 (pp. 429, 433).

CHAPTER 2

❖

The Three Rings:
Shevet Yehuda-Lessing /
Graetz-Fritz Ishaq Baer

Eleazar Gutwirth

I

At a conference delivered to the (then young) *Société des études juives* on 9 May 1885, Gaston Paris treated the story of doubt known as 'the three rings'.[1] Although Gaston Paris's field was Romance Philology, rather than Hebrew texts, the *Shevet Yehuda* (chapter 32) version was relatively prominent and was judged more authentic, closer to the original: 'la plus belle, la plus simple, la plus pure'. The version tells of a king who asks a Jew which is the best religion. The Jew answers by appeal to the parable of a father (a *lapidario*) who left his sons rings which were alike, the question is which is better. In the absence of the father it is found impossible to decide the question.

To be sure, Boccaccio's version in the *Decameron* (1353) and the later elaboration in *Nathan der Weise* (1779) were touched upon, as was an impressive array of less well-known sources. I mention the case of Paris not because he is the first to focus attention on the *Shevet Yehuda*'s rings story. Far from it: it had been touched upon in the previous decade, in 1871, by his colleague Hugo Schuchardt.[2] Moritz Steinschneider thought he had discovered a thirteenth-century analogue in Abulafia, ten years before Schuchardt, in 1861.[3] Long before the story was classified as Aarne-Thompson-Uther 920e, Steinschneider had pointed to its affinity with *sage* and *legende* and noted that the sons and servants are formal fixtures of folklore.[4]

Both romance philologists of the 1870s/80s argue for an ultimately 'Eastern' source. Both seem dependent on Wiener's translation published in Hanover as early as 1856.[5] Both lack apparatus and are not at their best when dealing with concrete issues of biography and historical context relating to the *Shevet Yehuda*. Both consider the chronicle *Shevet Yehuda* a work containing literary sections amenable to literary analysis. Archival research was equally foreign to both.

Gaston Paris is certainly an important figure in the history of scholarship on medieval texts. But the reason I mention him is that he is also the subject of numerous contextualizations which aim to situate or link his views to his biographical, political and psychological context. It may suffice to mention Bloch's work,[6] which relates repressed incestuous tendencies to Paris's theory of courtly love or that of Ursula Bähler, *Gaston Paris dreyfusard. Le Savant dans la cité*,[7] who sees him in the frame of, amongst other matters, the Dreyfus affair. That is to say that in recent decades there has been a development, namely that it is perfectly well understood that the historiography is relevant to the history. His decision to address the *Société des études juives* may now be interpreted as a show of solidarity and would explain the lengthy preface on Judeo-Christian polemical literature and the general air of a *plaidoyer* for toleration and coexistence between religions. This would also explain the choice of the particular theme and the special attention to the rings story in the *Shevet Yehuda*.

That the parable in the *Shevet Yehuda* shares traits with rings traditions — Arabic/Muslim and Christian — therefore, is an aspect of the Hebrew text that has been known and studied (at a conservative estimate) for more than 150 years. But there are some aspects which it does not share with them. There is a temptation to continue to divert or defer this as if the *Shevet Yehuda* story were merely concerned with a universal question of ethics or philosophy. Friedrich Niewöhner's very large study could be an example.[8] He sees it in a Maimonidean tradition, particularly the *Yemen Epistle* and the implications of prophets/messiahs as impostors. As the frame of the *Shevet Yehuda* story is a dialogue between a king and a Jew, one could, of course, argue that dialogue is a philosophical issue. In this vein one might recall Emmanuel Levinas's gloss on Buber to the effect that there is face-to-face dialogue and in face-to-face dialogue there is a question of *hauteur*: who is looking up and who is looking down.[9]

II

The precise formulations would be anachronistic but the preoccupation to emphasize such elements is clear in the story's frame. The king is represented as welcoming and at the same time, insulting; as innocent and yet as crafty. There are some micro-motifs almost imperceptibly interwoven into the fabric of the story: names and kings; the sarcasm at Jewish names; stories about above the waist and below the waist; the next-door neighbour — a *lapidario*.[10] Some attention to them might help us to understand the author's modus operandi and, therefore, how to read such texts. The *Shevet Yehuda* text is impoverished by a reading which sees it only as 'a version'. It presents the creative ambiguity[11] between, for example, ancient and 'modern', between Jewish and Christian.

After the anti-Jewish tirade of Nicolau of Valencia, the Christian Spanish king decides to call a Jew to the court. The first thing the king asks the Jew is: What is your name? And the Jew responds: Ephraim Ibn Sanchi. Kings and names are associated here. The numerous translations from Georgio Gentio,[12] M. de L(eón?)[13] and onwards might give the impression of a universalism where languages/cultures are immaterial because they can be substituted (near enough) by equivalents. But the original is highly allusive and book-haunted. In a Hebrew text, where the dependence on a Hebrew textual tradition beginning with the Bible (perhaps particularly the Book of Esther) is pronounced, one can hardly elude the question of, say, Midrash, Aggada or medieval exegesis.[14] Thus in the Bible we read: 'And the king of Egypt made Eliakim his brother king over Judah and Jerusalem, *and turned his name to Jehoiakim*.'[15] The commentary ascribed to Rashi explains ad loc: 'Thus is the way of kings and princes who name their servants as they wish (similar is the case of Pharaoh) And *Pharaoh called Joseph's name Zaphnathpaaneah*'.[16]

This influential view of Christian kings as interested in Jewish/Hebrew names is one of the possible and untapped resonances of a dialogue that begins with the king asking for a name. In addition, the realism noted in scholarly treatments of late medieval Hebrew poetry and prose narratives from Spain, would lead us to search for a real historical link between kings and Jewish names in the Spanish culture of the period. Here we are supported by a great deal of evidence, as legislation in the kingdom of Castile-León is frequently concerned with the issue. The Cortes de Jerez legislate about it in 1268, as do those of Palencia in 1313, and of Burgos in 1315; but here it suffices to recall the Cortes de Toro under Enrique III in 1371 where Jews are forbidden to bear Christian names.[17]

In the *Shevet* the question of names is associated with the question of authorship, as it appears in a story linked to Yehudah Ibn Verga. There — where the subject is the Name which serves to resuscitate — the kabbalistic character differentiates it from our more mundane reference to names. The ambiguities between mimesis (of kings' speech in this case) and *musar*/admonition reappear here as well. No less probable than a reference to Christian legislation would be a reading which understands it as a veiled critique of those Spanish Jews who did not follow strictly the older, internal opposition to adopting gentile names. It is clear in old Midrashic texts[18] where it is asserted that the Jews were redeemed from Egypt because they did not change their names.

III

The king introduces an analogy between composite names and bodies: a distinction between above the waist and below the waist. A royal connection in Spanish texts may be established. Indeed, one of the areas where this is a meaningful distinction is that of classical mythology. Triton has a body: above the waist that of a man, below it that of a dolphin. The coupling of Ixion and the cloud-woman gave birth to the centaurs, half men, half horses. The siren is another example. Centaurs and sirens in the *Shevet* have been recently analysed in the frame of the book's relation to medieval and Renaissance texts and cultures.[19] Here one may add the example of a work which is closely related to the king of Castile-León and waist stories: the *General estoria* attributed to King Alfonso X.[20] When writing about Erictonio the chronicle explains that he was the first to use chariots. When travelling, his legs were not seen. Therefore 'the Gentile authors' asserted that from the waist down he was fashioned like a dragon.

In the *Shevet*'s own century 'But to the girdle do the gods inherit / Beneath is all the fiend's' is probably the most famous connection between a king and 'waist lore'.[21] It is useful for us in that it makes the erotic/scatological import abundantly clear. It is, of course, decades later than the *Shevet*'s editio princeps and from a different culture, and yet, the Renaissance preoccupation with human dual nature is not exclusive to Shakespeare. Nor are Virgil's lines on Scylla in the *Aeneid*, where the waist is the border: she is a fair virgin to the waist.[22] In the *Lozana andaluza*'s sixteenth-century dialogue, it is made explicit in a post-coital conversation in Spanish: 'Sagüeso: De la cintura arriba dormíades, que estábades quieta'.[23] The late fifteenth-sixteenth century Polianthea fashion contributed its own angle. According to Mexia's *Silva*, Theodor of Gaza '[...] vió [...] nereyda [...] muger muy hermosa, y assí lo parescía hasta la cintura; y, de ay abaxo, fenecía en cola como de langosta, segun vemos pintada la que dize el pueblo serena de la mar'.[24] Here the interesting point is the parallelism between the *Shevet*'s formulation and that of Mexia's *Silva*. Neither is restricted to 'sirena'. Both add 'del(a) mar'.

In the case of the *Shevet*, the tradition which needs to be examined presents different possibilities. Thus, for example, we find repeated assertions to the effect that the symbolism of the High Priest's girdle (the *avnet*,) was understood as symbolic of atonement for erotic fantasies (lit. 'meditations of the heart', *hirhure ha-lev*).[25] Sa'adiah ben Yosef Gaon's exhortation to the readers of his prayer book was to wear a girdle to separate the heart from the genitalia in order to pray.[26] In late medieval Zaragoza, R. Behay Ben Asher (1255–1340) linked the Priest's girdle with Venus in his commentary on Leviticus.[27]

More evident and recognizable mainstream theologoumena come from texts which, though ancient, were nevertheless a staple of study and learning in medieval Hispano-Jewish communities as elsewhere. Thus the Talmud[28] alludes to Persian Zoroastrianism where our binaries are central. Amemar, on being told by one of the Magi, 'The upper half of thy body belongs to Ormuzd, the good principle; the lower to Ahriman, the evil principle', replies, 'Why, then, does Ahriman permit Ormuzd to carry the water (the excreta) through his province?' Possibly the most influential text refers to nothing less than the authorship of the Mishna, that is to say: why was the Mishna's authorship ascribed to Rabbi rather than to, say, R. Jose?

R. Jose said: I have never looked at my circumcised membrum. But that is not so, for Rabbi was asked, why were you called 'Our holy Teacher?' Said he to them, I have never looked at my membrum. In Rabbi's case there was another thing to his credit. He did not insert his hand beneath his girdle.[29]

The construction of the scene of Ibn Sanchi's embarrassment by way of names and waist lore should also be understood in the broader frame of the inner logic of story-telling. Indeed the rings' tale is here framed within a dialogue at court, between the king and the fantastic icon of medieval Christian scholasticism: 'Nicolau of Valencia'. The dialogue with Ephraim is a reaction to Nicolau's tirade and is carried out within Nicolau's hearing. The king has to establish his superiority and objectivity. He can refute Nicolau precisely because he is not a priori sympathetic to Jews. Also, such a frame serves to highlight the efficacy of the very matter of the *Shevet Yehuda*, namely Jewish arguments and reasoning even when confronting such unpromising beginnings. A minute — and yet radical — change occurs in this representation: the 'below' is pure and authentic, while the 'above' is hybrid and negative. In any case, we can now see the procedures at work in the chronicle.

IV

There are other components of the rings story in the *Shevet Yehuda* which are unparalleled in the rich traditions studied for more than 150 years by scholars of the rings parable. The appearance /absence of the personage known as 'the *lapidario*' is one of these and his role is emphasized by code switching from Hebrew into the *romance*. It may be argued that the resonances might reflect firstly a search for verisimilitude, a late medieval desire to offer some realistic background.

There is little doubt that there were Jewish or converso *lapidarios* in fifteenth-century Spain. Those familiar with Fritz Baer's documents will know about Juan Pardo *lapidario y mercader en piedras preciosas* or Pedro Alfonso de Córdoba *comerciante en piedras preciosas* who tried to leave Valencia for the Holy Land after 1453.[30] In fifteenth-century Spain, then, an anecdote in which there is a Jew whose neighbour was a Jewish (or converso) *lapidario* was not a fanciful notion. But the question of *lapidarios* is less transparent than it seems. The more obvious simile: (precious) stones/jewels/religions is barely a beginning in the work of recovering medieval/early modern resonances. In a *romance* work attributed to the bishop of Tuy,[31] we find a perspective on the possible resonances of 'precious stones' in the *imaginaire* of Spain and its speakers of *romance* at that particular period. They go far beyond simple equivalences: Moses is not presented here as a lawgiver or founder of a religion. He is imagined as a scholar of astrology and a great *lapidario*. He engraves two precious stones and one of them becomes the ring of memory and the other, the ring of oblivion.[32]

In a dialogue about identities or identifications by a king (cf. Ibn Sanchi's assertion to the Christian Spanish King: 'you wish to know *who I am*'), the theme of the extent of royal talent in judgment of character is evidently central. Could such a preoccupation be documented in late medieval Spain?

The *Castigos de Sancho IV* could be seen as evidence of royal mind-set or ideals. They have a chapter, the fifteenth, entitled 'Cómo debe ser el omne buen lapidario'. Apart from a praise of jewels and the injunction to the king to take pleasure in — and learn about — them, there is a transition to humans who are like jewels and a parallel injunction to achieve correct judgment and evaluation of humans in the way that the jeweller discerns between true and false. Theodosius should be a model; a studious king who achieved knowledge of the stones and was a good *lapidario*.

In addition, in a courtly context of a Jew addressing a medieval Spanish monarch, the mention of a *lapidario* would also and inevitably bring to mind Jews at court who had indeed composed *Lapidarios*, most notably Juda Ha-Cohen Mosca and his *Lapidarios* for Alfonso X.[33] The implications would be that previous kings addressed questions to Jews and were proffered reliable answers, that is, that there was a tradition of Spanish monarchs requesting Jews at court for knowledge, information, in the way that this king requests information about the best religion from the Jew at court in the *Shevet Yehuda*.

V

This fifteenth-/sixteenth-century representation of a Hispanic king as contradictory and unpredictable may have a contemporary, historical frame in similar contemporary representations of Hispanic Kings — particularly noticeable in Niccolò Machiavelli, Francesco Guicciardini and Baldassar Castiglione. In the first half of the sixteenth century there were representations of Spanish kings as cunning, hypocritical or deceitful. These representations drew attention and were understood by historians as early as William H. Prescott, in the 1830s,[34] or later, Ramón Menéndez Pidal.[35] I should also mention Robert Brian Tate's article on Isabella *magistra disimulationum / maestra de engaños*,[36] because it has a different approach and because it offers a balance to the male-centred discussions. Perhaps a stronger argument would be the feeling — by the immediate entourage of the Catholic Monarchs, the royal chroniclers, Hernando del Pulgar or Andrés Bernáldez — that there was a need to counteract such public opinions. The first needs to argue that Isabella was *verdadera en mantener su palabra*, while the second has to assert: *verdadera, clara, sin engaños*.[37] In any case, what these facts show us is that in this story we are dealing with specific representation and invective rather than universals, ethics or philosophy.

The rings parable in the *Shevet Yehuda* is not the only reply to the king's question, namely: which is the best religion. It is, in fact, a later, second and artful answer. The first, 'natural', visceral answer was rejected by the king. There is no intimation that the narrator of the story rejects it as well. The first, instinctive, reply is roughly: 'my religion serves me according to my interests (or needs), your religion serves you according to your needs'. The king rejects it outright.

In a sixteenth-century courtly frame where the interlocutors represent princes/ rulers/kings, scholastic counsellors and courtiers, such a 'functional' view of religion cannot but recall Machiavelli.[38] Baer intuited and understood — perhaps for the first time in the long history of *Shevet Yehuda* scholarship — that reading Machiavelli may help to understand the *Shevet Yehuda*.[39] But he did not consistently study the Machiavellism, anti-Machiavellism or 'Machiavellism before Machiavelli' of the *Shevet Yehuda*. There is also the question of which ideas of Machiavelli were to be found in the Hebrew book and which were not. Partly there was the problem of dates and places. The work of Helena Puigdomènech Forcada on Machiavelli in Spain had not yet appeared; nor had Howard published his book in 1948.[40]

Machiavelli has, of course, excited numerous and very different reactions, interpretations, readings. One of these is that he is treating religion, whatever its teachings, functionally 'as an instrument promoting desirable political behavior'.[41] In brief, the scepticism of the 'rings' second answer (namely that no one really knows which is the best religion) is the compliment to the 'Machiavellian' first answer, namely that religion is a functional tool in the quest for fame and power. We have other Hebrew chronicles of the period (some of them anonymous) which have been analysed as expressing views on, or assessments of, the character of Spanish monarchs which were current at the time, but these do not necessarily include the hypocrisy and deceitfulness of Ferdinand.[42] Of course neither Prescott nor Menéndez Pidal nor their followers had an interest in or, rather, access to these types of sources or anonymous Hebrew chronicles. They are however highly relevant in the case of a Hebrew chronicle such as the *Shevet*.

To support this reading one may adduce a text from the 1570s, authored in the Ottoman Empire where the insoluble (?) problems of authorship, date and place that we encounter in the *Shevet Yehuda* are obviated. Indeed, from our perspective, a closely similar representation of a Spanish king — (not Alfonso but) *Fernandico* — could be found in Onkeneira. In his *Ayuma Kanidgalot*, published in Constantinople in 1577, R. Isaac b. Samuel Onkeneira includes a story:

> [...] my grandfather the pious Hasid R. Yehuda Onkeneira told me that once there was an evil king Fernandico who reigned over the whole clime and they advised him to call all the elders and scholars and he also called eleven famous sages from our people saying that they should present themselves before him. And when they arrived he arose and received them with honour moving from the throne towards them as far as an arrow's throw, the king and the scholars who were with him.
>
> The Jews marvelled at this.
>
> And the king said: I love you like the daughter of my eyes and I wish you to be my guests. Choose whatever you like. All I ask is that you consume spiced (*mevusam*) pork and have sexual intercourse with an Aramean woman or drink wine of pagan libation.
>
> Wine is my honour. It raises my head. Thus will I know that I have found grace in your eyes and will grant you favour. Then a famous sage from our people arose and said: 'Oh, all powerful king give us three days and we shall see what is said in the books of the wise [...]'

The story is placed three generations before 1577 (that is, *c.* 1500), in the time of Onkeneira's grandfather. We note the *three days*,[43] the generic king's name in Spanish — neither Pedro nor Alfonso but — *Fernandico* with the slightly contemptuous suffix, the evil counsellor and most of all: the menace behind the vague air of politeness. These are only some of the parallels to the *Shevet Yehuda*, but they show clearly that one cannot speak of a general Sephardi mindset of unqualified appreciation of the Spanish kings.[44]

The role of the king (in the *Shevet Yehuda* story we are dealing with) is an 'interrogative statement' reminiscent of passages in other texts of the fifteenth and sixteenth centuries. I have recently referred to them as examples of 'scenes of identification'.[45] In these 'scenes', there is always a superior and an inferior/subaltern; so that the question or demand (of identification) implies superior strength, weapons or wealth. The questions are not symmetrical. In the 1430s, Pedro Tafur does not ask the sultan for identification. It is he, the foreign traveller, in Egypt in the fifteenth century, who is asked whether he is Catalan or not. Less than a century later, Ludovico di Varthema writes a passage to emphasize or caricature the incongruence of such apparent requests for information, these scenes of religious or other identifications. He does this by comparing the subordinate, the member of a minority, the traveller or foreigner, to an uncomprehending animal who cannot produce a correct answer to the question and is therefore beaten until he dies.

Perhaps beneath the underestimating of what I see as invective/satire, or at least a critical rather than naive view of politics and rulers, there lies the image of a medieval Jewry whose members are politically naive, who did not foresee the future events of 1391 or 1492, and whose interests were limited to questions of the philosophical ideal republics rather than the real ones. Bernard Lewis asserted this clearly. According to him 'politics (was) a subject of little concern to medieval Jewish scholars'.[46] Research does not support unequivocally such generalizing perceptions. One may refer to, for example, the Rosenthal–Pines discussion on Averroes's *Commentary on the Republic*. As may be recalled, Erwin Rosenthal, after many years of work, was able to complete a critical edition and English translation with commentary of Samuel ben Judah of Marseilles's (b. 1294) fourteenth-century Hebrew translation of Averroes's lost treatise on Plato's *Republic*.[47] It cannot be dismissed as an isolated, exceptional instance: apart from the eight scribes who worked to disseminate and perpetuate the work, we have (Parma, Palatina, 442) Joseph Caspi's extract of Averroes's *Commentary* entitled *Seder Hanhagah le-Aplaton* (1331). If that were not enough, there is also evidence of continued relevance or interest in the age of the *Shevet Yehuda*, in the case of the Latin version — which was achieved only after reading and studying the Hebrew version — by the Hispanic Jew, Jacob Mantinus in 1539.

Pines, in a by now classic review essay,[48] analysed the pertinent passages and terminology. For us, the interest lies in the resulting consequence, that is, the identification of the critique of non-ideal, 'present day rulers' originating in Averroes and its dissemination by this Hebrew translation circulating in Jewish communities at the time of the *Shevet Yehuda*. There is, in addition to Averroes, the question of Ibn Khaldun and, even more closely related, the question of Ibn Khaldun's contacts with and influence on Jewish thought in this (late medieval–early modern) period. As will be recalled, the idea of the Jews as a people of slaves mentioned in the *Shevet Yehuda*'s first answer is a fundamental component of Ibn Khaldun's ideology of Jewish history. I try to deal with the contacts between Ibn Khaldun and Hispano-Jewish scholars and texts elsewhere. For us this means that what late medieval Jews would learn or absorb from the Hebrew text was an attitude of criticism towards real governments. The prince or ruler or king cannot be reduced to the cipher *melekh hasid* pace Loeb and Baer and their emulators.[49]

In any case, the disinterest in politics is not supported by the evidence. Methodologically crucial here is to recognize that the genre of purely or formally philosophical essays or commentaries should not be confused with the field of political thought as a whole. That is to say that other forms, such as the epistle or the homily, need to be examined. Once this change of perspective is accepted, the way is clear for reading late medieval Hispano-Jewish texts which are not bibliographically, conventionally or formally described as treatises on politics such as Ephodi's *Epistle On Ahitophel* (*c.* 1400) or Joseph Ibn Shem Tov's *Sermon on the Qorah pericope* (*c.* 1450). The latter is not really a text concerned only with the ancient world of the Bible but, rather, a late medieval sustained meditation on the nature of government, ideal and bad rulers, necessary qualifications/disqualifications of the rulers, motivations for uprisings against such rulers. It has been argued that it draws on a repertoire of political ideas common also to scholastic treatises in Arabic or Latin, but does so transforming them in an individual way.[50] Today we know that the naive, folksy image of the *Shevet Yehuda* is a decoy or trick of the light concerning a work which draws on the Zohar, Bibax, Arama and other late medieval philosophical/theological texts.

VI

Alexander Altman believed that Moses Mendelsohn transmitted this particular Hebrew version of the rings parable to his friend Gotthold E. Lessing.[51] Lessing's version of 1779 cannot be addressed here except to say that there is no clear message of atheism (in an eighteenth-century sense) or scepticism or anti-religious argument but, on the contrary, his variation on the rings story is sufficiently unclear and ambiguous to stimulate numerous, different and differing interpretations.[52] What I should like to emphasize is Graetz's 'reading' of Lessing, because I suspect that he acts as a kind of subconscious of historians even today. Without copying all the long passages he wrote on Lessing, we may agree that they sound unambiguously like panegyrics. It suffices to recall his judgment of the play of the three rings, Nathan the Wise: 'The latest, most mature and most perfect offspring of his muse'.[53]

Graetz's attitude is, of course, not an individual quirk. It was shared by other German Jews, as has been abundantly proven by modern historians.[54] Baer had read Graetz's work and came out of this community. In his prologue to the Baer-Schochat edition of the *Shevet*, he claimed that the rings story was the 'programme', that is, the very centre of the whole work. Anyone who has read the *Shevet Yehudah* will realize that positing a centre and a margin in it is by no means self-evident and therefore that there is an element of individuality, subjectivity or interpretation in such postulates. Similar is the question of unity. Despite all the contradictions in the *Shevet Yehudah*, Baer (who was not oblivious to them, but had indeed pointed out many of them)[55] asserted that the author, a masterly craftsman, had achieved 'unity'.

The unity of a work of art was a concern in circles of literary criticism available at the time of Baer's writings. It was not a new, modernist attitude. In his 'On Poesy or Art', Samuel Taylor Coleridge (1772–1834), had written about the elements which make up the work of art: 'Art [...] stamps them into unity in the mould of a moral idea'.[56] Baer, obviously, thinks of unity as a useful, working category of criticism and seems to see it as an 'achievement' as did, for example, E. M. Forster, in his critical evaluation of Virginia Woolf's first novel (*The Voyage Out*): 'It is absolutely unafraid [...] Here at last is a book which attains unity as surely as *Wuthering Heights*, though by a different path'.[57] The direct implication would be that, not only the rings story but, the whole chronicle *Shevet Yehuda* is imbued with this sceptical stance which Baer calls 'Jewish averroism'.

It is not entirely clear that this type of 'unity' was a fifteenth-sixteenth century dominant concern. To be sure, there were Aristotelian concepts of unity which were becoming known in the sixteenth century. But, leaving aside the issue of the difference between dramatic and poetic unity, they have little relevance to the question of the unified scepticism of a prose work, a chronicle, in Hebrew such as the *Shevet Yehudah*. In very general terms, we may recall that the practice of grouping commentaries on verses of the Bible, or even fragments of verses, under *lemmata*, which is at the heart of medieval Jewish education and learning, is not conducive to unity. The same is the case with the division into *lemmata* of the Talmud in Rashi or Tosafot or in the then rising genre of super-commentaries for example on Rashi or Ibn Ezra, let alone in late medieval commentaries on the *Guide*.[58] In addition, it has recently been argued that in order to understand Hebrew chronicles of the fifteenth–sixteenth centuries such as Abraham Zacut's *Yuhasin* it is helpful to understand the tastes of the particular period and place which include the revival of the ancient polyantheas. It is not a genre which fosters unity.[59]

VII

The theme of unity is closely tied to that of authorship and, in this period, this is far from simple and not only in the case of the *Shevet Yehuda*. One need only recall (amongst so many others) the example of the *Celestina* and the body of studies which sees it as a work of two authors, i.e. of an author who composed a first section and another who expanded and completed it. Baer's own discovery of Alfonso de la Torre and Antonio de Guevara as sources was not treated by him with attention to its full implications. This 'humility' or misjudgement of the magnitude of his own discovery is followed more clearly by Schirman. After the publication of the discovery by Baer, Schirman penned an article about the impact of non–Jewish literature (including Baer's discoveries) on Jewish literature.[60] For us the implications of his approach is that Guevara's influence on the *Shevet Yehuda* is simply one more item in an indistinct list of ('Gentile') belletristic texts translated into Hebrew. The problem with the *Molad* article and its followers is that not all 'non-Jewish works' are the same. Similarly, Schirman does not dwell on the Hebrew author's fundamental artistic step: his precise and crucial option for one particular passage out of the enormous corpus of Guevara's *oeuvre*. Neither of them refers to the episode as 'el villano del Danubio'. This is a reflection of the *status quaestionis* at the time, before the full implications of the *Shevet*'s text had been realized. One might recall for example, that — at least some of — María Rosa Lida's views on Guevara's *villano* were only published posthumously.[61] Even though Celestina studies are clearly not *Shevet Yehuda* studies it is interesting for us here that according to her, Juan de Lucena had preceded Guevara in the fantastic tales about (classical, Greco-Roman) antiquities by half a century. Can there be an authorial unity in a work which at times consists of translations of de la Torre and Guevara and at times reads like a medieval Hebrew chronicle in the martyrological vein?

One characteristic feature of authorship in the *Shevet Yehuda* is stated at the very beginning, where Solomon Ibn Verga (or the editor) asserts that Yehuda Ibn Verga had collected accounts of persecutions and Solomon, it is implied, added some more. In other words, the account is like that of other Hispanic works of the period such as, say, the *Celestina*: according to Fernando de Rojas's Prologue, he found a text by another author and he, the second author added to it. Such analogies help us to understand not *one* idea or passage or fact in the book, but rather the book's conception of 'what is a historian' or 'what is a history book' as a whole. This is where it is useful to observe the notions of chronicle writing at the time and place where Solomon Ibn Verga and his family emerge.

We may mention, amongst numerous possible similar examples, the fifteenth century's *Refundición toledana de la Crónica de 1344*. There was a previous text of 1344, written by someone else, and, in the fifteenth century, *c.* 1440, it was enlarged by an anonymous Toledan converso author. An example of novelesque chronicles would be the *Cronica Sarrazina*. Here we are on even stronger grounds because recent identifications show that it was of interest to — and it was being read and commented by — Spanish Jews in the fifteenth century.[62] That is to say that the *Shevet Yehuda* stories which are usually described somewhat ironically as products of a peculiar individual's 'fertile imagination' are comprehensible within the frame of a well evidenced and established tradition of novelesque chronicles, interpolated texts and *refundiciones* where the authorship consists in continuing, abbreviating or expanding pre-existing texts, products of the labours of someone else.

In addition, in the case of a Hebrew chronicle such as the *Shevet Yehuda*, we may wish to recall another chronicle which, like the *Shevet*, has not been identified before as belonging in the *refundición* tradition: Abraham ben Solomon (b. 1482), the chronicler, penned his text as a 'continuation' or completion of Ibn Dawd. As in the case of the chronicler Abraham ben Shlomo, so too in the case of Yehudah Ibn Verga (who, as mentioned, is presented as the original author in the editio princeps's preliminaries) there has been no attempt to delineate a coherent authorial personality by reading the texts. Denying or asserting his authorship or link to the *Shevet* cannot proceed without such work. If we look at the works of Yehudah Ibn Verga, the first thing we notice is that they were in manuscript and not in print when *Shevet Yehuda* studies began and they remain in manuscript still. Of course, we are now fortunate in having access to history of science studies that were not available in Graetz's or Baer's time, but their relevance to a mainstream text such as *Shevet Yehuda* is practically nil.[63] On the contrary; the register of the language, the vocabulary, the style, let alone the concerns and contents of Yehudah Ibn Verga's writings — such as the astronomical tables in the British Library's manuscript — with their ideals of numerical precision seem to stand at the other pole of the *Shevet Yehuda*'s (rarely, if at all, correctly dated) engrossing, imaginative stories and fluent modernizing Hebrew. Perhaps more relevant are the paratexts. Their analysis reveals that Yehudah Ibn Verga shows his ability to present astronomy, that is, natural philosophy, as intrinsically relevant, indeed necessary to Jewish religion rather than irrelevant or opposed to it.[64] The *Shevet Yehuda* presents natural philosophy as providing topics of conversation, useful for Jewish arguments at royal courts, where they are represented by way of *oratio recta* as the subject matter of dialogues and discussions.

The 'rings story' is contiguous to a passage explicitly attributed to Joseph Ibn Verga — usually described as a Turkish rabbi who lived in Ottoman Adrianople and published around the time of the *Shevet*'s editio princeps in the mid-sixteenth century. The *Shevet Yehuda* and the *She'erit Yosef* [65] may have shared — apart from the family ties — the same printer at similar dates and the same place and yet *Shevet Yehuda* studies do not inquire about Yaavetz and vice versa. The question of his uncle Meir Ibn Verga may deserve to be taken into account elsewhere. The names 'Hamon' and 'Ibn Sanchi' in the passages immediately contiguous to the 'rings story', evoke the Jews at the Ottoman court in the first half of the sixteenth century. Recent finds at the Library of Congress in Washington DC, have uncovered a cache of letters by Abraham ben Ephraim Ibn Sanchi,[66] apparently the son of our story's protagonist (although there are theories of at least two Abraham Ibn Sanchis).[67] But a realistic historical contextualization is still a challenge, desideratum or lacuna. Thus, for example, there is no contemporary (that is, fifteenth- and not eighteenth-century) evidence concerning a putative Lisbon encounter with the king by Ibn Sanchi. Nor is the examination of Portuguese archival documents prominent or present in hypothetical accounts about Ephraim Ibn Sanchi's Portuguese past.

It is believed that in this same family Joseph Ibn Verga completed his father's work by adding a record of some of the events of his own time and of the age immediately preceding. Indeed, there was a time when Kaufman could assert that Joseph's addition of the Cairo Purim story — in the same book we are discussing — was more historically accurate than other accounts then available.[68] Reading or studying his *She'erit Yosef* (like reading Yehudah Ibn Verga's writings) is not a task that has attracted most writers on the *Shevet*. This is not entirely incomprehensible. Indeed the *She'erit* seems to belong to a different fifteenth-century Hispano-Jewish world: that of Campanton's *Darke ha- Gemara* or Shmuel b. Abraham Valensi's *Klale qal- wa- homer*. It is a world where the Talmud is at the centre and this centrality is not in question. This is not the attitude of the *Shevet Yehuda* to the Talmud and the 'talmudists'. The *Shevet Yehuda* is clearly *not* in the tradition of Campanton or other introductions to the Talmud. And yet, apart from a certain common stylistic fluency, there may be some unsuspected traces of other affinities between the *Shevet Yehuda* and the *She'erit Yosef*, between Solomon Ibn Verga and Joseph Ibn Verga. Thus, towards the end of the *She'erit Yosef* we find a chapter fully devoted to the history of scholarship or chain of tradition. It does not invoke Ibn Dawd, but rather (its 'offspring') the more astronomically inclined *Yesod 'Olam* by Isaac ben Joseph Israeli sometimes dated (questionably) to 1310. In this last work of the first half of the fourteenth century, there is also a chapter on the chain of tradition and Joseph Ibn Verga's avowed project is to bring that chapter up to date, to add to it, to 'complete' it. Here again, we may invoke the *refundiciones* template. Such contextualizations in the culture of the period and the family do not inform the average approaches to the chronicle.

VIII

Some time ago, attention was drawn to the Yiddish readings of the *Shevet Yehuda*.[69] At first glance, the more immediately obvious aspect of this phenomenon is the power of a Sephardi sixteenth-century prose text to inspire a poet, half a millennium later, in 1930s New York. But there is also a more relevant aspect, namely the Yiddish poem about the *Shevet* as an emblem of the trend to de-contextualize the *Shevet Yehuda* and deny it historical specificity. That is why there is a need for de-familiarization. This could be achieved in two related ways: Hispanicity and orality. As is well known, Baer put the question of disbelief on the agenda of studies on medieval and early modern Hispano-Jewish thought and history early on in his career with his extensive, dense article on Abner of Burgos/Alfonso de Valladolid.[70] Most of his critics or emulators on Averroism refer to the English translation of *A History of the Jews in Christian Spain*, but to my mind the important point is in another book, in his reading of the *Fortalitium fidei*, *c.* 1935. It is because of his experience in diplomatic that he could understand a section of it, for the first time in a long repetitive tradition, as the vestiges of a genuine and earlier inquisition file of Toledo, *c.* 1449.[71] It is typical that in reading such an inquisition file he was able to achieve that rare procedure of an original link between the Latin text and medieval Hebrew texts (the *Toldot Yeshu*) on the one hand and, on the other, a link to the medieval tradition of scepticism or *De tribus impostoribus* studied by Mario Esposito whom he explicitly cites. Esposito did not consistently ignore Spain: he mentions — albeit briefly — the *Fortalitium fidei*.[72] In other words, as we all know (for a later period) inquisition files are a rich — perhaps the richest — mine of evidence on disbelief, scepticism and religious doubt as could be understood as early as the time of Henry Charles Lea or Lucien Wolf and more seriously after Baer and, after him, in reading the abundant primary sources edited by the late Carlos Carrete Parrondo as well as in Encarnación Marín Padilla and numerous others.[73]

The question now is how to approach them. This is where the confrontation of primary sources sc. of *Shevet Yehuda* and inquisition material becomes crucial. Thus, around 1487–89, in a small village near Soria, a mill owner entered into an acrimonious discussion with a neighbouring farmer about irrigation during the drought. When the miller mentioned that the king's armies were defending the faith, the farmer replied: *Qué sabe ninguno de las tres leyes quál es la que Dios quiere más* [Who knows which of the three religions is most beloved of God].[74] Martín de San Pedro, a New Christian, *vecino de Descuellacabras*, was having an intimate conversation with Francisco de Cornago, the converso tailor, before 1502 and he asked him which was the better law and the reply was: *No ay dotor en el mundo que tal determine quál es la mejor* [No scholar/doctor in the world can determine which is the best].[75] Around 1492, two neighbours from Mamblilla were walking back home from the river and one asked, if their law/religion is better why are they being expelled and the other (Old Christian) replied *Por dónde sabré yo quál es mejor ley?* [How would I know which is better?].[76] Let us take the case of Juan Rodrigues, cura de Tajahuerce.[77] His formulation is near to the *Shevet*'s rings story. According to a testimony of 1491, his assertion was: *Tres leyes fizo dios, este es secreto que non sabe honbre qual es la mejor* [God made three laws/religions. This is the secret: no man knows which is the best]. A fuller comprehension would need to ponder on 'who is looking up'; on the difference between Soria and Tajahuerce; between a *cura* and a *capellán* and take account of the situation: just before the assertion, the *cura* had been told — and the formulation in Spanish leaves no doubt that it was an insult — that he was a *marrano*.[78] Juan Rodrigues did not print a book, so that the method of attending only to authors of books — in a largely illiterate society — would result in ignoring him. But the gossips — such as Martín de Ortega — disseminated his views and, by now, those interested can understand the power of gossip from the recent ample corpus of studies on this phenomenon. To be sure, the model would be from the school of *Annales* in the 1940s,[79] when Pierre Sardella showed the precise impact of rumours on insurance prices in late fifteenth- and early sixteenth-century Venice. The main directions of the work seem still to concentrate on Italy (or England) as in, say, Elisabeth Horodowich's article, which sees gossip as a factor in public life and political culture in early modern Venice.[80] But there is a wealth of evidence for the workings and mechanics of rumours in archival documentation from fifteenth- and sixteenth-century Spain where one can sometimes show precise chains of gossip in action at defined dates and places. They concern religion.

Of course, this approach differs from others such as to treat sayings about religion, doubt and scepticism according to the categories of theology or religion, hence Baer's 'Jewish averroism' or J. M. Millás Vallicrosa's 'agnostic fideism'[81] or the difference — introduced after Baer by F. Márquez Villanueva[82] — between averroism and popular averroism and numerous similar attempts to classify these phenomena of fifteenth–sixteenth-century Hispano-Jewish (or *judeo-converso*) thought. But for us, reading the *Staff of Judah* cannot be the same after these archival discoveries. Because what they reveal is that there is a world of orality outside the text which bears marked similarities to the *Shevet Yehuda*. Both speak of better rather than true religion, both place it within dialogues, both try to evade authorship as in Esposito's and his followers texts where it is usually someone else (for example the Stauffen Emperor, Friedrich II) who is responsible for articulating the doubt which is given a voice and disseminated in the text. In the *Shevet Yehuda* it is an absent neighbour. In the Tajahuerce inquisition case it is a *compadre* of the dead 'cura'. Rarely if ever do we have anyone taking full responsibility for scepticism. If the approaches of the nineteenth century saw it as a highly individualized, artistic tale leading to precise philological genealogies, the archival documentation would lead us to see it as a commonplace current even amongst rustics which erupts and appears in certain situations (anger, intimacy, tiredness, frustration). It could be seen as a case of etiological narrative, the phenomenon of creating stories to explain proverbs, dicta, idioms. The story in the *Shevet* transforms the common vernacular saying into a learned language story; the oral into the textual. The documented parallels do not come from royal courts so that the *Shevet* is elevating rumours — such as those of the small villages (Tajahuerce, Mamblilla, Descuellacabras, etc.) — to the royal courts of Spain, and by implication, the royal courts of Christian Europe.

Notes to Chapter 2

1. Gaston Paris, *La Parabole des trois anneaux* (Paris: A. Durlacher, 1885).
2. Hugo Schuchardt, 'Die Geschichte von den drei Ringen', *Im Neuen Reich*, 39 (1871), 481–85.
3. In a note in *Hebräische Bibliographie*, IV, 79 and *Hebräische Bibliographie*, XII, 21 but even then he makes reference to nineteenth-century predecessors in the task such as Isaac M. Jost, Adolf Jellinek, and others.
4. His idea was considerably amplified by Isidore Loeb, 'Le Folklore juif dans la chronique du Schebet Iehudah d'ibn Verga', *Revue des études juives*, 24 (1892), 1–29.
5. Solomon Ibn Verga, *Shebet Yehudah*, ed. by M. Wiener (Hanover: C. Ruempler, 1856); Ibn Verga, *Shevet Yehudah* (Hebrew), ed. by Azriel Shochat and Yitzhak Baer (Jerusalem: Bialik Institute, 1947).
6. R. Howard Bloch, 'Mieux vaut jamais que tard: Romance, Philology, and Old French Letters', *Representations*, 36 (1991), 64–86.
7. Ursula Bähler, *Gaston Paris dreyfusard. Le Savant dans la cité* (Paris: CNRS Editions, 1999).
8. It should be remembered that his main interest was Lessing and not Hispano-Jewish texts or cultures. See Friedrich Niewöhner, *Veritas sive varietas. Lessings Toleranzparabel und das Buch Von den drei Betrügern* (Heidelberg: Lambert Schneider, 1988). The notion that the story is inspired by Maimonides (*Epistle to Yemen*) appears in the notes to this chapter in the Baer-Shochat edition of 1947.
9. Emmanuel Levinas, *Totalité et infini. Essai sur l'extériorité* (Paris: Le Livre de Poche, 1991); Levinas, *Liberté et commandement (Transcendence et hauteur)* (Paris: Le Livre de Poche, 1999).
10. An interesting translation is (by Meir de L[eón]), Solomon Ibn Verga, *La vara de Judá* (Amsterdam: Mosseh d'Abraham Pretto Henriq, Jan de Wolf, 1744), p. 114: 'Dixo el Rey: llámese uno de los más sabios, y perguntárselo hemos, y como vino le dixo cómo te llamas, respondió Ephraim Aben Sancho, y el Rey dixo, parece que eres compuesto de cosas, de la mitad abaxo, donde está la señal de la circuncisión, Ephraim y de la mitad ariba xptiano, que muestra el nombre de Sancho; respondio el iudío: Rey y señor, Sancho es nombre de familia, como Sanchi, pero corrompióse en el vulgo; dixo el Rey: Pídote yo tu ija, qué me declaras tu familia? Respondió, señor, dixe Sancho, para diferenciar, porque ay muchos Ephraim en la tierra, y quieres saber quién soy, pues perguntaste cómo me llamo. Dixo el Rey: dexemos esto, que la razón porque te llamé es para que me respondas quál de las dos leyes es la buena, si la mía, ¡o la tuya! Respondió: mi ley es mejor para mí, segun mi caso, pues estuve en Egypt, siervo de siervos, y sacome de allí el Dio, con pruevas y milagros y tu ley es buena para ti, conforme el dominio continuo. Dixo el Rey: yo pergunto por las leyes en sí mismo, no en consideración de los recipientes. Dixo el sabio, después de estudiar tres días te responderé, si te parece: Respondió el Rey, sea assí, después dellos vino el sabio, y entró como hombre colérico y con la cara turbada, dixo el Rey, ¿de que vienes de tan mal humor?'.
11. E. Gutwirth, 'Creative Ambiguities and Jewish Modernity', in *Schöpferische Momente des europäischen Judentums in der frühen Neuzeit*, ed. by Michael Graetz (Heidelberg: Winter, 2000), pp. 63–73.
12. Solomon Ibn Verga, *Historia Judaica: res Judaeorum ab eversa aede Hierosolymitana, ad haec fere tempora usque, complexa. De Hebraeo in Latinum versa a Georgio Gentio* (Amsterdam: Petrum Niellium, 1651).
13. See above n. 10.
14. Amira Goldstoff-Frank, 'Shinuy ha-shem ba-miqra', *Mikhlol*, 16 (1998), 20–26.
15. II Chronicles 36. 4.
16. Genesis 41. 45.
17. 'et otrosí que fuese la nuestra merced de mandar que ningunos judíos, nin moros que non oviesen nombres de cristianos, e los que lo avíen que lo mudasen luego. A esto respondemos que en rasón que los judíos, nin los moros non ayan nombres de cristianos, que es servicio de Dios e que nos plase, e que de aquí adelante ningunt judío, nin moro non sea osado de se llamar nombre de cristiano, nin otrosí ninguno non sea osado de les llamar nombres de cristianos, et que non fagan ende al so pena de la nuestra mercet, e de las penas que en los derechos se contienen'.

Colección de Cortes de los reynos de León y de Castilla (Madrid: Real Academia de la Historia, 1836), p. 94.

18. Numbers rabbah 13.20

19. E. Gutwirth, 'The *Most marueilous historie of the Iewes*: Historiography and the "Marvelous" in the Sixteenth Century', in *In and Of the Mediterranean: Medieval and Early Modern Iberian Studies*, ed. by Nuria Silleras-Fernández and Michelle Marie Hamilton (Nashville, TN: Vanderbilt University Press, 2014), pp. 157–82.

20. 'Veemos en los libros de los autores de los gentiles que Vulcano ovo un fijo, e llamáronle Erictonio. [...] E fallamos que éste assacó primeramientre en Grecia la manera del carro [...] E porque cuando iva en él e seyé e nol paréciën los pies, e era aún allí cosa nueva el carro e ell andar en él, dixieron los autores de los gentiles que de la cintura ayuso avié fechura de dragón. E tod esto contaron d'él porque era muy sabidor, como leemos de Vulcano su padre, que diziën que non avié pies, e de la serpient otrossí que non á pies'. Alfonso X, *General Estoria, VI partes*, ed. by Pedro Sánchez-Prieto Borja (Madrid: Fundación José Antonio de Castro, 2009), 1st part, paragraph 17.q.

21. William Shakespeare, *King Lear*, Act IV, Scene 6, ll. 128–29.

22. Virgil, *Aeneid*, lib. 3.

23. Francisco Delicado, *La lozana andaluza*, ed. by Claude Allaigre (Madrid: Cátedra, 1985), p. 426. It continues: 'Divicia: La usanza es casi ley [...]'. I wonder whether *Lozana* readers have realized the parallelism to *minhag israel din hu* despite so many attempts at finding Jewish aspects.

24. Pedro Mexía, *Silva de varia lección*, ed. by Antonio Castro Díaz, 2 vols (Madrid: Cátedra, 1990), I, 376.

25. bZevahim 88a.

26. Simha Emanuel, *Sheelot W Teshuvot Ha-Geonim*, ed. by A. Shoshana (Jerusalem: Makhon Ofeq, 1995), no. 422. If one were to take account of *cordón* lore (as a possibility in explaining the representation/mimesis of a Spanish Christian of the late Middle Ages) the intensive work on it would lead us far afield to the cult of relics, its parody (cordón de Melibea), medicine, magic, the link between the rosary and the (knotted) girdle in Álvarez Gato, etc. See Santiago López-Ríos, ' "Señor, por holgar con el cordón no querrás gozar de Melibea". La parodia del culto a las reliquias en la Celestina', *Modern Language Notes*, 127 (2012), 190–207; Enrique Fernández, 'El cordón de Melibea y los remedios de amor en La Celestina', *La Corónica*, 42.1 (2013), 79–99; Jane Yvonne Tillier, 'Passion Poetry in the Cancioneros', *Bulletin of Hispanic Studies*, 62.1 (1985), 65–78.

27. Bahya ben Asher Ibn Halawa, *Perush al ha-Torah* (Bene Berak: Mishor, 2004), Tetzave Pericope.

28. bSanhedrin, 39a.

29. bGittin 59a.

30. Yitzhak Baer, *Historia de los judíos en la España cristiana*, trans. by José Luis Lacave, 2 vols (Madrid: Altalena, 1981), II, 540.

31. The translation of the *Chronica mundi* has been edited from Lucas de Tuy, *Text and Concordance of Obra sacada de las cronicas de Sant Isidoro, arcebispo de Sevilla, Kungliga Biblioteket, Stockholm MS. D 1272a*, ed. by Regina af Geijerstam and Cynthia M. Wasick (Madison, WI: The Hispanic Seminary of Medieval Studies, 1988). Lucas de Tuy, *Obra sacada de las crónicas de San Isidoro*, ed. by Juan Manuel Cacho Blecua (Zaragoza: Universidad de Zaragoza, 2003).

32. 'Por aquesto Moyses, como saujo astrólogo e grant lapidario, en dos piedras preciosas cauó dos ymágenes de tal ujrtut que la una daua memoria de las cosas passadas e la otra oblidança. E engastó aquestas dos piedras en dos anjellos e el anjello de oblidança dio a la muller Tarbis, e el otro se retuuo'. Lucas de Tuy, *Obra sacada de las crónicas*.

33. E. Gutwirth, ' "Entendudos": Translation and Representation in the Castile of Alfonso the Learned', *The Modern Language Review*, 93 (1998), 384–99.

34. W. H. Prescott, *Historia del reinado de los reyes católicos, D. Fernando y Doña Isabel*, 4 vols (Madrid: Rivadeneyra, 1846) IV, 315–16.

35. Ramón Menéndez Pidal, *Los reyes católicos según Maquiavelo y Castiglione* (Madrid: Universidad de Madrid, 1952), pp. 38–41; Miguel Saralegui, 'El príncipe afortunado. Fernando el Católico en la

obra de Maquiavelo', in *Virtudes políticas en el Siglo de Oro*, ed. by M. Idoya Zorroza (Pamplona: Eunsa, 2013), pp. 29–48.

36. Robert B. Tate, 'Políticas sexuales. De Enrique el Impotente a Isabel, maestra de engaños (*magistra dissimulationum*)', in *Actas del primer congreso anglo-hispano*, ed. by Richard Hitchcock and Ralph Penny, 3 vols (Madrid: Asociación de Hispanistas de Gran Bretaña e Irlanda, Castalia, 1994), III, 165–77.

37. Miguel Ángel Ladero Quesada, 'Isabel la Católica vista por sus contemporáneos', *En la España Medieval*, 29 (2006), 225–86 (p. 262).

38. J. Samuel Preus, 'Machiavelli's Functional Analysis of Religion: Context and Object', *Journal of the History of Ideas*, 40.2 (1979), 171–90.

39. Ibn Verga, *Shevet Yehudah* (Hebrew).

40. Helena Puigdomènech Forcada, 'Maquiavelo en las bibliotecas de algunos eclesiásticos españoles (siglos XVI y XVII)', *Anuario de filología*, 2 (1976), 425–32; Puigdomènech Forcada, 'Maquiavelo y maquiavelismo en España. Siglos XVI y XVII', in *Maquiavelo y España. Maquiavelismo y antimaquiavelismo en la cultura española de los siglos XVI y XVII*, ed. by Juan Manuel Forte and Pablo López Álvarez (Madrid: Biblioteca Nueva, 2008), pp. 41–60. Keith David Howard, *The Reception of Machiavelli in Early Modern Spain* (London: Tamesis, 2014).

41. Marcia L. Colish, 'Republicanism, Religion, and Machiavelli's Savonarolan Moment', *Journal of the History of Ideas*, 60.4 (1999), 597–616.

42. E. Gutwirth, 'Historians in Context: Jewish Historiography in the Fifteenth and Sixteenth Centuries', *Frankfurter Judaistischer Beiträge*, 30 (2003), 147–68.

43. The ultimate prototype of the 'three days' in both *Shevet* and *Ayuma* is probably the confrontation between Alexander the Great and the Jewish scholars in bSanhedrin 91a, where the scholars ask the king for three days before answering.

44. In Barcelona, Abraham Ibn Hasdai was the thirteenth-century author of *Ben ha-Melekh we-ha-nazir* (The Prince and the Hermit), a version of the stories known in the *romance* as 'Barlaam e Yosafat'. In it (Gate 16) he asserts that there are three things which have no credibility: the authorities, the sea, and Time. Shem-Tov ben Joseph Ibn Falaquera (*c.* 1225–95) is also believed to be Spanish. He offers a slightly more explicit version of this adage when writing in his *Iggeret Ha-Musar* that there are three things which are unreliable, lacking in credibility: the king, the sea, and Time. Abraham M. Haberman (ed.), 'Rabbi Shem Tov Falaquera's Iggeret ha-Musar', *Qoves 'al Yad*, 1 (1936), 43–90.

45. E. Gutwirth, 'Tres calas en la literatura de viajes del siglo XVI', in *Viajes a Tierra Santa. Navegación y puertos en los relatos de viajes judíos, cristianos y musulmanes (siglos XII–XVII)* ed. by Tania María García Arévalo (Granada: Universidad de Granada, 2014), pp. 67–90.

46. Bernard Lewis, 'E. I. J. Rosenthal (ed.), *Averroes Commentary on Plato's Republic*, Cambridge: University Press, 1956', *Die Welt des Islams*, 5.3 (1958), 300.

47. *Averroes' Commentary on Plato's Republic*, ed. by E. I. J. Rosenthal (Cambridge: University Press, 1956).

48. Shlomo Pines, 'Le- heqer torato ha-medinit shel Ibn Roshd', *'Iyyun*, 5 (1957), 65–84.

49. Loeb, 'Le Folklore juif', p. 5: 'Le roi est en general eclaire [...] il se montre bienveillant pour les juifs [...]'; Baer, Introduction to *Shevet Yehuda*, p. 13: 'Mitbarer lo ki ha- melakhim [...] ohavim et ha-yehudim' (he concludes that the kings love the Jews).

50. E. Gutwirth, 'El gobernador judío ideal. Acerca de un sermon inédito de Yosef Ibn Shem Tob', in *Actas del III Congreso Internacional Encuentro de las Tres Culturas (Toledo. 15–17 de octubre de 1984)*, ed. by Carlos Carrete Parrondo (Toledo: Ayuntamiento de Toledo, Universidad de Tel Aviv, 1988), pp. 67–75.

51. The theory is discussed by Niewöhner.

52. See for example Gabriele von Glasenapp, 'Vom edlen Freunde. Lessing in der jüdischen Historiographie', in *Lessing und das Judentum. Lektüren, Dialoge, Kontroversen*, ed. by Dirk Niefanger, Gunnar Och and Birka Siwczyk (Hildesheim, Zurich, New York: Olms, 2015), pp. 163–82. For Lessing's ambiguity, see, for example, Peter Heller, 'Paduan Coins: Concerning Lessing's Parable of the Three Rings', *Lessing Yearbook*, 5 (1973), 163–71.

53. Heinrich Graetz, *History of the Jews. Vol. V* (Philadelphia, PA: Jewish Publication Society of America, 1895), p. 323.

54. See, amongst others, Colin Walker, 'The Young Lessing and the Jews', *Hermathena*, 140 (1986), 32–54.
55. Baer, 'He'arot Hadashot la-Sefer Shevet Yehudah', *Tarbiz*, 6 (1935), 152–79.
56. Coleridge, *The Literary Remains of Samuel Taylor Coleridge*, vol. I (London: W. Pickering, 1836), p. 216.
57. Published in the *Daily News And Leader* in 1915.
58. E. Gutwirth, 'Ibn Ezra Supercommentaries as Historical Sources', in *Abraham ibn Ezra and his Age*, ed. by Fernando Díaz Esteban (Madrid: Universidad Autónoma de Madrid, Asociación Española de Orientalistas, 1990), pp. 147–54.
59. E. Gutwirth, 'The Historian's Origins and Genealogies: The Sefer Yuhasin', *Hispania Judaica Bulletin*, 6 (2008), 57–82.
60. Jefim Schirman, 'Translations of belles-letres in the Spanish Period' (Hebrew), *Molad*, 18 (1960), 105–09.
61. María Rosa Lida de Malkiel, 'Las sectas judías y los "procuradores" romanos. En torno a Josefo y su influjo sobre la literatura española', *Hispanic Review*, 39.2 (1971), 183–213.
62. E. Gutwirth, 'Le-toldot ha-sefer we-ha-qri'ah: qehilot yehude sefarad be-'eidan ha-dfus', in *Asufah le-Yosef*, ed. by Y. Ben-Naeh, J. Cohen, M. Idel and Y. Kaplan (Jerusalem: Shazar, 2014), pp. 263–84; Gutwirth, 'The Historian's Origins'.
63. Bernard R. Goldstein, 'The Astronomical Tables of Judah ben Verga', *Suhayl*, 2 (2001), 227–89.
64. E. Gutwirth, 'History and Jewish Scientific Study in Mediaeval Spain', in *La ciencia en la España medieval*, ed. by Lola Ferré, José Ramón Ayaso and Mª José Cano (Granada: Universidad de Granada, 1992), pp. 163–74.
65. Printed in Adrianopolis: Yaavetz, 1554; Mantua: Norzi, 1593.
66. Hebr. MS 31, Library of Congress.
67. Myron Weinstein, 'A Letter of 1510: Some Comments and Calculations', *Mizrah W-Ma'arav*, 6 (1995), 5–30; Weinstein, 'The correspondence of Dr. Abraham Ibn Sanchi', *Studies in Bibliography and Booklore*, 20 (1998), 145–76; Weinstein, 'Iggeret Shlomim me-ha-meah ha-shesh-esreh le-rabbaney yerushalayim ha-mistakhsekhim', *Shalem*, 7 (2002), 59–89. The articles concern a collection of nineteen Hebrew letters by the sixteenth-century physician-courtier at the Ottoman court in Istanbul.
68. David Kaufman, 'Joseph Ibn Verga's Extract from the Cairo-Megilla', *The Jewish Quarterly Review*, 11 (1899), 656–57; Kaufman, 'Miscellanea: The Egyptian Purim', *The Jewish Quarterly Review*, 8 (1896), 511–12.
69. E. Gutwirth, 'The Expulsion of the Jews from Spain and Jewish Historiography', in *Jewish History: Festschrift C. Abramsky*, ed. by Ada Rapoport-Albert (London: Peter Halban, 1988), pp. 141–61.
70. Yitzhak-Fritz Baer, 'Abner aus Burgos', *Korrespondenzblatt des Vereins zur Gründung und Erhaltung einer Akademie für die Wissenschaft des Judentums*, 10 (1929), 20–37.
71. Y. F. Baer, *Die Juden im christlichen Spanien*, vol. 2 (Berlin: Schocken, 1936), under that year.
72. Mario Esposito, 'Una manifestazione d'incredulità religiosa nel medioevo. Il detto dei "Tre impostori" e la sua trasmissione da Federico II a Pomponazzi', *Archivio Storico Italiano*, s.VII, 16 (1931), 3–48.
73. See for example Lucien Wolf, *Crypto-Jews in the Canaries* (London: Straker, 1910); Wolf, *The Jews in the Canary Islands* (London: Ballantine, 1926); Henry Charles Lea, *A History of the Inquisition of Spain* (New York: Macmillan, 1906); Carlos Carrete Parrondo, 'Dos ejemplos del primitivo criptojudaísmo en Cuenca', *El Olivo. Documentación y estudios para el diálogo entre Judíos y Cristianos*, 13.29/30 (1989), 63–69; Encarnación Marín Padilla, *Maestre Pedro de la Cabra, médico converso aragonés del siglo XV, autor de unas coplas de arte menor* (Madrid: E. Marín, 1998).
74. C. Carrete Parrondo, *Fontes iudaeorum Regni Castellae II: (1486–1502). El Tribunal de la Inquisición en el Obispado de Soria* (Salamanca: Universidad Pontificia, 1985), no. 272.
75. Carrete Parrondo, *Fontes iudaeorum*, no. 279.
76. Carrete Parrondo, *Fontes iudaeorum*, no. 304.
77. It was in the *Sexmo de Frentes* according to Juan Loperráez Corvalán, *Descripción histórica del*

obispado de Osma. Con el catálogo de sus prelados, 2 vols (Madrid: Imprenta Real, 1788), sv. Carrete Parrondo, *Fontes iudaeorum*, nos. 42, 53 and *passim*. Tajahuerce gained some notoriety thanks to González Palencia's linkage of a (later) sixteenth-century historical event there to the play 'Quien mal anda en mal acaba' by Ruiz de Alarcón. See Ángel González Palencia, *Historias y leyendas. Estudios literarios* (Madrid: CSIC, 1942).

78. Carrete Parrondo, *Fontes iudaeorum*, no. 98: 'anda para marrano'.

79. Pierre Sardella, *Nouvelles et spéculations à Venise au début du XVIe siècle* (Paris: Armand Colin, 1948).

80. Elizabeth Horodowich, 'The Gossiping Tongue: Oral Networks, Public Life and Political Culture in Early Modern Venice', *Renaissance Studies*, 19 (2005), 22–45.

81. José María Millás Vallicrosa, 'Aspectos filosóficos de la polémica judaica en tiempos de Hasday Crescas', in *Harry Austryn Wolfson Jubilee Volume on the Occasion of his Seventy-fifth Birthday* (Jerusalem: American Academy for Jewish Research, 1965), pp. 561–75.

82. Francisco Márquez Villanueva, 'El caso del averroísmo popular español. Hacia la Celestina', in *Cinco Siglos de Celestina. Aportaciones interpretativas*, ed. by Rafael Beltrán and José Luis Canet (Valencia: Universitat de València, 1997), pp. 121–32.

CHAPTER 3

❖

What Faith to Believe?
Vacillation, Comparativism and Doubt

Mercedes García–Arenal[1]

In 1611, Fr Jerónimo Gracián de la Madre de Dios published an interesting book titled *Diez lamentaciones del miserable estado de los atheistas de nuestros tiempos*. Fr Jerónimo was a well-known and prolific figure. A Carmelite friar, he had been the personal confessor of Therese of Jesus. Because of his reformist and Erasmian ideals and the internal strife in the order, he was expelled from the Carmelites and had to go to Rome to try to explain himself and get his expulsion overturned. He was taken captive by North African corsairs in 1593 and spent eighteen months in Tunis.[2] He was also later a missionary in Tétouan, in Northern Morocco. From 1608 until his death in 1614 he lived in Brussels, where he published *Diez lamentaciones*, a book that was censored and included in the 1632 Index of forbidden books, probably because it included detailed descriptions of the controversies around the beliefs of different Christian denominations. But what did Jerónimo Gracián understand by atheism? As he says:

> I call as atheism the depth of the evil that the heretics of our time have fallen into having abandoned the Roman Church. They do not end up in Luther's sect, or Calvin's or Menno Simons's; *instead they mock all laws, faiths and religions*, following their own private opinions and appetites, which are the only laws and beliefs they have.[3]

Thus atheists are not necessarily those who deny the existence of God or the afterlife, as in the modern sense of the term,[4] but those who do not believe in any religion, who challenge the authority or the universality of any *credo*, who are detached from and mock all faiths after having practised several or just after abandoning Catholicism. A prime example for Gracián were the New Jews of Amsterdam, who converted to Judaism from Catholicism and who, according to him, pretended to follow Jewish ritual in the synagogue, though most of them were atheists and believed in nothing.[5] Contemporary Portuguese preachers also address this question of 'atheism' in regard to descendants of converts from Judaism, linking atheism, as Gracián does, to the Judaizers' indecision in matters of religion and to their ignorance of both Laws or the mixing of elements from both.[6] Valério de São Raimundo, a Portuguese contemporary writing in 1622 and, like

Gracián, a Carmelite friar, addresses crypto-Jews in one of his sermons delivered at the occasion of an auto-da-fé, 'you are neither Christians nor Jews. You can be called atheists'. Estevão de Santana, likewise Portuguese and a friar of the *Ordinem Predicatorum*, declared, also in a sermon:

> You live like Atheists, without God, without Law [...] Receiving the Sacraments in the Church and practising yours in the Synagogue! This is not being a Christian or a Jew or a believer or a Catholic. So what is it? It is to be phantasms of religion, chimeras of faith, atheists of all laws because you are heretics of one and the other, hobbling in both.[7]

Gracián is not following in the tradition of the fifteenth-century anti-converso literature that spread the stereotype of conversos as not believing in either of the two religions. His main argument is that changing religion is conducive to unbelief: it entails vacillation and ambivalence, which are also forms of atheism.[8] Because what he labels as atheism is in fact 'irreligion', defined by Jean-Pierre Cavaillé as a negation, a detachment and doubt, implying criticism of a certain religious culture. According to Cavaillé, irreligion does not exist in the absence of religious authority, and that is what Gracián sees as most dangerous.[9]

Gracián implies that changing religion is voluntary. He never considers the circumstances of forced conversion; rather, he states that people who are forced to convert can always choose death. His 'Lamentación Sexta' is dedicated to hypocrites, the atheists who change their religion according to their circumstances and as a matter of convenience:

> This stratagem of changing laws like chameleons change colour, or like the cuttlefish that changes its colour to match the rocks it adheres to when it hunts, is used by many in our times. These (strictly speaking) are neither Catholics nor Lutherans nor Calvinists but atheist hypocrites; since they have no faith or law, although they pretend to keep the law that suits them, and although other heretics are bad and persecute Catholics [...] these heretics are incomparably worse because they not only persecute individual Catholics and go against particular books or beliefs, they go against God and against Christ and against all the authors and all the laws and beliefs and against all sacred scripture [...] The worst thing about this evil is that it is allayed with hypocrisy. Thus, it cannot be identified, discovered, punished or eradicated.[10]

Those atheists who change their religion are in fact against God and against all sacred scripture. According to Gracián, by changing religions they undermine their capacity for adhesion, loyalty and obedience. They have been uprooted from their faith and have relinquished their capacity for belief; they have put a distance between themselves and religion and cannot retrace their steps. Interestingly, Gracián links atheism to hypocrisy. In doing so, he shows that for him atheism is not so much about conceiving a world without God but rather being able to feign one faith or another because in fact there is no belief in any of them, no belief in religion per se.

From the brief biographical notes about Jerónimo Gracián at the beginning of this chapter, we can see that by 'atheists' he means not only converts to Judaism in Amsterdam but also 'renegades' — Christians who convert to Islam in North

Africa — and (after his experience in Flanders) heretics who waver between different Christian creeds. In fact, the controversies among different Christian sects are, according to him, a further inducement to atheism.[11] The renegades in North Africa are those chameleons whom Miguel de Cervantes describes in similar terms: Cervantes wrote the words *fino ateísta te muestras* [a fine atheist you show yourself to be] to describe a character in *La gran sultana* who is a renegade and who directly admits *yo ninguna cosa creo* [I do not believe in anything], who appears to be an atheist in the sense of conceiving a world without God.[12]

What interests me in Gracián's text is not so much his definition and use of the term 'atheist' but his diagnosis of what produces atheism. I will argue that the situation he saw as causing unbelief — the moving from one religion to another, the choosing between multiple religious 'truths' — had existed in Iberia for a century or a century and a half. Gracián would have found examples for his argument going back to the time of the forced conversions and expulsions of Jews and Muslims that took place in the fifteenth and sixteenth centuries. Through a series of royal decrees, Iberian society went from the religious pluralism of the Middle Ages to a mono-confessional state. This change had tremendous consequences and coincided with the establishment of the Inquisition and with the crisis produced by the Protestant Reformation, which questioned the sources of religious authority. Public indoctrination, evangelization, religious polemics, including attacks on Judaism and Islam — all became part of everyday life for the people of Iberia. I will suggest here that the confrontational method of comparing religious beliefs, which was the modus operandi of the Christian tradition of religious polemics, had the effect of contextualizing the idea of truth, which gave rise to vacillation, doubt and scepticism. In sum, it engendered a rejection of established hegemonic religion. Paradoxically, the circumstances produced by forced conversion ended up bringing to the fore the multiplicity of religious options, highlighting other religious faiths that had hitherto been contained within their own communities. There was also a profound change in the allegiance that religion demanded from the believer: it was now necessary to be knowledgeable about one's faith in order to be considered a true believer (*creer*);[13] the comfortable faith in the ancestral traditions of one's family or group was not enough anymore.[14] The previous members of non-Christian religions experienced at the same time forced evangelization but also marginality, persecution and abrupt changes in allegiance, experiences that are reflected in an array of irreligious attitudes that were often expressed as religious nonconformity.

In this chapter I will focus on the doubts and detachment from religion in general that were expressed by those who changed religion and the potential for these doubts to lead to unbelief. The Inquisition archives contain examples of attitudes toward religion that can best be described as mockery and aloofness. I propose to carry out a sort of anthropological study of these examples. I argue that, by attending closely to the accusations of the Inquisition, we find that the Holy Office was not so much concerned with heresy as with irreligion, as well as with any ambivalence or hesitation on the part of the accused that would challenge the categories that defined the work of the Inquisition. This essay also tries to show that irreligion was not the exclusive domain of educated elites steeped in philosophical thought.

Persecuting unbelief was a priority for the Inquisition. In the general Edicts of Faith, which were read out every year in the parishes of Spain's villages and cities and which exhorted the faithful to make denunciations, a brief description was made of the offences persecuted by the Inquisition. Particular mention was made of Judaism, Islam, and Lutheranism, which were included in the Instructions for Visitors of the Holy Office of the Inquisition (*c.* 1510–20) and were considered the principal heretical crimes. Other charges were specifically defined, and these officers were required by the Suprema to make the following inquiries: if anyone has heard somebody

> who has said or affirmed that there is no heaven for the good nor hell for the bad and that there is nothing more than birth and death, and who has said, in this world you will not see me suffer and in the next you will not see me punished or who has uttered heretical blasphemies like 'I do not believe', 'I cease to believe', 'I reject God our Lord and the virginity and purity of Our Lady the Virgin Mary' or who denied her virginity saying that Our Lady the Virgin Mary was not a Virgin before, during or after giving birth, or that she did not conceive by the Holy Spirit or who uttered heretical blasphemies against the heavenly saints [...] And if they know of anyone who claimed that simple fornication, or usury or perjury is not a sin, or who said that the soul of man is no more than a breath, and that blood is the soul, and who insulted or ill-treated images or crosses or that anyone did not believe in the creed or doubted any one of the articles of faith.[15]

In the Inquisition documents, both trials and *relaciones de causa*, we find numerous cases of persons belonging to the popular, uneducated classes who expressed repeatedly all the things described in this quotation from the Edict of Faith. There are also many — and this is the most interesting point for me in this chapter — who express total perplexity and frustration after having converted to Catholicism. They exhibit great anxiety due to their change of religion. For example, Alonso García El Blanco, a convert from Judaism who had returned to Guadalajara from Portugal after the expulsion and was tried in 1540, stated that now 'he was neither Christian, Moor, nor Jew: I don't know who I am; I am nothing and I wish to God I had suffered a bad death there (in Portugal) and not come back here to be a Christian for since I came back here I am blind to everything'.[16] Alonso is 'blind' also in the sense indicated by Gracián: unable to believe. Like many, Alonso has lost the comfort of the certainty of belief. The frustration and anger produced by enforced indoctrination following forced conversion is also very clear in the case of Álvaro Gómez, a Morisco from Granada who in 1575 was working in the vineyards of Campo de Montiel in La Mancha with Old Christian peasants who were trying to convince him of the benefits of papal bulls and indulgences for souls in Purgatory. Álvaro got very angry: 'the defendant responded angrily that he did not believe in God or in Saint Mary [...] nor did he believe in the articles of faith; he believed in nothing, nothing, nothing'.[17] Diogo Lopes Pinhanços, tried by the Inquisition of Coimbra in 1569, had been raised as a Catholic but in a family of Judaizers and it was because of Judaizing that he was detained by the Holy Office. He declared in front of the Tribunal that he had 'no faith or law', that it was all a lie, that there was no God in heaven. He did not believe in Jesus Christ or in the teachings of the Church. He had never seen God and he did not have to believe what he could not see. He could not believe that the consecrated host was God because he saw it was made of flour. He declared that he no longer wanted to live.[18]

Another Christian of Jewish origin from Daroca had less anxiety and had declared sarcastically before witnesses: 'I have had [i.e. lived under] the holy law of Moses, I have had the law of Jesus Christ and if a saint Muhammad were now to appear, by God! I would make it three and if so I would have no fear of God for I would have tried out all the laws'.[19] In about 1459, Bartolomé de Cetina was living in Calatayud with Juan Fierro, with whom he had been living for more than ten years. One day, Juan invited the merchant Juan Pérez de Santa Fe and Gonzalo de Arjarán — both neighbours from Ariza — to eat. After eating, but while still seated at the table, they began to discuss the Christian and the Jewish law, and after a long debate they said: 'We know not which of them is better; let us do what is right for he that does right will do well'.[20] That was also the attitude of Jerónimo de Torres, a shoemaker from Cartagena, who said that to be on the safe side he 'was a Lutheran, a Jew and a Moor',[21] though he neglected to hedge his bets completely by including Catholicism. Gaspar Vayazan 'said that he had and believed in three laws, that of Our Lord Jesus Christ, and that of Muhammad and that of Lord Moyssen, so that if one of them failed him, the other would not'.[22] Or Diego Peña, 'who made himself Jew, Moor and heretic'.[23] He is like a chameleon, changing his colours according to his surroundings, but he argued that 'he did it in jest'.[24]

A similar story, but with a slightly different nuance, took place in the marketplace in Calatayud, where one morning in about 1473, Simón de Santa Clara, Antón Ram and a group of Jews including Vidal Abenpesat were discussing the news of the day. Some said that the Turk was coming and 'would take and destroy all these lands'. Vidal said with mirth, 'Do not put on mourning clothes (for us), for if the Turk comes here, we'll have to make it three'. Vidal was clearly understood by the other people present to mean that 'they had once been Jews and had become Christians and would become Moors, if the Turk should come'. His insouciance is not only understood and shared but makes everyone present laugh at his repartee. This same Simón de Santa Clara was also denounced by another witness for having said to Mosse Alpastán: — 'What do you think, Mosse Alpastán? Neither from the law of the Christians, nor that of the Jews, nor that of the Moors, can the truth be known'.[25] The Jew Leon Quatorce knew Simón de Santa Clara very well and explained to him,

> As for me, I take God to be a kind of engraver: I have had the holy law of Moysen, I have had the law of Ihesu Christo and even if a Saint Muhammad were to appear and come. By God! That would make it three, and if this came to an end, I would not be afraid of God, since I had followed all the laws.[26]

The convert Simón de Santa Clara was in the habit of saying that he believed that what was said of Moses and Jesus Christ was true, but he also believed in Muhammad because 'in what way was Muhammad less than the others?' One day, talking to another, he said, 'The truth cannot be known from the law of the Christians nor that of the Jews nor that of the Moors: for me I say to you there is nothing more than being born and dying'. His fellow convert Hernando de la Rivera, 'as a man who doubted (*dudoso*) in the Faith and disbelieved, had dared to say and affirm that there was no more to life than being born and dying'.

The Jew Acach Xuen saw that the convert Juan de Sayas led such an evil life that he was neither a good Christian nor a good Jew. One day he asked him 'what he intended to do or which law he would follow: for I see that you do not have your law and you speak badly of the Jews and of their law and of the Moors and their law; I do not know, by God! What you will do in the world to come'. 'You are crazy', the convert replied, 'don't you know that in this world all is air except being born and dying and that the soul of a dog enters the soul of a man and that of a man in that of a dog? With all this I intend to commend my soul to all three laws and whichever has the greater right to it may take it'.[27] As in other parts of Europe, one of the recurring themes of the irreligious is to state that there is nothing but to be born and to die, that there is no afterlife.[28] This statement of *nascer e morir como bestias* is extremely frequent in Inquisition trials of converts and of Old Christians alike and has lately received much attention by historians, and so I will not go into it here.[29]

The testimony given by witnesses to Inquisition officers is extremely rich and expressive of the social and cultural context in which villagers, peasants, small artisans and parish priests lived and of the changes taking place in this context. Converts were not alone in expressing doubt about religion — far from it. This can be seen in the story of Pedro Navarro, an Old Christian who lived around the time of the expulsion of the Jews from Castile. One day, he was walking from the river to the village with other peasants after working in the fields, talking about how the Jews were leaving the land. Pedro Navarro remarked:

> the Jew said that he had a better law than ours, and the Moor said the same; and this witness and the other said: 'Well, if they have a better law than we do, why are they being cast out of the kingdom?' And this witness said: 'How do I know?' or 'How would I come to know which law is better?' and 'I don't know if God loves the Moor and the Jew!' And he did not say this because he doubted his faith but out of simplicity and ignorance, and he has always been steadfast in the faith and does not come from a Jewish or Moorish family.[30]

Then there is the story of Juan de Torme,

> a resident of Fuentealuilla de Valcorva, in Soria [...], [who] said that the previous Tuesday, on the fifth day of the month, two friars of the order of Saint Francis came to Fuentealuilla with their insignia to preach certain indulgences that they brought, and while one of the friars was preaching that Tuesday, to the church where he was preaching came Pedro Texero, a resident of that place, who commenced to talk about certain things such that he was disruptive to the friar who was preaching; and after the sermon was given and they went out of the church with the insignia, the friar asked Pedro Texero if he believed in God, and [...] Pedro Texero answered him saying that he did not believe in God; and then the friar answered him: 'Then, keep yourself from the fire, since the fathers are near'. And most of the town was present for this. He asked what

his reputation was and he said that of a bad Christian and that he never went to mass during the week and that on Sundays and Easter he would rather hunt than go to mass.[31]

Pedro Texero was disrupting the preaching of the Franciscans, did not believe in God and was cautioned that he should be careful about his behaviour since there were Dominicans, guardians of the Inquisition, in the vicinity and that could have fatal consequences for him.

Several witnesses heard the priest of Tajahuerce in Soria say 'that God had me three laws and that he did not know which of them was the best; and that at that point this witness said to him: "But my fellow, ours is of course the best"'. Another witness presented a different version: the priest had said: 'three laws or God; this is the secret that man doesn't know which is the best'.[32] He was presenting the choice between religion and a simple belief in God, maybe a sort of deism. Village priests were prone to doubts. Another witness, Pedro de Pynilla, a resident of Tajahuerce, 'said that he heard Juan Rodrigues, Tajahuerce's priest, say about three years earlier [...] that there were three laws, of the Moors, the Jews and the Christians and that each could be saved according to his law and that we do not know which is the best'.[33]

Therefore the statement 'let us practise the three laws, or the three religions' so as to be on the safe side because we cannot know which is the best, or because 'I have no preference for one or the other' can be related to the more frequent (and apparently contradictory) proposition that 'each is saved in his own law', as stated by Tajahuerce's priest. This could imply a certain degree of toleration or what Stuart B. Schwartz has called 'popular tolerance', but it also obviously suggests religious relativism and disaccord with the belief that only one religion can guarantee salvation. It probably reflects nostalgia for the past, a preference for the medieval religious regime in Iberia in which people belonged to and lived within their own religious community, following traditional rituals and ceremonial rhythms practised within the family.[34] It also implies a call for freedom of conscience, which is explicit in the case of the Moriscos who pointed to the Ottoman case as a model to be emulated. The Moriscos' demand for freedom of conscience — which made them similar to the *secta de los politicos*[35] — was repeatedly cited by the advocates for expulsion: 'They desired and greatly sought freedom of conscience, and to be left alone to live in their way, just as the Turk allows Christians in his realms to live according to their religion and some other princes who consent in their lands for each to follow whatever profession he likes'.[36] The proposition *cada uno se salva en su ley* was so frequent among Moriscos that many Christian polemicists affirmed that it was an Islamic tenet.[37]

Practising, or showing a willingness to practise, two or three laws was not about the relativity of truth and the equal value of the three laws, as *cada uno se salva en su ley* is; it was about the lack of certainty about which one was better. But both 'propositions' ('each one is saved in his own Law' or 'let us practise the three laws since we cannot know which is the true one') reject the imposition of a mono-confessional religious identity. Both reject the universality of just one Law, and the demand that such universality be accepted led many individuals who were prosecuted by the Inquisition to be sceptical of all three. In fact, there are cases in which the accused makes clear that his rejection of the three laws is because of the imposture of their founders, such as the man tried by the Portuguese Inquisition who claimed in 1587 that 'three men have deceived the world: Moses, Jesus and Muhammad'.[38] These doubts about the three religions led Pedro Cabrera, a farmer from Murcia, to the conclusion that there was no God, and the resulting anxiety almost made him lose his mind.[39]

Both propositions are reactions to the realization that there are too many truths, too many religions: it is difficult to choose and to be certain, and it is a cause of inner tension and unease. This is clear from remarks such as those made by Luis Borrico of Almansa, who was accused of publicly rebuking God for not having done his job properly, for having created three mutually exclusive Laws.[40] In the same vein, the converso Jaime de Santa Cruz, a merchant from Zaragoza, was accused of stating that if God were to give him His power for a fortnight, he would do things better. Among the changes he would make was to 'unite all beliefs and make Christians, Jews and Moors as one'; he also said that 'since [God] had created Moors and Jews who had been born into such beliefs, what fault was it of theirs when they were damned?' Santa Cruz admitted to having said that if he were granted God's power for a fortnight, he would make everyone a Christian, and he also questioned on occasion the guilt of the innocent children of 'Moors and Jews, for they die in a state of innocence and without having known the faith of Christ'. He had made such statements because he had heard it preached that these children were stained by the faith of their parents and went to hell for not having heeded the word of Jesus Christ. This was also the reason why he had said that 'a good Moor and a good Jew will go to hell but will be punished less than a bad Christian'. Santa Cruz also stated that, given God's power, he would have made 'the men and women from the new world [i.e. America] Christians to enable them to be saved, for he felt great pity and bitterness when he thought of the multitude of souls who went to hell there'. He insisted on his belief that 'the children of the Moors and Jews and other unbelievers were damned despite dying in a state of innocence, but that they would be spared most of the punishments of hell on account of their innocence, as would good Moors and Jews, who would receive more lenient punishments in hell than bad Christians'.[41] For many converts, the idea that there was no salvation outside the Catholic Church (which implied the damnation of one's fathers and forefathers) was hard to accept. Many Old Christians also found this belief unjust, including educated and learned men. An example is Francisco Marcilla, a twenty-three-year-old Latin student who appeared voluntarily before the Inquisition tribunal of Cuenca in 1609.[42] He was also against the plurality of religions and against the belief that only one of them, Catholicism, was the true one. He approved of the belief that there is but one God and that it was enough to follow natural law 'without forcing men to believe faithfully the other articles that we have and the evangelical precepts [...] he thought that it was enough to believe in one sole God and not to do to others that which one did not want for oneself'. Francisco thought this was best, 'and it made most sense to him because it seemed to him that it could be proven by natural demonstration'. He had arrived at these positions by comparing and seeing that 'there was such a wide variety of sects' and that the members of these sects all honoured God in their own way, just as he honoured God within the Catholic faith which he professed. For all these reasons he had reached the conclusion that 'the safest thing was to follow natural law'.

But Francisco was also periodically assailed by doubts about the existence of God. At times he did not know if there was a God or whether 'nature produced us', and at times he thought that 'there was no more than being born and dying like irrational animals'. And he considered that each found salvation in his own religion since it seemed to him impossible that so many Muslims and so many Lutheran Christians or so many Gentiles should be condemned if it were true, as he found it hard to accept, that there was only one true religion.

The physician Beltrán Campana, tried in Cuenca for Lutheranism, thought that the existence of multiple religions implied that each person could be saved in his own law. For that reason he was is in favour of freedom of conscience:

> He said that the religion of the Calvinists, the Roman [Catholics], the Lutherans were all a good, an excellent thing [...] and that each person could be saved through his own law: the Moor and the Turk in theirs, the Hebrew according to his, the Englishman in his, the Spaniard in his, and everyone else in theirs; and freedom of conscience is what is good, as has been said [...] the popes and priests are not necessary because they do inhumane things and want to raise themselves up and dominate all men and deny them their liberty and free will and they put on a good face to deceive and take everything for themselves, committing all manner of tyrannies and as for freedom of conscience, it is what matters, since everything else is false because there is nothing more than eating and fornicating and freedom and the latter is the glory of this world.[43]

Beltrán Campana died at the stake in Cuenca. There is a paradoxical association of fideism with free thought in his statements that can also be found in the New Jews of Amsterdam.[44] Seen from a different angle, maybe this is not so paradoxical, since different battles were being fought simultaneously: the battle for defined orthodoxies and the battle for freedom of conscience.[45]

Not all those who had doubts were able to allay them by practising or paying lip service to all three religions, or by concluding that salvation was assured in any of the three, or that all religion was wrong, as was the opinion of Lope de Vera, of whom I am are going to speak shortly. The Inquisition trials often included signs of vacillation between Catholicism and the religion of origin of the accused. For example, Román Ramírez, a Morisco from Deza who confessed to the Inquisition of Cuenca to being a Moor and availed himself of the Inquisition's Edict of Grace and became a good Christian. This was followed by a veritable religious crisis which left Ramírez in a state of vacillation between the two religions. He lived in this way for many years ('more than twenty', by his own account). He then became friends in Deza with a Turkish slave by the name of Muçalí, whom a captain with the surname Cabrera had brought with him, and as a result, Ramírez again began to observe Ramadan and to pray, in mispronounced Arabic, some of the *suras*. In the 1590 records of his trial, Ramírez comes across as a man who had grown old in doubting and vacillating between two religions.[46] Another example is the case of Hernán Sánchez de Castro in Uclés, Cuenca, in the 1490s. A witness saw how all the religious communities in the village started to pray for relief from the drought. 'He saw how Sánchez went out of the church of San Andrés with the other Christians in their procession, and when they passed by the plaza where the Jews stood with their Torah, waiting for the Christian procession to pass, Sánchez stayed there with the Jews and marched with the Torah, abandoning the procession of the Christians'.[47] Here, the vacillation is expressed even on the physical level, as Sánchez tries to decide whether to position with the Christians or the Jews.

The same kind of vacillation manifested itself a century later in an auto-da-fé that took place in 1632,[48] where it was revealed that Fray Ramairón, an Old Christian, had 'tried out' and/or professed the faith of Moses:

> The last of all those who came out was Fray Domingo Ramairón, a native of Genoa, a friar of the order of the very holy Trinity, who was an apostate atheist and inducer of heretics and said that he did not know if he was of the nation of Moors or Jews, and that he had taken up out of curiosity to save himself the Law of Moses.

He was planning to go to England to learn about Lutheranism when he was detained by the Inquisition. Many more cases could be mentioned, such as that of José Carreras, a Catholic priest who converted to Judaism in Amsterdam in 1655, preached his radical ideas there and afterwards went to England and converted to Protestantism.[49] Is this vacillation and doubt, or intellectual curiosity, or just refusing to adopt only one Law when there are several at hand, all of which have positive aspects? It is indeed religious non-conformity. In cases such as Carrera's we see people who have lost confidence in the Church's claim for the authority of the Vulgate, who doubt the reliability of the New Testament and the tradition that rests on such shaky foundations. We will look more closely at these issues with the case of Lope de Vera.

In 1604, in the Portuguese town of Evora, Custódio Nunes was accused by the Inquisition of being a *judaizante*, a crypto-Jew, but he defended himself by saying that he was both a Jew and a Christian,[50] that he abided by the Law of Moses but also believed in Jesus being God and in the message of the Gospels. People who tried to reconcile different religions or who vacillated were ambivalent, and this ambivalence prompted them to hedge their spiritual bets.[51] Custódio's position is close to the 'universal salvation' posited by those who held that Christians, Moors and Jews could each save their souls in their own faiths.

We can link the example of Custódio Nunes and others like him with cases of 'Judaizing Moriscos' such as Juan de Hortuvia, who travelled from Cuenca to Medina del Campo in the company of a Portuguese textile merchant who was a convert from Judaism. At some point during the days and nights that they spent together, the merchant observed that Juan did not eat pork or drink wine and asked him if he was a Morisco; he then explained to him at length that the Law of Muhammad was a good law and that he knew it well, but that it had certain flaws. The merchant explained these flaws and how Judaism deals with certain problems.

He taught the Morisco how the Jews fast and observe the Sabbath, something that Juan de Hortuvia practised thereafter and he was denounced to the Inquisition because of it. This and other cases of Judaizing Moriscos show individuals who feel attracted or at least sympathetic to other minority religions, and they look to them for inspiration for a new self-conception.[52] Whether they harbour doubts or not, their religious search is away from Catholicism. The Inquisition trials, in spite of themselves (and the inquisitors), reflect the fact that the faiths of both Judaizers and Moriscos were syncretic or at least contained elements of two or more religions. Groups, families, individuals fashioned their own faiths in the absence of the sacred text of their own religions — and established their own reference points, which varied according to time and place. These groups or individuals may well have, either knowingly or not, adapted their religious beliefs to suit their particular circumstances. There is a great deal of anxiety beneath what is, at the end of day, a lack of certainty.

Anxiety obviously manifests itself most clearly during certain extreme events in an individual's life. Expulsion from Spain was one of these events. Fray Damián Fonseca recounts the case of an old *alfaquí* from Valdigna who, as a sugar producer, could have stayed in Spain when the Moriscos were expelled in 1610 but decided to leave, 'doubtful over which of the two laws was best, for he had already heard a great deal from us, and wanted to dispute with scholars of the Qur'an and, after having heard both sides, make up his mind'.[53]

Doubt would surface and vacillation between the different religions would become more intense with the approach of death. Encarnación Marín has studied numerous cases of early fifteenth-century Aragonese Jews who were undecided at the time of death about which law they should follow or who were sceptics and, when faced with death, displayed total indifference towards the rites of one religion or another and indifference also towards belief.[54] One example was the converso Esperandeo Salvador, who on his death bed said to another converso that he did not have 'either one law or another'. Luis de Santangel was another Jewish New Christian who at the time of his death said he was 'in anguish for I know not in which law to die'. There were just as many cases among the Moriscos. One such doubter was Luis de Cebea, from Cuenca, who had practised Christianity his whole life but had held fast to Islam in his heart. At the time of his death he asked himself 'which was the true law in which he ought to save himself, whether that of the Christians or that of the Moors, to die in it'. His relatives and friends, who were by his side, encouraged him to die in his Muslim faith. His son 'had told him to die as he had lived, in the sect of Muhammad which was the right path to heaven and they brought him a Moor who was very well versed in his sect to help him die'. And last, there were irreligious people who converted when faced with serious illness and death, such as Manuel Rodríguez,

> who was among the most knowledgeable men in the world in all things and this witness never saw him or knew him to have anything to do with Christianity, nor did he have any knowledge of our faith, such that he knew nothing and had nothing as a Christian, and he did not know the Our Father nor the Ave

> Maria nor the Credo, he did not know how to cross himself nor did he ever go to mass or ever enter into a church nor did he have any part of our Catholic faith so that he had no faith. And when the inquisitors of this bishopric came to Aranda, he got sick and was yellow, half dead, unconscious, and he got worse and worse until he died shortly thereafter. And (while he was sick) everything that they told him about our faith [...] now, he believed it all [...][55]

Up to now we have considered people who vacillated between faiths and people who were faced with the impossibility of deciding which religion was the true one and reacted in various similar ways: feigning that they were willing to embrace all three of them (those whom Gracián calls hypocrites), saying that any of them is as good as the others, or navigating between them. In the last part of this chapter, I would like to focus on those who, in their doubts and in their quest for certainty, try out the different religions, without necessarily becoming fully convinced of any of the three or adopting a definitive religious identity. These are generally educated people of a higher social class than the ones we have considered up to now. In their quest for certainty, they attempt 'to open the eyes of their understanding', as one of them says.

There is, for example, the rather famous case of Eugenio de Torralba.[56] He was an Old Christian from Toledo who was accused of doubting the divinity of Christ and he appeared before the Inquisition to be interrogated:

> He was asked if he had ever believed and held that Christ was not God and was also asked how long he had been in that error. He said he had been in that error for a period of twenty years, sometimes believing it for as long as three years but then returning to faith in Christ, and when he said the words that witnesses claimed they had heard him say, he believed and held that Christ was not God and that a teacher called Alfonso who had been in Rome and was first a Jew and then a Moor and then a Christian talked to this penitent of his crimes and told him that everything in the Old and New Testament was deceit and that Christ did not die, denying that there were any apostles and denying all the other sacraments of the Church and that he believed in the law of Muhammad and that he persuaded him of this often in his younger days, for this was more than twenty years ago, telling him not to believe in the Old and New Testaments but in the law of Muhammad, but this penitent felt scruples in his heart and was made to leave and wander from the path of truth. He said he had been diverted from the faith by the teacher Alfonso and became ambiguous and doubtful whether to be a Jew or Moor for if he decided to do so he would not come to Spain but would rather go to Turkey or Barbary to become a Moor, but since he had drunk Christianity at his mother's breast he had never been completely determined nor had the intention to give up his true Redeemer.[57]

Although he had been 'doubtful, confused and perplexed', he had in some sense been saved by the milk drunk at his mother's breast, that is, by the belief he had imbibed as an ancestral inheritance. Or that is the argument he puts forward in his defence before the Holy Office, knowing his Old Christian background is to his advantage. The more interesting figure in this trial is this 'maestro Alfonso', whom the accused had met in Rome, who knew Arabic, and who had been a Muslim and a Jew and felt the contradictions in the sacred texts as an obstacle to belief.

This story has certain parallels with the one described by the protagonist of *The Marrakesh Dialogues*, a Spanish polemical text written in the form of a dialogue between a young man who converted to Judaism and his Christian brother.[58] Bernardo is a young Catholic from Antwerp in a Dutch ship bound for Morocco. During the long days of the passage he hears for the first time in his life a discussion of religion, specifically a discussion of different religions by Protestant sailors who attack Catholicism. His first contact with Protestantism thus becomes the *praeparatio mosaica*.[59] This introduction to religious doubt is expressed in the formula *abrir los ojos del entendimiento*. He says:

> when I sailed from Flanders on a ship bound for this land of Morocco, I overhead certain things that I had never heard before. Nobody had perhaps trusted in me over there, as these things were so criminal and I was of such a young age. I held my ears wide open and jointly the eyes of understanding.

Doubt, affirms Bernardo, is a duty for 'those who want to search for the truth like men ('como hombres').[60] Trying to open the eyes of his understanding, he then reads the Bible in vernacular for the first time:

> Then I started to read a Bible they [the Protestants] had brought with them, and when I read the Gospels, I found there so many things in so flagrant contradiction with each other that I came to cast doubt on them. I tried to guess which one of these stories was the true one, until I ended up considering them all as fabulous tales, unworthy of credit and not even well written, as are those found in Ovid or in Cicero's *On the Nature of the Gods* [...] As I noticed this, I went on to read the Holy Scripture where I found the truth of the Most Sacred Law given on Mount Sinai.[61]

He is following the Protestant principle of *sola scriptura*, but instead of becoming a Protestant he feels the truth lies in the Law of Moses: 'When I considered this to be the truth, as it actually is, I had left the dangerous harbour of the vain Christian faith. I was thrown into a raging sea of thoughts, riding upon the waves of my understanding and desire to arrive at an actual knowledge of the truth'. For Bernardo, the truth is to be found in Judaism and therefore he disembarks in Morocco, goes to the Mellah of Marrakesh where he becomes a proselyte with the name of Obadia ben Israel, dresses as a Moroccan Jew, marries, and stays to live there. Becoming a Jew gives the protagonist the licence to grow into adulthood and masculinity, to contradict his preachers and authorities, to mock what is presented as sacred. Following only the code of intellectual honesty, a Jew, in the words of Carsten L. Wilke, 'conceives the doubt, speculates the truth, discovers the lie', while clergymen evoke the principle of faith and obedience in order to take their lay folk by the bridle 'like horses and mules in which there is no understanding'.[62] The articles of faith are 'hoods imposed on you by those very people who consume hundreds of thousands of ducats' and who in addition mock their tithe-payers by abusing their wives and daughters. Bernardo's brother Andrés comes to Morocco years later to look for him and tries to convince him to return to Catholicism. The discussion that ensues is what is recorded in the *Dialogue*, a debate in which Judaism is of course victorious.

Another important trial is that of Lope de Vera, a case made famous by Miriam Bodian[63] and published in part by Kenneth Brown.[64] Lope de Vera was an Old Christian who converted to Judaism and died at the stake for maintaining and defending his beliefs. He was arrested by the Inquisition in 1639 while he was at the University of Salamanca, where he had studied Hebrew. He was an educated man, a university student who aspired to a post as professor of Hebrew. He had a deep love of the Hebrew language, which he considered the most ancient and the best, the tongue in which God had spoken to Adam. He was also familiar with other Oriental languages, including Arabic and Aramaic, and had been fond of reading forbidden books. His intimate acquaintance with the Hebrew Bible and his recognition of the inadequacy of the Vulgate, a conclusion he had arrived at by reading the forbidden works of Erasmus, along with his contacts with Portuguese conversos studying in Salamanca, had triggered his doubts about the tenets of the Catholic Church and about its foundations. He was struggling with doubt and trying out other religions with the aim of achieving certainty. He was a man of conscience. For him doubt appears to have been an intrinsic part of faith.

Before becoming a Jew (something that happened only after he had been in the Inquisitorial prisons for many months), Lope de Vera had vacillated for a time between the three faiths. I would like to quote directly from his trial records:[65]

> he read forbidden books such as the Annotations of Erasmus and the embassy and travels of David Reubeni and other Arabic texts and at that time he stopped confessing and following Church precepts and told some people he was a Jew or a Moor and he would have to go to Algiers or Constantinople to renege on his faith [...] and that he was a Jew and a Moor and that he would very willingly go to Algiers to forsake our holy faith [...] he especially enjoyed dealing with Jews and Moors and would willingly cross over (to North Africa) and read the Qur'an of Muhammad.[66]

He also said that he could easily be persuaded to follow the law of the Jews or the sect of the Moors and

> in communication with a Portuguese scholar concerning some of the articles of faith of the Roman Church he spoke against some of them and especially the Trinity, saying that it seemed impossible that God was Triune or that he had been incarnated or was present in the consecrated wafer [...] and that images should not be adored because God had commanded in the law of Moses that no images be made. He said that it was wrong to have religions, for it went against holy precept and natural blessing and that the miracles brought about by images and the people who performed them were all lies.[67]

According to the Inquisition prosecutor, Lope de Vera

> was of such a changeable and fragile nature that having learned the Hebrew and Arabic tongues he was easily inclined to follow the law of the Jews or the sect of the Moors and he was so confused by all his reading that he found himself among the Moors, not even knowing what his own law was and he exchanged the law of Christ for being excommunicated.[68]

The *calificador* of the Inquisition stated that 'it could not be denied that he was a prey to doubt and confusion'.[69]

Other witnesses testified that Lope had said that Catholicism required belief in 'many things that were difficult to believe'. He could profess the Law of Muhammad or the Law of Moses because their beliefs were 'more in conformity with natural reason'. This witness described Lope as a rationalist and sceptic who was analysing the comparative merits of Catholicism, Islam and Judaism. Lope himself testified before the Tribunal that he simply had a strong desire to talk with Jews and Moors and people of other 'naciones' and wanted to read the Qur'an. He said that all he had said and done was in a spirit of intellectual experimentation and that he liked to propose arguments by way of disputation. The *calificador* remarked that Lope de Vera: 'is an infidel and heretic and a confused Babel ('confusa babilonia'). He is wicked and an apostate from our holy Catholic faith and inclines to various other sects [...] He is a Jewish apostate, a Moor and a heretic and he is trying to avoid punishment by making frivolous excuses'. I cannot but wonder what this *calificador* would have said if he had read the letter that Cardinal Diego Hurtado de Mendoza, of the Mendoza family from Granada, ambassador in Trent and Venice, wrote to Cardinal Granvelle in May 1548 speaking of the struggle between the Church and the Empire, which stated, 'I speak as a philosopher or as a Moor from Granada or as a *marrano* [when I say] that the Inquisition has more to do today in Spain than it did on its first day'.[70]

In conclusion, the cases mentioned here could be divided into those individuals belonging to the popular classes and individuals who had access to education, knowledge of languages and books. But the perplexity, vacillation and doubt experienced by the two groups are the same and spring from the same religious context: the multiplicity of religious options that arose as a result of forced conversion. I have said before that the new religious situation in Iberia demanded of each person a knowledge of religious dogma in order to be considered a good Catholic. The Inquisition considered it imperative for the faithful to have undergone a sincere inner conversion and to adhere wholeheartedly to the whole corpus of Catholic belief. Doubt, inquiry, the search for certainty, were suspicious and dangerous because they called into question authority and also loyalty, adhesion, obedience. As Cavaillé, Wirth and Mothu have shown,[71] Catholicism gives value to the 'foi du charbonnier', the faith of the ignorant and the simple, but at the same time requires this *charbonnier*, when he is suspected of heresy or of irreligion, to demonstrate perfect theological orthodoxy and a complete absence of doubt, as in the cases of Lope de Vera, Francisco Marcilla and others that we have seen here.

Returning to Gracián, the starting point of this chapter, I have tried to show that his argument about conversion as engendering unbelief or irreligion was pertinent in Iberia at the end of the fifteenth century and throughout the sixteenth. The documents that have been examined here show how the contemporary concept of atheism as used by Gracián, which deals with people who are doubtful, perplexed or detached from religion and follow their own opinion (who verge, in fact, on 'libertinism' or pure scepticism), also included a more modern understanding of atheism, the absence of faith in any religion. But perhaps atheism was not the only hydra head the inquisitors had to deal with; lying beneath the statements and 'proposiciones' of many of the accused examined here is also the yearning for freedom of conscience.

Notes to Chapter 3

1. The research leading to these results has received funding from the European Research Council under the European Union's Seventh Framework Programme (FP7/2007–2013) / ERC grant agreement no. 323316, project CORPI, 'Conversion, Overlapping Religiosities, Polemics and Interaction. Early Modern Iberia and Beyond'.

2. About the experience of captivity, he wrote the *Tratado de la redención de cautivos*, ed. by Miguel Ángel de Bunes and Beatriz Alonso (Seville: Espuela de Plata, 2006).

3. 'llamo Atheismo a la profundidad de malicia a que llegan los hereges destos tiempos, que habiéndose apartado de la Iglesia romana, ya no siguen, ni paran en la seta de Luthero, Calvino ni Mennon, *sino que de todas las leyes, fees y religiones hacen burla*, siguiendo su particular opinión y apetito que solamente tienen por fee y por ley'. Jerónimo Gracián de la Madre de Dios, *Diez lamentaciones del miserable estado de los ateístas de nuestro tiempo*, ed. by Emilia Navarro de Kelley (Madrid: Editora Nacional, 1977), p. 319.

4. The historiographical debate on whether it was possible to be an atheist in the sixteenth and early seventeenth century (see Luca Addante's chapter in this volume) has relegated to the margins broader questions about popular expressions of scepticism and idiosyncrasy. See Nicholas Griffiths, 'Popular Religious Scepticism and Idiosyncrasy in Post-Tridentine Cuenca', in *Faith and Fanaticism: Religious Fervour in Early Modern Spain*, ed. by Lesley Twomey (Aldershot: Ashgate, 1997), pp. 95–128. Among the growing bibliography on this topic, see also: Thomas Lienhard, 'Athéisme, scepticisme et doute religieux au Moyen Âge. Notes de lecture à propos de trois publications récentes', *Revue de l'IFHA*, 3 (2012), 188–205.

5. 'El segundo daño del Atheísmo es en los mismos hereges, Moros y judíos, así en muchos que caen en estas heregías de nuestros tiempos (y todas ellas van mezcladas de Atheísmo) como en los que siendo ya hereges y cayendo en la cuenta que la secta que seguían de Luthero o Calvino etc. no es la verdadera, en lugar de volverse a la fee Cathólica, caen en el Atheísmo, como le ven seguido de tantos, así hereges como Cathólicos, y con esto se endurecen de tal suerte que se buelven inconvertibiles a la verdadera fee, si no díganlo los Judíos que moran en Amsterdam, donde les han hecho Synagoga, que los más dellos son Atheístas, aunque en lo exterior sigan el rito Judaico'. Gracián, *Diez lamentaciones*, p. 355.

6. David M. Gitlitz, 'Hybrid Conversos in the *Libro llamado el Alboraique*', *Hispanic Review*, 60 (1992), 1–17.

7. Valério de São Raimundo, *Sermão em o Auto da fee que se celebrou na Cidade de Evora em 12 de Novembro de 1662* (Lisbon: Domingo Carneiro, 1663); Estêvão Santana, *Sermão do Acto da fee que se celebrou na Cidade de Coimbra, na segunda Dominga de Quaresma, anno de 1612* (Lisbon: António Alvarez, 1618). Both quoted by Bruno Feitler, *The Imaginary Synagogue: Anti-Jewish Literature in the Portuguese Early Modern World (16th–18th Centuries)* (Leiden: Brill, 2015), pp. 90–91. On sermons delivered at *autos-da-fé*, see Edward Glaser, 'Invitation to Intolerance: A Study of Portuguese Sermons Preached at Autos-da-Fé', *Hebrew Union College Annual*, 27 (1956), 327–85.

8. There is an extensive bibliography (though not a specific monograph) on atheism in sixteenth- and seventeenth-century Spain starting with Marcelino Menéndez Pelayo, *Historia de los Heterodoxos españoles*, 3 vols (Madrid: Librería Católica de San José, 1880), and Julio Caro Baroja, *De la superstición al ateísmo. Meditaciones antropológicas* (Madrid: Taurus, 1974); also Caro Baroja, *Las formas complejas de la vida religiosa (religión, sociedad y carácter en la España de los siglos XVI y XVII)* (Madrid: Akal, 1978). A good synthesis is to be found in Natalia Muchnik, *Une vie marrane. Les Pérégrinations de Juan de Prado dans l'Europe du XVIIe siècle* (Paris: Honoré Champion, 2005), pp. 364 ff.

9. Jean-Pierre Cavaillé, 'La Question de l'irréligion populaire, à la rencontré de l'histoire et de l'anthropologie', *Institut d'histoire de la Réformation. Bulletin Annuel*, 36 (2014–15), 55–69. 'Irréligion comme doute, mécréance [...] mettant en évidence qu'il n'y a pas d' irréligion en soi

mais toujours relativement à une autorité religieuse donnée' (pp. 55–56), 'Ce que nous nommons irréligion est ce moment du négative, du détachement, du doute et de la critique interne (ou d'ailleurs externe) à une culture religieuse donnée, quelle que soit la finalité de la démarche, l'éloignement ou le refus des pratiques ou/et des croyances' (p. 57).

10. 'Este artificio de mudarse como Camaleones en diversas colores de leyes, o como la Xibia, que para pescar peces se muda de la color de la piedra, a que se apega, usan muchos de nuestros tiempos. Los quales (propiamente hablando) ni son Católicos, ni Luteranos, ni Calvinistas sino Atheístas Hypócritas: pues ninguna fee ni ley tienen aunque fingen guardar la que les está bien, y aunque los otros hereges son malos, y persiguen a los Cathólicos [...] estos hereges sin comparación son peores, porque no solo persiguen al particular Cathólico ni van contra un particular libro y opinión y fee, sino contra Dios y contra Christo y contra todos los autores y todas las leyes y fees y contra toda la sagrada escritura [...] Esta malicia, lo peor que tiene es paliarse con hipocresía. Porque así, ni se puede conocer, descubrir, castigar ni desarraigar'. Gracián, *Diez lamentaciones*, pp. 324 and 325. '

11. 'La quinta rayz de los Atheistas es ver las dissensiones y controversias que en lo essencial de la fee se hallan entre los mismos hereges de nuestros tiempos'. Gracián, *Diez lamentaciones*, p. 353.

12. Francisco Márquez Villanueva, *Moros, moriscos y turcos en Cervantes. Ensayos críticos* (Barcelona: Bellaterra, 2010), p. 157.

13. Jean-Claude Schmitt, 'Du bon usage du "Credo"', in *Faire croire. Modalités de la diffusion et de la réception des messages religieux du XIIe au XVe siècle* (Rome: École française de Rome, 1981), pp. 337–61.

14. *Belief in History: Approaches to European and American Religion*, ed. by Thomas Kselman (Notre Dame, IN: University of Notre Dame Press, 1991), especially John van Engen, 'Faith as a Concept in Medieval Christendom', pp. 19–67. See also Felipe Pereda's chapter in this volume.

15. Biblioteca Nacional de España [BNE], R/ 15114 ('[O] si sabeis o habeis oído decir otras algunas herejías, especialmente que no hay paraíso o gloria para los buenos ni infierno para los malos y que no hay más de nacer y morir. O algunas blasfemias hereticales como son: no creo, descreo reniego contra Dios Nuestro Señor y contra la virginidad y limpieza de Nuestra Señora la Virgen María o contra los santos y santas del cielo'. Archivo Histórico Nacional [AHN], Inquisición, Libro 1325, fol. 242 (Edict of Faith, 1607).

16. David M. Gitlitz, *Secrecy and Deceit: The Religion of the Crypto-Jews* (Albuquerque: University of New Mexico Press, 1996), p. 573.

17. 'El Reo había respondido con enojo que no creya en Dios ni en Santa María [...] ni creya en los artículos de la fee ni en nada, nada, nada'. AHN, Inq., leg. 2022, caja 1, exp. 20.

18. Miriam Bodian, *Dying in the Law of Moses: Crypto-Jewish Martyrdom in the Iberian World* (Bloomington: Indiana University Press, 2007), pp. 42–45.

19. Encarnación Marín Padilla, *Relación judeoconversa durante la segunda mitad del siglo XV en Aragón. La ley* (Zaragoza: E. Marín, 1986), p. 83.

20. — 'No sabemos qual dellas es la mejor; fagamos bien que quien bien fará bien habrá'. Marín Padilla, *Relación judeoconversa*, p. 84.

21. '[...] era lutherano, judío y moro'.

22. '[...] dijo que él tenía y creía en tres leyes, la de Nuestro Señor Jesuchristo, y la de Mahoma y la del señor Moyssen, porque si una le faltase, no le faltase la otra'. AHN, leg. 2022, caja 1, exp. 20.

23. '[...] que se hacía de judío, y de moro, y de herege'.

24. '[...] lo hacía por burla'. Julio Sierra, *Procesos en la Inquisición de Toledo (1575–1610). Manuscrito de Halle* (Madrid: Trotta, 2005), p. 162.

25. '¿Qué pensays, Mosse Alpastan? Ni de la ley de los christianos, ni de la de los judíos, ni de la de los moros, no se puede saber la verdat'. Marín Padilla, *Relación judeoconversa*, p. 86.

26. 'Yo, al Dio en un tallador lo tengo; yo he tenido la ley sancta de Moysen, yo he tenido la ley de Ihesu Christo y aun si agora salliese o viniesse un sant Mahoma, ¡Por el Dio! De tres la faría y si esto acabase no avría miedo al Dio, pues todas las leyes avía andado'. Marín Padilla, *Relación judeoconversa*, p. 87.

27. E. Marín Padilla, 'Relación judeoconversa durante la segunda mitad del siglo XV en Aragón. Enfermedades y muertes', *Sefarad*, 43.2 (1983), 251–344 (p. 306).

28. See, as an example among innumerable similar cases, Juan Rodríguez Melero who in 1524 said 'no creía aver buenaventura ni gloria en el otro mundo, y que mejor mundo era este que no el otro, y que ninguna ánima deste mundo salía no bolvía a dezir lo que avía en el otro'. AHN, Inq., leg. 101, 1. Cavaillé, 'La Question de l'irréligion populaire', p. 59, quotes similar cases all over Europe; see for example: 'Hell is nothing other than poverty and penury in this world and Heaven is nothing other than to be rich and enjoy pleasures; and [...] we die like beasts and when we are gone, there is no more remembrance of us'. Menochio also maintained the soul's mortality: Carlo Ginzburg, *The Cheese and the Worms: The Cosmos of a Sixteenth-Century Miller* (Baltimore: Johns Hopkins University Press, 1980).

29. In particular, Francisco Márquez Villanueva, '"*Nasçer e morir como bestias*" (criptoaverroísmo y cripto judaísmo)', included in his book *De la España judeoconversa. Doce estudios* (Barcelona: Bellaterra, 2006), pp. 203–28. Márquez follows Baer in linking the statement with Averroist tendencies in fifteenth-century Iberian Judaism. Yitzhak-Fritz Baer, *A History of the Jews in Christian Spain*, 2 vols (New York: Jewish Publication Society of America, 1961–66), II, 235–39, 270–77. See also John Edwards, 'Religious Faith and Doubt in Late Medieval Spain: Soria circa 1450–1500', *Past and Present*, 120 (1988), 3–25; and more recently, Stefania Pastore, 'Doubt in Fifteenth-Century Iberia', in *After Conversion: Iberia and the Emergence of Modernity*, ed. by Mercedes García-Arenal (Leiden: Brill, 2016), pp. 283–303 (pp. 290–95).

30. '[...] cómo desýa el judío que tenía mejor ley que nosotros, e el moro desía otro tanto; e desýan este testigo e el otro: "Pues sy mejor ley tyenen que nosotros, ¿cómo les echan del reyno?" E que este testigo dixo: "¿Eso cómo lo sabré yo?" o "¿Por dónde lo sabré yo quál es mejor ley?", "¡Qué sé yo sy querrá Dios al moro o al judío!" E que esto no lo dixo porque tenía dubda en la fee, saluo por synpleza e ynorançia, e que sienpre ha estado firme en la fee; e que no viene de linaje de judíos ni de moros'. Carlos Carrete Parrondo, *Fontes iudaeorum regni Castellae. II: (1486–1502). El Tribunal de la Inquisición en el Obispado de Soria* (Salamanca: Universidad Pontificia, 1985), p. 304.

31. '[...] dixo que el martes próximo pasado, que se contaron çinco días del dicho mes, vynieron a [...] Fuentealuilla dos frayles de la horden de Señor Sant Françisco e vn pendón a predicar çiertas yndulgençias que traýan; e que estando el dicho martes predicando vno de los dichos frayres, vyno a la yglesia donde el [...] frayre predicaua Pedro Texero, vezino del dicho logar, e començó a fablar çiertas cosas de manera que estorbaua al frayre que predicaua; e en después de dicho el sermón que sallaren de la [...] yglesia con el dicho pendón, el [...] frayre preguntara a [...] Pedro Texero sy creýa en Dios, e [...] Pedro Texero respondió e dixo que no creýa en Dios; e que entonçes el [...] frayre le respondió: "Pues guardaos del fuego, que çerca están los padres". E que a esto estauan presentes los más del pueblo. Preguntó qué fama tiene e dixo que de mal christiano e que nunca entre semana va a misa e quel día del domingo e las pascuas primero va a caçar que a misa'. Carrete Parrondo, *Fontes iudaeorum*, p. 105.

32. '[...] que tres leyes avía hecho Dios, e que non sabía quál era la mejor'; e que entonce que le dixo este testigo: 'Pues compadre, ¿quál ha de ser la mejor sino la nuestra?'. Carrete Parrondo, *Fontes iudaeorum*, p. 236.

33. '[...] puede aver tres años [...], que avýa tres leyes de moros, e de judíos e de christianos, e que cada vno se podía saluar en su ley, que non sabemos quál es la mejor'. Carrete Parrondo, *Fontes iudaeorum*, p. 101. See also the contribution of Eleazar Gutwirth to this volume.

34. Stuart B. Schwartz, *All Can Be Saved: Religious Tolerance and Salvation in the Iberian Atlantic World* (New Haven, CT: Yale University Press, 2008).

35. Jaime Bleda, *Coronica de los moros de España diuidida en ocho libros*, 2 vols (A Coruña: Órbigo, 2015) II, 924–25: '[...] el desseo que siempre tuvieron de que se les concediera libertad de conciencia, cosa tan prohibida por ley Diuina, aunque aprobada por la secta pestilencial de los Políticos'.

36. 'Deseaban y procurauan grandemente libertad de conciencia, y que los dexassen vivir a su modo de la suerte que el Turco permite en sus estados que los Christianos viuan en su Religión y algunos otros Príncipes que en sus tierras consiente que cada uno siga la profesión que quisiere'. Damián Fonseca, *Ivsta expvlsión de los moriscos de España* (Rome: Iacomo Mascardo, 1612), pp. 126–27.

37. M. García-Arenal, '"Mi padre moro, yo moro": The Inheritance of Belief in Early Modern

Iberia', in *After Conversion: Iberia and the Emergence of Modernity*, ed. by M. García-Arenal (Leiden: Brill, 2016), pp. 304–35, (pp. 312 ff).

38. António Baiao, *A Inquisição em Portugal e no Brasil. Subsídios para a sua história*, 10 vols (Lisbon: Archivo Histórico Português, 1910–16), VIII (1910), 426.

39. AHN, leg. 2022, caja 1, 'avía dubdado de la fee y la había perdido y había creído que los cristianos van errados y que no había Dios' during three years he 'había andado con muchas imaginaciones, casi fuera de juicio'.

40. AHN, leg. 2022, caja 1 (1567), 'que Dios pecó y que Dios no había hecho bien su oficio en hazer que unos fuesen christianos y otros moros y otros judíos'.

41. Marín Padilla, *Relación judeoconversa*, pp. 90–91.

42. Archivo Diocesano Conquese, leg. 380, exp. 5393, years 1609–12. See also Griffiths, 'Popular Religious Scepticism', pp. 95–128.

43. 'Dixo que la religión de los calvinistas, de los romanos, de los luteranos, toda es buena, es excelentísima cosa [...] y que cada uno se podía salvar en su ley, como el moro, el turco en la suya, el hebreo según su ley, el inglés en la suya, el español en la suya y todos los demás del mundo en su ley; y la libertad de conciencia es lo bueno, como lo tiene dicho'; 'los pontífices y sacerdotes no son necesarios porque hacen cosas inhumanas y se quieren levantar con todo y avasallar a todos los hombres y quitarles su libertad y libre albedrío y con buena capa engañan y se quedan con todo haciendo muchas tiranías y que en cuanto a la libertad de conciencia, es lo que vale, que lo demás es falso porque no hay más que comer y fornicar y beber y la libertad, y esta es la gloria de este mundo'. Adelina Carrión Mora, *Médicos e Inquisición en el siglo XVII* (Cuenca: Universidad de Castilla-La Mancha, 2006), p. 130.

44. Carsten L. Wilke "That Devilish Invention Called Faith': Seventeenth-Century Free-Thought and its Use in Sephardic Apologetics', in *Conversos, marrani e nuove comunità ebraiche in età moderna*, ed. by Myriam Silvera (Florence: Casa Editrice Giuntina, 2015), pp. 131–44.

45. Miriam Bodian, *Dying in the Law of Moses*, p. 182.

46. M. García-Arenal, *Inquisición y moriscos, los procesos del Tribunal de Cuenca* (Madrid: Siglo XXI, 1978); J. Caro Baroja, *Vidas mágicas e Inquisición*, 2 vols (Madrid: Taurus, 1967), I, 345.

47. Gitlitz, *Secrecy and Deceit*, p. 573.

48. *Auto de la fe, que se celebró, en la villa de Madrid corte de el católico Rey don Phelipe quarto, de este nombre en quarto de Julio de el año de mill seis cientos treinta y dos*, BNE, MS 2364, fols 35^r–45^r, on fol. 42^{r-v}.

49. Israël S. Révah, 'Aux origines de la rupture spinozienne. Nouvel examen des origines, du déroulement et des conséquences de l'affaire Spinoza-Prado-Ribera', *Annuaire du Collège de France*, 70 (1970), 562–68 (p. 563). Natalia Muchnik, *Une vie marrane*, p. 420.

50. François Soyer, ' "It is not possible to be both a Jew and a Christian": *Converso* Religious Identity and the Inquisitorial Trial of Custódio Nunes (1604–05)', *Mediterranean Historical Review*, 26.1 (2011), 81–97.

51. M. García-Arenal, 'A Catholic Muslim Prophet: Agustín de Ribera, "The Boy Who Saw Angels" ', *Common Knowledge*, 18.2 (2012), 267–91.

52. García-Arenal, *Inquisición y moriscos*, p. 113.

53. Fonseca, *Ivsta expvlsión*, p. 266.

54. Marín Padilla, 'Relación judeo-conversa durante la segunda mitad del siglo XV en Aragón. Enfermedades y muertes'. Marín Padilla, *Relación judeoconversa durante la segunda mitad del siglo XV en Aragón. Matrimonio* (Madrid: CSIC, 1983), pp. 305–06.

55. 'que era de los más sabidos honbres del mundo en todas las cosas, e que nunca vio este testigo ni conosçió en él que touiese cosa ni parte alguna de christiano, ni que touiese conosçimiento alguno de nuestra fee, de manera que no sabía cosa ninguna de christiano, ni lo tenía, e que no sabía Pater Noster, ni el Ave María, ni el Credo, ni se sabía santiguar, nin nunca yva a misa, ni entraua en yglesia, ni tenía cosa ninguna de nuestra santa fee católyca, de manera que no tenía fee ninguna. E que al tienpo que vinieron los ynquisidores deste obispado, a Aranda, que luego se paró como sentido, muerto, amarillo, e así se fue decayendo hasta que luego dende a poco tienpo morió. E que (mientras estaba enfermo) todo lo que le decían que hiziese de nuestra fee [...] agora, todo lo creýa[...]'. Carrete Parrondo, *Fontes iudaeorum*, p. 72.

56. Caro Baroja, *Vidas mágicas*, I, 248 ff, See also Fernando Bouza and José Luis Betrán, *Olvidados de la Historia. Enanos, bufones, monstruos, brujos y hechiceros: marginales* (Barcelona: Debolsillo, 2005), p. 141 ff.

57. 'Que un maestro Alfonso que estava en Roma, que antes fue judío y después moro y después christiano, hablando a este confesante le dixo que todas las cosas del testamento biejo y nuevo eran burlería y que Christo no murió y assí negava que no huvo apóstoles y todos los sacramentos de la Iglesia y que creya en la ley de Mahoma y que tantas vezes le persuadió aquesto en sus tiernos años [...] que con esto este confesante pasó escrúpulo en el ánimo y le hizo apartar y desbiar del camino de la berdad'; 'como en la leche mamó ser christiano'; 'aunque estuvo dudoso, confuso y perplexo [...] nunca enteramente se animó ni tuvo intención de dexar a su verdadero Redentor'. Caro Baroja, *Vidas mágicas*, I, 249.

58. Carsten L. Wilke, *The Marrakesh Dialogues: A Gospel Critique and Jewish Apology from the Spanish Renaissance* (Leiden: Brill, 2014).

59. Wilke, *The Marrakesh Dialogues*, p. 256.

60. Wilke, *The Marrakesh Dialogues*, and 'That Devilish Invention Called Faith', p. 138.

61. Wilke, *The Marrakesh Dialogues*, p. 134.

62. Wilke, *The Marrakesh Dialogues*, p. 235.

63. Miriam Bodian, *Dying in the Law of Moses*, chapter 6, 'A Hebrew Scholar at the University of Salamanca', pp. 153–77.

64. Kenneth Brown, *De la cárcel Inquisitorial a la sinagoga de Amsterdam (Edición y estudio del 'Romance a Lope de Vera' de Antonio Enríquez Gómez)* (Toledo: Consejería de Cultura de Castilla-La Mancha, 2007), Inquisitorial trial, pp. 370 ff.

65. AHN, Inq., leg. 2135, nos. 17–19.

66. AHN, Inq., leg. 2135, no. 17, fols 24–25. Brown. *De la cárcel inquisitorial*, p. 376.

67. AHN, Inq., leg. 2135, no. 17, fols 24–25. Brown. *De la cárcel inquisitorial*, p. 375.

68. AHN, Inq., leg. 2135, no. 17, fol. 25v. Bodian, *Dying in the Law of Moses*, p. 161.

69. 'que no se puede negar la duda y confusión en la que se hallaba'.

70. 'hablo como philósopho o como moro de Granada o como marrano, que aun tiene la Ynquisición que hazer en España más que el primer día'. Stefania Pastore, 'Una Spagna antipapale. Gli anni italiani di Diego Hurtado de Mendoza', *Roma Moderna e Contemporanea*, 15 (2007), 63–94 (p. 79).

71. Cavaillé, 'La Question de l' irréligion populaire', p. 68; Jean Wirth, 'La Naissance du concept de croyance (XII–XVII siècles)', *Bibliothèque d'Humanisme et Renaissance*, 45.1 (1983), 7–58; Alain Mothu, 'De la foi du charbonnier à celle du héros (et retour)', *Les Dossiers du Grihl* (2007) <https://dossiersgrihl.revues.org/3393 > [accessed 18 April 2017].

PART II

❖

Europe and the Iberian Connection

CHAPTER 4

❖

Dubius in fide, infidelis est:
Between Faith and Heresy,
Is There a Place for Doubt?

Isabelle Poutrin

The Gospels record few situations where one of Jesus's followers is struck by doubt. There is the episode of the storm on the Sea of Galilee, where Jesus takes hold of Peter and says to him 'O you of little faith, why do you doubt?' (Matthew 14. 31);[1] and another, where Thomas, seeing Jesus after his resurrection, makes sure of his identity by putting his finger into his side, an act which elicits these words from Jesus: 'Because you have seen me, you have believed; blessed are those who have not seen and yet have believed' (John 20. 29).[2] These situations are resolved by an affirmation of faith. In the sixteenth and seventeenth centuries, brief doubts like those of Peter and Thomas were not the concern of theologians, who were confronted by radical objections to Catholic doctrine. For those Christians who distanced themselves from the Church and wanted to escape the extreme punishment reserved for heretics, the doubtful stance (remaining silent on a doctrine, being neither for nor against) could appear a prudent and wise solution. But was being in two minds acceptable to confessors, theologians and Inquisitors?

Doubt (in Latin *dubitatio*) is a hesitation, an uncertainty. This attitude differs from *dubium* which meant a question to be examined by experts.[3] Here we propose considering this concept from the perspective of Catholic doctrine; our main guide will be the Jesuit Juan Azor (1536–1603), who addresses this issue in his *Moral Institutions* published in Rome in 1600.[4] With the development of spiritual direction, Catholic doctors aspired to a systematic approach to theology and canon law, which would provide confessors with useful instruments.[5] Azor's *Moral Institutions* are a major step in this evolution.[6] Azor deals with doubt in Book VIII which is dedicated to the first commandment of the Decalogue, faith in God. He first establishes that faith is outside the order of nature, the experience and the senses, but rather concerns the testimony and authority of God. He goes on to ask what the individual must believe in order to achieve salvation: is it enough to believe in what the Church believes in a general and implicit way? Azor gives a negative answer: the individual, even the 'common and coarse', must explicitly believe all the articles of faith that the Church teaches. To ignore the articles of faith is a sin. Other doctrinal elements which are not in the articles of faith (such as original sin, or the real presence in the Eucharist) may be believed only implicitly. The uneducated man may have a reduced knowledge of the Catholic profession of faith, but this profession must be known and affirmed explicitly. On this basis, Azor gives his own definition of the crime of heresy and asks the question: 'Is he who hesitates in the faith a heretic?' (*An dubius in fide sit hereticus*). Before giving his opinion, he refers to six writers who have dealt with the subject before him. These texts, which will form the body of this study, trace a collective route under the terms of which the Jesuit states his own view, following the scholastic method that remained dominant at this time among Catholic theologians and canonists.

The Church, Guardian of the Faith

Before undertaking this journey, the background should be laid forth. In the early seventeenth century, the separation between theology and canon law was not yet complete. Reflection on faith, doubt and heresy was not purely speculative but aimed to determine whether the doubter was guilty, not only before God but also in the eyes of the Church. The reference text on doubt was the canon *Dubius in fide* which opens title 7 (dedicated to heretics) of book 5 (dedicated to crimes and offenses) of the *Liber Extra* or *Decretals*, the great collection of canon law by the Dominican Raymond Peñafort, promulgated by Pope Gregory IX in 1234. This canon is a text attributed to Pope Étienne: 'He who hesitates/doubts in the faith is an infidel, and one absolutely cannot believe those who ignore the truth of the faith'.[7] The canon is introduced by the following summary: 'one who does not have the certainty of faith is an infidel and one must not believe the infidel to the detriment of another person'. At the time of the Council of Trent and subsequently, the *Decretals* remained a major resource for canonists and theologians.[8] The canon *Dubius in fide* set the framework of any reflexion about doubt by closely linking it with religious infidelity. The insertion of this canon in title 7 of Book 5 placed doubt within the scope of heresy and, more broadly, of crimes and offences, which gave it a negative connotation.

Struggling against the Protestants, theologians emphasized the link between faith and the authority of the Church, on the basis of the Pauline definition of faith: 'the confidence of what we hope for and assurance of what we do not see' (Hebrews 11. 1).[9] The theologians of the School of Salamanca, in particular, led extensive work to classify the content of the faith. They turned the spotlight on the articles of faith, that is, the truths revealed directly by God which cannot be demonstrated but which must be held to be true under the authority of the Church. 'In the sixteenth century, the Catholic faith is this set of truths which the Church laid forth to all as infallible, and which all are bound to believe explicitly'.[10] The material object of faith (its content, what one believes) is the truth; the formal object of faith (what inspires faith) is God: 'When a person believes, it is because God has presented the revelation to him immediately and is driven by [...] a spiritual consent'.[11] In other words, assenting to a truth of faith requires divine force (the action of the Holy Spirit) which leads the individual to inwardly believe. Faith is a supernatural gift without which the individual cannot find favour with God or be saved. The 'truth of faith' is not set out clearly and is very often obscure, unlike scientific statements which are imposed on reason through demonstration; these characteristics of faith are the very condition of human freedom. Faith also requires a specific mode of adhesion which concerns not only the reason but also the will of the individual who accepts the truth as the Church offers it to him.

However, the adjective 'Catholic' gained new importance in the sixteenth century because theologians insisted on the universality of the faith set forth by the Church. As the articles of faith come from God (through Holy Scripture), they are valid for all men, regardless of place and time. Since divine revelation is offered and guaranteed by the Church, it can and must be recognized as a truth of faith. The test of faith is not within the Christian (here, Catholic theologians differed from Lutherans), but in the Church which is the only rule of the faith, a safe rule because the Church, instituted by Jesus Christ, is infallible with the assistance of the Holy Spirit. If the Church is not the *efficient* cause of faith, it is she who, through preaching and teaching, promotes the faith.

The Church being the guardian of the faith, Catholic doctors engaged in a critical reflection on heresy; the practical viewpoint prevailed here, in conjunction with the development of inquisitorial criminal law.[12] In this respect, doctors followed the path made at the end of the twelfth century, towards the extension of the definition of heresy; for example, Huguccio of Pisa, in his *Summa* (1188) on Gratian's *Decretum*, included in the field of heresy disobedience to the Pope.[13] In the sixteenth century, the distinction was clearly established between formal heresy, which consisted in professing, knowingly and obstinately, an opinion different from the doctrine of the Church, and inquisitorial heresy, which covered all the opinions or behaviours that the institution qualified as an expression of the crime of heresy. Thus, the distinction was made between the work of theologians on faith and errors in faith, and the repression of doctrinal deviancies conducted by lawyers, judges and Inquisitors.

Among the increasing number of works dealing with the crime of heresy, the reference books were *On the just punishment of heretics* by Alonso de Castro (1495–1558), the *Catholic Institutions* by the Bishop of Zamora Diego de Simancas (1525–1583), and the *Treaty of heresy* by Prospero Farinacci (1554–1618).[14] These authors did not seek to refute theological errors, but rather to help ecclesiastical judges in detecting heretics and proving the crime of heresy through the external manifestations of inner convictions. Thus, determining whether he who doubts in the faith is guilty of heresy was an issue whose outcome entailed practical and dramatic applications. Between faith and heresy, was there a place for doubt?

Azor and his Authorities

Azor gives the following definition of heresy: it is an error of intellect, involving the deliberate and obstinate denial of an element of the faith.[15] Is he who hesitates in the faith a heretic? The question may be asked because, says Azor, whoever doubts does not make a mistake of the intellect since he neither agrees nor disagrees with the statement in question; therefore, he does not meet the definition of heresy. After quoting the canon *Dubius in fide*, the Jesuit states the scope of the question. The matter is to know if the doubter is really a heretic (guilty of the crime of heresy, according to legal definitions), and if he is subject to penalties prescribed for heretics.

The six authors mentioned by Azor are Augustine of Ancona (1243–1328), theologian of the Order of Augustinians and author of a *Summa of Ecclesiastical Power* published in Augsburg in 1479;[16] the Dominican cardinal Juan de Torquemada (1388–1468), author of a *Summa of the Church* (1433) published in Cologne in 1480;[17] the Dominican and Archbishop of Florence Antoninus (1389–1459), canonized in 1523, author of a *Summa of Moral Theology* published in 1477;[18] Arnau Alberti (1504–1544), a Majorcan who was Bishop of Patti in Sicily at the end of his career, and author of a treatise *On the distinction between Catholic and heretical statements* published in Palermo in 1544;[19] Alonso de Castro (1495–1558), a Franciscan theologian, jurist and professor at the University of Salamanca whose treatise *On the just punishment of heretics*, published in 1547 in Salamanca, quickly became a classic of inquisitorial law;[20] and the Dominican Melchor Cano (1509–1560), professor of theology at Salamanca and author of the treatise *Theological Method* published in this city in 1563.[21]

This is not an exhaustive list of the authors who have dealt with doubt. The reflections of Augustine of Ancona, Torquemada, and Antoninus of Florence were also cited in the margin of Cano's text in the 1593 edition, alongside other authors whom Azor, writing forty years later, did not mention, such as the Benedictine monk Nicolò de Tudeschi (1386–1445), a famous canonist of the same generation as Torquemada, and Gabriel Biel (*c.* 1420–95), a nominalist theologian from the University of Tübingen. The 1584 edition of Augustine of Ancona includes a reference to Juan López de Palacios Rubios (1450–1524), a canonist close to the Catholic Kings, and to Melchor Cano. As our goal is not to present an exhaustive study of texts on doubt, but to see how this issue was resolved in the early seventeenth century, we will follow the list given by Azor.

The Jesuit merely presents his list of authors without summarizing their explanations and opinions, and without detailing any disagreements between them. Apparently, the subject was not controversial. However, as we shall see at the end of this journey, the wording of Azor's own opinion is particularly concise and sharp. Each of these six authors sheds light on the various facets of doubt while leading to consistent or additional conclusions. How these texts are repeated or complement one another is a perfect illustration of how the consensus was established between doctors over successive generations.

The Five Modalities of Doubt

Augustine of Ancona opens his essay 28 entitled 'The resistance of the heretics' with the question: 'Are all those who doubt in the faith heretics?'.[22] True to the aim of his book, which was to present the powers of the Pope in accordance with his theocratic ideal,[23] he puts forth the statement 'All those who doubt in the faith should be considered by the pope as heretics' with reference to the canon *Dubius in fide*. Augustine of Ancona also quotes the apostle James, 'But the prayer must be made with faith, and with no trace of doubt, for he who doubts is like a wave of the sea driven and tossed by the wind' (James 1. 6),[24] which shows that he who doubts and hesitates in the faith is fickle, so 'such people are heretics because they do not believe consistently and firmly'. Moreover, says Augustine, 'one who believes all the articles of faith, and doubts one, becomes a heretic'.

The response, the second stage of reasoning, deepens the concept by distinguishing five modalities of doubt. The first, the 'surreptitious temptation', does not make the doubter a heretic. It is a fleeting thought which might be inspired by the devil. To escape from it, it is enough resolutely to turn one's thoughts to God and decide 'to believe what the Church believes'. The second modality, doubting in order to clarify the truth by reasoning through contradictory arguments as doctors do, is a way of perfecting one's faith and is, therefore, the opposite of a heretical approach. Neither does 'imperfect adherence', the third modality of doubt, make the individual a heretic, but rather a sinner and a bad Christian. With 'voluntary hesitation', the individual treads the path of error and infidelity, because he willingly chooses what to believe or not believe, ceasing to follow all the doctrine laid forth by the Church. Finally, 'the stubborn defence' makes the one who falls a heretic, since he stubbornly refuses to believe the articles of faith taught by the Church, which is a characteristic of heretics.

Thirdly, the theologian returns to the arguments presented at the beginning. He who doubts in the faith by willingly making choices between what he wants and does not want to believe is an infidel, and not a heretic, unless he stubbornly defends his opinion. He who hesitates, as mentioned by the apostle James, indulges in imperfect adherence and must be able to withstand the winds of temptation. He who doubts an article of faith is in error: he becomes heretical only if he begins to defend his error obstinately.

Faith Does Not Waver

A defender of the Pope's power against the Conciliarists during the reign of Eugene IV, Juan de Torquemada registered his treatise with a highly polemic perspective, which was not the case for Augustine of Ancona.[25] After dealing with the Church, papal primacy and councils, he dedicates book 4 of his *Summa of the Church* to schismatics and heretics. He firstly defines heresy as an opinion, false statement or false dogma contrary to Catholic truth in terms of what the Christian faith professes.[26] Catholic truth is universal, perpetual, infallible and necessary for all Christians to believe, explicitly or implicitly.[27] It comprises eight degrees, starting with what is contained in Scripture, which is the most important; the lowest degree includes truths that do not really belong to the faith but are added to it. Based on this scale, Torquemada defines types of heresy that deny the different degrees of Catholic truth, from the content of Scripture to the teaching derived from the Church Fathers' doctrine. This ranking allows him to list reprehensible statements, from heretical statements to what is merely reckless. Finally, Torquemada examines the various forms of heresy: simony, refusal of the general councils, opposition to the privileges of the Roman Church, etc. It is not until the end of this series of scales and lists that Torquemada sets his own definition, not of heresy, but of what is a heretic: 'A heretic is one who, having received the Christian religion in general and professing faith in Christ, supports and obstinately follows an opinion (or several) contrary to Catholic truth'.[28]

Doubt is one of the modalities of heretical behaviour: 'Anyone who hesitates in the faith may be said to be a heretic'.[29] Torquemada quotes the canon *Dubius in fide* but also the conclusion of Athanasius's 'rule of faith', 'This is the Catholic faith, without which no one can be saved without believing faithfully and firmly',[30] as well as Bernard of Clairvaux's saying: 'Faith does not waver, and if it does, it is a mistake which is repugnant to faith'.[31] These allegations are along the same lines, for the true faith must be firm, simple and unambiguous. However, Torquemada adds this detail: a heretic is one who doubts and continues to doubt voluntarily, remaining between both sides of the conflict. It is a different matter for the one who is tempted in his faith and feels pain and anguish in his heart. Thus, the Dominican takes into account the state of momentary weakness of the believer, who may waver in his faith by God's permission, but will overcome this temptation. Here we find the 'surreptitious temptation' as opposed to 'voluntary hesitation' and 'obstinate defence'. Torquemada then turns to the other modalities of heresy. Evidently, then, he did not attach great importance to the question of doubt which, he felt, did not require further attention.

Between Reflection and Adherence

Unlike other theologians, Antoninus of Florence placed doubt in the context of reflections on faith, not heresy. But like them, he inserted it into a typology, in this case a series of distinctions on the relationship between the act of thinking (*cogitare*) and of assenting (*assentire*). He who knows (*sciens*) reflects but does not adhere to anything; he reflects before agreeing. He who hesitates (*dubitans*) does not give his assent, he merely thinks. The suspicious (*suspicans*) think, but without making a firm commitment. The ignorant (*nesciens*) neither think nor adhere to anything. Those who speculate (*opinans*) think but their thoughts are not accompanied by perfect adherence. Finally, believers practise discursive thought while giving their firm approval. Therefore 'believing is halfway between knowing and speculating (*opinare*) and involves two steps'. Whoever hesitates is, strictly speaking, not 'faithful' (here Antoninus cites the canon *Dubius in fide*) but hesitation without willing stubbornness is not 'infidelity' (in the sense of withdrawal of faith).[32] Antoninus continues discoursing at length on the act of faith. He also distinguishes three kinds of hesitation or doubt (*dubitatio*):[33] that which identifies with infidelity and of which the Jews are examples; that which derives from sluggishness and lateness (thus the attitude of the Emmaus disciples hesitating to recognize Christ); and finally an attitude of piety or love, like that of John on learning that the Son of God descended into hell, and which is not really doubt. Here, Antoninus of Florence rather refers to amazement before something miraculous. In sum, the Dominican was less comprehensive than Augustine of Ancona in listing the modalities of doubt. However, he advanced the discussion by placing it at the crossroads of two activities, that of the understanding and that of the will, and by characterizing it as a non-committal thought process.

Limits of the Dispute

With Arnau Alberti, we come to so-called 'modern' authors, those whom the authors of the sixteenth and seventeenth centuries considered their contemporaries. The time of the great generalist *Summas* (like those of Torquemada and Antoninus of Florence) was coming to an end. Authors preferred to compose more specialized treaties. Arnau Alberti devoted his own to the distinction between Catholics and heretical statements, a subject which, in the 1540s, marked by the organization of Protestant churches and the convening of the Council of Trent, met a strong need for the Catholic Church. Of the book's thirty-six issues, doubt appears in three passages. In *quaestio* 3, devoted entirely to obstinacy in error or pertinacity (*pertinacia*), which is a component of heresy, Alberti briefly examines doubt.[34] He cites the canon *Dubius in fide*. He remarks that doubt also has a firmness of will and therefore a kind of obstinacy: he who perseveres in doubt (*dubitatio*), in questioning (*cogitatio*), is certainly a heretic. The case is different if this doubt is only fleeting, incidental and without perseverance, as noted by Augustine of Ancona.

Alberti returns to doubt when he asks in *quaestio* 13 if the faith can be disputed in public. From the beginning of the Protestant Reformation, disputes between theologians had been one of the major ways in which supporters of new ideas and the Catholic clergy had confronted one another.[35] The subject was therefore topical. Alberti states that it is not appropriate to dispute the faith by doubting it, for he who does so commits a sin — and here Alberti refers to the canon *Dubius in fide*. In his view the reason is obvious: since the Scripture and the Catholic faith are divine revelation and since by arguing in this way they are not assumed to be very clear, disputing matters of faith publicly is a grave offence against God, because it amounts to saying that Scripture might lie. However, one may contend for the faith against heretics, pagans, infidels and Jews to refute their errors, a work which is not only permissible but necessary. Questioning is only allowed in this context, to the extent that it helps to bring out the truth against heretics.[36] Through these reflections, Alberti warned clerics tempted to engage in disputes with the Protestants. They could do so if they were strong enough to attack them. In no event might the dispute be intended to cast serious doubt on Catholic dogma or to bring out a compromise position. On the other hand, disputing Scripture to explain it and bring out its truths is a meritorious work. 'The elucidation of truth' in an academic framework, as already reported by Augustine of Ancona, is very different from the deconstruction in which heretics indulged.

How is it possible to differentiate a preacher who attacks the faith with malice and obstinacy from a preacher who errs in ignorance — knowing that only the former is a heretic? The answer is given in *quaestio* 29 which deals with obstinacy as evidence of heresy.[37] The heretic is one who doubts the Catholic faith in a comprehensive way, raising doubts about what the Church believes and teaches. He shows his stubbornness because he refuses to be corrected. However, he who doubts an article taught by the Church which is not an article of faith, without knowing if this is addressed in Holy Scripture or in the general councils, should not be considered a heretic. He must still be carefully questioned to see if he is willing to be corrected on his mistake. Indeed, even he who doubts a point that is not an article of faith is suspicious, if he refuses to be corrected. Suspicious items are thus the subject of doubt (the questioning of faith as a whole, and not on points of detail) as is the will to remain in doubt and deny the Church's correction. Here, Alberti in turn cites St Bernard of Clairvaux: 'faith does not waver, and if it does, it is a mistake which is repugnant to faith'.

Nicodemus's Condemnation

Alonso de Castro dedicated his treatise to heresy, heretics and their punishment, as well as preventing heresies. Doubt is developed in chapter 7 of the first part entitled 'Who should be said to be a heretic?' The Franciscan extends his explanations over several chapters, insisting on the importance of the subject. The Inquisition should declare nobody a heretic without lengthy investigations.[38] The conditions of heresy are baptism made without true faith, error in the faith, and refusal of at least one part of the Catholic faith. It is in connection with error in the faith that Castro addresses the subject of doubt. As heresy is defined as error in the faith, 'he who doubts this very certain faith and this very firm truth' is mistaken, like he who says something contrary to the faith. Castro uses a quotation from St Augustine's *Enchiridion*: 'To err is nothing other than to think true what is false and to think false what is true, to think what is certain uncertain or what is uncertain certain, whether it is false or true'.[39] One who doubts the truth of the faith believes that Holy Scripture and the Church can be wrong, otherwise he would not be hesitating. Castro concludes that he who doubts abandons the faith through his lack of strength.[40] Among the array of authorities that follows, we find the canon *Dubius in fide*, but also St Athanasius's Rule of Faith and Bernard's 'unwavering faith'. One may certainly argue that he who doubts is not at odds with any article of faith, and therefore should not be considered a heretic. Castro takes the following example: in doubting the suggestion 'Christ is God', Peter remains indecisive, he does not dispute any article of faith, so he cannot be considered a heretic. To this argument, Castro replies that Peter was committing a grave sin against the tenet of the faith 'because, just as auricular confession is necessary for salvation, the credulity of the heart is necessary for justice'.[41] If the individual, knowing that the Church teaches that such an article of faith is necessary, questions this article, he commits a sin against the faith because he does not believe what he is obliged to believe; and he must, therefore, be considered a heretic. In other words, the sin lies not in the content of what is questioned, but in the very act of doubting when the Church requires the believer to be 'credulous', which is an act of faith.

At this point in the exposition, the Franciscan believes it necessary to warn the reader that he must not consider all forms of doubt sinful. Fleeting doubt caused by weakness does not make the doubter a heretic (we find here 'surreptitious temptation'). As for the intellectual approach to doubt, Castro contrasts two modalities. The act of doubting the words of Christ and Holy Scripture is prohibited, since it is contrary to the faith laid forth by the Church. Nicodemus, who questions the words of Christ about the resurrection (John 3), is an example, as are the Jewish disciples who question the words of Christ on the bread of life (John 6).[42] Here Castro attacks one of his contemporaries, the Franciscan François Titelmann (1502–1537) who, in his own commentary on the Gospel of John, interprets the questions of Nicodemus as evidence of an insatiable quest for truth. Titelmann considers that the disciple who never presents any objection to his master and accepts everything without understanding does not progress; he also digresses on the educational virtue of questioning.[43] Against this innovative and overly lenient reading, Castro prefers to stick to the traditional interpretation of Augustine, Cyril and John Chrysostom, who see Nicodemus as a disbeliever and an arrogant man. A second modality of intellectual doubt is to question the meaning of divine words without questioning their truthfulness in any way. Mary's question to the angel Gabriel (Luke 1) is one example, particularly given that the dialogue with the angel concludes with an act of obedience, '*Fiat voluntas eius*'. Castro draws an analogy between this question and the approach of scholastic theologians who propose questions for discussion in order to elucidate truth, and without doubting Scripture. In this case, methodical questioning is a meritorious act, especially since it is a good practice for refuting heretics.[44]

No Shades of Grey

The last stage of this journey, Melchor Cano's development on doubt, is by far the most successful.[45] His *Treatise on Theological Method (De locis theologicis)*, a monument of the Second Scholastic, establishes systematic foundations of theological arguments better to arm Catholic theologians in their struggle against the Protestants.[46] Book 12, the last one, occupies about a third of the whole treatise; it amply deals with theology, its purpose, its end, its principles and its conclusions. Cano then addresses extensively the definition of heresy, finally giving rules to judge the faith of an individual from the outside. A long piece of reasoning in two stages is devoted to heresy, which is defined initially as 'a stubborn error, by one who has professed faith, which manifestly contradicts a manifestly Catholic truth'. Against the various parts of this definition, the Dominican raises objections, the details of which we shall not enter into. At the heart of this demonstration lies the problem of hesitation in faith, to the point where it is a matter of knowing if heresy can be defined as an error. Cano cites the chapter *Dubius in fide*, 'He who hesitates in the faith is an infidel', with a syllogism: heresy is a type of 'infidelity' since the sceptic is an infidel and is also a heretic; but then, if hesitation in faith is heresy, then there can be heresy without error. Given that this hesitation is a suspension without assent, and that error is an assent that contradicts the truth, the sceptic commits no error, since he does not give his assent. This is the first part of the reasoning.

Nevertheless, taking up the issue of doubt in the second stage of his demonstration, Cano asks if it is heresy to doubt a Catholic truth. Again he proceeds in two parts, *pro* and *contra*. He argues firstly that doubt in faith is certainly heresy, an error incompatible with faith. The argument shows the equivalence between hesitation, infidelity and heresy, as well as authorities which are already well known such as the passage of St Augustine's *Enchiridion* and Bernard's 'faith is unwavering'. It also uses the criminal law of the Church, stressing that placing at the head of the title *On heretics* of the *Decretals* the canon '*Dubius in fide infidelis est*' clearly shows that he who wavers in the faith must be punished as a heretic. Continued strength is in the faith, while hesitation (*vacillatio*) and stubborn doubt (*dubitatio*) corrupt firmness of faith. Incidentally, Cano eliminates the transient modality of doubt as illustrated by Peter on the Sea of Galilee, for doubt does not totally eliminate faith in a weak man.

Secondly, Cano takes the opposite view: doubt in the faith is emphatically not heresy. This line of reasoning is surprising because scholastics usually place in second position any opinions consistent with their own. Now, given what we have read from Cano's predecessors, it is very unlikely that the rigorous Dominican did not consider doubt to be heresy. We must therefore consider this more closely. Other authors, says Cano, consider doubt to be lack of faith (the 'in' of 'infidelity' simply being a privative prefix) so that if heresy is contrary to faith, doubt cannot be considered a part of heresy. Indeed, heresy involves firm adherence to an opinion (false and contrary to the faith). Like faith or error, heresy is based on the consent of the individual, and the sceptic does not follow an opinion, he does not choose, and expresses neither agreement nor disagreement. Therefore, the sceptic is not a heretic and 'doubt is not a heresy'. Viewed in this way, doubt is midway between these two opposing extreme points, heresy and the Catholic faith.

At this point, Cano speaks again: for him, this way of posing the problem lies in how to define infidelity. As we have seen, infidelity can be defined in its relationship to faith either as a withdrawal or denial of faith or as the opposite of faith (refusal, opposition). In the first case, the infidel is simply one who has no faith, for example one who has never heard of the Catholic faith and cannot be blamed for his ignorance. In the second case, the infidel is one who contradicts the faith and despises it. If we seek to illustrate the theologian's argument, the first type of infidel may be embodied by the Indians, dear to the School of Salamanca, and the second by heretics in general, and Protestants in particular. There is still a third possible position, as an intermediate point between withdrawal and denial. It is a fluctuation between two parties, with no adherence to one or the other. Cano explains that it is in this sense that Pope Étienne declares that 'He who hesitates in the faith is faithless'.

In light of this explanation on the concept of religious infidelity, Cano goes on to refute the arguments raised in his first part, relying on what he advances in the second part. Firstly, hesitation is not error because the error is a false proposition, whether affirmative or negative, and implies firm assent. He who expresses an opinion (thus an uncertain proposition, not a certainty) is not necessarily wrong and is not necessarily heretical, since there are opinions which fall within the scope of faith. But he who doubts does not assert, nor does he deny, for he remains unsure. This is because he has no certainty, but nor does he have an opinion, choosing neither faith (true, certain) nor its opposite. As far as the meaning of words is concerned, he who doubts is not heretical.

Furthermore, doubt is not a corruption of the faith: only obstinate opponents should be regarded as heretics. To drive home this point, Cano uses a comparison with colours. It is not only black (heresy) which is contrary to white (faith), but also the intermediate colours. If we translate this comparison: grey (doubt) is not white, but nor is it black, and the sceptic is not really a heretic if he does not adhere to the faith. If Pope Étienne states that 'he who wavers in the faith is an infidel', it is that the undecided will not side with heretics, but nor does he strive to defend the faith; therefore he is not reliable and, 'according to legal fiction', he is punished as a heretic.

Gradually, Cano's reasoning hardens as one senses that doubt is losing ground. The text then reaches its final stage, where the author expresses his opinion. He continues by returning to the comparison of colours. White is 'expelled' not only by black, but also by the intermediate colours, beige, green, etc. Anything that is not faith (truth, perfection) is opposed to it. Thus doubt and opinion are also opposed to faith, even if in a far less radical way than heresy. As for the difference between doubt and error, Cano makes this nuanced. Error involves a false assent, a persistent error that is contrary to faith; it is the very definition of heresy. However, doubt, when stubborn, is also contrary to faith, not in the mind but in the will. However, is it ultimately possible to absolve obstinate sceptics, the perpetually indecisive? Are they so different from heretics? Cano here takes up his position personally ('In my view, no') by distinguishing two levels: that of metaphysical theology and that of moral philosophy (which will become moral theology). For the metaphysical theologian, doubt is without form or type, it has no independent existence. We can therefore situate it in relation to faith. However, 'under the laws of moral philosophy', that is, in normative terms, we cannot imagine that a man who persists in doubt is completely unfamiliar with any error of faith. This is because doubt covers not only certainties taught by the Church, but also the very foundations of Catholic doctrine. Cano asserts that the resolutely undecided man adheres to nothing and rejects nothing, which is totally implausible; the Dominican, then, makes this staggering assumption: 'unless one wants to imagine a man who subscribes to everything and who hesitates over everything, for whom all things are a boundless question, without there being anything constant anywhere or any stable truth'.[47]

The man who doubts is fictional, and imagining this untenable position leads us into unreality. Let us however accept, says Cano, that such a man who remains forever unresolved in this uncertainty may exist. Still, if he professes the Christian faith (which, needless to say, is a minimum requirement, otherwise the individual is an infidel in the sense of non-Christian), it is good that he accepts Christian doctrine. The theologian then only has to unravel the consequences of this adherence. Thus, Cano continues, the undecided man also accepts Holy Scripture and the authority of the Church. And if he doubts one of the points of faith, he needs simply to be shown the truth of the dogma defined by the Church or as arising from Scripture. The sceptic is therefore forced to take a stand: either he stops doubting, or he declares that the testimony of the Church and Holy Scripture is not certain, and, if he opts for that approach, he is a heretic. It is therefore right that the Inquisition, supported by theologians and canonists, condemn this kind of individual as heretical, in addition to 'all those who stubbornly doubt Catholic dogma'.

When Azor took up the question of doubt and heresy forty years after Cano, the debate was essentially over. The Jesuit gives his own opinion without developing the *pro* and *contra* arguments:

> My opinion is that he who hesitates in the faith wilfully and persistently is as much a heretic, because faith is true and certain adherence to something, even if obscure, but he whose faith remains willingly and obstinately uncertain does not give the assent that he should give: therefore, he is heretical or should be considered as such.[48]

Over the generations, the collective work of doctors has highlighted a set of attitudes vis-à-vis the claims of faith, from firm adherence to total refusal, to the desire to understand and to demonstrate, the fleeting temptation of disbelief, amazement at miracle and mystery, or distrustful distancing from the Church's statements. Hesitation, which at first seems innocent because of its very vagueness, does not stand up to scrutiny. For if faith is a gift of God, it is also a matter of free will, by which the believer relies on the Church's teaching to accept divine revelation — even if the Holy Spirit first prepares the will of the individual to believe.[49] Suspension of judgment and indecisive withdrawal are inseparable from a reduction or a lack of faith. Doubt, when settled permanently in the individual consciousness without being fought by the forces of the will, is a sign of disobedience to the Church and an inner resistance to the gift of faith. It could therefore only be condemned by defenders of Catholic orthodoxy, who saw this as the door opening to heresy and atheism.

Notes to Chapter 4

1. 'Modicae fidei, quare dubitasti?', *Biblia sacra iuxta Vulgatam Clementinam*, ed. by Alberto Colunga and Lorenzo Turrado (Madrid: Biblioteca de Autores Cristianos, 1994), p. 976.

2. 'Qui vidisti me Thomas, credisti; beati qui non viderunt, et crediderunt', *Biblia sacra*, p. 1064.

3. For example, questions raised on the validity of the sacraments: see 'Administrer les sacrements en Europe et au Nouveau Monde. La Curie romaine et les *dubia circa sacramenta*', ed. by Paolo Broggio, Charlotte de Castelnau-L'Estoile and Giovanni Pizzorusso, *Mélanges de l'École française de Rome, Italie et Méditerranée*, 121.1 (2009), 5–217; James Q. Whitman, *The Origins of Reasonable*

Doubt: Theological Roots of the Criminal Trial (New Haven, CT, and London: Yale University Press, 2008).

4. Juan Azor, *Institutionum moralium, in quibus universae quaestiones ad conscientiam recte aut prave factorum pertinentes breviter tractantur, pars prima* (Rome: Aloisio Zanetti, 1600). We use the Lyon edition, 1602; 'Azor, Juan', *Diccionario de Historia Eclesiástica de España*, ed. by Quintín Aldea Vaquero, 5 vols (Madrid: Instituto Enrique Flórez, CSIC, 1972–87), vol. 1 (1972), p. 166. On the expansion of moral theology linked to Tridentine reform, see John Mahoney, *The Making of Moral Theology: A Study of the Catholic Tradition* (Oxford: Oxford University Press, 1987).

5. See Miriam Turrini, *La coscienza e le leggi. Morale e diritto nei testi per la confessione della prima età moderna* (Bologna: Il Mulino, 1991); Adriano Prosperi, *Tribunali della coscienza. Inquistori, confessori, missionari* (Turin: Enaudi, 1996).

6. See Louis Vereecke, *De Guillaume d'Ockham à saint Alphonse de Liguori. Études d'histoire de la théologie morale moderne, 1300–1787* (Rome: Collegium S. Alfonsi de Urbe, 1986).

7. 'Dubius in fide infidelis est, nec eis omnino credendum est, qui fidem veritatis ignorant', Pseudo-Sixte, Ep. 1, chap. 3, in *Liber Extra* 5.7.1 in *Corpus Iuris Canonici*, ed. by Emil Friedberg, 2 vols (Leipzig: Tauchnitz, 1879–81), vol. 2 (1881), col. 778.

8. See Carlo Fantappiè, *Chiesa romana e modernità giuridica. Vol. I, L'edificazione del sistema canonistico (1563–1903)* (Milan: Giuffrè, 2008).

9. 'Est autem fides sperandarum substantia rerum, argumentum non apparentium'. Fantappiè, *Chiesa romana*, p. 1163.

10. Ignacio Jericó Bermejo, *La fe católica en los Salmantinos del siglo XVI. La vieja y la nueva problemática según los comentarios de Fray Luis de León, Juan de Guevara y Pedro de Aragón* (Madrid: Revista Agustiniana, 1999), p. 539.

11. Jericó Bermejo, *La fe católica*, p. 546.

12. Marie-Madeleine Fragonard, 'La Détermination des frontières symboliques. Nommer et définir les groupes hérétiques', in *Les Frontières religieuses en Europe du XVe au XVIIe siècle. Actes du XXXIe colloque international d'études humanistes*, ed. by Robert Sauzet (Paris: Vrin, 1992), pp. 37–49; Virgilio Pinto Crespo, 'Sobre el delito de la herejía (siglos XIII–XVI)', in *Perfiles jurídicos de la Inquisición española*, ed. by José Antonio Escudero (Madrid: Instituto de Historia de la Inquisición-Universidad Complutense de Madrid, 1989), pp. 195–204; Stefania Pastore, *Il vangelo e la spada. L'Inquisizione di Castiglia e i suoi critici (1460–1598)* (Rome: Edizioni di storia e letteratura, 2003).

13. Othmar Hageneder, 'Der Häeresie begriff bei den Juristen des 12. und 13. Jahrhunderts', in *The Concept of Heresy in the Middle Ages (11th.–13th. C.)*, ed. by W. Lourdaux and D. Verhelst (Louvain: University Press; La Haye: Martinus Nijhoff, 1976), pp. 42–103 (p. 65).

14. Alonso de Castro, *De Iusta Haereticorum punitione libri tres* (Salamanca: Juan de Junta, 1547), we use the Anvers edition of 1568; see 'Castro, Alonso de', in *Dictionnaire de Théologie catholique*, 36 vols (Paris: Letouzey et Ané, 1967–72), Vol. 4, t. II–2, col. 1835–36; Diego de Simancas, *Institutiones Catholicae* (Valladolid: Egidio de Colomies, 1552); José Luis Bermejo Cabrero, 'Apuntamientos sobre la vida y escritos de Diego de Simancas', in *El derecho y los juristas en Salamanca (siglos XVI–XX). En memoria de Francisco Tomás y Valiente*, ed. by Eugenia Torijano Pérez, Salustiano de Dios and Javier Infante Miguel-Motta (Salamanca: Ediciones Universidad de Salamanca, 2004), pp. 567–88; Prospero Farinacci, *Tractatus de haeresi* (Anvers: Ioannem Keerbergium, 1616); Virgilio Pinto Crespo, 'El apogeo del Santo Oficio (1569–1621). Los hechos y las actividades inquisitoriales en España: el último tercio del siglo XVI. La justificación doctrinal del Santo Oficio', in *Historia de la Inquisición en España y América*, ed. by Joaquín Pérez Villanueva, 3 vols (Madrid: Biblioteca de Autores Cristianos, 1984), 1, 880–86.

15. 'Heresis est error intellectus, sive mentis voluntarius ex electione et pertinacia contra aliquam sententia fidei'. Azor, *Institutionum moralium*, col. 1173.

16. Augustine of Ancona, *Summa de potestate ecclesiastica* (Rome: Ferrarius, 1584), q. 28, art. 1, 168–69.

17. Juan de Torquemada, *Summæ Ecclesiasticæ libri quatuor* (Salamanca: Juan María de Terranova, 1560).

18. Antoninus of Florence (saint), *Summa theologica*, part. 3, tit. 22, chap. 5 § 10 (Nuremberg: Antonius Koberger, 1477–79); Antoninus, *Prima [quarta] pars totius summe majoris beati Antonini*

(Lyon: Johannis Cleyn, 1506); Peter Francis Howard, *Beyond the Written Word: Preaching and Theology in the Florence of Archbishop Antoninus, 1427–1459* (Florence: L. S. Olschi, 1995).

19. Arnau Alberti, *Tractatus solemnis et aureus. De Agnoscendis Assertionibus Catholicis et Haereticis* (Venice: Candentis Salamandrae, 1571).

20. Castro, *De Iusta Haereticorum punitione*.

21. Melchor Cano, *De locis theologicis libri duodeci* (Salamanca: Matías Gast, 1563) [modern edition by Juan Belda Plans (Madrid, Biblioteca de Autores Cristianos, 2006) that we use for further quotations]; see Belda Plans, *La Escuela de Salamanca y la renovación de la teología en el siglo XVI* (Madrid: Biblioteca de Autores Cristianos, 2000).

22. Ancona, *Summa de potestate*, pp. 168–69.

23. Jean Rivière, 'Une première "Somme" du pouvoir pontifical. Le Pape chez Augustin d'Ancône', *Revue des Sciences Religieuses*, 18.2 (1938), 149–83.

24. 'Postulet autem in fide nihil hesitans: qui enim haesitat, similis est fluctui maris, qui a vento movetur et circumfertur'. James 1. 6.

25. See Javier López de Goicoechea Zabala, *Dualismo cristiano y estado modern. Estudio histórico-crítico de la 'Summa de Ecclesia' (1453) de Juan de Torquemada* (Salamanca: Universidad Pontificia de Salamanca, 2004).

26. Torquemada, *Summæ Ecclesiasticæ*, p. 561.

27. Torquemada, *Summæ Ecclesiasticæ*, pp. 569–70.

28. 'Hæreticus est, qui post susceptam religionem Christianam Christi fidem in generali profitens, aliquam, vel aliquas in speciali opinionem contrariam catholicæ veritati, pertinaciter tenet vel sequitur'. Torquemada, *Summæ Ecclesiasticæ*, p. 574.

29. 'Uno modo dicitur hereticus quicunque est dubius in fide'. Torquemada, *Summæ Ecclesiasticæ*, p. 574.

30. 'Hæc est fides catholica, quam nisi quisque fideliter, firmiterque crediderit, salvus esse non poterit'. Torquemada, *Summæ Ecclesiasticæ*, p. 574.

31. 'Fides ambiguum non habet: et si habet, fides non est'. Bernard of Clairvaux, *De consideratione*, 5, 3, PL: 40, 239.

32. Antoninus of Florence, *Summa theologica*, Pars 4, tit. 8, chap. 5.

33. Antoninus of Florence, *Summa theologica*, Pars 4, tit. 8, chap. 3, § 3.

34. Alberti, *Tractatus solemnis*, p. 9.

35. On the disputes in Switzerland from 1520 to 1530, see Fabrice Flückiger, *Dire le vrai. Une histoire de la dispute religieuse au début du XVIe siècle. Ancienne confédération helvétique, 1523–1536* (Neuchâtel: Alphil, Presses universitaires suisses, 2018).

36. Alberti, *Tractatus solemnis*, pp. 43–44.

37. Alberti, *Tractatus solemnis*, p. 183.

38. Castro, *De Iusta Haereticorum punitione*, fol. 37^r.

39. 'Errare est verum putare quod falsum est, falsum quod verum est, vel certum habere pro incerto, incertum vero pro certo, sive falsum, sive verum'; Augustine of Hippo, *Enchiridion ad Laurentium*, p. 17; Augustine, *The Augustine Catechism: The Enchiridion on Faith, Hope and Charity*, ed. and trans. by Bruce Harbert and Boniface Ramsey (New York: New City Press: 2008), p. 47.

40. Castro, *De Iusta Haereticorum punitione*, fol. 38^v.

41. 'Quia, sicut oris confessio ad salutem, ita cordis credulitas ad justitiam necessaria'. Castro, *De Iusta Haereticorum punitione*, fol. 39^r.

42. Castro, *De Iusta Haereticorum punitione*, fol. 39^v.

43. François Titelmann (Franciscus Titelmans), *Elucidatio paraphrastica in sanctum Christi evangelium secundum Joannem, cum annotationibus in aliquot capita* (Anvers: Symon Cock, 1543), fol. 27.

44. Castro, *De Iusta Haereticorum punitione*, fol. 41v.

45. Ignacio Jericó Bermejo, 'De propositionibus oppositis fidei non haereticis. Las exposiciones de Melchor Cano y Domingo Báñez (s. XVI)', *Communio. Commentarii internationales de Ecclesia et theologia*, 33.1 (2000), 33–104.

46. Juan Belda Plans, 'Introducción general histórico-teológica', in Cano, *De locis theologicis*, p. lxxxi.

47. '[...] nisi velimus hominem quempiam fingere haerentem ad omnia et nutantem, cui universarum

rerum infinita questio sit, et nullo loco constans et fixa veritas'. Cano, *De locis theologicis*, p. 429.

48. 'Meo iudicio quoties qui voluntarie et pertinaciter de fide haesitat, tot ipso est haereticus: quoniam fides est assensus verus et certus, licet obscurus; sed qui de fide voluntarie et pertinaciter ambigit, assensum non praestat, quem tamen pratestare deberet: ergo est haereticus, aut saltem tanquam talis habendus'. Azor, *Institutionum moralium*, col. 756.

49. See also Giacomo Pignatelli (1625–1698), *Novissima Consultationes Canonicae praecipuis controversias quae fidem, eiusque regulam spectant*, t. 1, consultatio 3 (Cologne: Gabrielis and Samuelis de Tournes, 1718), p. 4.

CHAPTER 5

❖

Pyrrhonism and Unbelief:
Diego Hurtado de Mendoza
and the Spanish Tradition

Stefania Pastore

'Almost Everyone Had a Copy of It'

In 1590, in his native Zafra, 'in extrema Baethica', the humanist Pedro de Valencia, who was not yet celebrated and had not yet been appointed to an official post, wrote his *Académica sive de iudicio erga verum ex primis ipsis fontibus*.[1]

During the complex transitional period in the kingdom, between the death of Philip II and the reign of Philip III, Valencia would rise to an important position, as the author of works about witches and Moriscos, about economic and colonial policy, and about biblical commentary and philology. His works, remarkable in their clarity and farsightedness and for their depth and critical independence, have yet to be comprehensively studied in their entirety. Appointed chronicler of the Indies and of the Crown, in recognition of his importance among Spanish cultural figures and in an attempt to mitigate his penury, Valencia moved to Madrid in 1607, and from that time forward he also played a leading role as a political adviser to the Spanish monarchy.

But during the spring of 1590, as he states in the dedication of his work, Valencia was still to be found in sleepy Zafra. There, at the urging of a group of friends, he was perusing the *Académica*, a sort of commented anthology of the principal sceptics from classical antiquity, with the intention of referring explicitly in his work's title to the Academic or Ciceronian school, with which he seemed to identify, albeit cautiously. Modesty led him to define the work as a mere academic exercise that had taken him no more than twenty days to complete. But its dazzling editorial success betrayed Valencia's false modesty. His *Académica* would be published in 1596 in Antwerp by Plantin, whose printing press was closely associated with Valencia's beloved teacher, the great humanist Benito Arias Montano. This lively compendium in folio must have had a remarkably wide circulation. A few years later, José de Sigüenza could quote from Valencia's work and easily have the reference understood when attempting to decipher the iconography of the El Escorial vaults and their representations of the philosophers of the School of Athens:

anyone reading Valencia's work could recognize the characters portrayed, explained Sigüenza, who was also a follower of Arias Montano and a close friend of Valencia.[2] Proof of widespread interest in ancient scepticism in late sixteenth-century Spain can be found not only in the refined iconography of the El Escorial, or in Sigüenza's remarks. Valencia himself illustrated how unnecessary it was during that period in Spain to go deeply into a description of Pyrrhonism of the opposing school, not Academic scepticism but the school deriving from the work of Sextus Empiricus, since

> Sexti Pyrrhonii commentaria omnibus prae manis sint, ex quibus hoc abunde liceat haurire, atque ii, qui non adeo vacarint, ut illa perlegant, ex Laertio commode id capere possint.[3]

Though he mentioned not being able to get his hands on a copy of the work in Greek, this was no great matter, because 'everyone had' a copy of Sextus Empiricus's commentaries, and the few who did not have access to them could always learn what they were about by consulting the biography of Sextus by Diogenes Laërtius.

Seen in the light of the decades-long historiographical debate about whether or not Michel de Montaigne and Francisco Sanches were indebted to the work of Sextus Empiricus and whether they should be included among the Pyrrhonian sceptics or the Ciceronian Academic sceptics,[4] Pedro de Valencia's composure is surprising and perhaps suggests that a less categorical approach to the question should be taken, and that the reading, the works and the life of an individual tend to engender a critical autonomy that is not reducible to trends and schools.

But this raises another issue: how, when, and to what degree were Spain and the Spanish empire affected by this far-reaching Pyrrhonian movement, which recast European knowledge and, according to what is now commonly believed, opened the door to European modernity? And, notwithstanding the debate among Pedro de Valencia scholars as to whether he was an adherent to scepticism,[5] how are we to understand the resurgence of sceptical doctrines from late Antiquity — whether of the Academic or the Pyrrhonian school — in a context like the Iberian one? Pedro de Valencia, a humanist hardly prone to hyperbole, spoke of Sextus Empiricus's *Outlines of Pyrrhonism* as if it were a best-seller that almost everyone had a copy of. Surprisingly, the ideas the work contained could be taken for granted in the Iberian world; even if one had not read Sextus himself, his ideas could be come by in any number of other ways, through similar authors or even through Sextus's critics and opponents, who frequently cited extracts from him in order to rebut his arguments.

But Valencia's words lead us to an Iberian tradition that is never mentioned in the well-known narrative about the history of European scepticism. And therefore perhaps it is necessary to take a step back, or rather two, in search of an attempted encounter that was later completely forgotten.

The Pyrrhonian Turn

In 1562 the famous French printer Henri Estienne published the first Latin edition of Sextus Empiricus's *Outlines of Pyrrhonism*, thereby placing at the disposal of a wider readership a text which had so far circulated only in manuscript and, moreover, in Greek. A man of wide knowledge and deep erudition, on this occasion Estienne also displayed a considerable flair for business. The work, a miscellany of texts and aphorisms from the non-Academic sceptic tradition, turned out to be highly successful and would from then on become a book no good library could afford to be without. Most importantly, however, it would come to represent a watershed in the history of European culture, helping to redefine the contours of French philosophical thought and lay the foundations of European scepticism.

In France, which at that time was being torn apart by wars of religion, Empiricus's work supplied a veritable arsenal of anti-dogmatic ideas. It eroded certainties and truth by reflecting on the frailty of human knowledge and of perceived forms. To a divided country, where Catholics and Huguenots slaughtered each other in their endeavour to assert the truths of their own faith, it became an instrument of conciliation and tolerance, introducing the balm of doubt into a war of certainties. Thus would the *Outlines* be perceived by the great philosopher Michel de Montaigne, who used it as a source of maxims from the classical sceptical tradition, the most significant of which he ordered to be transcribed onto the beams of his tower library.[6] Montaigne would repeatedly return to Sextus Empiricus as he compiled his *Essais*, freely borrowing from the text published by Estienne for the book-within-a-book that was his *Apologie de Raymond Sebond*, as well as for some of his most famous pages inviting Europeans to reflect upon the fragility of identity and doctrinal conflicts and to put aside dogmatic obsessions and religious beliefs. In these passages Montaigne underscored how central the *Outlines*, which he had read avidly from 1576 onwards, had been to his own development.

As Richard H. Popkin explained in the introduction to his final revision of *The History of Scepticism from Savonarola to Bayle*, the *Outlines of Pyrrhonism* helped to disseminate a selection of passages from the classical tradition, thereby inaugurating that important season of reflection on the appearance of forms and on doubt, which goes from Montaigne to Pierre Charron to the Sanches of *Quod nihil scitur* right down to the more famous cogitations of René Descartes.[7] The reading of Sextus Empiricus by Montaigne and by the French tradition was, however, not the only, or even the first, chapter in the history of the text's reception. As Popkin himself pointed out, it had already been rediscovered and used by certain Catholic theologians to demonstrate, from a fideistic perspective, the power and inscrutability of God as compared to the fragility and uncertainty of all rational knowledge. It was Girolamo Savonarola who ordered it to be transcribed for the first time, at the convent of San Marco, while Giovanfrancesco Pico, the nephew of the more famous Pico della Mirandola, reproduced large portions of it in his *De vanitate*.[8] It was from this same anti-rationalist standpoint that Hervé Gentian's 1569 edition of the *Adversus Mathematicos* emerged.

This theological reading of the text may be seen as opposite, indeed specular, to that which took place in France in the second half of the sixteenth century. But it was Estienne's edition, in the specific context of the wars of religion in France and the doctrinal conflicts that divided Europe, that would become the *livre de chevet* of succeeding generations. As Luciano Floridi has reminded us, that enthusiastic welcoming of the sceptical challenge was not so much (or at least not exclusively) a response to its epistemological component, which would assert itself later on, following Descartes's introduction of methodic doubt, but rather an ethical interpretation of scepticism, the search for a change in mental attitude.[9]

Spain: A Space for Doubt

The narrative about Estienne's successful translation contains all the ingredients that are traditionally associated with the development of modernity and of modern mind in Europe, according to a classical account that sees Luther's schism and the fragmentation of Western Christianity, the wars of religion in Europe, and the progressive erosion of all doctrinal certainty as the starting point for an anti-dogmatic reflection on the concept of tolerance. According to this narrative, doubt (both religious and epistemological), unbelief and the ability to question dogmas and certainties connected to one's religious identity become the fertile ground in which modern and tolerant proposals such as those of Montaigne, based on a cognitive and moral relativism, flowered. So, again, what is the place of Spain in all of this?

Most scholars of European intellectual history would struggle to make the case that there is one. The few Iberian names that emerge in connection with the impressive rebirth of scepticism in Europe belong to a history yet to be explored and certainly do not put one in mind of a movement comparable to those in Renaissance Italy and the France of Michel de Montaigne, or even later in Holland with Uriel da Costa and Baruch Spinoza.

Pedro de Valencia's anthology of scepticism represents almost a *unicum* in the context of Iberia, and outsiders and exiles such as the Portuguese physician and converso Francisco Sanches, praised by Pierre Bayle as a 'grand pyrrhonien', constitute exceptions that prove the rule. Sanches studied medicine in Rome and Montpellier and taught his entire life in France, in Toulouse. His masterpiece, *Quod nihil scitur*, published only a year before the *Essais* of Montaigne, left a deep impression on the epistemological debate in Europe. He insisted on the need for radical doubt, which would erase all certainty and lead to a re-establishing of all our knowledge. Sanches's influence was so important that many historians of philosophy have seen in him a brilliant precursor to Descartes's methodic doubt.

Sanches's treatise, published in Latin by Gryphe in 1581 and considered an essential work by Gabriel Naudé, has been published in an excellent English edition and analysed in various individual studies,[10] as well as in some illuminating pages in Richard H. Popkin, who characterized him as the most interesting sceptic of his day. However, there are still no studies that shed light on Sanches's Iberian and Italian education or analyse this Portuguese converso's unique combination of medical and philosophical training in an attempt to find points of contact between two spheres of knowledge that are usually considered to be unconnected.

Of course, if we think of France during the wars of religion as the principal setting for this development in the history of thought, it is important to emphasize how doubt, especially religious doubt, was understood and experienced in Spain and the Iberian empire. As a country that was torn apart and divided well before the Reformation began to spread in Europe, Spain experienced the effects of multiculturalism and the more or less forced coexistence of different religions before any other European country. A great deal has been written on the Golden Age of medieval Spain and on the more or less pacific 'convivencia' that characterized the coexistence of three faiths in the Iberian Peninsula. Only more recently has the focus turned to how the mixed and multi-confessional atmosphere in Spain — which gave rise to all manner of encounters, clashes and polemics between the three revealed religions — created a particularly receptive environment in which religious doubt had become an integral part of a tendency toward interreligious polemics and comparative thinking.[11] The traumatic experience of forced conversion, of religious dissimulation, of the passage from one faith to another and of the inevitable syncretisms and attempts to mediate between adherence to the old, inherited faith and the new, imposed one created the first, foundational laboratory for modern European critical consciousness. This is the insight behind the important volume *After Conversion: Iberia and the Emergence of Modernity*, as well as Stuart B. Schwartz's ground-breaking book, and the various contributions to this volume.[12] This is an important avenue for research, which opens up new ways to interpret European intellectual history and specifically the evolution of tolerance, making room for developments in places like Spain, which too often is ignored in traditional historiographical approaches to this topic because of its image as a bastion of the Counter-Reformation.

However, it is not to Spain in general between the fourteenth and the sixteenth century that I would like to direct my attention, nor to the many forms of doubt and disbelief experienced there. Rather, I will focus on one extraordinary figure and on his truly unique actions on the political and cultural stage, a man who was the product of that open and multicultural Spain whose contours I will attempt to trace, as well as being Charles V's political representative in Europe: Diego Hurtado de Mendoza. It is through Mendoza that I hope to reconstruct the uniqueness of medieval Spain's legacy within a European perspective and finally bring to light a possible Spanish contribution to the great French Pyrrhonian and sceptical tradition.

Granada's Legacy

It is difficult to introduce such an eclectic figure as Diego Hurtado de Mendoza. Known as one of the most brilliant humanists of Spain's Golden Age, a Petrarchan poet, the author of one of the classics of Spanish historiography, *Guerra de Granada*, and occasionally suspected of having penned one of the most famous works of Spanish literature, *El Lazarillo de Tormes*, Mendoza was also a voracious collector of books and codices. Last but not least, he was the Spanish ambassador to Italy and played a fundamental role on both the Italian and the European stage.[13]

Diego Hurtado was born, around 1503, into one of Spain's most illustrious families, the Mendoza, being the youngest son of Íñigo López de Mendoza, the Count of Tendilla.[14] His father was an ambassador and a humanist but also the hero of the war in Granada. In 1492, at the conclusion of the wars of Granada, when the city was ceded by the last Nasrid Muslim dynasty to the Catholic Monarchs of Spain, Mendoza's father was named governor of the city and of the kingdom. He was in charge of enforcing a series of agreements, the *Capitulaciones*, which in general allowed the city's Muslim inhabitants to continue to observe their religion and their customs.[15] Tendilla and Hernando de Talavera, confessor to Queen Isabella, had been put in charge of supervising the integration of the local Muslim residents, the conquering 'cristianos viejos' [old Christians], conversos from Toledo fleeing the new Inquisition and those who had newly converted from Islam, and help them build a peaceful coexistence on the basis of shared assumptions. Tendilla had undertaken the job with enthusiasm, adopting a highly personal approach and avoiding the new rules imposed by the Catholic Monarchs and the new *Consejos* of the monarchy: when Ferdinand's 'officials', who had been dispatched to Granada to oversee Talavera's and Tendilla's activities, violated the terms of the *Capitulaciones*, thereby triggering the first uprising of the Alpujarras, Tendilla repaired the rift by seeking a personal settlement with the rebels and even offering them, as a guarantee of his honest intentions, his wife and children as hostages.[16]

At the time, Diego had not been born, or was perhaps an infant, and was certainly not aware of the true importance of this event, but he had surely heard the story told a thousand times, as it was part of family lore celebrating the mythical 'caballero' Tendilla, his loyalty and his chivalry in dealing with the Moors, which eventually found its way into many Spanish stories.

The bond with the Muslim and Morisco world thus had deep roots in Diego's family. Just as the elder Mendoza resisted undue interference on the part of the court when it tried to break the capitulation agreements, his heirs also tried to protect the Moriscos as far as possible against the extremist zeal of the Spanish Inquisition and the Church. The Tendillas, much as the Morisco lords in Aragon were doing, requested and obtained Edicts of Grace that would shelter the Moriscos of Granada from the Inquisition and that would relieve them from an increasingly restrictive set of rules, protecting their right to wear traditional clothes and headwear and to maintain domestic traditions and rituals that set them apart from Christians.[17]

The lively and multi-cultural Granada that his father had helped to create, the last stronghold of tolerance in what was increasingly the uniformly Catholic Spain of the Counter-Reformation, left a strong impression on Diego. He had absorbed that cultural air, had made it his own, and remembered it often in his writings. The Granada of the early years of the *Capitulaciones* emerged from the limpid prose of his *Guerra de Granada* as the epitome of a lost world, a relic of an age at equal removes from the rigid dictates of Trent and the bureaucracy of the 'rey papelero', Philip II.

Famous and often quoted is his opinion of the Habsburgs' exasperating bureaucracy, in which ambitious 'letrados' corrupted the ancient and carefully balanced system on which the government so strongly depended during the *Capitulaciones*:

> The city and realm used to be governed, as among townsmen and companions, with a kind of arbitrary justice in which all thoughts were united, all resolutions intended for the common public good: this ended when the elders passed away. Jealousy crept in; rifts developed over petty matters between the ministers of justice and of war; written agreements backed by certificates became common practice, in which each party's understanding is reduced to his own opinion, one side determined not to suffer equally, the other determined to preserve its advantage, negotiated with more deceit than modesty.[18]

Long before writing *Guerra de Granada*, however, Diego had also carried his love for the last Nasrid kingdom with him to Italy. The Granada his father had idealized would fill the stories he told Italian humanists and courtiers. It was perhaps in Granada, or perhaps more plausibly in Salamanca, that the young Diego took up the study of Arabic, which would turn out to be the key to a faraway world, as important to his cultural education as the classical tradition of Greek and Roman antiquity was. Mendoza's solid knowledge of Arabic would be confirmed not only by the famous Venetian printer Paolo Manuzio and the humanist Ambrosio de Morales, but by the marginal notes he penned in his Arabic manuscripts, now in El Escorial. This knowledge was an unusual accomplishment for the time, and it was the cause of much astonishment among the Italian humanists, who greatly admired Mendoza's 'cultura estraña'. In Mendoza himself, this knowledge of the language inspired an enduring fascination with what was different, distant, other. This passion would never abandon him and would encourage him to search for new manuscripts, codices and printed books, whether from Spain, elsewhere in the Empire, Venice or Istanbul.[19] He had a similar passion for Greek texts, gradually building up a collection from various sources, ranging from North Africa to Turkey, his activity as a collector going hand in hand with his career as a man of arms and a courtier.[20] His passion for Arab history and philosophy went back at least to 1535, when he accompanied the emperor in his famous expedition to Tunis, where he was one of the group of Spanish 'philosophers' who took part in the dispute on Averroes with Muley Hacen, the king of Tunis. And it was to Mendoza — probably the most interested as well as the most informed member of this select group — to whom the dethroned monarch left some precious codices, saved from the fire that had almost entirely destroyed his library during the siege of Charles V.[21]

The Ambassador to Venice

Diego was appointed ambassador to Venice in 1539, with the thankless task of establishing closer ties to the republic, which was traditionally more inclined to friendship with France.[22] The card he chose to play was that of culture and patronage. His house became a frequent meeting place for Italian writers, humanists and artists, including Aretino, Bembo, Giovio, Titian, Sansovino, Beccadelli, and the Florentine protonotary Pietro Carnesecchi (the duke of Florence Cosimo de Medici's right-hand man, condemned to death for heresy in 1567). During his years in Italy he was the dedicatee of numerous works that the Inquisition would later brand as heretical and include in the Italian and Spanish Indexes of forbidden books.[23]

His political activities in Italy were highly particular. Firmly convinced that Charles V needed to reach an agreement with the Lutherans, he was the foremost representative of an anti-Roman and anti-curial policy in Italy. Neither Mendoza nor his entourage refused or avoided contact with representatives of the Reformation — on the contrary, they appeared to present themselves, at this strategic moment, as one of the most important and most authoritative points of contact. Later on, during his trial for heresy, Pietro Carnesecchi recalled that exciting world, teeming with ideas and heresies. He talked about 'a Flemish man of letters' — possibly Conrad Gessner, the author of *Bibliotheca Universalis* — whose ideas, Carnesecchi believed, smacked of heresy; Alfonso de Ulloa, Diego's private secretary, a free spirit who was tried by the Inquisition in 1558; Diego de Enzinas, author of a famous letter to Luther, who was burned in Rome in 1558; and a certain Ramírez, whose position Carnesecchi found hard to explain: 'More an atheist than anything else, like a man who combined aspects of the Marrano, considering his nationality, and of the Lutheran, considering his conversation'.[24]

In those years the Spanish ambassador's *salon* became an important cultural crossroads, open both northwards to Protestants and eastwards to Greek scholars and the precious codices they brought from Greece and Constantinople; it also became a significant point of contact between Venice and the New World (Diego's brother Antonio de Mendoza, another lover of books and curiosities, which he frequently sent to Venice, was Mexico's first viceroy). There were Protestant Greek scholars working in Mendoza's library, which according to Gessner, was one of the five largest in Italy, along with the Vatican and the Marciana Library in Venice. It was on the basis of Mendoza's codices that his librarian, Arnoldus Arlenius, published the *editio princeps* of Flavius Josephus (which was dedicated to Mendoza) and that of Polybius, with the Basel-based printer Johann Froben.[25] Arlenius also invited the erudite Protestant Conrad Gessner to come from Zwingli's Zurich to Venice, where he started working on his *Bibliotheca Universalis* in Mendoza's library. Indeed, it was in the dedicatory letter of this work, which would become the cornerstone text for the systematization of European knowledge,[26] that Gessner first publicly acknowledged (he would do so again in later years) his debt to Mendoza, the friend and patron who had been his host for three years, generously allowing him free access to his codices and books.

Two examples will suffice to give an idea of the importance of Mendoza's cultural practice: the rediscovery of Photius, and his remarkable catalogue of Greek works,[27] and the acquisition of Sextus Empiricus's codex of the *Outlines of Pyrrhonism* and the *Adversus mathematicos*, which Juan Páez de Castro began to translate into Latin in 1545.[28]

An Averroist in Trent

The discovery of ancient codices went hand in hand with Mendoza's long-standing enthusiasm for Averroes. During his years as Venetian ambassador, Mendoza maintained close ties with Italian Averroists and the Padua scholars.[29] He invited them to his Venetian *salon*, he started a Castilian translation of Aristotle's *Mechanics*,[30] and he prepared his *Paraphrasis totius Aristotelis*; when he was summoned to Trent as the representative of the emperor during the second phase of the Council, he first spent two months in Padua, the cradle of Aristotelian rationalism, gathering material to take to the Council. In Trent, he put his rich library at the disposal of the Council fathers and set up an 'Aristotelian Academy', gathering together numerous humanists and experienced Greek scholars.[31] Mendoza's political letters from Trent tell of the Council's painfully slow deliberations and of his impatience with the friars and their theological subtleties, which were the cause, in his view, of the failure to reach any agreement with the Lutherans. He repeatedly proclaimed himself an Averroist, rather an astonishing fact considering he was acting as the emperor's representative in the most important ecclesiastical council of the modern age. In his way of thinking — as he explained in the letter he wrote to the court to defend himself from the first accusation levelled against him — to support Averroes was also a way of circumventing the Thomistic rigidity of the friars and outflanking the authority of the pope and of Rome:

> that the confessor [Domingo de Soto] is not happy with me because I defended one Doctor Herrera in Trent, whom he falsely maligned, calling him a heretic in front of many bishops, and because I did not help him to print, at my own cost, a commentary on the Physics of Aristotle, and because in the disputes I always took Averroes's part, which I would not have done if I had known that he would become a confessor, and because I know more philosophy than he does.[32]

Diego was a voracious reader of Machiavelli, and Averroes must have represented for him not so much a philosophical system as the key to accessing a political perspective of religion proudly opposed to what Machiavelli had called 'the republic of clogs' ('la repubblica de zoccoli')[33] and more closely attuned to doubt than to Counter-Reformation certainties. Thus, his widely proclaimed Averroism was translated into an actual political position during the period of his embassy in Trent.

In later years, during the siege of Siena, when Mendoza's time of glory had passed, Italian pasquinades customarily depicted him as a Marrano, an arch-Marrano, a 'faithless' non-believer, mocking his physiognomy by calling him a white Moor ('un moro bianco') or joking that he was an 'uncircumcised Jew'. However, rather surprisingly, well before that time Mendoza himself had decided to poke fun at this prejudice of the Italians, and at their habit of equating Spaniards, Marranos and unbelievers. The joke on the 'Spanish peccadillo' was particularly familiar among the literati and intellectuals of Mendoza's circle, as was the association of Marranos with unbelievers.[34] Mendoza mocked the prejudices of the Italians, glorying in his Marrano image and exploiting his Spanish origins with all their implications.

As in the case of Averroism, the fact of being a Marrano and proclaiming himself a Marrano became a way of thinking, a way of behaving, and reflected a specific political position, in which the dialogue with Protestantism and the distancing from Rome, from the pope and from the conservative wing of Spanish Catholicism played an essential part. This is the only case in which the pejorative term *Marrano* became an intellectual category. For Mendoza, both terms — Marrano and

Averroist — have the same meaning: sceptic, unbeliever. Essentially, they denote a person who believes that religious conflict has to be tackled in an instrumental and political way.

'As a Moor, a Philosopher, a Marrano'

Mendoza continued to develop this image into a complex portrait that combined his personal history and attitude of mind and underscored his devotion to Averroes and his Spanish origins, his father's Granada and all the lessons that the intolerant Spain of the Inquisition had taught him.

Mendoza was convinced that Charles V needed to bypass the Roman authorities and reposition the issue of the confessional divide on a purely political level. In March 1548 the formulation of the *Interim* was complete and ready to be signed by the Germans. In mid-June, Charles took an even bolder step when he prepared a *Formula Reformationis* that also applied to the Catholic clergy; with it the emperor compelled the entire ecclesiastical body to carry out the long-awaited moral reforms. The reform of the Church and an agreement with the Protestants were at hand. But Rome's resistance would not be so easily overcome. Mendoza was constantly in contact with the great architect of the *Interim*, Antoine Perrenot de Granvelle, the mastermind of the imperial politics of the day. Mendoza expressed all his anger against the 'friars' who 'destroy us'[35] and, exasperated by the papal legates' continued obstructionism, presented a clear account of his position. Rome's firm will to control everyone's conscience, to extend its power even over people's thoughts, was a resounding failure.

The example of how little had been achieved by the Inquisition's policy of repression in Spain proved to everyone how difficult and useless it was to 'compel individual conscience' ('forçar a los yndividuos') in their private thoughts. He could only deplore the obstinacy with which people accused of crimes of opinion were prosecuted:

> [Rome] does not grant us the power to grant a general pardon but only an individual pardon, person by person, for those who wish to confess their error and receive pardon from the papal representatives; but it is impossible to force individuals one by one, and if I were one of them and did not wish to go to the house of the papal legate, and likewise the others, it is inconceivable to expect the policeman himself to go from house to house forcing us to do so; thus, the emperor may give general dispositions and the pope may forgive, but he cannot force consciences nor can he in a thousand years do so with an individual's conscience; and this I say as a philosopher, as a Moor of Granada, and as a Marrano, that today the Spanish Inquisition has even more work than it had the day it was created.[36]

At this point Mendoza's personal experiences and his intellectual persuasions crystalize into a strong decisive stance in favour of a particular brand of tolerance. His position stemmed from both his philosophical preferences and his Spanish roots. And as a 'philosopher', as a 'Marrano' and even as a 'Moor of Granada', he was convinced by what he had seen in Granada, in Spain and in the war-torn empire that a purely political solution was what was now needed — a radical change, that is, from Spanish confessional politics. The Inquisition had not been, nor could it be, a solution, because the conscience of the individual could not be subjected to any form of control and had nothing to do with loyalty or political stance.

Against Quarrellers: A Spanish Contribution to Pyrrhonism

It is perhaps useful to bear all this in mind as we return once more to the codex of Sextus Empiricus's *Outline of Pyrrhonism* that belonged to Mendoza. He had a copy in Greek in his own library in Venice, and, surprisingly, he decided to take it with him to Trent. We also know that Juan Páez de Castro discussed the *Outlines* in a letter sent to Jerónimo Zurita from Trent.[37] So, right in the middle of the Council of Trent, during the hectic days of the *De iustificatione* decree, Juan Páez de Castro and Mendoza were reading and discussing Sextus Empiricus's sceptical miscellany. It is moreover possible that, precisely at that time, they were planning a Latin translation. We know from a letter from Páez de Castro to Zurita that in 1549 the Latin translation was almost finished and ready to be published. Castro explained that they would use it to achieve great things for religion to ward off 'vitiligatores': 'I will write a preface in which I will put great things about this discipline and how useful it is for our religion, et *effugiam vitiligatores*'.[38]

I believe that the reference to the 'vitiligatores', the quarrellers, undoubtedly links the first translation of Sextus Empiricus to Mendoza's milieu and to his repeated efforts to find a political solution to the conflict with the Protestants. It is important, I think, to reflect on what Mendoza's decision to translate Sextus Empiricus might have meant. He was a keen bibliophile and was on the front line of imperial politics: what might Sextus Empiricus represent at this delicate historical moment, when imperial Spain and Europe were being torn apart by religious conflict? And why would its translation and dissemination be considered by Mendoza to be so important as to give it such high priority and assign it to none other than his personal secretary, Juan Páez de Castro, during such a crucial and complex time as the years of the Council of Trent and the *Interim*? Could it have been that reflecting on the mere appearance of all principles of truth, on the human inability to establish the veracity of one truth instead of and above another, might serve to overcome, in a political manner, the religious conflict that was tearing apart the empire of Charles V, where one theological truth confronted another in an endless series of debates and polemics? Could it have been part of a specific political agenda that Mendoza shared with part of the imperial entourage, and most certainly with the key figure in imperial politics during those years, Antoine Perrenot de Granvelle?

Páez de Castro's translation never actually saw the light of day. It remained a complete but unpublished Latin version. We do not know if Henri Estienne knew of this Spanish chapter in the history of Sextus's work. Floridi has argued that the French edition derived from another Italian copy, but in 1555, while he was in Venice, Estienne worked together with Giorgio Trifone, one of Mendoza's copyists. In any case, we cannot fail to note how Juan Páez de Castro's translation did not emerge, as has been said more than once, from a Catholic fideistic tradition but was instead undertaken with anti-dogmatic and tolerant intentions. Indeed, it emerged from a context that was very similar to that which produced the 1562 French edition. This was the first Latin translation of a text that, as Popkin has pointed out, would not only revolutionize the history of philosophy but also the history of religious tolerance in Europe, opening the way for religious relativism.

Unhappy Ending

Mendoza's good fortune in Italy waned rapidly. Appointed ambassador to Rome, he did not betray his reputation for 'andar al pelo con los Papas' [scuffling with the popes].[39] His first audience with Pope Paul III, which he attended dressed 'de capa y espada,' in layman's garb and with a sword at his side, caused an uproar and was interpreted by the cardinals as a sign of defiance. Mendoza defended it as an open act of defiance, continuing to dress in this manner, as portrayed by Titian, throughout all his years as ambassador.[40]

However, Italian politics and the alliances of Charles V quickly took a new direction. Mendoza's last move was to try to prevent the rise of the Inquisitorial party of Cardinal Gianpietro Carafa, the future Paul IV, and of the alliance formed by Leonor Álvarez de Toledo and Cosimo de Medici in Italy. Appointed governor of Siena and now deprived of aid and support, Mendoza was unable to cope with the anti-Spanish revolt. He was abruptly recalled by Charles V and relieved of all his duties in 1552. He left Rome in the dead of night, causing as much furore as when he had first arrived by breaking the nose of Julius II's personal servant.

And while the Roman Inquisition quickly devoured the lively Venetian world, condemning Mendoza's former protégés one after the other for heresy (the last of these, Cosimo de Medici's Florentine secretary Pietro Carnesecchi, burned as a Lutheran in 1567, after an Inquisition trial that provoked more outcry than any other in Italy), Mendoza languished in the shadows.

In 1568, after yet another fit of anger that led to a duel in the anteroom of the dying Don Carlos, he was exiled from court. Philip II banished him to his hometown of Granada. His status as a 'Marrano, a Moor, and a philosopher', as a critical witness of the politics of the times, only worsened matters. His last battle was on behalf of the Moriscos of Granada, who in 1568 rebelled against the cultural and religious restrictions imposed by Philip II and started a bloody two-year-long civil war in the heart of Spain. In somewhat puzzled terms that expressed his sense of alienation, Mendoza described Philip II's 'dirty war' and gave voice to that 'vanquished, conquered people, taken from their land and dispossessed of their homes and belongings', the Moriscos, who had seen their lands confiscated and redistributed by the letrados. Referring to them as 'A people without voice and out of favour', he put into their mouths a question that delegitimized years of political repression: why, if 'each nation, each profession and each state has its own specific dress, and all are Christians, [...] [are we] considered Muslims, because we dress according to the Morisco fashion, as if we carry the law in our clothes and not in our heart'.[41] This Spain was far removed from the Granada of Mendoza's childhood and from the country whose power he had dreamed of imposing over Europe; this was a country he no longer recognized.

His passions and his interests, however, were destined to produce fruit elsewhere. The *Bibliotheca Universalis*, which Conrad Gessner had pieced together thanks to Mendoza's extraordinary collections and vast knowledge, was destined to become a classic of European Reformation scholarship and an essential milestone in the rediscovery of the ancient classical tradition. And the famous Latin edition of the work of Sextus Empiricus, published in Lyon in 1562, was to mark the rebirth of Pyrrhonism in France, opening up the path towards doubt and relativism which, through Michel de Montaigne and Pierre Charron, would culminate in Descartes.

Yet this highly political scepticism had pointed the way to a different solution to the problems that would plague Spain, a country that was monoconfessional in name only, and to the conflicts that were brewing in Europe, where prolonged and devastating wars of religion would be fought both on the battlefield and through the clash of opposing dogmas. As a Marrano, Moor and philosopher, Mendoza had suggested that the Inquisition and the attempt at coercion of conscience had achieved nothing, and his repostulation of scepticism seemed to be more an anti-dogmatic proposition than a sign of adherence to a particular school. One also has to wonder whether his translation of Sextus circulated clandestinely in manuscript form — and not merely in a limited way, as Fernando Bouza has shown — and continued to nurture the passion for 'scepticism' in Spain through underground channels that were connected to those in France. Certainly a similar, though decidedly less radical, attitude can be found in the position of Pedro de Valencia, who like Mendoza would have occasion to reflect on the disastrous results of Spain's religious policies. In the pages of his treatise on the Moriscos, in which he complains bitterly of the inability of the Spanish empire to integrate the other — unlike what Seneca said had happened in the Roman Empire — the reasons for his scepticism are perhaps to be found. These are not the result of subscribing to a school or a choice arising from his own life experiences, but an anti-dogmatic proposition as an antidote to a confessional inflexibility that must be opposed fundamentally on the political plane. The solutions offered, on the eve of the expulsion, by the political advisor Pedro de Valencia to the problem of Morisco integration into Christian Spanish society are political solutions. And it is perhaps this political and instrumental variation on classical scepticism that constitutes Iberia's contribution to the long history of European scepticism.

Notes to Chapter 5

1. Pedro de Valencia, *Academica; sive, De iudicio erga verum. Ex ipsis primis fontibus* (Antwerp: Moretus, 1596). There are two recent editions of the text: Valencia, *Academica*, ed. by José Oroz Reta (Badajoz: Diputación Provincial de Badajoz, 1987) and Valencia, *Obras completas*. T. III, *Académica*, intr. by Juan Luis Suárez Sánchez de León, ed. by Juan Francisco Domínguez Domínguez (León: Universidad de León, 2006). I am quoting from the last one.
2. José de Sigüenza, *Historia de la orden de san Jerónimo*, ed. by Francisco J. Campos and Fernández de Sevilla (Valladolid: Junta de Castilla y León, 2000). On the iconographic choices at the El

Escorial and Sigüenza's important comment, see María M. Portuondo, 'The Study of Nature, Philosophy and the Royal Library of San Lorenzo of the Escorial', *Renaissance Quarterly*, 63.4 (2010), 1106–50.

3. Valencia, *Obras completas*. T. III, *Académica*, p. 232.

4. Miguel A. Granada, 'Francisco Sanchez et les courants critiques de la philosophie du XVIe siècle', *Bruniana e Campanelliana*, 15.1 (2009), 29–45. Emmanuel Naya, 'Renaissance Pyrrhonism: A Relative Phenomenon', in *Renaissance Scepticisms*, ed. by Gianni Paganini and José R. Maia Neto (Dordrecht: Springer, 2009), pp. 15–32; and Naya, 'Traduire les *Hypotyposes Pyrrhoniennes*. Henri Estienne entre la fièvre quarte et la folie chrétienne', in *Le Scepticisme au XVIe et au XVIIe siècle. T. II, Le Retour des philosophies antiques à l'âge classique*, ed. by Pierre-François Moreau (Paris: Albin Michel, 2001), pp. 48–101. See also, in the same volume Bernard Besnier, 'Sanchez à demi endormi', in *Le Scepticisme au XVIe et au XVIIe siècle*, pp. 102–20; and G. Paganini, 'Montaigne, Sanchez et la connaissance par phénomènes. Les Usages d'un paradigme ancien', in *Montaigne. Scepticisme, métaphisique et théologie*, ed. by Vincent Carraud and Jean-Luc Marion (Paris: PUF, 2004), pp. 107–35.

5. John C. Larsen, 'Pedro de Valencia's Academica and Scepticism in Late Renaissance Spain', in *Renaissance Scepticisms*, pp. 111–23. For a contrary view, see Juan Luis Suárez Sánchez de León, '¿Era escéptico Pedro de Valencia?', *Bulletin Hispanique*, 99.2 (1997), 393–408; Suárez Sánchez de León, 'Estudio preliminar', in Pedro de Valencia, *Obras completas*. T. III, *Académica*, pp. 15–88 (p. 75); Suárez Sánchez de León, *El pensamiento de Pedro de Valencia. Escepticismo y modernidad en el Humanismo español* (Badajoz: Diputación de Badajoz, 1997). See also Luis M. Gómez Canseco, *El humanismo después de 1600. Pedro de Valencia* (Seville: Universidad de Sevilla, 1993).

6. Luciano Floridi, *Sextus Empiricus: The Transmission and Recovery of Pyrrhonism* (Oxford: Oxford University Press, 2002), pp. 38–48, and more recently Manuel Bermúdez Vázquez, *The Skepticism of Michel de Montaigne* (Dordrecht: Springer, 2015).

7. Popkin would give this sceptical sylloge an increasingly prominent place in the successive editions of his history of scepticism, underscoring its centrality to the development of Western doubt and scepticism. In the final edition, he discusses Estienne's Empiricus in the Introduction itself. R. Popkin, *The History of Scepticism from Savonarola to Bayle* (New York: Oxford University Press, 2003).

8. See Walter Cavini, 'Appunti sulla prima diffusione in Occidente delle opere di Sesto Empirico', *Medioevo*, 7 (1977), 1–20; Gian M. Cao, 'Savonarola e Sesto Empirico,' in *Pico, Poliziano e l'umanesimo di fine Quattrocento*, ed. by Paolo Viti (Firenze: L. S. Olschki, 1994), pp. 231–45, and Cao, *Scepticism and Orthodoxy: Gianfrancesco Pico as a Reader of Sextus Empiricus* (Pisa: Serra, 2007); Floridi, 'The Diffusion of Sextus Empiricus's works in the Renaissance,' *Journal of the History of Ideas*, 56 (1995), 63–85, in particular pp. 66–70; and Floridi, *Sextus Empiricus*, pp. 70–72. Floridi's study is still the most complete account of the transmission of Sextus Empiricus, though it contains a number of small errors which I shall point out further on, that are nevertheless rather relevant to the present reconstruction.

9. I am referring here to the closing remarks in Floridi's 'The Grafted Branches of the Sceptical Tree: *Noli altum sapere* and Henri Stephanus' Latin Edition of *Sexti Empirici Pyrrhoniam Hypotyposeon libri III*', *Nouvelles de la République des Lettres*, 11 (1992), 127–66, at p. 162.

10. Francisco Sanches, *That nothing is known*, ed. and intro. by Elaine Limbrick, trans. by Douglas F. Thomson (Cambridge: Cambridge University Press, 1988). Naya, 'Quod nihil scitur. La Parole mise en doute', in *Libertinage et philosophie au XVIIe siècle. 7. La Résurgence des philosophies antiques* (Saint-Étienne: Université de Saint-Étienne, 2003), pp. 27–43; Damian Caluori, 'The Scepticism of Francisco Sanchez', *Archiv für Geschichte der Philosophie*, 89 (2007), 30–46, and the bibliography quoted above.

11. I discuss this issue at greater length in Pastore, 'Doubt in Fifteenth-Century Iberia', in *After Conversion: Iberia and the Emergence of Modernity*, ed. by Mercedes García-Arenal (Leiden: Brill, 2016), pp. 283–303.

12. Stuart B. Schwartz, *All Can Be Saved: Religious Tolerance and Salvation in the Iberian Atlantic World* (New Haven, CT: Yale University Press, 2008).

13. On Diego Hurtado de Mendoza, see Ángel González Palencia and Eugenio Mele, *Vida y obras de don Diego Hurtado de Mendoza*, 3 vols (Madrid: Instituto de Valencia de don Juan, 1941–43); Erika

Spivakovsky, *Son of the Alhambra: Don Diego Hurtado de Mendoza, 1504–1575* (Austin: University of Texas Press, 1970); David H. Darst, *Diego Hurtado de Mendoza* (Boston, MA: Twayne, 1987); Inés Rada, 'Un cadet de grande famille à l'epoque de la Renaissance. Don Diego Hurtado de Mendoza', in *Autour des parentés en Espagne aux XVIe et XVIIe siècles. Histoire, mythe et littérature*, ed. by Augustin Redondo (Paris: Université de la Sorbonne, 1987), pp. 31–42. On Mendoza's collections and on his library, see Anthony Hobson, *Renaissance Book Collecting: Jean Grolier and Diego Hurtado de Mendoza, their Books and Bindings* (Cambridge: Cambridge University Press, 1999); on his Italian period as ambassador, Pastore, 'Una Spagna anti-papale. Gli anni italiani di Diego Hurtado de Mendoza', *Roma Moderna e Contemporanea*, 15 (2007), 63–94. On his possible authorship of *Lazarillo*, see the recent study by Mercedes Agulló, *A vueltas con el autor del Lazarillo* (Madrid: Calambur, 2010).

14. An excellent synthesis on the Mendoza family is Helen Nader, *The Mendoza Family in the Spanish Renaissance, 1350–1550* (New Brunswick, NJ: Rutgers University Press, 1979), who also edited a volume on the women of the Mendoza household: *Power and Gender in Renaissance Spain: Eight Women of the Mendoza Family, 1450–1650*, ed. by Helen Nader (Urbana: University of Illinois Press, 2004). I should also like to remind the reader of Francisco Layna Serrano's *Historia de Guadalajara y sus Mendozas durante los siglos XV y XVI*, 4 vols (Madrid: Aldus, 1942).

15. David Coleman, *Creating Christian Granada: Society and Religious Culture in an Old-World Frontier City, 1492–1600* (Ithaca, NY: Cornell University Press, 2003).

16. It is one of the most famous episodes of the first uprising of the Alpujarras. See Miguel Ángel Ladero Quesada, *Los mudéjares de Castilla en tiempo de Isabel I* (Valladolid: Instituto Isabel la Católica, 1969); Antonio Domínguez Ortiz and Bernard Vincent, *Historia de los moriscos, vida y tragedia de una minoría* (Madrid: Revista de Occidente, 1978), pp. 18–23, and Juan Meseguer Fernández, 'Fernando de Talavera, Cisneros y la Inquisición en Granada,' in *La Inquisición española. Nueva visión, nuevos horizontes*, ed. by Joaquín Pérez Villanueva (Madrid: Siglo XXI, 1980), pp. 371–400, esp. 393–99.

17. On the Morisco policies of the Mendozas in Granada, see Domínguez Ortiz and Vincent, *Historia de los moriscos*; Rafael Benítez Sánchez-Blanco, *Heroicas decisiones. La Monarquía Católica y los moriscos valencianos* (Valencia: Institució Alfons el Magnànim, 2001); and Francisco Núñez Muley, *A Memorandum for the President of the Royal Audiencia and Chancery Court of the City and Kingdom of Granada*, ed. and trans. by Vincent Barletta (Chicago, IL: University of Chicago Press, 2007).

18. Diego Hurtado de Mendoza, *Guerra de Granada*, ed. by Bernardo Blanco-González (Madrid: Castalia, 1996), p. 100: 'Gobernábase la ciudad y reino, como entre pobladores y compañeros, con una forma de justicia arbitraria, unidos los pensamientos, las resoluciones encaminadas en común al bien público: esto se acabó con la vida de los viejos. Entraron los celos; la división sobre causas livianas entre los ministros de justicia y de guerra; las concordias en escrito confirmadas por cédulas; traído el entendimiento dellas por cada una de las partes a su opinión; la ambición de querer la una no sufrir igual, y la otra conservar la superioridad, tratada con más disimulación que modestia'.

19. Diego stated that he knew Arabic and could read it fluently; this is confirmed by Paolo Manuzio and Ambrosio de Morales in two dedicatory letters, which allow us more or less to reconstruct the early years of the life of Diego Hurtado de Mendoza and are reprinted in the appendix to González Palencia and Mele, *Vida y obras*, III, 271–75 and 470–74. On the study and dissemination of Arabic in Spain see Mercedes García-Arenal and Fernando Rodríguez Mediano, *The Orient in Spain: Converted Muslims, the Forged Lead Books of Granada and the Rise of Orientalism* (Leiden: Brill, 2013).

20. The catalogue of the library of Hurtado de Mendoza and the list of the Greek codices which he bought during his Venetian years may be found in Hobson, *Renaissance Book Collecting*, and Charles Graux, *Essai sur les origines du Fonds grec de l'Escorial* (Paris: Bibliothèque de l'École des Hautes Études, 1880).

21. The episode is recounted in Paolo Giovio, *Historiarum sui temporis*, ed. by Dante Visconti, 2 vols (Rome: Istituto poligrafico dello Stato, Libreria dello Stato, 1957), vol. II, chapter 34. See Spivakovski, *Son of the Alhambra*, p. 55, and Spivakovski, 'Lo de la Goleta', *Hispania*, 23 (1963),

366–79. On the 'supposed' donation of books, see Hurtado de Mendoza, *Guerra de Granada*, p. 96.

22. His official correspondence as Spanish ambassador in Venice is in AGS (Archivo General de Simancas), Estado, I-65–66. On his politics in Italy, see Michael J. Levin, *Agents of Empire: Spanish Ambassadors in Sixteenth-Century Italy* (Ithaca, NY: Cornell University Press, 2005), pp. 19–26 and 53–63.

23. See Pastore, 'Una Spagna antipapale?', pp. 69–73.

24. 'più presto atheo che altrimenti, come quello che haveva participatione di marano per natione et di lutherano per conversatione'. *I processi inquisitoriali di Pietro Carnesecchi (1557–1567)*, ed. by Massimo Firpo and Dario Marcatto, 2 vols (Vatican City: Archivio Segreto Vaticano, 1998–2000), II,1038.

25. Flavius Josephus, *Opera* (Basilea: Froben, 1544). On his activity as a printer in Basel, see Beat R. Jenny, 'Arlenius in Basel', *Basler Zeitschrift für Geschichte und Altertumskunde*, 64 (1964), 5–45.

26. Alfredo Serrai, *Conrad Gesner*, ed. by Maria Cochetti (Rome: Bulzoni, 1990), and, more recently, Fiammetta Sabba, *La 'Bibliotheca Universalis' di Conrad Gesner, monumento della cultura europea* (Rome: Bulzoni, 2012).

27. See Luciano Canfora, *Il Fozio ritrovato. Juan de Mariana e André Schott* (Bari: Dedalo, 2001), in particular pp. 9–28, and Canfora, *Convertire Casaubon* (Milan: Adelphi, 2002). The catalogue of books in Hurtado de Mendoza's library and the Greek codices acquired in the Greek years may be found in Hobson, *Renaissance Book Collecting*.

28. For a detailed description of the circulation of codices of the works of Sextus Empiricus before the 1562 Latin edition, see Floridi, *Sextus Empiricus*, in particular, for an account of the Latin translation by Páez de Castro, see pp. 70–72. Floridi, however, confuses Diego Hurtado de Mendoza with the Cardinal of Burgos, Francisco de Mendoza, who was Diego's cousin and also a famous collector.

29. Spivakovsky, 'Diego Hurtado de Mendoza and Averroism', *Journal of the History of Ideas*, 26.3 (1965): 307–26.

30. It was finished in 1545 and entitled *Mechanica de Aristotelis*. There is a modern edition published by Raymond Foulché-Delbosc, *Révue Hispanique*, 5 (1898), 365–405.

31. See the letter from Juan Páez de Castro to Jerónimo Zurita, dated 1 August 1545, in González Palencia and Mele, *Vida y obras*, I, 315–17.

32. 'que el confesor [Domingo de Soto] no está bien comygo porque defendí un doctor Herrera en Trento, a quien el deshonestamente tractava mal de palabras, llamándole en presençia de muchos obispos erege, y porque no le ayude ha imprimir a mi costa un comentario sobre la física de Aristótile, y porque en las disputas tenía siempre la parte de Averroe, el que no hiziera si penssara que havía de ser confessor, y porque sé más filosofía que él'. Diego Hurtado de Mendoza to Granvelle, 6 May 1549, in Hurtado de Mendoza, *Algunas cartas de don Diego Hurtado de Mendoza escritas 1538–1552*, ed. by Alberto Vázquez and R. Selden Rose (New Haven, CT, and London: Yale University Press, 1935), p. 124. There is a recent edition of Hurtado de Mendoza, *Cartas*, ed. by Juan Varo Zafra (Granada: Universidad de Granada, 2016).

33. The phrase was used for the first time by Francesco Guicciardini in a letter from Modena, dated 18 May 1521, in which he sarcastically commented on the fact that Machiavelli had been officially instructed to go to the general chapter of the Friars in Carpi in order to discuss matters of little importance. See Niccolò Machiavelli, *Opere. Vol. II Lettere legazioni e commissarie*, ed. by Corrado Vivanti (Turin: Einaudi, 1999), p. 377; the phrase was then recycled by Machiavelli in his reply to Guicciardini, ibid., p. 379.

34. On this image, see Pastore, 'From *Marranos* to *Unbelievers*: The Spanish Pecadillo in Sixteenth-Century Italy', in *Dissimulation and Deceit in Early Modern Europe*, ed. by Miriam Eliav-Feldon and Tamar Herzig (Basingstoke: Palgrave Macmillan, 2015), pp. 79–93.

35. Diego Hurtado de Mendoza to Granvelle, Rome, 23 May 1548, in Antonio Paz y Meliá, 'Cartas de don Diego Hurtado de Mendoza al cardenal Granvela (1548–1551)', *Revista de Archivos, Bibliotecas y Museos*, 3 (1899), 612–22.

36. '...no dan facultad para dispensar generalmente sino en particular per individuo, con cada uno de aquellos que quisieren confessar el error y yr a tomar penitençia y dispensación de los dichos

legados. Y es ynposible forçar a los yndividuos, porque si yo que soy un particular, no quiero yr a casa del legado y el otro y otro, no ha de andar el alguazil de casa en casa a forçarme que lo haga; así que el Emperador puede disponer en el general y el Papa dispensar; pero no puede forçar, ni es posible en millares de años dispensar con los yndividuos desta generalidad. Y esto hablo como philósopho, o como moro de Granada, o como marrano, que aun oy tiene la Ynquisiçión más que hazer en Spaña que el primer día'. Diego Hurtado de Mendoza to Granvelle, 1 September 1548, in Hurtado de Mendoza, *Algunas cartas*, pp. 119–20.

37. The manuscript is in the hand of Páez de Castro, with many corrections, addenda and notes in the margins. It was first described by Paul O. Kristeller, who saw it in H. P. Kraus's private collection, in his *Iter Italicum*, vol. v (London: The Warburg Institute; Leiden: Brill, 1990), p. 59. See also Floridi, *Sextus Empiricus*, pp. 70–72, and Arantxa Domingo Malvadi, *Bibliofilia humanista en tiempos de Felipe II. La Biblioteca de Juan Páez de Castro* (Salamanca: Universidad de Salamanca, 2011), pp. 298–99. In 2002, when Luciano Floridi wrote his book, the manuscript was up for sale and in 2003 part of it was auctioned at Sotheby's. My attempts to locate it have so far been fruitless. Part of the unbound volume is now in the Rare Book and Manuscript Library of the University of Pennsylvania; another part was auctioned by Maggs Bros in 2014.

38. 'Haré una prefación en que pondré grandes cosas de lo que toca a esta disciplina y del útil para nuestra religión, et effugiam vitiligatores'. Juan Páez de Castro to Jerónimo Zurita, 1 September 1549. Floridi's transcription, taken from Diego José Dormer, *Anales de Aragón* (Zaragoza: herederos de Diego Dormer, 1697) is slightly different. I quote the letter from the more reliable edition of Domingo Malvadi, *Bibliofilia humanista*, p. 386.

39. Diego Hurtado de Mendoza to Granvelle, 14 December 1549, in Hurtado de Mendoza, *Algunas cartas*, p. 145.

40. Titian, 'Portrait of Don Diego Hurtado de Mendoza', 1540, Pitti Gallery, Florence.

41. Hurtado de Mendoza, *Guerra de Granada*: 'cada nación, cada profesión y cada estado usa su manera de vestido, y todos son cristianos; y nosotros moros, porque vestimos a la morisca, como si trujésemos la ley en el vestido, y no en el corazón'. It was a very similar position (and it is a fact of great importance) to that of Núñez Muley, recently translated and edited by V. Barletta, see Núñez Muley, *A Memorandum for the President*. According to Javier Irigoyen García, *Moors Dressed as Moors: Clothing, Social Distinction and Ethnicity in Early Modern Iberia* (Toronto: University of Toronto Press, 2017), pp. 117–18, behind the Memorial there was not the voice of a downtrodden minority — the Moriscos — calling for a cultural revival, but that of the Marquis of Mondéjar, Captain General of Granada and an increasingly marginalized figure in the governance of that kingdom. I thank Trevor Dadson for drawing my attention to this book.

CHAPTER 6

Unbelief, Deism and Libertinism in Sixteenth-Century Italy

Luca Addante[1]

> Italy is full of libertines and atheists and people who do not
> believe in anything.[2]

This representation of the Italians — frequently cited in libertine studies — is a well-informed account (Gabriel Naudé) and refers to the first decades of the seventeenth century. Indeed, already in the sixteenth century a similar opinion was repeated throughout Europe by figures with diverse religious leanings and national backgrounds: Guillaume Farel, Melchor Cano, Gabriel Dupreau, Roger Ascham, Innocent Gentillet, Stanisław Reszka, and several others.[3] This vision was legitimized by the presence of radical-leaning Italian heretics who had spread across Europe, and by the dissemination of the audacious culture of the Renaissance. The uproar caused in Europe by Giulio Cesare Vanini and Tommaso Campanella consolidated this reputation in the seventeenth century, when Catholic apologists like François Garasse and Marin Mersenne denounced Italians such as Machiavelli, Pomponazzi, Cardano, Telesio, Vanini, Bruno, Campanella and others, grouping them together with the French libertine, deist and atheist thinkers they targeted in their works.[4] Such accusations were shared by the reformed churches: Dutch Calvinist Gijsbert Voet added to the list of culprits behind the spread of heretical Italian unbelief such figures as Lelio and Fausto Sozzini, Valentino Gentile and Bernardino Ochino, as well as the works of those who, like Campanella and Vanini, pretended to fight libertinism while in fact offering it an open door. Voet also wrote that in Italy, the insult 'good Christian' was used to call someone an idiot ('Vulgo Romae et in Italia, homines fatui et stolidi dicuntur boni christiani').[5]

Of course, these opinions echo religious divides and proto-nationalist sentiments, marked by racism and xenophobia. In the early modern period, negative stereotypes of Italians were a widespread phenomenon throughout Europe, and unbelief was one of the identifying features in the representations of Italians that circulated beyond the Alps, alongside their cunning and other less-than-edifying traits.[6] When reading contemporary sixteenth- and seventeenth-century accounts against Italians, one should therefore bear in mind the weight of stereotypical images from the spheres of politics and religion. Nevertheless, whereas such national traits are clearly exaggerated or outright made up, the issue of unbelief is another matter. Here, the distance between representation and reality is not so clear. While it is true, for example, that the period's anti-Machiavellianism was often deliberately founded on fabrications (as in the famous case of Gentillet's *Contre Machiavel*),[7] it is also undeniable that Machiavelli supported, in perfect libertine fashion, the political function of religion in *Discourses on the First Decade of Titus Livius*, not to mention his harsh critiques against Christianity.[8]

In fact, the ability for stereotype and reality to overlap is even easier to grasp if we shift our gaze from the champions of orthodoxy to its enemies: real heretics, libertines, sceptics, deists and atheists. We have seen the opinion of Naudé, and for his friend Guy Patin, Italy was 'a country of syphilis, poisonings and atheism, of Jews, of renegades and of the greatest swindlers of Christendom'.[9] A similar perception is voiced by the anonymous author of *De tribus impostoribus*, who commented that Italy, the 'principal seat of the Christian religion' ('principali religionis christianae sede'), was the land of 'many libertines' and 'many atheists' ('tot libertinos' and 'tot atheos').[10] Not to mention that other monument to unbelief, the *Theophrastus redivivus*, in whose *pantheon* the Italian culture of the sixteenth and seventeenth centuries played a key role.[11] After all, the Italians themselves provided much the same representations: Paolo Sarpi spoke of 'many atheists' and of the 'great atheism' that he saw all around him. Campanella described Italy as being full of 'Machiavellians' who were convinced 'that religion is the trickery of priests and monks to dominate the people'. Even Machiavelli himself had defined the Italians as being 'without religion' due to the influence of Rome's Christianity: 'Through the bad examples of that court, this land has lost all piety and religion'.[12] In short, the image of the unbelieving Italian was quite widespread during the early modern period, and not just among the learned classes. For example, Roman jester turned distiller Costantino Saccardino observed in the 1610s that 'the whole dovecote has opened its eyes' to the deceitfulness of religion.[13]

In the course of the seventeenth century, the representations of Italy as the land of unbelief were bolstered by the spread throughout Europe (from Poland to the United Provinces and England) of a movement with deep roots in Italy: the Unitarians or Socinians, whose name came from the Latin name (*Socinus*) of their founder, heresiarch Fausto Sozzini.[14] Another contributing factor to these images was without a doubt the progress of the Scientific Revolution, from Galileo Galilei to Academies such as the Accademia dei Lincei. Even years after Galileo's sentencing, in late seventeenth-century Naples, the Inquisition held the 'trial of the atheists', whose target was the Accademia degli Investiganti, successors to South Italian naturalism.[15] Not by chance, also at the turn of the eighteenth century, many innovators still held the stereotype that Italy was the home of unbelief. Similar perceptions are to be found throughout Pierre Bayle's notes to his *Dictionnaire historique et critique* — where one may read that 'most of the beautiful spirits and humanist scholars who shone in Italy [...] had no religion at all'[16] — as well as in the entries on figures such as Machiavelli, Sozzini and Pomponazzi.[17] This image of unbelieving Italians is even to be found lurking in Anthony Collins's *Discourse of Free-Thinking*, where one may read, 'For in ignorant Popish countries [first and foremost Italy, of course] where free-thinking passes for a crime, atheism most abounds'.[18] Naturally, similar representations abound in the field of apologetics, especially in the Lutheran world, where, for example, in *De dæmonologia*, the German writer Nathanael Falck's accusations of atheism lumped together figures such as Campanella, Vanini, Cardano and Telesio. For Falck, Italians, particularly through Italian naturalism, were at the origin of the many copies of real deists and atheists ('tam larga deistarum copia' and 'atheorum') to be found in France, in Germany, in England and in Holland, down to Thomas Hobbes and Baruch Spinoza, behind whom Falck saw the long shadow of the Italian unbelievers.[19] The theologian Johann Franz Budde, in much the same way, declared in *Theses theologicæ de atheismo et superstitione*, 'Italiam foecundam atheorum, aliorumque hominum impiorum, matrem esse'.[20] And the quotations could easily go on.

This sort image began to fade in the Age of Enlightenment proper, when the England of Newton and Locke, and the Holland of Grotius and Spinoza, became the new beacons that people turned to for a perspective on change, and no longer the Italy of the Renaissance or of heresy. However, this does not mean that Enlightenment thinkers ceased to be aware of unbelief in Italy during the early modern period. For example, Voltaire pointed out that during the Renaissance 'atheism was quite common in Italy'.[21] In Baron d'Holbach's *The System of Nature* (1770), one finds similar observations to those of Collins on the connection between repression and atheism, expressly in reference to the Italian Peninsula:

> They say that atheists are rarer in England and in the Protestant countries, where tolerance has been established, than in the Roman Catholic countries, where the princes tend to be intolerant, and are enemies of freedom of thought. In Japan, in Turkey, in Italy and especially in Rome, one finds many atheists. [...] It was Italy that gave rise to Giordano Bruno, Campanella, Vanini, etc.[22]

A similar sentiment is to be found in the *Encyclopèdie*'s entry on the *Unitaires*, by Jacques-André Naigeon, who saw in their ideas a privileged source of 'deism', of unbelief ('art de décroire'), of 'materialism' and of 'atheism'.[23] The same can be said of the Marquis of Condorcet, who reminded readers that, 'especially in Italy', there was 'a class of men who, rejecting all superstitions, indifferent to all forms of worship, subject only to reason, regarded religions as being human fabrications'.[24]

The image of an unbelieving Italy resounded even into the nineteenth century. Indeed, in the 'century of history', numerous lines of research attempted to add weight to this notion, laboriously negotiating the shift from images and myth to historiography. Many studies continued down this same path even as the twentieth century began to run its course. However, between the 1930s and '40s the situation changed completely, and historians swept such representations of Italians' unbelief under the carpet. And yet it is true that as late as 1939, in his *Eretici italiani del Cinquecento*, Delio Cantimori made a crucial contribution to the reconstruction of that world of religious dissidence, which he argued was at the root of freedom of religion, deism and the Enlightenment.[25] Nevertheless, shortly afterwards Lucien Febvre published *Le Problème de l'incroyance au XVIᵉ siècle* (1942), which was followed by René Pintard's *Le Libertinage érudit dans la première moitié du XVIIe siècle* (1943).[26] The co-founder of the *Annales* placed an enormous strain on the idea of sixteenth-century unbelief. For Febvre, in fact, the Europeans of the sixteenth century lacked the 'mental equipment', the very words and concepts, that would have enabled them to escape from the religious sphere, which he identified with Christianity. According to the French historian, 'in the sixteenth century, religion alone gave colour to the universe'; the 1500s were therefore 'a century that wants to believe', and that decidedly wanted to believe in Christianity: 'In the sixteenth century [...] Christianity was the very air people breathed in what we call Europe, and which was Christendom. It was an atmosphere in which man lived his life, his entire life'. All of the images of the apologists, all of the accusations of unbelief, were pure fabrications: the 'controversialists' knew that it was in their best interest 'to cry wolf'. As such, studies of the supposed unbelief of the sixteenth century had fallen for an 'anachronism' that was nothing more than a 'chimera'.[27]

While Febvre's book quickly consolidated a new paradigm, Pintard's book placed another strain on the idea of sixteenth-century unbelief. In the book's extraordinary ability to reconstruct the libertine networks of seventeenth-century France, it served to confirm Febvre's hypotheses by brushing aside the study of sixteenth-century libertines. Libertinism became a problem unique to seventeenth-century France that did not develop anywhere else in all the modern period.[28] Pintard's book — which was quickly applauded by Febvre[29] — was joined in 1950 by Giorgio Spini's *Ricerca dei libertini*. Spini was ostensibly drawing attention to the world of unbelief that had been left in the shadows of the two French historians' books. However, upon closer inspection, Spini too focused on the seventeenth century, and ruled out any relationship between libertine disbelief and the radical Reformation. Furthermore, Spini confirmed the idea that the libertines were a 'miscarriage', as they were scornfully termed by Febvre.[30]

Thus, by the second half of the twentieth century, historiography had silenced three centuries of decrying (or celebrating) Italian unbelief. And yet it is true that in the 1950s different opinions continued to circulate. Franco Venturi, for example, cited the heresies of the sixteenth century to explain the deistic conclusions of Piedmontese thinker Alberto Radicati, who lived between the seventeenth and eighteenth centuries.[31] And Henri Busson, in the second edition of his book *Le Rationalisme dans la littérature française de la Renaissance* (1957), proposed a full-fledged alternative paradigm to that of Febvre and Pintard. Through an investigation not without its limitations but broad in scope (from the Renaissance to the Radical Reformation), Busson demonstrated that the sixteenth century absolutely did have the words and concepts necessary for unbelief.[32] Nevertheless, by the 1960s the paradigm exemplified by Febvre and Pintard had reached the height of its success. It was aided by an essay by Alberto Tenenti published in 1963 in the *Annales*,[33] which proposed a typology of libertines. According to Tenenti, there was a first sixteenth-century libertinism that was anchored in heresy, the expression of a medieval and therefore Christian way of thought. This was followed by the *libertinage* of Jean Bodin's *Colloquium heptaplomeres*, which 'laid the foundations for the anti-

Christianity and deism of subsequent centuries',[34] and, above all, the libertinism exemplified by Pierre Charron, which Tenenti believed to have had much more historical weight. These last libertines corresponded to Pintard's *libertins érudits*.[35] Later on, in 1968, Paul Oskar Kristeller published *The Myth of Renaissance Atheism and the French Tradition of Free Thought*, seriously questioning so-called 'heterodox Aristotelianism', from Pomponazzi to Cremonini, which up till that point had been considered a privileged source for unbelief and freethinking.[36] Moreover, in the field of heresy studies itself (for example in George H. Williams's vast 1962 synthesis, *The Radical Reformation*)[37] the tendency was increasingly to make a clear-cut distinction between sixteenth-century heretics and real deists and atheists. For scholars like Williams, Servet, the Sozzini family, Castellio and the other key players in the Radical Reformation remained Christian theologians who were by no means unbelievers or the standard bearers of free thought.[38] In short, by the 1960s hardly anything was left of that image of unbelieving Italy that had been so widespread from the sixteenth century up to the early 1900s. Certain icons like Vanini or Machiavelli managed to hang on, but this was too little to lend credit to the representation of an Italy 'full of libertines and atheists'.

However, in the 1970s a new shift began to take shape, starting in the field of libertine studies. In 1970 Gerhard Schneider published *Der libertin*, a rich, close examination of historical semantics that expanded considerably on Busson's work, demonstrating that, at least as far as words were concerned, Febvre had been wrong. The terms needed in order to make unbelief conceivable in fact abounded in the sixteenth century.[39] Then, 1974 saw the publication of the proceedings of the conference *Aspects du libertinisme au XVIe siècle*, held in Sommières, which included several talks drawing attention to moments, movements and personages of a sixteenth-century libertinism that went beyond the divide between heresy and unbelief.[40] Later, in 1978, Jean Wirth published a ground-breaking essay, 'Libertins et épicuriens. Aspects de l'irréligion en France au XVIe siècle'. First of all, Wirth discovered, in the German Goliards' *Carmina burana*, a new way of interpreting the word 'libertine', with the connotation of loose morality, as opposed to the original Latin term (*libertinus*) meaning the son of a freed slave. Whereas up until then scholars had always repeated that John Calvin had been the first to alter the term's meaning, Wirth demonstrated that this change had already taken place in the Middle Ages. The historian also lingered on 1530s Strasbourg, and on authors such as Othon Brunfels and Agrippa von Nettesheim, showing how 'libertine' and 'epicurean' opinions and stances were to be found throughout the Christian world in the sixteenth century.[41] Meanwhile, in 1976 Carlo Ginzburg's extraordinary book *The Cheese and the Worms* was released, likewise criticizing Febvre's thesis and demonstrating, through the case of a miller known as Menocchio, that in the sixteenth century unbelief was widespread even in popular culture, and not just among the learned people.[42] To these important contributions of the 1970s we must add the 1978 Colloque de Strasbourg on *Croyants et sceptiques au XVIe siècle. Le Dossier des 'épicuriens'*; and François Berriot's 1976 study, *Athéisme et athéistes au XVIe siècle en France*.[43] These strong signs of revision were to be followed in the 1980s and

'90s by numerous other works. We might recall, as a symptom of these winds of change, David Wootton's essay, 'Lucien Febvre and the Problem of Early Modern Unbelief',[44] which was followed by the seminal volume directed by Wootton together with Michael Hunter, *Atheism from the Reformation to the Enlightenment*.[45] Within the latter, it is worth mentioning Nicholas Davidson's essay, 'Unbelief and Atheism in Italy 1500–1700',[46] although his study is not without its limitations. In particular, Davidson's numerous and interesting cases of unbelief appear disjointed, presented almost in juxtaposition to one another. Still, the essay was valuable in that it reopened the issue of an 'Italy full of libertines and atheists', with a methodologically fertile approach centred on observing phenomena of unbelief across a broad spectrum of categories and time periods, overcoming the boundaries between paradigms and disciplines through examples ranging from the Renaissance to the Radical Reformation.

The same years also saw scholars revisit libertinism, signalling a full-blown crisis for Pintard's paradigm. Even some who appeared to follow the same path as Pintard, such as Tullio Gregory and Françoise Charles-Daubert, in fact took a different stance on several key issues, such as the importance of libertinism in the development of the Scientific Revolution and the Enlightenment.[47] Moreover, especially starting with the reprinting of Richard Popkin's *History of Scepticism* in 1979, devout readings of the impious libertines began to circulate, under the category of 'fideistic scepticism', which made it possible to trace back to Christian origins even the *libertins érudits* of Pintard: Naudé, La Mothe le Vayer, Gassendi etc.[48] Also of note is Louise Godard de Donville's book *Le Libertin des origines à 1665. Un produit des apologètes*, in which the author went so far as to regard the libertine as a mere 'fictional being' made up by apologetics.[49] Another element that has contributed to the crisis of Pintard's paradigm is the recent discovery that the first modern shift in the meaning of the word 'libertine' dates back to the 1520s, in the Republics of Siena and Florence, twenty years prior to Calvin's anti-libertine treatises.[50] In the meaning that the term had in the Tuscan context (where the libertines were the most radical partisans of freedom), there have emerged stark differences with respect to the former dominant paradigm, according to which the libertines were rebels (or even impostors) in the religious sphere, but had absolutist leanings in the political sphere, positioning themselves against the people. However, both in Florence and in Siena, the libertines were the most extreme republicans, standing on the side of the people, thus making clear that the dominant paradigm no longer holds water.[51]

A long essay written in 2003 and published some years later in *Les Dossiers du Grihl* by Jean-Pierre Cavaillé signalled the end of the interpretive approach embodied by Pintard.[52] Cavaillé, who teaches at the École des hautes études en sciences sociales, is one of the leading names in the new trends in libertine studies. Through historical investigation, editions of texts, conceptual operations, and studies on personages, books, groups and identifying aspects such as simulation and dissimulation, today Cavaillé is one of the key figures behind a new way of understanding the libertines, and, more generally, dissidence, with an interdisciplinary approach applied over the long term and on a European level, going far beyond the rigid barriers of the schools of Febvre and Pintard. What emerges is the irreducibility of libertine phenomena to just one model, but also a number of constants, such as unbelief, the theory of religion being imposed by politics, and the centrality of the problem of freedoms, already conceived in a modern sense.[53] Lastly, one sign regarding this renewal of the late twentieth century has to do with heresy studies and new developments in the field of the Italian Reformation. In particular, Massimo Firpo's crucial research into Juan de Valdés and Valdesianism has demonstrated, among other things, how the teachings of this Spaniard in exile in Naples may in fact have had very radical consequences. With his Nicodemism, with his esoteric and gradual method, with his spiritualism based on an extreme reduction of the tenets of Christianity, on the devaluation of Scripture and on the emphasis of individual freedom, Valdés's religious ideas could have resulted (and in fact did result) in an extreme radicalism.[54]

Based on these premises and on the new directions in dissidence studies — which continued full force into the millennium — I have conducted various research projects on the Valdesian movement and on religious radicalism in the early modern period. I will be referring to them throughout the rest of this chapter, as I believe they contribute to proving that it was by no means impossible to leave Christianity in the sixteenth century. Indeed, following Valdés's death (1541), a sizeable group of people in Naples gathered around one of his close disciples, the Spaniard Juan de Villafranca, and set about sharing and promoting ideas that could hardly be defined as Christian.[55] Villafranca's method for converting his disciples was directly based on that of Valdés. This was true both in terms of his prudently gradual manner, as well as the first topic he insisted on with neophytes: justification through faith, the first step everyone had to take in order to form part of the Valdesian movement. Rather than transmitting doctrines, Villafranca, like his master, sowed the seeds of doubt and pushed his disciples toward personal reflection, guiding in Socratic fashion those he thought were prepared to taste 'God's secrets'.[56] Ready to step in as soon as his interlocutor had become riddled with doubt, he went on to arouse further problems, leading the novice step by step along a path that led further and further away from Christian dogma — a path that, according to first-hand accounts, snaked 'from one conclusion to the next'.[57] If the justification for sins had been given by Christ through his sacrifice, there was no place for indulgences, confessions, priests, fasting, Purgatory, prayer to the saints and the Virgin Mary, Jubilees, extreme unctions, worship of images, etc. Having pushed the novice to reach this distance from Catholicism, clearly Lutheran in origin (but not without its variants), the master left the person to reflect for several months. However, after this pause for reflection, Villafranca got back to work, leading the initiate toward radical positions. A first step was to raise doubts about the Eucharist, held to be a mere symbol, contrary to Luther and in accordance with Ulrich Zwingli. After this, the master moved on to full-fledged radical conclusions, casting doubt successively on the Trinity, the divinity of Christ, the virginity of Mary, the existence of Hell and the veracity of certain parts of the Gospels. At the end of the process, one might ask what was left of Christianity, whittled down to a set of ethical teachings.

Given the systematic doubt and individualism that Villafranca was pushing for, it is obvious that each follower might then continue past the purview of his teachings. In fact, there is evidence that this is exactly what happened. Whereas Villafranca had doubts as to certain passages of the Gospels, his disciple Girolamo Busale — a Calabrian born to *marranos* from Zaragoza, inheriting from them his leadership skills — went so far as to state that the entire New Testament was false, in addition to contesting the messianic nature of Jesus Christ, according to developments that were also clearly influenced by his roots in the converso world (from which Valdés himself in fact hailed). And, whereas Villafranca taught (as did Valdés) that the souls of the dead slept, and that only those of the elect would rise again on Judgment Day, while those of the damned would wither away in an 'eternal death', some, such as Giulio Basalù, pushed their doubt even further, altogether denying the immortality of the soul. This conclusion was drawn from the teachings of Villafranca and Busale, which had set him on the path away from all religion. As he himself would testify, appearing spontaneously before the Inquisition in Venice:

> Having taken up the opinion that after the body dies everyone's soul dies, every opinion crumbled, believing that all religions were made up by men in order to persuade men to lead good lives [...].
> I came to deny [...] all forms of religion, whether Christian, Jewish or anything else [...].
> I scoffed at everything [...]: I denied the Mass, Baptism, unction, the ecclesiastic religions and all of the sacraments, the creation of the world. I scoffed at Moses and the prophets, at David and at all the stories and said that in all religions, not just Christianity, there were miracles, and that Christ was a good man who taught people to lead good lives. And I said that concubinage was not a sin, and in short I scoffed at everything.[58]

It was a systematic demolition of every foundation of the faith, a libertine unbelief that is not some isolated case, given that others connected to these circles shared analogous opinions. One such person was the Neapolitan Tobia Citarella, a friend of Basalù whose ideas were even discussed on the streets of Venice, where the latter was tried along with some of his companions. In fact, in the mid-1500s some radical Valdesians migrated to the territories of the Venetian Republic, where they came into contact with the Anabaptist sect, made up of hundreds of women and men largely of humble social extraction: retailers, ragmen, bakers, blacksmiths, dyers, tailors, shop boys, butchers, etc. The man in charge of the Valdesians was Busale, who had shown his openness to the Anabaptists' ideas by being tactically rebaptized, while at the same time putting in place a strategy that, before long, would place him in a hegemonic position with respect to the Italian Anabaptists, converting the majority of them to Valdesian radicalism. Busale and his companions' attempt was squarely contested by the Anabaptist leader Tiziano, and the conflict between the two, and their respective followers, led to a synod held in Venice in 1550. The Venetian assembly sealed the Valdesians' victory, ratifying the key points of Villafranca's teachings: the Trinity was a chimera, Christ was not God but a man, Mary was not a virgin, Hell did not exist, and there were a number of doubts surrounding the Scriptures. However, among the Venetians, there were some who took a step even further. Silvio Rasonier — one of the Anabaptists from Vicenza, who were some of Busale's most fervent partisans — argued 'that faith is nothing more than man's opinion, insofar as the person imagines and constructs it in their brain, such that [Silvio] did not hold that one faith was truer or better than the other'. Therefore, as to Revelation, Rasonier exhibited the same lack of belief, given that 'he did not believe the Scriptures had been made by God's spirit, neither the New one, nor the Old one'.[59] Once again, these were ideas that strayed far from the banks of Christianity, spilling over into outright disbelief — anything but 'crying wolf', as Febvre argued.

Of course, one could object that Febvre's research was limited to the reality in France; however, the *Annales* co-founder held that his analyses were valid for all of Europe. Besides, in France too the same ideas circulated, spread by Italian religious exiles, who, starting in the 1550s, invaded Europe en masse to flee the Inquisition. Particularly in Lyon, between roughly 1560 and 1564, there was a sizeable group of dissidents who defined themselves as 'Deists'.[60] This is the first instance of a term with a long future ahead of it, which is a relevant piece of information in and of itself, and indicates how the links between religious dissidents in the 1500s and the developments in unbelief are much more closely connected than the historiography had previously held. Upon closer inspection, even Febvre was aware of the Lyonese origin of the term 'Deist', but he limited it to a single source, the Calvinist Pierre Viret, which allowed him to downgrade these first Deists to his category of 'crying wolf'. Closer scrutiny, however, has shown that multiple contemporaneous sources mention these Deists, both from the Reformed side and from the Catholic side. These sources reveal that all the Deist in Lyon denied the Trinity and that Christ was God, and there was a part of them who even denied the immortality of the soul, divine Providence and Revelation, declaring that what was written about Christ in the Scriptures was mere 'fantasies and dreams', with positions defined at times at 'Epicurean', if not outright 'atheist'. While there were surely some French people among the Deists active in Lyon, the key roles fell to various Italians: several protagonists from Cantimori's book, starting with Fausto Sozzini and others, including the Calabrian Valentino Gentile. The latter was a Valdesian propagandist in Italy who later took refuge in Geneva for religious reasons. There he joined those who had opposed the death sentence against Miguel Servet pushed by John Calvin (1553), taking part in the anti-Trinitarian propaganda. When he, too, was tried by Calvin and sentenced for his opinions (1558), he fled Geneva to spread religious radicalism alongside his Italian companions in France, Poland, Moravia, Transylvania and Austria, during which time he was arrested on several occasions, but each time managed to escape, until finally being sentenced to death in Bern in 1566, for which reason he was referred to as a 'second Servet'. Among the leading Deists in Lyon, Gentile belonged to the more radical wing, denying the divinity of Christ, his role as mediator, the immortality of the soul, resurrection and Judgment Day, in addition to having little regard for Revelation.[61]

As we have seen, the world of sixteenth-century Italian heresy witnessed several cases of people abandoning Christianity altogether, ceasing to believe. And the connections between these heretics and the culture of the Renaissance are worth highlighting. In fact, it was from the circles of Italian heretics that the first Latin translation of Machiavelli's *The Prince* was produced.[62] Several of these heretics had a background in humanism, not only the famous case of Celio Secondo Curione, but even Gentile himself, who was also from this milieu, as well as a number of other heterodox thinkers.[63] As already noted by Cantimori, behind the Italian heretics' systematic doubt regarding faith, the philological tradition of critical doubt from Lorenzo Valla to Erasmus of Rotterdam played a crucial role. This goes to show what great harm there is in maintaining a separation between research into heretical movements and into Renaissance schools of thought, as they are phenomena which are by no means impermeable to one another. Moreover, recent studies increasingly reveal the broad dissemination of Valdesian ideas, as well as heterodox opinions in general, within the Renaissance Academies (in Modena, Florence, Siena, Padua, Rovigo, Piacenza, Rome, etc.);[64] and in this case too the Kingdom of Naples stands out, with the Accademia Pontaniana, Accademia degli Ardenti and Accademia Cosentina.[65] Valdés himself frequented the Accademia Pontaniana, as did other Valdesians. In fact, a striking case of crossover between the heretical and Renaissance worlds is to be found in the last president of the Pontaniana, no less: the nobleman and jurist Scipione Capece. He had shared the positions of Busale's followers, not believing in the Trinity, the divinity of Christ, the virginity of Mary or the existence of Hell, in addition to doubting the veracity of the New Testament. However, like Basalù and others, Capece took a step further. In *De principiis rerum* (1546), a poem in the style of Lucretius which had a European circulation, he argued that the soul was material, and that the origin of all things was a material element: *aer* (something along the lines of the Stoics' and Epicureans' *pneuma*), indicative of a pantheistic stance inspired by ancient philosophy and by the Valdesians' destruction of the tenets of Christianity.[66]

The Valdesians also found their way into another Neapolitan *accademia*, the Ardenti, which, as with the Pontaniana, was quickly closed down by the authorities.[67] The circulation of Valdesian ideas even affected the Accademia Cosentina, led for a period by the satirical poet Niccolò Franco (later sentenced to death by the Inquisition), and then, most importantly, by the naturalist philosopher Bernardino Telesio, whose work would end up on the Index of forbidden books. Under Franco, the Cosentina was marked by distinct anticlerical leanings, by somewhat libertine manners, and of course by heterodox discourses as well. Later, during the period of Telesio's leadership, a young member of the Accademia, future physician, philosopher and religious exile Agostino Doni, was sentenced by the Inquisition (1568) in Cosenza for not believing in the immortality of the soul. These accusations spread to Telesio himself, who in 1570 was forced to defend himself against the attacks on the first edition of his *De rerum natura* (1565). The philosopher wrote that among the 'other statements counter to religion' he had been accused of, 'we can deduce that the soul is mortal'.[68] Thus, Telesio and other members of the Accademia must have had connections to the Valdesians, and, indeed, in the 1550s and 1560s Cosenza witnessed a series of arrests by the Inquisition, which revealed just how far

Valdesianism had penetrated into academic, noble, and ecclesiastic circles. Among the various aristocrats forced to recant were two brothers of Bernardino Telesio, the Abbot Paolo and the Baron Valerio. A third brother, Archbishop of Cosenza Tommaso Telesio, was threatened with arrest by the Holy Office after covering up the investigations opened in his diocese.[69]

These are just a few examples of the crossover in sixteenth-century Italy between the Radical Reformation and the Renaissance, as well as the reciprocal influences pushing in the direction of unbelief. In my opinion, it is a line of research that merits further study, given that relationships between these two worlds have also emerged in the case of Giordano Bruno.[70] They likewise show up in another of the greatest representatives of the late Renaissance: Tommaso Campanella,[71] who in 1599 encouraged a revolt aimed at proclaiming a 'republic' in Calabria and instituting 'natural freedom' with a 'new law'. In the religious sphere, more can be learned about this last concept thanks to the extensive documentation on the trials of Campanella and his numerous accomplices over their failed attempt at revolution. One of the most well-informed witnesses explained that, amidst the preparations for the rebellion, Campanella had given full voice to his unbelief:

> He said [...] that the sacrament of the Church [sc. the ecclesiastic order] was merely a matter of State [...]; as for the sacrament of the altar [sc. the Eucharist] he said it was meaningless and one would have to be mad to believe in it [...]. He went on to say that the other sacraments were not ordered by Christ. He also said of the crucifix that it was insane to worship [it]; that Mary Magdalene and Martha [...] received [Jesus], being his lovers; he moreover denied the virginity of the Virgin Mary. He said that the venereal act was licit, and said by way of example that, just as man can use an arm or a foot, he can use his member, and when I chided him and argued back through the authority of Scripture, he told me: you ass, you believe everything that is written [...]. And when I mentioned that Moses had crossed the Red Sea, he said that it was not true, because it was not that the sea had parted into two parts, but because the sea was subject to ebb and flow, and that in that moment there was an ebb tide, and that was how Moses crossed. He went on to say that he did not believe [that there] were demons, but that they are just madness [...]. He also said that [the body of] Christ was stolen and not resurrected, and that [...] it is a custom of lawmakers not to let their bodies be found: as did Moses, Pythagoras and others, so did Christ. And when I questioned him as to whether he believed in Christ's prophecies, he said that he had predicted the arrival of the Antichrist, and that this Antichrist was the Roman Pope. He also said that the Trinity is a chimera, a depiction of a body with three heads, and when I provided a number of reasons to the contrary, he told me: go join the devil, you ass. He also told me that the Pope's authority was usurped authority and tyranny, and this is all I have heard first-hand.[72]

This testimony is corroborated by a number of others, which incidentally reveal the degree to which Campanella's libertine propaganda had the support of another Dominican from Calabria: his close friend Dionisio Ponzio. Another accomplice testified that, at a meeting, 'brother Dionisio [...] began to discuss matters of God and of faith', setting the stage for the philosopher's remarks:

And in the discussion Campanella said that there was no such thing as God, only nature, and we have given to nature the name of God; and that there is no such thing as Paradise or Hell, but that it is all made up to scare the people into believing what [the powerful] want them to. And even that there was no such thing as demons, and he said to me: who has ever seen a demon? What is a demon, can you eat it? [...] He also said [...] that the sacraments and all of the things of the Church are made up by men, not God, and that they are mere reasons of State.[73]

Several other defendants confirmed that these were the ideas held by Ponzio himself (and not just Ponzio): he too dismissed the 'sacraments' as 'reason of State'; he said that Jesus 'is nothing and it's all a lot of bollocks ['coglionerie']'; 'that Christ was not really God and that he was a bum; and that while Christ did die, he was not resurrected; his body was stolen and he did the same thing as others who had given laws to the people, who did not let their bodies be found'. Dionisio described the Virgin Mary as 'black [...] but nice', 'denying her virginity'; and he added 'that there was no such thing as Purgatory, Hell or Paradise', 'and that when we die that's it, because the soul was a spirit, meaning a fleeting thing, and that we end up like stones'. In short, for Dionisio, too, 'the only God was nature'. All of this was peppered by varying sorts of blasphemy, from pummelling the crucifix to sticking the host in his private parts to demonstrate that it was not the body of Christ.[74]

Thus, the 1500s came to a close in such a peripheral region as Calabria with the spread of these libertine opinions and practices, which pushed the bounds of unbelief all the way to what Spinoza would call *Deus sive natura*. This is anything but a warped mirror of an Italy 'full of libertines and atheists', steeped in more than a century of doubts regarding the tenets of Christianity. An Italy where (as in other parts of Europe) that 'atmosphere' that Febvre saw as inescapably Christian, was actually host to winds — even gusts — of change that considerably altered the air quality.

Notes to Chapter 6

1. To Massimo Firpo, for his 70th birthday.
2. 'L'Italie est pleine de libertins et d'athées et de gens qui ne croyent rien'. Gabriel Naudé, *Naudæana et Patiniana, ou Singularitez remarquables* (Amsterdam: vander Plaats, 1703), p. 46, see also p. 8 and *passim*.
3. Guillaume Farel, *Le Glaive de la parole veritable* (Geneva: Girard, 1550), pp. 222–24; Melchor Cano, *De locis theologicis* (Salamanca: Matías Gast, 1563), p. 312; Roger Ascham, *The Scholemaster* (London: John Daye, 1570), p. 30; [Innocent Gentillet], *Discours sur les moyens de bien gouverner [...]. Contre Nicolas Machiavel [...]* ([n.p], 1579); Gabriel Dupreau (Prateolus), *Elenchus hæreticorum omnium [...]* (Köln: Quentelium, 1605), pp. 71–74, 141, 261, 488–90, 501 and *passim*; Stanisław Reszka, *De atheismis et phalarismis evangelicorum [...]* (Naples: Carlino, Pace, 1596), pp. 303–04, 308–09, 336, 344–46, 360–61 and *passim*. For more examples see J. Roger Charbonnel, *La Pensée italienne au XVIe siècle et le courant libertin* (Paris: Champion, 1919), p. 10 ff. and *passim*; Giorgio Spini, *Ricerca dei libertini [...]* (Florence: La Nuova Italia, 1983), p. 7 ff. and *passim*; Nicholas Davidson, 'Unbelief and Atheism in Italy, 1500–1700', in *Atheism from the Reformation to the Enlightenment*, ed. by Michael Hunter and David Wootton (New York: Clarendon Press, 1992), pp. 55–85.
4. François Garasse, *La Doctrine curieuse des beaux esprits de ce temps [...]* (Paris: Chappelet, 1623), pp. 43–45, 144–47, 247, 516, 650–53, 785–86, 852–58, 913–15, 986–89, 1007–10, 1013–16 and *passim*;

Marin Mersenne, *Quæstiones celeberrimæ in Genesim [...]* (Paris: Cramoisy, 1623), coll. 130–31, 279, 379–86, 392–96, 492, 496, 939–42, 1152, 1164 and *passim*; Mersenne, *L'Impieté des deistes, athees et libertins de ce temps [...]* (Paris: Bilaine, 1624), pp. 175, 210–39 and *passim*.

5. Gijsbert Voet, *Selectarum disputationum theologicarum pars prima* (Utrecht: Waesberge, 1648), p. 217, see also pp. 114–226 (*De atheismo*), pp. 643–44, 774, 852, 858, 863–64 and *passim*.

6. See Jean-François Dubost, *La France italienne. XVIe–XVIIe siècle* (Paris: Aubier, 1997), pp. 307–28 and *passim*; Henry Heller, *Anti-Italianism in Sixteenth-Century France* (Toronto: University of Toronto Press, 2003).

7. See Pamela D. Stewart, *Innocent Gentillet e la sua polemica antimachiavellica* (Florence: La Nuova Italia, 1969); Sydney Anglo, *Machiavelli: The First Century. Studies in Enthusiasm, Hostility, and Irrelevance* (New York: Oxford University Press, 2005), pp. 271 ff., 417 ff. and *passim*.

8. Niccolò Machiavelli, *Discourses on the first Decade of Titus Livius*, English trans., in *Machiavelli: The Chief Works and Others*, ed. and trans. by Allan H. Gilbert, 3 vols (Durham, NC, and London: Duke University Press, 1999), I, 223 ff., 330–31, 339–41, 422–23 and *passim*. On Machiavelli and religion see Emanuele Cutinelli-Réndina, *Chiesa e religione in Machiavelli* (Pisa and Rome: Istituti editoriali e poligrafici internazionali, 1998).

9. 'Un pays de vérole, d'empoisonnements et d'athéisme, de juifs, de renégats et des plus grands fourbes de la chrétienté'. Guy Patin, *Lettres choisies de feu monsieur Guy Patin [...]*, 3 vols (Paris: Petit, 1662), I, 265.

10. *De tribus impostoribus*, ed. by Germana Ernst, 2nd edn (Naples: La Scuola di Pitagora, 2009), p. 44.

11. *Theophrastus redivivus*, ed. by Guido Canziani and Gianni Paganini, 2 vols (Florence: La Nuova Italia, 1981–82).

12. Paolo Sarpi, *Lettere ai protestanti*, ed. by Manlio D. Busnelli, 2 vols (Bari: Laterza, 1931), II, 123, 127; Tommaso Campanella, *L'Ateismo trionfato, overo Riconoscimento filosofico della religione universale contra l'antichristianesmo macchiavellesco*, ed. by Germana Ernst, 2 vols (Pisa: Edizioni della Normale, 2004), I, 5 and *passim*; Machiavelli, *Discourses*, p. 228.

13. Carlo Ginzburg, 'The Dovecote has Opened its Eyes: Popular Conspiracy in Seventeenth-Century Italy', in *The Inquisition in Early Modern Europe: Studies on Sources and Methods*, ed. by Gustav Henningsen and John Tedeschi (DeKalb: Northern Illinois University Press, 1986), pp. 190–98 (p. 193).

14. For some of the most recent studies on Socinianism, see *Fausto Sozzini e la filosofia in Europa [...]*, ed. by Marta Priarolo and Elena Scribano (Siena: Accademia degli Intronati, 2006); *Socinianism and Arminianism: Antitrinitarians, Calvinists and Cultural Exchange in Seventeenth-Century Europe*, ed. by Martin Mulsow and Jan Rohls (Leiden: Brill, 2005); *Faustus Socinus and his Heritage*, ed. by Lech Szczucki (Kraców: Polska Akademia Umiejetnosci, 2006); Sarah Mortimer, *Reason and Religion in the English Revolution: The Challenge of Socinianism* (Cambridge: Cambridge University Press, 2010).

15. Luciano Osbat, *L'Inquisizione a Napoli. Il processo agli ateisti 1688–1697* (Rome: Storia e Letteratura, 1974).

16. 'La plupart des beaux esprits et de savans humanistes qui brillèrent en Italie [...] n'avaient guère de religion'.

17. Pierre Bayle, *Dictionnaire historique et critique*, 16 vols (Paris: Desoer, 1820), XIV, 22 ('Takiddin'), note A. See also the entries on 'Machiavel' (vol. X), 'Pomponace' (vol. XII), 'Socin' (vol. XIII) and *passim*.

18. [Anthony Collins], *A Discourse of Free-Thinking [...]* (London: [n. p.], 1713), p. 105.

19. Nathanael Falck, *Dissertationes quatuor de dæmonologia [...]* ([Wittenberg]: Schultz, 1694), pp. 2–5.

20. Johann Franz Budde, *Theses theologicæ de atheismo et superstitione [...]* (Jena: Joan. Felic. Bielckium, 1717), p. 111.

21. Voltaire, *Œuvres complètes de Voltaire, Correspondance générale*, vol. IX (Paris: Carez, Thomine et Fortic, 1822), p. 288, letter to the Marquis de Villevieille, 26 August 1768.

22. 'Les athées sont, dit-on, plus rares en Angleterre et dans les pays protestants, où la tolérance est établie, que dans les pays catholiques romains, où les princes sont communément intolérans

[*sic*] et ennemis de la liberté de penser. Au Japon, en Turquie, en Italie, et surtout à Rome, on rencontre beaucoup d'athées. [...] C'est d'Italie que sont sortis Jordano Bruno, Campanella, Vanini, etc'; Jean Baptiste de Mirabaud [Paul Henry Dietrich d'Holbach], *Système de la nature ou loix du monde physique et du monde moral*, 2 vols ([Amsterdam]: [Rey], 1770), II, 357–58.

23. Jacques-André Naigeon, 'Unitaires', in *Encyclopèdie [...]*, vol. XVII (Neufchastel: Faulche, 1765), pp. 387–401.

24. 'Une classe d'hommes qui, rejetant toutes les superstitions, indifférents à tous les cultes, soumis à la raison seule, regardaient les religions comme des inventions humaines'. Condorcet, *Esquisse d'un tableau historique des progrès de l'esprit humain*, ed. by Alain Pons (Paris: Flammarion, 1988), pp. 196–97. See also Condorcet, 'Notes sur Voltaire', in *Œuvres complètes de Condorcet*, vol. VII (Brunswick, Paris: Vieweg, Henrichs, 1804), p. 62 ('Athées').

25. Delio Cantimori, *Eretici italiani del Cinquecento e altri scritti*, ed. by Adriano Prosperi (Turin: Einaudi, 1992).

26. Lucien Febvre, *Le Problème de l'incroyance au XVIe siècle. La Religion de Rabelais* (Paris: Albin Michel, 1942); René Pintard, *Le Libertinage érudit dans la première moitié du XVIIe siècle* (Geneva: Slatkine, 2000).

27. Febvre, *Le Problème de l'incroyance*, pp. 126–27, 308, 324, 419–28 and *passim*.

28. Jean-Pierre Cavaillé, 'Libertinage, irréligion, incroyance, athéisme dans l'Europe de la première modernité (XVIe–XVIIe siècles). Une approche critique des tendances actuelles de la recherche (1998–2002)', in *Les Dossiers du Grihl* (2007) <http:/dossiersgrihl.revues.org/279> [accessed 21 April 2017]; Luca Addante, '"Parlare liberamente". I libertini del Cinquecento fra tradizioni storiografiche e prospettive di ricerca', *Rivista storica italiana*, 123.3 (2011), 927–1001.

29. Lucien Febvre, 'Aux origines de l'esprit moderne. Libertinisme, naturalisme, mécanisme', chapter in his *Au cœur religieuse du XVIe siècle* (Paris: SEVPEN-Bibliothèque générale de l'École pratique des hautes études, 1957), pp. 37–58.

30. Febvre, *Au cœur religieuse*, p. 348. Cfr. Spini, *Ricerca dei libertini*, pp. 41–42; Addante, 'Parlare liberamente', pp. 937–40.

31. Franco Venturi, *Alberto Radicati di Passerano* (Torino: Utet, 2005), pp. 189–205.

32. Henri Busson, *Le Rationalisme dans la littérature française de la Renaissance* (Paris: Vrin, 1971); Busson, 'Les Noms des incrédules au XVIe siècle', *Bibliothèque d'Humanisme et Renaissance*, 16 (1954), pp. 273–83.

33. Alberto Tenenti, 'Libertinismo ed eresia fra la metà del Cinquecento e l'inizio del Seicento', chapter in his *Credenze, ideologie, libertinismi tra Medioevo ed Età moderna* (Bologna: Il Mulino, 1978), pp. 261–85.

34. 'Preparato le basi dell'anticristianesimo e del deismo dei secoli successivi'.

35. Tenenti, 'Libertinismo ed eresia', pp. 275–76, 281. See Addante, 'Parlare liberamente', pp. 945–47.

36. Paul O. Kristeller, 'The Myth of Renaissance Atheism and the French Tradition of Free Thought', *Journal of the History of Philosophy*, 6.3 (1968), pp. 233–43 (note that the original essay dates from 1953).

37. George H. Williams, *The Radical Reformation* (Kirksville, MO: Sixteenth Century Journal Publishers, 1992).

38. See Luca Addante, 'Dal radicalismo religioso del Cinquecento al deismo (e oltre). Vecchie e nuove prospettive di ricerca', *Rivista storica italiana*, 127.3 (2015), 770–807.

39. Gerhard Schneider, *Der Libertin. Zur Geistes und Sozialgeschichte des Bürgertums im 16. und 17. Jahrhundert* (Stuttgart: Metzler, 1970).

40. *Aspects du Libertinisme au XVIe Siècle. Actes du Colloque International de Sommières* (Paris: Vrin, 1974).

41. Jean Wirth, 'Libertins et épicuriens. Aspects de l'irréligion en France au XVIe siècle', chapter in *Saint Anne est une sorcière et autres essais* (Geneva: Droz, 2003), pp. 25–67; see also Wirth, 'La Fin des mentalités', *Les Dossiers du Grihl* (2007) <http://dossiersgrihl.revues.org/284> [accessed 21 April 2017].

42. Carlo Ginzburg, *The Cheese and the Worms: The Cosmos of a Sixteenth-Century Miller* (Baltimore, MD: Johns Hopkins University Press, 1980).

43. *Croyants et sceptiques au XVIe siècle. Le Dossier des 'épicuriens'*, ed. by Marc Lienhard (Strasbourg: Libraire Istra, 1981); François Berriot, *Athéisme et athéistes au XVIe siècle en France*, 2 vols (Lille: Presses Universitaires de Lille, 1984); see also Berriot, *Spiritualités, hétérodoxies et imaginaires. Études sur le Moyen âge et la Renaissance* (Saint-Étienne: Université de Saint-Étienne 1994).

44. David Wootton, 'Lucien Febvre and the Problem of Unbelief in the Early Modern Period', *The Journal of Modern History*, 60.4 (1988), 695–730.

45. *Atheism from the Reformation to the Enlightenment*, ed. by Michael Hunter and David Wootton (New York: Clarendon Press, 1992).

46. Davidson, 'Unbelief and Atheism in Italy'.

47. Cavaillé, 'Libertinage, irréligion, incroyance, athéisme'.

48. Richard H. Popkin, *The History of Scepticism: From Erasmus to Spinoza* (Berkeley and Los Angeles: University of California Press, 1979).

49. Louise Godard de Donville, *Le Libertin des origines à 1665. Un produit des apologètes* (Paris, Seattle and Tübingen: Biblio 17, Papers on French Seventeenth Century Literature, 1989).

50. Jérémie Barthas, 'Retour sur la notion de libertin à l'époque moderne. Les Politiques libertins à Florence, 1520–1530', *Libertinage et philosophie au XVIIe siècle*, 8 (2004), 115–34; Barthas, 'Machiavelli e i 'libertini' fiorentini (1522–1531). Una pagina dimenticata nella storia del libertinismo. Col Sermone sopra l'elezione del gonfaloniere del libertino Pierfilippo Pandolfini (1528)', *Rivista storica italiana*, 120.2 (2008), 569–603; Luca Addante, 'Radicalismes politiques et religieux. Les Libertins italiens au XVIe siècle', in *Libertin! Usage d'une invective aux XVIe et XVIIe siècles*, ed. by Thomas Berns, Anne Staquet and Monique Weis (Paris: Classiques Garnier, 2013), pp. 29–50.

51. See Jean-Pierre Cavaillé, *Les Déniaisés. Irréligion et libertinage au début de l'époque moderne* (Paris: Classiques Garnier, 2014), pp. 358–59, 403–05, 497–98 and *passim*.

52. Cavaillé, 'Libertinage, irréligion, incroyance, athéisme'.

53. Among the great many works by J. P. Cavaillé, see *Dis/simulations. [...] Religion, morale et politique au XVIIe siècle* (Paris: Honoré Champion, 2002); Cavaillé, *Postures libertines. La Culture des esprits forts* (Toulouse: Anacharsis, 2011); Cavaillé, *Les Déniaisés*. For other contributions, see 'Les Dossiers de Jean-Pierre Cavaillé', in *Les Dossiers du Grihl* <https://dossiersgrihl.revues.org/261> [accessed 19 April 2017].

54. Among Massimo Firpo's numerous studies on Valdesianism, see *Juan de Valdés and the Italian Reformation* (Farnham: Ashgate, 2015).

55. For more on what follows, see Luca Addante, *Eretici e libertini nel Cinquecento italiano* (Rome and Bari: Laterza, 2010).

56. 'Los secretos de Dios'.

57. 'Di consequentia in consequentia'.

58. 'Essendo intrato in opinione che morto il corpo morisse l'anima di ognuno, ogni opinione andò per terra, credendo che tutte le religione fossero inventione di homini per indur li homini al ben vivere [...]'. 'Veni a negar [...] ogni sorte de religion, così christiana come ebrea et ogn'altra'. 'Mi ridevo d'ogni cosa [...]: negavo la messa, el battes[i]mo, l'untion, le religion ecclesiastiche et tutti li sacramenti, la creation del mondo. Me ridevo di Moysè et delli profeti, de David et de tutte le historie et dicevo che in ogni religion, oltra la christiana, si vedeva miracoli, et che Christo era stato homo da bene che haveva insegnato el ben viver. Et dicevo el concubinato non esser peccato, et in conclusion mi ridevo d'ogni cosa'. Addante, *Eretici e libertini*, pp. 30–31.

59. 'Che la fede non è altro che l'oppenione de l'huomo, secondo che la persona se l'immagina e fabrica nel suo cervello, di maniera che [Silvio] non afferma[va] l'una fede essere più vera né migliore dell'altra'; 'non crede[va] le Scritture essere stà[te] fatte per lo spirito di Dio, né la Nova né la Vecchia'. Addante, *Eretici e libertini*, pp. 86–116 and *passim*. On the synod (or council) of Venice, the key document is Pietro Manelfi, *I costituti di don Pietro Manelfi*, ed. by Carlo Ginzburg (Chicago, IL: The Newberry Library; Florence: Sansoni, 1970).

60. For more on what follows, see L. Addante, *Valentino Gentile e il dissenso religioso nell'Europa del Cinquecento. Dalla Riforma italiana al radicalismo europeo* (Pisa: Edizioni della Normale, 2014), pp. 162–84 and *passim*. See also Addante, 'Dal radicalismo religioso del Cinquecento al deismo'.

61. Addante, *Valentino Gentile*, pp. 196–98 and *passim*.

62. Leandro Perini, 'Gli eretici italiani del '500 e Machiavelli', *Studi storici*, 10.4 (1969), 877–918.

63. Cantimori, *Eretici italiani*; Silvana Seidel Menchi, *Erasmo in Italia, 1520–1580* (Turin: Bollati Boringhieri, 1987).

64. Firpo, *Juan de Valdés*, pp. 64–66 and *passim*.

65. Addante, *Eretici e libertini*, pp. 61 ff., 139–43 and *passim*; Addante, *Valentino Gentile*, pp. 42 ff., 68 ff.

66. Addante, *Eretici e libertini*, pp. 61–76 and *passim*.

67. Addante, *Valentino Gentile*, pp. 78–79.

68. 'Altre propositioni contra la religione'; 'si può cavar ch'io metto l'anima mortale'.

69. Addante, *Valentino Gentile*, pp. 70–100 and *passim*.

70. Addante, *Valentino Gentile*, p. 286; Addante, *Eretici e libertini*, pp. 163 and *passim*.

71. See Addante, *Tommaso Campanella. Il filosofo immaginato, interpretato, falsato* (Rome and Bari: Laterza, 2018), pp. 153–57, 226–27 and *passim*.

72. 'Disse [...] che il sacramento della Chiesa [*scil.* l'ordine ecclesiastico] era solo per raggion di Stato [...]; in quanto al sacramento dell'altare [*scil.* l'eucaristia] disse che è una bagatella et pazzia a crederlo [...]. Disse ancora che gli altri sacramenti non sono stati ordinati da Christo. Disse anche del crucifisso che è una follia di adorar[lo]; che Madalena et Martha [...] ricevevano [Gesù] ché erano sue inamorate; negava inoltre la virginità di Maria vergine. Dicea che era lecito l'atto venereo, et portava in questo essempio che, come l'homo po' usar un bracio o un piede, po' usar il membro, et io reprendendolo et argumentandoli con authorità di Scrittura in contrario, esso mi dicea: come sei asino tu, credi ogni cosa che si scrive [...]. Et io proponendoli che Mosè passò il Mare Rosso esso disse che non era vero, perché non fu che il mare si partì in due parti, ma perché quel mare patisce flusso et reflusso, et che allora patì reflusso et così passò Mosè. Mi disse ancora che non credeva [che ci] fussero gli demonij, ma che sono follie [...]. Disse anche che [il corpo di] Christo fu robato et non resuscitò, et che [...] è costume di legislatori di non lasciar trovar i loro corpi: come fece Mosè et Pitagora et altri, così fece Christo. Et interrogatolo io si credeva alle profetie di Christo, esso disse che havea predet[t]o la venuta dell'antichristo et che questo antichristo era il papa romano. Dicea anco che la trinità è una chimera, et così si dipinge un corpo con tre teste, et io portando molte raggioni in contrario, esso mi dicea: và col diavolo che sei un asino. Disseme anche che l'autorità del papa era authorità usurpata et tirannia, et questo è quanto ho sentito di bocca propria'. Luigi Amabile, *Fra Tommaso Campanella. La sua congiura, i suoi processi e la sua pazzia*, 3 vols (Naples: Morano, 1882), III, 200–01.

73. 'Et il Campanella nel ragionamento dicea che non c'era Dio ma solo la natura, et noi a questa gli havemo messo nome Dio; et che non c'è paradiso né inferno, ma che tutto questo sono fintioni per far credere con la paura alli populi ciò che vogliono [i potenti]. Come anco che non ci siano diavoli, et me dicea: chi ha mai visto gli diavoli? cosa è diavolo, si mangiano? [...] Dicea anche [...] che gli sacramenti et tutte le cose della Chiesa sono inventioni de homini et non di Dio et che sono solo ragioni di Stato'. Amabile, *Fra Tommaso Campanella*, III, 209; see also pp. 250, 394 and *passim*. For more on Ponzio, see L. Addante, 'Ponzio, Francesco, in religione Dionisio', in *Dizionario biografico degli Italiani*, vol. LXXXIV (2015) <http://www.treccani.it/enciclopedia/ponzio-francesco-in-religione-dionisio_(Dizionario-Biografico)/> [accessed 21 April 2017]; Addante, *Tommaso Campanella*.

74. '[Che Gesù] non è niente e sono tutte coglionerie'; 'Che Christo non fusse vero Iddio et che era un pezzente; et che se bene Christo morì, non resuscitò, ma il corpo suo fu robato et fece come altri che davano lege alli populi, che non lasciavano trovar gli corpi loro'; 'nigra [...] sed formosa'; 'negando la sua virginità'; 'che non ci era purgatorio, né inferno né paradiso'; 'et che morendo noi non c'è più niente, perché l'anima era un spirito, o sia cosa fugace, et che restamo come pietra'; 'non ci era altro Dio che la natura'. Amabile, *Fra Tommaso Campanella*, vol. 3, pp. 204–05, 238–41, 248, 256.

PART III

❖

Shifting Certainties in the Baroque

CHAPTER 7

All Things to All People: Baltasar Gracián, Dissimulation and the Question of Interpretation

Jeremy Robbins

What are we to make of Peter Paul Rubens's letter of 15 July 1626 to the French humanist, Pierre Dupuy, in which the artist talks of his grief following the death of his wife?[1] His grief is sharply evident throughout, his pain at his loss clear. Neo-Stoic thought infuses the letter, with references to Fate as an expression of the Supreme Power, to reason, and to Stoic equanimity, which Rubens says he does not pretend to attain, as well as being evident in the direct quotation from Tacitus and the Latin paraphrase from Seneca (the letter's other quotation is from the *Aeneid*). But there is a total and striking 'lack of any reference to God or to Catholicism'.[2]

Few would doubt Rubens's faith — and this is, of course, a letter from a learned artist to a humanist, and as such is shaped by humanist epistolary expectations and Classical sentiment. But where the Jesuit Baltasar Gracián is concerned, a writer very much a product of the same humanist culture and one similarly imbued with the Neostoic culture of his time, the absence of overt references to religion, which are otherwise so prevalent in Spanish contemporary moral and political writing, is deemed to be more problematic and symptomatic of a secular drift, if not an outright scission between morality and Christianity. And on the grounds that the norm was to convey morality through explicit Christian injunctions, a suggestion of immorality is often mapped onto this.

The core interpretative issue, then as now, is whether and when an absence is pregnant with meaning. In seventeenth-century terms, is Gracián's work an example of dissimulation, passing over in silence what cannot be openly expressed? And an affirmative answer here raises the further question of whether what is being concealed is something irreligious or immoral.

Gracián's deviations from contemporary discursive norms — that is to say, from the norms of contemporary Spanish moral and political discourses — can be broadly summarized: a relative absence of explicit references to God, of Biblical citations, of positing moral lessons by means of Christian *exempla* (whether from sacred history, Church history or the lives of the saints), of establishing a moral position through clear and unambiguous Christian injunctions. Human history and actions are rarely explicitly viewed through the lens of Christian teaching and only sporadically through the providential unfolding of God's plan, which was otherwise typical in seventeenth-century Spain. In brief, what marks Gracián out is his lack of overt religiosity. When set against Gracián's problems with the Jesuits that led him to being disciplined for disobedience in 1658 and to seek to leave the Society,[3] these discursive differences have occasioned very divergent interpretations of him as a writer and thinker: from the orthodox to the tacitly subversive, from the moral to the immoral.

With the singular exception of *El Comulgatorio* (1655), a series of Christian meditations that form a volume of spiritual exercises, the secularity of Gracián's texts and of his moral thought is widely acknowledged by critics. In terms of the *Oráculo manual y arte de prudencia* (1647), its existence and effects are neatly stated by Aurora Egido: 'in separating the divine from the human, Gracián establishes an autonomous field, one open to multiple readings according to situation and circumstance'.[4] Egido notes that within this work there is an 'ethical sense removed from the prevailing religiosity of the Society of Jesus',[5] and that, in contrast to the aphorisms in a work such as Fray Tomás Francés de Urritigoiti's *Idea de la prudencia, alivio de la fortuna* (1661), Gracián's are marked by 'profundity, secularism, universality and novelty'.[6] The result is that in Gracián's œuvre 'the process of secularity carried out by humanism reaches its highest point, clearly delineating the line that separates the divine from the human'.[7]

In a similar vein, Emilio Blanco has commented that Gracián's concept of prudence is itself fundamentally distinct from earlier traditions:

> *Art of Prudence.* Given this title, the frequency of references to this virtue is hardly surprising; [prudence] is no longer the virtue presented in Classical and Patristic authors but becomes rather a practical knowledge of how to live.[8]

And he tacitly endorses a view of the work's secular morality when he asserts that 'the Jesuit appears to be firmly in favour of an autonomous morality rooted in empirical observation of human nature, one which consciously dispenses with all theological support'.[9] Aranguren, whom Blanco cites in support of this view, writes in turn of Gracián's *prudencia mundana* [mundane or worldly prudence]. This he views as 'purely instrumental, neither good nor bad, but morally neutral'.[10] He argues that 'what happens is that [means] are simply placed in the service of an end which is good and, at the same time, the most convenient or useful', and that consequently Gracián's outlook is not Machiavellian, but rather syncretistic.[11] Gracián is held to thus deform Thomistic prudence by making it 'a virtue that is purely worldly in focus, simply functional and practical, and by tending to reduce it to caution, simulation and astuteness; but this deformation is never such as to entirely remove all similarity to traditional prudence'.[12]

Battlori in contrast takes an altogether different stance towards Gracián's secularity:

> There is no reason to believe, indeed far from it, that *El Comulgatorio* is a work cunningly written and published by Gracián to silence those who accused him

of writing 'frivoulous works' unworthy of a member of a religious order [...] I believe the opposite: that this is his most sincere work. In his other works, one can always perceive a *feigned* and deliberate literary stance, an effort to escape his context, to make his thought non-transcendent, to *feign* a secular morality and a naturalist deism.[13]

This tacitly sets out the various interpretative difficulties: not simply, or so much, the sharp difference in content and focus between the avowedly Christian *Comulgatorio* and the other works, as for Batllori, but rather how to interpret his *oeuvre*'s secularity and its clear deviation from standard discursive norms. Is such secularity genuine, or simply feigned, as Batllori has it? More broadly, what *is* secularity, and what might a manifestation of this mean in the early modern period? For there is an important difference between 'secular' in the sense of not being overtly concerned with religion, as indeed most of Gracián's work is not, and 'secular' as meaning avowedly non-religious or profane. And should one distinguish between secularity and the Jesuit worldliness that so many contemporaries claimed (whether sincerely or for their own political objectives) to find morally dubious and shocking? Which in turn raises the question of what ways (Jesuit) worldliness feeds off and into the initial phases of the rise of secularism.

Whilst a consideration of secularity is not my primary focus here, these questions are of course intimately connected with the broader issue of what is not said in Gracián and how to assess its hermeneutical significance. In looking at this, I wish to say something about Gracián and specifically about his collection of 300 aphorisms, the *Oráculo manual*. But I also wish to use Gracián as an example of a modern critical blind spot that the rise of interest in scepticism has occasioned: the nature of belief. My underlying suggestion is that we need to attend to the question of belief, as much as to the fraught and complex voicing of epistemological and sceptical doubt. For just as doubt is complex and multi-various, so is belief, and the history of one cannot be written without an assessment of the other.[14]

How does one interpret the significance of absence? And when studying writers in Catholic Spain, how does one move from acknowledging their pragmatic recommendations to deviate from absolute moral prohibitions such as that against lying — as both Machiavellian and anti-Machiavellian writers recommend — to seeing such recommendations as a sign of immorality, or as an expression of 'unbelief', when neither can be signalled overtly?

To complicate the puzzle of a writer such as Gracián, there are three interconnected dimensions that pose hermeneutical obstacles. The first of these is the broad philosophical tradition from Plato onwards of esoteric writing, that is to say, of philosophers writing for the few and therefore concealing what they are truly saying from the many. This is the subject of a recent study by Arthur Melzer who labels such esoteric writing 'philosophy between the lines'.[15] Gracián certainly advocates this approach, though whether to any end other than the strategic one of not alienating the majority is left unstated:

> *Think with the few and speak with the many.* To want to go against the current is as impossible for the wise as it is easy for the reckless. Only a Socrates could

> undertake this. [...] Truth is for the few; deception is as common as it is vulgar.
> The wise cannot be identified by what they say in public, since they never speak
> there with their own voice but following common stupidity, however much
> their inner thoughts contradict this.[16]

(As an aside, it is interesting to see Gracián here mentioning Socrates, the
figure with whom Melzer begins his study of the tradition of esoteric writing.)
This keeping-one's-true-thoughts-to-oneself is in turn linkable with a second,
specifically Christian dimension, namely Jesus's answer to the apostles' question as
to why he taught through parables, which was that he did so precisely so as not to
be understood by all (Matthew 13. 10–13). Such esotericism *a lo divino*, as it were,
sanctioned texts with a surface and a hidden message comprehensible to only an
intended audience. The third obstacle is a specifically Baroque one, and one very
pronounced in Spain in the seventeenth century, and that is the prizing of lexical,
conceptual and syntactical difficulty as a central component of the aesthetic of
wit. Gracián, of course, is synonymous with *agudeza*, and his prose, not least in
the *Oráculo*, embodies to an exceptional degree the difficulties associated with
the *conceptista* style. The cult of difficulty dominant in Baroque poetics is part of
the horizon of expectations, and further problematizes interpretation: to state the
obvious, what, *if anything at all*, do linguistic difficulty and the avoidance of the
expected through the pursuit of the unexpected mask? How does one discern when
or if style becomes part of the esoteric arsenal of concealment of a secret or hidden
agenda?

In the arena of moral, and in particular political treatises in the seventeenth
century, these critical issues and interpretative difficulties are brought into sharp
focus in contemporary attitudes towards dissimulation which was posited by many
as the acceptable face of non-truth telling, often in counter distinction to lying
(*mentira*) or deceit (*engaño*).[17] The concept of lying has a long and complex history in
Christian theology and morality, as does the accommodation early sought to square
the Biblical commandment against bearing false witness — the bed-rock of the
categorical Christian imperative against lying — with the pragmatic realization that
such an absolute prohibition caused danger and difficulty, and indeed seemed to fit
ill with occasions when Jesus appeared to be economical with the truth. The overall
picture in Western thought, and in theology in particular, has been examined
recently by Dallas Denery, so I will simply touch upon several key texts here.[18]

The Patristic and Scholastic positions both categorically prohibited lies and,
through careful analysis of concepts and choice of lexis, opened up the possibility
of acceptable non-telling of the truth. Thus Augustine in his *Contra mendacium*
(10:23) declared that it was not lying when the truth was hidden by simply not
being spoken.[19] This point was taken up by Aquinas who not only cites Augustine's
point approvingly ('one may, however, prudently mask the truth, as Augustine
explains'),[20] but elaborates on this, introducing the notion of simulation and when
this is and is not acceptable:

> a person lies verbally when he gives expression to what is not true, not when
> he is silent about what is true, a course sometimes permissible. Similarly,

there is deception when a person expresses what is not true through the
meaning of actions or objects, but not when he refrains from conveying what
is true. Consequently, it is possible for one to conceal his own sin without
deceiving.[21]

It is this context that the early modern period inherited and extended in the wake of
Machiavelli's 'infamous' advice on the necessary and acceptable feigning of virtue
in chapter 18 of *Il Principe*:

Since a ruler has to be able to act the beast, he should take on the traits of the
fox and the lion [...] Hence a sensible leader cannot and must not keep his word
if by doing so he puts himself at risk [...] If all men were good, this would be
bad advice, but since they are a sad lot and won't be keeping their promises to
you, you hardly need to keep yours to them. [...] So, a leader doesn't have to
possess all the virtuous qualities I've mentioned, but it's absolutely imperative
that he seem to possess them.[22]

Whether directly read or known only by reputation, this chapter was the most
discussed and contested by Catholic moralists and theorists of state as they attempted
to craft what Bireley calls the 'Counter-Reformation Prince'.[23] Machiavelli's point
about the duplicity of mankind — readily linked in Christian thought to the
consequences of the Fall and of the inherently sinful nature of humans — and the
inevitable failure awaiting any naively candid individual given this reality, was
echoed as a truism by moralists of whatever stripe.[24]

In Spain, there developed a complex but unsystematic lexis of deception to
distinguish the acceptable from the unacceptable. The problem was not simply that
there were those who found all forms of deviations from the truth unacceptable,
but that there was no uniformity of definition or usage amongst those who, taking
their lead from Augustine and Aquinas, accepted that some form of deception was
permissible and necessary in the Machiavellian world of contemporary political
life. This lexically rich field included *mentira*, *engaño*, *fraude*, *artificio*, *traza*, *simulación*,
disimulación, and *astucia*, with *mentira*, *engaño* and *simulación* being consistently
prohibited, *disimulación* the most acceptable form of concealing the truth, and *astucia*
the most conflictive term, sometimes being deemed acceptable, but more often
and by most writers, not.[25] The distinction between simulation and dissimulation
succinctly expressed by Torquato Accetto — 'dissimulation involves not letting
things be seen as they are. One simulates what is not, and dissimulates what is' —
was one broadly shared by the majority of theorists across Europe.[26]

On occasion Gracián condemns dissimulation, as when he writes that:

The astute draw fine distinctions with their much applauded sophistry, so
as not to offend reason or reason of state. But the steadfast man will judge
dissimulation a form of treason, pride himself more on tenacity than on
shrewdness, and always be found on the side of truth. (29)[27]

But elsewhere he certainly approves of its use, as is clear from a number of
aphorisms, as when he advises the reader:

Conceal your wishes. [...] The most practical kind of knowledge is dissimulation;
whoever plays their hand openly runs the risk of losing. (98)[28]

Or when he alludes with broad approval to one of the clichés of Baroque political theory, Louis XI's tag, 'he who doesn't know how to dissimulate, doesn't know how to rule' (*qui nescit dissimulare, nescit regnare*):

> A large part of ruling is dissimulation; you should pass over most things that occur among your family, your friends and particularly your enemies. (88)[29]

Squaring this circle of contradiction was easily done for most early modern moralists: whilst in an ideal world dissimulation would be wrong because unnecessary, in a fallen one it becomes acceptable because necessary for (social and political) survival — and success.

But are the practices of dissimulation used in his writing of the text? Is Gracián deploying, in other words, the lures and decoys he posits as necessary stratagems in misleading and thus besting an adversary? These are delineated in the drama of hermeneutical combat set out in aphorism 13:

> *Declared and undeclared intentions.* Life is a campaign against malice. Shrewdness fights by strategically using such intentions. It never does what it seems it will, taking aim, but only to mislead. It dextrously insinuates one thing, and then does what is completely unexpected, always careful to throw others off track. It gives out its intention so as to guarantee a rival's attention, and immediately does the opposite, triumphing with the unexpected. But penetrating intelligence, ever attentive, is prepared for this, cautiously lies in wait for it, understands the opposite of what it's intended to understand, and immediately detects any attempt at concealment. It passes over declared intentions, and waits for the real ones that lie beneath, and even the ones beneath those. Simulation increases when its artifice is discovered, and tries to deceive by using truth itself. It changes its game by changing its stratagem; its artifice is then its very lack of artifice, its astuteness based on total candour. Observation comes along and, recognizing this perspicacious strategy, uncovers the darkness beneath this veil of light. It deciphers the true intention, all the more hidden for being so simple. In this way, the craftiness of Python fights the candour of Apollo's penetrating rays.[30]

Gracián here offers a sharp portrayal of the feints and counter-feints as he sees it of all human — and not simply political or courtly — interaction. His choice of language conforms to the moral evaluation of terms typical of contemporary usage, *simulación, artificio, engañar, astucia*, all being portrayed negatively. And this suggests on which side of the moral debate over deception Gracián is positioning himself — unless, of course, and this is my point here, he is using such stratagems to say the opposite of what he appears to be saying...

The key point is, how would we know? For dissimulation is like *trompe l'oeil*: that is to say, if successful, we wouldn't recognize it, and if unsuccessful, then it has, in part, failed. This very Baroque paradox is subtly made by Accetto:

> Essentially, dissimulation is a profession that one cannot profess except to oneself [...] Of the excellent dissimulators that there have been and are, there is no evidence at all.[31]

Here, then, is the hermeneutical crux.

This leads us to a broader point made repeatedly in the seventeenth century following the rise in interest in Academic scepticism and Pyrrhonism at the end of the sixteenth century. The argument that our critical vision is inevitably and unavoidably distorted by our limited perspective applies self-evidently to the reader and the critic. But if our vision *is* distorted, then we (may) see what we (largely) want to see. The obvious example here is the turn in twentieth-century readings of Gracián from viewing him as orthodox to (in some form) heterodox. As the earlier cultural desideratum, indeed one might argue the expectation or need, for orthodoxy has receded, so the preference for a more 'subversive' Gracián has proven largely irresistible.

Gracián's world is profoundly dualistic, as indeed is Baroque culture itself, the binary terms *ser/parecer*, *engaño/desengaño*, reason/passion, *sabio/vulgo* profoundly informing his thought both conceptually and structurally. The dominance of such binary opposites encourages what one might call an anamorphic reading of Gracián — as of Baroque culture more generally — as clearly and categorically *either/or*. But in terms of belief and doubt, a reading polarized between binary opposites is a distortion of the reality, the lived experience, of both, for the distance between unquestioning belief at one extreme and absolute disbelief at the other is substantial and the positions between them numerous. Furthermore, one needs to avoid conflating religious belief and religious practice (including here expression): there is no ready or simple equation between the latter and the former, as the Golden Age itself needed reminding through such figures as Enrico in Tirso de Molina's *El condenado por desconfiado*, whose utterly depraved and immoral life nevertheless ends with his salvation. And similarly, of course, outward signs of religious belief and conformity do not necessarily signal sincerity, as Molière's Tartuffe and the Golden Age obsession with hypocrisy testify.

So how might one find where Gracián lies here? The Jesuit contexts in which he studied, trained, worked and lived establish a major horizon of expectation. So far, so obvious. And yet what is surprising here is that for the Jesuit Gracián, this Jesuit context is *the* unexplored context of his work. Indeed, perhaps the most understudied aspect of Gracián is the very fact that he *was* a Jesuit.[32] That is to say, precisely a member of an order whose critics accused it — as did some Jesuits themselves from its very inception — of having excessively *worldly* concerns, and thence of being immoral.[33] What should be self-evident is rarely followed: to interpret Gracián requires interpreting Jesuit culture. The problem of Gracián is often, in large part, the problem of how the Jesuits, specifically their behaviour and outlook, were perceived.

For Gracián is on the 'Jesuit spectrum', and at the worldly extreme. But that extreme is — or can certainly be read as — essentially Ignatian, that is to say, as an orthodox Jesuit stance, one that characterizes the Jesuits in the sixteenth and seventeenth centuries. Indeed, it would be provocative, though not too far from the truth, to argue that in some ways Gracián is actually more specifically Ignatian in mindset than many seventeenth-century Spanish Jesuits.

And of course the point here is that extreme worldliness need not preclude belief;

moral pragmatism and flexibility — accommodation to contingent circumstances being an essential part of 'our way of proceeding' (*nuestro modo de proceder*), as the Jesuit *Constitutions* and Ignatius's letters make crystal clear — were characteristic of Jesuit practice and Jesuit casuistry. But what was orthodox for Jesuits was shockingly unorthodox for many, not least — but certainly not only — Pascal and the Jansenists, who viewed it as immoral because they saw it as morally lax.[34] As so often in the early modern period, the issue is not so much one of belief or unbelief, but whether belief — and the morality this supposedly underpins — was held by others to be valid or acceptable or orthodox.

The greatest Ignatian debt in the *Oráculo* is found in aphorism 251, which is striking, and therefore most definitely accentuated, in its brevity:

> *Human means must be sought as if there were no divine ones, and divine ones as if there were no human ones.* The rule of a great master. No further comment is necessary. (251)[35]

The 'great master' is Ignatius who was repeatedly identified in Jesuit works with this approach to acting in the world.[36] (One may of course debate whether or how far Gracián neglects its spirit.) It is worth remembering here that although the Jesuits were an order, they were not a monastic order, and this ecclesiastical distinction, the being *in* the world, profoundly shaped their ethos — to the extent that the Society was often perceived as secular in the modern sense of the word.[37] The Jesuit Ribadeneira emphasized the stress Ignatius put on this dimension of the Society:

> [Ignatius] used to say that he who was not fit for the world was not fit for the Society, and he who had aptitude to live and thrive in the world was fit for our order.[38]

To exemplify the Jesuit and specifically Ignatian dimension I want very briefly to consider two contentious areas that may seem, to a modern reader, the most scheming and worldly. The first of these is the idea of being all things to all people:

> *Know how to be all things to all people.* A discreet Proteus: with the learned, learned, and with the devout, devout. A great art to win everyone over, since similarity creates goodwill. Observe each person's temperament and tune yours to it. Whether with a serious or a jovial person, go with the current, undergoing a transformation that is politic — and essential for those in positions of dependency. Such vital subtlety requires great ability. It is less difficult for the universal man with his wide-ranging intellect and taste. (77)[39]

It is easy now not to notice, not least because it is very typically not signalled by Gracián as it would have been by most other Golden Age moralists if making the same point, that the opening phrase which is expanded on across the aphorism is a Biblical injunction based on Paul's letter to the Corinthians:

> And unto the Jews I became as a Jew, that I might gain the Jews; to them that are under the law, as under the law, that I might gain them that are under the law; to them that are without law, as without law, (being not without law to

God, but under the law to Christ) that I might gain them that are without law.
To the weak became I as weak, that I might gain the weak: I am made all things
to all men, that I might by all means save some. (1 Corinthians 9. 20–22)[40]

And Paul's 'omnibus omnia' became a categorically Ignatian principle, one that
Ignatius repeats in his letters and that Ribadeneira, who knew Ignatius, cites as a
feature of his *modo de gobierno*.[41]

Gracián is clearly expanding the applicability of the principle to life in general, and
not simply applying it to actions in pursuit of conversion as Paul and then Ignatius
were applying it. (Though as an aside, it is perfectly reasonable to extrapolate from
Ignatius's letters that for him the notion of *omnibus omnia* was meant also as a general
principle of conduct for Jesuits.) But that does not necessarily mean that Gracián
countenances immorality. This is clear in his recommendation of accommodation.
Accommodation, itself obviously linked with the idea of being all things to all
people, was central to Jesuit practice, as already mentioned, and not surprisingly
therefore it is a major feature of Gracián's art of prudence:

> *Live as circumstances demand.* Ruling, reasoning, everything must be opportune.
> Act when you can, for time and tide wait for no one. To live, don't follow
> generalizations, except where virtue is concerned, and don't insist on precise
> rules for desire, for you'll have to drink tomorrow the water you shunned today.
> There are some so outlandishly misguided that they expect all circumstances
> necessary for success to conform to their own whims, not the reverse. But the
> wise know that the loadstar of prudence is to behave as circumstances demand.
> (288)[42]

Accommodation was central to Jesuit praxis because it was central to Ignatius's *modus
operandi*; as Ribadeneira records in his official and hugely influential biography of
the saint (published in 1572 in Latin, and then in a modified version in Spanish
in 1583), 'He used to say that anyone engaged with affairs mustn't accommodate
these to themselves, but rather themselves to those affairs'[43] — a saying that still
had currency in the mid-seventeenth century, being found for example in Daniele
Bartoli's 1650 *Vita* of Ignatius.[44]

The second contentious issue, one that is intimately connected with accommodation, is the dialectic between the few and the many — which returns me
to the issue of esoteric writing mentioned earlier. This idea is repeated across the
aphorisms, most explicitly in aphorism 43, already cited, and in aphorism 133:

> *Better mad with the crowd than sane all alone*, say politicians. For if everyone is
> mad, you'll be different to none, and if good sense stands alone, it will be
> taken as madness. To go with the flow is so important. The greatest form of
> knowledge is, on occasion, not to know, or to affect not to know. You have
> to live with others, and most are ignorant. To live alone, you must be either
> very like God or a complete animal. But I would modify the aphorism and say:
> better sane with the majority than mad alone. For some want to be unique in
> their fantastical illusions.[45]

It is easy to read this pragmatism as unprincipled and calculating. But it has a certain
Biblical precedent (Ecclesiasticus 4. 32) and is an early modern cliché found in

writers whose Christian beliefs and morality have always been far above suspicion, such as the virulently anti-Jesuit Pascal who writes in a similar vein to Gracián that:

> You must conceal your opinion, and judge all correspondingly, but speak along with the masses.[46]

Knowing this can, and I think should, put a very different inflection on Gracián.

This returns us to the question I asked at the outset, namely does Gracián's advocacy of speaking with the many indicate or suggest that he himself is dissimulating? The strikingly odd and critically neglected fact is that, in fact, Gracián does *not* follow this piece of advice repeated in different ways across the *Oráculo*; he does not 'write with the many' in one key respect, for his work is precisely *not* larded with explicit Biblical and religious injunctions found in virtually all other Spanish writers. This may be because he distinguishes writing from speaking; that is to say, that he distinguishes audiences, for it is one thing when one is communicating with the *vulgo*, another with the 'elite' who one assumes are the *Oráculo*'s intended readers. Nevertheless, his not writing as the majority did and as the majority might expect certainly indicates that he was not motivated by fear, one of Melzer's explanations for the use of esotericism (something he labels defensive esotericism).

Assuming for the moment that Gracián did have an ulterior motive for not explicitly and emphatically grounding his work in Christian teaching and Biblical precepts, in not dressing up his aphorisms as was standard and expected, we would need to ask if was he simply particularly daring in not hiding this. Or was his Spanish readership particularly obtuse in not seeing the hermeneutic significance of what was immediately apparent, namely the absence of what is consistently overtly signalled in the vast majority of Spanish political and moral works? Or was it simply that this was not, and was not perceived as, problematic, and his Spanish readers could accommodate the text's atypical discourse within the parameters of contemporary Christian morality? That is to say, they did not see anything odd or anything hidden here. Although it is a very rough-and-ready marker of critical reception, the Augustinian Gabriel Hernández's comment in his *aprobación* to the *Oráculo* that the aphorisms contain nothing against the Christian faith and do not pose any obstacle to this is not without significance here.[47]

Can one conclusively resolve what this writing about prudence in ways that are so untypical of Spanish moral and political discourse signifies? Ultimately no, for the deliberate cultivation of ambiguity that is occasioned largely by the avoidance of overt Christian markers, of standard Spanish Baroque religiosity, means the reader is left to ascertain Gracián's intentions and, more importantly, both the morality of the work and the relevance of its teaching to whatever particular set of circumstances one is confronted with. The reader of Gracián's art of prudence is left, in other words, to exercise prudence precisely as this Christian virtue was conceptualized by Gracián and by his contemporaries, namely as the virtue whose function was the choice of the morally correct course of action. As I have argued elsewhere, absence of the expected defamiliarizes a clichéd discourse and is thereby in theory a potential means of activating prudence, albeit that this is obviously something of a high-risk strategy.[48] Aphorisms as a form are both a symptom and an expression of fragmented knowledge in a sceptical world, and they require active absorption, thought, and application: they are isolated blocks to be built into a course of action. In the *Oráculo*, they express and in turn are activated by prudence, as signalled in the full title of the collection, as well as by Gracián's recurrent use of the Scholastic concept of synteresis, the only technical term defined within the work (aphorism 96).[49] Gracián takes to heart what Lipsius spells out, namely that circumstances are ever mutable and thus prudence is uncertain and unstable, and so he adopts a form suitable to this.[50] (And it is a short step from Lipius's cento — aphorisms in the making — to the *Oráculo*).

But having said that ultimately we cannot know Gracián's moral intentions, far less his beliefs, what makes me interpret the *Oráculo*, and thence Gracián, as I do here? First because, as I have suggested, Gracián is imbued with an Ignatian mentality that easily looks calculating, worldly, and thus secular, particularly when placed against the overt expressions of religiosity, Christian *exempla* and Biblical injunctions that characterize Spanish Baroque thought. I am not here precluding Gracián being on the extreme end of the spectrum of Jesuit worldliness, or indeed of belief; what I am arguing is that the existence of belief as a capacious and diverse category needs to be taken seriously in evaluating the moral and sceptical inclination of an early modern thinker like Gracián. If it is, then Gracián reads as an Ignatian Jesuit. (This leaves open, of course, how one regards early modern Jesuit mores.)

And secondly, the absence of explicit references and injunctions is *not* the same as an absence *per se*. For there is a marked Biblical and sapiential undercurrent across the *Oráculo*[51] — as also a marked Jesuit one, as I have indicated[52] — what Fumaroli snappily labels the collection's 'arrière-fond théologique' [theological backdrop].[53] The *Oráculo* may be different in degree, but that does not necessarily make it different in kind. And a comparison is telling here: the impact of Neostoicism and of Classical culture on the work is never critically ignored or downplayed, yet the myriad Classical and Stoic allusions and references are usually unsignalled too in the *Oráculo*. Gracián fully exhibits the syncretism, hybridity and 'flexibility with regard to discursive boundaries' that Braun signals as emblematic of a Baroque mode of thought.[54] Aranguren made a not dissimilar comment in contextualizing Gracián's thought:

> Gracián was transitional and thus syncretic. Like Montaigne and Descartes, he remained a Christian, but Christianity was not a fundamental inspiration for his work. Since he was unable to fuse them, he simply juxtaposed the distinct strata of his reflections, and especially the religious and the moral-philosophical. Both his life and his work consisted of a tension between these two, of a coming and going between one and the other.[55]

I am suggesting, then, that Gracián is not himself dissimulating; there is no hidden agenda. Rather, he recommends speaking with the many as a tactic of non-alienation necessary for social and thus personal success. The need for this masking is spelt out:

> *A man free from illusion*: a wise Christian, a worldly philosopher. But don't look like one, far less pretend to be one. Philosophy is discredited, although the

highest activity of the wise. The knowledge of sages is now without authority. Seneca introduced it into Rome; it survived amidst the elite for a while; and is now deemed irrelevant. But disillusion has always been the nourishment of prudence, the delight of integrity. (100)[56]

For such an individual, the *varón desengañado*, he is disarmingly open about the strategies necessary for surviving and thriving in court society, though one might see his style and form as a deliberate barrier to keep the *vulgo* from a full awareness of them. In his frankness, he is of course also offering a far from flattering view of that society, and of people in general.

It is important to stress that I am not wanting to downplay Gracián's differences vis-à-vis his contemporaries, or to whitewash him. He is no saint. To take one example, he gives a far more cynical take on the issue of excess credulity than the diplomat and political writer Saavedra Fajardo does. Fajardo carefully balances doxastic doubt (doubt concerning beliefs) and credence, emphasizing in so doing that doubt was not simply a component, but a necessary operative element of belief itself:

> The prince should trust and believe, but not without an element of doubt that he may be deceived. Such doubt shouldn't slow down his actions, but be a warning. If he didn't doubt, he would be negligent. Doubting is an act of caution and offers security; it is a weighing of all things. Whoever doubts nothing cannot know the truth. He should trust as if he believed everything, and doubt as if he didn't.[57]

Gracián's argument and tone are far more worldly and pointed:

> *Don't be completely dove-like.* Let the craftiness of the snake alternate with the simplicity of the dove. There's nothing easier than deceiving a good person. The person who never lies is more ready to believe, and one who never deceives is more trusting. Being deceived is not always the result of stupidity, but sometimes of simple goodness. Two types of people often foresee danger: those who have learnt from experience, very much to their own cost, and the astute, very much to the cost of others. Let shrewdness be as versed in suspicion as astuteness is in intrigue, and don't try to be so good that you create opportunities for someone else to be bad. Be a combination of the dove and the serpent; not a monster, but a prodigy. (243)[58]

This aphorism's overall point is made succinctly by La Rochefoucauld: 'The intention never to deceive lays us open to often being deceived'.[59] And it is a good example of the Biblical undercurrent of the *Oráculo* that I have just mentioned, for it explicates the New Testament injunction to be prudent, albeit without signalling that it is so doing:

> Behold, I send you forth as sheep in the midst of wolves: be ye therefore wise as serpents, and harmless as doves.[60] (Matthew 10. 16)

Nevertheless, whilst primarily focused on the idea that you can be too good for your own good, the cynical element in Gracián's aphorism comes in the pretence that in avoiding being too good you are not so much serving your own interests as someone else's, by preventing them being bad by deceiving you![61] Cynicism, certainly, but also, I think, a sort of wry wink to the reader, if not a touch of humour.

My overall point is a simple one: like doubt, belief as lived is complex, and often contradictory. Rather than viewing Gracián through a prism that simplifies belief and doubt into two self-contained and mutually exclusive categories, and seeing secularity as arising from the second, rather than potentially being a component of the first, we should rather acknowledge in him a list of characteristics or traits — Christian belief, moral practice profoundly inflected with Jesuit mores, pragmatism, worldliness, accommodation to circumstances, moral flexibility, cynicism, self-interest, existential pessimism — which, whilst from a rigidly binary point of view sit ill one with another if we expect unambiguous moral clarity, end up looking much like the complex morass of our own moral experiences, contradictions included. Critics reading a culture anamorphically (that is, in sharp terms as *either/ or*) too often tacitly conceive the world with the absolutism of a Pascal; most of us live rather with the worldliness, self-interest, and contradictions characteristic of the Jesuit Gracián.

Notes to Chapter 7

1. See Peter Paul Rubens, *The Letters of Peter Paul Rubens*, ed. and trans. by Ruth Saunders Magurn (Evanston, IL: Northwestern University Press, 1991), no. 84, pp. 135–36.
2. See catalogue entry by Bert Watteeuw in *Rubens in Private: The Master Portrays his Family*, ed. by Ben van Beneden (London: Thames and Hudson, 2015), p. 182 (with a facsimile of the letter on pp. 183–84).
3. See Miguel Batllori, *Gracián y el barroco* (Rome: Edizioni di Storia e Letteratura, 1958), pp. 96–100.
4. 'al separar lo divino de lo humano, Gracián acotó un territorio autónomo, susceptible de infinitas lecturas, a tenor de las ocasiones y las circunstancias'. See Aurora Egido, *La búsqueda de la inmortalidad en las obras de Baltasar Gracián* (Madrid: Real Academia Española, 2014), p. 92.
5. See Egido, *La búsqueda*, p. 92 n. 267: 'un sentido ético alejado de la religiosidad imperante en la Compañía de Jesús'.
6. See Egido, *La búsqueda*, p. 95 n. 276: 'profundidad, laicismo, universalidad y frescura'.
7. 'culminaba además el proceso de laicización llevado a cabo por el Humanismo, marcando con nitidez la línea que separaba lo divino y lo humano'. See Egido, *La búsqueda*, p. 346.
8. See Baltasar Gracián, *Oráculo manual y arte de prudencia*, ed. by Emilio Blanco (Madrid: Cátedra, 1995), p. 51: 'Arte de prudencia. No es extraño que, ante este título, menudeen en el Oráculo manual las referencias a esta virtud, que deja de ser la que presentaban los autores clásicos y los Padres de la Iglesia para convertirse ahora en un saber vivir a lo práctico'. For a counter view on this point, see J. Robbins, 'Prudence and Baltasar Gracián's *Oráculo manual*: Baroque Political Thought and the Thomistic Dimension', in *Artifice and Invention in the Spanish Golden Age*, ed. by Stephen Boyd and Terence O'Reilly (Oxford: Legenda, 2014), pp. 43–52 (pp. 48–49).
9. See Gracián, *Oráculo manual*, p. 66: 'el jesuita parece decidido partidario de una moral autónoma fundada sobre la base de un empirismo que arranca de la naturaleza humana y que prescinde deliberadamente de las ayudas teológicas'.
10. See José Luis Aranguren, 'La moral de Gracián', *Revista de la Universidad de Madrid*, 7 (1958), 331–54 (p. 338): 'meramente instrumental, ni bueno ni malo, sino moralmente neutral'.
11. See Aranguren, 'La moral de Gracián', p. 339: 'lo que procede es, pues, poner [los medios] sencillamente al servicio de un fin bueno que resulta ser al mismo tiempo [...] el fin más conveniente o útil'. Aranguren illustrates this outlook with two examples: (1) the dual presence in *El Héroe* of the 19 too worldly (demasiado humanos) chapters and the closing 20th chapter

with its assertion that greatness must be founded on God and that to be a hero in worldly matters amounts to little in comparison with being one in 'heavenly' ones; and (2) the *Oráculo*, whose 299 aphorisms are disconcertingly summarized in the final aphorism, no. 300, with 'In a word, a saint' [En una palabra, santo].

12. See Aranguren, 'La moral de Gracián', p. 343: 'una virtud puramente intramundana e incluso meramente funcional, técnica, y al tender a reducirla a cautela, simulación y astucia; pero su deformación no llega a tanto como a arrancarla toda semejanza con la prudencia tradicional'.

13. See Batllori, *Gracián y el barroco*, p. 87 (Batllori's emphases): 'No hay que creer, ni mucho menos, que *El Comulgatorio* sea una obra compuesta y publicada por Gracián con la taimada intención de tapar la boca a los que le acusaban de escribir 'libros poco graves' y poco dignos de un religioso [...] Yo creo que, por el contrario, es esta la obra más sincera de Gracián [...] En los demás libros suyos se nota siempre un esfuerzo por evadirse de su ambiente, por dessobrenaturalizar su pensamiento, por *fingir* una moral laicizante y un deísmo naturalista, como actitud literaria *fingida* e intencionada'.

14. Gregory makes two important observations: that 'secular confessional history [...] inevitably distorts the views of religious believer-practitioners' and that 'the mere fact that early modern Catholics and Protestants believed and did things noxious to current secular sensibilities [...] cannot in itself somehow render their motivations cynical instead of sincere, or secular rather than religious'. Whilst I am approaching Gracián from my secular perspective, my aim is to try not to fall unquestioningly into assumptions about motivations. See Brad S. Gregory, 'The Other Confessional History: On Secular Bias in the Study of Religion', *History and Theory*, 45 (2006), 132–49 (pp. 143, 145).

15. See Arthur M. Melzer, *Philosophy between the Lines: The Lost History of Esoteric Writing* (Chicago, IL, and London: University of Chicago Press, 2014).

16. See Baltasar Gracián, *The Pocket Oracle and Art of Prudence*, trans. by J. Robbins (London: Penguin, 2011), pp. 17–18, aphorism 43. English quotations from the *Oráculo* are to this translation, cited by aphorism number alone. See Gracián, *Oráculo manual*, in *Obras completas*, ed. by Emilio Blanco, 2 vols (Madrid: Biblioteca Castro-Turner, 1993), II, 208: '*Sentir con los menos y hablar con los más*. Querer ir contra el corriente es tan imposible al desengaño cuanto fácil al peligro. Sólo Sócrates podría emprenderlo. [...] la verdad es de pocos, el engaño es tan común como vulgar. Ni por el hablar en la plaza se ha de sacar el sabio, pues no habla allí con su voz, sino con la de la necedad común, por más que la esté desmintiendo su interior'. All Spanish quotations are from this edition.

17. The classic study here is Pérez Zagorin, *Ways of Lying: Dissimulation, Persecution, and Conformity in Early Modern Europe* (Cambridge, MA, and London: Harvard University Press, 1990). See also Jon R. Snyder, *Dissimulation and the Culture of Secrecy in Early Modern Europe* (Berkeley: University of California Press, 2009).

18. See Dallas G. Denery II, *The Devil Wins: A History of Lying from the Garden of Eden to the Enlightenment* (Princeton, NJ: Princeton University Press, 2015).

19. See Denery, *The Devil Wins*, pp. 117–18.

20. See *Summa theologiæ*, vol. 41, *Virtues of Justice in the Human Community (2a2æ 101–22)*, ed. and trans. by T. C. O'Brien (Cambridge: Cambridge University Press, 2006), II.II, 110 a.3, p. 161: 'licet tamen veritatem occultare prudenter sub aliqua dissimulatione, ut Augustinus dicit' (p. 160).

21. See *Summa theologiæ*, vol. 41, *Virtues of Justice*, II.II, 111 a.1, p. 173: 'Ad quartum dicendum quod sicut aliquis verbo mentitur, quando significat quod non est, non autem quando tacet quod est, quod aliquando licet, ita etiam simulatio est, quando aliquis per exteriora signa factorum vel rerum significat quod non est, non autem si aliquis prætermittat significare quod est' (p. 172).

22. See Niccolò Machiavelli, *The Prince*, trans. by Tim Parks (London: Penguin, 2009), pp. 69–70. And Machiavelli, *Il Principe*, ed. by Giorgio Inglese (Turin: Einaudi, 1995), pp. 116–18: 'Sendo dunque necessitato uno principe sapere bene usare la bestia, debbe di quelle pigliare la golpe e il lione [...] Non può pertanto uno signore prudente, né debbe, osservare la fede quando tale osservanzia gli torni contro [...] E se li uomini fussino tutti buoni, questo precetto non sarebbe buono: ma perché e' sono tristi e non la osserverebbono a te, tu etiam non l'hai a osservare a

loro [...] A uno principe adunque non è necessario avere in fatto tutte le soprascritte qualità, ma è bene necessario parere di averle'.

23. See Robert Bireley, *The Counter-Reformation Prince: Anti-Machiavellianism or Catholic Statecraft in Early Modern Europe* (Chapel Hill: University of North Carolina Press, 1990).

24. On Machiavelli and Spain, see Keith David Howard, *The Reception of Machiavelli in Early Modern Spain* (London: Tamesis, 2014).

25. See J. Robbins, *Arts of Perception: The Epistemological Mentality of the Spanish Baroque, 1580–1720* (Abingdon: Routledge, 2007), pp. 117–20.

26. See Torquato Accetto, *Della dissimulazione onesta*, ed. by Salvatore Silvano Nigro (Turin: Einaudi, 1997), ch. VIII, p. 27: 'la dissimulazion è una industria di non far veder le cose come sono. Si simula quello che non è, si dissimula quello ch'è'.

27. 'Abstraen los astutos con metafísica plausible por no agraviar o la razón superior o la del Estado, pero el constante varón juzga por especie de traición el disimulo, préciase más de la tenacidad que de la sagacidad, hállase donde la verdad se halla'.

28. '*Cifrar la voluntad*. [...] El más práctico saber consiste en disimular. Lleva riesgo de perder el que juega a juego descubierto'.

29. 'Es gran parte del regir el disimular. Hase de dar pasada a las más de las cosas entre familiares, entre amigos, y más entre enemigos'.

30. '*Obrar de intención, ya segunda, y ya primera*. Milicia es la vida del hombre contra la malicia del hombre; pelea la sagacidad con estratagemas de intención. Nunca obra lo que indica: apunta, sí, para deslumbrar; amaga al aire con destreza y ejecuta en la impensada realidad, atenta siempre a desmentir. Echa una intención para asegurarse de la émula atención, y revuelve luego contra ella, venciendo por lo impensado. Pero la penetrante inteligencia la previene con atenciones, la acecha con reflejas; entiende siempre lo contrario de lo que quiere que entienda, y conoce luego cualquier intentar de falso; deja pasar toda primera intención, y está en espera a la segunda, y aun a la tercera. Auméntase la simulación al ver alcanzado su artificio, y pretende engañar con la misma verdad. Muda de juego, por mudar de treta, y hace artificio del no artificio, fundando su astucia en la mayor candidez. Acude la observación, entendiendo su perspicacia, y descubre las tinieblas revestidas de la luz; descifra la intención, más solapada cuanto más sencilla. De esta suerte combate la calidez de Pitón contra la candidez de los penetrantes rayos de Apolo'.

31. 'In sostanza il dissimular è una professione, della qual non si può far professione, se non nella scola del proprio pensiero. [...] ma degli eccellenti dissimulatori, che sono stati e sono, non si ha notizia alcuna'. See Accetto, *Della dissimulazione*, V, 22.

32. The two major exceptions here are Batllori and Fumaroli. The former's biographically nuanced reading of Gracián's life as a Jesuit underplays his differences from cultural norms, whilst the latter's historically richer account of Gracián's work specifically in terms of its reception in France is thus not focused on the specificity, degree and range of Ignatian elements in his *oeuvre* and outlook. See Batllori, *Gracián y el barroco*; and Fumaroli, '1684. De l'homme de cour à l'homme de goût', in Marc Fumaroli, *Le Sablier renversé. Des Modernes aux Anciens* (Paris: Gallimard, 2013), pp. 17–254.

33. For an example of a Jesuit defence of Jesuit practice to a fellow Jesuit, see the letter sent on behalf of Ignatius in which he addressed and countered the concerns of Juan Álvarez that their recourse to powerful secular figures to defend and further their aims was 'bending the knee to Baal': Ignacio de Loyola, *Obras completas*, ed. by Ignacio Iparraguirre, with the *Autobiografía de San Ignacio*, ed. by Cándido de Dalmases (Madrid: Biblioteca de Autores Cristianos, 1963), pp. 719–21. For a nuanced view of early modern Jesuit worldliness, and of Ignatius as a 'worldly saint', see John W. O'Malley, *Saints or Devils Incarnate? Studies in Jesuit History* (Leiden: Brill, 2013), pp. 48–49, 117, 126–28.

34. On Jesuit casuistry and the Jansenists, see Robert A. Maryks, *Saint Cicero and the Jesuits: The Influence of the Liberal Arts on the Adoption of Moral Probabilism* (Aldershot: Ashgate; Rome: Institutum Historicum Societas Iesu, 2008).

35. '*Hanse de procurar los medios humanos como si no hubiese divinos, y los divinos como si no hubiese humanos*: regla de gran maestro, no hay que añadir comento'.

36. See Ribadeneira, *Vida del bienaventurado padre San Ignacio de Loyola*, in Pedro de Ribadeneira,

Historias de la Contrarreforma, ed. by Eusebio Rey (Madrid: Biblioteca de Autores Cristianos, 1945), V. 9, p. 364 and V. 11, p. 380; Ribadeneira, *Dichos y hechos de N. P. Ignacio*, in *Fontes Narrativi de S. Ignatio de Loyola*, vol. II: *Narrationes scriptae annis 1557–74*, ed. by Cándido de Dalmases (Rome: Monumenta Historica Soc. Iesu, 1951), I. 38, p. 477 and V. 52, p. 490 — this latter was taken from Gonçalves da Câmara, *Memoriale seu Diarium*, in *Fontes Narrativi de S. Ignatio de Loyola*, vol. I: *Narrationes scriptae ante annum 1557*, ed. by Dionisio Fernández Zapico and Cándido de Dalmases (Rome: Monumenta Historica Soc. Iesu, 1943), no. 234, pp. 663–64 — and Daniello Bartoli, *Della vita e dell'instituto di S. Ignazio della Compagnia di Gesù libri cinque* (Venice: Niccolò Pezzana, 1735), III. 35, p. 272. The closest to Gracián's formulation is Ribadeneira's in 'Tratado del modo de gobierno', *Historias*, VI. 14, p. 420. See also Lorenzo Ortiz, *Origen y instituto de la Compañía de Jesús, en la vida de San Ignacio de Loyola, su padre y fundador, que ofrece a las seis muy religiosas y apostólicas provincias de la Compañía de IESUS de las Indias Occidentales, que comprehende la Asistencia General en Roma, por la Corona de Castilla* (Seville: Colegio de San Hermenegildo de la Compañía de Jesús, 1679), III, 1, fols 88ᵛ–89ʳ. On aphorism 251, see Javier García Gilbert, 'Medios humanos y medios divinos en Baltasar Gracián (la dialéctica ficcional del aforismo 251)', *Criticón*, 73 (1998), 61–82; and, on its Ignatian roots, José María Andreu Celma, *Baltasar Gracián o la ética cristiana* (Madrid: Biblioteca de Autores Cristianos, 2008), pp. 347–50.

37. On the Jesuits' differences vis-à-vis monastic orders, see O'Malley, *Saints or Devils Incarnate?* pp. 126, 136, 147, 157, 162.

38. See Ribadeneira, *Vida*, V. 10, p. 378: 'decía [Ignacio] que el que no era bueno para el mundo, tampoco lo era para la Compañía, y que el que tenía talento para vivir y valerse en el siglo, ese era bueno para nuestra Religión'.

39. 'Saber hacerse a todos. Discreto Proteo: con el docto, docto, y con el santo, santo. Gran arte de ganar a todos, porque la semejanza concilia benevolencia. Observar los genios y templarse al de cada uno; al serio y al jovial, seguirles el corriente, haciendo política transformación, urgente a los que dependen. Requiere esta gran sutileza del vivir un gran caudal; menos dificultosa al varón universal de ingenio en noticias y de genio en gustos'.

40. Scripture quotations from The Authorised (King James) Version. Rights in the Authorised Version in the United Kingdom are vested in the Crown. Reproduced by permission of the Crown's patentee, Cambridge University Press. In the Vulgate: 'Et factus sum Iudaeis tanquam Iudaeus, ut Iudaeos lucrarer: iis qui sub lege sunt, quasi sub lege essem (cum ipse non essem sub lege) ut eos qui sub lege erant, lucrifacerem: iis qui sine lege erant, tanquam sine lege essem (cum sine lege Dei non essem: sed in lege essem Christi) ut lucrifacerem eos qui sine lege erant. Factus sum infirmis infirmus, ut infirmos lucrifacerem. Omnibus omnia factus sum, ut omnes facerem salvos'. See *Biblia Vulgata* (Madrid: Biblioteca de Autores Cristianos, 1994), p. 1113.

41. See Loyola, *Obras completas*, pp. 642, 741, 744, 765–66; Ribadeneira, 'Tratado del modo de gobierno', V, p. 416, and *Vida*, V.11, p. 385.

42. 'Vivir a la ocasión. El goberbar, el discurrir, todo ha de ser al caso. Querer cuando se puede, que la sazón y el tiempo a nadie aguardan. No vaya por generalidades en el vivir, si ya no fuere en favor de la virtud, ni intime leyes precisas al querer, que habrá de beber mañana del agua que desprecia hoy. Hay algunos tan paradojamente impertinentes, que pretenden que todas las circunstancias del acierto se ajusten a su manía, y no al contrario. Mas el sabio sabe que el norte de la prudencia consiste en portarse a la ocasión'. Compare the emphasis on virtue and morality in aphorisms 90 and 293.

43. See Ribadeneira, *Vida*, V.11, p. 385: 'Decía que el hombre que tiene negocios no ha de acomodar a los negocios a sí, mas antes él se ha de acomodar a los negocios'.

44. See Bartoli, *Vita*, III.37, p. 275: 'parlando delle cose pratiche, soleva dire, che per bene operare, conviene accomodar sè a'negozj, e non i negozj a sè'.

45. 'Antes loco con todos que cuerdo a solas', dicen políticos. Que si todos lo son, con ninguno perderá; y si es sola la cordura, será tenida por locura. Tanto importará seguir la corriente: es el mayor saber, a veces, no saber, o afectar no saber. Hase de vivir con otros, y los ignorantes son los más. Para vivir a solas ha de tener, o mucho de Dios, o todo de bestia; mas yo moderaría el aforismo, diciendo: 'Antes cuerdo con los más que loco a solas'. Algunos quieren ser singulares en las quimeras'. Compare aphorisms 143, 209, 270, 275.

46. 'Il faut avoir une pensée de derrière, et juger de tout par là, en parlant cependant comme le peuple'. See B. Pascal, *Œuvres complètes*, ed. by Louis Lafuma (Paris: Éditions du Seuil, 1988), p. 510 (n. 91).

47. See *Obras completas*, vol. 2, p. 187.

48. See Gracián, *Pocket Oracle*, pp. xliii–xliv.

49. On synteresis, see Robbins, 'Prudence and Baltasar Gracián's *Oráculo manual*', p. 46; and Fumaroli, '1684', p. 225.

50. See Lipsius, *Politica: Six Books of Politics or Political Instruction*, ed. and trans. by Jan Waszink (Assen: Royal Van Gorcum, 2004), IV.1, pp. 382–84.

51. See the listing of Biblical echoes and allusions, direct and indirect, in Andreu Celma, *Baltasar Gracián*, pp. 231–45. See also *Oráculo*, ed. Blanco, p. 67.

52. See the enumeration of Ignatian echoes in Andreu Celma, *Baltasar Gracián*, pp. 354–73. Celma describes the *Oráculo* as a distillation of the Ignatian spirit and as a sounding-board of Ignatian ideas (p. 346).

53. See Fumaroli, '1684', p. 223.

54. These terms are all Braun's. See Harald E. Braun, 'Baroque Constitution and Hybrid Political Language: The Case of Juan de Mariana (1535–1624) and Juan Márquez (1565–1621)', *Revista Canadiense de Estudios Hispánicos*, 33 (2008), 79–104 (p. 80).

55. 'Gracián [...] fue hombre de transición y, por tanto, sincretismo. Baltasar Gracián, como Montaigne y Descartes, siguió siendo cristiano, pero el cristianismo no inspiró ya fontanalmente su obra. Baltasar Gracián, al no poder fundir, se limitó a yuxtaponer los diversos planos de su meditación y, en especial, el plano filosófico-moral y el religioso; y su vida y su obra consistieron en una tensión entre uno y otro, en un instante pasar, ir y venir del uno al otro'. See Aranguren, 'La moral de Gracián', p. 351.

56. '*Varón desengañado*: cristiano sabio, cortesano filósofo; mas no parecerlo, menos afectarlo. Está desacreditado el filosofar, aunque es ejercicio mayor de los sabios. Vive desautorizada la ciencia de los cuerdos. Introdújola Séneca en Roma; conservóse algún tiempo cortesana; ya es tenida por impertinencia. Pero siempre el desengaño fue pasto de la prudencia, delicias de la entereza'.

57. See Diego Saavedra Fajardo, *Empresas políticas*, ed. by Sagrario López (Madrid: Cátedra, 1999), *empresa* LI, p. 612: 'Confíe y crea el príncipe, pero no sin alguna duda de que puede ser engañado. Esta duda no le ha de retardar en la obra, sino advertir. Si no dudase, sería descuidado. El dudar es cautela propia que le asegura; es un contrapesar las cosas. Quien no duda no puede conocer la verdad. Confíe como si creyese las cosas, y desconfíe como si no las creyese'. On such doxastic doubt, see Robbins, *Arts of Perception*, pp. 92–93.

58. '*No ser todo columbino*. Altérnense la calidez de la serpiente con la candidez de la paloma. No hay cosa más fácil que engañar a un hombre de bien. Cree mucho el que nunca miente y confía mucho el que nunca engaña. No siempre procede de necio el ser engañado, que tal vez de bueno. Dos géneros de personas previenen mucho los daños: los escarmentados, que es muy a su costa, y los astutos, que es muy a la ajena. Muéstrese tan extremada la sagacidad para el recelo como la astucia para el enredo, y no quiera uno ser tan hombre de bien que ocasione al otro el serlo de mal: sea uno mixto de paloma y de serpiente; no monstruo, sino prodigio'.

59. See François de La Rochefoucauld, *Œuvres complètes*, ed. by L. Martin-Chauffier (Paris: Gallimard, 2004), no. 118, p. 419: 'L'intention de ne jamais tromper nous expose à être souvent trompés'.

60. 'Ecce ego mitto vos sicut oves in medio luporum. Estote ergo prudentes sicut serpentes, et simplices sicut columbae' (*Biblia Vulgata*, p. 971). Not surprisingly, Ribadeneira also records Ignatius recommending this 'combination'. See *Vida*, V.11, p. 383.

61. Elsewhere when Gracián writes 'Don't be bad by being totally good' (No ser malo de puro bueno, aphorism 266) he is talking rather of not being coldly rational and emotionless: 'As someone is who never gets angry. Those who are insensible are hardly real people. This doesn't always stem from insensibility, but from stupidity. An opportunely expressed feeling is what makes us human. Birds quickly mock scarecrows. To alternate bitter and sweet is proof of good taste; sweetness alone is for children and fools. It's a great misfortune to lose yourself through being totally good in this state of insensibility' (Eslo el que nunca se enoja; tienen poco de

personas los insensibles. No nace siempre de indolencia, sino de incapacidad. Un sentimiento en su ocasión es acto personal. Búrlanse luego las aves de las apariencias de bultos. Alternar lo agrio con lo dulce es prueba de buen gusto; sola la dulzura es para niños y necios. Gran mal es perderse de puro bueno en este sentido de insensibilidad).

CHAPTER 8

The Concept of Doubt in the Trial of Miguel de Molinos (1687) and in the Controversy over Quietism

Fernando Rodríguez Mediano[1]

Miguel de Molinos (1628–96) is one of seventeenth-century Europe's best-known mystics. After a successful career as spiritual director at Rome, which brought him into contact with such important figures as Christina of Sweden,[2] his condemnation by the Roman Inquisition in 1687 involved, *inter alia*, an orthodox Catholic definition of Quietism, and of a series of propositions considered heretical. These would henceforth be used to label one or another belief or practice as 'Quietist', or — using an adjective newly minted for describing such heretical doctrines — as Molinosism. Before Molinos was put on trial, his spiritual teachings and practices as a guide to consciences could be identified with a type of spirituality whose expressions had developed mostly in Spain, France and Italy. The wide reach of these spiritual currents that culminated in Molinos's condemnation, and the repercussions caused by this negative judgement, show how important these affairs were in the context of religious controversy at the end of the seventeenth century.

During Molinos's trial the Roman Church declared 68 of his propositions to be heretical. This number was the result of a refinement process: the 68 propositions condemned on 28 August 1687 were a digest of 263 previous accusations. It is difficult to assess accurately the extent to which these 68 propositions faithfully reflect Molinos's actual thought.[3] Many are not found in his extant works (particularly the widely distributed *Guía Espiritual*), and his trial appears to have been set in motion primarily on the basis of his (and his followers') immoral behaviour, and of doctrinal material lifted mostly from 'old episodes, his former advice, the letters [written to his followers]'.[4] These letters, which were one of the principal bases for his condemnation, have been lost, which only exacerbates the problem of understanding Molinos's thought and of knowing how the inquisitorial trial was put together.[5] What does seem clear is that the 68 propositions constitute a list of what the Church at the end of the seventeenth century considered problematic about Quietist spirituality. This being so, one must see them not as defining what Molinos believed but as representing how the Church constructed the category of 'Quietism' in order to condemn it. Here we are face to face with a veritable 'construction of a heresy'.[6] After 1687, treatises condemning Quietism proliferated, using the propositions refined by the Roman Inquisition. These even served to condemn *a posteriori* books which had, in a former time, been seen as harmless treatises on Christian spirituality, but which now were included in a new range of teaching labelled Quietist.[7] The Spanish manifestation of anti-Molinosist literature has been partly studied by Jesús Ellacuría.[8] While the most serious accusation used against Quietism, and the one with the broadest application and distribution, was *alumbradismo* [illuminism], a more detailed look at the argumentation used in this controversy furnishes clues about concrete matters such as the cure of souls, and the authority of ecclesiastical institutions and the sacramental order — in sum, the problem of the 'Inner Forum' or Forum of Conscience. In this chapter, I shall attempt to explain not so much matters arising from Molinos's own teaching as those that emerge from the controversy surrounding Quietism. To do this, I shall begin with the concept of doubt as it appears in the 1687 trial.

'Doubt' in anti-Molinosist Polemic

Of the 68 propositions of Molinos condemned by the Inquisition, 'doubt' appears in number 11: 'An dubia, quae occurrunt, an rectè procedatur, nec ne, non est opus reflectere'[9] ['There is no need for reflection about doubts that arise regarding whether progress is being made rightly or not'].[10] Why does doubt occur in this proposition, and how is it understood in anti-Molinosist literature?

One of Molinos's main opponents in Spain was the Andalusian Dominican Pedro Sánchez (d. 1719), one of Seville's outstanding preachers of the seventeenth century. Towards the end of his life Sánchez composed some *Quodlibeta* to refute Molinos.[11] Sánchez's refutation of Molinos's eleventh proposition occurs within a discussion on the legitimacy of inducing young people to take religious vows.[12] Can a child be obligated to fulfil a vow made before reaching the age of consent? Is paternal consent enough? How can the obligation of a vow be reconciled with free will in the case of someone who does not have full use of his or her mental faculties, even when it is for a good purpose such as entry into the religious life? Sánchez explains the various possibilities of the case, and arrives finally at a kind of obligation not based on force but compatible to some extent with free will; it is the type of obligation entered into through vows, about which Saint Augustine said: 'Felix necessitas, quae in meliora compellit!' ['Happy necessity, that drives one toward better things!'].[13]

This discussion of the conditions under which vows and religious promises are obligatory leads Sánchez to reflect on the different conditions of those who enter the religious path. Those who come to religion are imperfect beings: some have a child's levity, while others are fearful or weak or have some other defect; nevertheless, by perseverance they can arrive at perfection. The critique against Molinos arises from this view of religious life as a road to perfection. Because it is essential to carry out tests and enquiries before taking up such a vocation — and having defined the religious life as a way of perfection — Sánchez concludes that it is therefore necessary to engage in reflection when doubts arise about whether one is walking in a good or an evil path: 'palpebrae tuae praecedant gressus tuos' ['let your eyelids look straight before you'] (Pr. 4. 25); or, as the Psalmist says, 'gressus meos dirige secundum eloquium tuum' ['Direct my steps according to Your word'] (Ps. 119 [118]. 133). These texts indicate that reflection (i.e., the 'eyelids') precedes walking. To not reflect when doubts arise is to abandon the use of reason: one may be walking well or ill, but failure to doubt means that one is thinking only of the verb ('walk') and not the adverb ('well' or 'ill'). Doubt is therefore an essential tool of the religious life which serves to bring about reflection and reasoning. The Psalms describe the person who abandons these: 'non est Deus in conspectu eius. Inquinatae sunt viae illius in omni tempore, auferuntur iudicia tua a facie eius' ['God is not in all his thoughts; his ways are always grievous; His judgements are far above out of his sight'] (Ps. 10. 4b–5a [9. 26]). This way of sadness is the lot of those who do not have the fear of God before their eyes and who do not know the way of peace; such is the way of the Molinosists.[14]

Another principal opponent of Quietism in Spain was Francisco Barambio, a Capuchin monk; he was confessor in the Capuchin monastery at Madrid, but little else is known about him.[15] Along with *Discursos philosóphicos, theológicos y morales*, written to condemn Molinos, Barambio was the author of *Casos reservados a su santidad*.[16] The eleventh of his *Discursos* was aimed at Molinos's eleventh proposition.[17] Barambio begins by defining doubt, as distinct from 'opinion', as:

> a type of knowledge in which the understanding, coming to know the reasons that are on each side, completely suspends judgement, and does not know which side to take hold of. There must be knowledge, else it would be ignorance and pure foolishness, and not at all *doubt*.[18]

This doubt can be either speculative or practical:

> The first speculates and explores only the truth of the matter, while the understanding remains in doubt. The second regards the truth that ought to be put into practice on certain occasions or in certain circumstances. And one must be aware that, in order to act well, it is unavoidably needful to have arrived at a practical and morally confident judgement that such an act is sure.[19]

For its part, the path can be that of the Commandments of the Law of God or of Prayer. In both cases one is faced with a moral problem: the 'doubt' that presents itself along the pathway ought to be resolved through reflection, which allows one to move beyond the suspension of judgement regarding whether the path is correct or not. This reflection should be done 'in consultation with holy and learned men who have experience of the way of the Law of God', or by returning to 'classical Authors'. In this way, the problem of reflection becomes a question of authority.

When walking the religious path, the passion appropriate for doubt is fear. In order to merit and retain grace, one ought always to be found in God's presence with fear:

> Therefore, you should fear when grace applauds you with its presence; fear when it increases for you; fear when it arrives once again; and know that this is always to have fear.[20]

Among the many biblical examples that illustrate fear arising from doubt, and the reflection that follows from it, we have the Virgin Mary, who, while at prayer, received the Angel's visit and was troubled, thinking: what greeting can this be? It was also the case of Saint Theresa of Jesus, who, 'because at this time women had experienced great imaginings and deceit worked by the Devil',[21] began to doubt her own prayers of quietude and union. Faced with such doubts, Saint Theresa sought conversation with a father of the Company of Jesus.

Thus, we find here a 'doubt-judgement-advice' construction that partially evokes the one Saint Thomas Aquinas built around the concept of 'prudence' (that is, 'right reason applied to action') as a fundamental virtue in the practice of governance, whose function it is to direct and command. Because of this, it is a virtue that fundamentally belongs to a man 'in so far as he has a share in ruling and governing'.[22] The potential parts of this principal virtue are: *eubolia*, 'good counsel', 'which concerns counsel'; *synesis*, 'which concerns judgement in matters of ordinary occurrence'; and *gnome*, 'which concerns judgement in matters of exception to the law'.[23] This is a conceptual field developed in order to integrate contingency into moral deliberation: faced with doubt as to how to apply a moral or judicial norm[24] (and not only these) to a particular situation, a set of interpretative and deliberative rules is constructed which includes the capacity for individual interpretation, or recourse to pertinent authorities. Thus the Forum of Conscience is turned, by means of doubt, into a space not only for moral judgement but also for constructing political and moral authority. It is not difficult to understand how and why doubt appeared in Molinos's prosecution: as with other aspects of the trial, the Roman Inquisition understood that Molinos's doctrine was attacking forms of authority and religious mediation when it advocated for unconditional abandonment to God. This was why critics insisted on the need to appeal to ecclesiastical or textual authorities when doubt arose.

In this way, Molinos's trial, in this specific aspect, appears as yet one more episode in the construction of conscience, in two senses: the conscience as moral and religious Subject carrying the capacity for judgement, and the conscience as a space for exercising forms of political government. Doubt is a fundamental tool for this construction, as indicated, for example, by the way in which moral theology developed the category of the 'doubtful conscience'.

The Conscience

Conscience is a key category for understanding how moral theology viewed the problem of practical moral judgement, and is therefore a preferred concept for understanding the type of conflict within which the trial of Molinos could take place. In order to show this relationship, I will give examples of moral theologians and casuists who were involved, like Barambio, in refuting Quietism.

Among them was Friar Martín de Torrecilla, one of Spain's leading casuists in the seventeenth century, and author of an immense work on matters of moral theology. One of his short works is dedicated to refuting Molinos's doctrine.[25] It is not a systematic refutation of Molinosist Quietism, but rather a defence of a point of Torrecilla's own moral doctrine which might be supposed to have similarities to Molinos — specifically to two of his propositions. The argument is as follows: in his *Suma* Torrecilla had developed his teaching on whether 'it was lawful not to impede upon awakening the pollution begun while asleep, when the danger of consent is past'. For Torrecilla it was indeed lawful not to impede pollution. What was more, some men might find by experience that sleeping in a certain position or eating hot food could be factors increasing the likelihood of pollution while asleep; yet a person should not in this case be obliged to sleep in a different position. Some might consider this teaching to be close to proposition 17 attributed to Molinos in the Roman sentence of condemnation:

> If the free will is given over to God, along with the care and governing of one's soul, one should no longer pay attention to temptations nor make any resistance to them, other than denial without striving; and if one's nature is resentful, one must let it be resentful, because it is nature.[26]

This proposition is very close to number 12:

> He who has given his free will to God ought not to have a care about anything else, neither from hell nor heaven, nor from a desire for one's own perfection, nor from the virtues, nor from one's holiness, nor from one's own salvation, the hope of which he should expunge.[27]

Torrecilla's tract is dedicated to pointing out the differences between the proposition attributed to Molinos and his own teaching, whose key phrase is 'cesando el peligro del consentimiento' ['when the danger of consent is past']. In fact, says Torrecilla, the central moral problem to be resolved was one of consent, which was linked to the Subject's will. When temptation or the danger of sinning presents itself, the Subject ought to seek divine aid through prayer.

Of course, Torrecilla makes the typical accusation of *alumbradismo* [illuminism] against Molinos, but he also finds an echo of Lutheran and Calvinist thought in these and other propositions regarding free will. What is more, he thinks that Molinos went further than Luther and Calvin dared to go, in his conception of the complete surrender of the will to God.[28] More generally, Torrecilla believes he can detect Calvin's doctrine in the teachings of Molinos when the latter writes:

> when God moves the human will by his divine grace, it is moved in such a way that everything it does proceeds from grace alone; and that the will should be only passive, so that it does not cooperate with grace, but *omnino nihil agit positiuè*.[29]

The category of 'conscience' was developed in order to define the Subject of moral judgement. Torrecilla himself presented a definition and classification of conscience in his works on casuistry. The conscience is defined as:

> an act of the understanding; not just any understanding, but one of judgement, by which it judges what the will ought to embrace or flee from, as being either in accordance with or against reason. [...] It should be distinguished from Synderesis, which judges universal principles, and from moral knowledge or

opinion, which judges universal conclusions, since the conscience only makes judgements about particular conclusions [...] And thus the conscience is the application of knowledge (*ciencia*) to the work that ought presently to be done; or it is a practical judgement of the understanding which says to the will: do this because it is reasonable, or do not do it because it is against reason.[30]

According to Torrecilla, the conscience can be differentiated by categories: *right*, 'that which calls truth, truth'; *erroneous*, 'that which calls error, truth'; *doubtful*, 'which is a suspension of the soul, in which, because there are insufficient reasons on one side or the other to move it to assent or dissent, or because there are equal difficulties in both sets of reasons, the understanding remains indifferent and unable to judge whether the matter is lawful or unlawful'; *probable*, 'which judges that something is probably lawful or unlawful, yet suspects that the opposite could be more true'; and *scrupulous*, which is 'a light suspicion born of insubstantial foundations, by which what is not sin is judged or believed to be sin, but always with the suspicion that the contrary might be true; thus it does not exclude the certain judgement or opinion of the opposite side, and it is more credulity than settled judgement; it is like a disturbance or suspicion which brings with it disquiet, fear, and spiritual alienation'.[31]

Here one can identify categories of conscience as they were exhaustively developed by casuistic and moral theology, as we shall see. Our interest for the purposes of this chapter is in the 'doubtful conscience' and the 'probable conscience'. Both imply doubt, but in different ways. The doubtful conscience refers to a 'suspension of assent' caused by doubt. This can be either negative, if there are no reasons in favour of one or another option, or positive, if there are reasons that favour both options but none is sufficiently strong to induce a choice. If, on the other hand, there are reasons that are sufficiently strong to support one of the options, one can no longer speak of rigorous doubt but rather of 'opinión probable o duda opinativa' ['probable opinion or opinionated doubt']. In other words, there is a distinction to be made between doubt that is incapable of forming an opinion (*conscientia dubia*) and the conscience that stands doubting between two choices, both of them valid (*conscientia probabile*).[32]

Martín de Torrecilla continued making distinctions that followed on from his initial classification of types of doubt. Besides positive or negative, doubts can be by right or in fact, speculative or practical. When a doubt arises, one should attempt to overcome it 'either by questioning or studying, or by searching for a sufficient motive' that will turn the doubt into probable opinion. If the conscience needs to act, either by urgency or necessity, there would be no sin even if the choice reached were improbable; and if the conscience needs to choose the lesser of two evils, there would be no sin in that either. Torrecilla repeats the well-known, apparently contradictory, pair of legal principles whose running argument is present throughout the whole of seventeenth-century polemics concerning moral laxism. The first is, 'melior est conditio possidentis' (that is, when doubt exists about property, the better right of the possessor was recognized); this was one of the basic principles of probabilism. The second was 'in dubiis tutior pars est eligenda' (that is, when in doubt, the more secure side should be chosen); this was the principle with which the rigorists opposed probabilism. Yet, according to Torrecilla, the two principles are morally complementary since the state of the property helps to define 'the more secure side'.[33] How should 'conditio possidentis' be understood morally? As an example, when faced with the question of whether a non-religious person ought to obey a prelate when such a person is in doubt about whether the command is lawful or whether it exceeds the churchman's authority, the answer is 'yes', because the superior possesses the right of commanding; and, in order for the Subject to excuse himself from obedience, he would have to demonstrate that the command is not rightly issued. However, if the Subject in question is a religious person, then the answer is 'no', because his vow does not obligate him, and he possesses freedom in this case.[34] In reality, the moral adoption of this legal principle implies that, when doubt exists, the balance should tip in favour of the person whose responsibility it is to make a judgement; that is, in favour of the conscience that is in possession of free will.

The categories of conscience, as Torrecilla received and reproduced them, were the product of a complex process. For example, the development of the 'scrupulous conscience' category, and its connection to the world of moral debate concerning probabilism, was not exempt from influence by the spiritual style of the Jesuits, forming part of a history that intimately connected the probabilist controversy to the Company of Jesus.[35] In this sense Torrecilla's book reflects the arrival point of intensive debates about the 'probable conscience' and the rules to which it is subject. Without going into detail regarding Torrecilla's explanations, I shall cite two of his chapters in which he explains his defence of probabilities. The first of these discusses 'the age, sufficiency, and utility of probabilities', concluding that they are very ancient, as old as Adam and Eve ('because they made excuses for certain great sins before the Fall'), Jacob, the Maccabees, the Apostles, and even the angels. On this point Torrecilla contradicted those who, like Prospero Fagnani (a renowned anti-probabilist), affirmed that probabilities were quite recent. Torrecilla attacked Fagnani's proposition, 'opinio probabilis non sufficit', which was also affirmed by Antonio Merienda (another famous anti-probabilist), and by Lutherans, Calvinists and Jansenists. It was a proposition whose orthodoxy was suspect, since Jansen inferred from it his 'Deus impossibilia iubet', which in turn produced several heretical propositions: 'Deus impossibilia praecipit' (this was heretical because there are rarely opinions of absolute certainty in moral affairs, and to oblige a person always to follow these would be to command the impossible), and 'Deus impossibilia potest et solet praecipere'. For Torrecilla, Jansenism leached into opinions such as 'peccant omnes qui in materia conscientiae sequuntur opinionem probabilem'.[36] On the other hand, when asking who has the right to debate probabilities, and who are those who have enlarged or narrowed people's consciences, Torrecilla responded that the Canonists had no right to speak about probabilities since they were ignorant of the philosophical subtleties of Moral Theology and worked mostly in the area of external rights. At the same time, in contrast to what their enemies thought, the Moderns had not relaxed people's consciences, but rather extraordinarily restricted them, for this reason: the old Catholics, faced with these two opinions — 'Ecclesia non vult suis legibus illigare Christianorum conscientias' and 'Ecclesia non potest eorundem illigare conscientias' — had chosen the first and rejected the second. Nevertheless, Luther had defended the second, and the 'common people' had followed him in it; for this reason, modern Catholics had seen the need to reinforce their power over consciences, 'and thus they said *iubet ergo potest*', a position which the Church afterward legitimized.[37]

The genealogy of Martín de Torrecilla's process of argument is clear. He himself explicitly cites Antonino Diana and Juan Caramuel. In fact, Torrecilla closely follows the latter in his *Apologema*.[38] The circumstances of this work have been studied by Julia Fleming.[39] It is a polemical work in which Caramuel defends probabilist doctrine against an attack by Prospero Fagnani, a canonist of the Roman Curia, who had made his assault on probabilism in a commentary on a chapter of the *Decretals Ne innitaris*. To a great extent it was an argument between the 'prince of rigorists' and the 'prince of probabilists'. In attacking probabilism (not only Caramuel), Fagnani had declared it to be a modern doctrine from the present century. Formerly, moral certainty had been the prerequisite for lawful behaviour, since moralists understood that probable opinion was insufficient.[40] Against this attack Caramuel defended the antiquity of probabilities and their use in the Bible and among the angels, and he made an assault on their true enemies, the Jansenists. Caramuel thought that Fagnani had unintentionally (being a canonist untrained in moral theology) defended a thesis from which the most damnable of Port-Royal's propositions could necessarily be derived — namely, that God could require impossible things of men. He believed that Fagnani's accusation that probabilists were *novatores* was unjust, recalling the label previously applied to Protestants.[41] In any case, probabilist theologians, far from being more lax than the canonists, had been more rigorous.[42] In reality, the fact that Fagnani found support for his position in texts produced in the environment of Port-Royal allowed the accusation of laxism launched against the probabilists to be understood in the context of Jansenist polemic.[43] A detailed (though not final) exposition of Caramuel's moral teaching is found in his *Theologia moralis*, whose third book is dedicated to matters of conscience.[44] The greater part of this book looks at the 'conscientia dubia',[45] a fact which is hardly strange given that the development of moral theology as its own discipline (clearly differentiated, as we have seen, from other areas of knowledge like canonistic science) had much to do with the importance given to the sacrament of confession. In fact, casuistic treatises were in principle written for confessors, to aid them in their work of guiding consciences. In large part, Caramuel was justified in feeling himself to be a 'modern', to the extent that he represented a kind of knowledge dedicated to the various forms of practical moral judgement, which could only be understood in the context of putting such forms into practice; with the consequent rejection of the idea of the perpetuity of the Faith as defended by Jansenism.[46]

In his *Apologema*, Caramuel defended Antonino Diana (who had died that same year) against an attack by Fagnani. Diana's name was linked to accusations of moral laxism. As we have seen, Torrecilla also used Diana as one of his main sources. Diana, in his exposition of the categories of 'conscientia dubia' and 'conscientia erronea', had explained that it was possible to act morally in practice even when speculative doubt existed, and he had suggested a moral application of the principle 'melior est conditio possidentis' — a principle that, as we have seen, would come to legitimize 'freedom of conscience'.[47] Undoubtedly, Torrecilla follows the probabilist tradition, reproducing the polemical context in which Diana and Caramuel produced their works. Nevertheless, we must keep in mind that, at the time when Torrecilla was writing against Molinos, probabilism had received a serious blow from Rome. Torrecilla himself had to write an exposition of the propositions condemned by Alexander VII and Innocent XI.[48] Following this papal condemnation of laxism, treatises on casuistry and moral theology normally included in their introductions the text of the condemnations.[49] In fact, as we have seen, Torrecilla's critique of Molinos had its starting point in a defence of his own teaching, in order to avoid any confusion with Molinosism regarding one critical point — namely, whether the conscience had resisted sin or not. This example indicated the dynamic context in which the process of defining moral doubt was carried on. To put it differently: building up a case against Molinos was the consequence of a long and deep conflict in which the conscience was a battleground for a confrontation between Jansenists and Jesuits, Reformed and Catholic, mystics and sceptics... Thus the definition of conscience arose from a need to conceptualize different positions that were — at least during the second half of the seventeenth century — in conflict, and that involved a complex process. An essential factor in all this was the Company of Jesus, whose position during the probabilist controversy is well known, and which enjoyed a fundamental role in the polemic against Molinos.

The Jesuits and Molinosism

One of the first polemicists against Miguel de Molinos was Fr Paolo Segneri, who in 1680 (that is, before the verdict against Molinos) published *Concordia tra la fatica e la quiete*.[50] The book was an argument against the Moderns who, in order to guide souls on the road to salvation, promoted the way of prayer over that of meditation. Segneri, beginning with a distinction between infused or mystic contemplation and acquired contemplation, criticized those teachers who conducted souls along the path of contemplation without showing any interest whatsoever in meditation — that is, in the exercise of interior abilities, the imagination, the understanding, or the will. According to them, once one had arrived at contemplation, there was no reason at all to return to meditation. Against this extreme view, Segneri proposed what he considered a middle way, in which the soul ought to return and again take up meditation after communication with God has ended. That is, if one loves God, then every means should be used to know him, both contemplation (near) and meditation (far). The surest rule for Segneri was:

> everything that is an object of faith is an object of contemplation [...] just as whatever is an object of contemplation [...] is an object of meditation. Meditation is not distinguished by its object, which is God first of all [...] but rather the two are differentiated by their methods of viewing that object.[51]

One consequence of the Modern contemplatives' ideas was that attention was given to a quite abstract idea of God, with a neglect of the human nature of Christ (so that theological reflection became distant from the sense-world), and a belittling of the mystery of the hypostatic union and the sacrament of the Eucharist.

At the end of the seventeenth century, Segneri's book was one of the most significant works of the anti-Quietist polemic through which a case against Molinos was being built up. Molinos responded to several of Segneri's attacks, specifically regarding the distinction between infused and acquired contemplation, and whether the soul ought to return to meditation once the state of contemplation had been reached.[52] This was an important question. The Jesuit Gottardo Bell'uomo, in his *Il pregio e l'ordine dell'oratione ordinarie e mistiche* — the first significant work against the Quietism of Molinos — explained the differences between ordinary and mystical prayer, the clearest of which was that it was possible 'to give precepts and relevant rules so that ordinary prayers can be perfectly made', whereas this was impossible with mystical prayers. This was so because:

> our powers, within the range of their natural ability, can act either well or badly when exercising themselves in prayer, so that they are open to being directed; and thus, *per regulas numquam fallentes* [...] we arrive at the desired result of praying and meditating rightly, just as happens when we exercise any other art, whether mechanical or intellectual.

In contrast, no precept or guide has any value for mystical prayer.[53] Here we find prefigured the problem of doubt: prayer can be exercised well or badly, and therefore it ought to be directed by a series of very precise rules. This is one of the key points of opposition between, on the one hand, abstract contemplation and the abandonment of the sensual world, which depends on direct communication between God and the soul, and, on the other hand, the way of meditation as discourse, which acts upon the soul's powers, imagination, memory, understanding and will. For the Jesuits, the principal model of this kind of meditation was, of course, the *Exercises* of Saint Ignatius.[54]

The works we have mentioned formed part of the reaction to the publication of the *Guía Espiritual* in 1675. In what seemed to be a victory for Quietism, Bell'uomo's and Segneri's books were condemned in 1681, before Molinos was put on trial.[55] Of course, we know that this was only an apparent victory, and that Segneri's work enjoyed a life well beyond the verdict against Molinos. In 1688 it was translated into Spanish, with the addition of 'a brief report on the sect of the Quietists, with the propositions of Molinos, which the Author impugns, and which His Holiness Innocent XI has condemned'.[56] The translator, himself a Jesuit, offered an *a posteriori* reconstruction of the anti-Molinosist quarrel, based on the propositions condemned by Rome, while emphasizing Segneri's role in defending Saint Ignatius's way of prayer against the pernicious doctrine of the Quietists. The latter taught that perfection was achieved through passivity of the powers and senses. The soul should be annihilated, neither considering nor contemplating nor remembering nor loving God. It should not be occupied with external devotion, but should repress all desire for movement or petitioning God (not even for one's own salvation or that of one's nearest and dearest). It should not resist temptations nor ask for God's aid in resisting them. Quietists despised images, not only physical ones but also those of the imagination. They called sins (no matter how serious) 'violencias del demonio' ['devilish forcefulness'], involving no consent or guilt of the will. In sum, the soul totally resigned its free will into God's hands, and everything that happened thereafter was due to the will of God. Unquestionably, Molinos taught — and this directly touches on the conceptualization of 'doubt' in the context of the verdict against him — that:

> those who walk in the *internal way* tread a path far removed from confession, confessionals, cases of conscience, theology and philosophy. And if doubts or scruples arise regarding actions, which they called forcefulness of the Devil, they should be despised. There was no authority on earth that could demand an account of what occurred between the soul and the Director.

The translation of Segneri's work into Spanish included a life of the author, originally written in Italian by Fr Joseph Massei. The volume was republished in 1705 with a new supplement: a 'response by the said Father Pablo Señeri to a great prelate's consultation regarding the probability of opinions'.[57] This was a defence of probabilism, with a definition of 'probable' and its rules of use. Segneri, one of the most important Jesuits of the latter part of the seventeenth century, was a defender of probabilism and one of the principal opponents of the probabiliorism of Tirso González de Santalla, General of the Jesuits at that time. This was a significant quarrel within the Company of Jesus, and it undoubtedly helps us to understand the position taken by many Jesuits with respect to Molinosism within the wider context of the problem of defining the frontiers between conscience and obedience.[58] Here I will point out just one aspect of Segneri's text: his focus on the field defined by the tension between rule and opinion, that is, the problem of freedom of conscience and the cure of souls. According to him, 'today's heretics' (meaning the Jansenists) not only tried to make certain that the common people were advised to follow the most probable opinion, but that they were obligated to do so, with the result that they caused them to fall into despair.[59] This tension is expressed in the proposition of the so-called 'benign opinion'; that is,

> that in a clash of opinions it is sometimes lawful to take the side of the less probable one, favouring liberty, against the more probable one, favouring the Precept.[60]

In fact, in terms of political government, the theory of probable opinion excludes those persons who are bound by norms: judges, the prince who must declare war, the bishop who distributes benefices, the physician who must heal... All these are subject to a 'Ley especial indubitabilísima' that limits universal law.[61] This same division between law and liberty of conscience can be found in the tension between canonical and non-canonical writers. Theology needs both: it takes 'efficient' — that is, necessary — arguments from the former, and from the latter it takes probable arguments that are nevertheless proper to their own field. For this reason, probability is linked to truth: not manifest truth ('which cannot shine except in Heaven'), but another, similar truth. Returning to the tension between the Ancients and the Moderns, Segneri defends the modern doctrine of probability, because the Ancients were themselves modern in their own time. To attack the Moderns was in some sense to act like the Jews who 'praised the prophets of the past and stoned their own contemporaries'.[62]

One can detect in Segneri's texts a common thread running through both his dispute with Quietism and his defence of probabilism: the problem of the conscience that, to the extent that it is a doubtful one, finds itself in need of moral or spiritual guidance. In the tension between meditation and contemplation, Segneri puts the emphasis on the problem of the 'spiritual guide'. And it is from this viewpoint that he criticizes another mystic, the Frenchman François Malaval, in his *Sette principii su cui si fonda la nuova oratione di quiete* (1682), 'non qual uomo, qual cristiano, qual cattolico, qual letterato, solo qual *direttore*'.[63] The insistence on the theme of confession and the directing of consciences runs throughout Molinos's trial,[64] and places it in the wider context of the topic of the development of instruments of modern discipline in the Catholic world, of 'tribunals of conscience', and the definition — following Trent — of a model of confession that in fact marks out a confessional frontier in Europe regarding the problem of conscience and individual responsibility.[65] The problem of probability is also centred on the issue of guiding consciences, as is evident from the whole of casuistic literature. It also raises, in a concrete way, the problem of the connection between morality and politics, as is shown by the cases of Antonino Diana or Juan Caramuel. For example, Diana, a Sicilian, wrote in defence of the legitimacy of Sicilian institutions against the political and financial pretensions of the Spanish monarchy.[66] For his part, Caramuel used the same method to uphold Spanish pretensions at the time of papal recognition of Portuguese independence in 1641.[67] In any case, we should keep in mind that one of the keys to understanding these theological controversies is the clash between national cultural and political forms, and the centralism and universalism of Rome.

The works of Fathers Segneri and Bell'uomo indicate that the polemic surrounding 'meditation' and 'contemplation' was centred on the Jesuit milieu and the method of Loyola's *Spiritual Exercises*. This fact is made explicit in Molinos's own *Defensa de la contemplación*, written to answer the Jesuit attacks, in which the Aragonese mystic declares that the *Exercises* of Loyola were holy and most useful, and had brought about many conversions, yet were not the immediate means for union with God and perfection.[68] Yet this same Jesuit setting, where the problem of how to act upon the Forum of Conscience is clearly represented by the *Spiritual Exercises*, was part of a much wider European context. First of all, as is well known, so-called Quietism was not a single spiritual school centred on the figure of Molinos, but an international movement with many adherents and varied expressions. I have already mentioned Malaval, but could also cite the names of other spiritual writers (Jeanne Guyon, Fénelon...) who defined a spiritual current in France that would eventually be condemned as Quietist.[69] In Italy, Molinos came to be received within circles that included, for example, Pier Maria Petrucci.[70] These were milieux where the works of the Almerían mystic Juan Falconi had already circulated in French and Italian translation.[71] At the same time, the French context points to one of the key disputes of the age respecting the problem of free will: Jansenism, whose hostile relationship with the Company of Jesus need not be detailed here. The 'construction of Quietist heresy' cannot be understood independently of this wider context, where the political, moral, and religious subjects were being dynamically defined. Evidence for this is found in interpretations of Quietism from beyond the borders of Italy and Spain, with their distinct perspectives regarding the intellectual or confessional territory at stake.

Quietism in Europe

Antoine Arnauld and Pierre Nicole were two key Port-Royal figures, if judged only by their joint authorship of *La logique ou l'art de penser*, an essential work in the history of sign theory in Europe. Both also displayed intensive theological activity, often of a polemical nature. Pierre Nicole published in 1667 *Les visionnaires*, a work directed against certain mystics of the age, in particular Jean Desmarets de Saint-Sorlin, a violent anti-Jansenist. Nicole sketched the profile of a spiritual type whom he called 'ilumminez', who, though driven by different forms of imagination, had a number of traits in common: they believed that Jesus reveals his secrets mainly to simple and ignorant people who do not know theology, and who receive every thought that comes to them, whether through reading or prayer, as internal illumination of the Holy Spirit. This was a dangerous path, from which arose most heresies,

> and especially all the different sects of the Anabaptists, among whom are the Socinians, who have ruined all the mysteries of our faith on the pretext of the text of Scripture alone, explained by itself, that is, by the particular spirit of all who wish to read it. Luther and Calvin gave birth to these monsters, but the unfortunate children have pushed their evil principles further than the parents. These Tremblers of England [i.e., Quakers] are still conducting themselves in the same way. They believe they are illumined (*éclairez*) in everything by the Holy Spirit, and that they speak and act only as moved by him.[72]

The difference between natural and supernatural prayer was really nothing more than different levels of elevation by the Spirit from God; yet these spiritual men believed they could be lifted to a higher grade of contemplation while being full of sin and ignorant of themselves, without ever distinguishing between 'thought and heart sentiment'.[73] Furthermore, they gave credence to every Scripture interpretation that came into their heads, and used allegory, not 'as an artificial *memoire* for retaining certain truths', but rather to explain extraordinary thoughts, to set down new opinions, or to prove false or uncertain things.[74]

Nicole's fierce diatribe against Desmarets and other mystics filters into the subsequent anti-Molinosist polemic, as Jacques Le Brun has clearly shown in relation to the work of Louis-Paul du Vaucel, *Breves considerationes in doctrinam Michelis de Molinos et aliorum quietistarum*, published anonymously at Cologne in 1688.[75] Du Vaucel was a Jansenist delegate to Rome between 1682 and 1700. His work was therefore the testimony of a contemporary witness to the trial of Miguel de Molinos, as well as an example of how news about the trial reached the rest of Europe. The work combines the arguments of the 'anti-Quietist Vulgate' put into circulation by Segneri, with others drawn from the previously cited Jansenist tradition of the *Visionnaires* and its anti-mysticism. In fact, as Le Brun indicates, there are clear traces here of the epistolary exchange between Du Vaucel and Antoine Arnauld concerning the affair. Thus the work is not only about the Quietism of Molinos, but also concerns the mystical tradition that includes Malaval and Petrucci.

Du Vaucel begins his attack on Quietism with a distinction between infused and acquired contemplation, and the problematic character of the latter in Quietist doctrine. The difficulty was in thinking that one could arrive at the contemplation of God not only by means of grace but by an act of the will, by 'human effort and the powers of free will',[76] without any intervention of divine grace.[77] Quietist doctrine reminded the author of several theological and philosophical reference points. On the one hand, a purely abstract contemplation of God that leaves aside all sense images put him in mind of the ancient Platonic philosophers, who attempted to know God by the light of reason alone.[78] On the other hand, Quietist impassibility smacked of the old *apatheia* of the Stoics, in the same way that Quietism on a moral level reminded him of the *impeccantia* of the Pelagians.[79] The problem of 'sinlessness' recalled not only the recurrent charge of Pelagianism but also the no less frequent one of *alumbradismo*.[80] For the Jansenists this was a fundamental moral problem. As one can see in the Du Vaucel–Antoine Arnault correspondence, the most infamous Quietist proposition was that the supposed mystic who fell into 'sordid disorderliness' could not blame his fall on the Devil, since it was God who had allowed it in order to purify him.[81] This was a central theme in which the moral conflict surrounding Quietism was amply expressed in terms of the tension between sin and free will.[82] The connection between moral laxism and the problem of sinlessness is clearly expressed in the phrase: 'Les Molinos et les Molina sont funestes à cette triomphante société' (i.e., the Jesuits).

The way in which these different themes are interconnected in the controversy surrounding Jansenism is illustrated in the work of John Sinnich, an Irish Jansenist theologian. For him, libertinism, spiritualism and probabilism shared the same 'perverse ambition for liberty'. In the wake of radical spiritualist movements, the probabilists had reclaimed the same 'arrogant confidence in their internal regeneration'. From the point of view of Augustinian theology, probabilists represented the arrogance of the human will in its desire to confront the will of God. The trouble with probabilism was not that it attempted to free the conscience from the fear of sin, but that it wanted to liberate it from every sort of scruple.[83]

One of the more interesting texts produced outside Spain concerning Molinos's trial was written by Jean Cornand de Lacroze,[84] a Huguenot who fled France after the revocation of the Edict of Nantes and took refuge first in Holland and then in England, and who collaborated with Jean Leclerc on the *Bibliothèque Universelle et Historique*. In 1688, Cornand de Lacroze published two works having to do with Molinos, in particular a collection of texts about Molinosism that included a French translation of the *Guía Espiritual* and the *Tratado de la comunión cotidiana*.[85] The introduction to this volume was in fact an apology in favour of Molinosism in the context of anti-Catholic polemic. Cornand de Lacroze began this apology speaking about the linguistic style of mysticism, whose obscure words and convoluted concepts seemed in principle to be far removed from Protestantism and its concept of the simplicity of grace. Yet there were reasons for such obscurity. It is true, he writes, that there are 'ideal' mystics who have not experienced contemplation and who speak about it out of vanity, trying to pass themselves off as wise men by mixing confused ideas from Aristotle's Metaphysics with their explanations. On the other hand, many people are incapable of understanding spiritual expressions. Mysticism is a science of the human heart and the love of God. As such, it uses specialized language that common people cannot understand, especially those who are sure that religion is an easy thing; that all it requires is a certain moral purity or the avoidance of actions one knows to be wrong, and that the pinnacle of spirituality is reached simply by doing certain external works of charity — while self-love continues to rule a heart full of 'self and the present age'. Such people are incapable of understanding expressions like 'renouncement', 'abandonment in God', or the true meaning of contemplation as expressed by authentic mystics like Saint John of the Cross, Herp, Molinos or Malaval.[86]

The wisdom of God, continues Cornand de Lacroze, often passes through madness; and thus the mystics are sometimes excessively reserved 'in order not to scandalize the weak, or expose the truth to persecution or to the mockery of the societies in which they live'.[87] There were no mystics in Holland because well-intentioned persons were able to live quietly there and publicly condemn the superstitions of the Roman Church without fear. Rather, mystics have arisen in Catholic countries, where, in most cases, they must shut themselves up in some monastery, unable to leave it without causing a scandal. Nor were mystics favourably looked upon among Protestants. Therefore they had to content themselves with revealing truth to a few chosen disciples, and could only write it in books with extreme care. In order to accomplish their object of correcting the abuses of the Roman Church, the mystics had used the same method that Descartes used to expose 'the false subtleties of Aristotle's philosophy'.

How can Quietist mysticism be compared with Cartesian philosophy? Philosophy's purpose is to push knowledge and the search for truth forward as far as possible. The purpose of mystical theology and Quietism is to purify the soul and unite it to God as far as is possible in this life. In both cases, it was necessary to free human beings from all the prejudices and false opinions they have embraced without examination. To do this, the Cartesians taught that one must begin the search for truth by doubting everything and rejecting all the old knowledge and judgements, in order to re-examine everything. That is why the Roman Church and the scholastics had brought a suit against them, accusing them of Pyrrhonism and of introducing doubt about everything, including God himself, and of mocking all the mysteries of religion and favouring Atheism and Deism. But these were mere calumnies.

Doubt is a disposition of the spirit to philosophize correctly, given that one does not philosophize except in order to stop doubting and assure oneself of the truth. Therefore God should not be offended at the search for rational proofs of his existence, but rather the opposite; and for the same reason, philosophy has never been closer to religion than with the Cartesians, who have proven the existence of God and the immortality of the soul. Besides this, they have applied themselves to reconciling Providence with human freedom and other mysteries of religion — except for Transubstantiation, which they have not been able to explain because it is in fact inexplicable.[88]

For their part, the mystics had faced the same opposition when establishing their system, opposed by superstitious people who worshipped images instead of the invisible Being, who invoked the saints instead of Jesus Christ, and who made divine worship to consist of eternal ceremonies, and the essence of piety to be indulgences, sackcloth, disciplines, and other extravagant practices. Unlike the Reformers, the mystics had not dared to cry openly against abuses and suffer the fury of the common people; rather, they had thought that some of those practices were not evil in principle, and that they might be useful for beginners, but that one need not spend a great deal of time with them, and should move from the state of meditation to that of contemplation in order to gaze on God directly, without shadows or figures, but divesting oneself of all images, forms and species. This was therefore a system that tended towards the destruction of Popery, since 'the stripping away of internal images involves doing the same with the external ones, and with the whole mass of ceremonies that only corrupts the spirit'.[89] The defenders of the Roman Church had realized the danger of this teaching, and had done everything they could to prohibit or censure it.

Thus Descartes and Molinos were similar in their method, destined to destroy, respectively, Scholastic prejudices and the abuses of the Roman Church. They were similar too in the great number of disciples that each was able to attract, and in the hatred they called forth from the Jesuits. The Company of Jesus had accused Descartes of introducing Pyrrhonism, and accused the Quietists of reducing the whole of religion to the contemplation of a vague and confused idea that was neither God nor any created thing, but rather an indeterminate principle, or nothing at all, with the purpose of bringing in atheism.

The Jesuits had used a 'subtle and malicious' trick to make Quietist doctrine hateful: they compared it to the teaching of Confucius's followers. Thus Cornand de Lacroze cites Fr Philippe Couplet's introduction to the work of Prospero Intorceta, *Confucius*.[90] Here Fr Couplet describes the different sects of Chinese philosophy, among whom were found the followers of Foe Kiao, characterized as political atheists. This sect taught that there are two types of doctrine. One consists of various precepts and external ceremonies for the common people; the other is internal, and Couplet describes it in the same terms in which the Quietists were described by their enemies: a sect that desired to reduce all religion to a contemplation of the void, without the use of reason or understanding; identified with a principle that is pure, eternal and immutable, that neither thinks, nor wishes, nor desires anything.[91]

In fact, as we have seen, *Confucius* was published in the same year as Molinos's trial, at a point when Europe — including Paris — was experiencing intense discussions about Quietism.[92] It is true that Couplet did not explicitly cite Molinos, but the Quietist reference in the description of Chinese philosophy would be clear to someone who, like Cornand de Lacroze, was thoroughly involved in the controversy. For example, Jean Leclerc and Jean Cornand de Lacroze, writing in about 1688, declared that Ignatius of Loyola had done things that were later condemned as heretical by the Jesuits themselves or by the Inquisition. He had taken evangelical poverty to an extreme; he seemed to have believed that the truths of the Faith could not be comprehended except through Scripture or interior illumination; he had believed that the flesh of the Virgin Mary was contained, substantially present, in the Eucharist in the flesh of the Son; and, finally, Ignatius of Loyola had had the same 'sentiments that the Inquisition has just condemned in Molinos'.[93] In any case, the way in which Fr Couplet presented Oriental philosophy in terms recognizable as 'Deist' or 'Atheist' in the European context was extended also to Spinozism, and thus attempted to identify the supposed 'interior' doctrine of the Buddha with the idea of the universe as a single substance whose modifications we perceive as our world.[94] Visible here is a cultural context in which internal spirituality was now understood not only with reference to the mystical tradition, but also in relation to the wider conflict in which interiority created a crisis for forms of religious and political authority, in a manner that harked back, in a general way, to Atheism. We may recall that, when the *Junta de Calificadores* met in Madrid in 1685 to pass judgement on the *Guía espiritual*, one of the accusers, the Jesuit Juan Cortés Osorio found a savour of Atheism in that model of perfection that tolerated no discussion, and that ended up denying external actions and expressions of devotion involving the senses. Modern heretics were those who, like Molinos, believed in a pure and universal faith, to the extent that it was now impossible to tell the difference between an Atheist and a Catholic.[95]

Jean Cornand de Lacroze alludes to other fundamental aspects of Molinos's doctrine, such as his advice that a person should not become upset or feel afflicted by sins committed — one of Molinosism's most controversial points from the viewpoint of morality, as we have seen. Lacroze interpreted this doctrine as referring to venial sins, not mortal ones. According to him, Molinos was thereby attempting to discredit confessors who imposed ridiculous penances and extravagant mortifications, things unknown in the primitive church. Once again we are faced with the crucial question of confession, the directing of consciences, and the relationship of Quietism to the problem of sin and free will.

Knowledge and the Eucharist

The issue of parallelism between Descartes and Molinos — each of them the inventor of a method for overcoming the prejudices of his epoch — might seem a little surprising, as Cornand de Lacroze himself affirmed. Naturally, within the serious religious conflicts of the time they can both be seen as enemies of the Catholic Church and common enemies of the Company of Jesus. In addition, it is possible to establish a relationship between them with respect to an all-pervasive theme that is central to the polemic surrounding Quietism: knowledge.

As Francisco Barambio wrote in his text about Molinos's condemnation, or as Torrecilla said in his work: doubt, whether speculative or practical, can be defined as 'a suspension of judgement'. The appearance of the sceptical 'epoché' in these texts can perhaps be understood as the result of the complicated process by which doubt, in the seventeenth century, had colonized the epistemological realm as a key tool of judgement.

One way of understanding this problem is from the viewpoint of mysticism as 'science'. We have already seen how the question of the various sciences and their specialized vocabularies arises at different points in the controversies described in the present text; as, for example, in the defence of Moral Theology by the casuists against the Canonists. As for mysticism, to consider it as 'the science of the knowledge of God and of the interior' is to see it as radically opposed to Theology as a science of 'experience'. In fact, one of the recurrent themes in the entirety of this polemic was the Quietists' affirmation that none but those with an experience of contemplation could make a judgement about it; furthermore, as one of Molinos's condemned propositions states: 'theologians are less disposed toward contemplation'. Thus the polemic surrounding contemplation can also be understood as yet one more expression of modern Europe's reorganization of the ways of knowing as they relate to experience.[96] From this point of view, the Quietist experience of contemplation also implied the undermining of the traditional theory of species, as a description of a process of knowing based on sense-experience. The polemic concerning how to articulate meditation and contemplation raises the question — a fundamental one — of whether the two can be compatible, and of whether a person can do without meditation forever once the state of contemplation has been reached. Is contemplation simply a single moment in time, so that it is not possible to reduce the whole of the believer's religious life to it? How to integrate contemplation into the Scholastic theory of knowledge was an old problem for mysticism, as it attempted to connect forms of sensate knowledge with the knowledge of God, which was not apprehensible via species. Saint John of the Cross had already rejected all ways of knowing God that rested on forms, rather than on 'the obscurity [*oscuridad*, 'darkness'] of faith'; in the same way, he had eschewed the use of images for approaching God, though hiding or softening his rejection perhaps out of 'fear of reprisals'.[97] In one of the first apologies for Saint John of the Cross, Fr José de Jesús María Quiroga spoke of 'conocimiento espiritual y sencillo en quietud de los actos de la razón' ['a spiritual and simple knowledge in the quietness of reason's acts'], and he attempted to explain, using an artistic metaphor, how one could reach a knowledge of God: the image of God can be formed by addition, as with painting, or by subtraction, as with sculpture; the latter is the contemplative method. This is negative knowledge (bringing to mind negative theology), which is brought about by 'stripping the understanding of all the known similitudes with which it, in its coarse and limited way, forms a concept of God'. In this way one can reach 'a greater knowledge of God than what a reasoned discourse can give us'.[98] Thus, here we have a super-substantial concept of God.[99]

Quiroga's text was written in a polemical context, in defence of his idea of contemplation, and is only one example of the way in which far-reaching controversies were reflected in the Molinosist condemnation. The debates surrounding mental prayer are well known, but I would like to stress one aspect of the Molinosist debate which is crucial to every one of the viewpoints raised throughout this chapter, and which is at the heart of the morality–epistemology nexus: the sacrament of the Eucharist.

The defenders of meditation had pointed out the problem of how contemplation of God without recourse to sense images could integrate the humanity of Christ into the way of mysticism. If contemplation was abstract, and the contemplation of God could not be done based on sensible species, what then should be done with the humanity of Christ, whose blood and body were, according to the doctrine of transubstantiation, made present in the Eucharist? Or, to put it the other way, could frequent communion be considered an instrument of permanent contact with God, beyond confession?

Both questions were central to an understanding of the context which produced the condemnation of Quietism, in its moral and epistemological aspect. A short treatise by Miguel de Molinos, *Breve tratado de la comunión frecuente*,[100] together with two chapters of his *Guía Espiritual*, give a complete picture of Molinos's ideas about the Eucharist, along with his defence of frequent communion for all who are not in a state of mortal sin. Interestingly, one of the passages from the *Guía espiritual* contains one of the few references in the book to the word 'doubt'.[101] After saying that many souls deprive themselves of 'this precious food' for fear of not being sufficiently prepared, he adds:

> on this reef of the desire to do the divine will, all difficulties will be broken, and all scruples, temptations, doubts, fears, revulsions and contradictions will be overcome.[102]

Frequent communion was a subject of great controversy at this time, and resulted in a 1679 bull of Innocent XI. The topic would explicitly come up again, even more clearly, in the verdict against Molinos, when the label 'Quietist' was given to the idea that contemplative souls ought not to receive the sacrament of penance before communion, or that while partaking of communion they should repress all feelings of humility, pleading or gratitude.[103]

Reflections about the Eucharist appear constantly in attacks upon Molinos. It is found, for example, in Du Vaucel's *Breves considerationes*, where the defence of daily communion is called 'lax', and weekly communion is advocated so that the believer might approach the heavenly meal with proper respect and preparation.[104] The theme of the Eucharist has a central role in defining a good part of the European theological and philosophical controversies of the day. Pierre Nicole, in his *Visionnaires*, had already had to defend himself against Desmarets's attack on the Jansenists, which claimed that they denied the presence of the body and blood of Christ in communion, leaving only 'a communion of the spirit by faith'. In thus abolishing the Eucharist, the Jansenists supposedly attempted also to abolish frequent masses, making communion a weekly thing only, a ceremony in which the host was eaten only by faith.[105] The Jesuits too accused the Jansenists of denying the presence of Christ's body and blood in the Eucharist — an accusation that provoked a response from Pascal in his Sixteenth Provincial Letter.

The Eucharistic question was fundamental to the Jansenists, and was one of the clear lines of demarcation with Protestantism that kept them within the Catholic camp. In large part, the positions adopted by Jansenism with respect to the Eucharist can be explained by their ongoing arguments with Calvinists, which impelled them, for example, to search the texts of the Oriental Church — such as the Coptic — for proofs of the continuity of Christian liturgy since antiquity, in order to demonstrate a continued belief in transubstantiation.[106] The centrality of the Eucharistic question also explains, for example, the fact that one of the largest obstacles that Cartesian philosophy encountered at Port-Royal had to do with the compatibility between its physical ideas and its doctrine of transubstantiation. In fact, one of its principal defenders among the Jansenists, Antoine Arnauld, only decided to take up the Cartesian cause when he became convinced that it was not incompatible with the Eucharist. Nevertheless, Du Vaucel, who wrote about Cartesian philosophy as well as Quietism, believed that the two were incompatible; he thought that Descartes's philosophy was particularly inadequate for explaining the real presence of Christ in the communion, especially because it made extension the essence of matter, which constituted the mark of Cartesianism.[107] On the Jesuits' side, this problem was fundamental to their opposition to Cartesianism and the condemnation of Descartes's works.[108] Thus the Jansenists made an enormous intellectual and theological effort regarding the Eucharist within the characteristic polemical environment in which they confronted Calvinists and Jesuits. By this effort they refined the doctrine of the real presence of Christ in the Eucharist, and also the significant forms of the remembrance of Christ and of prayer; this effort was crucial to the construction of Port-Royal's logic and the new theory of signs.[109]

Various central aspects of anti-Molinosist polemic come together in the issue of the Eucharist. One of the documents reproduced by Cornand de Lacroze in his *Recueil*, with the title 'Extraits d'une lettre angloise',[110] explains from a Reformed viewpoint Father Segneri's critique of Quietism with reference to the problem of remembering the humanity of Jesus Christ: meditation is reflection on His life, birth, miracles and passion; contemplation is a simple vision of God, a pure and momentary act of faith. By concentrating on the humanity of Christ, on his omnipotence and omniscience, the Roman theologians had committed the same error as the Socinians,[111] and had created a dogma that had produced, among other things, worship of the cross and of the Eucharistic bread, making an idol of Jesus. Only a few mystics like François Malaval had dared oppose 'this torrent of superstition' and the abuse that 'the Christians of his communion' gave to the humanity of Christ, to the detriment of his divine condition.[112] The Quietists' attempt to rise above the humanity of Christ had caused them to be accused of being anti-Trinitarians and Deists.[113]

The topic of frequent communion is in any case neither original nor specific to Molinos. The genealogy of spiritualist mysticism in late seventeenth-century Europe includes the outstanding figure of Juan Falconi de Bustamante (1596–1638), a theologian and mystic from Almería who pursued his career in Madrid, authoring a treatise entitled *El pan nuestro de cada día*, which enjoyed extraordinarily wide distribution in Europe and was translated into Italian and French.[114] The work belongs to a mystical and theological tradition related to this theme; it not only argues that daily communion is recommendable, but also defines the two conditions for participation in it: not to be in a state of mortal sin, and to receive the sacrament 'with the affection and devotion of which each one is capable'.[115] The theme of frequent communion, with its corollary of connected topics (like defining the 'disposition' of the communicant, the equating of the communicant with the priestly dignity, etc.) runs throughout the seventeenth century up to the *Tratado* of Molinos, which was condemned by the Spanish Inquisition in 1685.[116] At the same time, it is worth recalling here that several of Juan Falconi's works were censured in 1688–89, precisely because of his supposed nearness to Quietist propositions.[117] This was one of those examples of spiritual works being defined *a posteriori* as Quietist, and therefore censured.

Conclusion

One of the important points of Molinos's condemnation has to do with the relationship between obedience and spiritual guidance. Proposition 65 says:

> One should obey one's superior in what is external; and the latitude of the vow of obedience of Religious persons extends only to the exterior; the interior is a different matter, where only God and the guide enter.[118]

And 66 reads:

> There is a new doctrine in the Church of God that is laughable: that the soul, so far as the interior is concerned, ought to be governed by the Bishop; and if he is not able, the soul should go to him with its Director. I say 'new' because neither Holy Scripture, Councils, Canons, Bulls, Saints nor Authors have ever passed this down to us, nor could they do so, because *Ecclesia non iudicat de occultis*. And the soul has the right as well as the faculty to choose whomever it deems best.[119]

Proposition 67:

> to say that one ought to display what is internal to an external Tribunal of superiors, and that not to do so is a sin, is a manifest deception, because the Church *non iudicat de occultis*, and they endanger souls with these deceptions and fictions.[120]

And lastly, number 68:

> There is no faculty or jurisdiction in the world for commanding that one should make public the Director's letters regarding what is internal to the soul, and thus it is necessary to be aware that this is Satanic scoffing.[121]

All these propositions help to situate the legal attack upon Quietism within the wider context of the problem of constructing the Subject and of modern means of discipline. Barambio's response to these propositions is no surprise: obedience should be, at one and the same time, internal and external, since the commands of one's superiors compel the conscience; any obedience that is not also internal is poor obedience. The supposition, 'in the interior only God and me', is an outrageous doctrine, one which every heretic has attempted to introduce into the Church, and in particular the *alumbrados*.

Barambio's refutation of these condemned propositions constitutes a small treatise on interiority, or rather a treatise on how interiority is integrated into a system of canonical and political authority. What is internal (purely mental, related to confession or to prayer) is not actually distinct from what is external, and therefore it falls within the jurisdiction of canonical authority, as does the relationship between the Subject and his Director of conscience. On the other hand, when discussing Proposition 59 ('the internal way is separate from confession, confessors, cases of conscience, Theology and Philosophy'), Barambio affirms that the internal way is necessarily joined to confession — among other things — because the spiritual life is filled with pitfalls, both serious and minor, and with many doubts and difficulties that can only be resolved by confession, cases of conscience, Theology and Philosophy.[122] Here once again we are face to face with the concept of doubt, in a manner that explicitly links the 'Inner Forum', confession, and obedience.

The polemic surrounding moral laxism reproduces the same tension between affirming free will and obedience. Here is a key aspect in how the governing of souls was defined, and this explains why the clash between contemplation and meditation was seen as so important. This was an ancient dispute, but it became intensified during the trial of Quietism that began with the case against Molinos created by the Jesuits, and the reference to the *Spiritual Exercises*. To the extent that defining the Forum of Conscience was central to the entire process of moral reconfiguration in the seventeenth century, one can better understand how the case against Molinos was constructed. The repeated allusions to the problem of religious vows, their conditions and their reach were important also for understanding the aspects of this trial.

Is it true, as some thought, that it was possible to find a likeness between Cartesianism and Quietist mysticism? Both 'methods' were based on considering the distance between external and internal, and reflecting about the relationship between them — a relationship that belongs in principle to the order of knowledge, but that is also political, since it radically involves the forms in which authority is constructed. At the end of the seventeenth century, it was impossible to understand these processes without making reference to doubt. While it is true that doubt had been, since antiquity, a fundamental rhetorical tool of dialectic, at the historical moment we are discussing doubt inevitably contained the dissolvent power of scepticism, and of its importance in defining judgement. Certainly, mystical interiority and sceptical interiority are different. The modern sceptical tradition itself insisted on seeing them this way, and one of its mainsprings was the construction of a definition of faith far removed from any implication of mysticism, circumscribing the limits of all possible knowledge within the human sphere.[123] In any event, the case of Quietism allows us to add a significant element to the history of the controversy surrounding scepticism.

The relationship of Quietism to the development of other philosophical, logical, or scientific methods during the seventeenth century is, at any rate, far from simple or unambiguous. To give just one example: the sympathy with which Leibniz treated mysticism, especially Quietist mysticism, has been subject to varying explanations: certain affinities relative to the forms of knowing God and the Subject; a lack of confidence in the senses as the source of knowledge; a certain sort of idea about the absolute independence of substances...[124] One of the ways of approaching the knowledge question can be the crucial issue of the Eucharist. I have already cited the well-known example of the Logic of Port-Royal, which explains very well the development of a way of thinking about the relationship between language and truth. The exploration of the relationship between the body of Christ and the word of God constitutes an important theological problem at this moment in Catholic history, which can be studied from the perspective of the 'return to the sources' of Christianity.[125] We have also seen how the polemical framework of the confrontation between Ancients and Moderns appears continuously, as a constant questioning of the ways of constructing tradition in a context as dynamic as the one outlined here. On the other hand, the issue of religious vows requires the present work, in dealing with language and truth, to consider, on the one hand, the problem of constructing the Forum of Conscience, and, on the other, the problem of a logical grammatical system. These two problems are intertwined through their connection to the construction of the moral Subject.

Notes to Chapter 8

1. The research leading to these results has received funding from the European Research Council under the European Union's Seventh Framework Programme (FP7/2007–2013) / ERC grant agreement no. 323316, project CORPI 'Conversion, Overlapping Religiosities, Polemics, Interaction. Early Modern Iberia and Beyond', led by Mercedes García-Arenal.

2. Susanna Åkerman, *Queen Christina of Sweden and her Circle: The Transformation of a Seventeenth Century Philosophical Libertine* (Leiden: Brill, 1991), pp. 284–94.

3. José Ignacio Tellechea Idígoras, *Molinosiana. Investigaciones históricas sobre Miguel de Molinos* (Madrid: FUE, 1987), pp. 55–57.

4. 'viejos episodios, sus antiguos consejos, las cartas', Tellechea Idígoras, *Molinosiana*, p. 55. Tellechea Idígoras, *El proceso del doctor Miguel de Molinos* (Madrid: FUE-Universidad Pontificia de Salamanca, 2007).

5. For example, Francisco Trinidad Solano, 'Miguel de Molinos. La experiencia de la nada', in Miguel de Molinos, *Defensa de la contemplación*, ed. by F. T. Solano (Madrid: Editora Nacional, 1983), pp. 13–88 (p. 52).

6. This expression appears in Adelisa Malena, *L'eresia dei perfetti. Inquisizione romana ed esperienze mistiche nel Seicento italiano* (Rome: Edizioni di Storia e Letteratura, 2003), p. 1; and also in Marilena Modica, *Infetta dottrina. Inquisizione e quietisme nel Seicento* (Rome: Viella, 2009), p. 9. On the concept of 'heretical construct', see Jessica J. Fowler, 'Assembling Alumbradismo: The Evolution of a Heretical Construct', in *After Conversion: Iberia and the Emergence of Modernity*, ed. by M. García-Arenal (Leiden: Brill, 2016), pp. 251–82.

7. Malena, *L'eresia dei perfetti*, p. 4.

8. Jesús Ellacuría Beascoechea, *Reacción española contra las ideas de Miguel de Molinos (procesos de la Inquisición y refutación de los teólogos)* ([Bilbao]: [Gráf. Ellacuria], 1956).

9. The Latin text of this and other condemned propositions of Molinos is taken from Paul Dudon, *Le Quiétiste espagnol Michel Molinos (1628–1696)* (Paris: Gabriel Beauchesne, 1921), p. 293.

10. Contemporary Spanish translations of Molinos's propositions can be found in Francisco Barambio, *Discursos philosóphicos, theológicos, morales y místicos contra las proposiciones del Doctor Miguel de Molinos [...]*, 2 vols (Madrid: Juan García Infanzón, 1691–92), I, 172.

11. Pedro Sánchez, *Quodlibeta Divi Thomae Aquinatis, Doctoris Angelici, ad mysticas doctrinas applicata, reflexionibus aliquibus annexis pro securiori via spiritus [...]* (Seville: Francisco Sánchez Reciente, 1719). Ellacuría Beascoechea, *Reacción española*, pp. 266–353.

12. Sánchez, *Quodlibeta Divi Thomae Aquinatis*: 'Utrum liceat inducere Iuvenes ad Religionem voto, vel iuramento', 'Quodlibetum III, Articulus XI', p. 222.

13. Sánchez, *Quodlibeta Divi Thomae Aquinatis*, p. 224.

14. Sánchez, *Quodlibeta Divi Thomae Aquinatis*, pp. 226–27.

15. Ellacuría Beascoechea, *Reacción española*, pp. 117–228.

16. Antonio González Polvillo, *Análisis y repertorio de los tratados y manuales para la confesión en el mundo hispánico (ss. XV–XVIII)* (Huelva: Universidad de Huelva, 2009), no. 4435.

17. Barambio, *Discursos philosóphicos*, I, 172–87.

18. 'un conocimiento con el que el entendimiento, conociendo las razones que ay por una y otra parte, en una cosa, suspende de todo punto el juyzio, y no sabe a qué parte echarse. Ha de aver conocimiento, porque si no será ignorancia y pura nesciencia, y de ninguna suerte *duda*'.

19. 'la primera, especula y discurre solo sobre la verdad de la cosa, quedándose el entendimiento dudoso. La segunda es acerca de la verdad que se ha de practicar en tales ocasiones o circunstancias. Y se advierte, que para obrar bien, forçosamente es menester un juyzio práctico, moralmente cierto, de que tal obra es cierta'.

20. 'teme pues quando la gracia te aplaudiere con su presencia, teme quando se te aumente, teme quando de nuevo viniere, y sabe que esto es tener siempre miedo'.

21. 'como en estos tiempos avían sucedido grandes ilusiones en mugeres y engaños que les avía hecho el demonio'.

22. Aquinas, *Summa Theologiae*, 2a-2a, q. 47, a. 12.

23. Aquinas, *Summa Theologiae*, 2a-2a, q. 48, a. 1.

24. For example, Juan Cruz Cruz, 'Interpretación de la ley según Juan de Salas', *Cuadernos de Pensamiento Español*, 44 (2011), 9–103, (p. 88 and *passim*), which analyses the problem of the interpretation of the law.

25. Fray Martín de Torrecilla, 'En que se refutan las proposiciones del heresiarcha Molinos', in *Consultas, apologías, alegatos, questiones y varios tratados morales, y confutación de las más y más principales proposiciones del impío heresiarca Molinos*, 3 vols (Madrid: Jerónimo de Estrada, 1702), II, 552–62. Torrecilla is not one of the authors studied by Ellacuría Beascoechea.

26. 'Dado que sea el libre arbitrio a Dios, y el cuydado y gobierno de nuestra alma, no se deve hacer más caso a las tentaciones, no se debe hazer otra resistencia, sino negativa, sin usar industria; y si la naturaleza se resiente, es menester dexarla resentir, porque es naturaleza'; Barambio, *Discursos philosóphicos*, I, 272. 'Tradito Deo libero arbitrio et eidem relicta cura et cogitatione animae nostrae, non est amplius habenda ratio tentationum, nec eis alia resistentia fieri debet, nisi negativa, nulla adhibita industria, et si natura commovetur, oportet sinere ut commoveatur, quia est natura'; Dudon, *Le Quiétiste espagnol*, p. 294.

27. 'El que ha dado el libre arbitrio a Dios no debe dársele nada de cosa alguna, ni de infierno ni de gloria, ni de deseo de la propia perfección, ni de las virtudes, ni de la propia santidad, ni de la propia salud, que también debe perder la esperança'; Barambio, *Discursos philosóphicos*, vol. I, p. 188. 'Qui suum liberum arbitrium Deo donavit de nulla re debet curam habere, nec de inferno, nec de paradiso, nec debet desiderium habere propriae perfectionis, nec virtutum, nec propriae sanctitatis, nec propriae salutis cujus spem expurgare debet'; Dudon, *Le quiétiste espagnol*, p. 293.

28. Barambio also notes this, *Discursos philosóphicos*, I, 274.

29. Torrecilla, 'En que se refutan...', p. 558.

30. 'un acto del entendimiento, no qualquiera sino iudicativo, con que juzga qué es lo que la voluntad debe abraçar o debe huir, por ser conforme o contra razón [...] Diferénciase de la Sindéresis, que juzga los principios universales; y de la ciencia u opinión moral, que juzga de las conclusiones universales; porque la conciencia sólo juzga de las conclusiones en particular [...] Y así conciencia es aplicación de la ciencia a la obra que ahora se a de hazer; o un juizio práctico del entendimiento, que dize a la voluntad: Haz esto, porque es razón; o no lo hagas, porque es sinrazón'; Fray Martín de Torrecilla, *Compendio de la suma añadida del R. P. Fr. Martín de Torrecilla,*

con *Addiciones del tomo de proposiciones condenadas, y del de Obispos y otras* (Madrid: Antonio Román, 1698), p. 1.

31. *recta*, 'que dicta la verdad por verdad'; *errónea*, 'que dicta un yerro por verdad'; *dudosa*, 'que es una suspensión de ánimo, con que, por falta de razones que suficientemente la muevan, ni de una ni de otra parte al assenso ni al dissenso, o por hallar igual dificultad en sus razones, queda indiferente el entendimiento, sin poder juzgar si la cosa es lícita o ilícita'; *probable*, 'que es un juizio probable de que esto es lícito o ilícito, con rezelo de que lo contrario puede ser más verdadero'; *escrupulosa*, 'una leve sospecha, nacida de leves fundamentos, con la qual juzga o cree ser pecado lo que no lo es; pero siempre con rezelo de que lo contrario puede ser verdadero; y assí no excluye el juizio cierto o opinativo de la parte opuesta, y más es credulidad que juizio formado; es una como turbación o sospecha, que trae anexa a sí inquietud, temor y alienación de espíritu'. Torrecilla, *Compendio de la suma añadida*, pp. 1–2.

32. Torrecilla, *Compendio de la suma añadida*, pp. 4–5.

33. Torrecilla, *Compendio de la suma añadida*, p. 5.

34. Torrecilla, *Compendio de la suma añadida*, p. 16.

35. Jean-Pascal Gay, 'Doctrina Societatis? Le Rapport entre probabilisme et discernement des esprits dans la culture jésuite (XVIᵉ–XVIIᵉ siècles)', in *Le Discernement spirituel au dix-septième siècle*, ed. by Simon Icard (Paris: Nolin, 2011), pp. 23–46.

36. Torrecilla, *Compendio de la suma añadida*, p. 28.

37. Torrecilla, *Compendio de la suma añadida*, p. 29.

38. Juan Caramuel, *Apologema pro antiquisima et universalissima doctrina de probabilitate, contra nouam, singularem improbabilemque D. Prosperi Fagnani opiniationem* (Lyon: Laurent Anisson, 1663).

39. Julia Fleming, *Defending Probabilism: The Moral Theology of Juan Caramuel* (Washington, DC: Georgetown University Press, 2006), pp. 73ff.

40. Fleming, *Defending Probabilism*, pp. 74–75.

41. Fleming, *Defending Probabilism*, p. 80.

42. Fleming, *Defending Probabilism*, p. 80.

43. Fleming, *Defending Probabilism*, pp. 88–89.

44. Juan Caramuel, *Theologia moralis ad prima, eaque clarissima principia reducta* (Leuven: Petrus Zangrius, 1645), pp. 330–97.

45. Caramuel, *Theologia moralis ad prima*, pp. 332–94.

46. Jean-Robert Armogathe, 'Probabilisme et libre-arbitre. La Théologie morale de Caramuel y Lobkowitz', in *Le meraviglie del probabile. Juan Caramuel 1606–1682*, ed. by Paolo Posavino (Vigevano: Comune di Vigevano, 1990), pp. 35–40.

47. Antonino Diana, *Summa Diana* (Valencia: Claudio Macè, 1645), pp. 126–27.

48. Martín Torrecilla, *Consultas morales y exposición de las proposiciones condenadas por nuestros muy santos padres Inocencio XI y Alexandro VII* (Madrid: Juan García Infanzón, 1693).

49. Albert R. Jonsen and Stephen Toulmin, *The Abuse of Casuistry: A History of Moral Reasoning* (Berkeley: University of California Press, 1988), pp. 269–70.

50. Paolo Segneri, *Concordia tra la fatica e la quiete nell'orazione, espressa ad un Religioso* (Florence: Ipolito della Nave, 1680).

51. Segneri, *Concordia tra la fatica*, p. 38.

52. Tellechea Idígoras, 'Una apología inédita de Molinos. Scioglimento ad alcune obiettioni fatte contra i llibro della "Guida spirituale"', in *Molinosiana*, pp. 193–225.

53. Gottardo Bell'uomo, *Il pregio e l'ordine dell'oratione ordinarie e mistiche* (Modena: Soliani, 1678), pp. 34–36.

54. Bell'uomo, *Il pregio e l'ordine*, p. 46.

55. Dudon, *Le Quiétiste espagnol*, pp. 126ff.

56. 'una breve noticia de la secta de los quietistas, con las proposiciones de Molinos, que el Author impugna, y la Santidad de Innocencio XI ha condenado'; Paolo Segneri, *Concordia entre la quietud y la fatiga de la oración* (Barcelona: Rafael Figueró, 1688).

57. Paolo Segneri, *Concordia entre la quietud y la fatiga de la oración* (Barcelona: [n.p.], 1705).

58. Jean-Pascal Gay, *Jesuit Civil Wars: Theology, Politics and Government under Tirso González (1687–1705)* (Farnham: Ashgate, 2012), pp. 143–44 and *passim*.

59. Segneri, *Concordia entre la quietud y la fatiga*, pp. 219–20.
60. Segneri, *Concordia entre la quietud y la fatiga*, pp. 225–26. This explanation is included in a defence of probabilism against its condemnation by Innocent XI.
61. Segneri, *Concordia entre la quietud y la fatiga*, pp. 222–23.
62. Segneri, *Concordia entre la quietud y la fatiga*, pp. 235–36.
63. Malena, *L'eresia dei perfetti*, p. 119.
64. Among the condemned propositions of Molinos are the following: 'confession is useless and sometimes impossible'; 'one's superior is owed only external obedience'; 'it is deceptive to require the unburdening of the conscience to one's superior'; 'no one has the jurisdiction to require that letters written by one's Director of conscience referring to internal matters must be revealed; to say the opposite is an invention of Satan'; Ellacuría Beascoechea, *Reacción española*, pp. 53–54.
65. Adriano Prosperi, 'La confesione e il foro della coscienza', in *Il Concilio di Trento e il moderno*, Annali dell'Istituto storico italo-germanico, Quaderno 45, ed. by Paolo Prodi and Wolfgang Reinhard (Bologna: il Mulino, 1996), pp. 225–54; Prosperi, *Tribunali della coscienza. Inquisitori, confessori, missionari* (Turin: Einaudi, 1996), pp. 219 ff.
66. Santo Burgio, 'La decadenza como risorsa. Diana e il probabilismo in Sicilia negli anni Trenta e Quaranta', in his *Teología barocca. Il probabilismo in Sicilia nell'epoca di Filippo IV* (Catania: Società di Storia Patria per la Sicilia Orientale, 1998), pp. 17ff.
67. Burgio, 'La decadenza como risorsa', in *Teología barocca*, pp. 76–77.
68. Molinos, *Defensa de la contemplación*, p. 132.
69. Jacques Le Brun, *La Spiritualité de Bossuet* (Paris: Librairie C. Klincksieck, 1972), pp. 439–562.
70. For example, Dudon, *Le Quiétiste espagnol*, pp. 60–62.
71. Le Brun, *La Spiritualité de Bossuet*, pp. 442–43.
72. Pierre Nicole, *Les Visionnaires ou seconde partie des lettres sur l'hérésie imaginaire* (Liège: Adolphe Beyers, 1667), pp. 28–29.
73. Nicole, *Les Visionnaires*, p. 44.
74. Nicole, *Les Visionnaires*, p. 48.
75. Le Brun, *La Spiritualité de Bossuet*, pp. 445–49.
76. [Louis-Paul Du Vaucel], *Breves considerationes in doctrinam Michelis de Molinos et aliorum quietistarum* (Cologne: Nicolaum Shouten, 1688), p. 3.
77. [Du Vaucel], *Breves considerationes*, p. 29.
78. [Du Vaucel], *Breves considerationes*, p. 13.
79. [Du Vaucel], *Breves considerationes*, p. 31.
80. Stefania Pastore, *Un'eresia spagnola. Spiritualità conversa, alumbradismo e Inquisizione (1449–1559)* (Florence: L. S. Olschki, 2004), pp. 208ff.; J. Fowler, 'Assembling Alumbradismo'.
81. Le Brun, *La Spiritualité de Bossuet*, pp. 445–46.
82. To give just one example, see the previously cited Nicole, *Les Visionnaires*, p. 234.
83. Santo Burgio, 'Gnostici, libertini, probabilisti. La perversa genealogia di John Sinnich', in *Filosofia e storiografia. Studi in onore di Giovanni Papuli. II. Età Moderna*, ed. by S. Ciurla (Galatina: Congedo, 2008), pp. 5–15. On another way of approaching the relationship between libertinism and Molinosism, in the case of Christina of Sweden, see Åkerman, *Queen Christina of Sweden*, pp. 284–94; though Åkerman stresses Molinos's possible *marrano* origin.
84. Le Brun, *La Spiritualité*, 455–56.
85. [Jean Cornand de Lacroze], *Recueil de diverses pièces concernant le quiétisme et les quiétistes, ou Molinos, ses sentiments et ses disciples* (Amsterdam: A. Wolfgang and P. Savouret, 1688). The other work is *Trois lettres touchant l'état présent d'Italie écrites en l'année 1687. La première regarde l'affaire de Molinos et des quiétistes* (Cologne: [n. pub.], 1688).
86. [Lacroze], *Recueil de diverses pièces*, pp. 6–14.
87. [Lacroze], *Recueil de diverses pièces*, p. 14.
88. [Lacroze], *Recueil de diverses pièces*, pp. 14–18.
89. [Lacroze], *Recueil de diverses pièces*, p. 20.
90. Philippe Couplet and Prospero Intorceta, *Confucius, Sinarum philosophus, sive Scientia sinensis* (Paris: Daniel Horthemels, 1687), p. xxxii.

91. Couplet and Intorceta, *Confucius, Sinarum philosophus*, pp. 24–25.
92. Urs App, *The Cult of Emptiness: The Western Discovery of Buddhist Thought and the Invention of Oriental Philosophy* (Rorschach and Kyoto: University Media, 2012), pp. 178ff. Also well known is the reference to the Quietism of Molinos made by Pierre Bayle when he speaks, for example, of Hinduism as an experience of nothingness: Bayle, 'Brachmanes', in *Dictionnaire critique et universel. Nouvelle édition* (Paris: Desoer, 1820), IV, 100–02.
93. Jean Leclercq and Jean Cornand de Lacroze, *Bibliothèque Universelle et Historique de l'année 1688*, vol. XI (Amsterdam: Wolfgang, Waesberge, Boom and Van Someren, 1698), p. 131.
94. App, *The Cult of Emptiness*, p. 178. We may recall, too, how the use of contacts with the Oriental world to qualify European polemical categories (such as Jansenism v. Jesuitism) was also used at a later date in the context of the controversy over 'Chinese rites'. See, for example, [Jacques-Hyacinthe Serry], *La calunnia convinta, cioè Risposta ad un libello pubblicato da' difensori de' riti condannati della Cina* (Turin: Gio. Battista Fontana, 1709).
95. Modica, *Infetta dottrina*, pp. 25–26.
96. Modica, *Infetta dottrina*, p. 12. The problem was an old one, and it naturally appeared in the condemnation of *alumbrados*, in which the opposition between knowledge and experience played a fundamental role. Antonio Márquez, *Los alumbrados. Orígenes y filosofía* (Madrid: Taurus, 1972), esp. the chapter titled '¿Conocimiento o experiencia?', pp. 167–77.
97. Joaquín García Palacios, *Los procesos de conocimiento en San Juan de la Cruz. Estudio léxico* (Salamanca: Universidad de Salamanca, 1992), pp. 24–25, and 120 n. 24.
98. 'desnudando al entendimiento de todas las semejanzas conocidas con que a su modo grosero y limitado hace concepto de Dios'; 'mayor conocimiento de Dios de lo que nos podía dar el discurso de la raçón'.
99. José de Jesús María Quiroga, *Apología mística en defensa de la contemplación*, ed. by Jean Krynen (Madrid: Real Academia Española, 1992), pp. 61 and 103–06.
100. Printed as an appendix to: Pilar Moreno Rodríguez, *El pensamiento de Miguel de Molinos* (Madrid: FUE-Universidad Pontificia de Comillas, 1992), pp. 601–30.
101. Tellechea Idígoras, *Léxico de la 'Guía espiritual' de Miguel de Molinos* (Madrid: FUE-Universidad Pontificia de Comillas, 1991), *sub voce*.
102. 'en este escollo del deseo de hacer la divina voluntad se han de romper todas las dificultades y vencer todos los escrúpulos, las tentaciones, las dudas, los temores, las repugnancias y contradicciones', Miguel de Molinos, *Guía espiritual*, ed. by José Ángel Valente (Madrid: Alianza Editorial, 1989), p. 113.
103. Dudon, *Le Quiétiste espagnol*, pp. 80–92.
104. [Du Vaucel], *Breves considerationes*, pp. 60–61.
105. Nicole, *Les Visionnaires*, p. 111.
106. Alastair Hamilton, *The Copts and the West, 1439–1822: The European Discovery of the Egyptian Church* (Oxford: Oxford University Press, 2009), pp. 152–59.
107. Steven M. Nadler, 'Arnauld, Descartes, and Transubstantiation: Reconciling Cartesian Metaphysics and Real Presence', *Journal of the History of Ideas*, 49 (1988), 229–46.
108. Roger Ariew, 'Descartes and the Jesuits: Doubt, Novelty, and the Eucharist', in *Jesuit Science and the Republic of Letters*, ed. by Mordechai Feingold (Cambridge, MA: The MIT Press, 2003), pp. 158–94.
109. Louis Marin, *La Critique du discours. Sur la 'Logique de Port-Royal' et les 'Pensées' de Pascal* (Paris: Minuit, 1975), pp. 10–11.
110. Cornand de Lacroze, 'Extraits d'une lettre angloise écrite de Rome en Hollande au sujet des Quiétistes; le 15 de Février 1687', in *Recueil de diverses pièces*, pp. 262–332.
111. The problem of Socinian criticism of the Trinity, with its arguments regarding the concepts of 'person', 'substance', 'transubstantiation'…, were especially virulent in England at this precise moment, in the 1690s. Douglas Hedley, 'Persons of Substance and the Cambridge Connection: Some Roots and Ramifications of the Trinitarian Controversy in Seventeenth-Century England', in *Socinianism and Arminianism. Antitrinitarians, Calvinists and Cultural Exchange in Seventeenth-Century Europe*, ed. by Martin Mulsow and Jan Rohls (Leiden: Brill, 2005), pp. 225–40.

112. Lacroze, 'Extraits d'une lettre angloise', in *Recueil de diverses pièces*, pp. 274–75.

113. Lacroze, 'Extraits d'une lettre angloise', in *Recueil de diverses pièces*, p. 276.

114. Le Brun, *La Spiritualité de Bossuet*, p. 442.

115. 'cada uno con el afecto y devoción que pudiere'. Two chapters of the manuscript of this work are not included in the printed edition. One is titled: 'que no es tan pequeña disposición el estar en gracia como a algunos les parece' ('being in a state of grace is not such a minor disposition as some suppose'), and the other: 'que Cristo dio la Comunión a imperfectos y pecadores, y los Apóstoles también; y assí no emos de ser rigurosos en querer negarla a los que fueren' ('that Christ and his Apostles gave communion to imperfect people and sinners; and therefore we ought not to be rigorous in wishing to deny it to those who are such'), Elías Gómez, *Fr. Juan Falconi de Bustamante, teólogo y asceta (1569–1638)* (Madrid: Escuela de Historia Moderna-CSIC, 1956), p. 209.

116. Ellacuría Beascoechea, *Reacción española*, pp. 92–95.

117. Tellechea Idígoras, *El proceso del doctor*, pp. 251–61.

118. 'Praepositis obediendum est in exteriori, et latitudo voti obedientiae religiosorum tantummodo ad exterius pertingit. In interiori vero aliter res se habet, ubi solus Deus et director intrant'; Dudon, *Le Quiétiste espagnol*, p. 299; Barambio, *Discursos philosóphicos*, II, 418.

119. 'Risu digna est nova quaedam doctrina, in Ecclesia Dei, quod anima quoad internum gubernari debeat ab episcopo et quod si episcopus non sit capax, anima ipsum cum suo directore adeat. Novam dico doctrinam, quia nec S. Scriptura, nec Concilia, nec Canones, nec Bullae, nec Sancti, nec Autores, eam unquam tradiderunt, nec tradere possunt, quia Ecclesia non iudicat de occultis et anima jus habet et facultatem eligendi quemcumque sibi bene visum'; Dudon, *Le Quiétiste espagnol*, p. 299; Barambio, *Discursos philosóphicos*, II, 438.

120. 'Dicere quod internum manifestandum est exteriori tribunali praepositorum, et quod peccatum sit id non facere, est manifesta deceptio; quia Ecclesia non judicat de occultis, et propriis animabus praejudicant his deceptionibus et simulationibus'; Dudon, *Le Quiétiste espagnol*, p. 299; Barambio, *Discursos philosóphicos*, II, 453.

121. 'in mundo non est facultas nec jurisdictio ad praecipiendum ut manifestentur epistolae directoris quoad internum animae et ideo opus est animadvertere quod hoc est insultus Satanae'; Dudon, *Le Quiétiste espagnol*, p. 299; Barambio, *Discursos philosóphicos*, II, 454.

122. Barambio, *Discursos philosóphicos*, II, 341.

123. Sérgio Cardoso, 'On Skeptical Fideism in Montaigne's *Apology for Raymond Sebond*', in *Skepticism in the Modern Age: Building on the Work of Richard Popkin*, ed. by José R. Maia Neto, John Christian Laursen and Gianni Paganini (Leiden: Brill, 2009), pp. 71–82.

124. Donald Rutherford, 'Leibniz and Mysticism', in *Leibniz, Mysticism and Religion*, ed. by Allison P. Coudert (Dordrecht: Kluwert Academic Publishers, 1998), pp. 22–37.

125. Jean-Louis Quantin, *Le Catholicisme classique et les Pères de l'Église. Un retour aux sources (1669–1713)* (Paris: Institut d'Études Augustiniennes, 1999), pp. 515ff.

CHAPTER 9

❖

The *Art* of Believing in Golden Age Spain

Felipe Pereda[1]

To believe: In Latin CREDERE, to assent to something that we do not understand or feel, which is the distinctive response of faith. 2. In human affairs, those with little trust in others have this saying: 'Seeing is believing', which strictly speaking means *not believing*.

(*Creer: Latine* CREDERE, asentir con lo que no entendemos o sentimos, propio acto de la fe. 2. En las cosas humanas los que se fían poco de los demás tienen este refrán: 'Ver y creer', que en rigor es *no creer*.)

SEBASTIÁN DE COVARRUBIAS, *Tesoro de la lengua castellana o española* (1611)

However it is not possible for the same thing to be for the same person both an object of sight and an object of belief. Whence it follows that it is impossible for the same thing to be for the same person an object of knowledge and an object of belief.

(*Non autem est possibile quod idem ab eodem sit creditum et visum...*
Unde etiam impossibile est quod ab eodem idem sit scitum et creditum.)

THOMAS AQUINAS, *Summa Theologiae*, 2a-2a, q. 1, a. 5

'Pretence? No. Not pretence! That is not pretending!
"Dip your fingers in holy water, and you will end by believing",
as someone said.
And I, gazing into his eyes, asked him,
"And you, celebrating the mass, have you ended by believing?".
He lowered his gaze to the lake and his eyes filled with tears.

('¿Fingir? ¡Fingir no! ¡eso no es fingir!
Toma agua bendita, que dijo alguien, y acabarás creyendo.
Y como yo, mirándole a los ojos, le dijese:
"¿Y usted celebrando misa ha acabado por creer?"
él bajó la mirada al lago y se le llenaron los ojos de lágrimas'.)

MIGUEL DE UNAMUNO, *San Manuel Bueno, Mártir.*

FIG. 9.I. 'Christ and Two Followers on the Road to Emmaus' (*c.* 1630).
Oil on canvas, 51.5 × 66.7 cm. The Walters Art Museum, Baltimore, MD.

A Painting and an Argument in a Tavern

A small painting usually attributed to the Sevillian school and now in the Walters Art Gallery in Baltimore shows an episode from the Gospels that was rarely portrayed in the Spanish Baroque (Luke 24. 13–29) [**Fig. 1**]. The scene is set at the entrance to Emmaus, where two of Jesus's followers have just arrived after a long journey on foot (one is Cleopas, the other is unnamed). Three days have passed since their master's death, and as they walked the travellers had been expressing their concern about their master's announced resurrection. The men's spirits have begun to sink. A mysterious foreigner (*peregrino*) has joined them along the way, and taking an interest in their conversation he surprises them with a reproach for their lack of faith in the prophets. When the disciples reach their destination they have not recognized their fellow traveller because, according to Luke, their eyes have been 'holden'.[2]

The painting shows the exact moment when, at the entrance to the town, the master pretends (*finxit*) that he will continue on his way and one of the companions persuades him to stay and share their supper. The painter has approached the subject as a story about how the senses are challenged when faced with proof of the resurrection. The composition is carefully planned and the figures at the two sides are perfectly symmetrical.[3] Their bodies are twisted, as the apostle on the left hastens to enter the town while on the other side Jesus gestures with his hand in the opposite direction, preparing to walk toward the viewer. One is entering the painting while the other is hastening to leave it. Their bare feet are in similar positions but reversed, just before they set out on different paths. The artist painted them in identical fashion in order to dramatize the 'reversal' in the story: the very moment when events begin to unfold in exactly the opposite way as was expected. According to Aristotle's *Poetics*, this reversal (in Greek, *peripeteia*) is one of the two basic devices that tragedy uses to seize the attention of an audience.[4]

Between the two lateral figures is that of the second apostle. A good deal older, even elderly, he is dressed entirely in black, down to his shoes. Cleopas is bent awkwardly toward the anonymous pilgrim. His face is partially hidden by a deep shadow and his eyes, also shaded, look downward without meeting those of his master. In contrast to Jesus's open eyes, the disciple's are hardly more than a smear of dark pigment, as if they were dead. With his large left hand he is clutching Jesus's shoulder to oblige him to stay; but since his eyes have not recognized the Christ, his sense of touch will not help him either.

In a passage from the Gospel of Mark that drew the attention of some Baroque painters, the evangelist tells us that two of the disciples failed to recognize Jesus because he appeared to them *in alia effigie*, 'in another form', with a different aspect. (Mark 16. 12). Our painter has ignored this detail: Jesus's face, his frontal posture, and the luminous aura behind him all betray his identity. The Baltimore painting dramatizes the senses' limited ability to recognize the mystery of the resurrection, while at the same time making the viewer into a privileged witness. To what extent can our senses offer reasons, even evidence, that will allow us to believe? And to the contrary, to what extent is faith incompatible with sight? How does faith necessarily reside in those things that we do *not* see?

★　★　★　★　★

A tavern would not seem to be the best place to look for an answer to these questions and to the mysterious story shown in the painting; but it was in a tavern, and not in a church or a confessional — not even in a library — where a conversation took place that is recorded in one puzzling document in the Inquisition section of the National Archives in Madrid.

In 1582 the judges of the Holy Office in Madrid interrogated a French artisan who went by the name of Antón de Duay. Antón had become embroiled in a discussion with a certain Andrés Marquina (whom we will call simply Andrés). The latter had met a group of women and criticized the way that they spent their leisure time; he insisted that instead of chattering away they should employ themselves in something more useful. And he reminded them that in a recent bull the pope had declared that for every rosary said, the soul of a Christian would be released from Purgatory; therefore the women should be counting their beads. Antón the Frenchman, who had overheard, made a sour face and was unwise enough to disagree, and the resulting heated but weighty conversation is preserved for us thanks to the professional diligence of the Holy Office.

Antón and Andrés ended up quarrelling about the nature of faith and, eventually, about whether faith could be explained by the evidence of our senses. While each had a different opinion of the matter, each called on exactly the same authority to bolster his arguments. To begin at the beginning, these are the words that provoked the argument, according to the trial transcript:

> [...] and a man who was there, who seemed by his way of speaking to be French, said that he did not believe this for it had to be seen to be believed. And this witness [Andrés] replied that in a hospital in Madrid there were records of pardons [indulgences] and these had been published: and he believed this just as Holy Mother Church commands. And the aforementioned man [Antón] said that he would not believe it without seeing it, for God had not named anyone but Saint Peter and Saint Paul as pontiffs. And the other reproved him for his words, telling him that we are required to believe and follow what the supreme pontiff commanded according to the Catholic faith, and the man said that the other did not know what he was talking about [...]

So far, the issue seems to be a simple one. The Spaniard, Andrés, spoke relying on the papal bull that had been published in Madrid, while the Frenchman not only questioned the pope's authority to publish it but even doubted the existence of the bull. He would have to see it to believe it. At this point in the discussion the Spaniard, trying to prove that the senses are of no use and may even contradict our experience of faith, decided to bring in the most extreme example he could, that of the Eucharist. Then the argument grew heated:

> [...] and [Andrés] also told him that when the consecrated host was elevated he worshipped it as both God and true Man, for the Catholic faith says that we are to hold and believe that. Then the Frenchman said:
> — That is different [!] But *what I do not see I do not believe*, and Saint Thomas is Prester John of the Indies. [*see on this below*]
> And [Andrés] replied at once:
> — *You mean to say see and believe* like [Doubting] Thomas[!].
> And [Antón] said, '*Exactly: [that] what he doesn't see he doesn't believe.*' [emphasis added].[5]

So Andrés and Antón both identified themselves with the Thomas of the Gospel of John, the disciple who doubted the evidence of his own eyes and was encouraged to feel with his own hand the proof that Jesus had risen. But Andrés's Thomas and Antón's Thomas seem to be two different people. The Frenchman thought of Thomas as a sceptic who could only be convinced by the proof of his senses, but for Andrés the apostle was the symbol of total faith. For Antón, Thomas's story was one of unbelief; for Andrés it meant that the mysteries of the faith are within the reach of our fingers.

Their disagreement could be seen as just one more example of the early modern crisis of faith, a faith steadily eroded by secular attitudes of scepticism and the political fragmentation of the Church. But it also reveals a historic change in the forms and standards of belief during this period, both inside and outside the religious sphere. To follow their conversation we must be aware of two separate problems: the first, obviously, is why the story of Thomas meant such different things to the two men; and the second is what each of them understood by 'belief'. Although their argument may seem somewhat unnecessary or even hair-splitting, I will begin by taking up the second point.

Forms of *Believing*

It is important to note that with the terms 'having faith' and 'believing', Andrés and Antón were referring to two different things. Their statements even suggest that a person could profess either one of them without the other. One of the discussants showed an unshakable loyalty to the Catholic faith: 'That is different!' the Frenchman burst out when Andrés tried to show him the cracks that his faith revealed, but he also confessed to and even boasted of reasonable doubts about Church doctrine. Further, Andrés and Antón were in perfect agreement about the mystery of the Eucharist (which one of them defined, without being contradicted, as part of the 'Catholic *faith*'). They immediately disagreed, however, about how one should understand and believe the teachings of the Church. Had Jesus really instituted pontiffs other than Peter? Was the system of Indulgences legitimate?

In the words of Andrés and Antón we see the tension between faith as received and practised by members of the Church to which they both belonged as baptized Catholics, and the individual beliefs that each of them held. There is nothing new in this, of course; it is an experience no more typical of a man of the Reformation than of one of the Middle Ages or the twenty-first century.[6] But at the time when this tavern discussion was recorded — a time that has been described as characterized by a desperate search for certainty — something was changing.[7] Having faith was no longer enough; *believing*, and what and how one believed, had become a problem once again on both sides of the frontier laid down by the Reformation.

At this point we must make a brief digression about terminology. The original meaning of the concept and term *faith*, as it appears in Scripture, is found at the very origin of monotheism: it is the loyalty or trust that one places in God.[8] This is the sense of the Hebrew root *'mn'*, translated in the Septuagint as *pisteúein*, still within the semantic field of loyalty and full certitude (in Romance languages *confiar*, *confier*, *confidare*, etc.).[9] As Wilfred Cantwell Smith, who based all his work on an analysis of the term, was able to show, the word 'to believe', [*credo > credere*], referred to something similar;[10] its etymology leads us to Pascal's reasons of the heart, since it occurs in interpersonal relations. It is the act by which we put our faith in someone (a person) or something (an institution), offering him or it our loyalty at the same time.[11]

The protagonists of our document do not seem to have used the terms with this meaning, and they did not think of them as synonyms. If Andrés and Antón spoke of *faith* as the firm trust that they professed as Christians, they reserved *belief* for the specific doctrines of the Church — in this case, since they were debating the existence of a bull, even its judicial authority. For Andrés and Antón *faith* was the basis shared by the members of the community, but *belief* had what Smith called a 'propositional' meaning.[12]

We do not need to accept the conclusions of this American philosopher — that the act of believing in the monotheistic religions is not only recent but spurious, and that as a result religion is a 'modern' invention[13] — to recognize through his analysis the basic tension between two principles that originate in the New Testament, beginning with the Epistles of Paul.[14] As Bultmann showed in his classic work, in the Epistles — the first written document in Christianity — faith is no longer just *belief in* the existence 'of a hitherto unknown divine personage', a 'foreign divinity' (Acts 17. 18);[15] it is not merely an act of will by which one puts one's trust in him, because 'the figure of Jesus Christ cannot be separated from his "myth", i.e., from the history of the events of his life death, and resurrection'.[16]

If in the Old Testament the act of faith is an act of loyalty because of how God works in history, in the New Testament the object of faith is the content of God's prophetic message, what is known as his *Kerygma*. This distinction is important from both a historical and a cultural point of view. Martin Buber, in a famous essay, interpreted it as a sort of breach opened within the Pauline faith: a double principle, inherited from the Hebrew tradition on the one hand and Greek philosophy on the other. Buber reminds us that in Paul's most famous definition of faith, for the first time it has two aspects: it is not only 'the substance of things hoped for' but the 'proof [*elenchos*] of things not seen' (Hebrews 11. 1). It is both the object of belief and the proof of it.[17]

The breach between faith and the act of believing was thus initiated in the New Testament, but the tension between the two principles was destined to increase wherever any kind of doctrinal debate took place.[18] The advent of the Inquisition is both a symptom and a cause of this process.[19] As our example dramatizes, while religious conflicts were dismembering the unity of the Church, the elements that determined the content of each Church (the Roman and the Reformed) were acquiring new relevance.[20] The result could be none other than a continuous tension between the cognitive act of believing in something and faith as an act of allegiance and assent, loyalty and obedience.[21] The debate between Antón and Andrés in that Madrid tavern also shows that in sixteenth-century Spain this distinction was not only watched and spied on but that any deviation was followed up and potentially punished. The activity of the Church and its Tribunal of the Faith could therefore be seen as an effort to repair a unity that had been broken.[22]

Doubt and Certainty of the Apostle Thomas

Andrés and Antón, then, were living at a turbulent time in history when it was no longer enough to have faith; one had to know how to believe, so one's reasons for believing suddenly became relevant. It was natural for Andrés to fall back on the authority of the Roman Catholic Church and for both men to draw on Scripture for their arguments. What is interesting is that both actors in our anecdote should quote the same Bible story, the one about Doubting Thomas in the Gospel of John, and that they should interpret it in two very different — or worse, incompatible — ways. Furthermore, as we are about to see, neither way coincides exactly with how the great Scholastics had explained it — an explanation that, paradoxically, could be found in some of the manuals that the Inquisition supplied to its judges.

The conversation between the two men contains a hidden trap, a significant misunderstanding. For the sceptical Antón de Duay, Thomas's boldness in feeling Jesus's wound with his fingers justified his own doubt: only if Antón could see with his own eyes the indulgences under discussion could he believe in them. To judge by the words that the Inquisition notary carefully took down, Antón added a few ironic remarks to his account when he recalled the legend that linked the Apostle Thomas to Prester John of the Indies.[23] The medieval tale had been printed in Spanish a number of times: a sacred relic consisting of Thomas's arm and hand was kept in his mythical kingdom 'as fresh as if he were still alive'. But curiously, every time a successor to the throne was chosen it was the relic that made the decision by pointing toward the favoured candidate.[24] Antón was proud of sharing Saint Thomas's scepticism.[25] Just like Rabelais's Pantagruel — who, ironically, married the daughter of the mythical emperor of Ethiopia — the Frenchman insisted that if something was not self-evident he would need to see proof to be convinced of it: his words were reported as 'that's right, what he does not see he does not believe'.[26]

But we saw that Andrés replied at once, 'You mean to say seeing and believing, like Saint Thomas[!]'. The interlocutor had understood the story in exactly the opposite way. The Spaniard's retort might seem entirely orthodox — and the Holy Office seems to have taken it as such — but as we have just pointed out, it does not necessarily match the exegesis of this passage in Church teaching. Thomas Aquinas, for one, saw Saint Thomas's doubt as the classic example of the discontinuity between faith and vision, and therefore between faith and knowledge; the painting that we discussed at the beginning illustrates this principle perfectly.[27] For Aquinas the point of the story was that Thomas 'saw' one thing but 'believed' another: he saw a man but believed in God incarnate.[28] The thing seen is not a sufficient cause of faith; there must be a willing act of assent or adherence on the believer's part. Andrés, however, drew the opposite conclusion.

The disagreement between Andrés and Antón should not surprise us. During the Reformation period in which they lived, exegesis had reopened a problem of interpretation that had long lain dormant. A fascinating study has shown us how throughout the sixteenth century the exegesis of John 20. 24–29 followed two divergent paths.[29] Some Protestant theologians questioned whether Thomas had obeyed his master's command — whether he had only seen, but not touched, Jesus's body. (In the Gospel account the touch does not actually take place; Jesus merely invites it.) Calvin, for instance, criticized the Apostle's faith in his senses, a faith that needed to see — *quia vidisti me, Thomae, credidisti* — and even to touch, in order to believe; a faith that has been called 'epistemic' and which in Calvin's opinion was therefore imperfect.[30]

In the Roman Church, on the other hand, the authors of the Catholic Counter-Reformation could recognize in Jesus's words that we cannot come to faith through the evidence of our senses ('nor does it rely on what is seen', noted the Jesuit Jerónimo de Nadal); but they did not doubt that Thomas really placed his fingers on

Jesus's wound.[31] This compromise position preserved the ultimate, non-epistemic nature of their faith, its theological essence, without threatening the historical truth of the Gospels, which were based on the physical signs (*signa*) and proofs available to eye-witnesses. (Some of those proofs, such as the Holy Shroud, were relics that survived the Gospel era and would become crucial in figurative art.) In other words Catholic exegesis, while remaining rooted in the Scholastic tradition, was responding to the growing importance that empirical proof, testimony and autopsy were gaining in the human and natural sciences.[32] That is why Andrés's response is no less 'modern' than Antón's, or even incompatible with the Christian reception of Sceptical philosophy.[33] Andrés and Antón represent two different modes of dialogue between faith and reason in the early modern age.

The Spaniard's position in our tavern dispute accords with this new Catholic trend.[34] The Apostle's doubt did not undermine Andrés's faith in the least — on the contrary, it confirmed it.[35] Thomas, to Andrés, was not the symbol of a sort of scientific scepticism; rather he epitomized a deeply rooted faith, 'confirmed' by the senses. Far from interpreting, like Aquinas, that the wound the Apostle's fingers touched was the gulf between faith and experience, the Spaniard drew a far different conclusion: that what his eyes had seen provided the evidence he needed in order to believe. Translated into Scholastic terms this means that the senses may not be able to provide certainty, but do offer *credibility*: not the space where faith recognizes the ultimate truth[36] but the one occupied by what Aquinas called 'the evidence of signs' (*evidentia signorum*).[37]

That was the posture of the Inquisitor Diego de Simancas in his 1552 *Institutiones Catholicae*, which the members of Antón and Andrés's tribunal might well have consulted and which contains a long chapter on *De fide Catholica* that deals with the Doubting Thomas episode.[38] Simancas, after acknowledging that non-epistemic faith is superior and insisting with the Angelic Doctor that true faith does not require the help of the senses,[39] criticized what he saw as the radically subjective 'credulity' of the Lutheran faith.[40] And he immediately recalled that on one hand the truth of the Catholic faith was based on revelation, but on the other was 'confirmed' by 'innumerable miracles, Scripture, the learned and wise witnesses [of the Church]',[41] testimonies, reasoning and arguments in which truth was manifested, and before which man's understanding could only surrender.[42]

It should now be clear that Thomas's doubt, when placed in this context, played a role that was vital but diametrically opposed in the reasonings of Antón the sceptic and Andrés the firm believer. The two attitudes represent the complementary faces of a complex and progressive undermining of the medieval concept of *fides*, in which Faith now would have to be defined within the certainty of revelation; while 'belief', paradoxically, had entered into the realm of doubt.[43] Antón de Duay's interpretation of the passage on Saint Thomas's incredulity testifies eloquently to the fact. And the definition of 'believing' by Sebastián de Covarrubias, quoted as one of our epigraphs, is no less telling: 'seeing is believing, which strictly speaking means not *believing*'.

Doubt, Belief and the Art of Painting?

As Paul Veyne has written, the variety of modes of *believing* also reflects the full range of criteria for the nature of truth.[44] During the early modern age these criteria underwent an irreversible transformation. The impulse to decide how to discover and prove truths about nature, how to demonstrate one's discoveries, and how to convince one's audience produced a critical re-examination that would profoundly transform the structure of disciplines and their methods of proof.[45] The frontiers of faith were far from impermeable to this process. In the realm that Scholasticism would have called 'of credibility', an important dialogue took place between the areas of faith and science that would prove fundamental for defining early modern Catholicism. Thus began what Cardinal Newman termed 'The Age of Evidences', during which the Church would seek reasons for believing using the same tools and experimental methods as the natural sciences.[46] Throughout the seventeenth century autopsy and empirical observation played a decisive role in Biblical exegesis,[47] the defence of relics, processes of canonization, and the proving of miracles, as a growing number of studies have shown.[48] This process would soon affect the art of painting, turning it first into an instrument for providing evidences, before the status itself of this medium started to be questioned.

Before we summarize the answers that the present work will explore, we must first address the question: what end was the painter pursuing? Francisco Pacheco of Seville — one of the most important theoreticians of art in early modern Spain, and probably the most original — identified two objectives of this art: one general, which is imitation (he calls it the 'soul' of art), and one specific and proper to the Christian artist, which is persuasion, 'moving' men and leading them to piety. In Francisco Pacheco's [1649] opinion this was the 'principal' purpose of painting and of the Catholic painter.[49] The ultimate problem that faced the artist, for Pacheco, was not imitation but persuasion.

Pacheco of course borrows this comparison from rhetoric, in which convincing depends as much on the state of mind that the orator creates in his hearers (*pathos*) as on the signs or proofs that make up his argument (*logos*).[50] The painting's dramatic intensity 'moves' the viewer to share its characters' emotions, but the reasoning that his reactions provoke persuades him in equal measure — as Quintilian put it, *ad faciendam fidem* 'producing belief'.[51]

The painting of Spain's Golden Age, like rhetoric, exists between these two extremes of argumentation and emotion, between the 'what' and the 'how', between the evidence offered by the image portrayed and the persuasion it achieves through the art of imitation. On the one hand, the painter is a maker of images: in Seville, once an artist had passed the guild's examination he held the title of *pintor de imaginería*. In this sense the artist, whether painter or sculptor, is representing the 'truth' of religion. But on the other hand (as Pacheco informs us, paraphrasing the Italian Varchi) painting is the art of deception, so much so that its sister art, sculpture — whose reality we can assess through our sense of touch — is to painting 'as truth is to *falsehood*'.[52] Insofar as painting creates images, it is the art of truth; but paradoxically, insofar as it imitates it is the art of deceit and illusion.[53]

FIG. 9.2. Francisco de Zurbarán, 'La cena de Emaús', 1639. Oil on canvas.
Museo Nacional de San Carlos, Mexico.

The painting from the Walters Gallery with which we began embodies this apparent contradiction. The disciple touches his master and looks at him without seeing him, with eyes that are still veiled; but we, the viewers, are witnesses to the deception. Golden Age painting would explore this paradox with extraordinary creativity, as we shall see in a brief discussion of two more paintings. The Gospel account goes on to offer one of the themes that most attracted the interest of painters: Jesus finally accepts the invitation, and when all are seated together in Emmaus and Jesus breaks bread, only then, as a famous Catholic exegete would put it, 'would... their faith and virtues [be] firmed, their doubts dispelled'.[54]

An example that represents this episode can help to enrich our discussion. The *Supper at Emmaus* is not a common theme in Spanish Baroque painting, but we do have a superb example from the brush of Francisco de Zurbarán. Signed and dated in 1639, it was most likely painted in Seville to be sent to New Spain, where it would eventually hang in a Mexican monastery and form a pair with a Doubting Thomas that we are about to see. An analysis of these two paintings will serve as a perfect prelude to the dialectic of pictorial fiction to which our reading of Francisco Pacheco has introduced us.

The *Supper at Emmaus* describes what happened, according to the Gospel of Luke, on the same evening that the two disciples met the mysterious foreigner on the way to the town. In the Scriptural account Jesus blessed the bread, broke it, and gave it to his companions, 'and their eyes were opened, and they knew him; and he vanished out of their sight' (Luke 24. 31). In the narrative these three moments (after the earlier blessing) are simultaneous and exegesis insists on that fact, creating a challenge for the temporal unity of pictorial representation.[55]

Zurbarán's painting joins an ancient tradition, but his solution is especially original.[56] He has depicted the instant of 'recognition', which corresponds to the second medium available to tragedy to captivate its audience: *anagnorisis* (or 'agnition', as Baroque readers translated it; we saw how the first medium was *peripeteia* or 'reversal').[57] In Aristotle's description one recognizes a person with whom one was familiar but whose appearance has changed; he has therefore gone unrecognized but his identity is finally revealed.[58] The two disciples and Jesus are seated at the table with the foreigner in the centre, facing the viewer. Jesus has blessed the bread and is now breaking it with his hands.

In the painting we see how the disciples recognize their master in the 'sign' of his breaking the bread. But they are looking not at his hands but at his face, where now Jesus is in fact represented *in alia effigie*, as the Gospel of Mark has it: the brim of his large hat casts a partial shadow on his face, which is further obscured by a long, thick, dark beard, black like his hair. Darkness surrounds the figure, without any halo or light around the body that might betray his divine nature (Zurbarán paints two consecutive moments in one image).[59] Therefore the disciples recognize Jesus in his Eucharistic gesture of breaking bread — not *from* his appearance but *in spite of* it. Their eyes have been opened and they are learning to see 'through a glass, darkly'.[60] The painting invites the viewer to follow the disciples in this same exercise and to recognize what lies beyond appearances, making the meaning of the Supper at Emmaus a prefiguration of the Eucharist.[61]

Before its transfer to a museum the painting hung in the Augustinian monastery in Mexico City, in the crossing of the church.[62] There it formed a pair with a painting whose theme was also faith and doubt, *The Incredulity of Saint Thomas* by Sebastián López de Arteaga (1610–52). The works by Zurbarán and Arteaga are not only related narratively and dramatically but show other obvious stylistic and compositional similarities. Departing from the most recent tradition, Arteaga produced a monumental composition with full (as opposed to half) figures and in life size, as in the Supper. Jesus is also flanked by his disciples. The extreme simplicity of the clothing and the warm palette of colours, even the dimensions of the two paintings, are virtually identical.[63] Arteaga undoubtedly knew Zurbarán's painting and probably planned his own to act as its companion.

FIG. 9.3. Sebastián López de Arteaga, 'La incredulidad de Santo Tomás'. © D.R. Museo Nacional de Arte / Instituto Nacional de Bellas Artes y Literatura (Mexico) 2017.

What little we know about the painter's biography is unusual, and important for our purposes. Arteaga was born in Seville in 1610 and passed the examination there as a *pintor de imaginería* [maker of images] in 1630. He began his career by opening a workshop in Cádiz, and embarked for New Spain ten years later. He was already in Mexico City in 1643, for in that year he signed two important works: a monumental four-nail Crucifixion that was to hang in the Tribunal of the Holy Office, and the *Incredulity of Saint Thomas*. (Zurbarán's painting is dated 1639.) Both are signed with the recently granted title 'notary of the Holy Office', which Arteaga had sought ever since his arrival and which gained him important commissions by the Inquisition — indeed, most of his known works fall into that category.[64]

Following the typology of Northern origin that Caravaggio had made famous in his 'Incredulity of Saint Thomas' (Potsdam, 1601–02), Jesus holds the apostle by the wrist and makes him insert his fingers into the wound in his side.[65] The apostle then casts his eyes upward, indicating that his senses of sight and touch confirm each other. The painting is an eloquent illustration of the relationship of seeing to believing ('because thou hast seen me, thou hast believed', were His words), which is repeated in the Gospel of John more often and more clearly than in any of the synoptic Gospels.

Both paintings from the Augustinian monastery represent the act of believing. Zurbarán's, and Arteaga's painted to match it, draw their themes from Scriptural passages in which individuals must bear witness (*martyría*) to what they have seen with their own eyes — by no coincidence, one passage is from the Gospel of Luke and one from John.[66] Inspired by these two accounts, the paintings show the viewer two different ways in which belief is an exercise involving three separate steps: an initial state of mistrust; the moment when the senses receive a sign or demonstration, a 'piece of evidence'; and finally, access to the truth. In both cases 'belief' has an argumentative sense that we would call (with Wilfred C. Smith) 'propositional'. The paintings by Zurbarán and Arteaga display two different ways — perhaps contrasting but also complementary — in which Golden Age painting approached the connection between faith and sight, certainty and doubt.

★   ★   ★   ★   ★

Since the first discovery of Spanish painting in the middle of the nineteenth century, a still-flourishing historiographic tradition has considered such episodes as proof that Spanish Golden Age art was profoundly religious, sacred by definition. In this tradition faith and belief are simple synonyms.[67] But the paintings from the Augustinian monastery seem to tell a more complicated story. As I hope to have shown through Andrés and Antón's conversation in a Madrid tavern in 1582, the nature of faith was by no means a simple issue in Golden Age Spain and many voices joined in debating it. To ask oneself what, and especially how, Saint Thomas *believed* was to wonder what his testimony was based on. The question of faith had acquired an inescapably epistemological dimension.

The art of the Golden Age is inextricably linked to the question of *truth*, inside and outside the borders of painting, a question that made testimonies of paintings, while turning their spectators into witnesses. Against this 'forensic' background Golden Age artists' obsession with illusion, absence and deceit, on the one hand — all aspects present in the paintings we have been analysing — and the desperate quest for certainty in this same period's spirituality, on the other, emerge — I would argue — as two intimately related aspects, even complementary aspects, of one and the same phenomenon.

Notes to Chapter 9

1. The research leading to these results has received funding from the European Research Council under the European Union's Seventh Framework Programme (FP7/2007–2013) / ERC grant agreement no. 323316, project CORPI, 'Conversion, Overlapping Religiosities, Polemics and Interaction. Early Modern Iberia and Beyond', led by Mercedes García-Arenal. A Spanish version of this article appeared as part of the introduction to my book, *Crimen e Ilusión. La búsqueda de la verdad en el arte del Siglo de Oro* (Madrid: Marcial Pons, 2017); English version *Crime and Illusion: The Art of Truth in the Spanish Golden Age*, trans. by Consuelo López-Morillas (Turnhout: Brepols; London: Harvey Miller, 2018).

2. Luke 24. 16 (all English translations are from the King James Version (KJV)). In the Reina-Valera Spanish translation (1602), *velados*; in the Vulgate, *oculi autem illorum tenebantur*. In the later scene of the supper, 'and their eyes were opened, and they knew him'; Vulgate *aperti sunt oculi eorum et cognoverunt eum* (Luke 24. 31).

3. I thank Joaneath Spicer for having drawn my attention to this detail.

4. Aristotle, *Poetics* 1450a. 'Peripecia se dice mudanza súbita de la cosa en contrario que antes era [...]': Alonso López Pinciano, *Filosofía antigua poética* [1596], in *Obras completas*, ed. by José Rico Verdú (Madrid: Fundación José Antonio de Castro, 1998), p. 182. The other, the moment of recognition, occurs at a later point in this same story and is much more common in the painting of this period, as we shall see.

5. '... [E] un onbre que allí estava que le paresçió en el hablar ser françés dijo que él no creía tal, que avía menester vello para creello. Y este declarante le replicó que en el ospital de la corte avía cuentas de perdones e se publicava y este lo crehía como la santa madre yglesia lo manda y el dicho honbre dijo que si no lo viese que no lo crehía, que dios no avría echo pontífices más de san pedro e san pablo e este le reprehendió lo susodicho diziéndole que estávamos obligados a creher e cumplir lo que el sumo pontifice mandava conforme a la fe católica y el dicho honbre dijo que este no savía lo que dezía [...] y que tanbién le dijo este que quando alçavan la hostia consagrada este la adorava como a dios y honbre verdadero que hera fe católica que se avía de tener e creher ansí y el dicho honbre françés dijo: "Heso es otra cosa, mas lo que yo no veo no lo creo que santo tomás es preste juan de las yndias". Y este le dijo luego: "Querreys dezir ver y creher como santo thomás". E dijo el dicho honbre que sí, que lo que el no ve no lo cree'. Archivo Histórico Nacional (AHN), Inq., Leg. 206, 18. 'Antón de Duay [Douai] from Flanders, a carver, resident of Madrid' (Antón de Duay, flamenco, entallador, vecino de Madrid) [Madrid, 7 May 1582].

6. Sabina Flanagan, *Doubt in an Age of Faith: Uncertainty in the Long Twelfth Century* (Turnhout: Brepols, 2008); see also the material collected in John H. Arnold, *Belief and Unbelief in Medieval Europe* (London: Hodder Arnold, 2005). For Spain only specialized studies exist, for example, John Edwards, 'Religious Faith and Doubt in Late Medieval Spain: Soria circa 1450–1500', *Past & Present*, 120 (1988), 3–25.

7. Susan Schreiner, *Are You Alone Wise? The Search for Certainty in the Early Modern Era* (Oxford: Oxford University Press, 2011).

8. Jan Assmann, *Of God and Gods: Egypt, Israel, and the rise of Monotheism* (Madison: University of Wisconsin Press, 2008), p. 116.

9. 'Faith is always particular; and it lies in the realm of trust and loyalty among persons, of the giving of oneself and the finding of, being found by, the other. The word "believe" once

designated that': Wilfred C. Smith, *Believing: An Historical Perspective* (Oxford: Oneworld, 1998), p. 58. Needham defended the same analysis from an anthropological perspective, although he and Smith do not seem to have known of each other's statements; Rodney Needham's *Belief, Language, and Experience* (Oxford: Basil Blackwell, 1972) opens with a careful historical study of the term, pp. 40–50; he later asserts that 'Belief is not a discriminable experience, it does not constitute a natural resemblance among men, and it does not belong to the "common behaviour of mankind"', p. 188.

10. Smith, *Faith and Belief: The Difference between Them* (Oxford: Oneworld, 1998), p. 76. See a representation of his work and a criticism of his essentialism in Talal Asad, 'Reading a Modern Classic: W. C. Smith's *The Meaning and End of Religion*', *History of Religions*, 40.3 (2001), 205–22.

11. Emile Benveniste, *Le Vocabulaire des institutions indo-européennes* (Paris: Éditions de Minuit, 1969), pp. 171–79, where, however, the theory that it has the same origin as Latin *cor, cordis* is discussed and rejected.

12. The essential definition of a 'propositional' statement is that it may be either true or false and therefore falls within the realm of opinion (*opinio*); in the Thomist tradition that we will examine later on, this is wholly distinct from the realm of *fides*. 'Modern' history in which *credere* increasingly fell into the sphere of opinion ('drifting away from Faith') is the object of analysis in Smith, *Belief and History* (Charlottesville: University Press of Virginia, 1977), esp. pp. 36–65.

13. This thesis is developed in perhaps the most famous of Smith's works, *The Meaning and End of Religion: A New Approach to the Religious Traditions of Mankind* (New York: Macmillan, 1963). See a brilliant analysis of this debate that takes Smith as its starting point in Brent Nongbri, *Before Religion: A History of a Modern Concept* (New Haven, CT: Yale University Press, 2013), esp. pp. 3–5.

14. We follow here the criticism of Malcolm Ruel, *Belief, Ritual and the Securing of Life: Reflexive Essays on a Bantu Religion* (Leiden: Brill, 1997), pp. 36–59. I thank Yonatan Glazer-Eytan for this reference.

15. 'Strange gods', in KJV.

16. Rudolf Bultmann and Artur Weiser, *Faith* (London: Black, 1961), p. 75. Bultmann traces the origin of this new type of faith to a new construction (*pistis eis* in the accusative, rather than the dative, characteristic of the Septuagint, pp. 58–60, 68. There is a useful reconstruction of the problem in Salvador Pié-Ninot, *La teología fundamental* (Barcelona: Biblioteca de Autores Cristianos, 2006), pp. 175–92.

17. Martin Buber, *Two Types of Faith* (New York: Macmillan, 1950), p. 37. This important work is in need of a new and more careful edition. Kinneavy, in an analysis from the Greek perspective, has emphasized the rhetorical origin of *pistis*, 'faith', in the New Testament and especially the logical use of *elegchos*, as argument, proof, or evidence: James L. Kinneavy, *Greek Rhetorical Origins of Christian Faith* (Oxford: Oxford University Press, 1987), pp. 127–30.

18. In the Catholic Church's traditional formulation, *fides qua*, the act of believing, as opposed to *fides quae*, faith in a given proposition.

19. According to Wirth, 'the [Inquisition's] methods are incompatible with the traditional definition of *fides*. Now it is a matter of establishing an objective truth by means of evidence': Jean Wirth, 'La Naissance du concept de croyance', *Bibliothèque d'Humanisme et Renaissance*, 45.1 (1983), 7–58. See also Jean-Pierre Cavaillé, 'Les Frontiers de l'inacceptable. Pour un réexamen de l'histoire de l'incrédulité', *Les Dossiers du Grihl* <https://dossiersgrihl.revues.org/4746, accessed 18/04/2017>; Alain Mothu, 'De la foi du charbonnier à celle du héros (et retour)', *Les Dossiers du Grihl* <https://dossiersgrihl.revues.org/3393, accessed 18/04/2017>.

20. Jaroslav Pelikan, *Credo: Historical and Theological Guide to Creeds and Confessions of Faith in the Christian Tradition* (New Haven, CT: Yale University Press, 2005), pp. 53–92; J. Pelikan and Valerie R. Hotchkiss, *Creeds and Confessions of Faith in the Christian Tradition*, 3 vols (New Haven, CT: Yale University Press, 2003), vol. II, esp. pp. 3–25.

21. In Scholastic theology these are called respectively *fides explicita* and *fides implicita*. It is the second that would be the special object of criticism by the Reformation. For the Middle Ages I have benefited particularly from John Van Engen, 'Faith as a Concept of Order in Medieval Christendom', in *Belief in History: Innovative Approaches to European and American Religion*, ed.

by Thomas Kselman (Notre Dame, IN: Notre Dame University Press, 1991), pp. 19–67, (p. 36 ff). Jean-Claude Schmitt analyses the contradiction involved in explicit/implicit in 'Du bon usage du 'credo', in *Faire croire. Modalités de la diffusion et de la réception des messages religieux du XIIe au XVe siècle* (Rome: École Française de Rome, 1981), pp. 337–61. See also Steven Justice, 'Did the Middle Ages Believe in Their Miracles?' *Representations*, 103.1 (2008), 1–29, and by the same author in relation to the Eucharist 'Eucharistic Miracle and Eucharistic Doubt', *Journal of Medieval and Early Modern Studies*, 42.2 (2012), 307–32. For the Reformation's criticism of *fides implicita* see Ralf K. Wüstenberg, 'Fides implicita "revisited". Versuch eines evangelischen Zugangs', *Neue Zeitschrift für Systematische Theologie und Religionsphilosophie*, 49.1 (2007), 71–85.

22. Cf. T. Asad, 'The Construction of Religion as an Anthropological Category', in his *Genealogies of Religion: Discipline and Reasons of Power in Christianity and Islam* (Baltimore, MD: Johns Hopkins University Press, 1993), pp. 27–54 (p. 34), for a model of religion in which 'coercion was a condition for the realization of truth, and discipline essential to its maintenance'. This view contrasts with an interpretative tradition that ignores the disciplinary factor, emphasizing private religious experience while undervaluing religion's public dimension.

23. François Rabelais, *Pantagruel* (Paris: Fernand Roches, 1929), chapter 34.

24. 'Concerning how they choose Prester John of the Indies. All the presters [that is, priests] of mass in the city of Alves, which is called Edicia, walk in procession around the Apostle. And when it pleases God that one should be Prester and leader of the rest, the Apostle stretches out his arm toward him and opens his hand [...] and the one who is to be Prester John kisses Saint Thomas's hand and all the others kiss that of Prester John [...]' ('De cómo eligen al Preste Juan de las Indias. Alléganse todos los prestes de missa en la ciudad de alves, que es dicha Edicia, y andan todos en procession en derredor del Apóstol y aquél que le plaze a Dios que sea Preste y señor de los otros, el apóstol tiende el braço contra él y abre la mano [...] y aquél que a de ser Preste Juan besa la mano a Santo Thomás y todos los otros besan la suya del Preste Juan [...]'). See the full text in Elena Sánchez Lasmarías, 'Edición del Libro del infante don Pedro de Portugal, de Gómez de Santisteban', *Memorabilia*, 11 (2008), 1–30; there were editions in 1515, 1547, 1563 and 1596. The legend of Saint Thomas's incorruptible and active body in the mythical kingdom occurs as early as the first twelfth-century versions: see Keagan Brewer, *Prester John: The Legend and its Sources* (Farnham: Ashgate, 2015), p. 37. Surprisingly, Ginzburg's Menocchio would also be attracted by Prester John's story in Mandeville's book; Carlo Ginzburg, *The Cheese and the Worms: The Cosmos of a Sixteenth-Century Miller* (Baltimore, MD: Johns Hopkins University Press, 1980), pp. 41–43.

25. And he extended it, of course, to the legend about the relic of the saint's arm.

26. *Que sí, que lo que él no ve no lo cree*: cf. Lucien Febvre, *Le Problème de l'incroyance au XVIe siècle. La Religion de Rabelais* (Paris: Albin Michel, 1942).

27. Aquinas, *Summa Theologiae*, 2a 2a, q. 2 art. 4.

28. Aquinas, *Summa Theologiae*, 2a 2a, q. 1 art. 4.

29. Glenn W. Most, *Doubting Thomas* (Cambridge, MA: Harvard University Press, 2005), pp. 145–54.

30. Calvin, *Novum Testamentum Commentarii* III, pp. 368–69. In the Scholastic tradition there is concern that 'imperfect knowledge belongs to the nature of faith': *Summa Theologiae* 1a-2a, q. 67. See also Peter Lombard, *The Sentences Book 3*, Distinction XXIII.

31. Glenn W. Most finds only two pre-Reformation examples, Saint Augustine and the Greek Zigabenus: *Doubting Thomas*, pp. 139–41.

32. I borrow terms from the long commentary by the Jesuit Jerónimo de Nadal: 'And so He said, "Because you have seen Me, Thomas, you have believed. Blessed are those who have not seen and have believed." How well His words describe the Church's faith! At first, so many visible signs invited belief in His Resurrection — the vision and words of the angels, an empty tomb, the shroud and headpiece [*linteamina, sudarium*], the feel of His wounds, the food He ate — that the essence of faith might seem forgotten. No one would believe without an experience of those very events'; *Annotationes et meditationes*, p. 453, in the English translation of the 1607 edition: Nadal, *Annotations and Meditations on the Gospels. Vol. 3, The Resurrection Narratives*, trans. by Frederick A. Homann (Philadelphia, PA: St Joseph's University Press, 2005) p. 117.

33. One of its most distinguished figures, Pedro de Valencia, used the account in the same way: 'Let there be pious and blessed resistance, even if it is as extreme as that of the Apostle Saint Thomas in demanding the truth about the resurrection of Christ our Lord; it will be all to the good and even for the better'; Valencia, *Sobre el pergamino y láminas de Granada*, ed. by Grace Magnier (Oxford: Peter Lang, 2006), p. 9.

34. Alonso de Villegas in *Flos Sanctorum* (1588), for example, interprets John 20. 26–29 in the light of the first Epistle of John: 'That [...] which we have seen with our eyes, which we have looked upon, and our hands have handled [...] declare we unto you' (1 John 1–3). I quote the 1794 Barcelona edition p. 72.

35. For faith in the Middle Ages I have relied chiefly on Avery Dulles, *The Assurance of Things Hoped For: A Theology of Christian Faith* (Oxford: Oxford University Press, 1994). esp. pp. 33 ff; Van Engen, 'Faith as a Concept'; and Wirth, 'La Naissance du concept du croyance'.

36. Thomas Aquinas, *In Evangelium secundum Ioannem*, chapter 4, lectio 5; cited in Dulles, *The Assurance of Things Hoped For*, pp. 34–35.

37. Aquinas, *Summa Theologiae* 2a 2a, q. 1 art. 4.

38. Diego de Simancas, *Institutiones Catholicae* XXVIII; 'De Fide Catholica' on fols 16^{r-v}.

39. '*Blessed are they that have not seen, and yet have believed. It is as if he said, You believe, then, because you have seen and touched, but you do not rise above that. They shall be blessed who, without having seen, believed in me*' ('*Benditos los que no vieron y sin embargo creyeron. Como si dijese: tú crees entonces porque has visto, y porque has palpado, pero nada haces de mayor importancia. Beatos serán aquellos que no habiendo visto, creyeron en mí*').

40. A *monstruosa credulitas* that, according to Simancas, is born not *ratione divinae revelationis, sed propria voluntate* (Simancas, *Institutiones*, fol. 117). The faith of Luther maintains the cognitive meaning of the Scholastic one, but the doctrine of justification *sola fide* separates it from acts of charity. See a study of Luther's continuity and discontinuity with the Scholastic faith in Berndt Hamm, *The Reformation of Faith in the Context of Late Medieval Theology and Piety* (Leiden: Brill, 2004), esp. 'Why did "Faith" Become for Luther the Central Concept of the Christian Life?', pp. 153–78.

41. We must remember that ever since St Augustine, but especially with the Scholastics, theology had been bringing the domains of faith and reason ever closer together, thereby defining faith as an act of both will and understanding. Faith maintained its place between opinion (*opinio*) and knowledge (*scientia*) but also laid out the path that led to the ultimate truth revealed by Scripture. The scale was weighted toward the second half of Paul's formulation in Heb. 11. 1, 'the evidence of things not seen': *Summa Theologiae* 2a 2a, q. 5 art. 3; Dulles, *The Assurance of Things Hoped For*, pp. 33, 35.

42. 'Fidei Catholicae infallibilis est, quia innititur divinae revelationi, quae fallere nequit, aut falli. Praeterea nobis est confirmata stupendis, innumerisque miraculis, scripturis, & testibus sacratissimis, atque doctissimis: testimoniis etiam omnipotentis dei, angelorum, & omnium fere nationum, totque, ac tantis rationibus & argumentis eius veritas manifesta ostenditur, ut omnis intellectus, vitiis vacuus, non possit non assentiri'; fol. 166; see Simancas, *Institutiones*.

43. Smith, *Belief and History*, p. 60.

44. Paul Veyne, *Did the Greeks Believe in their Myths? An Essay on the Constitutive Imagination*, trans. by Paula Wissing (Chicago, IL: University of Chicago Press, 1988), p. 113.

45. Robert W. Serjeantson, 'Proof and Persuasion', in *The Cambridge History of Science,* vol. III: *Early Modern Science*, ed. by Roy Porter, Katharine Park and Lorraine Daston (New York: Cambridge University Press, 2006), pp. 132–75.

46. [Cardinal] Newman, *Fifteen Sermons*, in a critique of those who 'think that Faith is mainly the result of argument, that religious Truth is a legitimate matter of disputation, and that they who reject it rather err in judgment than commit sin'; p 140. I was led to this source by Peter Harrison's splendid *The Territories of Science and Religion* (Chicago, IL: University of Chicago Press, 2015), esp. pp. 105–08.

47. 'Biblical interpretation functioned not to silence or negate the operations of science, but in which natural philosophy emerged from and was imbricated with the practices of biblical exegesis'. Kevin Killeen and Peter J. Forshaw, 'Introduction', in *The Word and the World: Biblical*

Exegesis and Early Modern Science (Basingstoke: Palgrave Macmillan, 2007), pp. 1–22. See also the collected essays in the same volume.

48. I base my opinion on the following studies: for relics, *Reliques modernes. Cultes et usages chrétiens des corps saints des Réformes aux Révolutions*, ed. by Philippe Boutry, Pierre-Antoine Fabre and Dominique Julia (Paris: Éditions de l'EHESS, 2009). For the use of autopsies in canonizations, Fernando Vidal, 'Miracles, Science, and Testimony in Post-Tridentine Saint-Making', *Science in Context*, 20.3 (2007), 481–508; Katherine Park, 'Holy Autopsies: Saintly Bodies and Medical Expertise, 1300–1600', in *The Body in Early Modern Italy*, ed. by Julia L. Hairston and Walter Stephens (Baltimore, MD: Johns Hopkins University Press, 2010), pp. 61–73; Gianna Pomata, 'Malpighi and the Holy Body: Medical Experts and Miraculous Evidence in Seventeenth-century Italy', *Renaissance Studies*, 21.4 (2007), 568–86. For miracles see, for example, Paolo Parigi, *The Rationalization of Miracles* (Cambridge: Cambridge University Press, 2014). A more general introduction is Simona Cerutti and Gianna Pomata, 'Premessa', *Quaderni storici*, 36.108 (2001), 647–63 (monographical issue on 'Fatti: storie dell'evidenza empirica').

49. Francisco Pacheco, *Arte de la pintura* (Madrid: Cátedra, 1990), p. 253; the source is Gabriele Paleotti, *Discorso intorno alle immagini sacre e profane*, ed. by G. F. Freguglia (Vatican City: Libreria Editrice Vaticana, 2002).

50. In Chapters 3, 4 and 5 of my book *Crimen e Ilusión*, I deal with the proofs of rhetorical argument as they relate to the practice of painting.

51. Quintilian, *The Orator's Education (Institutio Oratoria)*, ed. by Donald A. Russell (Cambridge, MA: Harvard University Press, 2002).

52. Pacheco, *Arte de la Pintura*, p. 100; the source is Benedetto Varchi, *Due Lezzioni* (Florence: Lorenzo Torrentino, 1549).

53. Ernst H. Gombrich, *Art and Illusion: A Study in the Psychology of Pictorial Representation* (London: Phaidon, 1983), argues that deceit and illusion constitute the basic impulse of the Western artistic tradition.

54. Nadal, *Annotations*, p. 96.

55. Close attention has been paid to the iconographic tradition in the Early Modern period, particularly in regard to Caravaggio's highly original creation. Studies have focused on the purely iconographic, with Christ represented *in alia effigie* (Scribner); the proleptic (Lavin); and in a more complex way, the narrative (Pericolo). This literature is crucial for understanding Zurbarán's original interpretation, for which the most important studies are those of Charles Scribner, 'In Alia Effigie: Caravaggio's London Supper at Emmaus', *The Art Bulletin*, 59.3 (1977), 375–82; Irving Lavin, *Caravaggio e La Tour. La luce occulta di Dio*, trans. by Silvia Panichi and Daniele Francesconi (Rome: Donzelli, 2000), pp. 28–33; and Lorenzo Pericolo, 'Visualizing Appearance and Disappearance: On Caravaggio's London Supper at Emmaus', *The Art Bulletin*, 89.3 (2007), 519–39. Also by Pericolo, on Velázquez's response in an early painting now in the Metropolitan Museum in New York, see the chapter 'The Antichrist of Spanish Painting: Diego Velázquez's *Supper at Emmaus* and the two version of *La Mulata*', in *Caravaggio and Pictorial Narrative: Dislocating the Istoria in Early Modern Painting* (London: Harvey Miller, 2011), pp. 517–38.

56. The words of Nadal might almost have inspired this painting: 'When were those eyes opened? When did they recognize Christ? At the very moment when He broke the consecrated bread! And this, so that before they ate the celestial food their minds would be enlightened, their faith and virtues firmed, their doubts dispelled, if any remained. Once they received the Eucharist, Christ vanished, no longer in their sight. Clearly, no delay came [*nihil morae fuisse interpositum*] between their reception of the Eucharist and Christ's departure. Note also that He gave (the bread) to them. With that, Christ wanted the Church to be clear about His example of administering the Eucharist under the species of bread alone'. Nadal, *Annotations*.

57. 'Agnition or recognition is a sudden and abrupt piece of news about something, through which we enter into a great love or great hate for some other thing': López Pinciano, *Philosophía Antigua Poética* [1596], in *Obras completas*, p. 181.

58. Aristotle, *Poetics*, 1454b.

59. In the painting of the time Christ's *vera effigies* was usually shown with a short, divided beard

and chestnut or light-brown hair, as in the Walters Gallery example at the beginning of this chapter; such a description is also found in the popular and apocryphal Letter of Lentulus. See, for example, Alonso de Villegas, *Flos sanctorum y Historia general, de la vida y hechos de Iesu Christo* (Madrid: Pedro Madrigal, 1588), fols 10^v–11^v.

60. 1 Corinthians 13. 12.

61. See the commentary by Nadal, above.

62. Surprisingly, a replica in a private collection is also in Mexico: Francisco Vega Díaz, 'Sobre los *Peregrinos de Emaús* de Zurbarán', *Cuadernos hispanoamericanos*, 524 (1994), 85–98. The date at which it was sent to New Spain is unknown, although all critics agree that it was in the colonial period. On transfers of Zurbarán's paintings to New Spain, see Gonzalo Obregón, *Zurbarán en México* (Badajoz: Diputación Provincial, 1964), esp. pp. 7–8; Juan Miguel Serrera, 'Zurbarán y América', in *Catálogo de la exposición Zurbarán* (Madrid: Museo del Prado, 1988), p. 70 and the painting's description in the exhibition catalogue, pp. 392–94.

63. Arteaga's *Incredulity* in the National Museum of Mexico (MUNAL), 226 x 156.5 cm, Zurbarán's *Supper at Emmaus* in the Museo Nacional San Carlos (Mexico City), 228 x 154 cm.

64. For instance, nineteen portraits of Inquisitors (now lost), a Saint Dominic and a Saint Peter Martyr, all for the Hall of the Tribunal. For his relations with the Holy Office see Xabier Moysén, 'Sebastián de Arteaga (1610–1652)', *Anales del Instituto de Investigaciones Estéticas*, 15.59 (1988), 17–34, and Raquel Pineda Mendoza, 'Pintores novohispanos en el Tribunal de la Inquisición. Noticias documentales', *Imágenes* (2008) <http://www.esteticas.unam.mx/revista_ imagenes/dearchivos/dearch_pineda01.html, accessed 19/04/2017>. On his work see also Juana Gutiérrez Haces, '¿La pintura novohispana como una koiné pictórica americana? Avances de una investigación en ciernes', *Anales del Instituto de Investigaciones Estéticas*, 80 (2002), 47–99.

65. Gemäldegalerie, Sanssouci, Potsdam. In accordance with its theme the painting has been interpreted in two diametrically opposed ways: as an icon of faith — Maurizio Calvesi, *La realtà del Caravaggio* (Turin: Einaudi, 1990) — or as a declaration of scepticism — Ferdinando Bologna, *L'Incredulità di Caravaggio e l'esperienza delle 'cose naturali'* (Turin: Bollati Boringhieri, 1992). See a review and critique of these interpretations in Most, *Doubting Thomas*, pp. 161–65, and the bibliographic note at pp. 253–56. For a confessional reading see Gabriele Wimböck, 'Durch die Augen in das Gemüt kommen. Sehen und Glauben — Grenzen und Reservate', in *Evidentia. Reichweiten visueller Wahrnehmung in der Frühen Neuzeit*, ed. by Gabriele Wimböck, Karin Leonhard and Markus Friedrich (Berlin: Lit. Verlag, 2007), pp. 425–50. Ellen Spolsky's chapter, 'Is Touching Believing? What did Doubting Thomas Want to Know?', in *Satisfying Skepticism: Embodied Knowledge in the Early Modern World* (Aldershot: Ashgate, 2001), pp. 28–44, also begins with a citation of Luther's preference for *fides ex auditu*, although her conclusion is more ambiguous.

66. The term 'witness' is characteristic of Luke (Acts) and the Gospel of John, where we find 30 of its 37 occurrences in the entire New Testament. See Lothar Coenen, 'Testimonio', in *Diccionario Teológico del Nuevo Testamento* (Madrid: Sígueme, 1980), pp. 254–61.

67. See a proposal to re-examine this relationship in David Morgan, *Religion and Material Culture. The Matter of Belief* (New York: Routledge, 2010), esp. the introductory chapter 'The Matter of Belief', pp. 1–17.

PART IV

Marranisms:
Inside and Outside Iberia

CHAPTER 10

❖

Decircumcising the Heart: The Eucharist and Conversion in Calderón's *El socorro general*

Matthew Ancell

Introduction

In *El socorro general*, an *auto sacramental* by Calderón de la Barca from 1644, two armies face off, represented by the allegorized characters Iglesia and Sinagoga. Zabulón, a gracioso, fears for his life, enacting a Spanish Golden Age Jewish stereotype.[1] In the course of the battle, Sinagoga is routed, submits to Rome, and appeals to Gentilidad (the Gentiles) to protect itself from the Church.[2] At this point, Zabulón sides with the winner, declaring, without much conviction, that the notion of *viva quien vence* [long live the victor] is the wisest choice.[3] His stratagem is to present himself to the Church:

> because this way is simple,
> I will protect my 'individual',
> when I am with Jews, I'm a Jew,
> when I'm with Christians, a Christian.[4]

The Catalan Revolt, commencing in 1640, provides the nearly contemporary backdrop for *El socorro general*. Confronting open rebellion in the Principality of Catalonia, the Count-Duke of Olivares attempted to placate the Catalans by reversing recent offending policies. These efforts were too late, as matters quickly escalated with the murder of the Count of Santa Coloma at the hand of rioters. The *Diputació* and other local officials expelled the rebels from Barcelona, but the rebellion gained enough traction and controlled enough of the Principality to force Olivares to send troops. Pau Claris, head of the *Diputació*, had established a relationship with the French, and Richelieu offered help. In January of 1641, Catalonia was declared under the protection of the French Crown.[5] After some initial French victories, in 1643, Philip IV's army advanced in a campaign that retook Monzón, and then Lérida in 1644. The revolt was thus concurrent with the composition of the *auto*. Calderón and his brother José participated in the conflict as soldiers. The latter did not survive.[6]

The *auto sacramental* is a unique feature of Spanish drama, a type of religious play performed in the streets in celebration of the Feast of Corpus Christi, which reached the height of its popularity in the sixteenth and seventeenth centuries. Similar to medieval mystery and miracle plays, the autos sacramentales are allegorical sermons on a variety of doctrinal topics, but always pointing to the heart of Catholic worship, the Eucharist. In *El socorro general* the allegory superimposes a spiritual narrative onto the historical events, with the Army representing the Church militant, Sinagoga the Catalans, Gentilidad the French, and Toledo the Spanish Empire.

It is difficult to say whether this is a forced conversion, since Zabulón proleptically pronounces himself Christian, but it is certainly not a sincere one. It seems that he will preserve his religious identity by clandestinely practising Judaism with his community, while behaving as a Christian publicly. In this moment, Zabulón becomes both a converso and a crypto-Jew. The issue of Zabulón's motives is complicated by the fact that he is a *gracioso* in an allegory, although unlike others in the play, he has a fleshed-out personality and is a sympathetic character.

Another possibility is that his overall lack of conviction will allow him to oscillate between identities as his situation requires. By his own admission, what is at stake, what he aims to guard, is *el individuo mío*, or his 'individual'. Obviously his main goal is self-preservation. The *Diccionario de Autoridades* cites this passage from the play under the definition of 'Individuo', defines it as *própria persona*, and gives the etymology as 'Lat. *Individuum*'. The adjectival entry is 'Singular, particular, ù próprio, ò que no admite division ù distincion' [Singular, particular, or proper, or what does not permit division or distinction].[7] In this sense of 'indivisible', Zabulón's plan runs counter to his intention, since he will be of two minds and two masters, cutting himself in two to preserve himself. 'Individuo', however, also has vulgar connotations[8] — this is the *gracioso*, after all — and so on that level he intends to protect his male member, both as a synecdoche for his own self, but also in the sense of circumcision, and what we will refer to, as a metaphor for conversion, *de-circumcision*.

Cutting the Covenant

Before turning to *de-circumcision*, this seemingly impossible term, at least in its literal sense, it is helpful to trace the history of the rite of circumcision and its functions, from its pre-Hebraic origins to its Christian reinterpretation. Genesis 17 describes the inauguration of circumcision as a rite in Hebrew religion. God sets the terms of the covenant to Abraham, declaring:

> This is my covenant, which you shall keep, between me and you and your offspring after you: every male among you shall be circumcised. You shall circumcise the flesh of your foreskins, and it shall be a sign of the covenant between me and you. Throughout your generations every male among you shall be circumcised when he is eight days old, including the slave born in your house and the one bought with your money from any foreigner who is not of your offspring. Both the slave born in your house and the one bought with your money must be circumcised. So shall my covenant be in your flesh an everlasting covenant. Any uncircumcised male who is not circumcised in

the flesh of his foreskin shall be cut off from his people; he has broken my covenant.[9]

Circumcision becomes, then, the sign of the everlasting covenant, inscribed not only in Abraham's flesh, but in that of his male posterity and slaves. Many ancient cultures practised circumcision, including the Egyptians, but this material was important for later generations in forming a national identity, especially exilic Jews. Several functions of the practice precede the Abrahamic covenant and lie under the surface of the text. Initially, circumcision was a fertility rite, a benefit that manifests itself when Sarah becomes fertile after Abraham's circumcision. Since Abraham had sired Ishmael before then, it seems that the blessing extended to her barrenness, if not to his advanced age as well. Circumcision was also an apotropaic rite, intended to ward off violence and expulsion from the community. In its biblical uses, there is an accretion of metaphorical meanings: hearts, lips, ears, and even fruit trees are circumcised. In Deuteronomy 10. 16 the heart is the thinking, willing part of a human being and therefore a circumcised heart signifies an obedient mind and love of God through obedience, making one different from a Gentile, and allowing one to enter the temple and return from exile, for example. In Jeremiah 6. 10, uncircumcised ears cannot hear God's message. In Exodus, the circumcision of Moses's lips allows him to participate with God on behalf of the Israelites.[10]

These metaphorical usages are significant because when the meaning of circumcision changed in Christianity, its metaphorization was already embedded in the literal practice as well. In all his autos, Calderón follows the traditional tripartite division of laws that govern humanity: the Natural Law, from The Fall to Moses, a period of innocence in which humankind behaves according to divinely imposed principles; the second period is the Written Law, from Moses to Christ, governed by the legal code of the Pentateuch; and the third, the Law of Grace, from Christ until the end of times. As a 'sacrament' of the Ancient or Written Law that is superseded by baptism in the Law of Grace, circumcision reflects the Eucharistic debates between the literalness of Transubstantiation and the spectrum of more to fully figurative Protestant understandings, embodied in this auto in the character *Apostasía*.

In a different auto, *El Orden de Melquisedec* (1652–57? date unsure), Calderón provides a mini-catechism on the relationship between circumcision and baptism. Confused at the notion of rebirth, the characters' Judaism re-enacts the conversation between Nicodemus and Christ, with Emanuel:

> JUDAISM: Will an old man that receives it [baptism]
> return to the mother's womb
> to live again?
> EMANUEL: He will not.
> But being reborn of water
> to the Life of Grace,
> he will return to live again
> without the original stain
> of the first sin that was death. And thus is
> life in him that I offer.

> JUDAISM: Isn't our circumcision
> sufficient for that?
> EMANUEL: To clarify, it was sufficient, in faith,
> that there had to be time
> for Baptism to arrive,
> for even though there were sacraments
> in your Law, they were a schoolmaster,
> merely forerunners.[11]

For Christians, then, according to the *auto*, circumcision was only to teach about the greater Law. What was for the Israelites a sign of the covenant — that they were God's and He theirs — is folded into typological history, a literal practice (already with figurative associations) that becomes a type and a shadow.

Circumcision was deeply connected to the blood sacrifices of the law. Underlying verse 14 of Genesis 17, 'Any uncircumcised male who is not circumcised in the flesh of his foreskin shall be cut off from his people; he has broken my covenant', is the knife rite wherein parties to a covenant kill an animal and then swear by imprecation: 'if I fail to keep this covenant may the knife turn on me'. The expression was to 'cut a covenant' and the penalty was the turning of the knife on oneself, or the cutting off from the people, that is, exile. This strain continues through Hebrew literature.

During the Inquisition, even among judaizers, circumcision practically disappeared, along with other ostensible signs, since most crypto-Jews took a practical approach to appear as practising Christians.[12] Such caution was warranted, of course. While first-time offenders who readily confessed often received relatively lenient punishments, repeat offenders did not. As James Amelang explains: 'The court understood being caught committing the same offense twice as a mockery of its authority, as well as a refusal of the pardon offered the first time. Even genuinely penitent *relapsos* could expect to receive the death penalty, and many did'.[13]

Verpus Est

This history begins to set the stage for Zabulón's anxiety about what will happen to his 'individuo'. As he contemplates going into battle, likely to be killed, he begins a dialogue with his own life (the actor likely effecting different voices for each aspect of his now divided character).[14] Faced with death for fidelity to the covenant, or conversion for breaking it and entering into baptism, he comes to the conclusion already mentioned, conversion, a negating of circumcision or de-circumcision. This term is a curious one, and can only be taken metaphorically. Not that there are not ways to literalize it physiologically, of course. Since Greeks and Romans found the sight of a circumcised penis offensive, some Hellenized Jews practised epispasm, or the stretching of excess skin or a remnant of the foreskin over the glans and then infibulating themselves with a pin so as not to be associated with slaves and barbarians, as well as to be able to participate in public baths, athletics, or as dramatic actors. Even circumcised Greeks and Romans took care to avoid exposure by wearing sheaths. An epigram by Martial is instructive here:

So large a sheath covers Menophilus' penis that it would be enough by itself for all our comic actors. I had supposed (we often bathe together) that he was anxious to spare his voice, Flaccus. But while he was in a game in the middle of the sportsground with everybody watching, the sheath slipped off the poor soul; he was circumcised [Delapsa est misero fibula: verpus erat].[15]

The initial supposition that the purpose of the sheath is to spare Menophilus' voice depends on the notion that sexual expenditure weakens one's ability to perform. It is not clear that Menophilus is a Jew, but it is likely. What is clear is that what begins as an encomium to his manly girth ends with his complete emasculation, going from hero to buffoon.

It is rare to have a buffoon (*gracioso*) in an *auto sacramental*, but Zabulón allows for the indecorous subject of his circumcised *membrum virile* to appear in the allegory. The imperative to hide his circumcision would be necessary for him to be a Christian with Christians, as he puts it. That is, his conversion or de-circumcision will protect him from punishment and exile, allow him to establish a new covenant as a Christian, and form a new identity — all functions of circumcision. We should note that in 1 Corinthians 7. 18, Paul exhorts that a man should not seek epispasm but remain as God has called him. It is not circumcision, but faith in Christ that assures acceptance before God. But in the classical period, even ceasing to practise Judaism was not enough, as Rome levied a tax on the circumcised. Circumcision marked the impossibility of full political assimilation. Similarly, Zabulón will always be under suspicion, even if he did not intend to float expediently from one religious sphere to the other.

Baptism should, of course, allow Zabulón full entrance into the Christian community, as it did in the Primitive Church, comprised initially completely of Jews. After the conversion of Gentiles commenced, the famous disagreement about circumcision between Peter and Paul ended with Paul proclaiming that circumcision and the rest of the law should be spiritual. In Romans 2:

> Circumcision indeed is of value if you obey the law; but if you break the law, your circumcision has become uncircumcision. So, if those who are uncircumcised keep the requirements of the law, will not their uncircumcision be regarded as circumcision? Then those who are physically uncircumcised but keep the law will condemn you that have the written code and circumcision but break the law. For a person is not a Jew who is one outwardly, nor is true circumcision something external and physical. Rather, a person is a Jew who is one inwardly, and real circumcision is a matter of the heart — it is spiritual and not literal. Such a person receives praise not from others but from God.[16]

In *El socorro general*, Sinagoga and Bautismo have a dialogue on the same point:

> SINAGOGA: and regarding my circumcision,
>   you want to take away its efficacy.
>   [...]
> BAUTISMO: If before there was a benefit
>   in circumcision
>   of making you pure and clean
>   of Original Sin,

and now it is absolution of water
and not of blood, then it is clear,
as much as the shedding of blood
has claimed to excuse,
making clear that the Law
of Grace is a light yoke,
for without blood it returns us
to the first state
of Original Justice,
of which we were deprived at birth,
this merciful sacrament
stopping us from sinning,
baptized with water
and without blood **uncircumcised**.[17]

In Calderón's text, the converted are still described as uncircumcised rather than in terms of the spiritual circumcision in Romans. As Ignacio Arellano notes, *incirconcisos* could be an error for *circoncisos*, which would be the easier reading, but all the sources attest to the unexpected in-circoncisos reading. The new law does not obey that ancient 'sacrament' of circumcision, as it was referred to, so the baptized gentiles are uncircumcised. It is odd, though, for Calderón not to exploit the paradoxical figurative sense of 'circumcised'.[18] That is, 'sin sangre circuncisos', circumcised without the shedding of blood, would be an appropriately figurative trope. As it is, the 'incircuncisos' reading goes against all Baroque aesthetics, as we would expect the sense to be 'without blood, circumcised', not the unpoetic 'without blood, uncircumcised'.

By editorially excising the privative 'in' [un] we can preserve the literal sense (they are literally uncircumcised), while losing the poetic one. Perhaps in expressing the logic of being figuratively circumcised as a condition of conversion, while detesting the literal condition, has caused the privative to creep into the non-metaphor of *sin sangre incirconcisos*, metaphorizing the term into a positive sense of 'decircumcised' or converted. In effect, Calderón has decircumcised the figure, excising the figurative sense and exposing the literal. Adding a prefix both covers and converts the word, yet the sense of the circumcised member (of a religion) remains. This preposition, a grammatical prepuce, comes before the word, inscribing and protecting the member as part of a Christian community.

De/Uncircumcised

I have used the term de-circumcision, as distinct from uncircumcision, thus far without giving its origin, which we find in Michel de Montaigne's *Essays* (1588–92). As Katie Chenoweth has noted:

> Montaigne does not only *say* that strange and rare term, *se décirconcire*; he coins it [...]. The few modern French dictionaries to include this term cite this very passage from the *Essais* as the original usage. The first dictionary to officially recognize *se décirconcire* was the 1872 *Littré*, which did not fail to add this qualifying remark: 'Since circumcision is something physical that cannot

be undone, to decircumcise and decircumcision are not good words, able to be taken only in a figurative sense' [Comme la circoncision est quelque chose de physique qui ne peut être défait, décirconcire et décirconcision ne sont pas de bons mots, ne pouvant se prendre qu'en un sens figuré]. To decircumcise oneself is not a 'good word' because it has no proper sense, no sense in the body. In its most common figurative sense, the term has come to mean a forced act of conversion, specifically of a Jew or Muslim to Christianity. [Jacques] Derrida reminds us that such a conversion marks Montaigne's family history on his mother's side — making Montaigne's own maternal lineage 'decircumcised' in the very sense that Montaigne himself, for the first time, ascribes to this term. Montaigne coins the term [...] to describe that which *failed* to happen when death was found preferable to it, 'decircumcision' — when the alliance or ring of circumcision was espoused over life, at the cost of life ([as he says] 'to espouse at the cost of his or her life'). Meanwhile, through the mother who is mentioned not a single time in the *Essais*, Montaigne's own life was made possible because decircumcision, or conversion, was espoused *over* or *at the cost of* a belief more forceful than life.[19]

The passage from Montaigne is as follows:

Any opinion is strong enough to cause someone to espouse it at the cost of his or her life. The first article in that fair oath that Greece swore and kept in the war against the Medes was that every man would rather exchange life for death than Persian laws for their own. In the wars of the Turks and the Greeks, how many men can be seen accepting the cruelest of deaths rather than decircumcise themselves in order to be baptized? This is an example that no religion is incapable of.[20]

Zabulón does not choose death over de-circumcision, of course. Toward the end of the auto, Gentilidad asks Zabulón his name and he responds *No sé* [I don't know]. As a Jew he was Zabulón, as a Christian John, and as a gentile he says he could be Nero. He will become, in his words, *Zabulón Juan de Nerón*.[21] At this point, his *individuo* has been cut in three. Juan Carlos Garrot Zambrana argues that since the primary role of Judaism in *El socorro general* is to represent the Catalans, we shouldn't see the rebels as judaizers.[22] Indeed, Zabulón's falling away points precisely to heresy rather than a crypto-Judaism. His last lines in the play come just after Apostasía carries him off for leaving his religion:

APOSTASÍA: Whoever leaves
    the religion he has taken
    is mine.
ZABULÓN: Didn't I tell you
    that I have the face of a heretic?[23]

Apostasía in this auto represents Protestantism, and at the end of the plot, cannot get past St Peter for denying Transubstantiation. Ultimately, the Eucharist is the theme of all autos, and the folding of Zabulón's character into Apostasy links his conversion or de-circumcision with not only the sacrament of baptism but now the Eucharist as well.

The movement from Catholicism to heresy (Protestantism), however, does not efface the question of Judaism from Zabulón. In catechistically failing, Apostasía reveals Transubstantiation as a kind of Christian shibboleth. As a heretic, Zabulón is no longer Christian — from the Catholic perspective — but also remains a Jew, in that while the figurative decircumcision is no longer effective, his literal circumcision still obtains. Then again, as an allegory, none of this is literal. The substitution of names in *Zabulón Juan de Nerón* enacts the covering up of significations that persist: a heretic can recant, just as a Jew can convert, or a Christian can apostatize.

Part of Derrida's interest in Montaigne's maternal Jewish ancestry and familial conversion is his own (as he refers to it) *Marrano* lineage, and the theme of circumcision runs throughout his work. He connects circumcision and the Eucharist by examining the Orthodox Jewish rite in which the mohel draws blood from the wound of circumcised child with his mouth, mixing wine and blood in, as Derrida calls it, an 'incredible supper'.[24] Derrida's fascination with circumcision and de-circumcision should not be detailed here, but his own biographical and philosophical treatment gives insight into the operations of conversion in this auto and elsewhere, with the notion, as John Caputo describes, of 'a break that cannot be made cleanly, in virtue of what he elsewhere called the impossibility of the pure cut'.[25] The movement into the Law of Grace through baptism and the Eucharist, leaves a remainder behind. The blood sacrifices of the Ancient Law are transformed, but Christianity is tied to them. To be de-circumcised is not to be uncircumcised, nor is it necessarily the metaphorical circumcision of the heart. Rather, it is the bond that binds to what has been cut, the ligature of belonging still to a place where he does not belong, and thus speaks to the predicament of Jews embodied by Zabulón, already in diaspora then threatened with expulsion.

Bloodless Communities

Even in its conversion from the bloody rite of circumcision, baptism retains the trace of circumcision, 'con el agua bautizados / y sin sangre incircuncisos', in that it is now figured as the circumcision of the heart. The blood, however, is now that of the Eucharist, of the Real Presence. The Christian community is formed of literally uncircumcised gentiles, and metaphorically decircumcised (some literally circumcised) conversos. Gil Anidjar has analysed the connection between *limpieza de sangre* [purity of blood] and the Eucharist. He argues that in Western Europe the 'community of blood performed through the Eucharist, which Christians had only come to experience on a regular and massive way in the very recent past, is also the becoming-immanent of the community.'[26] He observes that as the *corpus mysticum* of the Church becomes the body politic of the Christian community in a movement of secularization, blood becomes conspicuously absent in representations of the body politic, even as it becomes the definitive feature of Old Christians.[27] The simultaneous obsession with blood and its absence from theories and representations of the body politic is a contradiction, but the bloodless body politics depends upon the religious community of blood:

> What is only apparently paradoxical is that the two moments (appearance and disappearance) are one and the same results of blood's motion, of the

> becoming-present of the community to itself as divine blood and through it. By realizing, rather than promising, the organic community, blood transforms the community into a theological (if 'secularized') body that is ultimately given rather than made [...] And whereas it used to be made *by* God, by the sovereign, and even by performing the ritual of *Corpus Christi*, the community is now already made *of* its members. And always already so. The community immanent, the community of blood, *lives as what it already is*.[28]

In this manner, the community of blood presupposes the bloodless body politic. The desire to represent the bloodless community reveals the same structure as 'without blood, uncircumcised'. The Christian community is tied together by blood lines, not by conversion or the 'circumcision of the heart', or by forced conversion, that is, decircumcision.

Unified by Communion, by sharing the flesh and blood of Christ, this 'community of blood', found its identity vulnerable to contamination. The community should be joined by the literal blood of Christ, yet New Christians, of course, were not really Christians at all, excluded by purity of blood statutes even as their Jewish ancestry, 'circumcision', ought to be irrelevant, according to Pauline theology: 'in Christ Jesus neither circumcision nor uncircumcision counts for anything'.[29] Baptism's insistence in *El socorro general* on bloodless uncircumcision occludes not only the Jewish foundations of Christianity, but also the literal Eucharistic blood of Christ that binds the baptized Christian community together. A figure such as Zabulón, while allegorical, speaks and behaves like a well-developed character, and embodies many of the anxieties that circle around issues of conversion. Ultimately, he no longer oscillates between religions, but is exiled as an apostate. Here, perhaps, we can invoke the Pauline pun on circumcision directed at defenders of circumcision as necessary, 'I wish those who unsettle you would castrate themselves!'[30] Wielded, rather disingenuously, by Archbishop Juan de Ribera in 1609 to justify the expulsion of the Moriscos, this verse dramatizes the plight of conversos as embodied by Zabulón.[31] A member of the community, a converso, is cut off after his initial decircumcision. His anxieties about his *individuo* were quite justified. As an individual character, he disappears from the text and stage.

A final note: as is well-known, by the mid-seventeenth century, the autos enjoyed lavish production values — employing four mobile carts, elaborate stage machinery, and visual and sound effects — resulting in an impressive spectacle, which at its best moved the audience emotionally as it educated them doctrinally. The perceived danger, though, was that the autos, as a purely metaphorical — that is, bloodless — supplement to the Eucharist and Real Presence, would overshadow and supplant the sacrament itself. The schoolmaster or forerunner, the type and shadow, meant to instruct, could replace the anti-type of the body of Christ, and not the other way around, in effect uncircumcising, in bloodless fashion, rather than converting the faithful caught in the spectacle and distracted from Mass. These concerns culminated in the mid-eighteenth century, when Charles III banned the *autos sacramentales* in 1765, excising the figurative from the literal, cutting them off and exiling them to history.

Notes to Chapter 10

1. Pedro Calderón de la Barca, *El socorro general*, ed. by Ignacio Arellano (Kassel: Reichenberger, 2001), vv. 631–46.
2. Calderón de la Barca, *El socorro*, vv. 692–98.
3. Calderón de la Barca, *El socorro*, v. 711.
4. 'porque así es llano / guardo el individuo mío, / con los judíos, judío, / con los cristianos, cristiano'. Calderón de la Barca, *El socorro*, vv. 720–22.
5. John H. Elliott, *Imperial Spain, 1469–1716* (New York: St Martin's Press, 1964), pp. 340–42. For extensive treatment of the Catalan uprising, see Elliott, *The Revolt of the Catalans* (London: Cambridge University Press, 1963).
6. Calderón de la Barca, *El socorro*, p. 8.
7. *Diccionario de autoridades* [Facsimile edition of *Diccionario de la lengua española* (1726–39)], 6 vols (Madrid: Gredos, 1963–69), vol. IV (1964), p. 255.
8. Calderón de la Barca, *El socorro*, p. 106n.
9. Genesis 17. 10–14, NRSV (New Revised Standard Version).
10. Exodus 6. 12, 30, NRSV.
11. 'J: el que le recibe anciano / ¿volverá al vientre materno / de nuevo a vivir? / E: No hará. / Mas del agua renaciendo / a la Vida de la gracia, / volverá a vivir de nuevo / sin la mancha original / de aquel pecado primero / que fue muerte; y así es / vida la que en él le ofrezco. / J: Pues nuestra circuncisión / ¿no bastaba para eso? / E: Distingo: bastaba en fe / de que había de haber tiempo / en que el Baptismo llegase; / porque aunque hubo sacramentos / en tu ley, fueron ensayos, / como prevenciones de estos / solamente'. Calderón de la Barca, *El orden de Melquisedec*, ed. by Ignacio Pérez Ibáñez (Kassel: Reichenberger, 2005), vv. 1099–17.
12. James S. Amelang, *Parallel Histories: Muslims and Jews in Inquisitorial Spain* (Baton Rouge: Lousiana State University Press, 2013), p. 117.
13. Amelang, *Parallel Histories*, p. 113.
14. Calderón de la Barca, *El socorro*, p. 102n.
15. Martial, *Epigrams*, ed. and trans. by D. R. Shakleton-Bailey, 3 vols (Cambridge, MA: Harvard University Press, 1993), vol. II, 7.82.
16. Romans 2. 25–29, NRSV.
17. 'Sinagoga: — y que a mi circuncisión, / quieres [Bautismo] quitarle el oficio [...] / Bautismo: — Pues si en la circuncisión, / antes era beneficio, / del original pecado / dejarlos puros y limpios, / y hoy es ablución de agua, / y no de sangre, está visto / cuanto sus derramamientos / excusar ha pretendido, / dando a entender que la ley / de gracia es yugo sencillo, / pues sin sangre nos reduce / al estado primitivo / de la original justicia / de que privados nacimos, / dejándonos de la culpa / este sacramento pío / con el agua bautizados / y sin sangre **incircuncisos**'. Calderón de la Barca, *El socorro*, vv. 297–99, 303–20. The emphasis is my own.
18. Calderón de la Barca, *El socorro*, p. 84n.
19. Katie Chenoweth, 'Cutting and Uncutting: A String Theory of Survival, from Derrida to Montaigne', manuscript in the author's possession.
20. Quoted in Jacques Derrida, *The Death Penalty, Vol. 1*, ed. by Geoffrey Bennington, Marc Crépon and Thomas Dutoit, trans. by Peggy Kamuf (Chicago, IL: University of Chicago Press, 2014), pp. 280–81.
21. Calderón de la Barca, *El socorro*, vv. 1400–05.
22. Juan Carlos Garrot Zambrana, *Judíos y conversos en Corpus Christi. La dramatugia calderoniana* (Turnhout: Brepols, 2013).
23. 'Apostasía: Porque cualquiera que deje / la religión que tomó / es mío. / Zabulón: ¿No lo dije yo / que tengo cara de hereje?'. Calderón de la Barca, *El socorro*, vv. 1454–57.
24. Geoffrey Bennington and Jacques Derrida, *Jacques Derrida* (Chicago, IL: University of Chicago Press, 1993), pp. 153–54.
25. John D. Caputo, *The Prayers and Tears of Jacques Derrida: Religion without Religion* (Bloomington: Indiana University Press, 1997), p. 283.
26. Gil Anidjar, 'Lines of Blood: *Limpieza de Sangre* as Political Theology', in *Blood in History and*

Blood Histories, ed. by Maricarla Gadebusch Bondio (Florence: Edizioni del Galluzzo, 2005), pp. 119–36 (p. 129).

27. Anidjar, 'Lines of Blood', pp. 127–28.
28. Anidjar, 'Lines of Blood', p. 130.
29. Galatians 5. 6, NRSV.
30. Galatians 5. 12, NRSV.
31. Seth Kimmel, *Parables of Coercion: Conversion and Knowledge at the End of Islamic Spain* (Chicago, IL: University of Chicago Press, 2015), pp. 157–58.

CHAPTER 11

❖

Marrano Emotions:
Francisco López de Villalobos

José Luis Villacañas

Introduction

Since the adjective *marrano* and its derivatives are central to this work, I think it is worthwhile to explain its theoretical meaning. Actually, I do not begin with the assumption of a collective *marrano* identity: nothing could be further from my intention. However, I do believe that this adjective has a breadth of meaning that is different from that of converso. Anyone with a thorough knowledge of the converso culture of Castilian authors from Alonso de Cartagena forward will easily understand that these authors yearned for integration within the church community and for an end to the caste system. This was the meaning for them of the theology expressed in the great Pauline epistles.[1] This converso experience is previous to or at least contemporaneous with the establishment of the Inquisition and can be seen in authors as late as Hernando de Talavera. It can even be seen in heroic authors who came later, such as Juan de Ávila.[2] Understandably, when the converso universe came into contact with the universe of the Reformation, beginning with Juan de Valdés, the converso community's aspiration for integration was channelled through the hope for a new reformed Church. Constantino Ponce de la Fuente is the most important author of this movement,[3] which was later carried on by Antonio del Corro.[4] In contrast to this converso movement, the *marrano* knows that this communitarian hope is an illusion. This knowledge directs his life toward a different horizon. It is my hope that, after reading this chapter, the reader will begin to be convinced of the general outlines of this horizon. He or she will then perceive in the *marrano* a general uneasiness with the identity options on offer in society during the first half of the sixteenth century, a will to separate oneself from the stable identity imposed from without, to sidestep the 'either/or' implicit in grand existential choices and to attempt to replace them with an evasive and reticent 'neither/nor'. This politics of existence creates an elective affinity between the *marrano* and the rhetoric of doubt, caution, distance, irony, etc. Therefore, I do not begin with a typological concept of the *marrano*, which is not only difficult to assert but also unproductive. Rather, I will try to establish in what sense Francisco López de Villalobos produced a literary work that we have to interpret as an expression of *marrano* emotions, which are incapable of offering the refuge of a fortified identity. From these assertions, it follows that *marrano* emotions, in my opinion, are most suited to a singularity that claims to be neither general nor universal. In this sense, and following Villalobos, it is a matter of taking the same precautions as historians take with respect to essentializing identities. Nothing could be further from my purpose than to affirm them. *Marrano* emotions are precisely what casts doubt on such identities. And it goes without saying that we are not talking about specifically racial factors. The members of Semitic groups in Spain, al-Andalus or Sepharad shared certain environmental circumstances that made them more likely to adopt the *marrano* option, but an Old Christian of noble and 'pure' lineage who had the appropriate cultural background could equally develop the *marrano* disposition. To prove this hypothesis, a suitable case study would be Diego Hurtado de Mendoza as a noble *marrano*.[5] We could even invoke López de Cortegana (who belonged to the previous generation and was Apuleyo's translator), who was a *hidalgo* but also had some features of critical culture. This would lead us to an additional hypothesis — not developed here — which is to see in the Hispanic *marrano* of the first half of the sixteenth century a precedent for the figure of the covert libertine defending his individuality. However, these additional hypotheses would need to be addressed elsewhere.

Here, I will deal solely with the work of Francisco López de Villalobos (1473–1549), the physician of Ferdinand the Catholic and later of the Queen Isabella, who treated her on her deathbed. Villalobos was a poet, court humourist, friend of Francesillo de Zúñiga, translator of Plautus's *Amphitryon*, editor of Pliny, author of the satirical letters that open *Lazarillo* and *Problemas naturales y morales* (which was published in multiple editions during his lifetime)[6] and quasi-mystic, and he is a proto-*marrano* in the sense that I have just described. To understand his work, I will first analyse the meaning of Plautus in the rhetoric of modernity, before briefly explaining the meaning of Villalobos's relationship to Plautus and the complex contextual significance of his version of *Amphitryon*. In my summary, I will analyse the rhetoric of the self that Villalobos presents to us and show the ambivalence inherent in this rhetoric, in order to deal in the last section with the existential scope of this rhetoric, the reason why it is useful to understand *marrano* emotions.

Plautus and Descartes

I will begin with a self-citation, which I hope will be the last. When Miguel Ángel Granada invited me to a conference organized on the occasion of the 350th anniversary of the *Discourse on the Method*, in 1987, I gave a talk about Descartes and Vico.[7] At that time, I argued that it was not by chance that in the first decisive challenge to the Cartesian era, made by Giambattista Vico, Descartes is accused of taking literally psychic processes that a sober Roman had made into an object of comedy. The substance of Vico's criticism was in seeing Cartesian modernity as a failure to comprehend classical rhetoric. Thus, Vico showed how similar methodical doubt was to the comic experiences of Sosia and Amphitryon in Plautus's play. The comparison between the character of Sosia in *Amphitryon* and Descartes's doubt was extremely consequential. Of course, Vico sought to condemn above all the cause of that rhetorical error, which he believed was the plebeian attitude that pays disproportionate attention to one's own thoughts in a quest for certainty ('vulgarem cognitionem, qua in indoctum quemvis cadat, ut Sosiam, non rarum verum et exquisitium').[8] I suggested that this obsession could only come from a kind of tormented subject — very common in the age of the Reformation — awaiting an unequivocal sign of Divine Grace amid its own private experiences. For a late Catholic such as Vico, who had a classical sense of objectivity, this anguish over inner doubt was rejected outright. Vico drew the conclusion that the correct approach was to curb the need for inner certainty in order to concentrate on the free search for objective truth. The thing that tormented the modern age of interiority — the certainty of the self — was roundly condemned by Vico as plebeianism. In this way, Vico proclaimed an era of objectivity known as Neoclassicism, in which one of the basic laws of good taste was the refusal to talk about one's self. Kant, with his maxim 'de nobis ipsius silemus', was part of this world.[9]

It was logical to think that what we call modern experience, centred in the access to the self and its certainties, would have affinities, parallels and correspondences with the contretemps of Plautus's work, and Vico understood this clearly. As Anna Castellani has shown,[10] we can see *Amphitryon* as an emblem of modernity, proof of the valence of Plautus's work. However, Plautus's comedy sought to lay bare the psychic complications that are hidden behind the anguish of identity. He did not seek to legitimize that anguish or to initiate the processes of self-affirmation that are typical of modernity. Instead, Plautus wished to show what was behind the doubts and their consequences. Comedy was the most appropriate cultural mechanism for experimenting with these problems; from ancient times, the popular procession known as *komos* was nothing more than a kind of licence for losing one's social and sexual identity through the inversion of the norms of society itself and liberation from repression and resentment. Just as the *komos* enacted the loss of identity, as in the *Saturnalia* festivals, the artistic treatment of the subject, which was a refinement of this popular custom, offered an appropriate space for an in-depth look at issues related to identity, its doubts and desires, its problematic consequences and ridiculous resolutions. One of these consequences was the problem of jealousy, which offered the inverse case of the traditional *komos*: it was not a question of actively losing one's identity but, on the contrary, of presenting an expansive identity, an identity that saw its own reflection in others to the point of confounding itself with them. Thus, jealousy presented an identity problem not because I harbour doubts about whether I will be one, but rather because, in order to overcome the trauma of extreme jealousy, I see myself as the other, as if it were my double. In focusing on this theme, Plautus introduced a productive, and fateful, innovation.

As we know, the classical Cartesian era presented a rhetoric of the self designed to assure its basic certainties and its self-affirmation through the method that organized the *cogito*'s chains of evidence. An escape from anguish was thus sought through the immanence of reflection. Vico's shrewd insight showed that Cartesian history had a prehistory in the rhetoric of the self in Plautus's comedy. The former could only be triumphant if the latter was forgotten. The basic difference between these two kinds of rhetoric was the distance between self-assurance through introspection and solitude — the foundation of Augustinian culture, which had been reactivated by the Reformation — and Plautus's public, ironic, spectacle-based and objective dimension, which is always staged by bringing into play the social fabric between observers and those who are observed, between characters and spectators, victims and witnesses. We need to give names to these two different kinds of rhetoric that will allow us to distinguish between the classical period and the modern period inaugurated by Descartes and that present all the illusions of liberalism and its substantial individual. If we pay heed to Vico, it is logical to call the rhetoric that comes from Descartes the modern rhetoric of the *cogito*, which defines an evidentiary path that unfolds in a way that is indefinitely self-affirming. Plautus's rhetoric would then be called classical rhetoric, scornful of the accidents of the mind, which it attempts to explain on the basis of the irrepressible metamorphosis of nature, the adventures of the *signatura rerum*, as both Foucault and Giorgio Agamben have made clear,[11] all of which is ironically limited by the social fabric. The opposition between these two kinds of rhetoric is irreconcilable. Let us not forget that all the modern versions of *Amphitryon* — whether by Rotrou, Molière, von Kleist or the rest, up to Girodoux[12] — refute the Cartesian rhetoric of modernity.[13]

I have the impression that there is also a split between *Amphitryon* and all its adaptations, on the one hand, and Descartes's *cogito*, on the other, that separates two opposing rhetorics of the body. Descartes's rhetoric is anchored in an ancestral deactivation of the body that goes back to the most archaic strata of early human experience — the shaman or magician — whereas Plautus's rhetoric resituates the body within the community and thereby offers the key to reestablishing functional distinctions between who we are for ourselves and the uniqueness of our bodies for the group that observes them. However, there is more. As a symptom of the profound resistance to the disbodying of human beings, later adaptations of *Amphitryon* exhibit a defensive rhetoric and emerge as fragments from a more complete universe that fell apart following modernity's excision of the body from the mind, of the individual from society. Francisco López de Villalobos enables us to recall this more intact cosmos, which links medicine, knowledge of the body, identity issues and social comedy and that offers us an integral, alternative image of human beings prior to the rhetoric of the *cogito*. He possesses a rhetoric that predates Cartesianism that we must also name. Let us say that the complex world of this rhetoric thrives on *marrano* emotions, on specific doubts about identity.

Plautus and Villalobos

I believe that the importance of one chapter in the reception of *Amphitryon*, the Spanish translation of the work by the physician Villalobos — the first known Romance version — has not been duly recognized. If we fail to take this translation into account, it is difficult to form an adequate conception of early Spanish modernity and the rhetoric of the self that it used as a vehicle for expressing certain anxieties. This rhetoric has a political dimension, which is only natural given that the text of the original comedy was thus. It would be easy to speak here of an 'ironic rhetoric' or a 'critical rhetoric', and this would be correct. In any case, not having identified this rhetoric we are in no position to highlight the centrality of *Amphitryon* or the work of Villalobos in Spanish culture, or to understand the issues that are at stake in his work. This would involve comparing it to the second Spanish translation of the work, which was produced soon afterward by Pérez de Oliva, who was neither a physician nor a *marrano*. But this is not the place for such a comparison. Let it suffice to say that Villalobos's version, in contrast to that of Pérez de Oliva, does not revel in the mythological aspects of the comedy, which he wants to recreate in all its classical grandeur, but neither does he establish a rhetoric of introspection and inner assurance through his own *cogitationes*. And yet, the naturalist scheme he brings to the work as a physician, comedian, philosopher of the body, poet and prophet will situate him in a position that helps us to identify what *marrano* emotion means, something that can only be expressed if we look at Villalobos's oeuvre as a whole.

Villalobos was a Jewish physician born in Zamora, near the border with Portugal, and by 1498 had already published *Sumario de Medicina*, which reveals an intimate familiarity with the students who constructed the narrative of *La Celestina*, as Gustavo Illades has shown.[14] It will be sufficient to give a brief summary in order to understand this work and familiarize ourselves with its vocabulary. In effect, Villalobos traces the genealogy of disease by describing a two-fold disturbance: 'mutations of animal [spirits]' and corrupt air (*SM*, p. 313).[15] Implied in this concept of corrupt air is a complex cosmos that includes everything from the influence of the stars to the degradation of the earth and the vices of mankind. Villalobos was, of course, among those who subscribed to the theory of the four humours in medicine,[16] to the idea that 'complexion' and 'temperament' were the result of the amalgamation of basic elements. However, when he analyses lovesickness — what the Greeks called 'hereos', a sickness related to the realms of family, society and politics — Villalobos is clear that it is an infirmity of the imagination. According to him, imagination needs to be distinguished from understanding. However, when defining the imagination, he speaks of it as 'bestial thinking'. Thus, imagination is a kind of thinking, which will later be the sphere of the *cogito*. In any case, it is a 'great power'. This is because the imagination is able to enlist the 'other powers' (*SM*, p. 322) for its own cause. Of course, it is what moves the senses, but it also affects 'memory and desire and eyes and ears'. Its extreme power consists of being able to bring all those organs and functions into its service in such a way that they take responsibility for the objective suggested to them by the imagination. With 'such thinking', imagination 'informs the other senses', concludes Villalobos. Hence the possibilities of the world of doubt that arises from the imagination and its *cogitationes*. When all the powers of memory and perception have been folded into imaginative thought, when they cease to see, remember and desire as they would naturally, then understanding, deceived by these false witnesses, is robbed of judgement and reason, 'counsel and prudence' (p. 322). 'They are all blind because of one that is blind'. The process culminates when thought and imagination manage to affect the heart, the dwelling place of the spirit. And they do so by placing in the heart 'burning fire / ever stoked and kindled by desire' (p. 323). The phenomenology of the lover is deployed in Villalobos's medical verses in the very same way as in *La Celestina*. The author of the latter, Rojas, must have read Villalobos's *Sumario de la Medicina*. Among the cures offered for lovesickness is of course this one: 'little old women must be brought to him / to unbound him, which they well know how to do' or 'go-betweens should lure him into loving other women to distract him' (p. 324).[17] But in any case, the destabilizing thing is thought and imagination. Distrust of the imagination will be a typical emotion among official converts who are unsure whether they can in good conscience adopt wholesale the ritual practices and iconology of their new religion. Cleary, authors with a Jewish background, like Villalobos, had an additional reason for their iconoclasm. But what is peculiar about our physician, as well as the author of *La Celestina*, is that he sees a strong link between idolatry, the imagination, obsessive identity and illness. In this we can discern an elective affinity between God, who prohibits images, and nature, which balances the relationship between the body and the spirit. What Descartes did when he entrusted himself to the *cogito*, leaving out the body, the organic foundation, was enter the fortress of the enemy so as to try to order it from the inside in an immanent way, a desperate move in Villalobos's opinion.

So, between 1515 and 1517, Villalobos translated and published Plautus's work, the only work from antiquity that contains the word *tragicomoedia*. Of course, students in Salamanca were already reading Plautus's work in Latin. The author of *La Celestina* was, therefore, one of an earlier generation of students who practised their Latin using this work by Plautus. It was for these students that Villalobos produced his translation, as he himself says, to help them understand the Latin text, which is difficult and obscure. However, it is interesting that Villalobos does not translate this prologue. Actually, he confesses to us that it vexes him. *Tragicomoedia* implies the juxtaposition of characters from both the upper and lower classes, and that is what Rojas duplicated in his work. However, the idea of mixing genres did not yet occur to him, only the mixing of characters. This is not important for Villalobos, who has his sights fixed on universal human nature. The physician — and this is another aspect of the *marrano* disposition — is not accustomed to seeing people as noble beings. He is too familiar with them, he has seen them urinate and defecate. As he once said, he visits their houses to examine their buttocks. For Villalobos, who was unsurpassed as a humourist before Quevedo, Plautus is an author of comedy and that is enough. His theatre offers us the spectacle of humanity, and his facts come from everyday life. His field of operation is the equality of the nature of things.

This is why Villalobos believes that Plautus is above all a philosopher. He provides apprentices with a philosophical exercise, although he does not offer the corpus of the truth, something that the physician presents in *Problemas*. Villalobos says that comedy is philosophy in the same way that sporting events are combat. Thus, comedy gives us a complete text. As a philosophical exercise, it can be read differently from the *corpus* of knowledge. Therefore, Villalobos provides glosses and a concluding treatise along with the text of *Amphitryon*, in which he presents the text of science. Here, in contrast to what Descartes does, medical science is marshalled to explain the rhetoric of comedy, which is a disruption in the functioning of the *cogitationes*. This neutralizes the possibility of idealizing imaginary rhetoric as a method, which will be Descartes's foundation for reducing medical science to a mechanistic understanding.

The crucial thing about Villalobos's project is that the text that he offers as a suitable complement to Plautus's comedy — apart from his detailed glosses — is a treatise on love, which is the key to the idolatrous power of the imagination. It is actually a treatise on jealousy and the destruction of the family as a body, which occurs when women are no longer honoured as they should be. We can see this as a metaphor for the destruction of the body politic. What is acted out in *Amphitryon* — a comedy about people who are eager for an expansive identity that is able to dominate the imaginary and induce the senses to project the self — is, medically speaking, a case of jealousy. The play presents the torments of a jealous wretch, but medical science explains their origins. This bears repeating: medical science is the hermeneutic key to the classical text; it is capable of reading both books and diseased bodies. Thus, the anxiety over identity that we see in the work is the consequence of love's complications, which in turn proceed from an idolatrous identity. Allow me to recall that underlying my entire analysis is the analogy between the individual body and the body politic, which is also apprehensive about its identity.

Of course, in the text of the comedy it does not say that *Amphitryon* is an exploration of jealousy, but that is what the work is actually about when looked at from the point of view of science and explained from a naturalist perspective. We will see shortly what the political equivalent of jealousy is. This is important because, as a result, it is in the complications of physical love and the supremacy of the imagination that Villalobos situates the origins of the idolatrous phantasmagoria of the gods and the delusions of grandeur and deification, and even of choice. I suspect that this is also how he saw the restless apprehensions of enlightened religious radicals. Of course, the *marrano* as a theoretical tool can be useful on many different levels: on the level of the family, the social and political spheres, but also the sphere of religion. In the glosses and in the philosophical explanation of the comedy, Villalobos allows himself to be carried away by his status as critic and sets forth an explanation of pagan polytheism — and of Christian Trinitarian polytheism — as an illusion and a manifestation of the amorous upheavals of the flesh, as a disturbance of human nature. This precursor of Nietzsche's[18] suggests that the meaning of this sublimated genesis of stories about gods resides in the fact that the supposed incarnations of the gods placate the fury of jealous men and their diseased and expansive sense of identity by both encouraging their masochism and amplifying their megalomania: they have been deceived not by men but by gods who took on their very bodies and faces. Their wives have been unfaithful but in doing so have produced little demigod heroes. In truth, they were chosen for this, and the agony of jealousy is offset by the megalomania of having been among the elect. This is tolerable. They have the children of the gods, but these children are so majestic that, in the end, they have showered us with grace, for which we must show gratitude. After all, we were chosen by them. After all, it was Providence that cuckolded us. As one might suppose, this explanation applies to Christianity as yet another pagan story, and Villalobos underlines the analogies expressly. Amphitryon is Saint Joseph. Christ's incarnation through the Spirit becomes the figure of a crazy old cuckold who proclaims the virginity of his wife despite the evidence. Later, in the work, the relationship between the Father and the Son in Christianity is presented to us as a variation of this sadistic/masochistic relationship between Jupiter and Mercury; Jupiter also subjects his son to torture and even threatens him with crucifixion. It is as if Jupiter is keeping at arm's length this Mercury pierced by hatred of the father and reacts with insufferable sadism to his impotent Oedipal hatred. Christ is not a Jewish story but a pagan one. In effect, Villalobos's translation and glosses underline all the correlations that make it possible to establish a parallel between the Passion of Christ and the ruthless and grotesque torture that Jupiter's cruelty inflicts on his son Mercury in order to be with the beautiful Alcmena. We can be almost sure that Villalobos astutely identified the parallel between the birth of Hercules and that of Christ, as the issue of a virgin impregnated by a god. Thus, the courteous physician, during the final days of his lord, King Ferdinand, in 1515, was working out his doubts regarding the Christian religion, to which he had officially converted, and he left us a text that is full of ironic hints about his suspicions, though free from any outright assertions. In this way, by showing the problems with all obsessive identity, the disease of jealousy, he presents the diagnosis of its origins, while at the same time giving us hints to his secret misgivings about a religious identity whose mythical beliefs reinforced that disease. Here, the physician's naturalism serves to support his critical attitude. I sincerely believe that this is a *marrano* perspective.

But *Amphitryon* is also a political story. This should not be forgotten.[19] Its hero is a *miles gloriosus* who, despite having founded an empire, is horrified to imagine that his sweet Alcmena has taken pleasure with another. Imperial conquest does not guarantee the faithfulness of his wife. We know that Hispania was traditionally likened to a wife. Isidore used this association in his *Laus Hispania*. When Charles V was received in Valladolid shortly after the publication of *Amphitryon*, a play dedicated to him was performed in the mud-caked plaza in which Spain, personified as a widow, was made young again in the joy of a young and vigorous husband. However, Amphitryon questions the constancy of the pure, serene, sensible and innocent Alcmena, and in the end everything gets resolved because Amphitryon assumes that she was visited by a god and will give birth to a great hero. In the treatise at the end of the work, Villalobos criticizes the nobility's misogyny and makes jealousy the capital offence of authentic Spanish culture. His impressive defence of women and mothers grows out of a profound concern for unambiguous filiation. For fifteenth-century Spanish Jews, Sepharad/Spain was the wife of these noble Goths and Franks, the descendants of nomadic races with no feeling for nature. The Jews saw themselves as the natural, millenary inhabitants of Spain, who settled there before the death of Christ, of whose Passion they were innocent. This is what Alonso de Cartagena had argued in his *Defensorium unitatis christianae*.[20] And he had done so using the familiar metaphor of the mixing of races through that archetypal marriage. They were Spain, virtuous and wise, and they offered the stability of their family and their ancestral home to the Goths from the north. And yet, the *miles gloriosus* distrusted that chaste wife and had therefore gone mad and sacrificed his judgement to an identity that could not brook the stain. As long as the boastful noble *miles* refused to reconcile with her — the bearer of nature, filiation and the familial and social path to healing — there would be no cure for his enraged isolation within his monstrous identity. This withdrawal into madness undoubtedly signified a relapse into paganism and its polytheistic stories, in opposition to a single God who was especially clear about one thing, and that was filiation.[21]

Defining a Rhetoric

Villalobos's rhetoric of the self — religious, scientific, political, erotic, medical — cannot be simplified. It is not the rhetoric of the *tragicomoedia*, the juxtaposition of nobility and the lower classes; it cannot be subsumed within a monotonous genre such as the confession or modern introspection. It is not abstract or pagan and yet that does not mean it is less philosophical. We could speak of a *clinical rhetoric*, but perhaps it would be better to call it a *marrano rhetoric* in order to identify, behind its ambivalences, the complexity of its emotions. First of all, its preferred emotion is analytical: those poor wretches adrift in their unbelievable upheavals, believing things but not knowing. Villalobos does not believe so much, but he knows. Intellectual superiority is one aspect of his disposition. Like Freud, he seeks to know more about others than they themselves do. When someone succumbs helplessly to a disease, he explains it to him triumphantly. We could define this as the rhetoric of someone who sees the world as theatre — perhaps where dreams or the imagination are performed — and who watches its action unmoved; but he sees it from the perspective of medical science, as a privileged spectator capable of explaining what is really going on among the characters, who do not know what they are about, while the spectators cannot decipher it by themselves. In his glosses and the treatise that he has appended to the work, Villalobos also deconstructs the storyline. The spectators laugh, but they do not know what they are laughing about. They are enjoying themselves, but only Villalobos's science can tell them why. This is not the same as Diderot's position in the *Paradox sur le comédien*. We are instead dealing with an observer who is both inside and outside the work; he translates it only in order to deconstruct it; he is involved with the world but outside the comedy of the world.

He knows that he is also subject to the possibility of believing what the crazed characters believe, because human nature is universal; but he is aware of the disorders that can operate in the mind and the spirit and lead one to see, think and believe as they do when they are mastered by their imaginations. In sum, he lives in a world of neurotics where he could also be one and probably is. The intellectual superiority of the physician also applies to himself. That is where the ironic aspect of his rhetoric comes in. Whatever he might say about himself, he may also be something else. Irony is a *marrano* emotion and reflects a contingent attitude toward identity. This is the *marrano* experience: one might be forced to share the madness of one's environment but must be firm in the knowledge of man provided by medicine and philosophy. With this knowledge, one will not adopt the madness completely, will not identify fully with it, will keep one's distance also from oneself.

From this perspective, the clinical rhetoric of the physician is tolerant and ironic. He does not view a person suffering from extreme and jealous identity with personal hostility but as a natural process of imbalance. It is only natural to go mad when filiation cannot be trusted! And how can there be trust when jealousy is present? Therefore, in a world of madmen the physician allows himself some of his own follies. He opens himself to comedy, but he does not abandon the firm ground from which he studies the social whole, the rock of medical science, transmitted to him by his father, who, according to some of Villalobos's letters, he never ceased to mourn. He does not reject the possibility of being one of the unhinged characters in Plautus's work, because he knows the influence and natural efficacy of the human mechanisms that are rooted in his body. When these mechanisms interact, their force is irresistible. We can be aware of them, but that does not mean we control them. However, at least we know *why* one thing happens rather than something else, and this is where Villalobos sees a final guarantee of freedom. No one is free to reject Catholic polytheism and the superstition of imagery that is necessary for establishing ironclad identities, but he knows that acceptance ultimately relies on an erotic and perceptual disorder that involves the worship of images, a somatic imbalance that anyone might suffer from if they do not have a family history that hinges on filiation and the transmission of the true idea of God. Without this, it is easy to succumb to the symptoms of doubt, of jealousy, the lack of valour and to come to believe in the fantasies they induce. However, the verisimilitude of this Catholic belief does not come from health but from serious bodily imbalances that condition perception and belief, fear, solitude, helplessness, indifference, trauma. Later, when Cervantes employs the medical science of one of Villalobos's heirs, Huarte de San Juan,[22] he will likewise do so in order to mock a *miles gloriosus* who is incapable of love and nurses a fantasy about Dulcinea that conceals his real desire for the discretely promiscuous Aldonza Lorenzo.

The physician, then, is in a position to understand the fragility of identity and its cultural by-products, because he understands the fragility of the body, to the point that, as a human being, he can also foresee these by-products in himself. But as a physician, he can still distance himself and explain to himself his own errancy from the perspective of the science of the body, which is his own. Thus, the *marrano* can explain the verisimilitude of Christianity as a man, given certain assumptions and notwithstanding certain bewilderments, as well as the impossibility of believing in it as a doctor. Socially he can be one of them, share in their comedy, but he will never be able to do so completely. This split, this being two things at once, not being either completely, is an aspect of the *marrano* disposition. This split has a foundation, one that makes it impossible to reconcile the past with the future.

The *marrano* knows who he was. This is the strongest *marrano* emotion, which has its origins in the issue of filiation. He does not dare to say that he still is what he was, in the middle of the farce. The mismatch, on the level of family and politics, is irreversible. But filiation is too. The *marrano*'s unique ambivalence has to do with these two different irreversibilities.

In Spain, Amphitryon's madness has not been cured. This is the theme of the radical criticism of the mentality of the nobility in the treatise appended to the translation. Alcmena has been wronged and there is no happy ending. And this is because the disorder in the body's systems — brought about by a love that is possessive and unhinged — produces a profound distrust of being loved under such circumstances. This possessive love intensifies one's sense of identity, which only leads to further rejection, which in turn produces jealousy and its delusions about abandonment and deception. The entire plot of *Amphitryon* spirals out of control because, upon returning from battle, Amphitryon suffers an imaginary loss of his naïve expectations due to the way his wife really received him. Her passion seems insufficiently intense to him. He suspects that his wife has been sated prior to his arrival. She answers him, yes, she was with him the night before. Amphitryon's hallucination resides in the fact that if his wife does not behave as vehemently when he arrives as he imagines she should, this is because another, a double, a ghost, has enjoyed the anticipated intensity of the reunion. This hallucination exposes subjectivity to an inexorable perceptual fragility. Plautus's genius lies in the fact that the jealous man who believes that his wife has been with another deep down only projects his identity. Jealousy leads to the destruction of the evidence for the limits of one's own identity and thus to the impossibility of orderly family life and social existence. That moment, when one's own ghosts seem to be everywhere, is the beginning of distrust, danger, violence, rage, loss of self-control, and hysterical, ridiculous, arrogant acts of unwarranted self-affirmation, which lead to an expansion of the cycle of infirmity, since the social order that should have cured the disease has been deactivated.

Amphitryon is thus the symbolic dénouement of the interracial marriage propounded by Cartagena, and it is the explanation of the nobleman's sadistic treatment of his wife in that marriage — Alcmena, Spain, Sepharad. Because within this disorder, it becomes impossible to attend to the discrete and balanced pleasures of the body and the calm and trusting enjoyment of them. And thus, violence and hysteria spread all around. That is why the existence of the Jewish physician is dangerous, since he has no community ties to the ailing nobleman. The physician must cure the man who might end up being his executioner. As a physician, he offers to treat the disease, but as a Jew he runs the risk of being killed. Throughout his correspondence, Villalobos repeatedly refers — in fearful and fateful terms — to this paradoxical situation in which the nobility puts to death the very people who could save them. He has to live in the midst of something that he knows is a volcano, the volcano of the non-culture of the nobility. Thus, the *marrano*'s duality is founded on science. He knows what he can explain, but he therefore has to fear being made into a scapegoat by the very person whose insanity he can cure. He applies pressure in order to allay and nuance ironclad identities and their hyper-affirmative megalomania, but the *marrano* physician contributes to them insofar as he excites feelings of distrust and strangeness. The basis of the hatred toward Jewish culture among the nobility is something beyond anti-Semitism: it is the fear of having to be otherwise. The metaphor of the family and the familial contract — between the Gothic male and the Jewish female — has been destroyed, and no other, better bond has been found to structure this duality, and thus there is no medicine to administer to the social body. Villalobos's *marrano* rhetoric is thus built on the conscious duality of cultures and its consequences, the impossibility of reunification and his complete removal from the social body, and therefore the possibility of becoming an animal hunted by those who need to be cured. This is the drama of the world of Spanish conversos.

The difference between this and the modern world of Descartes is key. In the latter, perceptual doubts about reality in general do not affect identity, because all bodily aspects have been excluded from identity. In Villalobos, by contrast, doubts about one's identity carry with them doubts about one's body and empty the subject of everything but doubt; they leave him in the unassailable realm of doubt, unless the body can be cured. This is what happens in Plautus's work. If, as Freud said, jealousy is characterized by blocked mimesis, we can be sure that one way it is manifested and falsely overcome is that there where another is I see myself or my double. To avoid this perceptual trick, we anxiously search for a solution, a simple way to eliminate the double without curing the need to project one's identity everywhere. This is the Spanish nobleman's experience. He does not accept the Jew's conversion, that he might become like him, that when looking at him he might see someone like himself;[23] but neither does he cease to project his identity or to inquire whether that double is like the self. To live in this situation means to abandon oneself to hallucination and madness. The only thing that I really see is that the other, the one who has overthrown me, is in my place. That where I should be he is. Lest he become my double and supplant me, it is necessary to enact a blood statute, to differentiate him, to mark him with a star. Then, as was the intention of Archbishop Silíceo, I can keep him from taking my place.

Thus, the difference between the rhetoric of Villalobos and Descartes is clear. Whereas the former wants to use medicine to destroy the figments of the imagination that lead to the polytheistic/Catholic religion as an illusory explanation of the self's delirium and the affirmation of that delirium that is the result of the will to impose an identity, the latter does not adopt a science capable of perceiving the illegitimacy of doubt and insists on the game of inner illusions as the proper base for reconstructing a systematized and ordered world. The *marrano* physician, therefore, employs a clinical rhetoric designed to eliminate mental illusions and redirect them toward the dysfunctions of the body. It makes us laugh but it also gets our attention. They could be us.

Rhetoric and Prophecy: *Marrano* Existence

This clinical rhetoric, based on a self-doubling of he who knows what he was (a Jew) but has to live in a world where what he was is not possible, prevents Villalobos from letting himself be carried along by any of the phenomena of everyday mental life, or be integrated into a community group. Neither has absolute value. His clinical rhetoric — ever divided between representations and the explanation that allows them to be described from the perspective of suspicion or doubt, truth or incertitude — expresses a complex narrative about capabilities and faculties, as opposed to the centralization in the *cogito*. This order of capabilities is the decisive one and the enjoyment of mental plurality is a *marrano* emotion. 'I have so many gulfs in my understanding', says Villalobos, 'that I don't know them myself'. The best place to study this is in *El sumario de la Medicina, con un tratado sobre las pestíferas bubas*, published in Salamanca in 1498, whence Rojas may have extracted the meaning of his *tragicomoedia*. Here Villalobos does not avoid a prophetic tone. The people who condemn the man who would cure them can only fall victim to plague. This fact allows us to identify another *marrano* emotion, which is complementary to the experience of having been: historical irreversibility, history as curse and plague, the true theological breadth of the God of Israel as a god of time who is also eternal nature. In the prose prologue that he puts forward in the *Tratado sobre las pestíferas bubas*, Villalobos recounts that while the monarchs were in Madrid, the kingdom experienced a 'general curse'. Recall that this book was published in 1498. This point is important as it relates to the painful circumstances in Spain toward the end of the fifteenth century (*OV*, p. 452) and more specifically in 1497, when the heir apparent died, casting a pall over the entire kingdom.

What we have here is Villalobos's prophetic dimension, where he puts himself in the 'person of God' and addresses the world saying that God himself has sent his angel. We know that it is the Angel of Death. His motive: that human beings are using the powers given to them by God in ways that do not further His ends. We should not forget that the prince's death was attributed to his frenzied lust. This violent, irate, unruly angel injures everyone it comes into contact with. And this is so because God was not able to repeat the care for His own as in Egypt. It is important to remember that there was a popular belief that Ferdinand the Catholic was of Jewish descent.[24] This is a solemn moment and leaves another *marrano* emotion: guilt, for the very events that are being suffered. 'At the time in Egypt God sought to kill / their enemies' first-born sons / he ordered the houses of Jews to be marked / lest the angel also come / and make combat against his own friends' (p. 454). Villalobos thus suggests that God has abandoned Spain for not allowing the houses of Jews to be marked so that the Angel of Death passed them by. Since the houses were not marked by the recent persecutions and prohibitions, there was general destruction and no one was spared the plague. But how could the Jewish houses be marked if the dissolution of that failed marriage between Goths and Jews, sown with mistrust and ruin, had already been come to pass; if forced conversion had already taken place? It is the *marrano* who sees that this conversion has resulted in tragedy because of Amphitryon, the *miles gloriosus*, and his lack of respect for Alcmena and filiation.

And yet, as would be recalled by Spinoza in his *Tractatus Theologico-Politicus*, in the seventeenth century,[25] and as Spanish scholars of the time knew,[26] these mixed marriages were common and had affected practically the entire Castilian nobility. Social synthesis was about to be achieved. The mixed-blood nobility, which was friendly to converts, was dominant and was responsible for setting Isabella and Ferdinand on the throne. Now he is blamed for the plague. There is no doubt what Villalobos is thinking about. The ultimate cause of the plague could very well be, as it is identified in his rhetoric, the fact that the sheep are being forced to atone for the shepherd's sins, that is, the King and the Church herself. At the end of this series of verses, Villalobos asserts, given the intensity of the disaster: 'I confirm this opinion as correct'. This is not just any historical moment, but one that is overburdened with pathos and anxiety. It was at this time that the Infante Don Juan died, who was the firstborn whose house was not preserved by the mark of the angel, the very son of Ferdinand, the shepherd of Jewish extraction. This is what Villalobos has in his sights. The explanation for the plague is 'to come because of the sinful lust of people today' (p. 545), the very vice for which it is said that Prince John died, which was condemned as *hereos* love in *La Celestina*, Amphitryon's vice.

However, the physicians say that the harm comes from an overabundance of the melancholy humour, of this knowledge that I was what I can no longer be, and that precisely because of this the value of what I now am is diminished. In contradistinction to this insufferable nihilism that demands new forms of worship, Villalobos the *marrano* glimpses a kind of health that goes beyond both idolatrous obstinacy and the guilt of betrayal. To fall into one of these two emotions, which lead to the experience of nothingness that is confirmed in jealousy, shapes the phantasmagoria of the many Amphitryons. The *marrano* knows that he can never again be a Jew. That time has passed. However, he feels no guilt because the irreversibility is not voluntary. All the same, he does not give in to pressure. That is why he conquers ways of being certain of his own value. Melancholy, which is not a *marrano* emotion, is the imbalance experienced by the man who knows only that he was. It is a moral infirmity and a curse. Or better: a curse confirmed by the disease that perturbs the body and the emotions. Thus, in the end, despite all the discussion of biological causes in medicine, especially in Avicenna, Villalobos comes to the conclusion that it is the Egyptian scab, 'which is as perverse and wicked as the scab / though sent by God as a punishment and a sentence' (p. 462). Egyptian scab, the Pharaoh's curse, the plague visited on those who abandon their God in one of those acts of faithlessness that were so frequent among his people. For Villalobos, the nascent Spanish empire was simply an imitation of the Egyptian empire and, at the time of the expulsion of the Jews, it was subjected to the same fate: the Plagues of Egypt.[27] Natural pestilence followed moral pestilence, because the God who was abandoned is also the Nature of things, Cartagena's and the Averroists' *Deus sive natura*, He who cannot be worshipped except through knowledge and rational Enlightenment. Therefore, another way of saying the cause is 'the bad impression of heavenly bodies / that made a harmful infection in the air' (p. 463). Since the earthly causes were found to be available, the result was the one that was due. It is a question of 'bad compound and constellation of unfortunate planets'. This is a 'presupposition of astrology' that of course is adopted into medicine. On earth, we have only the harmful air as a material copy of the melancholic spirit left by guilt, on which nature acts, giving rise to perverse effects. It should be recalled that, when the Inquisition was founded, it was legitimized as a way to ensure the eternal salvation of those whom it condemned and to obtain divine protection for the Spanish monarchy. However, nature carried out a different sentence despite human intentions, and Villalobos's *marrano* emotion is not able to detach itself from the superiority that he feels from knowing how things truly stand. This is important for the last point that I would like to make.

Marrano Rhetoric and Literature

In any case, a consequence of clinical rhetoric is that the physician — as a part of nature — also feels the effects of the distortion caused by melancholy and love, all the while knowing that he is doing so. This duality gives Villalobos's poems the double aspect that is characteristic of the ambivalence of things, a *marrano* emotion that is inseparable from his role as a physician. The Villalobos who translated and commented upon *Amphitryon* from the vantage point of medicine is the same Villalobos who is capable of loving as the play's characters love, but he maintains a distance from which he observes himself: 'I write jokes that are true / joking, I suffer truths / and I suffer while dissimulating / a thousand kinds of painful anguish', he says (*OV*, p. 271). The physician, because of the exclusive strength of knowing who he was, hides his suffering behind a smile by writing comedy and thereby overcomes melancholy with knowledge, a *marrano* emotion. By proposing this duality, this capacity for clinical rhetoric that translates immediate and painful experiences into something that is humorous and also removed, Villalobos offers a blueprint for *marrano* living, for a life that derives strength from translating suffering into laughter, without dispelling either — neither weeping nor laughter. This is the emotion behind the tragicomedy that Cervantes will put the finishing touches to.

In the ignorant, this melancholy generates a compensatory love for what was, which is the mechanism in *La Celestina*. In those who know, it generates a fitting sense of humour. Here it is sufficient to notice the analogy between the rhetoric of love and political rhetoric. Both spheres produce masters and lords. *Amphitryon* is also a work cut through by the vertical power differential between gods, masters and slaves. The rhetoric of love literature expresses the same condemnation that we have seen in political rhetoric. Even more, in this almost perfect analogy that equates the sovereign with the beloved, Villalobos perceives the same adaptability in the language whose meaning the master distorts to the point of turning it on its head. This is the language of power, and the basic *marrano* emotion is to resist it and denounce it according to the rules of the art of writing under persecution. 'Let him whom you condemn to death be saved by a sentence' — the way that Villalobos describes *hereos* love — is also what happens to someone who is burned by the

Inquisition, a tragedy similar to being burned by love unconnected to filiation. The reason in both cases is power: that 'it is you who commands'.

This contortion of language is also committed by physicians when they try to give hope to a patient: when they tell the truth and give great sorrow, they say that they give the best cure. This is also an experience of power, of another power. The lover can be described in an analogous way: he seems healthy when the beloved is near, but then she kills him. The political lord, the beloved, science — all force human beings to twist direct experience of pain into something else. Here, the *marrano* identifies analogous structures, which is one of the fundamental aspects of his inventiveness: to discover what is universal. 'It is when you bury the lance deepest / that I think you cure me' (*OV*, p. 272). The possibility of inverting experiences of pain into cure/salvation/pleasure is the work of thought, the *cogitatio*, which is therefore equipped with an impressive versatility for interpreting suffering and pain. 'With this thought / which I believe I don't deceive myself / there is no pain that is unknown to me'. But there is a difference, between the distortion of language under the rules of the imagination, on the one hand, and under the rules of the truth of nature, on the other. Credulity is thus the result of this versatile hermeneutic capacity of thought. But it is completely unrelated to understanding or judgement, which is based on knowing the nature of things. When we exercise judgement, all those constructions look like folly. 'But then I see my folly', Villalobos the poet concludes, as ever evoking an additional layer of reflection, an ironic distancing.

This scrutiny from the outside — the dispassionate view taken by judgement, by the *marrano*, the physician who talks to himself — understands everything as a comedy, only that it is now played out in the *cogitationes*. Just as the physician situates the explanation of the characters' folly in the glosses to Plautus's work, he imposes his judgement on the chain of *cogitationes* from a position in the transcendence of life, from the sidelines, the social margins that are the *marrano*'s place. It might be the very comedy of his thoughts, but he does not let himself be carried away by it, he does not lose understanding but explains it. Thought can play its games, caving in to the systems of social coercion and the inner pressure of love pierced through with melancholy, but judgement always constructs its gaze, which cannot be reconciled to the mad course of life and the work, but can only explain it. That is why the *marrano* emotion par excellence, the one that guarantees distance, separation, retraction, that imposes limits on identifying with the environment, the one that is truly constitutive of the *marrano*, is judgement. Therefore, the inquisitor aspires to one thing most of all: to occupy the seat of judgement, in such a way that the *marrano*'s confession to him and in him duplicates the customary words used by everyone else, and the *marrano* accepts a blessing and absolution, after the summary puts into the mouth of the accused precisely the thing that he is accused of in the end. The outside place, the soul's impenetrable stronghold, is then closed off and eliminated and with it the *marrano*'s possibilities are diluted.

The phenomenon of melancholy (whether Calixto's or Amphitryon's), which belongs to him who knows what he was, together with sublimated love and its reversions, has immense potential for destroying the equilibrium of the body and presenting the symptoms of a perceptual disorder. The *marrano*, who is highly susceptible to this danger, is his own physician. No need to recall Freud again. Melancholic love gives the inner world a weight that makes us pay closer attention to it than to the world of corporeality. In this inner world, it might seem to Villalobos that Descartes has put an arbitrary end to his methodical doubting about his *cogitationes*. Not even the *cogito* with all its *cogitationes* is free from this line of doubt, when what I was is already in the past. Actually, this is not so serious for Villalobos because the capacity for thought is not the most important or fundamental one. In a comical poem in which a lady asks her beloved what he is thinking about, Villalobos makes him answer, 'I'm thinking that my thought doesn't think what I'm thinking' (p. 281). How do we get from here to the foundational *cogito*? Nothing stable can be wrested from *cogitationes*, with their infinite reflections, not even an idea of the self. The *cogito* is a playing field for love and its disorders; it can be the foundation for nothing. I think my thought, but it is possible that the object of that thought thinks that it is not I who thinks. The *cogitationes'* continuous process of reflecting themselves can be prolonged indefinitely and always have the same outcome: the impossibility of recognizing oneself as an identity in the variations of thinking. Villalobos's path does not lead to Husserl, of course. Identity does not come from the imagination, from thought or from the body alone. As he says in the *Tratado del amor*, identity is the recognition of Alcmena's virtue, trust in filiation, a love that is not melancholic that assures you that you are still who you were. However, this is in the past because that serene love of the Jewish race is prohibited. Thus, what cannot be erased for the *marrano* is the memory of what he was. This will be the substance of his emotion. He knows that he can no longer be a Jew, but he knows he was one and this memory is at once a source of torture and pleasure. That is what the *marrano* is.

Thus, the fragility of identity is not external to the subject himself; rather it is necessary when he is alone. Filiation was more urgent for identity because of the fragility of the order of the body, which was incapable of being the foundation of identity by itself. In a poem called 'Al tiempo Bueno', Villalobos allows himself to be carried away by a moderate and controlled melancholy. 'Oh, memory of my life, / how you pain me, / pain that is never forgotten', he says unequivocally. The only true identity, the identity of the memory of the singular, is accompanied by pain. The continuity of the former is nothing but the conscious echo of the continuity of the latter. But instead of situating this pain and this loss in some deceptive devil or in an evil demon, as Descartes does, Villalobos places it in the body, whose form yields to time and prevents any possibility of a stable, objective identity. This is why memory is necessary and why there is no external sign that can serve as the basis for identity. 'They have made me so misshapen / that I do not recognize myself'. Paradox is insuperable and it is characteristic of the forced convert. I am myself, but I do not recognize myself because I have lost the shape that was once mine and that has now become a ghost, which despite its non-existence continues to be the basis of comparison of my identity, my memory. This memory does not aid the modern *cogito*, which is projected as a method of the future. The dissonance between my ghost and my current form is nothing but the consequence of time and the finitude of the 'graces' that human powers are equipped with. In any case, in the fullness of time, this physician can only find 'joy' in seeing himself 'free from all passions' (*OV*, p. 284), the corporeal basis of judgement, which thus reveals its dependence on the body as well, on a balanced body that does not allow itself to feel, a body capable of activating the medical knowledge that has been transmitted.

From this perspective, *marrano* emotions are rather human emotions, too human. The fragility of identity has its seat in the body's finitude and therefore the world's plenitude is rather an instant in the past. Time's fury in all its diversity does not offer anything in the future that can overcome the nuisance of existence. No longer capable of tying himself to a body deprived of its plenitude, to a deformation of its former shape, alone with his pain, this disconsolate man is able to see himself as living not so much because life consents to let him do so but because death 'has cast me off'. Man's surplus time, in which he is no longer wanted either by life or yet by death, in which there is no sufficient reason either to live or to die, *marrano* time, alien to and different from all things that are alive or dead, the enemy of both, the ally of both, Villalobos achieves uniqueness as the very consequence of an exception: he has been sidestepped by the dualities that make up the cosmos, including good and evil, love and lovelessness, identity and difference, life and death.

This *marrano* rhetoric not only does not abide identity; it sees life as an instantaneous gap that is maintained through the rejection of both life and death. Actually, this is how the *marrano* lives in society, neither integrated nor as *homo sacer*, and this is why he is hardly astonished. He can maintain his composure because he incarnates the universal human condition, which arises from his comprehension of the nature of things, and that is his consolation. At an instant that is equidistant from everything that is nameable in a binary order, inert time, time that is resistant to any difference, to evaluation, here we find the time in which the *marrano* finally discovers his own existential ground, his primary desire: to go unnoticed by life and death. However, such an existence understood in this way is part of the same lucidity that remembers the world's zenith, the fact of what was. Time experienced as ennui is the consequence of the fact that there was once a good time. Here also, duality and ambivalence — joy and tedium — are inevitable and are ruled by the fate of the body's time. The body enjoyed a good period and then came a tedious time, as also happened to the body of the Jewish people in Sepharad. But that time, the good one, was only the consequence of doing what is right. And this is something very concrete. 'The well-governed flesh / makes its owner agree'. Not the other way around. We are not in Cartesian rhetoric: the well-governed and well-tuned *cogito* will make it possible to understand the body's mechanisms and render it immortal. Nothing could be further from Villalobos than this scheme. The first thing to do is to eliminate the passions and govern well. Then, bliss. The passions are not of the soul: they are part of the order of the body. For the rest, for that which well-governed flesh cannot do, judgement has only one thing: patience, the ability to live with and in the tedium of time. This patience is part of identity, of memory and of pain, because like them it shares time with constancy. 'That our patience might do what the flesh cannot', says Villalobos. This is the principal component to the *marrano*'s *ethos* of life, the basis of his animal being, surpassed not by transcending its animal nature but by its ability to endure it consciously. And among the components of this consciousness of his animal nature there is one which we cannot linger over: that the *marrano* can always be hunted.

Notes to Chapter 11

1. See José Luis Villacañas, 'La ratio teológica paulina de Alonso de Cartagena', in *La primera escuela de Salamanca (1406–1516)*, ed. by Cirilo Flórez and Maximiliano Hernández (Salamanca: Universidad de Salamanca, 2012), pp. 75–95.

2. On this period, see Stefania Pastore's excellent book *Una herejía española. Conversos, alumbrados e Inquisición (1449–1559)* (Madrid: Marcial Pons, 2010).

3. On Constantino Ponce de la Fuente, see Villacañas, *¿Qué imperio? Un ensayo polémico sobre Carlos V* (Córdoba: Almuzara, 2008).

4. On Antonio del Corro, see Villacañas, 'La Tolleranza nel contesto ispanico del Cinquecento. Il caso di Antonio del Corro', in *Tracing the Path of Tolerance: History and Critique from the Early Modern Period to the Present Day*, ed. by Paolo Scotton and Enrico Zucchi (Newcastle: Cambridge Scholars, 2016), pp. 8–23.

5. See the contribution by Stefania Pastore in this volume.

6. *Libro intitulado los problemas de Villalobos, que trata de cuerpos naturales y morales, dos diálogos de medicina y el tratado de los tres grandes, una canción y la comedia Anphitrion* (Zamora: Juan Picardo, 1543; 2nd edn, Zaragoza: Jorge Coci, 1544). After the author's death, an edition was published in Seville in 1550 by Cristóbal Álvarez, and another in the same city in 1574, by Hernando Díaz. For a treatment of this figure, see my Introduction to López de Villalobos, *Tratado sobre las costumbres humanas* (Murcia: Biblioteca Saavedra Fajardo, 2012), and Consolación Baranda Leturio, 'El humanismo frustrado de Francisco López de Villalobos y la polémica con Hernán Núñez', *eHumanista*, 29 (2015), 208–39.

7. Villacañas, 'El estigma de Descartes y la búsqueda de la certeza: variaciones sobre un tema moderno', in *Actas del Symposium internacional sobre el 350 aniversario del Discurso del Método* (Barcelona: Universidad de Barcelona, 1987), pp. 907–28.

8. Giambattista Vico, *Opere Filosofiche*, ed. by Paolo Cristofolini (Florence: Sansoni, 1971), p. 73.

9. As we know, Kant takes this maxim from Bacon, who is the real precursor of Vico's *verum est factum*. In other words: interestingly, the sober, objective spirit of eighteenth-century Neapolitan Catholicism is the heir of Bacon, a Calvinist who was himself a driving force behind the struggle against the *idola* that dominate the human psyche. The project of liberation from these idols is decisively taken up by Vico. Here is yet another case of the influence that Calvinism had on Catholicism throughout its history.

10. *L'Anfitrione ovvero la modernità di Plauto*, ed. by Anna Castellani (Florence: Le Monnier, 1995), pp. 105–09.

11. On this topic, see Villacañas, 'Problemas de Método', in *Giorgio Agamben, filosofía, ética e política*, ed. by Ésio Francisco Salvetti, Paulo César Carbonari and Iltomar Siviero (Passo Fundo: Ifibe, 2015), pp. 77–113 and the bibliography.

12. See René Girard, 'Comedies of Errors: Plautus-Shakespeare-Molière', in *American Criticism in the Poststructuralist Age*, ed. by Ira Konigsberg (Ann Arbor: University of Michigan Press, 1981), pp. 66–86. Camões and Matías de los Reyes also wrote versions of the work. See Beth S. Tremallo, *Irony and Self-Knowledge in Francisco López de Villalobos* (New York: Garland P. I., 1991), p. 157.

13. In this sense, we might say that Descartes's rhetoric, as the object of mockery by the friends of *Amphitryon*, is the successor of everything that had previously earned Plautus's mockery. It is noteworthy that as early as the twelfth century, the work was used to ridicule the follies of the Scholastics. Vitalis of Blois, in his adaptation, titled *Geta*, shows that he who has learned enough logic from the universities is the slave, but of course he has not learned enough for

Archas, Mercury's counterpart, to be able to convince him that in reality he is no one: 'We have become two. Before, we were only one. / Everything that exists is unique / but I, who speak now am not unique / *ergo* it follows that Geta is no one' (verses 277–80). Cited by Richard F. Hardin, 'England's *Amphitruo* Before Dryden: The Varied Pleasures of Plautus's Template', *Studies in Philology*, 109.1 (2012), 45–62 (p. 49). It is important to note that mid-sixteenth-century English versions still present the work as a lesson against clever sophists. Descartes would have been one of them, though of course these English works were written especially against the sophistry that tries to impose a religious identity on rustics and simple men, that is, the sophistry of radical reformers. Doubtless, Descartes was reacting against this context of radical reform, but it remains inside his framework: he hopes to prevent the possibility of a personality being established from the outside, as in the practices of Catholic confessionalization, and thus he wants to offer an identity that is formed from the inside, self-referential and Augustinian.

14. Gustavo Illades Aguiar, *La Celestina en el taller salmantino* (Mexico: UNAM, Instituto de Investigaciones filológicas, 1999).

15. *Sumario de la medicina*, in Villalobos, *Algunas obras de Francisco López de Villalobos* (Madrid: Sociedad de Bibliófilos Españoles, 1886), p. 314. Hereafter cited as *SM*. When *SM* is not referred to, I give the citation as *OV* with a number.

16. Choler (yellow bile), phlegm, melancholy and blood. These are the four humours. Blood, 'before it goes on to nourish', changes into the four humidities through the capillaries. All body parts are made up of these humours. But the most important are the heart and the brain. After comes the liver and then the reproductive parts. All seek a balance between heat and humidity, so that they are not excessively cold or dry. The heart is the home of the vital virtues; the brain, of the animal virtues; and the liver, of nourishment. Virtues here are the ancient souls: life soul, animal soul, vegetal soul. Each virtue or soul has an instrument: the spirit (*OV*, p. 314), which has its seat in the heart. Illness can therefore be either simple or compound, the former due to bad complexion, bad composition or because it affects a body part.

17. Not only is the lover a case for medical explanation but also those who suffer from an 'incubus or strangler' (p. 325). The 'aluminados' have a special importance; they are those who 'suffer the malady of being male prostitutes'. Here, Villalobos allows a glimpse of his hatred toward Italy: 'And they say that in Italy there is a plague of this [disease]' (p. 400). It is a pity that this theory of Villalobos's has not been used to analyse the problem of the Castilian Enlightenment and the hidden eroticism underlying it.

18. I am not able to elaborate on this point here, but I hope to develop the analogy between the interpretations of Nietzsche and Villalobos in a book about the latter.

19. And one that is especially significant during the period the work was translated. We should recall that, at this same time, Ferdinand was poisoning himself with cantharides, a powder made from the Spanish fly, which was used as an aphrodisiac in the sixteenth century, simply because one of the effects of its ingestion was priapism. In large doses, fly powder was poisonous. Ferdinand was taking it because he wanted to have a son with Germana de Foix in order to break up the union of the crowns, or rather, to give this union an heir that was not a descendant of Joanna of Castile. Villalobos was Germana's physician and he must have thought it was ironic that Ferdinand went to such extreme lengths to leave an heir, while in Amphitryon's case it had been so easy for his wife to become impregnated. When we look at the comedy with this context in mind, it takes on a comic meaning that is unquestionably tragic. That the political fate of an entire society depended on a mythical obsession with impossible offspring is of course unsettling. If Ferdinand had had a looser notion of identity, it would not have mattered so much to him who the father was. It was indeed ironic that a people who believed the story about Saint Joseph's spurious paternity as the basis for their religion had such an uncompromising view of a situation that could have been easily resolved by imitating the mythical story of Christ.

20. See my analysis of this issue in the work cited in note 1.

21. Someday the issue of the Marian cult of the Immaculate Conception will need to be researched in this connection. As had been argued by converts such as Halevi, known after his conversion as Pablo de Santa María, Spanish Jews belonged to the same tribe as Mary and were close to her Davidic lineage. This can be seen in *Scrutinum scripturarum*, with Cristobal de Santotis's previous

biography, which was published by Filippo Giunta in Burgos, in 1591. It had been previously published in Mantua and Mainz, in 1478, which may have been the version that Luther read. It is no accident that those who were most hostile to the cult of the Inmaculada were Dominicans and especially the most typical anti-Semites, such as Quevedo. In convert communities, all kinds of symbolic representations of the Jewish period in Christ's life were common, with an emphasis on the role of his mother, who it should be recalled was never baptized or became a Christian. It is paradoxical and ironic to think that this Marian cult was a form of resistance for converts of Hebrew lineage, and in this sense, it is an example of a specific, 'neither ... nor' identity. In effect, the Virgin Mary cannot be considered either as a Jew or as a Christian. As someone who lived during the interregnum between the old law and the new, she enjoyed her own unique and archetypical status, a status that those who are deeply devoted to her reproduce in their singularity. These traditions came to be represented in art, such as in the Luzón Reredos by Juan de Soreda — now in Torremocha del Pinar — which represents Jesus's life as a Jew and which dates back to precisely this period, the first decade of the sixteenth century. See Francisco Javier Ramos Gómez, 'Juan Soreda y las tablas del antiguo retablo de Luzón', *Archivo Español del Arte*, 75.299 (2002), 293–322. I would like to thank José Ramón Álvarez Layna for pointing this out to me.

22. On the relationship between the two, see Gustavo Illades Aguiar, 'Dos pacientes virtuales del médico Francisco de Villalobos. Anselmo y Carrizales', *Bulletin of the Cervantes Society of America*, 19.2 (1999), 101–12. Cf. Juan Huarte de San Juan, *Examen de Ingenios* (Baeza: Juan Bautista Montoya, 1575; Madrid: Cátedra, 1989). It is extremely interesting that the work that Illades suggests as a link between Villalobos and Huarte de San Juan is none other than Juan Luis Vives's *De anima et vita* (Basel: Roberti Vinter, 1538).

23. See the book by Christina H. Lee, *The Anxiety of Sameness in Early Modern Spain* (Manchester: Manchester University Press, 2016).

24. See Rabi Eliyahu Capsali, *El judaísmo hispano según la crónica hebrea de Rabí Eliyahu Capsali, traducción y estudio del 'Seder Eliyahu Zuṭa' (capítulos 40–70)*, ed. and trans. by Yolanda Moreno Koch (Granada: Universidad de Granada, 2005). On this topic see my *Monarquía hispánica* (Madrid: Espasa Calpe, 2008), pp. 586–87, 667–79.

25. See this text in Spinoza, *Tractatus Theologico-Politicus*, chapter 3, 'Of the vocation of the Hebrews': 'That they have been preserved in great measure by Gentile hatred, experience demonstrates. When the king of Spain formerly compelled the Jews to embrace the State religion or to go into exile, a large number of Jews accepted Catholicism. Now, as these renegades were admitted to all the native privileges of Spaniards, and deemed worthy of filling all honourable offices, it came to pass that they straightway became so intermingled with the Spaniards as to leave of themselves no relic or remembrance. But, exactly the opposite happened to those whom the king of Portugal compelled to become Christians, for they always, though converted, lived apart, inasmuch as they were considered unworthy of any civic honours'. For an analysis, see my article 'Spinoza. Democracia y subjetividad marrana', *Política Común*, 1 (2011), 53–84.

26. See Francisco de Mendoza y Bobadilla, *Tizón de la nobleza de España* (Cuenca: Francisco Gómez, 1852).

27. For Spanish objections to the empire of Charles V, see Villacañas, *¿Qué imperio?*

CHAPTER 12

❖

Literary Discourse between the Eternal Validity of the Torah and Philosophical Doubt: The Polemical Writings of Abraham Gómez Silveira (1656–1741)

Harm den Boer

This chapter discusses the polemical work written by the Amsterdam Sephardic Jew Abraham Gómez Silveira (1656–1741), extant in a series of seven manuscript volumes written in Spanish. Initially conceived as a Jewish refutation of Isaac Jacquelot's *Dissertations sur le Messie*,[1] Silveira argues with a large number of Christian theologians, relying both on a canon of contemporary Jewish apologists and on his own arguments. Although his ideas, rooted in fideistic rationalism, seem straightforward and repetitive, he nonetheless merits attention for three reasons: a) his progressive openness towards other religions and his plea for religious tolerance; b) his self-fashioning as a commonsensical Jewish bystander, even as a fool; and c) his uncontainable literary urge to alternate serious discourse with displays of humour and wit.

The impressive literary production of Abraham Gómez Silveira, all in Spanish, is relatively unknown when compared to that of fellow contemporary Sephardim of converso origin living in Amsterdam. Among the writers of secular literature, Daniel Levi (Miguel) de Barrios, Jacob (Manuel) de Pina, and Joseph Penso have been more widely received, mainly because of the printed fortune of their works; the same can be said of the authors of a specifically Jewish literature, such as Isaac Cardoso or Menasseh ben Israel. On the other hand, authors of Jewish apologetics like Saul Levi Mortera and Isaac Orobio de Castro, who could only resort to manuscript circulation of their work, enjoyed a significantly wider reception and consequently have also received more critical attention. One could argue that his manuscripts appear somewhat dispersed in different collections, but the presence of Silveira's works in the *Catalogue of the manuscripts of Ets Haim/Livraria Montezinos*[2] — many volumes, thousands of pages — should be enough to draw attention to this author.[3] Perhaps this sheer extension, its repetitiveness and also the particular *jocoserio* style of Silveira, alternating between serious arguments and playful interruptions, have relegated the author to a secondary role in the study of Jewish apologetics.[4]

I want to argue that it is precisely the literary element of his polemical texts that makes them an interesting and innovative contribution to the genre. In his impressive edition of the *Marrakesh Dialogues* between Obadia ben Israel and his Catholic brother, Andrés, the scholar Carsten Wilke has rightly stressed the novelty and relevance of the literary element in early modern Sephardi polemics, referring to the adoption of humanist dialogue and all kinds of rhetorical and narrative devices in a genre hitherto conceived as purely argumentative.[5] In Silveira's case, it is not so much the use of new persuasive strategies mentioned by Wilke, but rather his self-fashioning as a simple believer and even as a jester, together with his seemingly arbitrary whimsical interludes in the middle of his serious arguments, that provide a new dimension in Jewish polemics. Not only does this style serve an audience of Jewish laymen, its literary character has also a potential of irreverence — 'subversion' is perhaps too strong a term here — that goes beyond the author's purported fideistic scepticism. In this sense, he shows a remarkable resemblance to some Iberian Jewish authors. Like Sem Tob de Carrión, he cultivated a genre of philosophical poetry rooted in Castilian popular tradition — in the case of Silveira, through his *coplas filosóficas* or 'Silveiradas' — and like Sem Tob, he fashioned himself as a humble subject; indeed he went even further, adopting the role of a fool and a jester, recalling the *poetas locos* of fifteenth-century Spain.[6] This is all the more remarkable, as Silveira came to Amsterdam at a young age and must have acquired the larger part of his formation outside Iberia.

Biographical Profile

Abraham was born Diego Silveira, in Arévalo in 1656.[7] Although the Castilian town is known for its Jewish medieval past, Diego had Portuguese roots. He belonged to an important converso family, among whose members figure the royal chronicler Rodrigo Méndez[8] and Miguel de Silveira[9] the physician and author of the famous epic poem *El Macabeo*, published in Naples in 1638. Silveira informs us in two of his works that his mother, Ana Jiménez, when still twelve years old, was rounded up together with other family members by the Inquisition, supposedly in the middle of a secret synagogue service in the house of his maternal great-uncle Diego Jiménez, in Madrid, in the year 1635.[10] Sent to Cuenca, all were eventually sentenced to wear sambenitos. If a passage in one of his poems is to be read as an autobiographical hint, Diego himself would have lived in Madrid for some time as well,[11] before going to France. What is known for sure is that around 1671 he arrived in Amsterdam where he and his family entered the Portuguese Jewish community. Diego, now Abraham,[12] was admitted to Abi Yetomim, a charitable society within the Sephardic community of Talmud Torah which provided young orphans with a three-year Jewish education, with the possibility of a rabbinical training for its most promising students. Abraham proved to be an excellent pupil and upon completing his education over a further three years, he was offered the honour of delivering a sermon on the occasion of the inauguration of the *medras* of Talmud Torah.[13] In 1677, AGS had seven of his sermons published in a small volume that contained effusive laudatory poems, in Hebrew, Portuguese, and Spanish, and an approbation in prose by outstanding members of the congregation, among whom should be mentioned the leading rabbis or *hahamim* Isaac Aboab de Fonseca, Moses Raphael Aguilar, and Solomon de Oliveira.[14] In his sermons, AGS showed a considerable literary talent which he was also able to cultivate at the literary Academia del Temor Divino, founded in 1676 by the wealthy Sephardic merchant and diplomat Isaac Núñez, alias Don Manuel de Belmonte.[15]

In 1682 AGS published a *Vejamen*, a witty text that reflects his activities in another literary society, this time among the Portuguese Jews of Antwerp.[16] He resided for some time in the Spanish Netherlands, although his presence there cannot have been continuous. In 1694 he married Ester Franco da Silva in Amsterdam. By 1700 he started to write the first volumes of his polemical work against Isaac Jacquelot. In 1705, he was still living in Antwerp, as can be inferred from letters he wrote to the Mahamad, the seven-member governing board of the Portuguese Jewish Community of Amsterdam, in that year; in 1718 he appeared as a 'friend of the author', the Portuguese-born Samuel Mendes de Sola, when the latter's first sermon was printed.[17] In 1732, he lamented the death of his daughter Sara Gomes Silveira. According to the records of the Portuguese Jewish Cemetery at Ouderkerk, he died on 19 Adar 5501 (7 March 1741), at the very respectable age of 85 years.[18]

From this biographical sketch it would seem that Abraham successfully effaced his Catholic Iberian Christian past and succeeded in creating for himself a new and promising future at Amsterdam. Aged fifteen, he was provided with a sound Jewish education, acquainting himself with Hebrew and rabbinical literature — but also enjoying a curriculum that included the study of rhetoric and dialectics;[19] he fits the model of the 'modern' Jew, conversant in both Jewish and secular culture, well integrated into society.[20]

But the rest of Silveira's life does not obey this myth of redemption that is provided in a 'New Jerusalem narrative' fashioned by Sephardim of converso origin.[21] Shortly after having been launched as a promising young scholar, Abraham Gómez Silveira left Amsterdam for Antwerp. We do not know the reasons for this departure, neutrally registered in the archives of Abi Yetomim with the remark *foise a Amberes*. It is possible that Abraham harboured ambitions of securing a rabbinic appointment at Amsterdam and that he did not succeed: by the 1670s competition was huge. During the second half of the seventeenth century Talmud Torah exported rabbis and Talmidim that would occupy prestigious posts at Sephardic congregations such as Hamburg, London and Bayonne. Perhaps there was family business to attend to; another explanation for the departure would be a conflict. We know in fact that, from Antwerp, he addressed himself on two occasions to his former Amsterdam congregation, distancing himself from rumours that identified him as the author of a text apparently titled *El judío reformado* that the authorities of Talmud Torah had been made aware of, and consequently prohibited, threatening the author with the most serious sanctions (confiscation of copies, *herem*). Abraham had known that certain individuals attributed those works to him, an accusation he vehemently denied. He complained that the rumours in fact greatly damaged his reputation, his 'honour', and thereby threatened his family. He begged the authorities to find the true author of these texts and burn all of them.[22]

From these letters we learn the despair of a person who considered himself and his family destroyed upon losing their honour. We also learn that he was associated with heterodox literature. Possibly, the polemical texts AGS had started to write from 1700 onwards earned him an unforeseen reputation among his fellow Sephardim.

The Polemical Oeuvre of Abraham Gómez Silveira

A closer look at Silveira's manuscript work can provide us with some clues regarding the purported heterodoxy attributed to the writer. AGS was the (anonymous) author of a *Fábula burlesca de Jesucristo y Magdalena*, a poem written in the vein of parodic mythography, where Jesus appears as a true *pícaro*, and even as a libertine.[23] He is also the author of an equally parodic poem on the life of the false Messiah of the Jews, Sabbatai Zevi, who had gathered many fervent adepts among the Sephardim of Amsterdam (as in other Jewish communities, of course).[24] If the latter subject might have been controversial because it opened up old wounds, the poem on Jesus was potentially harmful to relations with the Christians. It can be doubted, however, if such poems would have been censored. For one, they were written in a language Dutch society largely ignored, and, more importantly, they only circulated in manuscript form. There existed, in fact, a huge corpus of polemical literature in Spanish and Portuguese, circulating among Sephardim of converso past, a semi-clandestine literature that was tolerated and even encouraged (or written) by the rabbis of the community.[25]

Another such work was the *Diálogos theológicos en versos jocoserios para deleitar aprovechando. Interlocutores. Un sabio ministro reformado, presidente; un doctor cathólico apostólico romano; un turco mahometano, herudito; un judío desapasionado.*[26] In this work, of which several copies are extant, AGS displays in witty poetical style and the 'coplas' form — that is, the popular *romance* — his opinions on the eternal validity of the Law (Torah) against the 'novelties' introduced by Christianity and Islam, but also an attack on religious coercion and persecution (represented by the Catholic Church, most notably by the Inquisition) together with a plea for religious tolerance. Although the poem is not as satirical and playful as the aforementioned parodies on Christ and Sabbatai, its title is somewhat reminiscent of the work prohibited by the Mahamad in 1705, by the presence of the word 'reformado' and the syntagm 'Dios y el sabio contra el necio' [God and the wise against the fool]. Perhaps the *Diálogos theólogos* had been misinterpreted or a converted Sephardi (*judío reformado*) had launched a provocative work imitating AGS's style. As long as we do not find more information on the issue, we will not know. However, the fact alone that Silveira, someone who must have been well known in the congregation, was regarded as a potential heterodox cannot be dismissed as irrelevant.

Let us therefore examine Silveira's main polemical work more closely. As its initial title informs us, it was addressed to the French protestant theologian and preacher Isaac Jacquelot (1647–1708),[27] in reaction to the latter's *Dissertations sur le Messie* (1699). Silveira's reply occupies thousands of handwritten pages debunking the Christian Messiah and defending Judaism, collected in a series of volumes with different titles, although the leading title could be *Disertaciones sobre el Mesías donde se prueva a los christianos que J. C. no es el Mesías prometido y vaticinado en el viejo Testamento*. These volumes also called *Silveiradas* were written, according to their author or copyist, between 1700 and 1738, occupying thereby a considerable life span.

They start with two volumes kept in The Hague, called *Disertaciones sobre el Mesías... con su respuesta en diálogos, Libro primero* and *Libro segundo*. The subsequent volumes are present in Ets Haim as *Libro Terzero* or *Silveiradas*, the *Libro Quarto* titled *El juez de las controversias*, the *Libro quinto* called *Quinta piedra del Zurrón de David, que arroja el autor a la testa de los gigantes que mantienen los dominantes errores* (1725). They were followed by a work that was meant to be the introduction to all: *Preluminarias que deven anteceder a todo género de controversias en materia de religión*, also called *Libro anteprimero*. The final volume, copied posthumously, bears the title *Libro mudo*.[28] As one can appreciate from these titles, they include a literary and ludic element, which was increasingly displayed by the author: whereas the first 'books' had been conceived as translations and replies, the third already included a play with the author's name (*Silveiradas*) and the following works received alternative titles in a progressive display of literary awareness.

Each of these volumes or parts has between 230 and 280 folios written on both sides, that is, in total about 3800 pages of handwritten text.[29] The first two books contain a summarized translation of Jacquelot's text, chapter by chapter, each one followed by the author's replies, refuting one by one the thesis launched by the French theologian. Written in the form of dialogues, this arrangement by AGS already contains an element of fiction. Of course, these dialogues do not reflect a real dialogue between Jacquelot and Silveira; but they introduce some fictional elements suggesting an oral interchange and a setting of playful rivalry:

> S[ilveira]. Monsieur Jacquelot. Here we are all together. My first book, as you have seen, is already finished and contains the first part of yours, answered part by part. Well, as we have nothing to do, let us get down to work, and dispute again. M[onsieur] J[acquelot]. I am provided with such a harvest of prose to straighten the greatest difficulties that if you want to free yourself of the spiderwebs that your sight has created in your study's loom, truth will reveal itself and will not be crawling along the floor rubbing against lies. With this fox tail you can shake the dust off your ignorance. Here we will have to play all the keys so that there will not be any tails left to skin. To persuade your insufficiency is a victory for a man of my letters, of little substance. Call up a gathering of rabbis and you will see that I will have a stiff beard to all of them and they will know that one should speak only of what one understands.[30]

A real dialogue never took place: Jacquelot was not living in the Netherlands anymore when his *Dissertations sur le Messie* were published in 1699. Such interchanges as had taken place between Menasseh ben Israel and Christian scholars, including António Vieira, or an 'amicable conversation' Limborch had entertained with Orobio de Castro were perhaps no longer fashionable at the turn of the eighteenth century.[31] In any case, AGS presented himself, time and again, as a marginal person, a Jew living in exile, who was excluded from such encounters, afraid of openly exposing himself to the criticism of Christian society:

> Letter / To the very learned Ishac Jacquelot
>
> Monsieur, after putting myself humbly at your service, I wish to inform you that I have sent you two books with the latest post, wherein by way of dialogue I answered the book made by your zeal for our instruction. And when I was awaiting acknowledgement of receipt, I found out that my care left the books hidden... Let the idea suffice that I wanted to send you the books in order to write again; I recognize there is no safe truth of opinions, each wise man has his hobby, it is impossible to wash off the colour of a black man with a hundred turns of bleach, he who opens his eyes to 'what will they say?' better keep his mouth shut, many Esaus will sell their birthright for a bowl of stew... for all this foolishness I have to believe that until God, as he promises, offers the remedy, nor you nor I can solve anything. You can write that you are in retreat in your land and in your house: I cannot breathe, as I am captive without a span of earth. However, as I don't have anything at hand, just to do something that serves nothing, I will pick up the principal arguments from your book and from my answers and one by one I will go on reflecting and answering every one. If this letter arrives at your hand in the Valley of Josaphat you will tell me personally if the Jews are as ugly as they are depicted.[32]

This evident rhetorical stance of the author might reflect, or not, a reality of impossible dialogue; what Jewish readers of AGS's works would recognize, however, was their position of a priori inferiority in such encounters. For the moment, battles could only be won on paper, and out of public sight.

Silveira's arguments in this controversy are quite straightforward and are exclusively based upon his unconditional faith in the Scriptures, the Eternal Truth of the Torah.[33] For him, truth is simple: the Torah was given by God and is eternal. This, Silveira argues, is agreed by Christians and Muslims alike; each of these religions is respectable, but has introduced 'novedades', novelties, that contradict the immutable character of God's Law. What this law is, is mostly very clear, and one should not seek hidden truths: only the literal sense permits man to know Divine Will. Silveira rejects allegories and thereby invalidates all typological readings of the Old Testament. He calls the searches for hidden truths — those who look for the obscure texts — 'Gongorismos'. The Scriptures contain, of course, figurative or literary passages, but when it comes to precepts, what God wants from men, the text is always clear and unambiguous. Therefore, far-fetched interpretations, such as those introduced by Christian theologians (Doctores), have to be dismissed. AGS admits Jesus as a Jewish teacher and points to all the passages in the New Testament where Jesus upholds the validity of the Law given to Moses.

AGS's other main argument is the indivisible unity of God. Time and again, Silveira considers Christianity, and above all, Catholicism, as idolatry. The divine nature of the Christian Messiah is not to be found in the Scriptures, neither in the so-called Ancient Testament nor in the New Testament. Silveira relies on a vast corpus of Jewish polemical literature to prove that the Messiah has not come — the main argument of Jacquelot's *Dissertations*. He frequently mentions Isaac of Troki and also refers to Saul Levi Mortera, Isaac Orobio de Castro, and Menasseh ben Israel. The author himself insists that the world has been and still is in such a state, an iron age full of conflicts, that the Messiah cannot have come. The latter's immediate and overall acceptance by mankind announced in the Scriptures was lacking during the time of Jesus Christ. In AGS's own world, with his awareness of the state of political and religious division in Europe, Asia, and America, such a moment does not seem to be on the horizon, either. The most imminent threat is represented by the libertines, those who, according to Silveira, deny God's existence.

There is, however, comfort: Silveira has an increasing awareness of a climate in which religious dialogue seems to become possible. AGS argues repeatedly and extensively against religious coercion, defended by such (Catholic) authors as Augustine and contemporary Iberian Catholic theologians. Persecution on religious grounds cannot be admitted and AGS continuously exposes and ridicules the archetype of intolerance, the Inquisition. In the third volume of his *Disertaciones* he laments the fact that free interchanges on religious matters are not possible, they have no chance of being permitted.[34] However, by the time he writes the *Preluminarias*, from 1723 onwards,[35] in a work largely dedicated to tolerance and dialogue, he insistently calls upon the celebration of 'conferences' in matters of religion, free from threats, as a great opportunity; although he ends by conceding that they would probably remain a mere wish, he nevertheless keeps mentioning their necessity.[36] Finally, he feels hopeful and is strengthened by the fact that such gatherings apparently are taking place; through the *Gazzette d'Amsterdam* he has learned of the freemasons in London, in 1737.[37]

AGS's stance is therefore extremely straightforward and traditional, but not dogmatic: 'I propose what I believe and I do not order people to believe me' [propongo lo que creo y no mando que me crean]. He follows the fideistic scepticism of Cornelius Agrippa — whom he mentions.[38] As man cannot find the truth by himself, and human philosophy leads only to doubt, one should have faith in God and rely upon the authority of the Torah and the sages. The fideism advocated by Silveira is, however, not anti-rationalistic. Silveira finds religious truth compatible with reason and with natural law, and the core of his argument defending Judaism leans on its rationality. Only if such does not seem to be the case should one simply rely upon God's superior truth and authority. Science that does not conform with Scripture is called 'ignorant':

> Very learned ignorance
> is what my Muse calls
> the sciences that do not conform
> with Scripture.
> When God speaks clearly,
> follow the Letter,
> and leave to God only
> the mysterious parts.[39]

> [...]
> God speaks clearly, the obscure
> does not touch upon salvation,
> it contains mysteries; let us
> leave the hidden to God.[40]
> [...]
> In the clear part, I must follow
> the letter in everything and for everything,
> not say anything on the obscure;
> to reason otherwise
> is no way to reason.[41]

It would seem that Silveira's position is hardly audacious, and does not seem to bear any relation to the reputation as a deviant or heretic that he had according to the accusation made against him around 1705. AGS manifests himself as a traditional Jew with unreserved confidence in God and Torah, and also with an expressed obedience and loyalty to the rabbis (*mis rabinos*),[42] by which he means probably both Oral Law and the rabbis or authorities of his community. Nonetheless, I think there are some remarkable features in his purportedly traditional position of unshakable tradition.

To begin with, and continuing the last argument, AGS hardly mentions rabbinic judaism and the value of Oral Law. He certainly does not dispute them — he clearly attacks the so-called Sadducees — but makes no point of insisting on the importance of rabbinical judaism either, whereas the latter had been a central preoccupation of the rabbis dealing with communities of converso origin. One could argue that this question had lost urgency among Western Sephardim by the eighteenth century, but the subject certainly calls for more attention.

Secondly, AGS's fashioning of a simple man, of *bobo, poeta rocín, simple* or *loco*, etc. is both in line with his purported scepticism — man's nullity against God — but also creates freedom to challenge and mock adversaries:

> In Spain they respond with blood and fire, and here, as they are so witty, they will answer whatever is convenient to them. I myself am a fool, I can answer to anything if they let me allegorize, bend and lie at liberty. They think that we here are all fools and unaware of these pitfalls. In Dialectics fallacies also are taught to prevent us being misled by lewd wittiness.[43]

The fool Silveira challenges Jacquelot, attacks Catholic theologians and the Inquisition, and even laughs at Sabbatai Zevi. His straightforward belief in the uncomplicated clarity, that is literality, of the Law not only attacks Christian — Catholic — sophists (*agudos, gongorinos, doctos*) but also marks a clear distance with those Jewish sages who delve into deeper and hidden meanings. Answering Jacquelot's criticism of some rabbis, AGS simply states that not all rabbinic opinions are to be considered.

A third argument for singling out AGS as more in line with modern, enlightened forms of scepticism — I would avoid 'radical' — than would appear from his fideistic stance is indirect. If his position of traditional Jewish allegiance was so clear and straightforward, why did the author feel the need to repeat himself over and again, and, above all: why had he to read and comment so much more than Jacquelot's *Dissertations sur le Messie*? Reading the vast work produced by AGS, one cannot but be impressed by the sheer number of sources he mentioned and commented upon. He was of course versant in rabbinical literature, Medieval Jewish and contemporary Iberian Jewish authors. Scriptures are extensively quoted, Silveira apparently modernizing the Ferrara translation. As for Christian Scriptures, it seems to me that few other Jewish apologists have mentioned New Testament sources so extensively and repeatedly as Silveira. The Gospels (Matthew, Luke, John), but also Letters to the Corinthians, Letters to the Romans, Ephesians, Hebrews, etc.: they are not only commented upon in the *Libro Mudo*,[44] which pretends to be a catalogue of sources where a reader can find his own truth, but everywhere in AGS's polemics. There is no lack of patristic literature and of medieval Christian theologians: Augustine, Origenes, Pierre d'Aylli, John Hus, Jerome of Prague, Raimundo Llull, Thomas Aquinas. Among contemporary Christian authors, some 100 Catholic names are commented upon, many Iberian, but also many French. The most striking feature is the host of Protestant — mainly French — authors read and mentioned by AGS: Abbadie, Basnage, Bayle, Calvin, Coulan, Jacquelot, Jurieu, Mandeville, Mesnard, Moulin, Senault or Cipriano de Valera. Silveira was informed about many of the early newspapers and journals published in the Netherlands and was aware of the latest novelties in religion and thought.[45] At the age of eighty-two, only a few years before his death, he read or was informed of the *Relation apologétique et historique de la Société des Francs-maçons*, published in Dublin in 1738. He deemed it 'a very nice and true history of the Masons' ('una muy linda y cierta Historia de los Albañiles').

To sum up: AGS read with an exceptional eagerness, a 'bulimic'[46] attitude that somehow contradicts the image of the peaceful and retired 'wise fool' he wanted to convey to the reader. Perhaps Silveira was desiring an epoch of true religious tolerance that would leave the times of persecution and Inquisition definitively in the past, a space where Jews would be truly respected. Reading his later works, however, one is struck by his curiosity for all matters in religion, whether they regard Judaism, Christianity, Islam (he mentions 'Turcos', that is Muslims, and the *Alcorán* frequently) or even the religion of the Chinese or the Amerindians.

Finally, there is the literary spirit of AGS's writings: the need to interrupt serious arguments with playful asides. He combines a form of explicitly Castilian popular wisdom — expressed in *refranes* and *dichos*, with Spanish literary intertextuality — alluding to, for instance, Don Quixote, or with pastiches of the witty parodies in the style of Jacinto Polo de Medina. He further departs from normal, serious, polemical discourse founded on reasoning, by frequent exclamations, apostrophe, and puns (*paranomasia, dilogía...*). Irony — presenting himself as the simple, sometimes as the marginal, or as the jester — alternates with mockery — directed against the Catholic Church and the Inquisition. Thus, he calls his polemical work *Silveyradas*, or he introduces chapters in his text, parodying Cervantes in his Quixote: 'Cap. 1. Donde el autor dize, lo que dize el capítulo'; '[Cap. 2.] Donde se dize lo que en ello se contiene'; 'Cap. 3. Donde el autor dize unas cosas y calla otras...'.[47]

Thus, frequently he passes from prose to poetry, to a traditional form of wisdom poetry the *coplas*, that take up the serious questions treated before introducing numerous variations:

> The Pope they hold infallible:
> But the Mufti deserves more credit,
> or which gentle priest,
> or which priest of the gentiles?
> I stick to Pero Grullo ['Mr. Self-Evident'],
> who knew more than Merlin.
> A commentary of yes, is not no,
> a commentary of no, is not yes.[48]

He frequently introduces a festive, carnivalesque argument in the middle of his serious passages. Here is a particularly interesting one:

> The sacrilegious impropriety of calling the Law 'Testament' caused the idea of calling the Gospels a codicil. Such a name of Testament is not to be found in the Scripture. Here we use the term to refer to the disposition people make of their goods for their heirs. The Author of the Law is the creator of all, without beginning or end. The author of the Gospels is J. C. who died and as he had nothing left when he died, his Gospel is neither testament nor codicil. A friar told me yesterday that if I did not believe the new testament, the Devil would come to get me, I gave him 'a Dios' and said that I did not believe in the new and the old whereupon he called me Libertine, and I with this liberty told him I only believe the Law of the living God, and not the testament of any dead God. 'Oh, these friars!', another spoke to his brother comrade, 'Did the devil *Patillas* tempt you some time to become a Jew?' 'God forbid!' he replied, crossing himself, 'such a temptation I never had!' The other answered: 'I was tempted by a legion of Lucifers to become a Christian and a friar and, as you see, I gave in to the temptation!' Consider it a joke.[49]

One would think that, through voracious readings and irrepressible, irreverent humour, Silveira enjoyed a very pleasurable form of doubt.

Notes to Chapter 12

1. Isaac Jacquelot, *Dissertations sur le Messie. Où l'on prouve aux Juifs que Jesus-Christ est le Messie promis et predit dans l'Ancien Testament* (The Hague: Etienne Foulque, 1699).
2. Lajb Fuks and Rena G. Fuks-Mansfeld, *Catalogue of the Manuscripts of Ets Haim, Livraria Montezinos, Sephardic Community of Amsterdam* (Leiden: Brill, 1975), nn. 200, 201, 207, 235, 236, 246; not mentioned, but also present at Ets Haim are MS 48 A 23 and 48 A 22.
3. One of the first scholars to consider the importance of the polemical works of Silveira has been Yosef Kaplan, who identified Gómez Silveira as the author of the mockery poem on Sabbatai Zevi, of Amsterdam, 'The Attitude of the Leadership of the Portuguese Community in Amsterdam to the Sabbatian Movement, 1665–1671' (in Hebrew), *Zion*, 39 (1974), pp. 198–216 (p. 215). The article by Shalom Rosenberg and Alexander Even-Chen, 'Coplas filosóficas de Abraham Gómez Silveyra', *Revue des Études Juives*, 153 (1994), 327–51, contains useful information. See also Henry Méchoulan, 'A propos de la liberté de conscience. Remarques sur un manuscrit d'Abraham Gomes Silveyra', in *Nature, croyance, raison. Mélanges offerts à Sylvain Zac*, ed. by P. F. Moreau, J. Lagrée, and M. Crampe-Casnabet (Saint-Cloud: École Normale Supériure Fontenay, 1992), pp. 25–41.
4. Rena G. Fuks-Mansfeld, having described copies of his works in the *Catalogue of the manuscripts of Ets Haim*, together with her husband Leo Fuks, called for a study of Silveira's work and of Spanish and Portuguese polemical literature as a whole in *De Sefardim in Amsterdam tot 1795.*

Aspecten van een joodse minderheid in een Hollandse stad (Hilversum: Uitgeverij Verloren, 1989), pp. 177–78. Further references in Harm den Boer, *La literatura sefardí de Amsterdam* (Alcalá de Henares: Instituto Internacional de Estudios Sefardíes y Andalusíes, 1995), esp. pp. 91, 97, 119, 295; Boer, 'Le "contre-discours" des nouveaux juifs. Esprit et polémique dans la littérature des juifs sépharades d'Amsterdam', in *Les Sépharades en littérature. Un parcours millénaire*, ed. by Esther Benbassa (Paris: PUPS, 2005), pp. 47–65; and Kenneth Brown and Harm den Boer, *El barroco sefardí: Abraham Gómez Silveira, Arévalo 1656–Amsterdam 1740* (Kassel: Reichenberger, 2001).

5. Carsten L. Wilke, *The Marrakesh Dialogues: A Gospel Critique and Jewish Apology from the Spanish Renaissance* (Leiden: Brill, 2014), pp. 114–16.

6. Magnificently explored by Francisco Márquez Villanueva, 'Jewish "Fools" of the Spanish Fifteenth Century', *Hispanic Review*, 4 (1982), 385–409.

7. A more extensive biographical profile — still in need of updating with further information on his family — is found in Brown and Den Boer, *El barroco sefardí*, pp. 13–23.

8. Rodrigo Mendes da Silva was born in Celorico da Beira, Portugal, in 1606. He was at the Spanish Court at Madrid between 1635 and 1659. Royal chronicler of Spain and Minister of the Supremo Consejo de Castilla, he was arrested by the Inquisition in 1659. Tortured, sentenced to abjure his 'mosaic faith', he fled to Venice where he entered the Jewish Community. There, he died in 1670. See Abraham Gómez Silveira, *Libro Mudo*, fols 218^v–219^r; Israël S. Révah, 'Le Procès inquisitorial contre Rodrigo Méndez Silva, historiographe du roi Philippe IV', *Bulletin Hispanique*, 67 (1965), 225–52; and Brown and Den Boer, *El barroco sefardí*, p. 14.

9. Miguel de Silveira, also originally from Celorico da Beira, Portugal, studied Law in Coimbra between 1599 and 1604 and afterwards Medicine and Natural Sciences in Salamanca, receiving his degree in 1608. He lived for twenty years in Madrid. In 1636 he took the precautionary step of accompanying his friend the Viceroy Ramiro Felipe de Guzmán to Naples; there he published his epic poem *El Macabeo*, recreating the story of Judah Maccabee and the restauration of Jerusalem. According to Abraham Gómez Silveira, Miguel de Silveira was nephew and cousin of Diego Jiménez, the author's maternal great uncle (Preluminarias, 48 A 18, fol. 21^v).

10. Diego was the brother of Abraham Gómez Silveira's maternal grandfather (*hermano de su abuelo* [*Libro mudo*, 48 B 18, fol. 218^v]; *su sobrina y mi madre Ana Ximénez* [*Preluminarias*, 48 A 18, fol. 21^v]).

11. *Diálogos Theológicos...*, MS Ets Haim/Livraria Montezinos (Amsterdam), 48 B 17, fol. 185^r.

12. From here on, we will refer to Abraham / Diego Gómez Silveira as 'AGS', an acronym the author himself used frequently.

13. It is likely that the education was paid for by Abi Yetomim, enabling AGS to study at Ets Haim, the rabbinical seminar of the Sephardic congregation of Amsterdam. Silveira appears in a list of pupils of Isaac Aboab. The list was published in Joaquim Mendes dos Remédios, *Judeus em Portugal* (Coimbra: Amado, 1895), pp. 222–25.

14. A. Gómez Silveira, *Sermones compuestos por Abraham Gomes Silveira* (Amsterdam: Moséh Díaz, 5437 [1675–76]). The book was financed by the author, as he informs us on the title page.

15. The Academia is described by Daniel Levi (Miguel) de Barrios. Abraham Gómez Silveira is mentioned as one of its *aventureros*, meaning 'voluntary participants' in the literary competitions. See Den Boer, *La literatura sefardí*, p. 138.

16. The text of the printed *Vejamen* is described and edited in Brown and Den Boer, *El barroco sefardí*, pp. 220–35.

17. On Samuel Mendes de Sola, see H. den Boer, 'Perfil literario de Samuel Mendes de Sola', in *A Sefardic Pepper-Pot in the Caribbean: History, Language, Literature, and Art*, ed. by Michael Studemund-Halévy (Barcelona: Tirocinio, 2016), pp. 327–61.

18. Records of the Portuguese Jewish Cemetery of Ouderkerk, P.I.B., 9148.

19. The unpublished MA Thesis of Arts in Jewish Studies, by Ari Bergmann, 'Ets Haim: Tradition and Innovation in Jewish Education' (Columbia University, 2006) describes the curriculum introduced by Ets Haim, and already admired in its time by Jewish travellers. I am grateful to the author for having provided me with a copy of his thesis.

20. Richard H. Popkin, 'The Historical Significance of Sephardic Judaism in 17th Century Amsterdam', *The American Sephardi*, 5 (1971), 18–27; Popkin, 'Some Aspects of Jewish–Christian Theological Interchanges in Holland and England, 1640–1700', in *Jewish–Christian Relations in*

The Seventeenth Century: Studies and Documents, ed. by J. van den Berg and E. G. E. van der Wall (Leiden: Brill, 1988), pp. 3–32.

21. In the texts composed by Sephardic authors of converso origin there are not so many expressions of nostalgia one would expect among exiles. Their return to Judaism made many of them silent about their Iberian (Christian) past. In the Sephardic 'community discourse' the migration from the Iberian Peninsula is regarded as an escape and a liberation, and exile is most commonly transferred to Jewish Diaspora. See Harm den Boer, 'Exile in Sephardic Literature of Amsterdam', *Studia Rosenthaliana*, 35.2 (2001), 187–99.

22. The text referred to was apparently titled 'Judío reformado, Dios y el sabio contra el necio', which the Mahamad (governing board) of the Portuguese Jewish Congregation of Amsterdam characterized as containing 'perjudicial doctrina e heréticos discursos'. See Daniel M. Swetschinski, 'The Portuguese Jewish Merchants of Seventeenth Century Amsterdam: A Social Profile' (unpublished doctoral thesis, Brandeis University, Waltham, MA, 1979), p. 429. The two letters have been edited by Brown and Den Boer, *El barroco sefardí*, pp. 252–55.

23. On the genre, and Silveira's particular contribution, see Harm den Boer, 'Ovid und die verspotteten Götter des spanischen Barock', in *Carmen perpetuum. Ovids Metamorphosen in der Weltliteratur*, ed. by H. Harich-Schwarzbauer and and A. Honold (Basel: Schwabe Basel, 2013), pp. 131–49. Text and commentary in Brown and Den Boer, *El barroco sefardí*, pp. 253–55.

24. 'Historia del famoso Don Sabatay Seví'. Brown and Den Boer, *El barroco sefardí*, pp. 133–98.

25. On the genre of Jewish apologetics and anti-Christian controversy as a whole, see Wilke, *The Marrakesh Dialogues*, 'Invention of a Literary Genre', pp. 113–50.

26. Title according to the copy held in Ets Haim/Livraria Montezinos, 48 B 14, Fuks, Catalogue, p. 246. Another copy of the MS, extant at the Jewish Theological Seminary of New York, bears the title 'Entretenimientos gustozos o diálogos burlescos entre un judío, turco, reformado y católico'.

27. Isaac Jacquelot was a theologian and Protestant minister (Vassy, 1647–Berlin, 1708). Appointed as Minister at Vassy in 1668, he was forced to leave France in 1685, as a consequence of the revocation of the Edict of Nantes. He was a minister at Heidelberg, and from 1687 at the Hague, where he was appointed as preacher to the Walloon congregation. In 1702 he joined the French church in Berlin, where he died in 1708. Jacquelot embraced the Enlightenment, but warned and wrote against the new philosophical and scientific ideas — condensed in Spinoza — that denied the revealed truths of religion. Jacquelot countered with his idea of 'design' (purpose) by an intelligent Creator, thus proving the necessity of God's existence (*Dissertation sur l'existence de Dieu*, 1697). Although Silveira reacted against Jacquelot's *Dissertations sur le Messie*, published in 1699, he found an ally in Jacquelot in their common rejection of libertine philosophers. See Otto Zöckler, *Geschichte der Apologie des Christentums* (Gütersloh: Bertelsmann, 1907); *Nieuw Nederlandsch Biografisch Woordenboek*, 10 vols (Amsterdam: A. W. Sijthoff's uitgevers-maatschappij, 1911–37), vol. II (1912), p. 633; *Biographisch woordenboek van protestantsche godgeleerden in Nederland*, 6 vols (Utrecht: Nijhoff, 1907–49), vol. IV (1931), pp. 529–30; *Biographisch-Bibliographisches Kirchenlexicon*, 37 vols (Hamm: Bautz, 1975–2016), vol. II (1990) pp. 1423–24. See also: Jonathan Israel, *Radical Enlightenment: Philosophy and the Making of Modernity, 1650–1750* (Oxford: Oxford University Press, 2001), pp. 459–61.

28. Its full title reads *Libro mudo. Donde se alegan muchas authoridades divinas y humanas para todas las controvercias en materia de religión. Con estos materiales, los juiciosos conozerán lo bueno y lo malo y apartarán la luz de la obscuridad. El autor repite las agenas opiniones y calla*. The scribe defines it as the 'Libro duodécimo y póstumo de los cinco de la primera parte y de los seis de la parte segunda que compuso el autor'. As it mentions a *Gazzette* of 1737, it is very possible that the work was in fact copied after the author's death. The number twelve seems a hyperbole as no second part had been previously mentioned and the seven extant volumes — in several copies — seem hard to surpass.

29. *Disertaciones*, vol. I, fols 318 ff; *Disertaciones*, vol. II, fols 237 ff; *Disertaciones*, vol. III, fols 316 ff; *Libro Quarto*, fols 246 ff; *Libro Quinto*, fols 232 ff; *Preluminarias*, fols 268 ff; *Libro mudo*, fols 282 ff.

30. 'S[ilveira]. Monsieur Jacquelot. Acá estamos todos. Ya mi primero libro, tal qual lo hauéis visto, está acabado, en él queda la primera parte del vuestro, de medio a medio respondido. Pues, no

tenemos que hazer: manos a la obra, bolvamos a disputar. M[onsieur]. J[acquelot]. Yo me hallo en contado con tal cosecha de prosa para apear las mayores dificultades que si queréis desollinar los ojos de las telarañas que urde la vista en el telar de vuestros estudios, quedará la verdad de par en par patente y no andará ras con ras rozándose con la mentira. Con este rabo de zorra podéis sacudir el polvo a vuestras ignorancias. Aquí havemos de tocar todas las teclas sin que nos queden por desollar los rabos. El convencer vuestra insuficiencia es victoria para un hombre de mis letras, de poquísima substancia. Convocad un concilio de rabinos y veréis que a todos juntos les tengo la barba tiesa y conocerán que solo quien las sabe las tañe'. *Disertaciones*, Libro segundo, fol. 318^r.

31. Antonio José Saraiva, 'Antonio Vieira, Menasseh ben Israel et le cinquième empire', *Studia Rosenthaliana*, 6.1 (1972), 24–57 ; Yosef Kaplan, *From Christianity to Judaism: The Story of Isaac Orobio de Castro*, trans. by Raphael Loewe (Oxford: Littman-Oxford University Press, 1989); Peter van Rooden and Jan W. Wesselius, 'The Early Enlightenment and Judaism: The "civil dispute" between Philippus van Limborch and Isaac Orobio de Castro', *Studia Rosenthaliana*, 21.2 (1987), 140–53; and the studies of Richard H. Popkin, see above, note 20.

32. 'Carta / Doctíssimo señor Ishac Jaquelot. Monsieur, después de ponerme con el mayor rendimiento a vuestra obediensia, paso a poner en vuestra noticia, vos embié el coreo pasado dos libros, donde por vía de diálogo, dava respuesta al que vuestro celo compuso para nuestra enseñanza. Y quando esperava avizo del resivo, hallé que my cuidado dexó los libros escondidos... Basta la idea de quererlos imbiar para bolver a escrivir, conosco no ay verdad segura de opiniones, cada sabio con su tema, es imposible quitar con cien legías la color a un negro, el que abre los ojos por el qué dirán, cierra la boca, muchos Esaus por un vil potage venden la mejor primogenitura... por todas estas sinrazones, devo creer que hasta que Dios, como lo promete, lo remedie, ni yo, ni vos, lo podemos remediar. Vos podéis escrivir que estáis con descanso en vuestra tierra y en vuestra casa, yo no puedo respirar, que estoy cautivo sin casa ni palmo de tierra. No obstante, como no tengo qué hazer, por hazer algo que servirá de nada recogeré de vuestro libro y de mis repuestas los principales puntos y uno por uno los iré aquí ponderando y respondiendo, si esta carta llegara a vuestra mano en el valle de Josephat, me diréis al oido si son los Jidíos [*sic*] tan feos como los pintan'. *Disertaciones sobre el Mesías*, Libro terzero, fol. 1^v.

33. On this perspective on the Scriptures as Law, similar to a Confession, see Yosef Hayim Yerushalmi, *From Spanish Court to Italian Ghetto. Isaac Cardoso: A Study in Seventeenth-century Marranism and Jewish Apologetics* (New York: Columbia University Press, 1971), pp. 214–18.

34. To give but one example: 'Cada gallo canta en su muladar. La religión dominante en su país aborreze y si puede apremia, ynquisida y castiga sin piedad a todas las otras religiones. No se permiten las comferencias, ni valen razones'. *Disertaciones*, Libro terzero, fol. 314^v.

35. The date is mentioned.

36. *Preluminarias*, fols 5^r, 5^v, 47^v, 77^v, 91^v–92^r, 94^r, 247^v, 252^r.

37. *Libro mudo*, fols 253–56^r.

38. For instance, 'Cornelio Agripa en el prólogo de su libro *Paradoxa sobre la vanidad de las humanas ciencias*, "Más vale en el mundo la opinión de los hombres que apellidan doctos que la autoridad divina".' *Libro quinto. Zurrón...*, fol. 5^r.

39. 'Doctísima ignorancia / llama mi Musa / las ciencias inconformes / con la Escriptura. / Quando Dios habla claro / sigan la letra, / y dexen a Dios sólo / las encubiertas.' 'Romancillo', text edited in Brown and Den Boer, *El barroco sefardí*, pp. 216–17.

40. 'Dios habla claro, lo obscuro / no toca a la salvación, / tiene misterio y dexamos / las encubiertas a Dios.' 'Romance', Brown and Den Boer, *El barroco sefardí*, p. 218.

41. 'Debo en lo claro seguir / la letra en todo y por todo, / nada en lo obscuro decir, / que discurrir de otro modo / no es modo de discurrir.' 'Quintillas', Brown and Den Boer, *El barroco sefardí*, p. 201.

42. 'Aunque nací en España, aprendí acá la lengua hebrea, según las constantes rabínicas tradiciones, sabiendo esto, sé todo lo bueno. Quien sabe más, sabe menos [...]'. *Disertaciones*, Libro terzero, fol. 254^v.

43. 'En España responden con sangre y fuego, acá como son agudos, responderán lo que ellos fueron servidos. Yo mismo que soy un tonto, todo lo sé responder si me dexan a mis anchas alegorizar,

torzer y mentir. Piensan que acá somos bobos y que ignoramos estas trampas. En la Dialéctica también se enseñan las falacias para que no engañen las torpes agudezas.' *Disertaciones*, Libro terzero, fol. 254^v.

44. *Libro Mudo*, fols 15–22^v.

45. The *Gazettes* of Amsterdam and of Paris, *Le Journal des Savants*, the *Bibliothèque Raisonnée des Ouvrages des Savants de l'Europe, Mémoires secrets de la République des Lettres*, etc.

46. The adjective comes from Carsten Wilke, from the abstract of a conference on Silveira held at the Katz Center for Advanced Judaic Studies, Philadelphia, on 28 April 2014. Wilke and I are planning a study and edition of AGS's polemical work.

47. *Libro quarto El Juez de las controversias*, MS Ets Haim/Livraria Montezinos, 48 B 17, fols 2^r, 38^v, fol. 65^r respectively.

48. 'Al Papa creen infalible, / más fe mereze el Mophti, / ¿o qué gentil sacerdote, / o qué sacerdote gentil? / Yo me atengo a Pero Grullo, / que supo más que Merlín / comento de sí, no es no, / comento de no, no es sí'.

49. 'La impropiedad sacrílega de llamar a la Ley testamento, ocasionó la idea de que llaméis al Evangelio codicilio. Tal nombre de testamento no se halla en la Escritura. Acá llamamos assí a la disposición que hazen los hombres de sus bienes para sus herederos. El Autor de la Ley es el criador de todo, sin principio ni fin. El Autor del Evangelio es J. C. que murió y como no tenía sobre qué caer muerto, su Evangelio ni es testamento ni codicilio. Un frayle me dixo ayer que si no crehía el nuebo testamento, me llevava el Diablo, yo le di a Dios, y le dixe que no dava fee al nuebo ni al viejo, me llamó Libertino, y yo con esta Libertad, le dixe crehía solo en la Ley de Dios vivo, y no en el testamento de ningún Dios muerto. "¡Vaya de frayles!", otro dixo a su hermano compañero, "¿Vos tentó alguna vez el satán Patillas para ser Judío?" "¡Dios nos libre, dixo haziéndose cruzes, tal tentacion nunca la tube!" Respondió el otro. "A mí me tentó una legión de Luziferes, para que fuese cristiano y frayle y cahí, como lo veis, en la tentación". Pase por chiste'. *Disertaciones sobre el Mesías*, MS KB 75F7, fol. 28^v. Ibid., fol. 22^r.

CHAPTER 13

❖

Uriel da Costa's Career:
An Interpretation

Miriam Bodian

In the spring of 1640, at the age of about fifty-six,[1] the Amsterdam Portuguese Jew Uriel da Costa, humiliated and defeated, took his own life. Before he did so, however, he wrote an essay, known as *Exemplar humanae vitae*,[2] in which he sketched the anguished course of his life, excoriated the Jewish community of Amsterdam, and laid out his radical beliefs about religion. He argued that Scripture and all positive religions were fraudulent; the 'law of nature' was the only law of God.

We will never know how many Portuguese Jews in the early modern Atlantic world harboured consciously sceptical views about rabbinic tradition.[3] The few who openly challenged rabbinic authority undoubtedly voiced the doubts of many others who, even if they were articulate and self-aware, had little incentive to violate communal norms of expression. And those who harboured private doubts concerning the fine points of rabbinic law probably still accepted rabbinic authority as a given — a necessary anchor of identity and belonging, a bridge to the wider Jewish world, and a symbol of the core truths of ancestral tradition. Overall, given the complexity of Portuguese Jews' outlook (and the silence of most of them, outside the traditionalist elite), we are largely in the dark about the mental morphology beneath the surface of conformity.

Uriel da Costa, a familiar figure to anyone who has studied the Western Sephardi diaspora, has attracted abundant scholarly attention, due above all to the account of his life in the *Exemplar*. Scholars have sought to place Da Costa within an intellectual tradition, scholars — among them, Carl Gebhardt, Richard Popkin and Yirmiyahu Yovel — have sought to place Da Costa within an intellectual tradition, often taking the *Exemplar* more or less at face value. A few scholars have published major works seeking to thoroughly document his life and work — most importantly, Carl Gebhardt, I. S. Révah (and Carsten Wilke), H. P. Salomon and Omero Proietti. Yet while a great deal of evidence has been accumulated, a close reading of Da Costa's writings incorporating that evidence remains a desideratum. This essay seeks to take a closer look at the way Da Costa actually expressed himself — his imagery, his terminology, and his description of his own emotional states — to piece together a plausible narrative of his psychic and intellectual path, particularly during the years of his life about which we have good corroborating evidence, that is, from his birth around 1585 to his first Amsterdam excommunication in 1624. It also considers what may have been an outside source for Da Costa's 'deistic' views toward the end of his life.

★   ★   ★   ★   ★

Let me first summarize the problems any scholar must deal with in making use of the *Exemplar*. The full text is known only in the form of a document first published in 1687, almost a half century after Da Costa's death. It appeared as an appendix to a work by the Dutch Remonstrant (moderate Calvinist) theologian Philipp van Limborch — a work in which Limborch reconstructed a 'friendly [theological] debate' he had engaged in with Isaac Orobio de Castro, a learned Portuguese Jew in Amsterdam.[4] Limborch wrote that he had found the original manuscript of Da Costa's *Exemplar* among the papers of his great-uncle Simon Episcopius, a Remonstrant theologian and innovative thinker who died in 1643. Episcopius, he asserted, had received the manuscript from 'a distinguished man' of Amsterdam, whose identity he (or Limborch) may have concealed because of its scandalous nature.[5] Limborch was certainly familiar with the papers left by Episcopius, many of which he published. Episcopius must have received the Da Costa manuscript shortly after Da Costa's death in 1640, since Episcopius himself died only three years later. Limborch probably found the manuscript around 1662, when he was preparing the second volume of Episcopius's theological works — that is, about twenty-five years before he published the text that has come down to us; in any case, we know he had already seen the manuscript by March of that year.[6]

It is conceivable that Da Costa composed his text in Latin, so that it could be read by the widest educated public. But scholars familiar with the text have doubted that Da Costa, whose other writings are in Portuguese, could have written his anguished final testament in Latin — indeed, in *elegant* Latin.[7] In any case, in 1898 Siegmund Seligmann discovered, in the library of the University of Amsterdam, a Latin manuscript that had apparently been prepared to serve as the basis for Limborch's published version.[8] Analysing this manuscript, Gebhardt came to the conclusion that it was a translation from another language, presumably Portuguese. But this conclusion has been challenged by Omero Proietti, who maintains Da Costa wrote the original in Latin.[9]

Complicating the transmission story is the fact that another copy of the Latin text of the *Exemplar* existed in the 1640s, a fragment of which has survived. The Lutheran theologian Johannes Müller, a pastor in Hamburg, published an anti-Jewish polemical work in 1644 entitled *Judaismus oder Jüdenthumb*, in which he wrote that a 'wretched letter' written by 'Uriel Jurista, ein Sadduceer dieses Orthes' — a Saducee of 'this town', that is, Hamburg — had come into his hands.[10] He quoted a passage that corresponds almost verbatim to the first half of the final paragraph of the *Exemplar* published by Limborch, though there are a few significant discrepancies.[11]

Despite warranted suspicions about the composition of the *Exemplar*, evidence indicates that a significant substrate of the text was Da Costa's. I. S. Révah and other scholars have shown that the account the *Exemplar* gives of Da Costa's early life in Portugal is factually accurate, with details that a later tinkerer would not have known.[12] To be specific, archival documents have confirmed the accuracy of the following points made in the early pages of the text: Gabriel da Costa (later Uriel) *did* grow up in a well-to-do converso family in Porto, and his father *was* apparently a sincere Catholic. It was a great exaggeration to say that his parents were 'of noble rank' (*ex ordine nobilium*); still, his father, a merchant, *was* able to obtain the minor titles of *cavaleiro fidalgo da casa da Infante Dona Maria* in 1578, and of *cavaleiro da casa del Rey* in 1584.[13] Da Costa *did* study canon law at the University of Coimbra.[14] He *did* obtain an ecclesiastical benefice as church treasurer — specifically (as the inquisitorial testimony of his relative Leonor de Pina reveals) in the church college of São Martinho de Cedofeita.[15] And he *did* play a role in persuading his family to judaize, as is also confirmed by inquisitorial testimony.[16]

The corroboration of these facts about Da Costa's childhood and early adulthood in Portugal seemed to confirm that at least this first part of the *Exemplar* was Da Costa's handiwork. Yet concerning the aspect of the passages that most interest us — the narration of Da Costa's conversion from practising Catholic to crypto-Jew — the account is quite problematic. Da Costa wrote that his doubts about Catholicism arose from his anxiety about salvation. This is not remarkable in itself. Everywhere in early modern Europe, the intensified awareness of multiple religious traditions — religions that taught different and mutually exclusive paths to salvation — raised discomfort among believing Christians about any creed's monopoly on salvation. There were those, in Spain and Portugal as well as elsewhere, who resolved the difficulty posed by the Church's claim to an exclusive path to salvation by implicitly denying Church teaching and asserting that a person could be saved in any faith.[17] Such a laissez-faire attitude would not, however, have appealed to Da Costa, whose personality inclined him throughout his life toward a single dogmatic truth.

By his account in the *Exemplar*, Da Costa lost his belief in Catholicism in a process that was entirely internal and independent of his environment, an environment he portrayed as being uniformly and normatively Catholic. By his account, it was his inner anxiety about the Church's path to salvation, and that anxiety alone, that impelled him to delve into the (for him) unexplored terrain of unmediated Scripture-reading.[18] As he began to grasp, during this period of intensive study, how the Old Testament differed from the Gospels, he started to form affirmative ideas about the Law of Moses.

Scholars began questioning the plausibility of this conversion account even before there was clear evidence to challenge it. 'Not every Christian who doubts', two French scholars wrote pithily in 1926, 'necessarily becomes a Jew'.[19] While Da Costa described his father with pride,[20] he made no mention of his mother as a presence in his childhood. Was she too a conforming Catholic? And even if she were (as seems to have been the case), could it be that Da Costa's awareness of judaizing among Portugal's New Christian population played no role in his thinking about Judaism? Just about everyone in Portugal — Old Christians as well as New — knew something about key crypto-Jewish practices, which the Church itself publicized at autos-da-fé and in Edicts of Faith. Did it contribute nothing to Da Costa's anxiety about his ultimate fate to know that men and women who shared his Jewish ancestry took great risks to observe the Law of Moses because they believed salvation could be attained only in that way?

I. S. Révah, while he confirmed certain facts about Da Costa's early life that are mentioned in the *Exemplar*, also unearthed evidence that validated suspicions about Da Costa's account, showing that Da Costa had lived in an environment in which judaizing was an ineluctable reality.[21] Since there was a large New Christian population in Porto, quite a few of whose members were sentenced for judaizing, Da Costa's experience must have included reports of arrests and autos-da-fé, perhaps even among families he knew.[22] Some New Christian merchants of Porto had even visited the Jewish community in Amsterdam and, upon their return, taught their families ceremonies they had learned in that city.[23] Closer to home, there had been inquisitorial prosecutions in his family. An aunt of Da Costa's mother, arrested in 1566, was burned at the stake in 1568. A half-sister of Da Costa's mother, arrested in the same year, was condemned to relaxation but was reconciled.[24] The Inquisition had also investigated family members on the paternal side. Between 1597 and 1618, it had repeatedly scrutinized the widows and children of Da Costa's two paternal uncles. One of the widows, Beatriz Nunes, fled Portugal with her daughter in the late sixteenth century and settled in Amsterdam.[25] Moreover, Révah showed that by the time of Da Costa's crisis of conscience, between 1600 and 1608, a number of members of his mother's family had escaped Portugal and were living as Jews in Pisa, Venice and Amsterdam.[26]

Further challenging the account in the *Exemplar*, Révah uncovered concrete evidence showing that Da Costa's understanding of the Law of Moses did *not* rely solely on Scripture. His relative Leonor de Pina, who was already involved in a simple form of judaizing when Da Costa began instructing her further, remained in Portugal after Da Costa's departure and gave detailed testimony before the Inquisition in 1619 about practices she had learned from Da Costa. Notably, some of those practices had their source in crypto-Jewish traditions with post-biblical, rabbinic origins — for example, observing the three-week mourning period between the seventeenth of Tammuz and the ninth of Av, and the 'taking of challah' (*hafrashat challah*).[27] Leonor de Pina's testimony, analysed with great care by Révah, reveals that in reality Da Costa participated in a form of crypto-Judaism that Révah has called *marranisme normal*.[28]

We can only speculate about other external catalysts that may have stimulated Da Costa first to commit himself to the Law of Moses, then to convert members of his family and depart with them for Amsterdam. It is at least worth mentioning that during his years as a student of canon law at Coimbra, he attended the lectures of Dr António Homem, who led an organized crypto-Jewish circle in the years after Da Costa abandoned his studies.[29] The scholar who studied this 'confraternity' has speculated that Homem may have had an influence on Da Costa's spiritual development; however, there is no evidence for this.[30]

Certainly Da Costa would have experienced the negative stimulus that led so many conversos to seek an affirming counter-ideology — the stigma of tainted blood. With his exquisite sensitivity to affronts to his honour (which will be discussed further on), Da Costa would have felt keenly the humiliations of simply being a New Christian in Iberian society. Escape abroad had already offered a way out for many. He and his family clearly knew something about the growing Portuguese-Jewish community in Amsterdam. That city offered the promise of a livelihood for his merchant brothers; it also symbolized a great collective spiritual liberation and rebirth, with biblical overtones that would not have been lost on Da Costa.

While Da Costa's experiences in his complex Iberian environment clearly played a role in his conversion to the Law of Moses, the fact that he eliminated those experiences from his narrative does not entirely invalidate the account he gave of his conversion. There is no reason to doubt that his study of the Bible led to discoveries that had a profound effect on his thinking. Yet even as a description of a solitary intellectual upheaval, the conversion account in the *Exemplar* is not always consistent or coherent.

Let us examine that account more closely. Da Costa's initial doubts arose, the text tells us, out of anxieties about whether he could achieve salvation through the means prescribed by the Church — that is, through absolution of his sins and scrupulous Catholic observance. If such doubts were indeed the driving force, one would expect that his conversion to the Law of Moses had something to do with *resolving* those anxieties. But just at this point in the text where we would expect to see this, the *Exemplar* takes an odd turn. It tells us that as Da Costa came to the conclusion that the Church did not offer salvation — and as he then struggled, at the age of about twenty-two, to 'shake off' his deeply rooted Catholic conditioning, he began wondering whether belief in an afterlife was not after all a fraud, since it seemed to him inconsistent with reason.[31]

Such a radical conclusion seems at odds with what we know about the nature of Da Costa's subsequent judaizing. Salvation 'in the Law of Moses' was an integral theme of 'marranisme normal', and it seems to have been an element of Da Costa's proselytizing. Leonor de Pina, in her testimony, declared that Da Costa had taught her that 'one could not be saved in the law of the Christians but only in that of Moses'.[32] Moreover, the *Exemplar* itself seems immediately to contradict the 'bombshell' it just dropped, reverting to Da Costa's earlier anxiety that he 'would not find salvation *in the path I was in*'[33] — suggesting that his thinking was indeed still dominated by a search for a secure road to salvation. A passage further on in the *Exemplar* seems to confirm this conclusion, stating that it was only when he was preparing to write the *Exame das tradições Phariseas*, many years later in Hamburg, that he began to doubt the immortality of the soul.[34] This corresponds to what other evidence would suggest about the emergence of his doubts about the afterlife: his 'Propostas' of 1616, a bitter attack on rabbinic Judaism, lacked any mention of the doctrine of the immortality of the soul, whereas an attack on that doctrine was central to his *Exame* of 1623.[35]

It seems reasonable to conclude that personal anxieties about salvation — anxieties that he also mentioned in the *Exame*[36] — were critical in propelling Da

Costa toward a commitment to the Law of Moses. Yet in the passage describing his conversion, the *Exemplar* scrupulously avoided mentioning such a resolution of his anxieties. Instead, it provided a set of rather dry and abstract rationalizations for his transfer of loyalty from Catholicism to the Law of Moses. First, it stated, he was seeking an alternative to the Church, for he 'felt a need to attach himself to some other [religion]'.[37] Second, he saw that many things in the New Testament were contradicted by the Old. And third, the Old Testament had the virtue of being accepted as revealed Scripture by both Jews and Christians. This is a passage that describes a life-changing moment, yet it lacks all drama, and the conversion comes across as the practical result of cool calculation. Could such a tepid catalogue of reasons have motivated this intense young man to pursue the transformative venture of committing himself to crypto-Judaism, converting members of his family to the Law of Moses, and fleeing to Amsterdam?[38]

There is no easy way to account for the inconsistencies and blandness of the *Exemplar*'s conversion story, but there would seem to be two general avenues of explanation. First, it is possible that another hand — perhaps that of Limborch — tampered with the passage. As Limborch emphasized in his preface to the *Exemplar*, as well as in the *Refutatio* that follows it, his reason for publishing the text was to defend Christianity against the attacks against revealed religion of 'atheists or deists' like Da Costa. (Similarly, his 'friendly discussion' with the Amsterdam Jew Orobio de Castro, to which the *Exemplar* was appended, was intended to defend Christianity against Jewish claims.)[39] Suppose, then, that Da Costa's reasons for abandoning Christianity in favour of Judaism, as actually articulated, included sharply negative evaluations of Christianity — a standard feature of crypto-Judaism. Limborch might well have been tempted to modify material that was offensive (and that undermined his objectives). Such a hypothesis would explain why, despite Da Costa's exceptional capacity for strident language, the *Exemplar* describes his withdrawal from Christianity without a word of criticism for the Church.

But there is a second possibility. There are distortions in the *Exemplar* that can best be understood in light of Da Costa's concern for his self-image — for example, the text's silence about his family's history of judaizing, or its silence (at a later point) about his continuing contact with, and support from, members of his family, even after his radical ideas had created challenges for them.[40] Not just in the *Exemplar* but in his other writings as well, Da Costa cultivated a self-image as a solitary truth-seeker who spurned conventional attachments to tradition and relied entirely on his own powers of reason. (Révah aptly referred to the 'exaggerated personalization' of his 'spiritual drama'.)[41] The complete lack of emotionally charged elements — familial, ethnic, or spiritual — in the passage describing his conversion to the Law of Moses might reflect Da Costa's wish to suppress the actual nature of his conversion experience many years later. Overall, the evidence suggests that as a young man Da Costa turned to the Law of Moses with the reassuring conviction that it offered the best path to salvation — relying, like other judaizers, on crypto-Jewish traditions that emphasized the exclusive salvific efficacy of the Law of Moses.[42] (Even Bible-literate judaizers like Da Costa were typically unaware that their hopes for salvation, nurtured by an Iberian environment, had little basis in Jewish Scripture. It was only later that Da Costa 'discovered' how little Jewish Scripture actually had to say about immortality of the soul.) He may have avoided admitting to his youthful folly (as it must have seemed to him late in his life) by filtering it out, and representing his conversion as rational, dispassionate, and entirely self-generated.

The self-image Da Costa cultivated as he constructed his narrative was consistent with a certain ideal type that emerged in early modern European societies. Among crypto-Jews in the Iberian Peninsula, the particular variation of this type was the so-called '*dogmatista*' — the crypto-Jewish activist who was able, by virtue of his learning, to challenge Church teachings with confidence. These men assumed positions of religious authority in their families or in a wider circle of judaizers. When arrested by the Inquisition they were likely to adopt a defiant position. Some became widely known martyrs of the Inquisition. Their audacious displays of independence and intellect allowed them to triumph psychologically and polemically — at least in their own eyes — over the tribunals they faced, despite their objective position of extreme weakness.[43] Like the heroic martyrs of the Reformation, with whom they had much in common, they attained a place in popular martyrological lore, where they were portrayed in the posture they assumed so effectively: as men driven purely and exclusively by theological conviction, oblivious to the everyday concerns of living. Carsten Wilke has aptly termed this ideal type as a 'walking religious conscience'.[44] I do not mean to suggest that Da Costa consciously modelled himself after celebrated crypto-Jewish martyrs. Rather, such a male ideal would have resonated with him because of aspects of his personality that are evident throughout his career: a consuming preoccupation with religious truth and personal honour (which were related in his thinking); an idealized notion of his motivations; and a need to stand out rather than join in.

Let us return to events in Portugal. In May 1608, when his father died, the now Jewishly committed Da Costa apparently had to abandon his studies at Coimbra (and perhaps his career plans), taking up a church benefice to help support his family.[45] It was during this period, according to his account, that he began examining Scripture closely. His reading of the Old Testament probably served for him what it served for other educated conversos. Like them, he would have focused on those passages that confirmed the central elements of crypto-Jewish belief and practice, unconsciously minimizing the discrepancies between a simplified, crypto-Jewish notion of 'the Law of Moses' and the complex body of precepts and narratives in the Old Testament.

The death of his father may have marked the turning point at which Da Costa began to proselytize members of his family, persuading them to convert to the Law of Moses or, in the case of a few of them, to 'reconvert' to a higher level of observance.[46] Da Costa was well-placed to assume this role. His university education gave him unique authority to expound on the Law of Moses (this was generally the case for *dogmatistas* in Iberian lands, where direct access to Scripture required a knowledge of Latin).[47] With his father now deceased, his new role as religious guide would have given him a position of leadership in the family, despite the fact that he had an older brother. (Da Costa's brother-in-law and disciple Álvaro Gomes Bravo, in later Inquisition testimony, noted this special status of Da Costa:[48] the *Exemplar* also mentioned it.[49]) Given the dangers of judaizing in Portugal, flight and resettlement in a free Jewish community was an obvious next step. It is hard to imagine Da Costa envisioning or actually bringing about the emigration of his family if he were inspired only by the conversion experience described in the *Exemplar*. It is even less plausible that he was able to convert his mother, brothers, and others in his family, relying only on an intellectual inquiry stripped of the dynamic, animating qualities of myth. It is more likely that he and his family shared a crypto-Jewish vision according to which the journey to freedom was a re-enactment of a biblical narrative of oppression, escape, and redemption with mythic, transcendent dimensions.

★   ★   ★   ★   ★

In the next and much longer part of the *Exemplar* — a narrative of Da Costa's life after his flight from Portugal — the textual problems multiply. The most glaring peculiarity of this part of the essay is its omission of any mention of Hamburg — the town to which Da Costa proceeded with one of his brothers, his mother and his wife, shortly after he arrived in Amsterdam (where the family disembarked no later than April 1615). We know he was living in Hamburg when the first *herem* [ban] was issued against him by Venetian rabbis in 1618, after he refused to renounced his 'Propostas' (discussed below); he continued to live there until he moved to Amsterdam in 1623.[50] Johannes Müller, the Hamburg pastor who had seen a copy of Da Costa's 'wretched letter' not long after his death in 1640, knew that he had lived in Hamburg. It is thus puzzling that the *Exemplar* published by Limborch in 1687 placed Da Costa in Amsterdam from his first days on northern soil to his death thirty-five years later, and attributed all of his sufferings to the Jews of that city alone.

The first antagonistic step Da Costa took within the Jewish community occurred not long after his arrival. Here too, however, there are discrepancies between the *Exemplar* and other evidence. The *Exemplar* states that Da Costa had been in Amsterdam only a few days when he saw 'that the customs and ordinances of the Jews did not agree in the least with those prescribed by Moses'.[51] This sudden discovery, he wrote, aroused his indignation and zeal. Since Scripture held that its Law 'was to be strictly observed', it seemed evident to him that the rabbis — the 'so-called Jewish sages' — had corrupted it, and he 'saw it as a service to God' to defend the Law as it was written.[52] The *Exemplar* does not offer particulars about the only important action of his of which we are aware: in Hamburg in 1616, at least eight months after his arrival on northern soil, Da Costa sent a document to the Western Sephardi congregation in Venice, enunciating eleven theses (known as his 'Propostas'). These proved, in his view, that rabbinic law was contrary to, and indeed violated, the Law of Moses. He asked that these theses be either refuted or acknowledged as correct. The Sephardi leaders in Venice turned Da Costa's theses over to a leading Venetian rabbi, Yehudah Aryeh (Leon) de Modena, whose summary of Da Costa's theses, in the first part of his formal reply (*responsum*), along with quotations from the 'Propostas' in the body of the responsum, offer the only version we have of the original document.[53]

Scholars have paid scant attention to the particular line of attack Da Costa adopted to support his overall contention that rabbinic law was a human fabrication. His selection of laws to analyse and criticize was somewhat curious, and if there was a method behind his choices, it went unexplained. However, the overarching argument was simple: there was no Torah except the written Torah, and it was heresy (Modena's term in his Hebrew summary: כפירה) to modify or augment divine law by means of human law. Da Costa stated this as his seventh 'proposta'; Modena sensibly chose to address it first — as did Da Costa himself in its subsequent iteration in the *Exame*.

The 'Propostas' open with criticism of the detailed rabbinic laws concerning the wearing of *tefillin* [phylacteries] during prayer, which was done to fulfil the commandment (Exodus 13. 9), 'And it shall be to you as a sign on your hand and as a memorial between your eyes, that the law of the Lord may be in your mouth'.[54] Presumably the biblical source had been mentioned to Da Costa as he was shown how to lay on *tefillin* in the synagogue. He may have been immediately struck by the rabbinic concretization of a precept he had understood, as a Bible-reading judaizer, as a purely mental one. Scripture, he now wrote in the 'Propostas', said nothing about a physical object that was to be constructed in such-and-such a way. It violated Scripture's explicit prohibition of adding to the commandments (Deuteronomy 4. 2). Moreover, he wrote, the practice of putting on these rabbinically devised objects gave an opening to the Gentiles to ridicule the Jews. This was no doubt an indirect expression of his own discomfort. It may have reflected sentiments experienced privately by other ex-converso neophytes as well, even if they did not channel their discomfort into the development of a dogmatic programme.

In similar fashion, Da Costa held that certain surgical and ceremonial aspects of the rabbinic practice of circumcision were a violation of the Torah. Here, too, he saw a violation of the prohibition of adding to the literal word of Scripture, and he viewed the rituals around a special piece of furniture known as Elijah's chair as exposing the Jews to Gentile ridicule. He maintained that if God had intended that the Jews follow these practices, he would have explicitly commanded them to do so in the Torah. The broader principle, as Da Costa put it (in Modena's Hebrew translation/summary), was that in Scripture 'nothing essential has been left out or unexplained'.[55] For the same reason, Da Costa rejected the practice of keeping a second day of the major holidays (*yom tov sheni shel galuyot*). The final three theses of the 'Propostas' echoed the same theme. In them, Da Costa criticized: a) the rabbinic procedure for releasing a person from a scripturally based vow; b) the rabbinic precepts that form a 'fence' around the Law;[56] and c) the imposition of the benediction 'Blessed be the Lord...who sanctified us with his commandments and commanded us' to perform a certain action, even in cases when that action had been commanded not by God but by the rabbis.

These aspects of observance were ones Da Costa either would have, or might well have, experienced in the months after his arrival in Amsterdam and settlement in Hamburg.[57] In contrast, the fourth, fifth and sixth theses pertained to talmudic rulings that had long since lost any practical significance. All three served to mitigate corporal punishments ordained by Scripture. Leviticus 20. 14 stated that for incest involving a man and his mother-in-law the culprits should be 'burned by fire'. This meant, Da Costa argued, that they should be reduced to ashes. He held that the rabbis deviated from the Torah by concluding that death 'by fire' should be carried out by pouring molten lead in the culprit's mouth.[58] If the Torah had intended this to be the method, Da Costa reiterated, it would have said so explicitly.[59] Likewise, Exodus 20. 29 required that in the case of an ox that gored a person, and subsequently gored another person to death, the negligent owner of the ox be put to death; the rabbis, Da Costa wrote, ignored the clear meaning of the verse by ruling that the owner merely had to pay monetary compensation. Similarly, Leviticus 24. 19–20, requiring 'an eye for an eye, a tooth for a tooth': once again the rabbis disregarded the clear meaning of Scripture by interpreting the verse to mean only a proportionate monetary compensation.[60]

The point Da Costa wanted to make was clear: rabbinic rulings could not be 'the Law' if they contradicted the explicit language of Scripture. But it is a matter of speculation why, given the vast corpus of rabbinic rulings that modify scriptural injunctions, Da Costa homed in on these three particular cases. Perhaps he wanted to show just how absolute the Jews' fidelity to the literal meaning of Scripture had to be, in his opinion. But did Da Costa really imagine, prior to his emigration, that it was the practice in Jewish communities to blind the eye of a Jew who caused the loss of another's eye? More generally, how could he possibly have imagined that contemporary Jewish life, in an urban European setting, proceeded according to the literal word of Scripture? In the absence of a Temple with its priests, for example, what would Jewish institutional life look like? As Yosef Hayyim Yerushalmi has noted, Da Costa knew perfectly well that the Christianity practised in seventeenth-century Portugal was quite different from that of the time of Jesus; why should he have expected the Judaism of his time to be that of Moses?[61] In any case, it is inconceivable, given what we know about Da Costa's circumstances in Porto and news he would have received from abroad, that he did not know even then about such things as rabbinic authority, synagogue services and Talmud study — that is, essential aspects of normative Jewish life that were absent in Scripture.

Given its aggressive tone, Da Costa's letter must have been viewed not as a set of 'questions' (as Modena referred to it) but as a scandalous attack. That Da Costa sent it to Venice is not surprising; at the time, the Amsterdam community was still in the early stages of development, and the so-called 'Ponentine' community in Venice was the major European centre of the Portuguese-Jewish diaspora.[62] The question is what prompted him to compose this document in the first place. Da Costa was a newcomer in a community of men and women who were not likely to be sympathetic to a challenge to the very foundations of their community and to the tradition to which they had 'returned'. The community's wealthy merchants — natural leaders of this patriarchal group, who from the start provided the lay leadership — strongly supported the rabbis, for a variety of religious, ideological and practical reasons. (Indeed it was they who made the effort to attract to Amsterdam well-qualified rabbis from established Mediterranean Sephardi communities.)[63] Even those émigrés who had been startled to discover rabbinic law in all its minutiae may have found its expression in Jewish communal life to be rich and meaningful, or at least a tolerable element of Portuguese-Jewish collective life. Why, given his relative youth, his middling socioeconomic status, and his minimal Jewish knowledge would Da Costa, so shortly after his arrival, openly challenge rabbinic authority?

There were undoubtedly multiple factors that led him to take such a provocative action. It is reasonable to think that he *was* shocked when he discovered the sheer enormity of Jewish law, with its labyrinthine underpinning of talmudic argumentation. While it is true that in the *Exemplar* he exaggerated his ignorance of post-biblical Judaism before his arrival in Amsterdam, the number of rabbinic practices in 'marranisme normal' was nevertheless quite limited. Especially for an educated converso who turned to the Vulgate as *the* source for the Law of Moses, the discovery that contemporary Jews engaged in a profusion of unrecognizable practices may well have generated the feelings of repugnance and alienation that Modena's summary of Da Costa's objections conveys.

Da Costa was not the only Portuguese-Jewish émigré in early seventeenth-century Amsterdam to raise questions about the authority and reasonableness of rabbinic traditions. Hector Mendes Bravo, testifying before the Inquisition after he returned to the Iberian Peninsula, reported that sometime between 1612 and 1617 he had spoken to Rabbi Isaac Uziel in Amsterdam, arguing that the rabbinic interpretation of Isaiah 53 was wrong, because it interpreted collectively what was clearly a single 'suffering servant'. This was a self-serving statement, given that he was addressing the Inquisition, for whom the 'suffering servant' was indeed a single person — a very particular one. But Bravo continued with the interesting remark that Uziel had instructed him to 'remove himself from the views of the Karaites' — a group (mentioned further below) that broke off from rabbinic Judaism in the eighth century, seeking an independent reading of the Hebrew Bible.[64]

Even more suggestive is a case from 1615, the year after Da Costa and his family arrived in Amsterdam. A member of the Amsterdam community — probably the physician David Farar — insisted that the Torah could be interpreted properly only according to the plain meaning of the text (*peshat*). In response, a member of the communal elite turned to Leon da Modena in Venice for a rabbinic opinion. Interestingly, Modena ruled that Farar's position was a legitimate one, and implicitly criticized those who questioned it.[65] One wonders whether Da Costa, alert to rationalist and biblicist undercurrents among the émigrés as well as Modena's ruling), may have turned to Venice in hopes of generating momentum and support for his own, far more radical position.

Da Costa's formulation of a radical biblicist creed out of consternation over the 'aberrations' of rabbinic tradition could scarcely have developed without an awareness of the parallel dynamic of the Protestant Reformation. Protestants had successfully liberated themselves from a centuries-old Catholic tradition, dismantling the entire authority structure of late medieval Christianity and returning, as they saw it, to the authentic teachings of the Gospels. They had minimized outward ceremonies — the Catholic equivalents, one might say, of *tefillin* and Elijah's chair — in favour of a practice that emphasized the moral teachings of the Gospels. They had also dispensed with some of the more fanciful christological readings of the Old Testament, preferring a more literal interpretation. It is true that Da Costa did not mention the Protestant Reformation as reforming his thought. One would not expect a Jewish 'reformer' to do so. But he was clearly aware of Protestant theology,[66] and central aspects of his experience — his training in canon law, his flight from Porto to Amsterdam/Hamburg, his discovery (one can assume) of Protestant biblicism — must have underscored the possibilities for a transformation of Judaism. Is it going too far to suggest that his eleven 'Propostas' took their cue from Martin Luther's ninety-five theses?

The structure of Da Costa's argumentation also betrays a sensitivity to the Reformation. He was by no means singular in this respect; educated conversos and Portuguese Jews were quite attentive to the upheaval in Western Christianity. Among crypto-Jews in particular, Reformation rhetoric about the autonomy of individual conscience and the abuses of the clergy resonated strongly. The adoption of such rhetoric is evident in the testimony of crypto-Jewish dogmatistas, a category that, as mentioned, included Da Costa in the years prior to his departure from Portugal in 1614. These dogmatistas often refuted Catholic theology by relying on a selective and literal reading of Scripture, supported by arguments from reason.[67] One of the arguments marshalled by both Protestants and crypto-Jews against Catholicism had to do with the authority of Scripture: if God had wanted to establish the various extra-biblical interpretations and practices prescribed by tradition, he would have set them down clearly and explicitly in Scripture.[68] What distinguished Da Costa was not his adoption of this argument, but his turning it against rabbinic authority. Why he alone among his Portuguese-Jewish contemporaries took this step has to do less with intellectual conditioning than with psychological predisposition.

It may be that a disillusioned Da Costa 'reactivated' in Hamburg a familiar role, now pitting himself not against the Church but against the new authority structure with power over him, the rabbinic establishment. It is of more than passing interest that his *Exame*, published eight years after he sent his 'Propostas' to Venice, opens with a declamation depicting him in a biblical role defending God's truth. 'Joshua and Caleb', he opened, 'said to the people that they should not listen to the false and harmful voice of those who, speaking against God, obstruct and impede their own well-being'.[69] The biblical passage in question portrays Joshua and Caleb taking a stand against an angry mob, a stand for which they were eventually vindicated. Such a dramatic opening to his work was clearly a way of framing Da Costa's own heroism vis-à-vis the rabbis and the Jewish 'mob'.

Naturally, the dogmatista's role as zealot for the truth against established authority had a different valence when it was turned against the authorities of the dogmatista's own social group. Da Costa's defiant, religiously autonomous stance toward the rabbis could only have excited anger and dismay, at least publicly. For most of the émigrés, the rabbis played a crucial role in creating a workable and stable identity and way of life, after the turmoil of the Iberian experience. If Da Costa aspired to a role of leadership within the Portuguese-Jewish community, with the objective of leading it in a radical return to elemental biblical law, he grasped the practical, psychic and religious needs of the community very poorly indeed.

A final factor that prompted Da Costa to defy the rabbinic establishment in a seemingly reckless way was his hypersensitivity to affronts to his honour. Carsten Wilke — following Révah, who was always alert to Da Costa's psychic vulnerabilities — has suggested that loss of status and an inability to adapt to his new situation in Hamburg contributed to his rapid turn against rabbinic authority.[70] In Portugal, his position as church treasurer had given him a place of dignity both within his family and in Portuguese society. His self-esteem had been reinforced in a non-public way by his role within his family as spiritual authority and mentor. When he took up residence in Hamburg, he entered a world in which he possessed neither intellectual nor professional distinction. As a merchant in a Lutheran town, his training in canon law counted for nothing, and in commerce he was less prepared than his brothers. Moreover, in the Jewish community he had been so determined to join, he quickly learned he had no hope of playing a role of spiritual and intellectual leadership. His family would now have looked to others for instruction. It must have been daunting, indeed humiliating, to discover in Amsterdam and Hamburg a vast corpus of rabbinic learning that, at his age and in his circumstances, was beyond his reach.

The difficulties Da Costa experienced in making the transition from life in Porto to life in Hamburg may help explain the aggressiveness of the 'Propostas'. His psychic makeup no doubt exacerbated the crisis he experienced: rather than making the best of a difficult situation, he sought a principled way to rise above it, as it were. That he could 'see through' the rabbis' fabrications liberated him from any need for rabbinic training. I do not mean to be overly reductive about Da Costa's motivations. There can be no doubt that a genuine cognitive shift occurred in Da Costa's thinking as he rejected rabbinic Judaism. But he was not able, like more influential truth-seekers of his age, to accept the need for prudence and dissimulation. Everything in his writing and actions points to a need to stand out as a superior soul, to thrust himself in the limelight. While this impulse may have served him well during the brief heroic phase of his life, it was unlikely to ease his transition to life in the Jewish communities of Hamburg and Amsterdam.[71] Yet even at this juncture, his defiant posture may have satisfied a paramount drive, allowing him to invert the intellectual hierarchy that had placed him, with his 'naïve' reading of Scripture, at the bottom of the scale.

Let us pick up the narrative. In 1618, the Hamburg communal leaders received Modena's ruling that if Da Costa did not recant, he would be placed under a ban.[72] This was accompanied by Modena's detailed and lengthy responsum in reply to 'the abovementioned *epikoros* [unbeliever]'.[73] In it, Modena rejected Da Costa's arguments on grounds that had been elucidated by rabbinic authorities over many centuries, explaining why rabbinic interpretation was necessary, given the difficulties presented by the raw text of Scripture. When Da Costa refused to retract his claims — as the *Exemplar* puts it, 'I resolved that it was better to endure everything and insist upon my opinion'[74] — he was placed under a ban in Venice and Hamburg. According to the *Exemplar*, the ban prevented Da Costa from having any contact with other Jews — even his brothers. Scholars have been puzzled by the evidence that in the years 1618–23, Da Costa continued living in Hamburg and engaged in commercial transactions with his brother Mordecai/Jerónimo and other Portuguese Jews.[75] It appears that the ban was not fully enforced — as a passage in a work by a contemporary strongly suggests.[76] Even so, it stood as a rebuke — one that Da Costa was not inclined to ignore. It was the ban, according to the *Exemplar*, that impelled Da Costa to write a book 'to demonstrate the justice of my position' and to prove, on the basis of Scripture, that the 'traditions and institutions of the Pharisees' contradicted the Law of Moses.[77]

★　★　★　★　★

The book Da Costa eventually produced in 1624, which named the author as 'Uriel Jurista Hebreo', was the aforementioned *Exame das tradições Phariseas*, published by the Amsterdam printer Paul van Ravesteyn.[78] While he was working on the book, Da Costa wrote, he also sought to convert members of the community to his view. However, he met with such resistance that he gave up the idea of publishing the work — until Samuel da Silva, a Hamburg physician who had got hold of three chapters, published a counter-attack in 1623. As the title of his work, *Tratado da immortalidade da alma*, suggests, Da Silva's attack concerned not Da Costa's views on the Oral Law (at least not primarily), but a new development in Da Costa's thinking: a repudiation of the rabbinic doctrine of the immortality of the soul.[79] In response, Da Costa proceeded to publish his *Exame*.[80]

It is true that the first fourteen chapters of the *Exame* are mostly a revised and expanded version of the 'Propostas'. Da Costa no doubt wished to bring to a wider audience his reasons for rejecting the Oral Law. But these chapters are by no means just a rehash. They, too, reveal a new and important element of Da Costa's thinking: an explanation in human, historical and political terms of the rabbis' enterprise of fabrication. Fundamental to that explanation was a conception of the Pharisees and Sadducees as camps that reflected not so much conflicting principles as conflicting motivations. It was, for Da Costa, quite simple: the Pharisees were driven by self-interest, the Sadducees by noble-minded aims. Da Costa drew support from the brief discussions of Josephus (accessible to him in Latin translation), while imposing his own absolute moral criteria. The Pharisees, he maintained, gained the upper hand by luring the common people with *doçuras* [sweet words], offering lenient rulings and promising immortality of the soul.[81] Their great insight was that pandering to the people gave them power over the people. Opposing them were the Sadducees and Boethians, who had been instructed by Antigonus, in a line of tradition that went back to Ezra; they were supported by the 'most important, learned, and noble' element of the people. But the Pharisees, with their appeal to simple minds, won out.[82] Once in power, they became tyrannical and favoured the wealthy over the poor. Rabbinic law concerning the redemption of sold property, for example, was 'false, tyrannical, and hostile to the poor'.[83] Similarly, the rabbinic limitation on plucking grapes or corn from another's field was 'false, absurd, and hostile to the poor'.[84]

Da Costa's interpretation of the Pharisees' behaviour (and that of their successors, the rabbis, whom he also referred to as 'Pharisees') echoed negative characterizations of religious elites in both popular and learned Reformation discourse. As an effort to historicize Judaism, however, it showed little sophistication. He did not so much as mention the historical developments over the seventeen centuries that separated the Pharisees of Josephus's time from the rabbis of his own time, and was perhaps quite ignorant of them. There is a cartoonish quality about his argumentation: when rabbinic laws struck him as being more lenient than the Law of Moses, he argued that they were motivated by the Pharisees' aim of gaining the people's favour; when they struck him as more stringent, he argued that they revealed the Pharisees' hunger for power. For Da Costa, then, 'Pharisees' and 'Sadducees' were more rhetorical categories than historical entities; it was as such that he was able to identify himself as a 'Sadducee'. In sum, the *Exame* may hint at things to come in its historical approach to religious phenomena; but in its lack of an underlying anthropology, and in its one-dimensional portrayal of the rabbis, the *Exame* is here (as elsewhere) more popular screed than learned treatise.

Yet Da Costa wanted historical legitimation for his lonely quest, and he deployed his limited resources as well as he could, possibly with some inadvertent help from Modena.[85] As mentioned, his reconstruction of the early schism between the Saducean defenders of the Torah and the Pharisaic falsifiers of it relied in important respects on 'the histories of Josephus', which he reported having read 'in the past [*antigamente*]' — perhaps a reference to his time in Portugal.[86] It is also possible, though the evidence is indirect, that his conception of the 'Sadducees' as strict biblicists drew from contemporary discourse. When Da Costa mistakenly claimed that the Sadducees did not wear *tefillin* or practice *periah* as part of circumcision, he was conflating the Sadducees with the later Karaites, who were also strict biblicists in their own way, and who in fact did not follow these practices.[87] The seventeenth century had seen a renewed interest in the Karaites among both Christians and Jews; the Jesuit scholar Nicolaus Serarius, like Da Costa, identified them as latter-day Sadducees, as the great linguist Joseph Justus Scaliger had once done.[88] The primary issue at stake was the accessibility of religious truth through an unmediated reading of Scripture.[89] Certain Protestants looked favourably on the Karaites, as they imagined them, seeing them as the Jewish equivalents of Protestants in their faithfulness to Scripture and their opposition to a falsified tradition. The Scottish theologian John Dury articulated this idea vividly in a letter to Thomas Thorowgood published by the latter in 1650:

> [T]he Pharisees, as the Papists, attribute more to the Authoritie and traditions of their Rabbies and Fathers, than to the word of God; but the Caraits will receive nothing for a rule of faith and obedience but what is delivered from the

word of God immediately [...]. These two Sects are irreconcilably opposite to each other, and as the Papists deale with Protestants, so do the Pharisees with the Caraits, they persecute and suppres them and their profession by all the meanes they can possibly make use of [...] the Pharisees are full of superstitious imaginary foolish conceits, and thalmudicall questions and nicities in their Sermons and Bookes; the Caraits are rationall men that take up no doctrines but what the Scriptures teach.[90]

By the same token — if we look at the issue from Limborch's perspective — Da Costa's rejection of rabbinic tradition must have struck the Remonstrant theologian as useful for substantiating the rationalist Protestant critique of traditional Judaism.

But the biblicism in the *Exame* leads in a direction that was as shocking to Protestants as it was to rabbinic Jews: a denial of the immortality of the soul. Scripture as it was revealed to the Jewish people said nothing about a world to come. It was all a delusion, Da Costa concluded, adding his own theological arguments for why the soul must be mortal. The *Exemplar* describes briefly how Da Costa came to embrace this view. After he had begun work on the book, he wrote,

> it happened (I must report the whole sequence of events straightforwardly and truthfully) that I came to adhere resolutely and persistently to the opinion of those who understand reward and punishment in the Old Law as applying to this world only, and do not even imagine an afterlife or immortality of the soul. Among other things, I relied on the fact that the Law of Moses is silent on this matter, and those who observed or violated the Law were promised [in Scripture] only temporal rewards or punishments.[91]

H. P. Salomon has suggested that Da Costa's progression to a disavowal of the afterlife may have been prompted or encouraged by a remark in Modena's formal response to the 'Propostas'. At one point in the responsum Modena asked the rhetorical question, 'Where [in Jewish Scripture] do we find clearly set out the survival of the soul, posthumous reward and punishment, Paradise and Gehenna, etc?'[92] Modena's aim was to make the point that if something as self-evident as the immortality of the soul lacked a clear basis in Scripture, the Written Law alone was obviously insufficient. But for Da Costa, thinking against the grain as he was inclined to do, this might have triggered awareness of a whole new possible realm of rabbinic falsification. Not fortuitously, the same Sadducees who rejected Pharisaic law believed, as Josephus put it, that 'the soul perishes along with the body'. Da Costa would also have been aware that the New Testament mentions the Sadducees' denial of resurrection.[93]

How, then, to explain those biblical passages that *did* seem to allude to reward and punishment in a world to come? It was to solve this problem that Da Costa first made claims about the partial falsification of Scripture. The Pharisees, he argued, eager to win people over and accumulate power, introduced this idea. (Josephus had suggested as much.)[94] To achieve their end, they took the extraordinary step of corrupting revealed Scripture, planting passages that hinted at or promised future reward, promising resurrection or immortality of the soul. The Sadducees, he believed, had rejected these falsified passages, to little avail.

While Da Costa's theories about scriptural falsifications might be thought to anticipate biblical criticism, he lacked the theoretical and linguistic tools to make convincing scholarly arguments of the kind humanists were able to make. His 'method' was little more than a form of circular reasoning: his conclusion that any given passage (or book) of the Jewish Bible was fabricated by the Pharisees was based on the certain conviction that 'true' Scripture (which he referred to as 'the Law') could never speak of or even hint at resurrection or immortality of the soul. He plainly states this modus operandi in comments on the biblical passage in which Saul experiences Samuel as coming back from the dead to speak to him:

> Since this passage [I Sam. 28. 7–20] contradicts the true doctrine of the Law, it is necessarily false, like other glosses established by the Pharisees but rejected by the Sadducees. We take the Law as our guide and principal foundation, and we judge accordingly, separating the false from the true.[95]

Although Da Costa wrote that he could not always be sure which books the Pharisees had invented, 'never having been in communication with the Sadducees',[96] he felt sure they had produced the Book of Daniel, with its explicit allusion to resurrection,[97] and possibly the twelfth chapter of Ecclesiastes.[98] Without specifying his criteria, he also offered his opinion that three pseudepigraphical works, the Book of Judith and 3 and 4 Ezra, as well as the canonical Book of Esther, were texts fabricated by malicious men (if not Pharisees).[99]

Regardless of what Jewish Scripture might have to say (or not say) about the world to come, it is evident that by 1623 Da Costa firmly believed there was no such thing. Popular scepticism about the existence of heaven and hell was probably more widespread than sources indicate.[100] But in the early seventeenth century, it was unheard of to publish an explicit attack on the immortality of the soul, whether one was Christian or Jew. Samuel Da Silva, in his pre-emptive attack on Da Costa's position, accused Da Costa of being an Epicurean, and ridiculed him for following a pagan source regarding the nature of the soul.[101] In the *Exame*, Da Costa vigorously objected, denying he had any affinity with a sensualist like Epicurus.[102] It seems reasonable to take Da Costa at his word that he was driven to his rejection of the soul's immortality primarily by his radical biblicism. But there is another, very interesting personal element to his thinking on the subject, one that seems to run like a red thread through his biography: his search for a way to eliminate anxieties around salvation.

Three chapters of the *Exame* (3, 18, and 20) offer insight into the role anxiety about salvation played in his dawning conviction that the hope for salvation was a deception. 'For a time', he wrote,

> I found myself in the same darkness in which I see that many exist, bewildered and filled with doubts produced by the false writings and teachings of illusion-spinning men. I was unable to achieve the certainty of arriving at the eternal life that so many proclaimed [...] seeing that the Law was entirely silent on such great matters.[103]

This passage goes on to describe how Da Costa resolved this problem: he overcame 'the fear of men' and, driven only by his love of truth and fear of God, achieved a state of inner peace that echoes the Stoics (as well as some important contemporary thinkers), and seems strangely out of place in this tempestuous work. 'Thus I live', he wrote, 'content to know my end and the conditions of the Law that God has given me to observe, not building castles in the air, not gladdening (or deceiving) myself with false hopes of imagined blessings. Nor do I sadden or perturb myself with the dread of great evils'.[104]

It was, he reported, returning to the theme of anxiety around salvation, a hard-won truth:

> In truth, the thing that has most afflicted and wearied me in this life was believing or imagining that a time of eternal bliss or misery awaited a man, and that according to his works he would earn that bliss or that misery. If I had but been given the choice, I would have responded with no hesitation that I did not want such a risky reward, and would rather content myself with a lesser reward. In the end God permits these [fraudulent] ideas to torment the consciences of those who abandon him and his firm truth.[105]

The passage in chapter 3 is unfortunately all too brief. In the final chapters, however, Da Costa developed at some length the practical consequences of his insight. One of the evils of believing in a future reward was, he believed, the attendant contempt for the blessings of this world.[106] It was a natural, if provocative, next step to repudiate practices of self-mortification and the act of martyrdom, both of which were predicated on a belief in reward in the world to come. In response to Da Silva, who had defended the rabbinic ruling that one must endure death rather than commit idolatry, based on the biblical dictum that one must love God 'with all your heart and with all your soul' (Deut. 6. 5), Da Costa defined a position that bears a closer look.

It is worth mentioning that his simplified view of rabbinic opinion on this, as in other matters, was either uninformed or hostile (possibly both). In fact, rabbinic discussions of martyrdom show considerable flexibility and a preference for life over death. In a classic dictum, for example, the Talmud permitted violating the Sabbath to save a life, on the grounds that Scripture enjoined Jews to 'live by them', the commandments, and not, the Talmud added, 'die by them'.[107] Yet there can be no question that acts of martyrdom (*kiddush ha-shem*) were highly valued in rabbinic literature. Among crypto-Jews and Portuguese Jews, admiration for acts of steadfast martyrdom was a deep-seated feature of collective culture, and this reverence translated easily into the rabbinic language of memorialization. The Portuguese-Jewish rabbis acted to curb excessive preoccupation with this theme, but what they sought was balance, not suppression.[108]

Da Costa, however, hard-wired as he was for provocation, denied *any* value even to the acts of men and women who had been burned alive at the stake. Especially notable was his justification, in absolute terms, of the practice of dissimulation and equivocation by a person faced with coercion. In a striking passage, he elaborated his position, opening with a syllogism:

> As to what he [Da Silva] notes, namely that the Law requires us to love God with all our heart and soul, this [verse] does not support his claim [that

martyrdom is required]. Rather, one might derive proof from this [verse] of the contrary, because to love is the act of a living person; the dead cannot love. It follows that human beings are commanded to love God by living. And while committing idolatry is an act contrary to love [of God], one must consider the difference between a free act and a coerced act. If I commit idolatry of my own free will, I show that I have abandoned that love, but if I am being forced to commit idolatry on pain of torture and death, no one can say I have abandoned a love that is rooted in my heart, even though in the face of evil the root has remained concealed.[109]

Da Costa did concede that the *courage* of the martyr was worthy of admiration. This is not surprising, given his concern with honour and his personal conviction that voicing his beliefs, rather than concealing them, was a matter of honour. But the only reward for such courage, he insisted, was the martyr's recognition among men.[110]

In the final chapter of the *Exame*, Da Costa returned to his central concern: the human longing for salvation and the severe problems it caused. Persons who were raised to believe in eternal punishment suffered great anguish and despair, seeing that they could not desist from committing sins. But the very notion of eternal punishment was absurd, given God's justice. Men were finite and limited creatures, capable neither of the evil that would merit eternal damnation nor of the virtue that would merit eternal reward. The Pharisees, the papists and Luther had all sought in their own way to alleviate the anxiety produced by the erroneous teaching of eternal reward and punishment. In so doing, they had perpetuated belief in an unjust and cruel God, as well as in a doctrine that has no basis in Scripture.[111]

At the end of the *Exame*, Da Costa briefly offered an alternative understanding of life, predicated on the mortality of the soul. Human beings, he concluded, must 'take stock of themselves, and realize that God gave them this life to live, and that they should live it well, and that to achieve a good death is their bliss'. What, in the absence of the promise of future reward, would persuade them to lead moral lives? Nothing further, Da Costa asserted, than the wish to live and die well, 'considering how great is human self-love and people's natural tendency to seek their own welfare'.[112] This very brief passage is nevertheless very important from the scholar's point of view, because it establishes that in 1623 Da Costa was harbouring ideas that anticipated some of the concluding passages of the *Exemplar*. Had he been reading and absorbing the sixteenth-century French sceptics (or re-reading the ancient ones), for whom the main goal of life was to free oneself from the emotional turmoil that moral and religious beliefs caused? The brief passage in question is at least very suggestive of such exposure.

With the exception of this terse advice about how to live a good and tranquil life, Da Costa's prose in the second part of the *Exame* is unremittingly vitriolic. To be sure, Da Silva's preface to his pre-emptive attack on Da Costa, to which Da Costa was replying, was strongly accusatory, but it did not display the acrimony of Da Costa's rejoinder. Echoing the image with which Da Costa opened the book — that of Joshua and Caleb confronted by a threatening mob — he envisaged himself in these pages in the guise of a biblical hero confronting powerful enemies. He was Jacob, facing Laban's false accusation of idolatry. He was Moses confronted by Korach and his self-seeking followers. Like Moses, he was defending himself against the accusation that he was 'seeking to raise himself up by seizing political power [*de se querer levantar com o senhorio*]'.[113] He was Joseph, assailed by his brothers: 'It seems to me', he wrote, 'that [Pharisaism] is an inheritance from those ancient wolves of brothers, who, abandoning all humanity, conspired to stain themselves with the blood of that pious, innocent, and meek lamb who had come looking for them, wandering through the hills just to know if they were well'.[114] Here, as elsewhere, the structure of his thinking reflected his antagonistic personality, with its emotionally distorted and dualistic perception of human motivations; he seems to have been unable to sustain for long the philosophically informed serenity he sought.

★   ★   ★   ★   ★

One of the important questions about Da Costa is how his thinking on religion shifted between the publication of the *Exame* in 1623 and his death in 1640. Although we know important facts about his life in those years, the *Exemplar* is our only source of information about the evolution of his thought. Even if we could be sure he had written every word of the text published by Limborch, we would be left with serious questions. Da Costa seems not to have been in touch with non-Jewish intellectuals. (It is unlikely, given his personality, his intellectual limitations, and his radical beliefs, that he would have been welcome.) Yet the ideas about natural law sketched in the *Exemplar* echo a rapidly developing new conception of natural law in early modern Europe.[115] In my opinion, there is little reason to doubt that Da Costa was the author of the passages that have convinced scholars he was a 'deist' by the time he died. Limborch or Episcopius may have altered the text when it suited their purposes,[116] but Limborch would hardly have turned Da Costa into an 'atheist' just so that he would have an atheist to refute. A more compelling reason to accept these passages as genuinely his is, as mentioned above, that striking passage in Da Costa's *Exame*, a work published seventeen years earlier, that anticipates the embrace of natural law in the *Exemplar*.

One might read the *Exemplar* and almost overlook the important step in Da Costa's thinking that preceded his championing of a vision of natural law — Da Costa's rejection of all positive religion, including the Law of Moses. His account of this step is, like previous such accounts, brief and vague:

> It was some time after this [that is, after Da Costa's arrest and release in 1624] [...] that I came to doubt that the Law of Moses should be considered the law of God, since there were many things that seemed to persuade — or rather require — [one to believe] the contrary. Finally I was fully convinced that it [the Law of Moses] was nothing but a human invention, like many others in the world. In fact, it contained many things contrary to the law of nature. And God, who was the creator of nature, could not contradict himself, which he would have done if he had proposed that men act contrary to the nature of which he was the creator.[117]

A seventeenth-century thinker could conceptualize the 'law of nature' in a variety of ways. A summary of the passages in which Da Costa elaborated his thinking about this concept will be helpful if we want to form an idea of how he positioned himself at the time of his death. Da Costa declared that in the pursuit of truth, he was asserting 'the true and natural rights of men [*naturali hominum libertate*], who deserve to live a life worthy of men, free of false superstitions and vain ceremonies'.[118] In a digression, he berated the 'Pharisees', with no little sarcasm, for disregarding a rabbinic teaching that, by this period, some Christian scholars (and at least one other Amsterdam Jew) had come to associate with the law of nature, namely the so-called Noahide laws.[119] But after taking another opportunity to ridicule contemporary rabbinic Jews in this way, he returned to the exposition of his beliefs. Of particular interest was his statement that the 'true standard of that law of nature' was 'the rule of right reason [*recta ratio*]'.[120] And he continued:

> Since we have mentioned the law of nature, let me dwell on it a little, so as to take notice of the excellence of this original law. I affirm, then, that this law is common and innate in all men, by virtue of the fact that they are men. It binds them together in mutual affection, and is alien to discord, which is the cause and the root of all hatred [...] It teaches us to live well, distinguishing between right and wrong, between the hateful and the beautiful.[121]

Insofar as the positive religions deviated from the law of nature, he argued, they led to divisions and turmoil. The 'most useful precepts in the Law of Moses or any other religion' were those dictated by the law of nature and inherent in our natural sociability and self-interest:

> What is best in the law of Moses or in any other religion regarding human society, that makes possible among men a serene and peaceful life? First of all, the commandment to honour one's parents; then, not to take possession of the goods of others, whether they be life, honour or other goods necessary for life. Which of these norms, I ask, is not already contained in the law of nature and the inherent rule of right reason [*norma recta mentibus inhaerens*]? We naturally love our children, and children their parents; brother loves brother, a friend loves his friend. By nature we desire that everything that we possess be kept safe, and we hate those who disturb our peace, or who want to steal what is ours by violence or deception. From this it follows that we must not commit actions that we condemn in others.[122]

The ceremonies and other 'impositions' of positive law are a source of misfortune; they should be done away with, leaving 'only those things which assist us in leading a good moral life; for we cannot be said to live well, when we observe many vain ceremonies, but only when we live like rational creatures'. He concludes,

> In a word, if men would follow right reason [*rectam rationem*], and live according to human nature, they would all mutually love and have compassion for one another. Everyone, to the degree possible, would relieve the suffering of others, or at least no one would injure another without reason, for that would be contrary to human nature.[123]

Did Da Costa develop these ideas independently? Was this the fruit of years of solitary reflection? I think not. From a textual point of view, these passages stand out somewhat oddly; one is struck by the contrast in tone between Da Costa's impassioned and choleric attacks on the 'Pharisees' (which occupy the lion's share of the last part of the *Exemplar*) and the serene, reasonable tone of these somewhat dispersed endorsements of a life lived according to natural law. Moreover, Da Costa seems unconcerned about any systematic foundation for his ideas, or with the many questions his brief exposition would raise in an educated contemporary reader. (If this law 'is common and innate in all men, by virtue of the fact that they are men', why do human beings — and *how can* human beings — choose to live otherwise?)

In my opinion, Da Costa has drawn his thinking about natural law from an external source, one whose intellectual heft reassured him that his own undeveloped (and modified) borrowings were correct. He had probably, I believe, read and been influenced by the great Dutch jurist Hugo Grotius's work *De jure belli ac pacis* [The Rights of War and Peace].[124] Let me explain.

Da Costa recounted that it was 'some time after' his arrest and release in 1624 that he began to see that the Law of Moses was not consistent with the law of nature. It was very shortly thereafter, in 1625, that Grotius's *De jure belli ac pacis* was published in Paris. A second edition was published in Frankfort in 1626, and a third in Amsterdam in 1631. Grotius soon gained an international reputation. The fact that he was forced to flee the Netherlands twice (permanently in 1632) because of his support for religious toleration and Christian unity may have endeared him to the excommunicated Da Costa. More importantly, the earlier passage in the *Exame* which, with its neo-Stoic theme, seems to anticipate the *Exemplar*, indicates that by 1623 Da Costa was already interested in the notion of a good life lived in this world, one that could be achieved by following one's natural inclination to rational self-love.

But Grotius offered a compelling contemporary model that among other things aimed to dispel the scepticism of the French neo-Stoics. While Da Costa had entertained doubts in the course of his life, he had always moved to a new dogmatism; and on the face of it this is what he did by embracing a notion of natural law toward the end of his life. In any case, the similarity to Da Costa's terminology in the early pages of *De jure belli ac pacis* is striking. The 'true standard' of the law of nature was, Da Costa wrote, 'the rule of right reason [*recta ratio*]'. 'Natural right', wrote Grotius, 'is the rule and dictate of right reason' (*Ius natural est dictatum rectae rationis*).[125] Likewise, the primary dictates of natural law, as Da Costa laid them out in the *Exemplar*, also appear strikingly close to those of Grotius. Consider, for example, this passage in *De jure belli ac pacis*:

> This sociability, which we have now described in general, or this care of maintaining society in a manner conformable to the light of human understanding, is the fountain of right, properly so called; to which belongs the abstaining from that which is another's, and the restitution of what we have of another's, or of the profit we have made by it, the obligation of fulfilling promises, the reparation of a damage done through our own default, and the merit of punishment among men.[126]

Finally, in the course of his discussion of natural law, Grotius alludes several times to the rabbinic concept of Noahide Law that Da Costa accused the rabbis of ignoring. It is perhaps not important that Grotius did not, like Da Costa, regard Noahide Law as *being* the law of nature; what mattered would have been his view of this law as *consistent* with the law of nature, and antithetical to 'wicked customs'. As he wrote,

> Therefore, both the Law of Moses, and the Law given to Noah, tend rather to explain and renew the law of nature, obscured, and, as it were, extinguished by wicked customs, than to establish anything new.[127]

This does not constitute proof that Da Costa had read Grotius. But such an explanation might help understand why we find cropping up in the *Exemplar* ideas that were crystallizing in European learned circles in answer to problems faced by jurists and political theorists in the post-Reformation era — and not by Da Costa. For Da Costa, the primary issues had always been intensely personal. What seems to have appealed to him in the new discourse of natural law was its offer of a belief that relieved his personal doubts and anxieties. And yet Da Costa had no sooner formulated that new belief than he took his life. Was it perhaps a position he would have *liked* to be able embrace fully, rather than one that held him in its grip? Perhaps his stance was at least in part a rhetorical means to claim superiority over the members of the Jewish community and uphold his honour — that is, brave last words before he took his life in despair. In the end, there is no way to know whether Uriel da Costa died in a new dogmatic certainty or not.

Notes to Chapter 13

1. Israël S. Révah calculated that Da Costa was born sometime between November 1583 and March 1584. See Révah, 'Du "marranisme" au judaïsme et au déisme. Uriel da Costa et sa famille', *Annuaire du Collège de France*, 68 (1968), 562–72 (p. 568). The date for Da Costa's death in April 1640 was reported by Johannes Müller; see *Die Schriften des Uriel da Costa* , ed. by Carl Gebhardt (Amsterdam: Menno Hertzberger, 1922), p. 203.

2. In his preface to the *Exemplar*, Philipp van Limborch stated that Da Costa himself had written the title *Exemplar Humanae Vitae* at the head of the manuscript that was found among Simon Episcopius's papers. See Philipp van Limborch, *De Veritate Religionis Christianae amica collatio cum erudito Judaeo* (Gouda: Justus van Hoeve, 1687), p. 654.

3. It is worth noting that the great Dutch jurist Hugo Grotius, in a work of 1615, expressed his concern that 'among the Jews as well as among those of other religious convictions, there are often some atheists and impious people who should not be tolerated in any good republic'. See Hugo Grotius, *Remonstrantie nopende de ordre dije in landen van Hollandt ende Westvrieslandt dijent gestelt op de Joden*, ed. by Jacob Meijer (Amsterdam: [n. pub.], 1949), p. 122; translation from Jacob Meijer, 'Hugo Grotius' *Remonstrantie*', *Jewish Social Studies*, 17 (1955), 91–104 (p. 98). See the contribution in this volume by Mercedes García-Arenal.

4. Limborch, *De Veritate Religionis*, pp. 657–70.

5. Limborch, *De Veritate Religionis*, p. 655.

6. Limborch wrote to Theodor Graswinckel concerning a voluminous dossier Episcopius kept, with material about the Jewish community, to advance his cause of limiting the right of religious authorities to excommunicate. See the extract from Limborch's letter to Graswinckel published in Gebhardt, *Die Schriften*, pp. 198–200; a German translation follows. For a French translation, see Jean-Pierre Osier, *D'Uriel da Costa à Spinoza* (Paris: Berg, 1983), pp. 185–86.

7. See Gebhardt, *Die Schriften*, p. 261.

8. MS Amsterdam, Bibl. Univ. III E 3 83. Seligmann noted his discovery in a review, *Zeitschrift für hebraïsche Bibliographie*, 15 (1911), 41–43 (p. 42).

9. See Gebhardt, *Die Schriften*, pp. 260–61; Omero Proietti, *Uriel da Costa e 'l'Exemplar humanae vitae'* (Macerata: Quodlibet, 2005), pp. 109–16.

10. Müller may have had a special interest in the text because of his fears about people from abroad bringing libertine ideas to German lands. See Jonathan Israel, *Radical Enlightenment: Philosophy and the Making of Modernity, 1650–1750* (Oxford: Oxford University Press, 2001), p. 61.

11. Johannes Müller, *Judaismus oder Jüdenthumb, das ist: außführlicher Bericht von des jüdischen Volckes Unglauben, Blindheit und Verstockung* (Hamburg: J. Rebenlein, 1644), p. 71. The two passages from Müller's work that discuss Da Costa (the first of which contains the quotation from the 'wretched letter') have been republished by Gebhardt, *Die Schriften*, pp. 202–04. For Gebhardt's discussion of the fragment Müller quoted, see *Die Schriften*, p. 261. For a comparison of Müller's quoted passage with the same passage in Limborch's version, see Proietti, *Uriel da Costa*, pp. 45, 105–08.

12. See Israël S. Révah, 'La Religion d'Uriel da Costa, Marrane de Porto (d'après des documents inédits)', *Revue de l'histoire des religions* (1962), 45–76, republished in Révah, *Des marranes à Spinoza* (Paris: J. Vrin, 1995), pp. 77–108, as well as further material in Révah, *Uriel da Costa et les Marranes de Porto, Cours au Collège de France, 1966–1972*, ed. by Carsten Wilke (Paris: Calouste Gulbenkian, 2004), pp. 77–88. For a summary of the factual discrepancies and omissions in the *Exemplar* that have been brought to light by archival material, some of them minor, see Proietti, *Uriel da Costa*, pp. 189–91.

13. For the statement in the *Exemplar*, see Gebhardt, *Die Schriften*, p. 105; on the granting of the titles, see Révah, *Uriel da Costa*, pp. 235–36.

14. For the statement in the *Exemplar*, see Gebhardt, *Die Schriften*, p. 105. For the archival source, see Révah, *Uriel da Costa*, pp. 253–55.

15. For the statement in the *Exemplar* see Gebhardt, *Die Schriften*, p. 106; for the archival source see Révah, *Uriel da Costa*, p. 398.

16. Da Costa's role in the conversion of his family should not, however, be exaggerated; as Révah has found, other members of the family were also reportedly engaged in crypto-Jewish initiation and teaching among themselves. See Révah, 'La Religion', pp. 53–54.

17. See especially Stuart B. Schwartz, *All Can Be Saved: Religious Tolerance and Salvation in the Iberian Atlantic World* (New Haven, CT: Yale University Press, 2008), and the contribution in this volume by Mercedes García-Arenal.

18. He does mention other 'Catholic writings' as well but he made it clear that it was his searching of Scripture that enlightened him. Gebhardt, *Die Schriften*, pp. 105–06.

19. Abraham Beer Duff and Pierre Kahn, introduction to Uriel da Costa, *Une vie humaine*, trans. by A. B. Duff and P. Kahn (Paris: F. Rieder, 1926), pp. 73–74. Cited in Révah, *Uriel da Costa*, p. 84.

20. Révah followed the family of Bento da Costa Brandão from 1563.

21. For the findings, see Révah, 'La Religion', pp. 45–76; Révah, 'Du "marranisme" au judaïsme at au déisme. Uriel da Costa et sa famille', *Annuaire du Collège de France*, 67 (1967), 515–26; 68 (1968), 562–72; 69 (1969), 578–85; 70 (1970), 569–77; 72 (1972), 653–62, republished in Révah, *Des marranes à Spinoza*, pp. 119–68; Révah, *Uriel da Costa*. Among these works there is much repetition; I will not give further multiple citations.

22. Révah counted more than 150 conversos from Porto who were tried for judaizing in Coimbra or Lisbon between 1618 and 1625. See Wilke's introduction, Révah, *Uriel da Costa*, pp. 22–23.

23. See Wilke's introduction, Révah, *Uriel da Costa*, p. 31.

24. Révah, 'La Religion', pp. 56–58.

25. Révah, *Uriel da Costa*, p. 134.

26. Révah, *Uriel da Costa*, pp. 392–94. See also Wilke's introduction, in Révah, *Uriel da Costa*, p. 4.

27. Révah, *Uriel da Costa*, p. 490; pp. 511–29.

28. Révah, 'La Religion', p. 74.

29. We know Homem to have been leading the group from 1609 to 1618. On this episode, see Révah, *Uriel da Costa*, pp. 53–54, 258–59.

30. João Manuel Andrade, *Confraria de S. Diogo. Judeus secretos na Coimbra do séc. XVII* (Lisbon: Nova Arrancada, 1999), p. 65 n. 10.

31. Gebhardt, *Die Schriften*, p. 106.

32. 'q' se não podia salvar na ley dos xpãos senão na de Mouses, na qual cresse'; Révah, *Uriel da Costa*, p. 63. All translations are my own, unless otherwise noted. I have, however, consulted John Whiston's English translation and Carl Gebhardt's German translation of the *Exemplar*, as well as H. P. Salomon and I. S. D. Sassoon's English translation of the *Exame*.

33. 'Hoc in dubium vocato animo, quievi, & quicquid effet, tandem statuebam me non posse tali viâ incedendo salutem animae assequi'; Gebhardt, *Die Schriften*, p. 106 (Italics mine).

34. Gebhardt, *Die Schriften*, p. 108.

35. These two texts are discussed further below.

36. Uriel da Costa, *Examination of Pharisaic Traditions*, trans. and intro. by H. P. Salomon (Leiden: Brill, 1993), pp. 96–97 [hereinafter, Da Costa, *Exame*].

37. 'cuperem alicui inhaerere'; Gebhardt, *Die Schriften*, p. 106.

38. Révah believed Da Costa was 'strongly exaggerating' when he reported such early doubts about the immortality of the soul. In his view, fear of damnation was the driving force behind Da Costa's conversion, and the meagre account of that conversion years later had to do with his loss of interest in that episode of his life. See Révah, *Uriel da Costa*, pp. 535–36.

39. For the preface, see Limborch, *De Veritate Religionis*, pp. 653–54, 672–73. For a French translation of Limborch's preface and *Refutatio* to the *Exemplar*, see Osier, *D'Uriel da Costa*, pp.168–84.

40. After what can only be understood as a reference to his first excommunication, in Venice and Hamburg (1618), the *Exemplar* states that Da Costa's brothers took no notice of him when they passed him in the street (Gebhardt, *Die Schriften*, p. 108). Yet notarial records show that Da Costa was actively engaged in commercial activities with his brother Mordecai/Jerónimo/Miguel as late as June 1623 (H. P. Salomon, introduction to Da Costa, *Exame*, p. 12 n. 25). Similarly, the *Exemplar* recounts that Da Costa was arrested and imprisoned by the Dutch authorities for eight or ten days and fined 300 gulden for publishing the *Exame*, and states, 'I was released after posting bail' (Gebhardt, *Die Schriften*, p. 109); it fails to mention that it was his brothers Mordecai and Joseph/João who bailed him out (see the document published in Gebhardt, *Die Schriften*, p. 184). Finally, the *Exemplar* describes Da Costa's isolation and separation from his family with pathos, failing to mention that his mother lived with him in exile, probably up to her death in 1628; we know this from a rabbinic query as to whether this situation made her ineligible for a Jewish burial (for details see H. P. Salomon, introduction to Da Costa, *Exame*, p. 18).

41. Révah, *Uriel da Costa*, p. 76. Overall, Révah was 'profoundly persuaded' that Da Costa sought to 'completely dissociate his emotional metaphysical adventure from the general history of Portuguese New Christians'; Révah, 'Du "marranisme" au judaïsme', *Annuaire*, 70 (1970), 569–77 (p. 569).

42. Cf. Wilke in Révah, *Uriel da Costa*, p. 63.

43. On the dogmatista martyrs, see M. Bodian, *Dying in the Law of Moses: Crypto-Jewish Martyrdom in Iberian Lands* (Bloomington: Indiana University Press, 2007).

44. Carsten L. Wilke, 'Conversion ou retour? La Metamorphose du nouveau chrétien en juif portugais dans l'imaginaire sépharade du XVIIe siècle', in *Mémoires juives d'Espagne et du Portugal*, ed. by Esther Benbassa (Paris: Publisud, 1996), pp. 53–67 (p. 57).

45. The financial difficulties of the family are reflected in documents showing that Da Costa's mother sought to borrow 319,000 *réis* in November 1608, six months after her husband's death. The father was also owed a large sum for which he was suing at the time of his death, which Uriel da Costa sought to recover in 1611. Révah, 'Du marranisme au judaïsme', *Annuaire*, 70 (1970), 575–76.

46. This is Révah's term, in reference to Leonor de Pina. See Révah, *Uriel da Costa*, p. 497.

47. Two judaizing dogmatista martyrs, Luis Carvajal and Francisco Maldonado da Silva, even converted Old Christians who were fellow prisoners to 'the Law of Moses'. See Bodian, *Dying in the Law*, pp. 62–63, 135–37.

48. Révah, *Uriel da Costa*, p. 64. Da Costa's relative Leonor de Pina likewise suggested the special status that Da Costa, being 'a great Latinist', enjoyed, since this gained him access to the Bible. Révah, *Uriel da Costa*, p. 512.

49. Da Costa wrote (assuming the passage in the *Exemplar* is his) that after his excommunication, 'my own brothers, who in the past had taken me as their teacher [*praeceptor*], out of fear

pretended not to see me and did not greet me in public'; Gebhardt, *Die Schriften*, p. 108.

50. We know this from notarial documents published by Abraham de Mordechai Vaz Dias, *Uriel da Costa. Nieuwe bijdrage tot diens levensgeschiedenis* (Leiden: Brill, 1936), pp. 15–17.

51. Gebhardt, *Die Schriften*, p. 107.

52. Gebhardt, *Die Schriften*, p. xx.

53. While the original text he sent to Venice has been lost, Da Costa restated and expanded his theses in his *Exame* published in 1624. In that later version, he made some revisions in light of Modena's response; see H. P. Salomon's introduction to Da Costa, *Exame*, pp. 25–27. For Modena's responsum, see Yehudah Aryeh da Modena, *Magen ve-tzinah* (Breslau: H. Sulzbach, 1856), fols 1ʳ–10ᵛ.

54. Cf. Ex. 13. 16; Deut. 6. 8; Deut. 11. 18 RSV (Revised Standard Version).

55. In Modena's translation, כי לא הניחה דבר עיקרי בלי ביאור

56. For example, the rabbinic prohibition of handling an implement used for work on the Sabbath, lest one haphazardly perform work prohibited by the Torah on that day.

57. In the *Exemplar*, he mentions being circumcised as one of his first acts upon arrival (see Gebhardt, *Die Schriften*, p. 107); he would have been introduced to the other two precepts as routine matters of practical observance.

58. For the rabbinic discussion on this point, see Babylonian Talmud [BT], 52a.

59. In Modena's translation,

שלא כן דברה תורה, ואילו רצתה בכך ביארה דבריה, ואין לנו אלא מה שדברה תורה

60. For the rabbinic discusson, see BT Bava Kama, chapter 8.

61. Y. H. Yerushalmi, 'Marranos Returning to Judaism in the Seventeenth Century: Their Jewish Knowledge and Psychological Readiness' [in Hebrew], in *Proceedings of the Fifth World Congress of Jewish Studies*, 5 vols (Jerusalem: World Union of Jewish Studies, 1969), II, 208.

62. On the Ponentine community in Venice, see *The Jews of Early Modern Venice*, ed. by Robert Davis and Benjamin Ravid (Baltimore, MD: Johns Hopkins University Press, 2001), pp. 86–94.

63. On the complex way in which community was forged among the Portuguese Jews of Amsterdam, see Miriam Bodian, *Hebrews of the Portuguese Nation: Conversos and Community in Early Modern Amsterdam* (Bloomington: Indiana University Press, 1997).

64. Cecil Roth, 'The Strange Case of Hector Mendes Bravo', *Hebrew Union College Annual*, 18 (1944), 221–45 (pp. 242–43).

65. The responsum is published in Yehudah Aryeh da Modena, *She'elot ve-teshuvot ziknei yehudah*, ed. by Shlomo Simonsohn (Jerusalem: Mosad Ha-Rav Kook, 1956), p. 99.

66. In the *Exame*, Da Costa makes an explicit reference to Luther in reference to Luther's concept of the soul. He assumes the reader's familiarity with Luther. See Da Costa, *Exame*, p. 153.

67. See Bodian, *Dying in the Law*.

68. On the dovetailing of Protestant and crypto-Jewish thinking along these lines, see Miriam Bodian, 'The Geography of Conscience: A Seventeenth-Century Atlantic Jew and the Inquisition,' *The Journal of Modern History*, 89.2 (2017), 247–81 (pp. 264–65).

69. Da Costa, *Exame*, p. 53. (Salomon facsimile). For the biblical episode, see no. 14. 7–10.

70. Wilke introduction to Révah, *Uriel da Costa*, pp. 64–65. As Wilke notes, Révah saw a similar phenomenon in the career of Juan de Prado.

71. I have discussed possible Peninsular conditioning behind the behaviour of insistently heterodox ex-conversos in the Amsterdam community in Bodian, *Dying in the Law*, pp. 180–82. On the rabbinic leaders' discouragement of a too-active and continued martyrdom ideal among the émigrés, see Bodian, *Dying in the Law*, pp. 183–84.

72. Published in Gebhardt, *Die Schriften*, pp. 150–51.

73. Modena, *Magen ve-tzinnah*, fol. 3ʳ.

74. Gebhardt, *Die Schriften*, p. 108.

75. For a summary of sources and opinions about this problem, see Proietti, *Exame das tradições phariseas*, pp. 14–17.

76. Samuel da Silva (whose work will be discussed shortly) wrote of the Hamburg community's behaviour toward Da Costa in the period between 1618 and 1623: 'muyto se trabalhou por não chegar a rigor, não bastou nada, & ainda assi se procedeu com toda a brandura a que o feo caso

deu lugar consentindo que ficasse na terra por ver se tornava em contriçam & emenda de seus erros'. This lenience ended, he wrote, only when Da Costa's 'scandalous and insolent' writings — that is, chapters from the *Exame* — came into the hands of Da Silva and others. Samuel da Silva, *Tratado da immortalidade da alma* (Amsterdam: Paul van Ravesteyn, 1623), p. 3.

77. Gebhardt, *Die Schriften*, p. 127.

78. A facsimile copy of Da Costa's *Exame* was published shortly after the volume's discovery in 1990, in Da Costa, *Exame*. Recently an annotated edition has appeared: Uriel da Costa, *Exame das tradições phariseas, Esame delle tradizioni farisee (1624)*, ed. and trans. by Omero Proietti (Macerata: Università di Macerata, 2014).

79. Silva, *Tratado da imortalidade da alma*. An English translation was published by H. P. Salomon and I. S. D. Sassoon in their edition of the *Exame*, pp. 427–551. It incorporates the three chapters of Da Costa's that had come into his hands. For a detailed comparison of the two published texts, see Da Costa, *Exame* (Salomon edn), pp. 32–38, and Da Costa, *Exame* (Proietti edn), pp. 67–73; the differences are not significant for this essay.

80. Da Costa, *Exame*, p. 53.

81. Da Costa repeats the theme of Pharisaic pandering to the mob by promising immortality of the soul, noting Josephus as his source, later in Da Costa, *Exame*, 152. For the source in Josephus, see his *Antiquities of the Jews*, trans. by William Whiston, 1737) book XVIII, 1,3. See <http://penelope.uchicago.edu/josephus/ant-18.html> [accessed 18 April 2019].

82. Da Costa, *Exame*, p. 59. On the noble and learned character of the Sadducees and Boethians, Da Costa is echoing Josephus, *Antiquities*, book XIII, 10,6; book XVIII, 1,4: 'but this doctrine is received but by a few, yet by those still of the greatest dignity'. And see Da Costa, *Exame*, p. 152, where Da Costa mentions his source as Josephus.

83. Da Costa, *Exame*, p. 76. This is in reference to Lev. 25. 26.

84. Da Costa, *Exame*, p. 94. This is in reference to Deut. 23. 25–26.

85. It may have been the Venetian rabbi Leon da Modena who originally (and inadvertently) suggested to Da Costa that he had intellectual ancestors in the ancient Sadducees. In his 1616 letter to the Hamburg communal leaders, Modena wrote sarcastically that he did not know whether Da Costa was 'a Sadducee, a Boethusian or a Karaite'. Gebhardt, *Die Schriften*, p. 150.

86. Da Costa noted his reliance, in reconstructing the schism that concerned him, on the *Antiquities* of Josephus (see Da Costa, *Exame*, p. 60), and he followed Josephus's remark that the Pharisees 'are not apt to be severe in punishments' (*Antiquities*, XIII. 10,6). For the rabbinic text connecting Antigonus with the origins of the Sadducees and Boethusians, see *Avoth de Rabbi Nathan* 5:2. For Da Costa's remark about his reading of Josephus, presumably in Portugal, see Da Costa, *Exame*, p. 235.

87. Da Costa wrote: 'It would appear that the differences among the Jews themselves in putting on [*tefillin*] — that the Ashkenazis wear them during the intermediate days of festivals, but without saying the required blessing, whereas the Levantines do not, and the Karaites do neither one nor the other...' Gebhardt, *Die Schriften*, p. 4. Incidentally, the identification of Karaites with Sadducees was not unknown among medieval Jews. For example, Yom-Tov Lipmann Muhlhausen's *Liber Nizahon Rabbi Lipmanni*, a fifteenth-century polemical work aimed at Christians and Karaites, makes the connection explicitly. See Ora Limor and Israel Jacob Yuval, 'Skepticism and Conversion: Jews, Christians, and Doubters in Sefer ha-Nizzahon', in *Hebraica veritas? Christian Hebraists and the Study of Judaism in Early Modern Europe* , ed. by Allison Coudert and Jeffrey S. Shoulson (Philadelphia: University of Pennsylvania Press, 2004), pp. 159–80 (p. 161).

88. On Christians' identification of Karaites with Sadducees, see Johannes van den Berg, 'Proto-Protestants? The Image of the Karaites as a Mirror of the Catholic-Protestant Controversy in the Seventeenth Century', in *Jewish–Christian Relations in the Seventeenth Century: Studies and Documents*, ed. by Johannes van den Berg and Ernestine G. E. van der Wall (Dordrecht, Boston and London: Kluver, 1988), pp. 33–49 (pp. 35–36).

89. On the issue of early modern 'Karaism,' see Marina Rustow, 'Karaites Real and Imagined: Three Cases of Jewish Heresy,' *Past and Present*, 197.1 (2007), 58–70; Yosef Kaplan, '"Karaites" in the Early Eighteenth Century', in Kaplan, *An Alternative Path to Modernity: The Sephardi*

Diaspora in Western Europe (Leiden: Brill, 1996), pp. 234–79; Van den Berg, 'Proto-Protestants?', pp. 33–49.

90. John Dury, 'An Epistolicall Discourse of Mr. Iohn Dury to Mr. Thorowgood', in Thomas Thorowgood, *Iewes in America, or, Probabilities that the Americans are of that race* (London: W. H. for Tho. Slater, 1650), unpaginated.

91. Gebhardt, *Die Schriften*, p. 108.

92. See Da Costa, *Exame*, p. 28. For the Hebrew passage in the responsum, see Modena, *Magen ve-Tzinnah*, fol. 4ʳ.

93. On the ancient sources identifying the Sadducees with denial of resurrection, including Josephus and the New Testament, see C. D. Elledge, *Resurrection of the Dead in Early Judaism, 200 BCE–CE 200* (Oxford: Oxford University Press, 2017), pp. 101–06.

94. *Antiquities*, XVIII, 1,3. Exploitation of this kind, Da Costa noted, was also recognized by the first-century Roman writer Pomponius Mela. Mela ascribed ulterior motives to the wise men of certain barbarian cultures, who taught the existence of the soul's return after death in order to encourage their warriors' fearlessness in battle. Da Costa, *Exame*, pp. 151–52.

95. 'Assi sendo a tal escritura contraria á verdadeira doutrina da lei, he força que seia falsa, e commentada como outros escritas, e reçibidas pellos Phariseus, e reprovadas pellos Saduçeus. E no temos a lei por guia, e fundamento principal, e por ella avemos de julgar, a apartar o falso do verdadeiro'; Da Costa, *Exame*, p. 126, and p. 169.

96. Da Costa, *Exame*, p. 130.

97. Da Costa, *Exame*, p. 141.

98. Though verses in this chapter might, he wrote, be explained metaphorically. *Exame*, pp. 173–74.

99. Da Costa, *Exame*, p. 143.

100. Denial of an afterlife has been documented for late medieval and early modern Iberia, especially among conversos. The classic work on this is Francisco Márquez Villanueva, ' "Nascer e morir como bestias" (criptojudaísmo y criptoaverroísmo)', in *Los judaizantes en Europa y la literatura castellana del Siglo de Oro*, ed. by Fernando Díaz Esteban (Madrid: Letrúmero, 1994), pp. 273–93.

101. '& se os epycuros primeiros authores desta mà seita tiveram ley & creram nella eu fico que nunca tal lhe passara pola imaginacam, que nam eram tam faltos de juyzo & philosophia, que negassem a força dos argumentos' of tradition proving the immortality of the soul. Samuel da Silva, *Tratado da immortalidade da alma*, p. 71.

102. Da Costa, *Exame*, pp. 159–61, 194–96, 207–09. A passage in the *Exemplar*, presumably written by Da Costa, revised this negative opinion of Epicurus. Gebhardt, *Die Schriften*, pp. 108–09.

103. Da Costa, *Exame*, p. 148.

104. Da Costa, *Exame*, p. 148.

105. Da Costa, *Exame*, pp. 148–49.

106. Da Costa, *Exame*, p. 146.

107. BT Yoma 85b, on Lev. 18. 5.

108. On the memorialization of martyrdom in the Portuguese-Jewish diaspora, see Bodian, *Dying in the Law*.

109. Da Costa, *Exame*, p. 246. For a quite parallel expression of this idea by a Portuguese Jew facing the Inquisition, see Bodian, 'Geography of Conscience', p. 264.

110. Da Costa, *Exame*, p. 247.

111. Da Costa, *Exame*, pp. 254–59.

112. See Da Costa, *Exame*, pp. 258–59.

113. Da Costa, *Exame*, p. 105.

114. 'Pareçeme que he herença, que herdaram daquelles antigos irmaons lobos, que esqueçidos de toda a humanidade se deliberavam a contaminarse, e mancharse no sangue da piadosa, innoçente, e mansa ovelha, que viha a buscalos, desguerrada [sic] pellos montes, só por saber de sua saude'; Da Costa, *Exame*, p. 236; the theme appears again on p. 250. Cf. Gen. 37: 12–18.

115. On this development, see, inter alia, Richard Tuck, 'The "Modern" Theory of Natural Law', in *The Languages of Political Theory in Early Modern Europe*, ed. by Anthony Pagden (Cambridge: Cambridge University Press, 1987), pp. 99–119.

116. This essay will not deal with possible tampering with the text, with the aim of exaggerating the persecution of Da Costa by the 'Pharisees', or of magnifying Da Costa's vengefulness. For a detailed effort to analyse the textual problems of the *Exemplar* in linguistic and literary terms, see Proietti, *Uriel da Costa*. Proietti's documentation of textual parallels to New Testament passages (pp. 47–48; 99–103) is in some cases compelling, but his conclusions are by no means the last word.

117. Gebhardt, *Die Schriften*, pp. 109–10.

118. Gebhardt, *Die Schriften*, p. 116.

119. Gebhardt, *Die Schriften*, pp. 117–18. In his defence before the Lisbon Inquisition in the 1640s, a young Portuguese Jew from Amsterdam made a point of discussing Noahide Law, which he identified with natural law. See Miriam Bodian, 'Geography of Conscience', p. 267.

120. '...secundum rectam rationem, quae vera norma est illius naturalis legis...' Gebhardt, *Die Schriften*, p. 118.

121. Gebhardt, *Die Schriften*, p. 118.

122. Gebhardt, *Die Schriften*, pp. 118–19.

123. Gebhardt, *Die Schriften*, p. 122.

124. Hugo Grotius, *De jure belli ac paci libri tres* (Paris: Nicolaum Buon, 1625). For the English translations I have used Grotius, *The Rights of War and Peace*, ed. by Richard Tuck, trans. by A. C. Campbell (Indianapolis: Liberty Fund, 2005).

125. Grotius, *De jure belli ac pacis*, I, 1, x.

126. Grotius, *Rights of War and Peace*, 'Prolegomena'.

127. Grotius, *Rights of War and Peace*, I, 2, v. See also I, 1, xvi.

BIBLIOGRAPHY

❖

Accetto, Torquato, *Della dissimulazione onesta*, ed. by Salvatore Silvano Nigro (Turin: Einaudi, 1997)

Ackerman, Ari, ed., *The Sermons of R. Zerahya Halevi Saladin* [in Hebrew] (BerSheva: Ben Gurion University Press, 2012)

Addante, Luca, 'Dal radicalismo religioso del Cinquecento al deismo (e oltre). Vecchie e nuove prospettive di ricerca', *Rivista storica italiana*, 127.3 (2015), 770–807

——*Eretici e libertini nel Cinquecento italiano* (Rome and Bari: Laterza, 2010)

——'"Parlare liberamente". I libertini del Cinquecento fra tradizioni storiografiche e prospettive di ricerca', *Rivista storica italiana*, 123.3 (2011), 927–1001

——'Ponzio, Francesco, in religione Dionisio', in *Dizionario biografico áegli Italiani*, vol. LXXXIV (2015) <http://www.treccani.it/enciclopedia/ponzio-francesco-in-religione-dionisio_(Dizionario-Biografico)> [accessed 21 April 2017]

——'Radicalismes politiques et religieux. Les Libertins italiens au XVIe siècle', in *Libertin! Usage d'une invective aux XVIe et XVIIe siècles*, ed. by Thomas Berns, Anne Staquet, and Monique Weis (Paris: Classiques Garnier, 2013), pp. 29–50

——*Tommaso Campanella. Il filosofo immaginato, interpretato, falsato* (Rome and Bari: Laterza, 2018)

——*Valentino Gentile e il dissenso religioso nell'Europa del Cinquecento. Dalla Riforma italiana al radicalismo europeo* (Pisa: Edizioni della Normale, 2014)

Agulló, Mercedes, *A vueltas con el autor del Lazarillo* (Madrid: Calambur, 2010)

Aillet, Cyrille, *Les Mozarabes. Christianisme, islamisation et arabisation en péninsule Ibérique (IXe–XIIe siècle)* (Madrid: Casa de Velázquez, 2010)

Åkerman, Susanna, *Queen Christina of Sweden and Her Circle: The Transformation of a Seventeenth Century Philosophical Libertine* (Leiden: Brill, 1991)

Alberti, Arnau, *Tractatus solemnis et aureus. De Agnoscendis Assertionibus Catholicis et Haereticis* (Venice: Candentis Salamandrae, 1571)

Albo, Joseph, *Sefer ha-Ikkarim/Book of Principles*, ed. by Isaac Husik, 4 vols (Philadelphia, PA: Jewish Publication Society of America, [1929] 1946)

'Aleph Forum on the Knowability of the Heavens and of Their Mover (*Guide*, 2: 24)', *Aleph. Historical Studies in Science & Judaism*, 8 (2008), 151–339

Alfonso X, King of Castile, *General Estoria. VI partes*, coord. by Pedro Sánchez-Prieto Borja, 10 vols (Madrid: Fundación José Antonio de Castro, 2009)

Amabile, Luigi, *Fra Tommaso Campanella. La sua congiura, i suoi processi e la sua pazzia*, 3 vols (Naples: Morano, 1882)

Amelang, James S., *Parallel Histories: Muslims and Jews in Inquisitorial Spain* (Baton Rouge: Lousiana State University Press, 2013)

Andrade, João Manuel, *Confraria de S. Diogo. Judeus secretos na Coimbra do séc. XVII* (Lisbon: Nova Arrancada, 1999)

Andreu Celma, José María, *Baltasar Gracián o la ética cristiana* (Madrid: Biblioteca de Autores Cristianos, 2008)

ANGLO, SYDNEY, *Machiavelli. The First Century: Studies in Enthusiasm, Hostility, and Irrelevance* (New York: Oxford University Press, 2005)

ANIDJAR, GIL, 'Lines of Blood: *Limpieza de Sangre* as Political Theology', in *Blood in History and Blood Histories*, ed. by Maricarla Gadebusch Bondio (Florence: Edizioni del Galluzzo, 2005), pp. 119–36

ANTONAZZI, GIOVANNI, *Lorenzo Valla e la polemica sulla donazione di Costantino* (Rome: Edizioni di Storia e Letteratura, 1985)

ANTONINUS OF FLORENCE, *Prima [quarta] pars totius summe majoris beati Antonini* (Lyon: Johannis Cleyn, 1506)

——*Summa theologica* (Nuremberg: Antonius Koberger, 1477–79)

APP, URS, *The Cult of Emptiness: The Western Discovery of Buddhist Thought and the Invention of Oriental Philosophy* (Rorchach and Kyoto: University Media, 2012)

ARANGUREN, JOSÉ LUIS, 'La moral de Gracián', *Revista de la Universidad de Madrid*, 7 (1958), 331–54

ARENDT, HANNAH, *Men in Dark Times* (New York: Harcourt Brace, 1993)

ARIEW, ROGER, 'Descartes and the Jesuits: Doubt, Novelty, and the Eucharist', in *Jesuit Science and the Republic of Letters*, ed. by Mordechai Feingold (Cambridge, MA: The Massachusetts Institute of Technology Press, 2003), pp. 158–94

ARISTOTLE, *Poetics* 1450a, in *Aristotle in 23 Volumes*, vol. XXIII, trans. by W. H. Fyfe (Cambridge, MA: Harvard University Press; London: William Heinemann, 1932) <http://www.perseus.tufts.edu/hopper/text?doc=Perseus%3Atext%3A1999.01.0056%3Asection%3D1450a> [accessed 23 September 2018]

ARMOGATHE, JEAN-ROBERT, 'Probabilisme et libre-arbitre. La Théologie morale de Caramuel y Lobkowitz', in *Le meraviglie del probabile. Juan Caramuel 1606–1682. Atti del convegno internazionale di studi, Vigevano 29–31 ottobre 1982*, ed. by Paolo Posavino (Vigevano: Comune di Vigevano, 1990), pp. 35–40

ARNOLD, JOHN H., *Belief and Unbelief in Medieval Europe* (London: Hodder Arnold, 2005)

ASAD, TALAL, 'Reading a Modern Classic: W. C. Smith's *The Meaning and End of Religion*', *History of Religions*, 40.3 (2001), 205–22

——*Genealogies of Religion: Discipline and Reasons of Power in Christianity and Islam* (Baltimore, MD: Johns Hopkins University Press, 1993), pp. 27–54

ASCHAM, ROGER, *The Scholemaster* (London: John Daye, 1570)

Aspects du Libertinisme au XVIe siècle. Actes du colloque international de Sommières (Paris: Vrin, 1974)

ASSMANN, JAN, *Of God and Gods: Egypt, Israel, and the Rise of Monotheism* (Madison: University of Wisconsin Press, 2008)

——*Religio Duplex: How the Enlightenment Reinvented Egyptian Religion* (Cambridge: Polity Press, 2014)

AUGUSTINE OF ANCONA, *Summa de potestate ecclesiastica* (Rome: Ferrarius, 1584)

AUGUSTINE OF HIPPO, *The Augustine Catechism: The Enchiridion on Faith, Hope and Charity*, ed. and trans. by Bruce Harbert and Boniface Ramsey (New York: New City Press, 2008)

AZOR, JUAN, *Institutionum moralium, in quibus universae quaestiones ad conscientiam recte aut prave factorum pertinentes tractantur, pars prima* (Rome: Aloisio Zanetti, 1600)

BAER, YITZHAK-FRITZ, 'Abner aus Burgos', *Korrespondenzblatt des Vereins zur Gründung und Erhaltung einer Akademie für die Wissenschaft des Judentums*, 10 (1929), 20–37

——'Die Disputation von Tortosa (1413–1414)', *Spanische Forschungen der Görresgesellschaft. 1. Reihe: Gesammelte Aufsätze zur Kulturgeschichte Spaniens*, 3 (1931), 307–36

——'He'arot Hadashot la-Sefer Shevet Yehudah', *Tarbiz*, 6 (1935), 152–79

——*Die Juden im christlichen Spanien*, 2 vols (Berlin: Schocken, 1936) [English trans. by Louis Schoffman, *A History of the Jews in Christian Spain*, 2 vols (New York: Jewish

Publication Society of America, 1961–66)] [Spanish translation by José Luis Lacave, *Historia de los judíos en la España cristiana*, 2 vols (Madrid: Altalena, 1981)]

BÄHLER, URSULA, *Gaston Paris dreyfusard. Le Savant dans la cité* (Paris: Centre National de la Recherche Scientifique Editions, 1999)

BAIAO, ANTÓNIO, *A Inquisição em Portugal e no Brasil. Subsídios para a sua história*, 10 vols (1910–16), vol. VIII (1910)

BARANDA LETURIO, CONSOLACIÓN, 'El humanismo frustrado de Francisco López de Villalobos y la polémica con Hernán Núñez', *eHumanista*, 29 (2015), 208–39 <http://www.ehumanista.ucsb.edu/sites/secure.lsit.ucsb.edu.span.d7_eh/files/sitefiles/ehumanista/volume29/10%20ehum29.viv.baranda.pdf> [accessed 10 May 2017]

BARAMBIO, FRANCISCO, *Discursos philosóphicos, theológicos, morales y mýsticos contra las proposiciones del Doctor Miguel de Molinos, diuididos en dos partes, la primera hasta la Proposicion XXX, la segunda concluye la obra*, 2 vols (Madrid: Juan García Infanzón, 1691–92)

BARTHAS, JÉRÉMIE, 'Machiavelli e i 'libertini' fiorentini (1522–1531). Una pagina dimenticata nella storia del libertinismo. Col Sermone sopra l'elezione del gonfaloniere del libertino Pierfilippo Pandolfini (1528)', *Rivista storica italiana*, 120.2 (2008), 569–603

——'Retour sur la notion de libertin à l'époque moderne. Les Politiques libertins à Florence, 1520–1530', *Libertinage et philosophie au XVIIe siècle*, 8 (2004), 115–34

BARTOLI, DANIELLO, *Della vita e dell'instituto di S. Ignazio della Compagnia di Gesù libri cinque* (Venice: Niccolò Pezzana, 1735)

BATLLORI, MIGUEL, *Gracián y el barroco* (Rome: Edizioni di Storia e Letteratura, 1958)

BAYLE, PIERRE, *Dictionnaire critique et universel. Nouvelle édition*, 16 vols (Paris: Desoer, 1820–24)

BELDA PLANS, JUAN, *La Escuela de Salamanca y la renovación de la teología en el siglo XVI* (Madrid: Biblioteca de Autores Cristianos, 2000)

——, ed., MELCHOR CANO, *De locis theologicis* (Madrid, Biblioteca de Autores Cristianos Maior, 2006)

BELL'UOMO, GOTTARDO, *Il pregio e l'ordine dell'oratione ordinarie e mistiche* (Modena: l'Heredi del Soliani, 1678)

BEN ASHER IBN HALAWA, BAHYA, *Perush al ha-Torah* (Bene Berak: Mishor, 2004)

BENEDEN, BEN VAN, ed., *Rubens in Private: The Master Portrays his Family*. Rubenhuis (Antwerp, 28 March–28 June 2015) (London: Thames & Hudson, 2015)

BENÍTEZ SÁNCHEZ-BLANCO, RAFAEL, *Heroicas decisiones. La Monarquía Católica y los moriscos valencianos* (Valencia: Institució Alfons el Magnànim-Diputació de València, 2001)

BENNINGTON, GEOFFREY, and JACQUES DERRIDA, *Jacques Derrida* (Chicago, IL: University of Chicago Press, 1993)

BEN-SASSON, HAIM H., 'Jewish-Christian Disputation in the Setting of Humanism and Reformation in the German Empire', *Harvard Theological Review*, 59.4 (1966), 369–90

BENVENISTE, EMILE, *Le Vocabulaire des institutions indo-européennes* (Paris: Éditions de Minuit, 1969)

BERGMANN, ARI, 'Ets Haim. Tradition and Innovation in Jewish Education' (unpublished MA thesis, Columbia University, 2006)

BERMEJO CABRERO, JOSÉ LUIS, 'Apuntamientos sobre la vida y escritos de Diego de Simancas', in *El derecho y los juristas en Salamanca (siglos XVI–XX). En memoria de Francisco Tomás y Valiente*, ed. by Eugenia Torijano Pérez, Salustiano de Dios and Javier Infante Miguel-Motta (Salamanca: Ediciones Universidad de Salamanca, 2004), pp. 567–88

BERMÚDEZ VÁZQUEZ, MANUEL, *The Skepticism of Michel de Montaigne* (Dordrecht: Springer, 2015)

BERRIOT, FRANÇOIS, *Athéisme et athéistes au XVIe siècle en France*, 2 vols (Lille: Presses Universitaires de Lille, 1984)

——*Spiritualités, hétérodoxies et imaginaires. Études sur le Moyen Âge et la Renaissance* (Saint-Étienne: Université de Saint-Étienne, 1994)

BESNIER, BERNARD, 'Sanchez à demi endormi', in *Le Scepticisme au XVIe et au XVIIe siècle. II, Le Retour des philosophies antiques à l'âge classique*, ed. by Pierre-François Moreau (Paris: Albin Michel, 2001), pp. 102–20

Biblia sacra iuxta Vulgatam Clementinam, ed. by Alberto Colunga and Lorenzo Turrado (Madrid: Biblioteca de Autores Cristianos, 1994)

Biographisch woordenboek van protestantsche godgeleerden in Nederland, 6 vols (Utrecht: Nijhoff, 1907–49)

Biographisch-Bibliographisches Kirchenlexicon, 37 vols (Hamm: Bautz, 1975–2016)

BIONDI, ALBANO, 'La giustificazione della simulazione nel Cinquecento', in *Eresia e riforma nell'Italia del Cinquecento: miscellanea I* (Florence: Sansoni; Chicago, IL: The Newberry Library, 1974), pp. 7–68

BIRELEY, ROBERT, *The Counter-Reformation Prince: Anti-Machiavellianism or Catholic Statecraft in Early Modern Europe* (Chapel Hill: University of North Carolina Press, 1990)

BLEDA, JAIME, *Corónica de los moros de España diuidida en ocho libros* (Valencia: Felipe Mey, 1618; A Coruña: Órbigo, 2015)

BLOCH, R. HOWARD, 'Mieux vaut jamais que tard: Romance, Philology, and Old French Letters', *Representations*, 36 (1991), 64–86

BODIAN, MIRIAM, *Dying in the Law of Moses: Crypto-Jewish Martyrdom in the Iberian World* (Bloomington: Indiana University Press, 2007)

——*Hebrews of the Portuguese Nation: Conversos and Community in Early Modern Amsterdam* (Bloomington: Indiana University Press, 1997)

——'In the Cross-Currents of the Reformation: Crypto-Jewish Martyrs of the Inquisition, 1570–1670', *Past and Present*, 176 (2002), 66–104

——'The Geography of Conscience: A Seventeenth-Century Atlantic Jew and the Inquisition', *The Journal of Modern History*, 89.2 (2017), 247–81

BOER, HARM DEN, 'Exile in Sephardic Literature of Amsterdam', *Studia Rosenthaliana*, 35.2 (2001), 187–99

——'Le 'contre-discours' des nouveaux juifs. Esprit et polémique dans la littérature des juifs sépharades d'Amsterdam', in *Les Sépharades en littérature. Un parcours millénaire*, ed. by Esther Benbassa (Paris: PUPS, 2005), pp. 47–65

——'Ovid und die verspotteten Götter des spanischen Barock', in *Carmen perpetuum. Ovids Metamorphosen in der Weltliteratur*, ed. by Henriette Harich-Schwarzbauer and Alexander Honold (Basel: Schwabe Basel, 2013), pp. 131–49

——'Perfil literario de Samuel Mendes de Sola', in *A Sefardic Pepper-Pot in the Caribbean: History, Language, Literature, and Art*, ed. by Michael Studemund-Halévy (Barcelona: Tirocinio, 2016), pp. 327–61

——*La literatura sefardí de Amsterdam* (Alcalá de Henares: Instituto Internacional de Estudios Sefardíes y Andalusíes, 1995)

BOLOGNA, FERDINANDO, *L'Incredulità di Caravaggio e l'esperienza delle 'cose naturali'* (Turin: Bollati Boringhieri, 1992)

BOURETZ, PIERRE, *Lumières du Moyen Âge. Maïmonide philosophe* (Paris: Gallimard, 2016)

BOUTRY, PHILIPPE, PIERRE-ANTOINE FABRE and DOMINIQUE JULIA, eds, *Reliques modernes. Cultes et usages chrétiens des corps saints des Réformes aux Révolutions*, 2 vols (Paris: Éditions de l'EHESS, 2009)

BOUZA, FERNANDO, and JOSÉ LUIS BETRÁN, *Olvidados de la Historia. Enanos, bufones, monstruos, brujos y hechiceros: marginales* (Barcelona: Debolsillo, 2005)

BRAUN, HARALD E., 'Baroque Constitution and Hybrid Political Language: The Case of Juan de Mariana (1535–1624) and Juan Márquez (1565–1621)', *Revista Canadiense de Estudios Hispánicos*, 33 (2008), 79–104

BREWER, KEAGAN, *Prester John: The Legend and its Sources* (Farnham: Ashgate, 2015)

BROGGIO, PAOLO, CHARLOTTE DE CASTELNAU-L'ESTOILE, and GIOVANNI PIZZORUSSO, eds, 'Administrer les sacrements en Europe et au Nouveau Monde. La Curie romaine et les *dubia circa sacramenta*', *Mélanges de l'École française de Rome, Italie et Méditerranée*, 121.1 (2009), 5–217

BROWN, KENNETH, *De la cárcel Inquisitorial a la sinagoga de Amsterdam (Edición y estudio del 'Romance a Lope de Vera' de Antonio Enríquez Gómez)* (Toledo: Consejería de Cultura de Castilla-La Mancha, 2007)

BROWN, KENNETH, and HARM DEN BOER, *El barroco sefardí. Abraham Gómez Silveira, Arévalo 1656–Amsterdam 1740* (Kassel: Reichenberger, 2001)

BRÜLL, NEHEMIAH, *Jahrbücher für Jüdische Geschichte und Literatur*, 7 vols (Frankfurt am Main: W. Erras, 1874–85)

BUBER, MARTIN, *Two Types of Faith* (New York: Macmillan, 1950)

BUDDE, JOHANN FRANZ, *Theses theologicae de atheismo et superstitione variis observationibus illustratae et in usum recitationum academicarum editae* (Jena: Joan. Felic. Bielckium, 1717)

BULTMANN, RUDOLF, and ARTUR WEISER, *Faith* (London: Black, 1961)

BURGIO, SANTO, 'Gnostici, libertini, probabilisti. La perversa genealogia di John Sinnich', in *Filosofia e storiografia. Studi in onore di Giovanni Papuli. II. Età Moderna*, ed. by S. Ciurla, E. De Bellis. G. Iaccarino, A. Novembre and A. Paladini (Galatina: Congedo, 2008), pp. 5–15

—— *Teologia barocca. Il probabilismo in Sicilia nell'epoca di Filippo IV* (Catania: Società di Storia Patria per la Sicilia Orientale, 1998)

BUSSON, HENRI, 'Les Noms des incrédules au XVIe siècle', *Bibliothèque d'Humanisme et Renaissance*, 16 (1954), 273–83

—— *Le Rationalisme dans la littérature française de la Renaissance*, 3rd edn (Paris: Vrin, 1971)

CALDERÓN DE LA BARCA, PEDRO, *El orden de Melquisedec*, ed. by Ignacio Pérez Ibáñez. Autos Sacramentales Completos de Calderón, 49 (Kassel: Reichenberger, 2005)

—— *El socorro general*, ed. by Ignacio Arellano. Autos Sacramentales Completos de Calderón, 33 (Kassel: Reichenberger, 2001)

CALUORI, DAMIAN, 'The Scepticism of Francisco Sanchez', *Archiv für Geschichte der Philosophie*, 89 (2007), 30–46

CALVESI, MAURIZIO, *Le realtà del Caravaggio* (Turin: Einaudi, 1990)

CAMPANELLA, TOMMASO, *L'Ateismo trionfato, overo Riconoscimento filosofico della religione universale contra l'antichristianesmo macchiavellesco*, ed. by Germana Ernst, 2 vols (Pisa: Edizioni della Normale, 2004)

CANFORA, LUCIANO, *Il Fozio ritrovato. Juan de Mariana e André Schott* (Bari: Dedalo, 2001)

—— *Convertire Casaubon* (Milan: Adelphi, 2002)

CANO, MELCHOR, *De locis theologicis libri duodeci* (Salamanca: Matías Gast, 1563)

CANOVAN, MARGARET, 'Friendship, Truth, and Politics: Hannah Arendt and Toleration', in *Justifying Toleration: Conceptual and Historical Perspectives*, ed. by Susan Mendus (Cambridge: Cambridge University Press, 1988), pp. 177–98

CANTIMORI, DELIO, *Eretici italiani del Cinquecento e altri scritti*, ed. by Adriano Prosperi (Turin: Einaudi, 1992)

CANZIANI, GUIDO, and GIANNI PAGANINI, eds, *Theophrastus redivivus*, 2 vols (Florence: La Nuova Italia, 1981–82)

CAO, GIAN M., 'Savonarola e Sesto Empirico,' in *Pico, Poliziano e l'umanesimo di fine Quattrocento*, ed. by Paolo Viti (Florence: L. S. Olschki, 1994), pp. 231–45

—— *Scepticism and Orthodoxy: Gianfrancesco Pico as a Reader of Sextus Empiricus. With a facing text of Pico's Quotations from Sextus* (Pisa and Rome: Serra, 2007)

CAPSALI, ELIYAHU, *El judaísmo hispano según la crónica hebrea de Rabí Eliyahu Capsali, traducción y estudio del 'Seder Eliyahu Zuṭa' (capítulos 40–70)*, ed. and trans. by Yolanda Moreno Koch (Granada: Universidad de Granada, 2005)

CAPUTO, JOHN D., *The Prayers and Tears of Jacques Derrida: Religion without Religion* (Bloomington: Indiana University Press, 1997)

CARAMUEL, JUAN, *Apologema pro antiquisima et universalissima doctrina de probabilitate, contra nouam, singularem improbabilemque D. Prosperi Fagnani opiniationem* (Lyon: Laurent Anisson, 1663)

——*Theologia moralis ad prima, eaque clarissima principia reducta* (Leuven: Petrus Zangrius, 1645)

CARDOSO, SÉRGIO, 'On Skeptical Fideism in Montaigne's *Apology for Raymond Sebond*', in *Skepticism in the Modern Age: Building on the Work of Richard Popkin*, ed. by José R. Maia Neto, John Christian Laursen and Gianni Paganini (Leiden: Brill, 2009), pp. 71–82

CARO BAROJA, JULIO, *De la superstición al ateísmo. Meditaciones antropológicas* (Madrid: Taurus, 1974)

——*Las formas complejas de la vida religiosa (religión, sociedad y carácter en la España de los siglos XVI y XVII)* (Madrid: Akal, 1978)

——*Vidas mágicas e Inquisición*, 2 vols (Madrid: Taurus, 1967)

CARRETE PARRONDO, CARLOS, *Fontes iudaeorum Regni Castellae II: (1486–1502). El Tribunal de la Inquisición en el Obispado de Soria* (Salamanca: Universidad Pontificia, 1985)

——'Dos ejemplos del primitivo criptojudaísmo en Cuenca', *El Olivo. Documentación y estudios para el diálogo entre Judíos y Cristianos*, 13.29–30 (1989), 63–69

CARRIÓN MORA, ADELINA, *Médicos e Inquisición en el siglo XVII* (Cuenca: Universidad de Castilla–La Mancha, 2006)

CASTELLANI, ANNA, ed., *L'Anfitrione ovvero la modernità di Plauto* (Florence: Le Monnier, 1995)

CASTRO, ALONSO DE, *De Iusta Haereticorum punitione libri tres* (Salamanca: Juan de Junta, 1547)

CÁTEDRA, PEDRO, *Sermón, sociedad y literatura en la Edad Media. San Vicente Ferrer en Castilla (1411–1412)* (Valladolid: Junta de Castilla y León, 1994)

CAVAILLÉ, JEAN-PIERRE, 'La Question de l'irréligion populaire, à la rencontré de l'histoire et de l'anthropologie', *Institut d'histoire de la Réformation. Bulletin Annuel*, 36 (2014–15), 55–69

——'Les Frontiers de l'inacceptable. Pour un réexamen de l'histoire de l'incrédulité', *Les Dossiers du Grihl* (2007) <https://dossiersgrihl.revues.org/4746> [accessed 18/04/ 2017]

——'Libertinage, irréligion, incroyance, athéisme dans l'Europe de la première modernité (XVIe–XVIIe siècles). Une approche critique des tendances actuelles de la recherche (1998–2002)', *Les Dossiers du Grihl* (2007) <http:/dossiersgrihl.revues.org/279> [accessed 21 April 2017]

——*Dis/simulations. Religion, morale et politique au XVIIe siècle. Jules-César Vanini, François La Mothe Le Vayer, Gabriel Naudé, Louis Machon et Torquato Accetto* (Paris: Honoré Champion, 2002)

——*Les Déniaisés. Irréligion et libertinage au début de l'époque moderne* (Paris: Classiques Garnier, 2014)

——*Postures libertines. La culture des esprits forts* (Toulouse: Anacharsis, 2011)

CAVINI, WALTER, 'Appunti sulla prima diffusione in Occidente delle opere di Sesto Empirico', *Medioevo. Rivista di Storia della Filosofia Medievale*, 7 (1977), 1–20

CERUTTI, SIMONA, and GIANNA POMATA, 'Premessa', *Quaderni storici*, 36.108 (2001), 647–63

CHARBONNEL, J. ROGER, *La Pensée italienne au XVIe siècle et le courant libertin* (Paris: E. Champion, 1919)

CHIFFOLEAU, JACQUES, ' "Ecclesia de occultis non iudicat". L'Eglise, le secret et l'occulte du XIIe au XVe siècle', *Micrologus. Nature, Sciences and Medieval Societies*, 13 (2006), 359–481

COENEN, LOTHAR, 'Testimonio', in *Diccionario Teológico del Nuevo Testamento* (Madrid: Sígueme, 1980), pp. 254–61

Colección de Cortes de los reynos de León y de Castilla (Madrid: Real Academia de la Historia, 1836)

COLEMAN, DAVID, *Creating Christian Granada. Society and Religious Culture in an Old-World Frontier City, 1492–1600* (Ithaca, NY: Cornell University Press, 2003)

COLERIDGE, SAMUEL TAYLOR, *The Literary Remains of Samuel Taylor Coleridge*, vol. I (London: W. Pickering, 1836)

COLISH, MARCIA L., 'Republicanism, Religion, and Machiavelli's Savonarolan Moment', *Journal of the History of Ideas*, 60.4 (1999), 597–616

Collected Works of Erasmus (Toronto: University of Toronto Press, 1974)

[COLLINS, ANTHONY], *A discourse of free-thinking, occasion'd by the rise and growth of a sect call'd Free-Thinkers* (London: [n. pub.], 1713)

CONDORCET, MARQUIS DE (Jean-Antoine-Nicolas de Caritat), *Esquisse d'un tableau historique des progrès de l'esprit humain; (suivi de) Fragment sur l'Atlantide*, ed. by Alain Pons (Paris: Flammarion, 1988)

——*Œuvres complètes de Condorcet*, vol. VII (Brunswick: Vieweg; Paris: Henrichs, 1804)

COPELAND, RITA and INEKE SLUITER, eds, *Medieval Grammar and Rhetoric: Language Arts and Literary Theory, AD 300–1475* (Oxford: Oxford University Press, 2009)

Corpus Iuris Canonici, ed. by Emil Friedberg, 2 vols (Leipzig: Tauchnitz, 1879–81)

COUPLET, PHILIPPE, and PROSPERO INTORCETA, *Confucius, Sinarum philosophus, sive Scientia sinensis* (Paris: Daniel Horthemels, 1687)

CRUZ CRUZ, JUAN, 'Interpretación de la ley según Juan de Salas (1553–1612)', *Cuadernos de Pensamiento Español*, 44 (2011), 9–103

CUTINELLI-RÈNDINA, EMANUELE, *Chiesa e religione in Machiavelli* (Pisa and Rome: Istituti editoriali e poligrafici internazionali, 1998)

DA COSTA, URIEL, *Exame das tradições phariseas, Esame delle tradizioni farisee (1624)*, ed. and trans. by Omero Proietti (Macerata: Università di Macerata, 2014)

——*Examination of Pharisaic Traditions*, trans. and intro. by H. P. Salomon and Isaac S. D. Sassoon (Leiden: Brill, 1993)

——*Une vie humaine*, trans. by Abraham B. Duff and Pierre Kahn (Paris: F. Rieder, 1926)

DARST, DAVID H., *Diego Hurtado de Mendoza* (Boston, MA: Twayne, 1987)

DAVIDSON, NICHOLAS, 'Unbelief and Atheism in Italy, 1500–1700', in *Atheism from the Reformation to the Enlightenment*, ed. by Michael Hunter and David Wootton (New York: Clarendon Press, 1992), pp. 55–85

DAVIS, ROBERT and BENJAMIN RAVID, eds, *The Jews of Early Modern Venice* (Baltimore, MD: Johns Hopkins University Press, 2001)

DELICADO, FRANCISCO, *La lozana andaluza*, ed. by Claude Allaigre (Madrid: Cátedra, 1985)

DENERY II, DALLAS G., *The Devil Wins: A History of Lying from the Garden of Eden to the Enlightenment* (Princeton, NJ: Princeton University Press, 2015)

DERRIDA, JACQUES, *The Death Penalty*, vol. 1, ed. by Geoffrey Bennington, Marc Crépon and Thomas Dutoit, trans. by Peggy Kamuf (Chicago, IL: University of Chicago Press, 2014)

DIANA, ANTONINO, *Summa Diana: in qua R.P.D. Antonini Diana... Clerici Regul... opera omnia, Diana ipso committente [et] approbante, Ausonio verò Noctinot Siculo Tertii Ordinis S. Francisci operam dante, in vnicum volumen, duabus partibus distinctum, arctantur: cum additionibus cruce notatis ...: accessit in marginibus Breuiarium* (Valencia: Claudio Macè, 1645)

Dictionnaire de Théologie catholique: contenant l'exposé des doctrines de la théologie catholique, leurs preuves et leur histoire, ed. by Alfred Vacant and Eugène Mangenot, 36 vols (Paris: Letouzey et Ané, 1967–72)

Diccionario de Historia Eclesiástica de España, ed. by Quintín Aldea Vaquero, 5 vols (Madrid: Instituto Enrique Flórez, Consejo Superior de Investigaciones Científicas, 1972–87)

DOMINGO MALVADI, ARANTXA, *Bibliofilia humanista en tiempos de Felipe II. La Biblioteca de Juan Páez de Castro* (Salamanca: Universidad de Salamanca, 2011)

DOMÍNGUEZ ORTIZ, ANTONIO, and BERNARD VINCENT, *Historia de los moriscos, vida y tragedia de una minoría* (Madrid: Revista de Occidente, 1978)

DORMER, DIEGO JOSÉ, *Anales de Aragón: desde el año MDXXV ... hasta el de MDXL* (Zaragoza: herederos de Diego Dormer, 1697)

DUBOST, JEAN-FRANÇOIS, *La France italienne, XVIe–XVIIe siècle* (Paris: Aubier, 1997)

DUDON, PAUL, *Le Quiétiste espagnol Michel Molinos (1628–1696)* (Paris: Gabriel Beauchesne, 1921)

DULLES, AVERY, *The Assurance of Things Hoped For: A Theology of Christian Faith* (Oxford: Oxford University Press, 1994)

DUPREAU, GABRIEL (Prateolus), *Elenchus haereticorum omnium, qui ab orbe condito ad nostra vsque tempora veterumque and recentium auctorum monimentis prodidi sunt: vitas, sectas and dogmata complectens: alphabetico ordine digestus: cum eorundem haereticorum origine* [...]. 3rd edn (Köln: Arnold Quentell, 1605)

DURY, JOHN, 'An Epistolicall Discourse of Mr. Iohn Dury to Mr. Thorowgood', in Thomas Thorowgood, *Iewes in America, or, Probabilities that the Americans are of that race* (London: T. Slater, 1650)

[DU VAUCEL, LOUIS-PAUL], *Breves considerationes in doctrinam Michelis de Molinos et aliorum quietistarum* (Cologne: Nicolaum Shouten, 1688)

EDWARDS, JOHN, 'Religious Faith and Doubt in Late Medieval Spain: Soria circa 1450–1500', *Past & Present*, 120 (1988), 3–25

—— *Religion and Society in Spain, c.1492* (Aldershot: Variorum, 1996)

EGIDO, AURORA, *La búsqueda de la inmortalidad en las obras de Baltasar Gracián* (Madrid: Real Academia Española, 2014)

ELLACURÍA BEASCOECHEA, JESÚS, *Reacción española contra las ideas de Miguel de Molinos (procesos de la Inquisición y refutación de los teólogos)* ([Bilbao]: [Gráf. Ellacuria], 1956)

ELLEDGE, C. D., *Resurrection of the Dead in Early Judaism, 200 BCE–CE 200* (Oxford: Oxford University Press, 2017)

ELLIOTT, JOHN H., *Imperial Spain, 1469–1716* (New York: St Martin's Press, 1964)

—— *The Revolt of the Catalans* (London: Cambridge University Press, 1963)

EMANUEL, SIMHA, *Sheelot W Teshuvot Ha-Geonim*, ed. by A. Shoshana (Jerusalem: Makhon Ofeq, 1995)

ERASMUS, DESIDERIUS, *Collected Works of Erasmus. 3. Letters 298 to 445*, trans. by R. A. B. Mynors and D. F. S. Thomson (Buffalo, Toronto: University of Toronto Press, 1976)

—— 'Enchiridion militis Christiani', in *Ausgewählte Werke*, ed. by Annemarie Holborn and Hajo Holborn (München: C. H. Beck, 1933), pp. 1–136

—— *Moria de Erasmo Roterodamo. A Critical Edition of the Early Modern Spanish Translation of Erasmus's Encomium Moriae*, ed. by Jorge Ledo and Harm den Boer (Leiden: Brill, 2014)

—— *Opera omnia Desiderii Erasmi Roterodami* (Amsterdam: [n.p], 1969)

ERNST, GERMANA, *Tommaso Campanella. The Book and the Body of Nature* (Dordrecht: Springer, 2010)

——, ed., *De tribus impostoribus*, 2nd edn (Naples: La Scuola di Pitagora, 2009)

ESPOSITO, MARIO, 'Una manifestazione d'incredulità religiosa nel medioevo. Il detto dei "Tre impostori" e la sua trasmissione da Federico II a Pomponazzi', *Archivio Storico Italiano*, s.VII, 16 (1931), 3–48

FALCK, NATHANAEL, *Nathanaelis Falcken, d. ss. theol. in gymn: dissertationes quatuor, de dæmonologia recentiorum autorum falsa, anno 1692. Wittebergæ habitæ, nunc vero præfixis literis Schomerianis ibidem recusæ*, 2nd edn ([Wittenberg]: M. Schultz, 1694)

FANTAPPIÈ, CARLO, *Chiesa romana e modernità giuridica. Vol. II, L'edificazione del sistema canonistico (1563–1903)* (Milan: Giuffrè, 2008)

FAREL, GUILLAUME, *Le Glaive de la parole veritable* (Geneva: Jean Girard, 1550)

FARINACCI, PROSPERO, *Tractatus de haeresi* (Anvers: Ioannem Keerbergium, 1616)

FEBVRE, LUCIEN, *Au cœur religieuse du XVIe siècle* (Paris: SEVPEN-Bibliothèque générale de l'École pratique des hautes études, 1957)

—— *Le Problème de l'incroyance au XVIe siècle. La Religion de Rabelais* (Paris: Albin Michel, 1942).

FEITLER, BRUNO, *The Imaginary Synagogue: Anti-Jewish Literature in the Portuguese Early Modern World (16th–18th Centuries)* (Leiden: Brill, 2015)

FERNÁNDEZ, ENRIQUE, 'El cordón de Melibea y los remedios de amor en La Celestina', *La Corónica*, 42.1 (2013), 79–99

FIRPO, MASSIMO, *Juan de Valdés and the Italian Reformation* (Farnham: Ashgate, 2015)

——, and DARIO MARCATTO (eds), *I processi inquisitoriali di Pietro Carnesecchi, 1557–1567*, 2 vols (Vatican City: Archivio Segreto Vaticano, 1998–2000)

FLANAGAN, SABINA, *Doubt in an Age of Faith: Uncertainty in the Long Twelfth Century* (Turnhout: Brepols, 2008)

FLEMING, JULIA, *Defending Probabilism: The Moral Theology of Juan Caramuel* (Washington, DC: Georgetown University Press, 2006)

FLORIDI, LUCIANO, *Sextus Empiricus: The Transmission and Recovery of Pyrrhonism* (Oxford: Oxford University Press, 2002)

—— 'The Diffusion of Sextus Empiricus's Works in the Renaissance', *Journal of the History of Ideas*, 56 (1995), 63–85

—— 'The Grafted Branches of the Sceptical Tree: *Noli altum sapere* and Henri Stephanus' Latin Edition of *Sexti Empirici Pyrrhoniam Hypotyposeon libri III*', *Nouvelles de la République des Lettres*, 11 (1992), 127–66

FLÜCKIGER, FABRICE, *Dire le vrai. Une histoire de la dispute religieuse au début du XVIe siècle. Ancienne confédération helvétique, 1523–1536* (Neuchâtel: Alphil-Presses universitaires suisses, 2018)

FONSECA, DAMIÁN, *Ivsta expvlsión de los moriscos de España, con la instrvcción, apostasía, y trayción dellos, y respuesta a las dudas que se ofrecieron acerca desta materia* (Rome: Iacomo Mascardo, 1612)

Fontes Narrativi de S. Ignatio de Loyola. Vol. I, Narrationes scriptae ante annum 1557, ed. by Dionisio Fernández Zapico and Cándido de Dalmases (Rome: Monumenta Historica Societatis Iesu, 1943)

Fontes Narrativi de S. Ignatio de Loyola. Vol. II, Narrationes scriptae annis 1557–74, ed. by Cándido de Dalmases (Rome: Monumenta Historica Societatis Iesu, 1951)

FOULCHÉ-DELBOSC, RAYMOND, 'Mechanica de Aristotiles', *Révue Hispanique*, 5 (1898), 365–405

FOWLER, JESSICA J., 'Assembling Alumbradismo: The Evolution of a Heretical Construct', in *After Conversion: Iberia and the Emergence of Modernity*, ed. by M. García-Arenal (Leiden: Brill, 2016), pp. 251–82

FRAGONARD, MARIE-MADELEINE, 'La Détermination des frontières symboliques. Nommer et définir les groupes hérétiques', in *Les frontières religieuses en Europe du XVe au XVIIe siècle. Actes du XXXIe colloque international d'études humanistes*, ed. by Robert Sauzet (Paris: Vrin, 1992), pp. 37–49

FRIMER, NORMAN E., and DOV SCHWARTZ, *The Life and Thought of Shem Tov Ibn Shaprut* (in Hebrew) (Jerusalem: Ben-Zvi Institute, 1992)

FUKS, LAJB, and RENA G. FUKS-MANSFELD, *Catalogue of the Manuscripts of Ets Haim, Livraria Montezinos, Sephardic Community of Amsterdam* (Leiden: Brill, 1975)

FUKS-MANSFELD, RENA G., *De Sefardim in Amsterdam tot 1795. Aspecten van een joodse minderheid in een Hollandse stad* (Hilversum: Uitgeverij Verloren, 1989)

FUMAROLI, MARC, *Le Sablier renversé. Des Modernes aux Anciens* (Paris: Gallimard, 2013)

GAMPEL, BENJAMIN, 'A Letter to a Wayward Teacher: The Transformations of Sephardic Culture in Christian Iberia', in *Cultures of the Jews: A New History*, ed. by David Biale (New York: Schocken Books, 2002), pp. 389–447

GARASSE, FRANÇOIS, *La Doctrine curieuse des beaux esprits de ce temps ou prétendus tels* (Paris: Chappelet, 1623)

GARCÍA-ARENAL, MERCEDES, 'A Catholic Muslim Prophet: Agustín de Ribera, "The Boy Who Saw Angels"', *Common Knowledge*, 18.2 (2012), 267–91

—— *Inquisición y moriscos, los procesos del Tribunal de Cuenca* (Madrid: SigloXXI, 1978)

—— 'L'Estompe des identités en situation de conversion. Isaac Pallache, un converti insincère?', in *Les Musulmans dans l'histoire de l' Europe*, ed. by Jocelyne Dakhlia and Wolfgang Kaiser, 2 vols (Paris: Albin Michel, 2013), II, 35–60

—— '"Mi padre moro, yo moro": The Inheritance of Belief in Early Modern Iberia', in *After Conversion. Iberia and the Emergence of Modernity*, ed. by M. García-Arenal (Leiden: Brill, 2016), pp. 304–35

——, ed., *After Conversion: Iberia and the Emergence of Modernity* (Leiden: Brill, 2016)

GARCÍA-ARENAL, MERCEDES, and FERNANDO RODRÍGUEZ MEDIANO, *The Orient in Spain: Converted Muslims, the Forged Lead Books of Granada and the Rise of Orientalism* (Leiden: Brill, 2013)

GARCÍA-ARENAL, MERCEDES, and GERARD WIEGERS, eds, *Polemical Encounters: Christians, Jews and Muslims in Iberia and Beyond* (University Park: Pennsylvania State University Press, 2018)

GARCÍA GILBERT, JAVIER, 'Medios humanos y medios divinos en Baltasar Gracián (la dialéctica ficcional del aforismo 251)', *Criticón*, 73 (1998), 61–82

GARCÍA PALACIOS, JOAQUÍN, *Los procesos de conocimiento en San Juan de la Cruz. Estudio léxico* (Salamanca: Universidad de Salamanca, 1992)

GARROT ZAMBRANA, JUAN CARLOS, *Judíos y conversos en Corpus Christi. La dramatugia calderoniana*. Etudes Renaissantes, 10 (Turnhout: Brepols, 2013)

GAY, JEAN-PASCAL, '*Doctrina Societatis*? Le Rapport entre probabilisme et discernement des esprits dans la culture jésuite (XVIe–XVIIe siècles)', in *Le Discernement spirituel au dix-septième siècle*, ed. by Simon Icard (Paris: Nolin, 2011), pp. 23–46

—— *Jesuit Civil Wars: Theology, Politics and Government under Tirso González (1687–1705)* (Farnham: Ashgate, 2012)

GEBHARDT, CARL, ed., *Die Schriften des Uriel da Costa* (Amsterdam: Menno Hertzberger, 1922)

[GENTILLET, INNOCENT], *Discours sur les moyens de bien gouverner et maintenir en bonne paix un royaume ou autre principauté. Divisez en trois parties: asavoir, du conseil, de la religion, et police que doit tenir un prince. Contre Nicolas Machiavel Florentin. A treshaut et tres-illustre prince François duc d'Alençon, fils et frère de roy*, 3rd edn ([n.p.], 1579)

GILBERT, ALLAN H., ED. and TRANS., *Machiavelli: The Chief Works and Others*, 6th edn, 3 vols (Durham, NC, and London: Duke University Press, 1999)

GINZBURG, CARLO, 'The Dovecote Has Opened its Eyes: Popular Conspiracy in Seventeenth-Century Italy', in *The Inquisition in Early Modern Europe: Studies on Sources and Methods*, ed. by Gustav Henningsen and John Tedeschi (DeKalb: Northern Illinois University Press, 1986), pp. 190–98

—— *The Cheese and the Worms: The Cosmos of a Sixteenth-Century Miller* (Baltimore, MD: Johns Hopkins University Press, 1980)

—— *Il Nicodemismo. Simulazione e dissimulazione religiosa nell' Europa del 500* (Turin: Einaudi, 1970)

GIOVIO, PAOLO, *Historiarum sui temporis*, ed. by Dante Visconti, 2 vols (Rome: Istituto poligrafico dello Stato, Libreria dello Stato, 1957)

GIRARD, RENÉ, 'Comedies of Errors: Plautus-Shakespeare-Molière', in *American Criticism in the Poststructuralist Age*, ed. by Ira Konigsberg (Ann Arbor: University of Michigan Press, 1981), pp. 66–86

GITLITZ, DAVID M., 'Hybrid Conversos in the *Libro llamado el Alboraique*', *Hispanic Review*, 60 (1992), 1–17

—— *Secrecy and Deceit: The Religion of the Crypto-Jews* (Albuquerque: University of New Mexico Press, 1996)

GLASENAPP, GABRIELE VON, 'Vom edlen Freunde. Lessing in der jüdischen Historiographie', in *Lessing und das Judentum. Lektüren, Dialoge, Kontroversen*, ed. by Dirk Niefanger, Gunnar Och and Birka Siwczyk (Hildesheim, Zurich, and New York: Olms, 2015), pp. 163–82

GLASER, EDWARD, 'Invitation to Intolerance: A Study of Portuguese Sermons Preached at Autos-da-Fé', *Hebrew Union College Annual*, 27 (1956), 327–85

GODARD DE DONVILLE, LOUISE, *Le Libertin des origines à 1665. Un produit des apologètes* (Paris, Seattle and Tübingen: Biblio 17-Papers on French Seventeenth Century Literature, 1989)

GOLDSTEIN, BERNARD R., 'The Astronomical Tables of Judah ben Verga', *Suhayl*, 2 (2001), 227–89

GOLDSTOFF-FRANK, AMIRA, 'Shinuy ha-shem ba-miqra', *Mikhlol*, 16 (1998), 20–26

GOMBRICH, ERNST H., *Art and Illusion: A Study in the Psychology of Pictorial Representation* (London: Phaidon, 1983)

GÓMEZ, ELÍAS, *Fr. Juan Falconi de Bustamante, teólogo y asceta (1569–1638)* (Madrid: Escuela de Historia Moderna-CSIC, 1956)

GÓMEZ CANSECO, LUIS M., *El humanismo después de 1600. Pedro de Valencia* (Seville: Publicaciones de la Universidad de Sevilla, 1993)

GÓMEZ SILVEIRA, ABRAHAM, *Sermones compuestos por Abraham Gomes Silveira* (Amsterdam: Moséh Díaz, 5437 [1675–76])

GONZÁLEZ PALENCIA, ÁNGEL, *Historias y leyendas. Estudios literarios* (Madrid: Consejo Superior de Investigaciones Científicas, 1942)

——, and EUGENIO MELE, *Vida y obras de don Diego Hurtado de Mendoza*, 3 vols (Madrid: Instituto de Valencia de don Juan, 1941–43)

GONZÁLEZ POLVILLO, ANTONIO, *Análisis y repertorio de los tratados y manuales para la confesión en el mundo hispánico (ss. XV–XVIII)* (Huelva: Universidad de Huelva, 2009)

GRACIÁN, BALTASAR, *Obras completas*, ed. by Emilio Blanco, 2 vols (Madrid: Biblioteca Castro-Turner, 1993)

—— *Oráculo manual y arte de prudencia*, ed. by Emilio Blanco (Madrid: Cátedra, 1995)

—— *The Pocket Oracle and Art of Prudence*, trans. with introduction and notes by Jeremy Robbins (London: Penguin, 2011)

GRACIÁN DE LA MADRE DE DIOS, JERÓNIMO, *Diez lamentaciones del miserable estado de los ateístas de nuestro tiempo*, ed. by Emilia Navarro de Kelley (Madrid: Editora Nacional, 1977)

—— *Tratado de la redención de cautivos*, ed. by Miguel Ángel de Bunes and Beatriz Alonso (Seville: Espuela de Plata, 2006)

GRAETZ, HEINRICH, *History of the Jews. Vol. V* (Philadelphia, PA: Jewish Publication Society of America, 1895)

GRANADA, MIGUEL A., 'Apologétique platonicienne et apologétique sceptique. Ficin, Savonarole, Jean-François Pic de la Mirandole', in *Le Scepticisme au XVIe et au XVIIe siècle. Le Retour des philosophies antiques à l'âge classique, vol. II*, ed. by P. F. Moreau (Paris: Albin Michel, 2001), pp. 11–47

—— 'Francisco Sanchez et les courants critiques de la philosophie du XVIe siècle', *Bruniana e Campanelliana*, 15.1 (2009), 29–45

GRAUX, CHARLES, *Essai sur les origines du Fonds grec de l'Escorial* (Paris: Bibliothèque de l'École des Hautes Études, 1880)

GREGORY, BRAD S. 'The Other Confessional History: On Secular Bias in the Study of Religion', *History & Theory*, 45 (2006), 132–49

——— *The Unintended Reformation: How a Religious Revolution Secularized Society* (Cambridge, MA: Belknap Press of Harvard University Press, 2012)

GRIFFITHS, NICHOLAS, 'Popular Religious Scepticism and Idiosyncrasy in Post-Tridentine Cuenca', in *Faith and Fanaticism: Religious Fervour in Early Modern Spain*, ed. by Lesley Twomey (Aldershot: Ashgate, 1997), pp. 95–128

GROTIUS, HUGO, *De jure belli ac paci libri tres* (Paris: Nicolaum Buon, 1625)

——— *Remonstrantie nopende de ordre dije in landen van Hollandt ende Westvrieslandt dijent gestelt op de Joden*, ed. by Jacob Meijer (Amsterdam: [n. pub.], 1949)

——— *The Rights of War and Peace*, ed. by Richard Tuck, trans. by A. C. Campbell (Indianapolis: Liberty Fund, 2005) <http://oll.libertyfund.org/titles/1425>

GUTAS, DIMITRI. *Greek Thought, Arabic Culture: The Graeco-Arabic Translation Movement in Baghdad and Early Abbasid Societ (2nd–4th/8th–10th centuries)* (London and New York: Routledge, 1998)

GUTIÉRREZ HACES, JUANA, '¿La pintura novohispana como una koiné pictórica americana? Avances de una investigación en ciernes', *Anales del Instituto de Investigaciones Estéticas*, 80 (2002), 47–99

GUTWIRTH, ELEAZAR, 'Creative Ambiguities and Jewish Modernity', in *Schöpferische Momente des europäischen Judentums in der frühen Neuzeit*, ed. by Michael Graetz (Heidelberg: Winter, 2000), pp. 63–73

——— 'El gobernador judío ideal. Acerca de un sermon inédito de Yosef Ibn Shem Tob', in *Actas del III Congreso Internacional Encuentro de las Tres Culturas (Toledo, 15–17 de octubre de 1984)*, ed. by Carlos Carrete Parrondo (Toledo: Ayuntamiento de Toledo / Tel-Aviv University, 1988), pp. 67–75

——— ' "Entendudos": Translation and Representation in the Castile of Alfonso the Learned', *The Modern Language Review*, 93 (1998), 384–99

——— 'Historians in Context: Jewish Historiography in the Fifteenth and Sixteenth Centuries', *Frankfurter Judaistischer Beiträge*, 30 (2003), 147–68

——— 'History and Jewish Scientific Study in Mediaeval Spain', in *La ciencia en la España medieval. Musulmanes, judíos y cristianos. Actas del VII Congreso internacional 'Encuentro de las Tres Culturas'*, ed. by Lola Ferré, José Ramón Ayaso and María José Cano (Granada: Universidad de Granada, 1992), pp. 163–74

——— 'Ibn Ezra Supercommentaries as Historical Sources', in *Abraham ibn Ezra and his Age*, ed. by Fernando Díaz Esteban (Madrid: Universidad Autónoma de Madrid-Asociación Española de Orientalistas, 1990), pp. 147–54

——— ' "Le-toldot ha-sefer we-ha-qri'ah: qehilot yehude sefarad be-'eidan ha-dfus', in *Asufah le-Yosef*, ed. by Y. Ben-Naeh, J. Cohen, M. Idel and Y. Kaplan (Jerusalem: Shazar, 2014), pp. 263–84

——— 'The Expulsion of the Jews from Spain and Jewish Historiography', in *Jewish History: Festschrift C. Abramsky*, ed. by Ada Rapoport-Albert (London: Peter Halban, 1988), pp. 141–61

——— 'The Historian's Origins and Genealogies: The Sefer Yuhasin', *Hispania Judaica Bulletin*, 6 (2008), 57–82

——— '*The Most marueilous historie of the Iewes*: Historiography and the "Marvelous" in the Sixteenth Century', in *In and Of the Mediterranean: Medieval and Early Modern Iberian Studies*, ed. by Nuria Silleras-Fernández and Michelle Marie Hamilton (Nashville, TN: Vanderbilt University Press, 2014), pp. 157–82

——'Tres calas en la literatura de viajes del siglo XVI', in *Viajes a Tierra Santa. Navegación y puertos en los relatos de viajes judíos, cristianos y musulmanes (siglos XII–XVII)*, coord. by Tania María García Arévalo (Granada: Universidad de Granada, 2014), pp. 67–90

HABERMAN, ABRAHAM M., ed., 'Rabbi Shem Tov Falaquera's Iggeret ha-Musar', *Qoves 'al Yad*, 1 (1936), 43–90

HAGENEDER, OTHMAR, 'Der Häeresie begriff bei den Juristen des 12. und 13. Jahrhunderts', in *The Concept of Heresy in the Middle Ages (11th.–13th. C.)*, ed. by W. Lourdaux and D. Verhelst (Louvain: University Press; La Haye: Martinus Nijhoff, 1976), pp. 42–103

HAMES, HARVEY J., *Like Angels on Jacob's Ladder: Abraham Abulafia, the Franciscans and Joachimism* (Albany: State University of New York Press, 2007)

HAMILTON, ALASTAIR, *The Copts and the West, 1439–1822: The European Discovery of the Egyptian Church* (Oxford: Oxford University Press, 2009)

HAMM, BERNDT, *The Reformation of Faith in the Context of Late Medieval Theology and Piety* (Leiden: Brill, 2004)

HARDIN, RICHARD F., 'England's *Amphitruo* before Dryden: The Varied Pleasures of Plautus's Template', *Studies in Philology*, 109.1 (2012), 45–62

HARRISON, PETER, *The Territories of Science and Religion* (Chicago, IL: University of Chicago Press, 2015)

HAZARD, PAUL, *La Crise de la conscience européenne, 1680–1715*, 2 vols (Paris: Boivin, 1935)

HEDLEY, DOUGLAS, 'Persons of Substance and the Cambridge Connection: Some Roots and Ramifications of the Trinitarian controversy in Seventeenth-Century England', in *Socinianism and Arminianism: Antitrinitarians, Calvinists and Cultural Exchange in Seventeenth-Century Europe*, ed. by Martin Mulsow and Jan Rohls (Leiden: Brill, 2005), pp. 225–40

HEINEMANN, ISAAK, *Three Jewish Philosophers, Philo, Saadya Gaon, Jehuda Halevi* (New York: Meridian Books, 1960)

HELLER, HENRY, *Anti-Italianism in Sixteenth-Century France* (Toronto, Buffalo and London: University of Toronto Press, 2003)

HELLER, PETER, 'Paduan Coins: Concerning Lessing's Parable of the Three Rings', *Lessing Yearbook*, 5 (1973), 163–71

HOBSON, ANTHONY, *Renaissance Book Collecting: Jean Grolier and Diego Hurtado de Mendoza, their Books and Bindings* (Cambridge: Cambridge University Press, 1999)

HORODOWICH, ELIZABETH A., 'Civic Identity and the Control of Blasphemy in Sixteenth-Century Venice', *Past and Present*, 181 (2003), 3–34

——'The Gossiping Tongue: Oral Networks, Public Life and Political Culture in Early Modern Venice', *Renaissance Studies*, 19 (2005), 22–45

——'The Unmannered Tongue: Blasphemy, Insults, and Gossip in Renaissance Venice' (unpublished PhD thesis, University of Michigan, 2001)

HOWARD, KEITH DAVID, *The Reception of Machiavelli in Early Modern Spain* (London: Tamesis, 2014)

HOWARD, PETER FRANCIS, *Beyond the Written World: Preaching and Theology in the Florence of Archbishop Antoninus, 1427–1459* (Florence: L. S. Olschi, 1995)

HUARTE DE SAN JUAN, JUAN, *Examen de Ingenios* (Baeza: Juan Bautista Montoya, 1575; Madrid: Cátedra, 1989)

HUNTER, MICHAEL, and DAVID WOOTTON, eds, *Atheism from the Reformation to the Enlightenment* (New York: Clarendon Press, 1992)

HURTADO DE MENDOZA, DIEGO, *Algunas cartas de don Diego Hurtado de Mendoza escritas 1538–1552*, ed. by Alberto Vázquez and R. Selden Rose (New Haven, CT, and London: Yale University Press, 1935)

——*Cartas*, ed. by Juan Varo Zafra (Granada: Universidad de Granada, 2016)

——*Guerra de Granada*, ed. by Bernardo Blanco-González (Madrid: Castalia, 1996)

HUSIK, ISAAC, *A History of Mediaeval Jewish Philosophy* (New York: Meridian Books, [1916] 1958)

—— *Philosophical Essays: Ancient, Mediaeval & Modern*, ed. by Milton C. Nahm and Leo Strauss (Oxford: Blackwell, 1952)

IBN VERGA, SOLOMON, *Historia Judaica: res Judaeorum ab eversa aede Hierosolymitana, ad haec fere tempora usque, complexa. De Hebraeo in Latinum versa a Georgio Gentio* (Amsterdam: Petrum Niellium, 1651)

—— *Shevet Yehudah*, ed. by M. Wiener (Hanover: C. Ruempler, 1856) [Hebrew edn by Azriel Shochat and Yitzhak Baer (Jerusalem: Bialik Institute, 1947)] [Spanish trans. by Meir de León, *La vara de Judá* (Amsterdam: Mosseh d'Abraham Pretto Henriq, Jan de Wolf, 1744)]

IDEL, MOSHE, 'The Pearl, the Son and the Servants in Abraham Abulafia's Parable', *Quaderni di Studi Indo-Mediterranei*, 6 (2013), 103–35

ILLADES AGUIAR, GUSTAVO, 'Dos pacientes virtuales del médico Francisco de Villalobos: Anselmo y Carrizales', *Bulletin of the Cervantes Society of America*, 19.2 (1999), 101–12

—— *La Celestina en el taller salmantino* (Mexico: UNAM, Instituto de Investigaciones filológicas, 1999)

IRIGOYEN GARCÍA, JAVIER, *Moors Dressed as Moors: Clothing, Social Distinction and Ethnicity in Early Modern Iberia* (Toronto: University of Toronto Press, 2017)

ISRAEL, JONATHAN I., *European Jewry in the Age of Mercantilism, 1550–1750*, 3rd edn (London: Littman Library of Jewish Civilization, 1998)

—— *Radical Enlightenment. Philosophy and the Making of Modernity, 1650–1750* (Oxford: Oxford University Press, 2001)

JACQUELOT, ISAAC, *Dissertations sur le Messie: Où l'on prouve aux Juifs que Jesus-Christ est le Messie promis et predit dans l'Ancien Testament* (The Hague: Etienne Foulque, 1699)

JARDINE, LISA, 'Lorenzo Valla and the Intellectual Origins of Humanist Dialectic', *Journal of the History of Philosophy* 15.2 (1977), 143–64

—— 'Lorenzo Valla: Academic Skepticism and the New Humanist Dialectic', in *The Skeptical Tradition*, ed. by Myles Burnyeat (Berkeley: University of California Press, 1983), pp. 253–86

JENNY, BEAT R., 'Arlenius in Basel', *Basler Zeitschrift für Geschichte und Altertumskunde*, 64 (1964), 5–45

JERICÓ BERMEJO, IGNACIO, 'De propositionibus oppositis fidei non haereticis. Las exposiciones de Melchor Cano y Domingo Báñez (s. XVI)', *Communio. Commentarii internationales de Ecclesia et theologia*, 33.1 (2000), 33–104

—— *La fe católica en los Salmantinos del siglo XVI. La vieja y la nueva problemática según los comentarios de Fray Luis de León, Juan de Guevara y Pedro de Aragón* (Madrid: Revista Agustiniana, 1999)

JONSEN, ALBERT R., and STEPHEN TOULMIN, *The Abuse of Casuistry: A History of Moral Reasoning* (Berkeley: University of California Press, 1988)

JOSEPHUS, FLAVIUS, *Opera* (Basilea: Froben, 1544)

—— *Antiquities of the Jews*, ed. by William Whiston (London: [n. pub.], 1737) <http://penelope.uchicago.edu/josephus/index.html> [accessed 24 May 2017]

JUSTICE, STEVEN, 'Did the Middle Ages Believe in Their Miracles?' *Representations*, 103.1 (2008), 1–29

—— 'Eucharistic Miracle and Eucharistic Doubt', *Journal of Medieval and Early Modern Studies*, 42.2 (2012), 307–32

KAHN, VICTORIA ANN, *Rhetoric, Prudence, and Skepticism in the Renaissance* (Ithaca, NY: Cornell University Press, 1985)

KAPLAN, BENJAMIN J., *Divided by Faith: Religious Conflict and the Practice of Toleration in Early Modern Europe* (Cambridge, MA: Belknap Press of Harvard University Press, 2007)

KAPLAN, YOSEF, *An Alternative Path to Modernity: The Sephardi Diaspora in Western Europe* (Leiden: Brill, 1996)

—— 'The Attitude of the Leadership of the Portuguese Community in Amsterdam to the Sabbatian Movement 1665–1671' [in Hebrew], *Zion*, 39 (1974), 198–216

—— *From Christianity to Judaism: The Story of Isaak Orobio de Castro*, trans. by Raphael Loewe (Oxford: Littman-Oxford University Press, 1989)

KAUFMAN, DAVID, 'Joseph Ibn Verga's Extract from the Cairo-Megilla', *The Jewish Quarterly Review*, 11 (1899), 656–57

—— 'Miscellanea: The Egyptian Purim', *The Jewish Quarterly Review*, 8 (1896), 511–12

KILLEEN, KEVIN, and PETER J. FORSHAW, eds, *The Word and the World: Biblical Exegesis and Early Modern Science* (Basingstoke: Palgrave Macmillan, 2007)

KIMMEL, SETH, *Parables of Coercion: Conversion and Knowledge at the End of Islamic Spain* (Chicago, IL: University of Chicago Press, 2015)

KINNEAVY, JAMES L., *Greek Rhetorical Origins of Christian Faith* (Oxford: Oxford University Press, 1987)

KOZODOY, MAUD, *The Secret Faith of Maestre Honoratus: Profyat Duran and Jewish Identity in Late Medieval Iberia* (Philadelphia: University of Pennsylvania Press, 2015)

KRISTELLER, PAUL OSKAR, 'The Myth of Renaissance Atheism and the French Tradition of Free Thought', *Journal of the History of Philosophy*, 6.3 (1968), 233–43

—— *Iter Italicum. Accedunt Alia Itinera: a Finding List of Uncatalogued or Incompletely Catalogued Humanistic Manuscripts of the Renaissance in Italian and other Libraries*, vol. V (London: The Warburg Institute; Leiden: Brill, 1990)

KSELMAN, THOMAS, ed., *Belief in History: Innovative Approaches to European and American Religion* (Notre Dame, IN: University of Notre Dame Press, 1991)

—— . *Conscience and Conversion: Religious Liberty in Post-Revolutionary France* (London and New Haven, CT: Yale University Press, 2018)

KUTTNER, STEPHAN, 'Ecclesia de occultis non iudicat. Problemata ex doctrina poenali decretalistarum a Gratiano usque ad Gregorium P. IX', in *Acta congressus iuridici internationalis VII saeculo a decretalibus Gregorii IX et XIV a codice iustiniano promulgatis*, 5 vols (Rome: Pont. Instituti Utriusque Iuris, 1934–37), vol. III (1936), pp. 225–46

LA ROCHEFOUCAULD, FRANÇOIS DE, *Œuvres complètes*, ed. by L. Martin-Chauffier, rev. by Jean Marchand (Paris: Gallimard, 2004)

[LACROZE, JEAN CORNAND DE], *Recueil de diverses pièces concernant le quiétisme et les quiétistes, ou Molinos, ses sentiments et ses disciples* (Amsterdam: A. Wolfgang and P. Savouret, 1688)

—— *Trois lettres touchant l'état présent d'Italie écrites en l'année 1687. La Première Regarde l'affaire de Molinos et des quiétistes* (Cologne: [n. pub.], 1688)

LADERO QUESADA, MIGUEL ÁNGEL. 'Isabel la Católica vista por sus contemporáneos', *En la España Medieval*, 29 (2006), 225–86

—— *Los mudéjares de Castilla en tiempo de Isabel I* (Valladolid: Instituto Isabel la Católica, 1969)

LANDAU, LEO, *Das Apologetischen Schreiben des Josua Lorki an den Abtrünnigen Don Salomon Ha-Lewi (Paulus de Santa Maria)* (Antwerp: Teitelbaum & Boxenbaum, 1906)

LARSEN, JOHN C., 'Pedro de Valencia's *Academica* and Scepticism in Late Renaissance Spain', in *Renaissance Scepticisms*, ed. by Gianni Paganini and José R Maia Neto (Dordrecht: Springer, 2009), pp. 111–23

LAVIN, IRVING, *Caravaggio e La Tour. La luce occulta di Dio*, trans. by Silvia Panichi and Daniele Francesconi (Rome: Donzelli, 2000)

LAYNA SERRANO, FRANCISCO, *Historia de Guadalajara y sus Mendozas durante los siglos XV y XVI*, 4 vols (Madrid: Aldus, 1942)

LEA, HENRY CHARLES, *A History of the Inquisition of Spain* (New York: Macmillan, 1906)

LE BRUN, JACQUES, *La Spiritualité de Bossuet* (Paris: Librairie C. Klincksieck, 1972)

LECLERC, JEAN, *L'Amour des lettres et le désir de Dieu. Initiation aux auteurs monastiques du Moyen Âge* (Paris: Les Éditions du Cerf, 2008)

——, and JEAN CORNAND DE LACROZE, *Bibliothèque Universelle et Historique de l'année 1688*, vol. XI (Amsterdam: Wolfgang, Waesberge, Boom & Van Someren, 1698)

LEE, CHRISTINA H., *The Anxiety of Sameness in Early Modern Spain* (Manchester: Manchester University Press, 2016)

LEVIN, MICHAEL J., *Agents of Empire: Spanish Ambassadors in Sixteenth-Century Italy* (Ithaca, NY: Cornell University Press, 2005)

LEVINAS, EMMANUEL, *Liberté et commandement (Transcendence et hauteur)* (Paris: Le Livre de Poche, 1999)

——— *Totalité et infini. Essai sur l'extériorité* (Paris: Le Livre de Poche, 1991)

LEWIS, BERNARD, 'E. IJ. Rosenthal (ed.), *Averroes Commentary on Platos' Republic*, Cambridge: University Press, 1956', *Die Welt des Islams*, 5.3 (1958), 300

LIDA DE MALKIEL, MARÍA ROSA, 'Las sectas judías y los "procuradores" romanos. En torno a Josefo y su influjo sobre la literatura española', *Hispanic Review*, 39.2 (1971), 183–213

LIENHARD, MARC, ed., *Croyants et sceptiques au XVIe siècle. Le Dossier des 'Epicuriens'. Actes du Colloque organisé par le GRENEP, Strasbourg, 9–10 juin 1978* (Strasbourg: Librarie Istra, 1981)

LIENHARD, THOMAS, 'Athéisme, scepticisme et doute religieux au Moyen Âge. Notes de lecture à propos de trois publications récentes', *Revue de l'IFHA*, 3 (2012), 188–205 <http//ifha.revues.org/194>

LIM, RICHARD, *Public Disputation, Power, and Social Order in Late Antiquity* (Berkeley: University of California Press, 1995)

LIMBORCH, PHILIPP VAN, *De Veritate Religionis Christianae amica collatio cum erudito Judaeo* (Gouda: Justus van Hoeve, 1687)

LIMOR, ORA, and ISRAEL JACOB YUVAL, 'Skepticism and Conversion: Jews, Christians, and Doubters in *Sefer ha-Nizzahon*', in *Hebraica veritas? Christian Hebraists and the Study of Judaism in Early Modern Europe*, ed. by Allison Coudert and Jeffrey S. Shoulson (Philadelphia: University of Pennsylvania Press, 2004), pp. 159–80.

LIPSIUS, JUSTUS, *Politica: Six Books of Politics or Political Instruction*, ed. and trans. by Jan Waszink (Assen: Royal Van Gorcum, 2004)

LOEB, ISIDORE, 'Le Folklore juif dans la chronique du Schebet Iehudah d'ibn Verga', *Revue des Études Juives*, 24 (1892), 1–29

LOPERRÁEZ CORVALÁN, JUAN, *Descripción histórica del obispado de Osma, con el catálogo de sus prelados*, 2 vols (Madrid: Imprenta Real, 1788)

LÓPEZ DE GOICOECHEA ZABALA, JAVIER, *Dualismo cristiano y estado modern. Estudio histórico-crítico de la 'Summa de Ecclesia' (1453) de Juan de Torquemada* (Salamanca: Universidad Pontificia de Salamanca, 2004)

LÓPEZ DE VILLALOBOS, FRANCISCO, *Libro intitulado los problemas de Villalobos, que trata de cuerpos naturales y morales, dos diálogos de medicina y el tratado de los tres grandes, una canción y la comedia Anphitrion* (Zamora: Juan Picardo, 1543; 2nd edn, Zaragoza: Jorge Coci, 1544)

——— *Tratado sobre las costumbres humanas*, ed. by José Luis Villacañas (Murcia: Biblioteca Saavedra Fajardo, 2012) <http://www.saavedrafajardo.org/Archivos/LIBROS/Libro00788. pdf> [accessed 10 May 2017]

———*Algunas Obras de Francisco López de Villalobos* (Madrid: Sociedad de Bibliófilos Españoles, 1886)

LÓPEZ PINCIANO, ALONSO, *Obras completas*, ed. by José Rico Verdú (Madrid: Fundación José Antonio de Castro, 1998)

LÓPEZ-RÍOS, SANTIAGO, '"Señor, por holgar con el cordón no querrás gozar de Melibea". La parodia del culto a las reliquias en la Celestina', *Modern Language Notes*, 127 (2012), 190–207

LOYOLA, IGNACIO DE, *Obras completas*, ed. by Ignacio Iparraguirre, with the *Autobiografía de San Ignacio*, ed. by Cándido de Dalmases, 2nd edn (Madrid: Biblioteca de Autores Cristianos, 1963)

LUCAS DE TUY, *Obra sacada de las crónicas de San Isidoro*, ed. by Juan Manuel Cacho Blecua (Zaragoza: Universidad de Zaragoza, 2003)

—— *Text and Concordance of Obra sacada de las crónicas de Sant Isidoro, arcebispo de Sevilla, Kungliga Biblioteket, Stockholm MS. D 1272a*, ed. by Regina af Geijerstam and Cynthia M. Wasick (Madison, WI: The Hispanic Seminary of Medieval Studies, 1988)

MACCOBY, HYAM, *Judaism on Trial: Jewish-Christian Disputations in the Middle Ages* (London: The Littman Library of Jewish Civilization, [1982] paperback 1993)

MACGREGOR, GEDDES, 'Doubt and Belief', in *The Encyclopedia of Religion*, ed. by Mircea Eliade, 16 vols (New York: Macmillan Publishing Company, 1987)

—— *Doubt and Faith* (London: Longmans-Green, 1951)

MACHIAVELLI, NICCOLÓ, *Il Principe*, ed. by Giorgio Inglese (Turin: Einaudi, 1995) [English trans. by Tim Parks, *The Prince* (London: Penguin, 2009)]

—— *Opere. Vol. II Lettere legazioni e commissarie*, ed. by Corrado Vivanti (Turin: Einaudi, 1999)

—— *Machiavelli: The Chief Works and Others*, ed. and trans. by Allan H. Gilbert, 3 vols (Durham, NC, and London: Duke University Press, 1999)

MAHONEY, JOHN, *The Making of Moral Theology: A Study of the Catholic Tradition* (Oxford: Oxford University Press, 1987)

MALENA, ADELISA, *L'eresia dei perfetti. Inquisizione romana ed esperienze mistiche nel Seicento italiano* (Rome: Edizioni di Storia e Letteratura, 2003)

MANEKIN, CHARLES, 'Belief, Certainty, and Divine Attributes in the *Guide for the Perplexed*', *Maimonidean Studies*, 1 (1990), 117–41

—— 'Hebrew Philosophy in the Fourteenth and Fifteenth Centuries: An Overview', in *History of Jewish Philosophy*, ed. by Daniel H. Frank and Oliver Leaman (London: Routledge, [1997] 2003), pp. 350–78

MANELFI, PIETRO, *I costituti di don Pietro Manelfi*, ed. by Carlo Ginzburg (Chicago, IL: The Newberry Library; Florence: Sansoni, 1970)

MARIN, LOUIS, *La Critique du discours. Sur la 'Logique de Port–Royal' et les 'Pensées' de Pascal* (Paris: Minuit, 1975)

MARÍN PADILLA, ENCARNACIÓN, *Maestre Pedro de la Cabra, médico converso aragonés del siglo XV, autor de unas coplas de arte menor* (Madrid: E. Marín, 1998).

—— 'Relación judeoconversa durante la segunda mitad del siglo XV en Aragón: enfermedades y muertes', *Sefarad: Revista de Estudios Hebraicos y Sefardíes*, 43.2 (1983), 251–344

—— *Relación judeoconversa durante la segunda mitad del siglo xv en Aragón. La ley* (Zaragoza: E. Marín, 1986)

—— *Relación judeoconversa durante la segunda mitad del siglo XV en Aragón. Matrimonio* (Madrid: Consejo Superior de Investigaciones Científicas, 1983)

MÁRQUEZ, ANTONIO, *Los alumbrados. Orígenes y filosofía* (Madrid: Taurus, 1972)

MÁRQUEZ VILLANUEVA, FRANCISCO, 'El caso del averroísmo popular español. Hacia la Celestina', in *Cinco Siglos de Celestina. Aportaciones interpretativas*, ed. by Rafael Beltrán and José Luis Canet (Valencia: Universitat de València,1997), pp. 121–32

—— 'Jewish "Fools" of the Spanish Fifteenth Century', *Hispanic Review*, 4 (1982), 385–409

—— *De la España judeoconversa: Doce estudios* (Barcelona: Bellaterra, 2006)

—— *Moros, moriscos y turcos en Cervantes. Ensayos críticos* (Barcelona: Bellaterra, 2010)

—— '"Nascer e morir como bestias" (criptojudaísmo y criptoaverroísmo)', in *Los judaizantes en Europa y la literatura castellana del Siglo de Oro*, ed. by Fernando Díaz Esteban (Madrid: Letrúmero, 1994), pp. 273–93

MARTIAL, *Epigrams*, ed. and trans. by D. R. Shakleton-Bailey, 3 vols, Loeb Classical Library, 95 (Cambridge, MA: Harvard University Press, 1993)

MARYKS, ROBERT A., *Saint Cicero and the Jesuits: The Influence of the Liberal Arts on the Adoption of Moral Probabilism* (Aldershot: Ashgate; Rome: Institutum Historicum Societas Iesu, 2008)

MAS, ALBERT, *Les Turcs dans la littérature espagnole du Siècle d'Or*, 2 vols (Flers: Follope, 1967)

MÉCHOULAN, HENRY, 'A propos de la liberté de conscience. Remarques sur un manuscrit d'Abraham Gomes Silveyra', in *Nature, croyance, raison. Mélanges offerts à Sylvain Zac*, ed. by P. F. Moreau, J. Lagrée and M. Crampe-Casnabet (Saint-Cloud: École Normale Supériure Fontenay, 1992), pp. 25–41.

MEIJER, JACOB, 'Hugo Grotius' *Remonstrantie*', *Jewish Social Studies*, 17 (1955), 91–104

MELZER, ARTHUR M., *Philosophy between the Lines: The Lost History of Esoteric Writing* (Chicago, IL: University of Chicago Press, 2014)

MENDES DOS REMÉDIOS, JOAQUIM, *Judeus em Portugal* (Coimbra: Amado, 1895)

MENDOZA Y BOBADILLA, FRANCISCO DE, *Tizón de la nobleza de España* (Cuenca: Francisco Gómez, 1852)

MENÉNDEZ PELAYO, MARCELINO, *Historia de los Heterodoxos españoles*, 3 vols (Madrid: Librería Católica de San José, 1880)

MENÉNDEZ PIDAL, RAMÓN, *Los reyes católicos según Maquiavelo y Castiglione* (Madrid: Publicaciones de la Universidad de Madrid, 1952)

MERSENNE, MARIN, *L'Impiété des déistes, athées et libertins de ce temps combattue et renversée de point en point par raisons tirées de la philosophie et de la théologie* (Paris: Bilaine, 1624)

—— *Quæstiones celeberrimæ in Genesim, cum accurata textus explicatione* (Paris: Cramoisy, 1623)

MESEGUER FERNÁNDEZ, JUAN, 'Fernando de Talavera, Cisneros y la Inquisición en Granada', in *La Inquisición española. Nueva visión, nuevos horizontes (I Symposium Internacional sobre la Inquisición Española Cuenca 1978)*, ed. by Joaquín Pérez Villanueva (Madrid: Siglo XXI, 1980), pp. 371–400

MEXÍA, PEDRO, *Silva de varia lección*, ed. by Antonio Castro Díaz, 2 vols (Madrid: Cátedra, 1990)

MIGNANA, ALPHONSE, and RENDEL HARRIS, 'Woodbrooke Studies: Christian documents in Syriac, Arabic, and Garshūni, edited and translated with a critical apparatus. Fasciculus 3: The apology of Timothy the Patriarch before the Caliph Mahdi', *Journal of the John Rylands Library*, 12.1 (1928), 137–298

MILLÁS VALLICROSA, JOSÉ MARÍA, 'Aspectos filosóficos de la polémica judaica en tiempos de Hasday Crescas', in *Harry Austryn Wolfson Jubilee Volume on the Occasion of his Seventy-fifth Birthday* (Jerusalem: American Academy for Jewish Research, 1965), pp. 561–75

MIRABAUD, JEAN BAPTISTE DE [PAUL HENRY DIETRICH D'HOLBACH], *Système de la nature ou loix du monde physique et du monde moral*, 2 vols ([Amsterdam]: [Rey], 1770)

MITTLEMAN, ALAN, 'Tolerance, Liberty, and Truth: A Parable', *Harvard Theological Review*, 95.4 (2002), 353–72

MODENA, YEHUDAH ARYEH DA, *Magen ve-tzinah* (Breslau: H. Sulzbach, 1856)

—— *She'elot ve-teshuvot ziknei yehudah*, ed. by Shlomo Simonsohn (Jerusalem: Mosad Ha-Rav Kook, 1956)

MODICA, MARILENA, *Infetta dottrina. Inquisizione e quietisme nel Seicento* (Rome: Viella, 2009)

MOLINOS, MIGUEL DE, *Guía espiritual*, ed. by José Ángel Valente (Madrid: Alianza Editorial, 1989)

MOREAU, PIERRE-FRANÇOIS, ed., *Le Scepticisme au XVIe et au XVIIe siècle. Le Retour des philosophies antiques à l'âge classique*, 2 vols (Paris: Albin Michel, 2001)

MORENO RODRÍGUEZ, PILAR, *El pensamiento de Miguel de Molinos* (Madrid: Fundación Universitaria Española-Universidad Pontificia de Comillas, 1992)

MORGAN, DAVID, *Religion and Material Culture: The Matter of Belief* (New York: Routledge, 2010)

MORTIMER, SARAH, *Reason and Religion in the English Revolution: The Challenge of Socinianism* (Cambridge: Cambridge University Press, 2010)

MOST, GLENN W., *Doubting Thomas* (Cambridge, MA: Harvard University Press, 2005)

MOTHU, ALAIN, 'De la foi du charbonnier à celle du héros (et retour)', *Les Dossiers du Grihl* (2007) <https://dossiersgrihl.revues.org/3393> [accessed 18 April 2017]

MOYSSÉN, XABIER, 'Sebastián de Arteaga (1610–1652)', *Anales del Instituto de Investigaciones Estéticas*, 15.59 (1988), 17–34

MUCHNIK, NATALIA, *Une vie marrane. Les Pérégrinations de Juan de Prado dans l'Europe du XVIIe siècle* (Paris: Honoré Champion, 2005)

MÜLLER, JOHANNES, *Judaismus oder Jüdenthumb, das ist: außführlicher Bericht von des jüdischen Volckes Unglauben, Blindheit und Verstockung...* (Hamburg: J. Rebenlein, 1644)

MULSOW, MARTIN, and JAN ROHLS, eds, *Socinianism and Arminianism: Antitrinitarians, Calvinists and Cultural Exchange in Seventeenth-Century Europe* (Leiden: Brill, 2005)

NADAL, JERÓNIMO DE, *Annotations and Meditations on the Gospels. Vol. 3, The Resurrection Narratives*, trans. by Frederick A. Homann (Philadelphia, PA: St Joseph's University Press, 2005)

NADER, HELEN, *The Mendoza Family in the Spanish Renaissance, 1350–1550* (New Brunswick, NJ: Rutgers University Press, 1979)

——, ed., *Power and Gender in Renaissance Spain: Eight Women of the Mendoza Family, 1450–1650* (Urbana: University of Illinois Press, 2004)

NADLER, STEVEN M., 'Arnauld, Descartes, and Transubstantiation: Reconciling Cartesian Metaphysics and Real Presence', *Journal of the History of Ideas*, 49 (1988), 229–46

NAIGEON, JACQUES-ANDRÉ, 'Unitaires', in *Encyclopédie, ou, Dictionnaire raisonné des sciences, des arts et des métiers* (Neufchastel: S. Faulche, 1765), XVII, 387–401

NAUDÉ, GABRIEL, *Naudæana et Patiniana, ou Singularitez remarquables*, 2nd edn (Amsterdam: vander Plaats, 1703)

NAYA, EMMANUEL, 'Renaissance Pyrrhonism: A Relative Phenomenon', in *Renaissance Scepticisms*, ed. by Gianni Paganini and José R Maia Neto (Dordrecht: Springer, 2009), pp. 15–32

——'Traduire les *Hypotyposes Pyrrhoniennes*. Henri Estienne entre la fièvre quarte et la folie chrétienne', in *Le Scepticisme au XVie et au XVIIe siècle. II, Le Retour des philosophies antiques à l'âge classique*, ed. by Pierre-François Moreau (Paris: Albin Michel, 2001), pp. 48–101

——'Quod nihil scitur. La Parole mise en doute', in *Libertinage et philosophie au XVIIe siècle. 7. La Résurgence des philosophies antiques* (Saint-Étienne: Université de Saint-Étienne, 2003), pp. 27–43

NEEDHAM, RODNEY, *Belief, Language, and Experience* (Oxford: Basil Blackwell, 1972)

NICLÓS ALBARRACÍN, JOSÉ VICENTE, 'La Disputa religiosa de D. Pedro de Luna con el judío D. Shem Tov Ibn Shaprut en Pamplona (1379). El contexto en la vida y la predicación de Vicente Ferrer', *Revue des Études Juives*, 160.3/4 (2001), 409–33

NICOLE, PIERRE, *Les Visionnaires ou seconde partie des lettres sur l'hérésie imaginaire* (Liège: Adolphe Beyers, 1667)

Nieuw Nederlandsch Biografisch Woordenboek, 10 vols (Amsterdam: A. W. Sijthoff's uitgevers-maatschappij, 1911–37)

NIEWÖHNER, FRIEDRICH, *Veritas sive varietas. Lessings Toleranzparabel und das Buch Von den drei Betrügern* (Heidelberg: Lambert Schneider, 1988)

NISBET, HUGH, *Gotthold Ephraim Lessing: His Life, Works, and Thoughts* (Oxford: Oxford University Press, 2013)

NONGBRI, BRENT, *Before Religion: A History of a Modern Concept* (New Haven, CT: Yale University Press, 2013)

NÚÑEZ MULEY, FRANCISCO, *A Memorandum for the President of the Royal Audiencia and Chancery Court of the City and Kingdom of Granada*, ed. and trans. by Vincent Barletta (Chicago, IL: University of Chicago Press, 2007)

O'MALLEY, JOHN W., *Saints or Devils Incarnate? Studies in Jesuit History* (Leiden: Brill, 2013)

OBREGÓN, GONZALO, *Zurbarán en México* (Badajoz: Diputación Provincial, 1964)

ORTIZ, LORENZO, *Origen y instituto de la Compañía de Jesús, en la vida de San Ignacio de Loyola, su padre y fundador, que ofrece a las seis muy religiosas y apostólicas provincias de la Compañía de IESUS de las Indias Occidentales, que comprehende la Asistencia General en Roma, por la Corona de Castilla* (Seville: Colegio de San Hermenegildo de la Compañía de Jesús, 1679)

OSBAT, LUCIANO, *L'Inquisizione a Napoli. Il processo agli ateisti, 1688–1697* (Rome: Storia e Letteratura, 1974)

OSIER, JEAN-PIERRE, *D'Uriel da Costa à Spinoza* (Paris: Berg, 1983)

PACHECO, FRANCISCO, *Arte de la pintura* (Madrid: Cátedra, 1990)

PACIOS LÓPEZ, ANTONIO, *La Disputa de Tortosa, II, Actas* (Madrid, Barcelona: CSIC-Instituto Arias Montano, 1957)

PAGANINI, GIANNI, 'Montaigne, Sanchez et la connaissance par phénomènes. Les Usages d'un paradigme ancien', in *Montaigne. Scepticisme, métaphisique et théologie*, ed. by Vincent Carraud and Jean-Luc Marion (Paris: Presses Universitaires de France, 2004), pp. 107–35 [republished in Paganini, *Skepsis. Le Débat des Modernes sur le scepticisme, Montaigne, Le Vayer, Campanella, Hobbes, Descartes, Bayle* (Paris: J. Vrin, 2008), pp. 15–60]

PAGDEN, ANTHONY, *The Fall of Natural Man: The American Indian and the Origins of Comparative Ethnology* (New York: Cambridge University Press, 1982)

PALEOTTI, GABRIELE, *Discorso intorno alle immagini sacre e profane*, ed. by G. F. Freguglia (Vatican City: Libreria Editrice Vaticana, 2002)

PARIGI, PAOLO, *The Rationalization of Miracles* (Cambridge: Cambridge University Press, 2014)

PARIS, GASTON, *La Parabole des trois anneaux* (Paris: A. Durlacher, 1885)

PARK, KATHERINE, 'Holy Autopsies: Saintly Bodies and Medical Expertise, 1300–1600', in *The Body in Early Modern Italy*, ed. by Julia L. Hairston and Walter Stephens (Baltimore, MD: Johns Hopkins University Press, 2010), pp. 61–73

PASTORE, STEFANIA, 'Doubt in Fifteenth-Century Iberia', in *After Conversion: Iberia and the Emergence of Modernity*, ed. by Mercedes García-Arenal (Leiden: Brill, 2016), pp. 283–303

——'From *Marranos* to *Unbelievers*: The Spanish Pecadillo in Sixteenth-Century Italy', in *Dissimulation and Deceit in Early Modern Europe*, ed. by Miriam Eliav-Feldon and Tamar Herzig (Basingstoke: Palgrave Macmillan, 2015), pp. 79–93

——*Il vangelo e la spada. L'Inquisizione di Castiglia e i suoi critici (1460–1598)* (Rome: Edizioni di storia e letteratura, 2003)

——'Una Spagna antipapale. Gli anni italiani di Diego Hurtado de Mendoza', *Roma Moderna e Contemporanea*, 15 (2007), 63–94

——*Un'eresia spagnola. Spiritualità conversa, alumbradismo e Inquisizione (1449–1559)*, (Florence: L. S. Olschki, 2004) [Spanish translation, *Una herejía española. Conversos, alumbrados e inquisición (1449–1559)* (Madrid: Marcial Pons, 2010)]

PATIN, GUY, *Lettres choisies de feu monsieur Guy Patin. Dans lesquelles sont contenuës plusieurs particularités historiques, sur la vie & la mort des scavans de ce siècle, sur leurs ecrits & plusieurs autres choses curieuses depuis l'an 1645*, 3 vols (Paris: Petit, 1662)

PAZ Y MELIÁ, ANTONIO, 'Cartas de don Diego Hurtado de Mendoza al cardenal Granvela (1548–1551)', *Revista de Archivos, Bibliotecas y Museos*, 3 (1899), 612–22

PELIKAN, JAROSLAV, *Credo: Historical and Theological Guide to Creeds and Confessions of Faith in the Christian Tradition* (New Haven, CT: Yale University Press, 2005)

PELIKAN, JAROSLAV, and VALERIE R. HOTCHKISS, *Creeds and Confessions of Faith in the Christian Tradition*, 3 vols (New Haven, CT: Yale University Press, 2003)

PEÑA DÍAZ, MANUEL, 'Cultura escrita, escrúpulos y censuras cotidianas (siglos XVI–XVIII)', *Estudis. Revista de historia moderna*, 37 (2011), 73–90

PEREDA, FELIPE, *Crimen e Ilusión. El arte de la verdad en el Siglo de Oro* (Madrid: Marcial Pons, 2017) [English trans., *Crime and Illusion: The Art of Truth in the Spanish Golden Age*, trans. by Consuelo López-Morillas (Turnhout: Brepols; London: Harvey Miller, 2018)]

—— 'True Painting and the Challenge of Hypocrisy', in *After Conversion: Iberia and the Emergence of Modernity*, ed. by Mercedes García-Arenal (Leiden: Brill, 2016), pp. 358–94

PERICOLO, LORENZO, 'Visualizing Appearance and Disappearance: On Caravaggio's London Supper at Emmaus', *The Art Bulletin*, 89.3 (2007), 519–39

—— *Caravaggio and Pictorial Narrative: Dislocating the Istoria in Early Modern Painting* (London: Harvey Miller Publishers, 2011)

PERINI, LEANDRO, 'Gli eretici italiani del '500 e Machiavelli', *Studi storici*, 10.4 (1969), 877–918

PIÉ-NINOT, SALVADOR, *La teología fundamental* (Barcelona: Biblioteca de Autores Cristianos, 2006)

PIGNATELLI, GIACOMO, *Novissima Consultationes Canonicae praecipuis controversias quae fidem, eiusque regulam spectant* (Cologne: Gabrielis and Samuelis de Tournes, 1718)

PINEDA MENDOZA, RAQUEL, 'Pintores novohispanos en el Tribunal de la Inquisición. Noticias documentales', *Imágenes* (2008) <http://www.esteticas.unam.mx/revista_imagenes/dearchivos/dearch_pineda01.html>

PINES, SHLOMO, 'Le- heqer torato ha-medinit shel ibn Roshd', *'Iyyun*, 5 (1957), 65–84

—— 'The Jewish Christians of the Early Centuries of Christianity According to a New Source', *The Israel Academy of Sciences and Humanities, Proceedings* (separatum), 2.13 (1966), 1–72

PINTARD, RENÉ, *Le Libertinage érudit dans la première moitié du XVIIe siècle* (Geneva: Slatkine, 2000)

PINTO CRESPO, VIRGILIO, 'El apogeo del Santo Oficio (1569–1621). Los hechos y las actividades inquisitoriales en España. El último tercio del siglo XVI. La justificación doctrinal del Santo Oficio', in *Historia de la Inquisición en España y América*, ed. by Joaquín Pérez Villanueva, 3 vols (Madrid: Biblioteca de Autores Cristianos, 1984–2000), vol. I (1984), pp. 880–86

—— 'Sobre el delito de la herejía (siglos XIII–XVI)', in *Perfiles jurídicos de la Inquisición española*, ed. by José Antonio Escudero (Madrid: Instituto de Historia de la Inquisición-Universidad Complutense de Madrid, 1989), pp. 195–204

POLIZIANO, ANGELO, *Commento inedito alle Satire di Persio*, ed. by Lucia Cesarini Martinelli and Roberto Ricciardi (Florence: L. S. Olschki, 1985)

—— *Una ignota Expositio Suetoni del Poliziano*, ed. by Vincenzo Fera (Messina: Centro di Studi Umanistici, 1983)

POMATA, GIANNA, 'Malpighi and the Holy Body: Medical Experts and Miraculous Evidence in Seventeenth-century Italy', *Renaissance Studies*, 21.4 (2007), 568–86

POPKIN, RICHARD H., 'Some Aspects of Jewish-Christian Theological Interchanges in Holland and England 1640–1700', in *Jewish–Christian Relations in The Seventeenth Century. Studies and Documents*, ed. by J. van den Berg and E. G. E. van der Wall (Leiden: Brill, 1988), pp. 3–32

—— 'The Historical Significance of Sephardic Judaism in 17th Century Amsterdam', *The American Sephardi*, 5 (1971), 18–27

——— *The History of Scepticism: From Erasmus to Spinoza* (Berkeley: University of California Press, 1979)

——— *The History of Scepticism from Savonarola to Bayle* (New York: Oxford University Press, 2003)

PORTUONDO, MARÍA M., 'The Study of Nature, Philosophy and the Royal Library of San Lorenzo of the Escorial', *Renaissance Quarterly*, 63.4 (2010), 1106–50

PRESCOTT, WILLIAM H., *Historia del reinado de los reyes católicos, D. Fernando y Doña Isabel*, 4 vols (Madrid: Rivadeneyra, 1846)

PREUS, J. SAMUEL, 'Machiavelli's Functional Analysis of Religion: Context and Object', *Journal of the History of Ideas*, 40.2 (1979), 171–90

PRIAROLO, MARTA, and ELENA SCRIBANO, eds, *Fausto Sozzini e la filosofia in Europa. Atti del Convegno (Siena, 25–27 novembre 2004)* (Siena: Accademia degli Intronati, 2006)

PRODI, PAOLO, *Una storia della giustizia. Dal pluralismo dei fori al moderno dualismo tra coscienza e diritto* (Bologna: Il Mulino, 2000)

PROIETTI, OMERO, *Uriel da Costa e 'l'Exemplar humanae vitae'* (Macerata: Quodlibet, 2005).

PROSPERI, ADRIANO, 'Confessione e dissimulazione', *Les Dossiers du Grihl* (2009) <https://dossiersgrihl.revues.org/3671>

——— 'La confesione e il foro della coscienza', in *Il Concilio di Trento e il moderno*, Annali dell'Istituto storico italo-germanico, Quaderno 45, ed. by Paolo Prodi and Wolfgang Reinhard (Bologna: il Mulino, 1996), pp. 225–54

——— *Tribunali della coscienza. Inquisitori, confessori, missionari* (Turin: Einaudi, 1996)

PUIGDOMÈNECH FORCADA, HELENA, 'Maquiavelo en las bibliotecas de algunos eclesiásticos españoles (siglos XVI y XVII)', *Anuario de Filología*, 2 (1976), 425–32

——— 'Maquiavelo y maquiavelismo en España. Siglos XVI y XVII', in *Maquiavelo y España. Maquiavelismo y antimaquiavelismo en la cultura española de los siglos XVI y XVII*, coord. by Juan Manuel Forte and Pablo López Álvarez (Madrid: Biblioteca Nueva, 2008), pp. 41–60

QUANTIN, JEAN-LOUIS, *Le Catholicisme classique et les Pères de l'Église. Un retour aux sources (1669–1713)* (Paris: Institut d'Études Augustiniennes, 1999)

QUINTILIAN, *The Orator's Education (Institutio Oratoria)*, ed. by Donald A. Russell (Cambridge. MA: Harvard University Press, 2002)

QUIROGA, JOSÉ DE JESÚS MARÍA, *Apología mística en defensa de la contemplación*, ed. by Jean Krynen (Madrid: Real Academia Española, 1992)

RABELAIS, FRANÇOIS, *Pantagruel* (Paris: Fernand Roches, 1929)

RADA, INÉS, 'Un cadet de grande famille à l'epoque de la Renaissance. Don Diego Hurtado de Mendoza', in *Autour des parentés en Espagne aux XVIe et XVIIe siècles. Histoire, mythe et littérature*, ed. by Augustin Redondo (Paris: Université de la Sorbonne, 1987), pp. 31–42

RAMOS GÓMEZ, FRANCISCO JAVIER, 'Juan Soreda y las tablas del antiguo retablo de Luzón', *Archivo Español del Arte*, 75.299 (2002), 293–322

RESZKA, STANISŁAW, *De atheismis et phalarismis evangelicorum libri duo, quorum prior de fide, posterior tractat de operibus eorum* (Naples: Carlino, Pace, 1596)

RÉVAH, ISRAËL S., 'Aux origines de la rupture spinozienne. Nouvel examen des origines, du déroulement et des conséquences de l'affaire Spinoza-Prado-Ribera', *Annuaire du Collège de France*, 70 (1970), 562–68

——— 'Du "marranisme" au judaïsme at au déisme. Uriel da Costa et sa famille', *Annuaire du Collège de France*, 67 (1967), 515–26; 68 (1968), 562–72; 69 (1969), 578–85; 70 (1970), 569–77; 72 (1972), 653–62.

——— 'La Religion d'Uriel da Costa, Marrane de Porto (d'après des documents inédits)', *Revue de l'histoire des religions* (1962), 45–76 [republised in Révah, *Des marranes à Spinoza* (Paris: J. Vrin, 1995), pp. 77–108]

—— 'Le Procès inquisitorial contre Rodrigo Méndez Silva, historiographe du roi Philippe IV', *Bulletin Hispanique*, 67 (1965), 225–52

—— *Uriel da Costa et les Marranes de Porto, Cours au Collège de France, 1966–1972*, ed. by Carsten Wilke (Paris: Calouste Gulbenkian, 2004)

RIBADENEIRA, PEDRO DE, *Historias de la Contrarreforma*, ed. by Eusebio Rey (Madrid: Biblioteca de Autores Cristianos, 1945)

RIVIÈRE, JEAN, 'Une première "Somme" du pouvoir pontifical. Le Pape chez Augustin d'Ancône', *Revue des Sciences Religieuses*, 18.2 (1938), 149–83

ROBBINS, JEREMY, *Arts of Perception: The Epistemological Mentality of the Spanish Baroque, 1580–1720* (Abingdon: Routledge, 2007)

—— 'Prudence and Baltasar Gracián's *Oráculo manual*: Baroque Political Thought and the Thomistic Dimension', in *Artifice and Invention in the Spanish Golden Age*, ed. by Stephen Boyd and Terence O'Reilly (Oxford: Legenda, 2014), pp. 43–52

ROSENBERG, SHALOM, 'The Concept of *Emunah* in Post-Maimonidean Jewish Philosophy', in *Studies in Medieval Jewish History and Literature*, ed. by Isadore Twersky, 2 vols (Cambridge. MA: Harvard University Press, 1984), II, pp. 273–307

ROSENBERG, SHALOM, and ALEXANDER EVEN-CHEN, 'Coplas filosóficas de Abraham Gómez Silveyra', *Revue des Études Juives*, 153 (1994), 327–51

ROSENTHAL, E. I. J., ed., *Averroes' Commentary on Plato's Republic* (Cambridge: Cambridge University Press, 1956)

ROTH, CECIL, 'The Strange Case of Hector Mendes Bravo', *Hebrew Union College Annual*, 18 (1944), 221–45

RUBENS, PETER PAUL, *The Letters of Peter Paul Rubens*, ed. and trans. by Ruth Saunders Magurn (Evanston, IL: Northwestern University Press, 1991)

RUBIÉS, JOAN-PAU, *Travellers and Cosmographers: Studies in the History of Early Modern Travel and Ethnology* (Aldershot: Ashgate, 2007)

RUEL, MALCOLM, *Belief, Ritual and the Securing of Life: Reflexive Essays on a Bantu Religion* (Leiden: Brill, 1997)

RUSTOW, MARINA, 'Karaites Real and Imagined: Three Cases of Jewish Heresy', *Past and Present*, 197.1 (2007), 58–70

RUTHERFORD, DONALD, 'Leibniz and mysticism', in *Leibniz, Mysticism and Religion*, ed. by Allison P. Coudert, Richard H. Popkin and Gordon M. Weiner (Dordrecht: Kluwert Academic Publishers, 1998), pp. 22–37

SAAVEDRA FAJARDO, DIEGO, *Empresas políticas*, ed. by Sagrario López (Madrid: Cátedra, 1999)

SABBA, FIAMMETTA, *La 'Bibliotheca Universalis' di Conrad Gesner, monumento della cultura europea* (Rome: Bulzoni, 2012)

SANCHEZ, FRANCISCO, *Quod nihil scitur* (Lyon: Gryphe, 1581) [English trans. by Douglas F. Thomson *That nothing is known*, ed. and intro. by Elaine Limbrick (Cambridge: Cambridge University Press, 1988)]

SÁNCHEZ, PEDRO, *Quodlibeta Divi Thomae Aquinatis, Doctoris Angelici, ad mysticas doctrinas applicata, reflexionibus aliquibus annexis pro securiori via spiritus. In quibus omnes propositiones molistinarum de verbo ad verbum impugnantur* (Seville: Francisco Sánchez Reciente, 1719)

SÁNCHEZ LASMARÍAS, ELENA, 'Edición del Libro del infante don Pedro de Portugal, de Gómez de Santisteban', *Memorabilia*, 11 (2008), 1–30

SANFORD, EVA M., 'Juvenal', in *Catalogus Translationum et Commentariorum: Mediaeval and Renaissance Latin Translations and Commentaries*, ed. by Paul Oskar Kristeller (Washington, DC: Catholic University of America Press, 1960), pp. 175–238

SANTANA, Estêvão, *Sermão do Acto da fee que se celebrou na Cidade de Coimbra, na segunda Dominga de Quaresma, anno de 1612* (Lisbon: Antonio Alvarez, 1618)

SÃO RAIMUNDO, VALÉRIO DE, *Sermão em o Auto da fee que se celebrou na Cidade de Evora em 12 de Novembro de 1662* (Lisbon: Domingo Carneiro, 1663)

SAPERSTEIN, MARC, *'Your Voice Like a Ram's Horn': Themes and Texts in Traditional Jewish Preaching* (Cincinnati, OH: Hebrew Union College Press, 1996)

SARAIVA, ANTONIO JOSÉ, 'Antonio Vieira, Menasseh ben Israel et le cinquième empire', *Studia Rosenthaliana*, 6.1 (1972), 24–57

SARALEGUI, MIGUEL, 'El príncipe afortunado. Fernando el Católico en la obra de Maquiavelo', in *Virtudes políticas en el Siglo de Oro*, ed. by M. Idoya Zorroza (Pamplona: Eunsa, 2013), pp. 29–48

SARDELLA, PIERRE, *Nouvelles et spéculations à Venise au début du XVIe siècle* (Paris: Armand Colin, 1948)

SARPI, PAOLO, *Lettere ai protestanti*, ed. by Manlio D. Busnelli, 2 vols (Bari: Laterza, 1931)

SCHECHTER, RONALD, ed., *Nathan the Wise by Gotthold Ephraim Lessing, with Related Documents, Translated, Edited, and with an Introduction by Ronald Schechter* (Boston Bedford; New York: St Martin's, 2004)

SCHIRMAN, JEFIM, 'Translations of Belles-lettres in the Spanish Period' (Hebrew), *Molad*, 18 (1960), 105–09

SCHMITT, CHARLES B., *Cicero scepticus: A Study of the Influence of the Academica in the Renaissance* (The Hague: Martinus Nijhoff, 1972)

SCHMITT, JEAN-CLAUDE, 'Du bon usage du "Credo"', in *Faire croire. Modalités de la diffusion et de la réception des messages religieux du XIIe au XVe siècle. Actes de table ronde de Rome (22–23 juin 1979)* (Rome: École française de Rome, 1981), pp. 337–61

SCHNEIDER, GERHARD, *Der Libertin. Zur Geistes und Sozialgeschichte des Bürgertums im 16. und 17. Jahrhundert* (Stuttgart: Metzler, 1970)

SCHREINER, SUSAN, *Are You Alone Wise? The Search for Certainty in the Early Modern Era* (Oxford: Oxford University Press, 2011)

SCHUCHARDT, HUGO, 'Die Geschichte von den drei Ringen', *Im Neuen Reich*, 39 (1871), 481–85

SCHWARTZ, STUART B., *All Can Be Saved: Religious Tolerance and Salvation in the Iberian Atlantic World* (New Haven, CT, and London: Yale University Press, 2008)

——, ed., *Implicit Understandings: Observing, Reporting and Reflecting on the Encounters between Europeans and Other Peoples in the Early Modern Era* (Cambridge and New York: Cambridge University Press, 1995)

SCRIBNER, CHARLES, 'In Alia Effigie: Caravaggio's London Supper at Emmaus', *The Art Bulletin*, 59.3 (1977), 375–82

SELIGMANN, SIEGMUND, *Zeitschrift für hebräische Bibliographie*, 15 (1911), 41–43

SEGNERI, PAOLO, *Concordia tra la fatica e la quiete nell'orazione, espressa ad un Religioso in una risposta da Paolo Segneri* (Florence: Ipolito della Nave, 1680).

—— *Concordia entre la quietud y la fatiga de la oración* (Barcelona: Rafael Figuerò, 1688) (Barcelona: [n. p.], 1705)

SEIDEL MENCHI, SILVANA, *Erasmo in Italia, 1520–1580* (Turin: Bollati Boringhieri, 1987)

SERJEANTSON, ROBERT W., 'Proof and Persuasion', in *The Cambridge History of Science: Vol. 3, Early Modern Science*, ed. by Roy Porter, Katharine Park and Lorraine Daston (New York: Cambridge University Press, 2006), pp. 132–75

SERRAI, ALFREDO, *Conrad Gesner*, ed. by Maria Cochetti (Rome: Bulzoni, 1990)

SERRERA, JUAN MIGUEL, 'Zurbarán y América', in *Catálogo de la exposición Zurbarán* (Madrid: Museo del Prado, 1988), p. 70

[SERRY, JACQUES-HYACINTHE], *La calunnia convinta, cioè Risposta ad un libello pubblicato da' difensori de' riti condannati della Cina* (Turin: Gio. Battista Fontana, 1709)

SHAGRIR, IRIS, 'The Parable of the Three Rings: A Revision of its History', *Journal of Medieval History*, 23.2 (1997), 163–77

SIERRA, JULIO, *Procesos en la Inquisición de Toledo (1575–1610). Manuscrito de Halle* (Madrid: Trotta, 2005)

SIGÜENZA, JOSÉ DE, *Historia de la orden de san Jerónimo*, ed. by Francisco J. Campos and Fernández de Sevilla (Valladolid: Junta de Castilla y León, 2000)

SILVA, SAMUEL DA, *Tratado da immortalidade da alma* (Amsterdam: Paul van Ravesteyn, 1623)

SIMANCAS, DIEGO DE, *Institutiones Catholicae* (Valladolid: Egidio de Colomies, 1552)

SMITH, WILFRED C., *Belief and History* (Charlottesville: University Press of Virginia, 1977)

—— *Believing: An Historical Perspective* (Oxford: Oneworld, 1998)

—— *Faith and Belief: The Difference between Them* (Oxford: Oneworld, 1998)

—— *The Meaning and End of Religion: A New Approach to the Religious Traditions of Mankind* (New York: Macmillan, 1963)

SNYDER, JON R., *Dissimulation and the Culture of Secrecy in Early Modern Europe* (Berkeley: University of California Press, 2009)

SOSA MAYOR, IGOR. *El noble atribulado. Nobleza y teología moral en la Castilla moderna (1550–1650)* (Madrid: Marcial Pons, 2018)

SOYER, FRANÇOIS, ' "It is not possible to be both a Jew and a Christian": *Converso* Religious Identity and the Inquisitorial Trial of Custódio Nunes (1604–05)', *Mediterranean Historical Review*, 26.1 (2011), 81–97

SPINI, GIORGIO, *Ricerca dei libertini: la teoria dell'impostura delle religioni nel Seicento italiano*, 2nd edn (Florence: La Nuova Italia, 1983 [1950]).

SPIVAKOVSKY, ERIKA, 'Diego Hurtado de Mendoza and Averroism', *Journal of the History of Ideas*, 26.3 (1965), 307–26

—— 'Lo de la Goleta', *Hispania*, 23 (1963), 366–79

—— *Son of the Alhambra: Don Diego Hurtado de Mendoza, 1504–1575* (Austin: University of Texas Press, 1970)

SPOLSKY, ELLEN, *Satisfying Skepticism: Embodied Knowledge in the Early Modern World* (Aldershot: Ashgate, 2001)

STEWART, PAMELA D., *Innocent Gentillet e la sua polemica antimachiavellica* (Florence: La Nuova Italia, 1969)

STROUMSA, GUY G., *A New Science: The Discovery of Religion in the Age of Reason* (Cambridge, MA, and London: Harvard University Press, 2010)

STROUMSA, SARAH, *Maimonides in his World: Portrait of a Mediterranean Thinker* (Princeton, NJ: Princeton Unniversity Press, 2009)

SUÁREZ SÁNCHEZ DE LEÓN, JUAN LUIS, '¿Era escéptico Pedro de Valencia?', *Bulletin Hispanique*, 99.2 (1997), 393–408

—— 'Estudio preliminar', in Pedro de Valencia, *Obras completas. T. III, Académica*, ed. by Juan Francisco Domínguez Domínguez (León: Universidad de León, 2006), pp. 15–88

—— *El pensamiento de Pedro de Valencia. Escepticismo y modernidad en el Humanismo español* (Badajoz: Diputación de Badajoz, 1997)

SWETSCHINSKI, DANIEL M., 'The Portuguese Jewish Merchants of Seventeenth Century Amsterdam: A Social Profile' (unpublished PhD thesis, Brandeis University, Waltham, MA, 1979)

SZCZUCKI, LECH, ed., *Faustus Socinus and his Heritage* (Kraców: Polska Akademia Umiejetnosci, 2006)

TALMAGE, FRANK E., *Disputation and Dialogue: Readings in the Jewish-Christian Encounter* (New York: Ktav Publishing House, 1975)

TATE, ROBERT B., 'Políticas sexuales. De Enrique el Impotente a Isabel, maestra de engaños (*magistra dissimulationum*)', in *Actas del primer congreso anglo-hispano*, ed. by Richard Hitchcock and Ralph Penny, 3 vols (Madrid: Asociación de Hispanistas de Gran Bretaña e Irlanda, Castalia, 1994), III, 165–77

TELLECHEA IDÍGORAS, JOSÉ IGNACIO, *El proceso del doctor Miguel de Molinos* (Madrid: Fundación Universitaria Española-Universidad Pontificia de Salamanca, 2007)

——, JUAN CARLOS SÁNCHEZ, and JAVIER SANTA CLOTILDE, *Léxico de la 'Guía espiritual' de Miguel de Molinos* (Madrid: Fundación Universitaria Española-Universidad Pontificia de Comillas, 1991)

——*Molinosiana. Investigaciones históricas sobre Miguel de Molinos* (Madrid: Fundación Universitaria Española, 1987)

TENENTI, ALBERTO, *Credenze, ideologie, libertinismi tra Medioevo ed Età moderna* (Bologna: Il Mulino, 1978)

THOMAS AQUINAS, *Summa theologiæ, Vol. 41, Virtues of Justice in the Human Community (2a2æ 101–22)*, ed. and trans. by T. C. O'Brien (Cambridge: Cambridge University Press, 2006)

TILLIER, JANE YVONNE, 'Passion Poetry in the Cancioneros', *Bulletin of Hispanic Studies*, 62.1 (1985), 65–78

TITELMANS, FRANCISCUS, *Elucidatio paraphrastica in sanctum Christi evangelium secundum Joannem, cum annotationibus in aliquot capita* (Anvers: Symon Cock, 1543)

TORQUEMADA, JUAN DE, *Summæ Ecclesiasticæ libri quatuor* (Salamanca: Juan María de Terranova, 1560)

TORRECILLA, MARTÍN DE, *Compendio de la suma añadida del R.P.Fr. Martín de Torrecilla, con Addiciones del tomo de proposiciones condenadas, y del de Obispos y otras* (Madrid: Antonio Román, 1698)

——*Consultas, apologías, alegatos, questiones y varios tratados morales, y confutación de las más y más principales proposiciones del impío heresiarca Molinos*, 3 vols (Madrid: Jerónimo de Estrada, 1702)

——*Consultas morales y exposición de las proposiciones condenadas por nuestros muy santos padres Inocencio XI y Alexandro VII* (Madrid: Juan García Infanzón, 1693)

TOUATI, CHARLES, *Le Kuzari. Apologie de la religion méprisée par Juda Hallevi* (Paris: Verdier, 1994)

TREMALLO, BETH S., *Irony and Self-Knowledge in Francisco López de Villalobos* (New York: Garland P. I., 1991)

TRINIDAD SOLANO, FRANCISCO, 'Miguel de Molinos. La experiencia de la nada', in *Miguel de Molinos, Defensa de la contemplación*, ed. by F. T. Solano (Madrid: Editora Nacional, 1983), pp. 13–88

TRUMAN, RONALD W., *Spanish Treatises on Government, Society and Religion in the Time of Philip II* (Leiden: Brill, 1999)

TURRINI, MIRIAM, *La coscienza e le leggi. Morale e diritto nei testi per la confessione della prima età moderna* (Bologna: Il Mulino, 1991)

TUTINO, STEFANIA, *Shadows of Doubt: Language and Truth in Post-Reformation Catholic Culture* (Oxford: Oxford University Press, 2014)

VAJDA, GEORGES, 'Études sur Saadia', *Revue des Études Juives*, 109 (1948–49), 1–37 [republished in: *Mélanges Georges Vajda. In Memoriam*, edited by G. E. Weil (Hildesheim: Gerstenberg Verlag, 1982), pp. 68–102]

VALENCIA, PEDRO, *Academica; sive, De iudicio erga verum. Ex ipsis primis fontibus. Opera Petri Valentiae Zafrensis in extrema Baetica* (Antwerp: Moretus, 1596)

——*Academica*, ed. by José Oroz Reta (Badajoz: Diputación Provincial de Badajoz, 1987)

——*Obras completas. T. III, Académica*, intro. by Juan Luis Suárez Sánchez de León, ed. by Juan Francisco Domínguez Domínguez (León: Universidad de León, 2006)

——*Sobre el pergamino y láminas de Granada*, ed. by Grace Magnier (Oxford: Peter Lang, 2006)

VAN DEN BERG, JOHANNES, 'Proto-Protestants? The Image of the Karaites as a Mirror of the Catholic–Protestant Controversy in the Seventeenth Century', in *Jewish–Christian Relations in the Seventeenth Century: Studies and Documents*, ed. by Johannes van den Berg and Ernestine G. E. van der Wall (Dordrecht, Boston and London: Kluver Academic Publishers, 1988), pp. 33–49

VAN ENGEN, JOHN, 'Faith as a Concept of Order in Medieval Christendom', in *Belief in History: Innovative Approaches to European and American Religion*, ed. by Thomas Kselman (Notre Dame, IN: Notre Dame University Press, 1991), pp. 19–67

VAN ROODEN, PETER, and JAN W. WESSELIUS, 'The Early Enlightenment and Judaism: The "civil dispute" between Philippus van Limborch and Isaac Orobio de Castro', *Studia Rosenthaliana*, 21.2 (1987), 140–53

VARCHI, BENEDETTO, *Due Lezzioni* (Florence: Lorenzo Torrentino, 1549)

VAZ DIAS, ABRAHAM DE MORDECHAI, *Uriel da Costa. Nieuwe bijdrage tot diens levensgeschiedenis* (Leiden: Brill, 1936)

VEGA DÍAZ, FRANCISCO, 'Sobre los *Peregrinos de Emaús* de Zurbarán', *Cuadernos hispanoamericanos*, 524 (1994), 85–98

VENTURI, FRANCO, *Alberto Radicati di Passerano*, 2nd edn (Turin: Utet, 2005)

VEREECKE, LOUIS, *De Guillaume d'Ockham à saint Alphonse de Liguori. Études d'histoire de la théologie morale moderne, 1300–1787* (Rome: Collegium S. Alfonsi de Urbe, 1986)

VEYNE, PAUL, *Did the Greeks Believe in their Myths? An Essay on the Constitutive Imagination*, trans. by Paula Wissing (Chicago, IL: University of Chicago Press, 1988)

VICO, GIAMBATTISTA, *Opere Filosofiche*, ed. by Paolo Cristofolini (Florence: Sansoni, 1971)

VIDAL, FERNANDO, 'Miracles, Science, and Testimony in Post-Tridentine Saint-Making', *Science in Context*, 20.3 (2007), 481–508

VILCHES, ELVIRA, *New World Gold: Cultural Anxiety and Monetary Disorder in Early Modern Spain* (Chicago, IL: University of Chicago Press, 2010)

VILLACAÑAS, JOSÉ LUIS, 'El estigma de Descartes y la búsqueda de la certeza. Variaciones sobre un tema moderno', in *Actas del Symposium internacional sobre el 350 aniversario del Discurso del Método* (Barcelona: Universidad de Barcelona, 1987), pp. 907–28

——'La ratio teológica paulina de Alonso de Cartagena', in *La primera escuela de Salamanca, 1406–1516*, ed. by Cirilo Flórez and Maximiliano Hernández (Salamanca: Universidad de Salamanca, 2012), pp. 75–95.

——'La Tolleranza nel contesto ispanico del Cinquecento. Il caso di Antonio del Corro', in *Tracing the Path of Tolerance, History and Critique from the Early Modern Period to the Present Day*, ed. by Paolo Scotton and Enrico Zucchi (Newcastle: Cambridge Scholars, 2016), pp. 8–23.

——*Monarquía hispánica* (Madrid: Espasa Calpe, 2008)

——'Problemas de Método', in *Giorgio Agamben, filosofía, ética e política*, ed. by Ésio Francisco Salvetti, Paulo César Carbonari and Iltomar Siviero (Passo Fundo: Ifibe, 2015), pp. 77–113

——*¿Qué imperio? Un ensayo polémico sobre Carlos V* (Córdoba: Almuzara, 2008)

——'Spinoza. Democracia y subjetividad marrana', *Política Común*, 1 (2011), 53–84

VILLEGAS, ALONSO DE, *Flos sanctorum y Historia general, de la vida y hechos de Iesu Christo [...] conforme Breuiario Romano, reformado por decreto del santo Concilio Tridentino, junto con las vidas de los santos propios de España, y de otros extrauagantes: quitadas algunas cosas apócrifas è inciertas, y añadidas muchas figuras y autoridades de la Sagrada Escritura* (Madrid: Pedro Madrigal, 1588)

VIO, TOMMASO DE, *Reverendissimi D. Thomae de Vio Caietani, cardinalis sancti Sixti perquam docta, resoluta, ac compendiosa de peccatis Summula, nuper diligentissime recognita* (Lyon: Vaeneunt in vico Mercuriali, apud Vincentium de Portonariis, 1528)

VIVES, JUAN LUIS, *De anima et vita* (Basel: Robert Winter, 1538)

VOET, GIJSBERT, *Selectarum disputationum theologicarum pars prima* (Utrecht: Waesberge, 1648)

VOLTAIRE, FRANÇOIS-MARIE AROUET, *Œuvres complètes de Voltaire. Correspondance générale*, vol. IX (Paris: Carez, Thomine et Fortic, 1822)

WALKER BYNUM, CAROLINE, *Christian Materiality: An Essay on Religion in Late Medieval Europe* (New Yok: Zone Books, 2011)

WALKER, COLIN, 'The Young Lessing and the Jews', *Hermathena*, 140 (1986), 32–54

WEINSTEIN, MYRON, 'A Letter of 1510: Some Comments and Calculations', *Mizrah W Maarav*, 6 (1995), 5–30

—— 'Iggeret Shlomim me-ha-meah ha-shesh-esreh le-rabbaney yerushalayim ha-mistakhsekhim', *Shalem*, 7 (2002), 59–89

—— 'The Correspondence of Dr. Abraham Ibn Sanchi', *Studies in Bibliography and Booklore*, 20 (1998), 145–76

WHITMAN, JAMES Q., *The Origins of Reasonable Doubt: Theological Roots of the Criminal Trial* (New Haven, CT, and London: Yale University Press, 2008)

WILKE, CARSTEN L. 'Conversion ou retour? La Metamorphose du nouveau chrétien en juif portugais dans l'imaginaire sépharade du XVIIe siècle', in *Mémoires juives d'Espagne et du Portugal*, ed. by Esther Benbassa (Paris: Publisud, 1996), pp. 53–67

—— *The Marrakesh Dialogues: A Gospel Critique and Jewish Apology from the Spanish Renaissance* (Leiden: Brill, 2014)

—— ' "That Devilish Invention Called Faith": Seventeenth-Century Free-Thought and its Use in Sephardic Apologetics', in *Conversos, marrani e nuove comunità ebraiche in età moderna*, ed. by Myriam Silvera (Florence: Casa Editrice Giuntina, 2015), pp. 131–44

WILLIAMS, GEORGE H., *The Radical Reformation*, 3rd edn (Kirksville, MO: Sixteenth Century Journal Publishers, 1992)

WIMBÖCK, GABRIELE, '*Durch die Augen in das Gemüt kommen*. Sehen und Glauben — Grenzen und Reservate', in *Evidentia. Reichweiten visueller Wahrnehmung in der Frühen Neuzeit*, ed. by Gabriele Wimböck, Karin Leonhard and Markus Friedrich (Berlin: Lit. Verlag, 2007), pp. 425–50

WIRTH, JEAN, 'La Fin des mentalités', *Les Dossiers du Grihl* (2007) <http://dossiersgrihl.revues.org/284> [accessed 21/04/2017]

—— 'La naissance du concept de croyance', *Bibliothèque d'Humanisme et Renaissance*, 45.1 (1983), 7–58 [republished in *Sainte Anne est une sorcière* (Geneva: Droz, 2003), pp. 113–76]

—— *Saint Anne est une sorcière et autres essais* (Geneve: Droz, 2003)

WOLF, LUCIEN, *Crypto-Jews in the Canaries* [*Paper Read before the Jewish Historical Society of England, in the Mocatta Library, University College, December 12, 1910*] (London: Straker, 1910)

—— *The Jews in the Canary Islands: Being a Calendar of Jewish Cases Extracted from the Records of the Canariote Inquisition in the Collection of the Marquess of Bute* (London: Ballantyne, 1926)

WOOTTON, DAVID, 'Lucien Febvre and the Problem of Unbelief in the Early Modern Period', *The Journal of Modern History*, 60.4 (1988), 695–730

WÜSTENBERG, RALF K., 'Fides implicita "revisited". Versuch eines evangelischen Zugangs', *Neue Zeitschrift für Systematische Theologie und Religionsphilosophie*, 49.1 (2007), 71–85

YERUSHALMI, Y. H., *From Spanish Court to Italian Ghetto. Isaac Cardoso: A Study in Seventeenth-century Marranism and Jewish Apologetics* (New York: Columbia University Press, 1971)

—— 'Marranos Returning to Judaism in the Seventeenth Century: Their Jewish Knowledge and Psychological Readiness' [in Hebrew], in *Proceedings of the Fifth World Congress of Jewish Studies*, 5 vols (Jerusalem: World Union of Jewish Studies, 1969), ii, 201–09

YOVEL, YIRMIYAHU, *The Other Within. The Marranos: Split Identity and the Emerging Modernity* (Princeton, NJ: Princeton University Press, 2009)

ZAGORIN, PÉREZ, *Ways of Lying: Dissimulation, Persecution, and Conformity in Early Modern Europe* (Cambridge, MA, and London: Harvard University Press, 1990)

ZÖCKLER, OTTO, *Geschichte der Apologie des Christentums* (Gütersloh: Bertelsmann, 1907)

INDEX

❖

www.ingramcontent.com/pod-product-compliance
Lightning Source LLC
Chambersburg PA
CBHW080540090426
42734CB00016B/3164